Law of
Employment

Eleventh edition

Norman Selwyn

LLM, Dip Econ (Oxon), Barrister at Law

Butterworths
London, Edinburgh, Dublin
2000

United Kingdom	Butterworths, a Division of Reed Elsevier (UK) Ltd, Halsbury House, 35 Chancery Lane, LONDON WC2A 1EL and 4 Hill Street, EDINBURGH EH2 3JZ
Australia	Butterworths, a Division of Reed International Books Australia Pty Ltd, CHATSWOOD, New South Wales
Canada	Butterworths Canada Ltd, MARKHAM, Ontario
Hong Kong	Butterworths Asia (Hong Kong), HONG KONG
India	Butterworths India, NEW DELHI
Ireland	Butterworth (Ireland) Ltd, DUBLIN
Malaysia	Malayan Law Journal Sdn Bhd, KUALA LUMPUR
New Zealand	Butterworths of New Zealand Ltd, WELLINGTON
Singapore	Butterworths Asia, SINGAPORE
South Africa	Butterworths Publishers (Pty) Ltd, DURBAN
USA	Lexis Law Publishing, CHARLOTTESVILLE, Virginia

A CIP Catalogue record for this book is available from the British Library.

ISBN 0 406 91357 9

Printed and bound in Great Britain by the Bath Press, Bath

Visit Butterworths LEXIS *direct* at: http://www.butterworths.com

Law of
Employment

Preface

The aim of this book is to state the modern law of employment in a manner which is readable, accurate and up to date, for the benefit of employers and employees generally and, in particular, for lawyers, students, personnel specialists and others who have to advise on the subject.

This edition takes account of the considerable number of substantial legislative changes which have been made in recent years, in particular those stemming from the Employment Rights Act 1999. These include the new rights on maternity leave of absence, the right to have time off work to care for dependants, time off work for parental leave, and the right to be accompanied at disciplinary and grievance hearings. The Act also introduced new concepts in trade union law, including a statutory recognition procedure, protected industrial action, and amendments to the balloting provisions. Compensation limits have been increased, and other minor changes made to unfair dismissal rights. Other changes noted stem from the Human Rights Act 1998 (particularly with regard to its effect on the right of a worker to privacy).

New regulations have been introduced on gender reassignment, part-time workers, European Works Councils, methods of collective bargaining, health and safety etc. There are new Codes of Practice on Industrial Action Ballots, Access to Workers during Recognition and Derecognition Ballots, and Disciplinary Practices and Procedures.

There has been the usual crop of significant decisions from British and European courts (some of which have generated more heat than light), and new problem areas (references, sexual orientation etc) have brought forward new solutions.

All in all, it has been a busy time for employment law, and it is likely to be even busier for employment lawyers in the future!

I have tried to state the law in accordance with the sources available to me at 1 August 2000.

Norman Selwyn
Solihull, West Midlands
August 2000

Contents

CHAPTER 1

The institutions of employment law   1

CHAPTER 2

The nature of a contract of employment   27

CHAPTER 3

The formation of a contract of employment   58

CHAPTER 4

Discrimination in employment   87

CHAPTER 8

Protection of wages   185

CHAPTER 9

Transfer of undertakings   198

CHAPTER 10

Performance of the contract of employment   213

CHAPTER 11

Health and safety at work   245

CHAPTER 23

Law relating to industrial relations   483

Appendices

APPENDIX H

Codes of Practice   543

APPENDIX I

European Commission recommendation No 92/131/EEC on the protection of the dignity of women and men at work   683

Table of statutes

References in the right-hand column are to paragraph numbers.
Those references in *italics* are to page numbers.

Table of statutory instruments

References in the right-hand column are to paragraph numbers.
Those references in *italics* are to page numbers.

Table of cases

PARA

PARA

F

G

H

PARA

PARA

X

Y

Z

Decisions of the European Court of Justice are listed below numerically.
These decisions are also included in the preceding alphabetical list.

CHAPTER I

The institutions of employment law

Advisory, Conciliation and Arbitration Service

1.1   The Advisory, Conciliation and Arbitration Service (ACAS) was placed on a statutory basis by the Employment Protection Act 1975 and continued by virtue of the Trade Union and Labour Relations (Consolidation) Act 1992 (TULR(C)A s 247). It is charged with the general duty of promoting the improvement of industrial relations. Its work is directed by a Council, which consists of a chairman and up to nine other members appointed by the Secretary of State. Three of these are to be appointed after consultations with employers' organisations, three after consultation with workers' organisations, and three 'neutral' (usually academic) appointments are usually made. Additionally up to three deputy chairmen may be appointed. The Secretary of State may appoint two further members of the Council, after consultation with both sides of industry. The appointments will be initially for a period of five years, and may be renewed for a further period (TULR(C)A s 248).

1.2   ACAS will appoint its own staff, including a secretary, and will also provide staff for the Certification Officer and the Central Arbitration Committee. Although it will perform its functions on behalf of the Crown, it shall not be subject to any directions from any minister as to the manner in which it is to exercise any of those functions. It is this complete independence from government control which is a distinguishing feature of ACAS. It will make an annual report on its activities and those of the Central Arbitration Committee to the Secretary of State, which will be laid before Parliament and published.

Whenever it thinks appropriate to do so, ACAS may charge a fee for its services, and also the Secretary of State may direct ACAS to charge fees, either at a full economic cost or a specified proportion or percentage of the economic cost. However, ACAS must notify the person concerned that a fee may or will be charged (TULR(C)A s 251A).

1.3   The function of ACAS can be examined under the following headings:

A. Advice

1.4   ACAS may, on request or otherwise, give employers, employers' associations, workers and trade unions such advice as it thinks appropriate on matters connected with or likely to affect industrial relations. General advice on this topic may also be published (TULR(C)A s 213).

B. Conciliation

1.5 Where a trade dispute exists or is apprehended, ACAS may offer its assistance to the parties, either on its own volition or at the request of any party, with a view to bringing about a settlement. This may be achieved by conciliation or other means, and by the appointment, if necessary, of someone outside ACAS whose assistance may be used. Due regard will be had to the desirability of encouraging the parties to use any appropriate agreed procedures (TULR(C)A s 210).

1.6 It should be noted that for conciliation purposes, the definition of 'trade dispute' is the old definition (based on the Employment Protection Act 1975), now contained in s 218 of TULR(C)A, not the more restricted definition (based on the Trade Union and Labour Relations Act 1974) now contained in s 244 of TULR(C)A. The effect is to give ACAS a wider conciliation brief.

1.7 Conciliation officers will also be appointed for the purpose of settling by conciliation certain matters which are, or could be, the subject of proceedings before an employment tribunal under any legislation, whenever passed (TULR(C)A s 211), provided the relevant legislation so indicates (see Employment Tribunals Act 1996 s 18). When a complaint is presented to an employment tribunal, a copy will be sent to a conciliation officer, who is an officer of ACAS, and who has a duty to try to promote a settlement without the matter having to be dealt with by the tribunal. He will intervene for this purpose if requested to do so by the claimant or the person against whom the complaint has been made (ie, the respondent), and also in the absence of such request, if he thinks he could act with a reasonable prospect of success. He may also conciliate at the request of either party in respect of a matter which could be the subject of tribunal proceedings, but before a complaint has been presented. In practice, a large number of claims made to employment tribunals are disposed of as a result of the intervention of the conciliation officer. The majority of these will be settled on the basis of the employer making some financial payment to the claimant, and the rest will be withdrawn or a private settlement reached.

ACAS will not conciliate in the following disputes: written statements of terms and conditions of employment, claims for interim relief, time off work for safety representatives, and appeals against the imposition of prohibition and improvement notices.

1.8 There is a continuing obligation on ACAS to act until all questions of liability and remedies have been determined by an employment tribunal (*Courage Take Home Trade Ltd v Keys*).

1.9 Anything communicated to the conciliation officer in connection with the performance of his functions shall not be admissible in evidence in any proceedings before the tribunal without the consent of the party who communicated it. So far as dismissals are concerned, he shall try to promote the re-engagement or reinstatement of the claimant by the employer or by a successor or associated employer on terms appearing to him to be equitable or, if this is not possible, to try to promote a settlement on the sum to be paid by way of compensation. Apart from certain specific instances (see para 20.66), it is not possible for a person to contract out of his statutory rights, and any agreement to this effect is generally void, but this rule does not apply to any agreement reached through the intervention of the conciliation officer, and any such settlement agreed between the parties will be legally binding (Employment Rights Act 1996 s 203(2)(e)). However, although a conciliation officer may try to effect a settlement in respect of claims brought before an employment tribunal under most legislative provisions, he can only draw up a legally binding settlement in respect of those claims specified in s 18 of the Employment Tribunals Act 1996. There are, therefore, some disputes on which he can conciliate, but cannot draw up a legally binding settlement.

1.10 There is no obligation on the conciliation officer to advise or inform the employee of his statutory rights. How he performs his functions is a matter for his discretion, and in the absence of bad faith, or adopting unfair methods, an agreement reached under his auspices cannot be set aside (*Slack v Greenham Plant Hire*). However, the conciliation officer must take care not to give the impression that he favours the views of one side to the dispute. Thus, if the parties have reached an agreement, he should not get involved with its merits, but merely record it on the appropriate form and obtain the parties' signatures (*Moore v Duport Furniture Products*). Indeed, an agreement reached orally between the parties under the auspices of the conciliation officer is equally binding (*Gilbert v Kembridge Fibres*).

1.11 In *Hennessy v Craigmyle & Co Ltd* the claimant was told that he would be dismissed summarily but, provided he signed an agreement which had been prepared by the conciliation officer giving up his rights to bring a complaint before an employment tribunal, he would be treated as having been made redundant, and would be given certain monies. After taking legal advice, he signed the agreement, but subsequently brought a claim for unfair dismissal. He alleged that his consent had been obtained by economic duress, and hence was void. The argument was dismissed by the employment tribunal, the EAT and the Court of Appeal. Economic duress was a ground for avoiding an agreement only if the claimant's will was so overborne that his consent was vitiated because he had no real alternative. In this case there was such an alternative, for he could have refused to sign the agreement and taken his chance in the employment tribunal. In any case, whether economic duress exists is a question of fact for the employment tribunal to determine.

1.12 As a result of a recent change in policy, ACAS have indicated that they will no longer act as a 'rubber stamp' to an agreement, but will only draw up form COT3 (which records the agreement) when they have 'taken action' with regard to a settlement, in accordance with their statutory powers.

C. Arbitration

1.13 At the request of one or more parties to a trade dispute, but with the consent of all of them, ACAS may refer any matter to arbitration for settlement, either by a person appointed from outside ACAS, or by the Central Arbitration Committee. However, arbitration is not to be used unless the parties have exhausted agreed procedures for negotiation or the settlement of disputes, unless there is a special reason which justifies arbitration as an alternative to those procedures (TULR(C)A s 212). With the consent of all the parties, ACAS may decide to publish the award. The Arbitration Act 1996 does not apply to any arbitration under this section, and thus the award is not capable of being legally enforced in a court of law.

ACAS may also prepare a scheme, approved by the Secretary of State, for providing arbitration facilities in cases of disputes involving claims or proceedings which could be brought before an employment tribunal in respect of unfair dismissal, and arising out of any other enactment specified in an Order to be made by the Secretary of State (see Trade Union and Labour Relations (Consolidation) Act 1992 s 212A). The scheme may provide for enforceable re-employment orders. If both parties agree in writing so to refer the dispute, ACAS will appoint a person for that purpose (not being an officer or employee of ACAS). The arbitrator's decision will be binding. To date, no such scheme has been prepared.

D. Enquiries

1.14 ACAS may enquire into industrial relations generally, or in a particular industry, or in a particular undertaking. After taking into account the views of the parties, such findings may be published (TULR(C)A s 214).

E. Codes of Practice

1.15 ACAS may issue Codes of Practice containing such practical guidance as it thinks fit for the purpose of promoting the improvement of industrial relations (TULR(C)A s 199). The old Code of Practice issued under the Industrial Relations Act 1971 has been revoked, and three Codes are currently in force (see Appendix H), namely:
(a) Disciplinary and Grievance Procedures;
(b) Disclosure of Information for Collective Bargaining purposes;
(c) Time off work for trade union duties and activities.

1.16 In addition, an Advisory Handbook entitled 'Discipline at Work' has been issued which contains useful guidance on the handling of disciplinary and dismissal situations.

1.17 The codes are first prepared and published in draft form, and then ACAS shall consider any representations made about them (and if necessary modify them) before they are finally submitted to the Secretary of State. If he approves, he shall lay them before Parliament. If he does not approve, he will give reasons for withholding his approval. After completing the Parliamentary procedure, the code will be issued in the form of a draft by ACAS and will come into effect on a day appointed by the Secretary of State. A failure on the part of any person to observe a code shall not of itself make him liable to any proceedings, but in any proceedings before an employment tribunal or the Central Arbitration Committee the code will be admissible in evidence, and any relevant provision shall be taken into account in determining the issue (TULR(C)A s 207) (see *Lock v Cardiff Rly Co*).

1.18–1.25 A code of practice may be revised or revoked with the approval of the Secretary of State (TULR(C)A ss 201–202). The Code of Practice 'Disciplinary and Grievance Procedures' has recently been revised, with certain additions and refinements, particularly with the inclusion of guidance on the new statutory right to be accompanied at grievance and disciplinary hearings.

Certification officer (TULR(C)A s 254)

1.26 The post of Certification Officer was originally created to take over certain administrative functions exercised in connection with trade unions, although nowadays he has wide powers of investigation and supervision over matters such as register of members, accounting records, elections, breaches of union rules, funds for political objects, and so on (see Chapter 22). He is appointed by the Secretary of State, and will make an annual report to him and also to ACAS. Although the staff of the Certification Officer is provided by ACAS, he is completely independent of that organisation.

Since TULRA 1974 (now TULR(C)A s 2) the Certification Officer has kept a list of organisations which are trade unions and employers associations within the legal definition. Since the Employment Protection Act 1975 (now TULR(C)A s 6) he has issued certificates of independence to those trade unions which have applied, and meet the necessary criteria (see Chapter 22). He has issued a booklet entitled 'Guidance for trade unions wishing to apply for a certificate of independence'. He has taken custody of all documents held by his predecessors since 1871, and will keep these for public inspection, along with the list of trade unions and records of all applications for certificates of independence (TULR(C)A ss 255–258). Following the abolition of the office of the Commissioner for the Rights of Trade Union Members many of the functions of that office have been transferred to the Certification Officer (Employment Relations Act 1999 Sch 6). The Certification Officer now has wide powers in respect of complaints by trade union members of alleged breaches of trade union law and trade union rules, and can now make declarations and orders on a number of matters, which may be enforced in the same manner as an order of the courts. An appeal from his decisions may be made on a point of law to the Employment Appeal Tribunal.

Central Arbitration Committee

1.27 This body replaced the Industrial Arbitration Board (formerly known as the Industrial Court) and consists of a chairman (and deputy chairman) appointed by the Secretary of State (after consultation with ACAS) and other persons appointed from representatives of employers and workers who are experienced in industrial relations. The appointments may be for up to five years, and are renewable. CAC will exercise its functions on behalf of the Crown, but will not be subject to directions of any kind from any ministers as to the manner in which those functions are to be exercised. CAC has a central role in the new statutory scheme for the recognition of trade unions, created by the Employment Relations Act 1999 (see Chapter 23). In performing its functions, CAC must have regard to the object of encouraging and promoting fair and efficient practices and arrangements in the workplace, although it will remain neutral on the issue of collective bargaining. CAC will continue to exercise its former statutory functions to adjudicate on claims relating to disclosure of information for collective bargaining purposes brought under TULR(C)A s 183 (see para 23.28) and to hear references under ss 5 and 7 of the Equal Pay Act 1970. CAC also acts as a voluntary arbitration panel and will also adjudicate on certain disputes arising out of the provisions of the Transnational Information and Consultation of Employees Regulations 1999 (see para 23.261).

Employment Appeal Tribunal (Employment Tribunals Act 1996 ss 20–37)

1.28 This tribunal consists of judges of the High Court nominated by the Lord Chancellor in England, and the Lord President of the Court of Session in Scotland, plus other members (appointed on the joint recommendations of the Lord Chancellor and the Secretary of State) who have special knowledge or experience of industrial relations as representatives of employers or of workers. The EAT will be a superior court of record, with a central office in London, but it may sit anywhere in the country, and one or more divisions of the EAT may sit at the same time. In practice, appeals are heard either in London or Edinburgh.

A party may appear before the EAT either in person, or be represented by a solicitor or barrister, or a representative of a trade union or employers' association, or any other person whom he desires to represent him. The procedure before the EAT is now governed by the Employment Appeal Tribunal Rules 1993 (as amended), and subject to those Rules, the EAT will generally regulate its own procedure. Costs will not normally be awarded against either party unless the proceedings were unnecessary, improper or vexatious, or there has been unreasonable delay or unreasonable conduct in bringing or conducting the proceedings. Further details of the procedure before the EAT can be found in the various Practice Directions issued by the President of the EAT.

Appeals will be heard by a judge and either two or four members, so that in either case there is an equal number of persons whose knowledge or experience of industrial relations is as a representative of employers and workers respectively. With the consent of the parties, however, an appeal may be heard by a judge and one or three members. If the appeal is from a decision of an employment tribunal chairman sitting alone (see para 1.42), the appeal may be heard by the judge alone, unless the judge directs that one or more appointed member should sit also.

A restriction on proceedings order may be made to prevent vexatious litigants wasting court time (rr 13–17), and a restricting reporting order may be made in cases where sexual misconduct is alleged (r 23) or disability discrimination (r 23A). It is an offence, punishable by a fine not exceeding level 5 on the standard scale (currently £5,000) to act in contravention of such an order.

1.29 The jurisdiction of the EAT is as follows:
(a) to hear appeals on points of law from decisions of employment tribunals (see para 1.45) except decisions relating to improvement and prohibition notices, which are heard by the Divisional Court (see para 11.29);
(b) to hear appeals on questions of law from the decisions of the Certification Officer given under the provisions of Pt VI of TULR(C)A (restrictions on the use of trade union funds for political objects) (see TULR(C)A s 95);
(c) to hear appeals on points of law from decisions of the Certification Officer given under s 103 of TULR(C)A (resolutions approving instruments of amalgamation) (see s 104);

(d) to hear appeals on points of law and fact from decisions of the Certification Officer given under TULR(C)A ss 2–6 (entry on the list of trade unions, and applications for certificates of independence) (see s 9);

(e) to hear appeals on a point of law arising from a decision of the Certification Officer made under TULR(C)A s 25 (failure of trade union to maintain register of names and addresses of members), s 31 (rights of members to have access to accounting records) and s 45C (duty to ensure that union posts are not held by certain offenders);

(f) to hear original applications for compensation in respect of unreasonable exclusion or expulsion from a trade union (TULR(C)A s 176) and similar applications in respect of unjustifiable disciplinary action by a trade union (TULR(C)A s 67);

(g) to hear complaints of a failure to establish a European Works Council (as required by the Transnational Information and Consultation of Employees Regulations 1999, see para 23.261).

1.30–1.40 An appeal can only be entertained by the EAT if there is a genuine dispute between the parties (*IMI Yorkshire Imperial Ltd v Olender*) and appeals should not be pursued with other ulterior motives (*Baker v Superite Tools Ltd*). A further appeal will lie on a point of law to the Court of Appeal or, in Scotland, to the Court of Session, and a final appeal will lie to the House of Lords. At any time, however, a tribunal or court can refer a case to the European Court of Justice in Luxembourg, if a question arises as to the application of European law (see para 1.157).

Employment tribunals

1.41 The constitutional basis for employment tribunals can be found in the Employment Tribunals (Constitution and Rules of Procedure) Regulations 1993, and the Employment Tribunals (Constitution and Rules of Procedure) (Scotland) Regulations 1993. A Central Office of Employment Tribunals (COET) has been set up in Bury St Edmunds and Glasgow, with 11 regional offices in England and Wales, and three offices in Scotland. Employment tribunals may also sit at other locations. An employment tribunal is an inferior court, for the purpose of the law of contempt (*Vidler v UNISON*).

1.42 An employment tribunal consists of a legal chairman and two lay members. The chairman can be either a barrister or solicitor, and may be full-time or part-time. The lay members, who are all part-time, are selected from a panel drawn up after consultation with representatives of employers' organisations and trade unions. There is also a self-nomination procedure, designed to attract women, ethnic minorities, and persons with disabilities. At an actual hearing, there will always be a representative from each side of industry, although a chairman can sit with one lay member only if both parties to the dispute agree. Each member of the employment tribunal has an equal vote, and although decisions can be reached by a majority vote, in practice it appears that, despite the somewhat diverse backgrounds, 96 per cent of all decisions reached are unanimous. In the remaining cases, the 'wingmen' are just as likely to unite in outvoting the legal chairman as the latter is likely to have the support of one or the other member. In cases of sex discrimination, it is desirable to have one member of either sex, and in race discrimination cases, a member who has special experience of race relations, but there is no absolute legal requirement that an employment tribunal should be so composed (*Habib v Elkington & Co Ltd*).

Although, generally speaking, an employment tribunal will consist of a chairman and two members, in the following circumstances a chairman may sit alone. These are:

(a) applications for interim relief (Employment Rights Act 1996 ss 128–132, TULR(C)A ss 161, 165, 166);
(b) employee's rights on employer's insolvency (ERA s 188);
(c) unauthorised deductions from wages (ERA s 23);
(d) damages for breach of contract of employment (Employment Tribunals Extension of Jurisdiction (England and Wales) Order 1994, and Employment Tribunals Extension of Jurisdiction (Scotland) Order 1994, see para 1.55);
(e) proceedings in which the parties have given their written consent to be heard by the chairman alone;
(f) where the person bringing the proceedings has given written notice withdrawing the case;
(g) proceedings in which the person against whom the proceedings were brought does not contest the case;
(h) unauthorised or excessive trade union subscription deductions (TULR(C)A s 68A);
(i) failure by employer to pay a protective award (TULR(C)A s 192);
(j) failure to give a written statement of terms and conditions of employment (ERA s 11);
(k) failure by employer to make a guarantee payment (ERA s 34);
(l) failure by employer to make a medical suspension payment (ERA s 64);
(m) reference on the right or amount of a redundancy payment (ERA s 163);
(n) liability of the Secretary of State to make a redundancy payment (ERA s 170);
(o) employment tribunal proceedings by the estate of a deceased employee (ERA s 206(4));
(p) compensation claims in respect of employer's failure to inform or consult on a transfer of an undertaking (TUPE Regs reg 11(5));
(q) failure to give a worker access to records, or permit him to be accompanied, (National Minimum Wage Act 1998 s 11);
(r) appeal by employers against enforcement notices and penalty notices (National Minimum Wage Act 1998 ss 19, 22).

1.43   However, in any of the above circumstances, the chairman may at any stage decide to have the case heard by a full tribunal
(a) where there is a likelihood of a dispute arising from the facts,
(b) where there is a likelihood of an issue of law arising,
(c) having taken into account the views of any of the parties,
(d) where there are other proceedings which might be heard concurrently and which do not come within the above categories which enable a chairman to sit alone.

1.44   Indeed, a chairman should not sit alone, even if all the parties agree to him so doing, where there is a likelihood of a dispute on the facts (*Sogbetun v Hackney London Borough*).

1.45 The jurisdiction of employment tribunals is as follows:

a. Industrial Training Act 1982 s 12—appeals against assessment of industrial training levies;

b. Equal Pay Act 1970 s 2—complaints of breach of equality clauses in contracts of employment;

c. Health and Safety at Work etc Act 1974 s 24—appeals against improvement and prohibition notices;

d. Safety Representatives and Safety Committees Regulations 1977—time off work with pay for safety representatives;

e. Pension schemes—decisions on whether an independent trade union is recognised for collective bargaining purposes or whether consultation requirements have been observed (Occupational Pension Schemes (Disclosure of Information) Regulations 1986;

f. Occupational or personal pension schemes—failure by the Secretary of State to make payments on an employer's insolvency (Pension Schemes Act 1993 s 126);

g. Sex Discrimination Act 1975 s 63—complaints of discrimination on grounds of sex or marital status; s 68—appeals against non-discrimination notices; s 72(3)(a)—applications by the Equal Opportunities Commission relating to discriminatory advertisements; s 73—applications by the Equal Opportunities Commission prior to county court actions;

h. Sex Discrimination Act 1986 s 6—complaints of discriminatory collective agreements;

i. Race Relations Act 1976 s 54—complaints of race discrimination; s 59— appeals against non-discrimination notices; s 63—applications by the Commission for Racial Equality relating to discriminatory advertisements; s 64—applications by the Commission for Racial Equality prior to county court actions;

j. Disability Discrimination Act 1995 s 8—complaints of unlawful discrimination on grounds of disability;

k. Employment Rights Act 1996 s 11—failure to give written statement under s 1 or failure to give itemised statement under s 8; s 23—unlawful deductions or unlawful payments from wages, unlawful deductions or unlawful payments in respect of cash shortages; s 34—guarantee payments;protection from suffering detriment; s 44—health and safety cases; s 45—shop workers; s 45A—working time cases; s 46—trustees of occupational pension funds; s 47—employee representatives; s 47A—time off work for studying; s 47B— protected disclosures; s47C—leave for family or domestic reasons; s 50— time off work for public duties; s 52—time off work to look for work or arrange retraining; s 55—time off work for ante-natal care; s 57A—time off work to care for dependants; s 58—time off work for pension scheme trustees; s 61— time off work for employee representatives; s 63A—time off work for study or retraining; s 64—suspension on medical grounds; s 66—suspension on maternity grounds; s 80—right to parental leave; s 92—written reasons for dismissal; ss 94–107—unfair dismissals; s 128—applications for interim relief; s 163—claims for redundancy payments; s 170—Secretary of State's liability to make redundancy payments on the employer's insolvency; s 177—applications for equivalent payments made by certain office holders; s 188—payments to be made on an employer's insolvency;

l. Transfer of Undertakings (Protection of Employment) Regulations 1981— failure to inform or consult with trade unions or employee representatives, failure to pay compensation;

m.   Local Government (Compensation) Regulations 1974, British Transport (Compensation to Employees) Regulations 1970 —compensation payments for loss of office on reorganisation;

n.   Employment tribunals have jurisdiction to apply EC law to claims made under UK law, ie as laid down in specific UK legislation (eg ERA, SDA etc). But there is no jurisdiction to hear or determine 'free-standing' claims based on the Treaty of Rome or an EC Directive, outside the domestic statutory framework (*Biggs v Somerset County Council*), and there is no jurisdiction to hear '*Francovich*' style claims (*Secretary of State for Employment v Mann*);

o.   Pensions Act 1995 s 63—equal treatment in pension schemes;

p.   The following complaints can be brought under the provisions of the Trade Union and Labour Relations (Consolidation) Act 1992; s 64—complaints of unjustified discipline; s 68—unauthorised check-off; s 86—unauthorised deduction from wages for the political fund; ss 137–138—refusal of employment on the ground on trade union membership or non-membership; s 146—detriment on the ground of trade union membership or non-membership; ss 152–3—dismissal on the ground of trade union membership or non-membership; s 161—interim relief; s 168—time off work for trade union duties; s 170—time off work for trade union activities; s 174—exclusion or expulsion from a trade union; s 189—failure by employer to arrange the election of employee representatives and failure to consult representatives on redundancies; s 192—failure to pay protective award; s 238A—unfair dismissal of participants in official strike action;

q.   Right to have time off work, not to suffer a detriment, not to be unfairly dismissed, because of membership of activities or as a member of a European Works Council (Transnational Information and Consultation of Employees Regulations 1999);

r.   Applications made by the Secretary of State for an order prohibiting a person from carrying on an employment agency because of misconduct or other evidence of unsuitability (Employment Agencies Act 1973 as amended);

s.   Claims for breach of contract of employment (Employment Tribunals Act 1996, see para 1.55);

t.   Complaints under the National Minimum Wage Act 1998 relating to a failure by the employer to produce relevant records, or failing to permit a worker to inspect and copy them or be accompanied by someone; claims for remuneration equal to the national minimum wage (whether as a breach of contract claim or a claim in respect of a deduction in wages); appeals by employers in respect of an enforcement notice and by an employer against financial penalties imposed; the right of a worker not to suffer a detriment and the right of an employee not to be unfairly dismissed because he took action to enforce his right to a national minimum wage;

u.   Complaints under the Working Time Regulations 1998;

v.   Right to be accompanied at disciplinary and grievance hearings – Employment Relations Act 1999 s 10;

w.   Claims brought under the Part-time Workers (Prevention of Less Favourable Treatment) Regulations 2000.

1.46   The procedure before employment tribunals is governed by the Employment Tribunals (Constitution and Rules of Procedure) Regulations 1993, and the Employment Tribunals (Constitution and Rules of Procedure) (Scotland) Regulations 1993. These regulations provide for the making of original applications, appearance by respondents, disclosure and information, further information, witness attendance orders, pre-hearing review, procedure at the hearing, applications for review, award of costs, extension of time, joinder of parties, and other miscellaneous matters. Generally speaking the tribunal has a wide discretion in operating its procedures, and its decision can only be challenged on appeal where the discretion was wrongly exercised because of a mistake of law, a disregard of principle, a misapplication of the facts, or the tribunal took into account irrelevant matters or failed to take into account relevant matters, or where the decision was outside the generous ambit within which a reasonable disagreement is possible (*Noorani v Merseyside TEC Ltd*).

1.47 The 1993 Regulations contain five schedules, which lay down the procedure to be followed, depending on the issues involved. Schedule 1 deals with procedural matters generally, Sch 2 is for use when dealing with an equal value claim, Sch 3 is for use when hearing appeals against the imposition of an industrial levy, Sch 4 deals with appeals against the imposition of prohibition and improvement notices, and Sch 5 applies to appeals against non-discrimination notices.

1.48 Proceedings are quite informal, for employment tribunals have the power to conduct them in whatever manner they consider to be most suitable (see Chapter 20). The parties may represent themselves, or be represented by a solicitor or barrister, or a representative of a trade union or employers' association, or any other person whom they desire to represent them. Costs are not normally awarded (although there is now an absolute discretion to do so) unless a party has acted frivolously, vexatiously, abusively, disruptively, or otherwise unreasonably in bringing or conducting proceedings (*ET Marler Ltd v Robertson*). However, under para 12 of Sch 4, a tribunal may make an award of costs in cases of appeals from the imposition of an improvement or prohibition notice issued under the Health and Safety at Work etc Act 1974 (see Chapter 11), on the appropriate County Court Scale.

1.49 In cases which involve allegations of sexual misconduct or disability discrimination the employment tribunal may make a restricted reporting order, prohibiting the publication of any identifying matter, ie the names of the parties until a decision on liability has been reached and entered into the register, when the order ceases to have effect (*A v B, ex p News Group Newspapers Ltd*). Such an order cannot be made to protect the identity of a corporate employer who may be vicariously liable for the acts of its employees, even though its commercial reputation may suffer (*Leicester University v A*). However, there is no power in such cases to exclude the press or members of the public (*R v Southampton Industrial Tribunal, ex p INS News Group Ltd*).

It is an offence punishable by a fine not exceeding level 5 on the standard scale to act in contravention of any such restricted reporting order.

1.50 An employment tribunal may only sit in private if:
(a) it would be against the interests of national security to allow evidence to be given in public;
(b) a person is giving evidence which he could not disclose without contravening a prohibition imposed by an enactment;
(c) the evidence has been communicated to a person in confidence; or

(d) the evidence is information which if disclosed in public, could cause substantial injury to an undertaking of the witness or in which he works for reasons other than its effect on collective bargaining (see para 8, 1st Schedule).

If a private hearing is ordered, this does not preclude the presence of the applicant's representative (*Fry v Foreign and Commonwealth Office*).

1.51 An employment tribunal has the power to issue attendance orders for the purpose of compelling a witness to attend, they may require a party to disclose documents to the other side, and to give further information of any claim or defence (see Chapter 20). Documents which are produced in order to comply with an order for discovery may only be used for the purpose of the hearing, and not for any other cause or action. In *Riddick v Thames Board Mills Ltd*, an employee of the defendants wrote a confidential memorandum about the manner of the claimant's dismissal, which was allegedly defamatory. The claimant got to know about the documents as a result of a court order for discovery, made during the course of a legal action brought against the employer. The action was settled, but the claimant brought a further action for defamation. It was held that the public interest required that documents which were compulsorily disclosed on discovery should be used only for the purpose of the action in which they were disclosed, and that each party impliedly undertook not to use them for any other ulterior or improper motive.

1.52 If there are High Court proceedings between the employer and employee in which there are issues in common with an application for unfair dismissal, the tribunal chairman has a discretion to order that the latter claim be postponed, pending the outcome of the High Court proceedings (*Carter v Credit Change Ltd*). He should take into account the convenience, expedition and cost when exercising his discretion (*First Castle Electronics Ltd v West*). The test to be applied is 'In which court is this action most conveniently and appropriately to be tried, bearing in mind all the surrounding circumstances, including the complexity of the issue, the amount involved, the technicality of the evidence and appropriateness of the procedure?' Thus, where a managing director was alleging a repudiatory breach of contract by the employers which was claimed to be a wrongful and unfair dismissal, the Employment Appeal Tribunal ordered that employment tribunal proceedings should be adjourned until after the hearing of the High Court action (*Bowater plc v Charlwood*).

1.53 An award made by an employment tribunal will now attract interest, on a day-to-day basis, at the stipulated rate of interest, after 42 days from the date when the decision has been sent to the parties. Interest is not payable on costs awarded, nor on any part of the award which is subject to the recoupment provisions.

1.54 Interest is still payable if the tribunal's decision is subject to appeal or review, but if the amount of the award is subsequently varied, interest is payable on the amount as varied (Employment Tribunals (Interest) Order 1990).

An employment tribunal is an inferior court, exercising the judicial powers of the state for the purpose of the Contempt of Court Act 1981 s 19, and contempt of court proceedings may be brought if there is an attempt to pervert the course of justice or any other breach of the Act (*Peach Grey & Co v Sommers*).

Claims for breach of contract

1.55 The Employment Protection Act 1975 contained an enabling power whereby employment tribunals could deal with claims for breach of contract arising out of the employment relationship. For various technical reasons, this power was not exercised until 1994, when the Employment Tribunal Extension of Jurisdiction (England and Wales) Order was passed (a similar Order has been passed in respect of Scotland). Employment tribunals now have jurisdiction to hear claims for damages for breach of a contract of employment, or any other contract (subject to certain exceptions, see below) connected with employment, including a claim for a sum due under such a contract, and a claim for the recovery of a sum in pursuance of any enactment relating to the terms or performance of such a contract. The claim must be outstanding on the termination of the employee's employment, and the maximum award which can be made in respect of any number of claims is £25,000. The claim must be brought within three months from the effective date of termination of the contract of employment (or within three months from the last day when the employee worked in the employment which has been terminated) with the usual extension of time if it was not reasonably practicable to bring the claim within that time (see also para 20.2).

1.56 Once an employee has lodged such a claim, the employer may lodge a counterclaim in respect of breach of contract by the employee, within six weeks (or, if not reasonably practicable to do so, within such further time as the employment tribunal considers to be reasonable). The counterclaim is not limited by the amount of the original claim, and may be continued irrespective of what happens to the original claim, as long as it has been presented before the employee's claim has been settled or withdrawn. Indeed, if the employee's breach of contract claim fails because it was not presented within the appropriate time limits, the employer's counterclaim, validly presented, can still proceed (*Patel v RCMS*).

1.57 Neither the employee nor the employer can bring a claim or counterclaim in respect of:
(a) damages for personal injuries;
(b) breach of a term requiring the employer to provide living accommodation for the employee, or a term imposing an obligation on either of them in connection with the provision of living accommodation;
(c) a term relating to intellectual property;
(d) a term imposing an obligation of confidence;
(e) a term which is a covenant in restraint of trade.

1.58 One effect of the Order is to give an alternative route for claims (other than the above exceptions) which would otherwise have to be brought in the county court, although it should be noted that there are a number of differences in the respective jurisdictions and procedures (see para 8.3). Another effect of the Order is to enable employment tribunals to deal with matters which hitherto were not within the scope of the Wages Act 1986 (now Employment Rights Act 1996 ss 13–22, see para 8.11), in particular claims for payments in lieu of notice, holiday pay, advances etc. Again, there are differences between the Order and the Act, and it will be necessary to scrutinise the nature of a claim very carefully in order to bring it under the appropriate heading.

1.59   However, there appears to be a further development (which is probably unintentional) which needs to be considered. A claim for constructive dismissal (see para 17.23) is essentially based on a claim for breach of contract (breach of an implied term of respect etc). There thus appears to be no reason why such a complaint could not be brought under the Order, rather than under the provisions of the Employment Rights Act 1996. The advantage to the employee of using this route is that he does not need to have the requisite one year continuous employment.

1.60–1.70   It could also be argued that those employees who are dismissed in breach of contractual disciplinary procedures could bring breach of contract claims, as opposed to claims for unfair dismissal although such a claim was turned down in *Janciuk v Winerite Ltd*. Indeed, since legal ingenuity knows no bounds, one may expect the Order to be utilised in a number of circumstances which were not envisaged when it was passed.

Industrial training boards

1.71   The Industrial Training Act 1982 enables the minister to set up training boards in any industry in order to provide for industrial and commercial training of persons who are over school-leaving age. A board will consist of a chairman, with an equal number of persons from either side of industry, educational representatives and additional persons appointed by the Secretary of State, although only the employers' representatives may vote on the imposition of a levy. A board may provide courses for training purposes, or approve courses run by other institutions, and has wide powers relating to the making or recommendations for training, laying down training standards, and to assist persons to find facilities for being trained for industry. It can pay fees, maintenance allowances, and make grants or loans to organisations providing courses or other facilities which are approved by the board. At the present time, seven such boards are still in operation.

1.72–1.80   To meet its expenses a board may impose a levy on employers in the industry, which is assessed by reference to a percentage of the payroll. For this purpose a board may require employers to furnish returns and information, and keep and produce records. An employer who has been assessed for a levy may appeal to an employment tribunal, which may rescind or reduce or increase it as the tribunal determines (see Sch 3 Employment Tribunals (Constitution and Rules of Procedure) Regulations 1993).

Equal Opportunities Commission

1.81   The Sex Discrimination Act 1975 established the Equal Opportunities Commission (EOC), consisting of between eight and 15 members. It will work towards the elimination of discrimination on grounds of sex, generally promote equality of opportunity between men and women, keep the Sex Discrimination Act 1975 and the Equal Pay Act 1970 under review, and, where necessary, draw up and submit proposals for amendments, and review the relevant statutory provisions relating to health and safety at work in so far as they require different treatment for men and women. The Commission also has power to draw up codes of practice giving practical guidance on ways to eliminate discrimination and promote equality of opportunity between men and women. Such codes will have the same standing as those issued by ACAS. A code entitled 'For the elimination of sex and marriage discrimination, and the promotion of equality of opportunity in employment' has been approved and a code on equal pay is also in force (see Appendix H). The EOC may carry out formal enquiries (see Chapter 4) and can give financial or other support to actual or potential claimants.

Commission for Racial Equality

1.82 The Commission for Racial Equality (CRE) was established by the Race Relations Act 1976, and consists of between eight and 15 members. It will work towards the elimination of racial discrimination, promote equality of opportunity and good relations between persons of different racial groups, and keep under review the workings of the 1976 Act and, where necessary, draw up and submit proposals for its amendment. The CRE has issued a code of practice entitled 'For the elimination of racial discrimination and the promotion of equality of opportunity in employment' (see Appendix H). The CRE may give financial or other assistance to any organisation which has for its objects the improvement of community relations, undertake or promote research or educational activities and has like powers of holding enquiries and giving assistance to claimants as the EOC.

Health and Safety Commission

1.83 The Health and Safety at Work etc Act 1974 established the Health and Safety Commission to take over the general supervision of the promotion of health and safety at work. The Commission consists of a chairman, three members representing employers' organisations, three members representing trade unions, and three other members appointed after consultation with local authorities and other interested parties. The duty of the Commission is to do such things and make such arrangements as it considers appropriate:

a. to assist and encourage persons concerned with matters relevant to any of the general purposes of Part I of the Health and Safety at Work etc Act 1974 to further those purposes. Since the bulk of the Act is contained in Part I, this is the widest possible duty of the Commission;

b. to make such arrangements as it considers appropriate for the carrying out of research, the publication of results, the provision of training and information in connection therewith, and to encourage research and the provision of training and information by others;

c. to make arrangements for securing that government departments, employers, employees, employers' organisations and trade unions are provided with an information and advisory service;

d. to submit proposals for the making of regulations.

1.84 The Commission must report from time to time to the Secretary of State (who retains overall responsibility), act in accordance with proposals approved by him, and give effect to any directions made by him.

1.85 The enforcement and day-to-day supervision of the Act is in the hands of the Health and Safety Executive. This consists of three persons; the Director is appointed by the Commission with the approval of the Secretary of State, and two assistant directors appointed by the Commission with the approval of the Secretary of State after consultation with the Director. The powers of the Executive are wide. Generally, it must exercise on behalf of the Commission such of the Commission's functions as the Commission directs, and give effect to any direction given to it by the Commission, but the Commission may not direct the Executive to enforce any statutory provision in any particular case. At the request of any Minister of the Crown, the Executive must provide him with information concerning activities in which he has an interest, and provide him with advice on such matters.

1.86–1.95 In particular, the Commission may direct the Executive or authorise any other person to hold an enquiry into any accident, occurrence, situation or other matter, and regulations have been published concerning the conduct of such enquiries or investigation.

Disability Rights Commission

1.96 The Disability Rights Commission was created by the Disability Rights Commission Act 1999, with powers and functions similar to the CRE and EOC. The Commission will work towards the elimination of discrimination against disabled persons, promote the equalisation of opportunities, take such steps as it considers appropriate with a view to encouraging good practice in the treatment of disabled persons, and keep the working of the Disability Discrimination Act 1995 under review. The Commission may make proposals or give advice to the Minister, or any other Government agency or public authority as to the practical application of any law, and undertake (or arrange for support of) the carrying out of research or the provision of advice or information.

1.97–1.105 The Commission may prepare Codes of Practice (which must be approved by the Secretary of State and laid before Parliament), in order to give practical guidance to employers and other service providers, give assistance to persons who propose to bring claims for unlawful discrimination, carry out formal investigations, and issue non-discrimination notices.

Low Pay Commission

1.106 This body, which consists of a chairman and eight other members appointed by the Secretary of State, was put on a statutory basis by the National Minimum Wage Act 1998, and is responsible for recommending to the Secretary of State the level of the national minimum wage. Before making regulations establishing the national minimum wage, the Secretary of State will refer the following matters to the LPC, ie:
(a) what single hourly rate should be prescribed as the national minimum wage;
(b) what shall be the pay reference period;
(c) what methods should be used for determining the hourly rate at which a person is remunerated;

(d) whether persons under the age of 26 should be excluded from the right to a national minimum wage, or be entitled to a different hourly rate;
(e) whether any other persons should be excluded, and if so, what hourly rate should be prescribed.

The role of the government

1.107 Following a Government reshuffle, the Department of Employment was abolished, and its various functions were reallocated to other departments. Responsibility for industrial relations policy and legislation, pay issues, redundancy payments, employment tribunals and ACAS has been taken over by the Department of Trade and Industry; the Department of Education and Employment is responsible for the Employment and Careers Service, adult and youth training, European social policies and programmes, work permits, women's issues, helping the unemployed back to work, and sponsoring the Equal Opportunities Commission. Responsibility for health and safety at work has been transferred to the Department for the Environment, and employment statistics and labour market surveys transferred to the Central Statistical Office.

1.108–1.115 The Secretary of State has power to issue Codes of Practice (TULR(C)A s 203), and codes have been issued on Picketing, Industrial Action Ballots and Notice to Employers, and Access to Workers during Recognition and Derecognition Ballots (see Appendix H). It is of interest to note that whereas codes of practice issued by ACAS, EOC, CRE and DRC are admissible before employment tribunals, those issued by the Secretary of State and DRC are also admissible in the courts.

The impact of the European Union

1.116 As from 1 January 1973, the United Kingdom became a member of the European Union, and by the European Communities Act 1972 (s 2) all obligations arising out of the various treaties which set up the EU are to be given legal effect in this country without further enactment. European law is thus of particular importance in the study of domestic employment law, for it will override domestic provisions. In order to understand European Union law, we must examine the treaties, the institutions and the nature of the legal rules which take effect.

A. Treaty of Rome

1.117 This Treaty was signed in 1957 by the original six founding states (France, West Germany, Italy, Belgium, the Netherlands and Luxembourg). The UK, Ireland and Denmark acceded to the Treaty in 1973, Greece in 1981, Spain and Portugal became full members in 1992 and Austria, Finland and Sweden joined in 1995. The original Treaty required unanimity between all the member states before laws could be passed. So far as is relevant, art 140 of the Treaty stated that one of the objects of the Community was to harmonise laws relating to 'employment, labour law and working conditions, basic and advanced training, social security, protection against occupational accidents and diseases, occupational hygiene, law of trade unions, and collective bargaining between workers and employers'.

1.118   In 1986, the Single European Act was signed in The Hague and Luxembourg, making certain amendments to the Treaty of Rome. These amendments were given effect in this country by the European Communities (Amendment) Act 1986. One significant change made was the introduction of a system of 'qualified majority voting' on certain issues. Each state has been allocated a certain number of votes (Germany, Italy, France and the UK have 10 votes each, Spain has 8, Belgium, the Netherlands, Portugal and Greece have 5, Austria and Sweden have 4, Denmark, Finland and Ireland have 3 and Luxembourg has 2). A qualified majority decision requires 62 out of the 87 votes available to pass a particular proposal. The significance is that qualified majority voting can be used to pass proposals relating to health and safety matters in the working environment under art 139 of the Treaty.

B. The Maastricht Treaty

1.119   In 1992 the Treaty of European Union (the Maastricht Treaty) was signed, expanding the scope of the Community's existing responsibilities, and introducing new policy areas. The ultimate aim is to create European citizenship, a single currency as part of economic and monetary union, a common foreign policy and a common defence policy. The concept of 'subsidiarity' was also introduced so that matters which could more usefully be dealt with at local or national level would not be the subject of Community action unless there was no other way the objectives could be achieved.

C. Treaty of Amsterdam

1.120   Originally, the UK Government opted out of certain social policy provisions which were contained in the Single European Act of 1986, set out in the Social Rights Charter in 1989, and implemented by a protocol to the Maastricht Treaty in 1991, as the 'Social Chapter'. However, by the Treaty of Amsterdam in 1997 the new UK Government announced its acceptance of the Social Chapter, and measures to implement directives so far approved have recently been introduced. In particular, the UK Government has implemented the European Works Councils Directive (94/45/EC), the Working Time Directive (93/104/EC) and the Parental Leave Directive (96/34/EC). Other directives due to be implemented shortly will deal with the rights of part-time workers, burden of proof in sex discrimination cases, and posted workers.

1.121   The Treaty of Amsterdam also brought about a renumbering of the Articles of the Treaty of Rome. Thus, freedom of movement is now art 39 (formerly art 48); the principle of equal pay for equal work is now art 141 (formerly art 119), and so on.

D. EU institutions

1.122   *Council of Ministers*   This is the supreme policy making body of the EU. Each meeting of the Council is attended by a minister from each member state. Usually, this will be the respective prime ministers or foreign secretaries, but sometimes, when specific detailed proposals are being discussed, the respective 'portfolio' ministers will attend. One member of the Council will hold the presidency for six months and then the position rotates. The Council is assisted by a Secretariat (comprising a staff of some 2,000) and preparatory work for the meetings is undertaken by frequent meetings of senior civil servants from the respective countries, known as the Committee of Permanent Representatives (Coreper).

1.123 *The Commission* This is sometimes described as being the 'bureaucracy' of the Union, but perhaps a more accurate description would be the 'engine room'. There are 20 commissioners (Germany, France, Italy and the UK each appoint two commissioners, the other member states each appoint one.) However, although appointed by their respective countries, commissioners are totally independent of them. Each commissioner has certain departmental responsibilities and is assisted by a cabinet and directorate general. Decisions are taken on a collegiate basis.

1.124 The Commission has the responsibility of initiating and drafting proposals for approval by the Council. It acts as a mediator between states, and as a 'watchdog' to ensure that EU rules are being observed. Indeed, if the Commission considers that a member state is failing to comply with an EU law, it can take enforcement action by referring the alleged breach to the European Court of Justice for a ruling (see para 1.157).

1.125 *European Parliament* This body sits in Strasbourg and Brussels and consists of 626 members of the European Parliament (MEPs) elected directly from each member state. It can express an opinion to the Council of Ministers on proposals which emanate from the Commission, can submit questions to both institutions, and can, as a final sanction, dismiss the Commission on a vote of censure passed by a two-thirds majority. The Single European Act introduced a co-operation procedure, whereby the views of the Parliament must be established prior to the Council of Ministers reaching a common position on any particular proposal.

1.126–1.135 *European Court of Justice* This Court sits in Luxembourg, and comprises 15 judges and nine advocates general. Appointments are made for six years. The Court gives rulings on the interpretation of European law, either on a reference from the Commission, at the request of the courts of a member state or on a claim brought by an individual person or corporation in a member state. Once it has given its ruling the matter is then referred back to the courts of the member state for compliance.

European Union law

1.136 For the purpose of this book, the law of the European Union consists of (a) Articles of the Treaty of Rome, (b) Directives passed by the Council of Ministers, (c) Recommendations, and (d) Decisions of the European Court of Justice. It must be borne in mind that any common law or statutory rule which is contrary to European law is void, and if there is any conflict between European law and British law, the former is to be applied. Indeed, if, in any preliminary proceedings, it appears that the sole obstacle towards granting interim relief is a rule of national law which is in conflict with European law, that national law has to be set aside (*R v Secretary of State for Transport, ex p Factortame (No 2)*). Further, the UK courts have now held that an organisation (*R v Secretary of State for Employment, ex p Equal Opportunities Commission*) or a private individual

(*R v Secretary of State for Employment, ex p Seymour-Smith and Perez*) can bring an action for a declaration that UK law does not correctly implement EU law.

A. Articles of the Treaty

1.137   If an article of the Treaty of Rome is clear, precise, unconditional, requires no further implementation, and does not give any discretion to member states, it is directly applicable and becomes an integral part of the law of member states (*Defrenne v Sabena*). For example, art 141 (formerly 119) of the Treaty of Rome provides 'Each Member State shall ensure and maintain the application of the principle that men and women should receive equal pay for equal work ...' This article has been invoked in a number of cases, and has been held to confer a distinct legal right on an individual, which can be enforced in national courts, in addition to any legal right conferred by national law (*Garland v British Rail Engineering Ltd*). Similarly, art 39 (formerly 48) of the Treaty provides that member states shall ensure the free movement of workers within the Community without discrimination as regards employment, remuneration and other conditions of work and employment, and this too has a direct legal effect (*Van Duyn v Home Office (No 2)*). Thus if a national of a member state wishes to obtain employment in the United Kingdom, he does not need a work permit, and he must be given equal access to social security benefits, holidays, equal pay, etc.

B. Directives

1.138   A Directive, passed by the Council of Ministers, is binding as to the result to be achieved, but the national authorities are given a choice of form and methods. However, as Directives are binding on member states, it is the duty of those states to implement them, and if the state fails to do so, an individual may seek to enforce the terms of the Directive against a state in its capacity as an employer (*Marshall v Southampton and South West Hampshire Area Health Authority*). For this purpose, 'the state' includes any body which is an emanation of the State (eg a nationalised industry) or which provides a public service under the control of the state. In other words, a State cannot take advantage of its own failure to comply with European law (*Foster v British Gas*).

In *Doughty v Rolls-Royce plc* the Court of Appeal laid down three criteria to be applied in considering whether or not any particular body is 'an emanation of the State', following principles laid down by the European Court in *Foster v British Gas*. These are:
(a)   whether the entity was made responsible, pursuant to a measure adopted by the state, for providing a public service;
(b)   whether the service it provided was under the control of the state; and
(c)   whether it possessed or claimed to exercise any special powers.

Thus, although Rolls Royce was 100 per cent owned by the state, it was a commercial undertaking rather than a state body for the purpose of enforcing the provisions of a Directive.

1.139   In strict legal theory, a Directive is not enforceable against a non-state body or a private individual. Thus, if there are no national rules on a subject, it is not permissible to rely on the provisions of a Directive as the basis of a claim. However, the European Court of Justice has gone a great deal further in two recent cases. In *Dekker v Stichting Vormingscentrum voor Jong Volwassenen (VJV-*

Centrum) Plus (see para 4.65), it was held that it is permissible to rely on the provisions of a Directive in order to interpret national law, and in particular those provisions of national law which were designed to implement a Directive. Thus the European Court will interpret national law in the light of the language and aims of the Directive. In *Marleasing SA v La Comercial Internacional de Alimentación*, the Court went still further. They stated 'It follows from the obligation on member states to take all measures appropriate to ensure the performance of their obligation to achieve the results provided for in Directives, that in applying national law, whether it was a case of provisions prior to or subsequent to the Directive, the national court called on to interpret it was required to do so as far as possible in the light of the wording and purpose of the Directive in order to achieve the result sought by the Directive.'

Finally, in an historic decision, the European Court has stated that if a member state fails to take the necessary steps to achieve the results required by a Directive, an individual who suffers damage thereby may sue the State for the loss suffered which results from that failure. In *Francovich v Italy*, the Italian Government had failed to implement EC Directive 80/987 on the protection of employees on an employer's insolvency. In consequence, an employee was unable to recover wages owed to him following his employer's insolvency, and he sued the Italian Government for compensation. It was held that his claim could succeed as long as three conditions were satisfied. These were that: (a) the result required by the Directive includes the conferring of rights for the benefit of individuals, (b) the contents of those rights may be determined by reference to the provisions of the Directive, and (c) there is a causal link between the breach of the obligation of the state and the damage suffered by the person affected.

Since these three conditions were met, the claim succeeded. However, the European Court appeared to suggest that a claim could be made not only when a member state fails to implement the terms of a Directive, but also when it incorrectly implements a Directive. Further, national courts are the appropriate forum for such claims, without the necessity of seeking a remedy in the European Court. However it should be noted that in *R v Secretary of State for Transport, ex p Factortame*, the Advocate-General expressed the view that such liability would only arise if the breach was 'manifest and serious', which suggests that inadvertent or unwitting breaches of European law may not necessarily attract such a remedy.

Thus, although Directives are addressed to member states, and can be enforced by intended beneficiaries against the state, there now appears to be an interesting remedy against a state which fails to implement or incorrectly implements a Directive by persons who suffer damage thereby.

It should be noted that '*Francovich*' style claims arising from an alleged failure by a state properly to implement a Directive must be brought in the High Court, not an employment tribunal (*Secretary of State for Employment v Mann*).

In a recent decision (*Brasserie du Pecheur SA v Germany*), the European Court of Justice gave guidance on the principles and approach to be adopted when national courts deal with *Francovich* type claims. The three issues considered were liability, damages and retrospection.

So far as liability was concerned, the Court stated that there was no difference in principle between those EU rights which were directly or indirectly applicable. Thus a right arising out of the Treaty (eg art 141) or a right against a state body by a state employee (*Foster v British Gas*) is to be treated in the same way as those rights which were indirectly applicable (*Marleasing SA v La Comercial Internacional de Alimentación*). Further, the state was to be considered as a single entity, and thus it did not matter if the breach was attributable to the executive, the legislature or the judiciary.

If the EU rule confers a wide discretion (as do most Directives), it must be established that it was intended to confer rights on an individual. If so, the next question to answer is whether the breach was 'sufficiently serious' in that there was a manifest and serious disregard of the discretion. This is for the national courts to decide, taking into account the clarity and precision of the rule that has been breached, the measure of the discretion given to national authorities, whether the breach was voluntary or involuntary, whether any error of law was excusable or inexcusable, whether it was caused or contributed to by any position taken by an EU institution, and the general adoption or retention of national measures which are contrary to EU law. A breach will be sufficiently serious if it has continued despite a judgment finding that there has been a breach, or where there has been a previous legal ruling from the ECJ making it clear that there has been an infringement.

So far as damages are concerned, the Court stated that national rules must not make it impossible or extremely difficult for an individual to obtain reparation, and damages awarded must be commensurate with the loss suffered. The criteria should not be less favourable than those applicable to similar claims based on domestic law. However, a national court is entitled to enquire into the steps taken by a complainant to mitigate the loss, in particular having regard to available legal remedies.

Finally, so far as retrospection was concerned, the ECJ was of the opinion that the main issue was whether the breach was sufficiently serious. If it was, then there was no temporal limit on the effect of an ECJ judgment. However, claims could be subjected to substantive and procedural limitations imposed by national law, which could take into account principles of legal certainty by applying time limits on claims.

1.140 Currently, there are a number of Directives in force which have a particular bearing on employment law, and which have been implemented by UK legislation.

1.141 (i) *Directive 75/117/EEC* (the Equal Pay Directive). This states that the principle of equal pay means, for the same work or for work to which equal value has been attributed, the elimination of all discrimination on grounds of sex with regard to all aspects and conditions of remuneration. Member states shall take the necessary measures to ensure that provisions appearing in collective agreements, wage scales, wage agreements or individual contracts of employment which are contrary to the principle of equal pay shall be declared null and void or may be amended. The Equal Pay Act 1970 and the Equal Pay (Amendment) Regulations 1983 implement this Directive.

1.142 (ii) *Directive 76/207/EEC* (the Equal Treatment Directive). This states that men and women shall be entitled to equal treatment as regards access to employment, including promotion, and also to vocational training and working conditions. There shall be no discrimination on grounds of sex, either directly or indirectly by reference to marital or family status. To comply with this Directive, reference may be made to the Sex Discrimination Acts of 1975 and 1986. Equal access to occupational pension schemes is now provided for in the Pension Schemes Act 1993, and equal benefits will come within the provisions of the Pensions Act 1995. The dismissal of a transsexual for a reason relating to a sex change is precluded by the Directive (see *P v S* para 4.102).

1.143 (iii) *Directive 75/129/EEC* (Collective Redundancies Directive). This Directive requires employers to consult with workers' representatives before making collective redundancies, and also requires that prior notification be given to the competent public authorities. The provisions of TULR(C)A ss 188–194 (as amended) are designed to meet this Directive.

1.144 (iv) *Directive 77/187/EEC* (Acquired Rights Directive). This Directive provides for the safeguarding of the rights of employees when their employment is transferred from one employer to another. The transferor and transferee are also required to consult with employees' representatives about the consequences of the transfer. The Transfer of Undertakings (Protection of Employment) Regulations 1981 (as amended) were passed to implement the Directive.

1.145 (v) *Directive 79/7/EEC* (Equal Treatment in Social Security Matters). This Directive requires that there should be no discrimination on grounds of sex (either directly or indirectly by reference to marital or family status) in the scope of social security schemes (ie sickness, invalidity, old age, occupational accidents and diseases, and unemployment benefits), the conditions of access thereto, contributions, the calculation of benefits (including benefits for spouses and dependants) and the duration of benefits. However, excluded from this Directive are benefits which arise from the determination of pensionable age. At the present time, women are permitted to receive the state pension at 60, whereas men receive it when they are 65 although the Pensions Act 1995 makes provisions for the progressive equalisation of state pensions at age 65 for both sexes, and this is permissible under the Directive. Other social security legislation has been passed to conform to its provisions.

1.146 (vi) *Directive 86/613/EEC* (Equal Treatment in Occupational Pension Schemes). This Directive requires that there shall be no discrimination between men and women in access to and benefits from occupational pension schemes. The Social Security Act 1989 was designed to implement the Directive, but further problems have arisen as a result of the decision in *Barber v Guardian Royal Exchange Assurance Group* (see para 4.112).

1.147 (vii) *Directive 86/613/EEC* (Equal Treatment for Self-employed). This Directive requires that the laws of member states relating to self-employment shall not contain any discriminatory provisions, that there shall be protection for self-employed persons and their wives during pregnancy and motherhood, and that discrimination does not arise from the establishing of businesses or other self-employed activities.

1.148 (viii) *Directive 80/987/EEC* (Employers' Insolvency). This Directive requires member states to guarantee the payment of certain outstanding claims due to an employee when his employer becomes insolvent, subject to certain limits. The provisions of the Insolvency Act 1986 meet the terms of this Directive.

1.149 (ix) *Directive 91/533/EEC (Proof of Employment Relationship)* requires employers to inform employees on the terms and conditions which apply to the employment relationship. This Directive has been given effect by ss 1–10 of ERA.

1.150 (x) *Directive 93/104/EEC* concerns aspects of the organisation of working time, with compulsory rest periods, and a maximum working week of 48 hours. This Directive was passed under the provisions of art 139 of the Treaty of Rome, which permits health and safety matters to be passed by a qualified majority vote. The lawfulness of this Directive was challenged by the UK Government (*UK v EU Council*) but the ECJ held that it was properly a health and safety matter, and in consequence, the Working Time Regulations 1998 were introduced.

1.151 (xi) *Directive 94/45/EC (European Works Councils)*. This Directive requires works councils to be set up in Community-scale undertakings, ie an undertaking with at least 1,000 employees in a member state and at least 150 employees in at least two member states. The Transnational Information and Consultation of Employees Regulations 1999 implement this Directive.

1.152 (xii) *Directive 96/34/EC (Parental leave)*. Men and women have an individual right to parental leave on the grounds of the birth or adoption of a child to enable them to take care of that child, for at least three months, until the child reaches the age of eight. The right is 'non-transferable' ie either a man or woman can take leave in respect of a child, but not both of them, and not alternatively. The Directive leaves it to member states to decide the details of how the scheme for parental leave should be implemented, eg on a full time or part-time basis, in a piecemeal way, or in the form of a time credit system. There is to be protection against dismissal for applying for or taking parental leave, and, at the end of the leave, workers will have the right to return to their old job, or to a similar or equivalent job. The Directive also requires states to provide that workers are to be permitted to take time off work in the event of *force majeure* for urgent family reasons in cases of sickness or accident. This Directive has led to the new provisions on parental leave (see para 7.89) and time off work to care for dependants (see para 7.81).

1.153 (xiii) *Part-time Work Directive (97/81/EC)*. This Directive requires the removal of less favourable treatment in respect of part-time workers. It has been implemented by the Part-time Workers (Prevention of Less Favourable Treatment) Regulations 2000.

1.154 A number of other Directives relating to health and safety at work have also been passed by the Council of Ministers, and these will be referred to in Chapter 11.

C. Recommendations

1.155 A Recommendation made under Community law has no binding effect, and cannot be relied upon to enforce a legal right in a national court. However, in *Grimaldi v Fonds des Maladies Professionnelles*, the European Court of Justice held that national courts are bound to take recommendations into account when determining disputes which are referred to them, in particular when they clarify the interpretation of laws passed to implement them, or when they are designed to supplement binding Community measures.

1.156 Recommendations have been made on such topics as the employment of disabled persons, hours of work and holidays generally, flexible retirement, vocational training for women and sexual harassment (see Appendix J).

D. Decisions of the European Court of Justice

1.157   The Court has jurisdiction under art 234 (formerly 177) of the Treaty of Rome to give rulings concerning the interpretation of the Treaty or Regulations or Directives made by the Council of Ministers. A member state may be taken to the Court by another state or by the European Commission (see *EC Commission v United Kingdom*, para 18.111). A British court may, but is not bound to, make a reference to the Court if it is necessary to enable a decision to be made (see *Macarthys Ltd v Smith*, para 5.93). Once the Court has given its opinion, the matter is referred back to the national court for the application of the opinion to the facts of the case (see *Jenkins v Kingsgate (Clothing Productions) Ltd*).

1.158   It should be noted that there are no specified time limits for bringing a claim under European law, as the provisions of the Treaty of Rome came into force upon accession (see *Stevens v Bexley Health Authority*). Time will start to run against a state body from the day the state makes good its failure to comply with the objectives laid down in the Directive (*Cannon v Barnsley Metropolitan Borough Council*). However, the European Court may, when giving a ruling, indicate that this shall only apply to claims lodged at the date of the ruling (*Barber v Guardian Royal Exchange*).

1.159–1.165   However, if a person is seeking to enforce a private right which has come to light as a result of the interpretation of EC law by the ECJ, national domestic procedures relating to time limits must be adhered to. Thus in *Biggs v Somerset County Council* the applicant was a teacher who worked for 14 hours per week. She was dismissed in 1976 but, relying on the House of Lords decision in *R v Secretary of State for Employment, ex p Equal Opportunities Commission* (which held that the 'hours' requirement was discriminatory and contrary to the EC Equal Treatment Directive), brought a claim for unfair dismissal in 1994. It was held that her claim was out of time. She was not seeking to enforce a Community right (there is no EC right to be unfairly dismissed), and there is no separate procedure for bringing claims under EC law (see also *Setiya v East Yorkshire Health Authority* and Chapter 20).

Human Rights Act 1998

1.166   In order to prevent a repetition of the horrors and atrocities which took place before and during the Second World War, the European Convention for the Protection of Human Rights and Fundamental Freedoms was signed in 1950. Many countries incorporated the Convention into their domestic law, but British citizens who wished to assert a Convention right were forced to petition the European Court of Human Rights in Strasbourg. The Government would always give effect to any ruling from the Court, but the Convention itself was not enforceable in British courts.

1.167   Nonetheless, the Convention did have an impact on the British legal system, and indeed, some notable decisions have been given against the British Government, where the ordinary legal system could not or would not provide a remedy. For example, in *R v Admiralty Board of the Defence Council, ex p Lustig-Prean*, the Court of Appeal refused to interfere with a decision to discharge the claimant from the Royal Navy on the ground that he was a homosexual, with the result that proceedings were instituted in the European Court of Human Rights.

That court held (*Lustig-Prean v United Kingdom*) that a decision to discharge homosexuals from the armed forces on grounds of their sexual orientation was a violation of their right to respect for their private lives, and thus contrary to art 8 of the Convention. The outcome was the lifting of the ban on homosexuals and lesbians joining or staying in the armed forces. A similar outcome was reached in three other cases (see *Smith v United Kingdom*).

1.168 The Human Rights Act 1998 is thus designed to give effect to the rights and freedoms guaranteed under the Convention, although it has to be admitted that the effect of the Act is at this stage somewhat unpredictable. In theory, it could have far-reaching implications for all branches of the law. Much will depend on the approach taken by the judiciary, in response to legal ingenuity.

1.169 The Human Rights Act 1998 came into force from October 2000, and provides that in determining a question which arises in connection with a Convention right, a court or tribunal must take into account the jurisprudence of the European Court of Human Rights. New legislation must contain a statement of compatibility with the Convention, and read in a way which is compatible with it. If this is not possible, the court can make a declaration of incompatibility, although this will not affect the validity of the provision, nor the outcome of the case.

1.170 There are a number of possible implications arising from the Act so far as employment law is concerned, although it should be noted that the Act is targeted against the powers of the State (including public bodies) and thus has no effect on the actions of private employers and/or individuals. Articles which may have some relevance include art 4 (slavery, servitude, forced or compulsory labour), art 6 (right to a fair and public hearing within a reasonable time by an independent and impartial tribunal), art 8 (respect for private and family life and correspondence), art 9 (freedom of religion), art 10 (freedom of expression), art 11 (right to freedom of association, and to join trade unions), and art 14 (prohibition of discrimination).

1.171 Although the Act was not in force at the time, it was considered by the EAT in *Smith v Secretary of State for Trade and Industry*, where an application was made to an employment tribunal against the decision of the Secretary of State refusing to make a redundancy payment. It was pointed out that art 6(1) of the Convnetion requires a person's civil rights to be heard by an impartial and independent tribunal. However, the rules of the employment tribunal are made by the Secretary of State, he appoints and pays the lay members and can terminate their appointment, and his Department funds the Employment Tribunal Service. Thus, although it was not suggested that the members of the employment tribunal would in any way act improperly or incorrectly, there is an apparent lack of impartiality when they are called upon to adjudicate in cases involving the Secretary of State. The EAT gave the applicant leave to appeal to the Court of Appeal, so that the matter could be argued more thoroughly.

1.172 The implications of the Human Rights Act on the employee's right to privacy is considered at para 10.39.

CHAPTER 2

The nature of a contract of employment

2.1 The complex form of modern industrial and commercial organisation enables people to work under a variety of legal arrangements which may be entirely satisfactory to all concerned, but which are difficult to rationalise into well-defined categories necessary for the purpose of legal analysis. Legal rights and responsibilities are frequently at the mercy of verbal distinctions, for modern terminology does not assist in the process of drawing precise lines between different economic relationships. The nineteenth century concept of 'master and servant', though somewhat servile by today's standards, at least had the merit of elegant simplicity.

Workers

2.2 Consider the term 'worker'. This can mean 'anyone who works for a living', and would thus include all from a managing director of a large public company to a machine operator in an engineering factory; a bookmaker's clerk on a race track to a surgeon in a hospital. Nowadays it is surely a mistake to use the term with a socio-economic undertone. On the other hand, the term 'workman' has, in the past, been given a more precise legal meaning, though it appears to be falling into legislative disuse as legal rights are given a wider scope.

2.3 Whatever the currently acceptable meaning of these terms may be, the law can place within its ambit anyone it wishes. Thus there are two current definitions of the term 'worker'. Section 296 of TULR(C)A states that a worker is an individual who works or seeks to work:
(a) under a contract of employment; or
(b) under any other contract whereby he undertakes to do or perform personally any work or services for another party to the contract who is not a professional client of his; or
(c) in employment under or for the purposes of a government department (otherwise than as a member of the armed forces) in so far as such employment does not come within (a) or (b) above.
  The Employment Rights Act 1996 (s 230) defines the term as an individual who has entered into or works under (or worked under):
(a) a contract of employment, or

(b) any other contract whereby the individual undertakes to do or perform personally any work or services for another party to the contract whose status is not by virtue of the contract that of client or customer of any profession or business undertaking carried on by the individual.

The reason the latter Act does not deal with Crown employment is because there are other specific provisions which take effect (see ss 191–192).

Although these two Acts define 'an employee' in almost identical terms, in the Sex Discrimination Act, the Race Relations Act and the Disability Discrimination Act the term is not defined, but 'employment' is defined as employment under a contract of service or apprenticeship or a contract personally to execute any work or labour, and thus both employment and self-employment are covered. The point is that the terms 'employment' and 'worker' are wider than 'employee', and thus employment rights are extended to a wider group of persons. This is in line with the modern trend to extend employment protection to all but the genuinely self-employed.

As we shall see, these terms do not cover certain 'office holders', and policemen and other members of the constabulary are also excluded. The point is that a worker is not necessarily an employee. It is a much wider term, though apparently not wide enough to extend to writers who submitted scripts to the BBC (who were 'selling' the right to perform completed dramatic scripts, see *Writers' Guild of Great Britain v BBC*). Nor does the term include a Church of England clergyman, because he is not a person whose rights and duties are defined by contract (*Housman v Bishop of Ely*). Thus all employees are workers, but not all workers are employees (*Broadbent v Crisp*).

2.4–2.10 As noted above, ERA s 230 defines an employee as an individual who has entered into or works under (or, where the employment has ceased, worked under), a contract of employment. The bulk of the legal rights to be discussed will be applicable to employees only, though a few apply also to workers. From one point of view, a person may be legally classified as an employee, and yet the same person may be a self-employed person from another standpoint. The 'economic man' refuses to be placed in neat legal pigeon-holes.

Employers

2.11 Thus the language of the lawyer, the economist, the politician and the layman tends to become confused in overlapping situations. In this book we are mainly dealing with the legal rights and duties of the employer and the employee. The employer is usually a readily identifiable entity, and may be defined as any person, partnership, corporate body or unincorporated association who (or which) employs one or more persons under a contract of employment, although this definition is not particularly helpful. In the building industry, for example, an 'employer' is the term used for someone who 'engages' a main contractor, whereas he ought properly to be described as 'the client'. Frequently, the 'acts' of the employer are in reality done by various levels of management, who are themselves employees, yet it is 'the employer' who will be called to account (eg *Courtaulds Northern Textiles v Andrew*). If the employer is an unincorporated association, a person employed by it will be employed by the members of the management committee for the time being (*Affleck v Newcastle Mind*).

Directors

2.12 A person who is a director of a limited company is not an employee of that company by virtue of his directorship, but he will be an employee if he had a service contract with the company, which can be express or implied. Every company must keep a copy of every written service agreement, or a written memorandum of a service agreement which is not in writing (Companies Act 1985 s 318). As a director, he can be voted out of office at any time by a simple majority of shareholders' votes at a general meeting of the company, but as an employee he will have all the protections afforded either by his service agreement or the rules of modern employment law. However, a company may not give a director security of employment for more than five years, unless the arrangement has been approved by a resolution of the company in general meeting (Companies Act 1985 s 319).

2.13 A service contract between a company and a director can be either express or implied. In the absence of a written agreement or memorandum, it must be ascertained if the person concerned worked as a director, and only occasionally worked in the capacity as an employee, or if he kept regular working hours, or worked full-time, and spent only short or insignificant periods on his duties as a director (*Folami v Nigerline (UK) Ltd*). Thus, if remuneration is by way of director's fees, rather than by a salary, if tax and national insurance contributions are not paid on the remuneration, and if there is an absence of a service agreement as required by s 318 of the Companies Act, it is unlikely that a director will be regarded as an employee of the company (*Parsons v Albert J Parsons & Sons Ltd*). It is also possible for the law to change a person's legal status in accordance with the circumstances. In *Road Transport Industry Training Board v Readers Garage Ltd* the question was whether industrial training levy could be assessed on the earnings of a controlling director who also worked as an employee, and the court held that if there was a contract of service implied between him and the company, the employment tribunal must assess how much of his drawings from the company were in respect of that service, and assess the levy on that amount. Any sum he received in his capacity as a director would not be assessed for levy purposes.

2.14 Technically, a limited company is a separate legal entity, distinct from the persons who control it. It follows that in legal theory there is no reason why a sole shareholder of a company cannot be regarded as an employee of the company. Thus in *Lee v Lee's Air Farming Ltd*, Lee owned all the shares in a company bar one. He was killed while piloting an aircraft, and it was held that his widow was entitled to benefit under a New Zealand statute which dealt with workman's compensation. However, this dichotomy does not appear to apply in respect of UK employment law, because a person who is a controlling director in fact controls the company, rather than the company controlling him. Thus in *Buchan v Secretary of State for Employment* the applicant had a 50 per cent shareholding in a private company. He worked for the company on a full time basis, was in receipt of an annual salary, paid tax and national insurance contributions, and was entitled to five weeks' holiday each year. However, he did not have a written service agreement. When the company went into liquidation, he applied to the Secretary of State for arrears of wages, a redundancy payment and a payment in lieu of notice. An employment tribunal dismissed his claim, holding that he was not an employee, and the decision was upheld by the

EAT. A controlling shareholder cannot be an employee for the purpose of ERA because he is able to prevent his own dismissal, and the EAT thought that it would be inconsistent with the purpose of the Act to extend its protection to a person who could not be dismissed from his employment. It followed that if he had no remedy against the company over which he had control, he cannot have any claim against the guarantor of the company's liability, ie the Secretary of State. The appointment of a receiver did not alter the applicant's status; if he was not an employee before the receiver was appointed, he did not become one after that appointment. The EAT thus distinguished *Lee v Lee's Air Farming Ltd*, on the ground that that case involved a claim for compensation under insurance arrangements.

2.15–2.25 There are a number of legal decisions by the EAT which confirm the approach taken in *Buchan*, including the Scottish EAT in *Fleming v Secretary of State for Trade and Industry*, although it was stressed that there was no rule of law involved in such a finding, the issue being one of fact. If a limited company is indeed a distinct legal entity, logic would suggest that in law it is separate from its directors, even if in practice the latter does control the former. Indeed, in *Secretary of State for Trade and Industry v Bottrill* the Court of Appeal disagreed with the reasoning in *Buchan* and held, on the special facts of the case, that a managing director who was also the sole shareholder of a limited company was an employee, and entitled to recover redundancy and other payments from the Secretary of State when the company went into liquidation.

Business consultants

2.26 A person who works in a consultancy or advisory capacity is capable of being an employee, depending on the legal and factual arrangements which are made. In *Bromsgrove Casting and Machining Ltd v Martin*, the applicant was a managing director of a company. He ceased to hold office, but continued to work as a director and consultant. There was no provision as to the number of hours to be worked, and his salary was unchanged. He was then dismissed, and he brought a complaint of unfair dismissal. It was held that in his capacity as a consultant, he was retained, not employed. His employment only came into being when he was actually called upon to give advice. Therefore, the employment tribunal should have enquired into the number of hours he was normally required to give advice, to see whether or not his contract was for the requisite number of hours per week in order to qualify for protection from unfair dismissal (nb: this is no longer a prerequisite for such a claim: see para 2.167).

Partners

2.27 A partner is a self-employed person in business who is remunerated by taking a share of the profits. Cases can be found where 'salaried partners' are known to exist. This is clearly a contradiction in terms. Architects and dentists frequently engage 'associates', and may make contractual arrangements which suit all concerned, but in law such persons, however designated, are probably employees. However, the contract of engagement may specify to the contrary. A junior partner, however, is a partner with (usually) a lesser share of the profits and/or a smaller say in the conduct of the partnership business. The modern vogue for co-partnership and profit-sharing schemes may well throw up further problems in the future, for although the mere fact of sharing profits is not evidence that a partnership exists (Partnership Act 1890 s 3), it could together with other relevant circumstances, lead to that conclusion (see *Glasgow v Independent Printing Co*).

2.28–2.35 If an employee is employed by a partnership, which ceases to trade, he may be able to recover a redundancy payment from the National Insurance Fund if he can show that he has taken all reasonable steps to recover the payment (ERA s 166). But in order to obtain arrears of pay, notice money, holiday pay and compensation for unfair dismissal under s 182 of ERA, he would have to show that the employer is insolvent, which means that each and every one of the partners must be adjudged bankrupt. As long as there is a partner who is solvent, it is from such a person that the employee must first seek payment (*Secretary of State for Trade and Industry v Forde*).

Office holders

2.36 A special category of persons exists who are technically known as office holders. They are not employed by virtue of a contract of employment, and therefore have certain privileges attached to their position. A judge, for example, holds office during good behaviour and may only be dismissed on a resolution passed by both Houses of Parliament. A magistrate is also an office holder (*Knight v A-G*). However, some office holders may also have a contract of employment, eg a stipendiary reader in the Church of England (*Barthorpe v Exeter Diocesan Board of Finance Ltd*). In *102 Social Club and Institute v Bickerton*, a club secretary was paid an honorarium of £225 per year. The EAT held that the employment tribunal should consider whether the money was paid by way of a salary for services rendered, or whether it was an honorarium for work done as a member of the club in his capacity as an office holder. In the former case only would he be regarded as being an employee.

2.37 Regular earnings received by an office holder are more akin to remuneration for work done than by way of honorarium for tenure of office. Thus his claim for the money is closely analogous to a claim for a salary due under a contract of employment. It follows that the office holder must be willing and able to render the services required of him, and that if he refuses to perform his duties (as a form of industrial action) his paymaster is entitled to withhold the relevant part of his remuneration (*Miles v Wakefield Metropolitan District Council*).

2.38 In *Johnson v Ryan*, the EAT held that there were three categories of office holders, namely:
(a) an office holder whose rights and duties are defined by the office they hold, and not by any contract (such as a police officer),
(b) persons who have the title of office holder, but who are in reality employees with a contract of service, and
(c) workers who are both office holders and employees, such as company directors.

2.39–2.45 Indeed, there is a fourth category of office holder, namely a worker who is not necessarily an employee. In *Perceval-Price v Department of Economic*

Development, the Northern Ireland Court of Appeal held that full-time holders of judicial posts in tribunals were 'workers' for the purpose of art 141 of the Treaty of Rome, and hence provisions in domestic law which provided that statutory officers were not to be regarded as employed under a contract of service had to be disapplied. So far as EU law is concerned, the criterion was the existence of an employment relationship, regardless of the legal nature of that relationship and its purpose.

There is little doubt that the categories of people who nowadays could properly be described as 'office holders' is declining, because formerly the offices in question were attached to incorporeal hereditaments, and many such titles are nowadays largely obsolete. In *R v BBC, ex Lavelle*, Woolf J commented: 'The distinctions which previously existed between pure cases of master and servant and cases where a person holds an office are no longer clear.'

Ministers of religion

2.46   Generally speaking, ministers of religion cannot be said to be employed under a contract of employment (*President of the Methodist Conference v Parfitt*). Although, in the past, employment tribunals have held that rabbis, Granthis and Inmans are employees, it is likely that those decisions are wrong (*Singh v Guru Nanak Gurdwara*). Thus in *Diocese of Southwark v Coker* it was held that an assistant curate was the holder of an ecclesiastic office, and not a person whose rights and duties were defined by a contract of employment.

Crown employees

2.47   The precise legal nature of the relationship between the Crown and civil servants has long been a moot point, but it now appears that since such arrangements have an intention to create legal relations, a contract of employment exists, enforceable by private law remedies (*R v Lord Chancellor's Department, ex p Nangle*). The provisions of the Equal Pay Act 1970 (see s 1(8)), the Race Relations Act 1976 (see s 72(2)) and the Sex Discrimination Act 1975 (see s 85(2)) do apply to the Crown. Most of the provisions of the Employment Rights Act 1996 apply to Crown employees, except those relating to rights to minimum periods of notice, redundancy payments, Sunday working for shop and betting office workers, and rights on insolvency! There are restrictions on the disclosure of information based on grounds of national security, but a Minister can no longer exclude the rights of certain employments on that ground (Employment Relations Act 1999 Sch 8). The provisions of TULR(C)A similarly apply, except the power of the court to make an order against an employer in respect of a failure to ensure that a check-off arrangement excludes a payment to the political fund of a trade union (s 87), failure to comply with a declaration of the Central Arbitration Committee requiring an employer to disclose information for collective bargaining purposes (s 184), and the procedure for consulting with trade unions on redundancies (ss 188–194).

2.48   Members of the staff of the House of Commons have been accorded the same statutory protection in most fields as that enjoyed by Crown employees by virtue of ERA s 195, with the House of Commons Commission (or Mr Speaker) being the employer. Staff employed by the House of Lords also have a similar full range of protections, except in relation to time off work for public duties connected with political activities and other minor exceptions (see ERA s 194 and TULR(C)A s 277).

2.49–2.55   However, where a person holds any office or employment under the Crown, which does not constitute a contract of employment, those terms shall be deemed to be such a contract for the purpose of the law relating to the liability in tort of any person who commits an act which induces another to break a contract, or interferes with the performance of any contract (or induces the interference), or consists of a threat that a contract will be broken, or its performance interfered with. In other words, Crown servants will be deemed to have contracts of employment for the purpose of tort liability arising out of industrial action, unless the protections of s 219 of TULR(C)A apply.

Armed forces

2.56   Various provisions in the Employment Rights Act apply to members of the naval, military or air forces of the Crown. These include written particulars, ante natal care, suspension on medical and maternity grounds, rights to maternity leave of absence, written reasons for dismissal, and unfair dismissal. The Sex Discrimination Act, Equal Pay Act and Race Relations Act also apply, but nothing is to be rendered unlawful if it was done for the purpose of ensuring combat effectiveness. Although there is a general rule that a member of the Armed Forces should go through service redress procedures before complaining to an employment tribunal, this is no longer always so (see Race Relations (Complaints to Employment Tribunals) (Armed Forces) Regulations 1997, Equal Pay (Complaints to Employment Tribunals) (Armed Forces) Regulations 1997, and Sex Discrimination (Complaints to Employment Tribunals) (Armed Forces) Regulations 1997).

Health Service employees

2.57   Employees of the National Health Service have the full range of employment protection rights (now including the right to redundancy payments, see National Health Service and Community Care Act 1990 s 60).

Police

2.58   A person is employed in the police service if he serves as a member of any constabulary maintained by virtue of an enactment, or in any capacity by virtue of which he has the powers or privileges of a constable. This includes special constables, but not police cadets (*Wiltshire Police Authority v Wynn*), nor prison officers, who are now 'workers' for the purpose of ERA and TULR(C)A (see Criminal Justice and Public Order Act 1994 s 126(1)). Otherwise, policemen, even though they may be engaged under a contract of employment in the police service, have few employment law rights. Thus, they are not entitled to an itemised pay statement, guarantee pay, rights under the Working Time Regulations, protection

33

for employee representatives, rights in protected disclosure cases, leave for domestic reasons, time off work for public duties, time off work as an employee representative, suspension from work on medical or maternity grounds, right to return to work after childbirth, written reasons for dismissal, and unfair dismissal (except in health and safety cases), even in respect of conduct which occurs when he is not exercising the privileges or powers of a constable (*Home Office v Robinson*). Nor can they claim in respect of unlawful deductions from wages (*Metropolitan Police Comr v Lowrey-Nesbitt*). A policeman does have the right to have written particulars of his terms and conditions of employment, minimum periods of notice, and redundancy pay.

2.59 A policeman is deemed to be employed by the chief constable or the police authority for the purpose of the Sex Discrimination Act (s 17) and the Race Relations Act (s 16) in respect of any act done by him, or the authority in relation to discrimination in employment, but not acts committed outside the course of employment (*Waters v Metropolitan Police Comr*). The Police (Health and Safety) Act 1997 applies the provisions of the Health and Safety at Work etc Act 1974 (see Police (Health and Saftey) Regulations 1999) to holders of the office of constable (ie police, including police cadets), even though they are not employed under a contract of employment. The Police Federation is to be treated as a recognised trade union for the purpose of appointing and consultation with safety representatives.

2.60–2.70 A policeman cannot be dismissed without a proper hearing in accordance with the rules of natural justice (*Ridge v Baldwin*) (see Police Act 1996 ss 84–85), and, in the event of wrongful dismissal, he has the right to be reinstated. Police cadets are persons training to become policemen, and are not employees (*Wiltshire Police Authority v Wynn*).

Status

2.71 Over the years a number of different groups of employees had additionally acquired a special legal status which overrode the existence of their contracts of employment (see, eg *McClelland v Northern Ireland General Health Services Board*), but 'status' relating to a person's occupation is now in decline, and in this sense it may be truly said that in employment law, 'there is a movement from status to contract'. Thus registered dock workers no longer enjoy the special protection which they had under the dock labour scheme (see Dock Work Act 1989), and tenure for all university staff appointed or promoted after 20 November 1987 has been abolished (Education Reform Act 1988 s 203). In respect of university academic staff appointed prior to that date, regard must be had to the terms of their appointment. If these state that dismissal is only possible for 'good cause' then it is not possible to dismiss for any other reason, eg redundancy (*Pearce v University of Aston in Birmingham*).

2.72–2.80 On the other hand, there are many groups of workers who have special protections and advantages by virtue of their situation, including pregnant women, trade unionists, safety representatives etc, and in this respect, therefore, 'status' still retains a certain significance.

Employees

2.81 An employee, though easy to define, is not so easy to describe, for the relationship between A (the employer) and B (the employee) is complicated by the fact that there is also a relationship between B and the state. It is possible that a person can be an employee for one purpose, but not an employee for another. Thus in *Challinor v Taylor* a taxi driver was the night driver of a cab which was used during the day by the owner. The latter paid for the fuel, insurance and maintenance of the car, and took 65 per cent of the gross takings. He also paid the cost of the employer's contribution towards the driver's national insurance stamp. The driver, however, was assessed for income tax purposes as a self-employed person under Schedule D. The owner sold the taxi and the driver was thus redundant. It was held that he was not an employee, and therefore not entitled to a redundancy payment.

2.82–2.90 There is no reason in principle why an employee cannot have more than two employers, and, provided he is within the appropriate protection of the law, pursue his legal remedies against either of them. Indeed, it is possible for an employee to have two contracts of employment with the same employer, so that if he is dismissed from his employment under one contract, he may pursue his remedy whilst still leaving the other contract subsisting (*Throsby v Imperial College of Science and Technology*).

Contract of service

2.91 The basic division for our purposes is between those who are employed persons and those who are self-employed, and the distinction between these categories is that the employed person works under a contract *of* service, whereas the self-employed person works under a contract *for* services. Again, it is easy to state this distinction, but in practice it has proved difficult to draw it, and over the years the courts have developed a number of tests designed to produce a given result. Also, under the Conduct of Employment Agencies and Employment Businesses Regulations 1976 (made under the Employment Agencies Act 1973) if a person is employed otherwise than under a contract of service or apprenticeship, he is deemed to be self-employed. To rebut this presumption, all the terms of the contract must be examined in detail (*Ironmonger v Movefield Ltd* and see *McMeechan v Secretary of State for Employment*, para 2.156).

2.92–2.100 It is possible for Parliament to ignore the distinction altogether; for example, the Sex Discrimination Act defines 'employment' as meaning employment under a contract of service ' ... or a contract personally to execute any work or labour ...' which definition clearly includes self-employed persons (see *Quinnen v Hovells*, para 5.4). It must thus be clear that the law may categorise workers as it wishes in accordance with the objectives to be achieved.

Control test

2.101 In the nineteenth century the determining factor was stated to be the control which was exercised by the employer over the manner in which the employee could do his work. Thus if the employer could tell the employee not only what to do, but how to do it, then a contract of service existed (*Yewens v Noakes*). In modern conditions the application of such a test is clearly unreal. An employee may be highly skilled and qualified, and employed specifically because he has professional training and competence, so that the employer is frequently unable (as well as being unwilling) to instruct the employee as to how the work is to be done. Despite this difficulty, some modern decisions have added to the control test, a refinement which looks for *the right to control* as being the determinant factor (*Gibb v United Steel Companies Ltd*), or even the existence of the right to control, even though this is seldom if ever exercised in practice. It is clear that the greater the degree of control which is exercisable by the employer, the more likely it will be that the contract is one of service (*Whittaker v Minister of Pensions and National Insurance*), but 'the greater the skill required for an employee's work the less significant is control in determining whether the employee is under a contract of service' (*Beloff v Pressdram*).

2.102–2.110   But the exercise of a degree of control is not conclusive. In *Hitchcock v Post Office*, the applicant ran a sub-post office as part of a shop he owned. Although the Post Office exercised control over many of its activities, it was held that this was because of the need to ensure financial control and security, rather than being a control over managerial functions. Consequently, the sub-post master was not an employee of the Post Office.

Organisational test

2.111   In *Stevenson, Jordan and Harrison Ltd v MacDonald and Evans*, Denning LJ suggested a more up-to-date test. 'Under a contract of service', he said, 'a man is employed as part of the business and his work is done as an integral part of the business'. This 'organisational' test has certain advantages, particularly in relation to skilled employees who are 'integrated' into an enterprise, eg doctors, nurses etc, in respect of whom the control test is inappropriate. In *Whittaker v Minister of Pensions and National Insurance* a trapeze artiste broke her wrist as a result of a fall in her act. It was held that she was an integral part of the circus business and thus an employee for the purpose of claiming industrial injuries benefit.

Multiple test

2.112   But these problems are too complex to be capable of being resolved by the application of any single simple test, and the courts nowadays will look at all the surrounding features, thus applying what is in fact a multiple test. Certainly the power of selection, the payment of wages, national insurance stamps, income tax, holiday monies and pensions, and the power to suspend and dismiss are all relevant features which need to be taken into account. In *Ready Mixed Concrete (South East) Ltd v Minister of Pensions and National Insurance* a firm dismissed its drivers, sold all the lorries to them and re-employed them under a contract which contained obligations capable of leading to the conclusion that they were both employed and self-employed persons. The drivers had to wear the company's uniforms, place their lorries at the company's disposal for a certain number of hours, only use them for the company's business, obey the orders of the foreman, and sell the lorries back to the company at an agreed current market valuation. On the other hand, the drivers had to maintain the lorries at their own expense and pay all running costs. In addition, they could employ a substitute driver, and could own more than one lorry. They paid their own income tax and national insurance contributions, had no set hours or meal breaks, and made their own decisions as to how to drive the lorries and which routes to take. MacKenna J held that there were three conditions necessary to establish that a contract of service existed. The first was that the employee agreed to provide his own work and skill in the performance of a service for his employer, the second was that there must be some element of control exercisable by the employer, and the third was that the other terms of the contract must not be inconsistent with the existence of a contract of employment. The fact that the drivers could (and did) employ a substitute was clearly crucial in deciding that they were self-employed haulage contractors.

2.113   As a general principle, it can be said that if a person is not contractually bound to perform the contract personally, he is not an employee. It is what is stated in the contract that will determine this, not what actually occurs in practice (*Express and Echo Publications v Tanton*).

2.114   More recently the entrepreneurial test seems to be the dominating feature. The problem is looked at from a self-employed person's point of view, and the question asked 'Is he in business on his own?' Again, no exhaustive list of considerations can be formulated. Does he provide his own equipment? Hire his own helpers? Is there any degree of financial responsibility for investment or degree of risk? Does he undertake any other sort of commission, business or employment? Is there any opportunity to profit from sound management? These questions were raised in *Market Investigations Ltd v Minister of Social Security*, where a company employed women on a part-time basis to do market research. They could work as they chose, but according to a set pattern. It was held that the women were employees, and not employed in business 'on their own'. The more unskilled and untrained a person is, the less likely it will be that the employment tribunal will hold that he is running his own business. In *Airfix Footwear Ltd v Cope* the applicant was a home-worker making heels for shoes manufactured by the respondent company. She was provided with the necessary equipment and material, and worked in accordance with instructions given to her. The EAT upheld a finding that she was an employee. On the other hand, in *Argent v Minister of Social Security* an actor taught drama on a part-time basis at a school. It was held that he was a self-employed lecturer.

2.115   In *Withers v Flackwell Heath Football Supporters' Club*, the EAT stated that difficult cases could be resolved by using industrial, rather than legal, terminology. Hence, the person could be asked a simple question, 'Are you your own boss?'

2.116   This pragmatic approach was taken even further in *Davis v New England College of Arundel*, where the claimant was engaged as a lecturer on a yearly renewable contract. He specifically asked to be treated as being self-employed as he wished to retain that status for income tax and national insurance purposes. He was not re-engaged, and claimed that he had been unfairly dismissed. It was held that to determine whether or not he was an employee, the matter had to be looked at objectively. His request to be treated as being self-employed, and the fact that the college so regarded him, did not alter the nature of the contractual relationship between him and his employer. In reality, he was an employee of the college, and hence he was entitled to bring a claim. It is the essence of the arrangement, rather than the form, which is the determinant factor (*Tyne and Clyde Warehouses Ltd v Hamerton*).

2.117 The difficulties inherent in such cases can be seen in *Massey v Crown Life Insurance Co* where the claimant was an employee of the respondents. It was then agreed that he should be treated as being self-employed, and a new agreement to this effect was signed. Although his actual duties were identical, the claimant was taxed under Schedule D, and paid self-employed insurance. He was then dismissed, and claimed unfair dismissal. It was held that he was employed under a contract for services. While the parties cannot alter the nature of their relationship by putting a different label on it, where the situation was in doubt, or was ambiguous, an agreement which stipulated the nature of the relationship affords strong evidence of what it is. In this case, there was a genuine attempt to change the legal situation to that of an independent contractor. There was no attempt to deceive the Inland Revenue. It was a genuine agreement to enable the applicant to be treated as being self-employed. Consequently, he could not claim that his dismissal was unfair. The Court of Appeal distinguished the case of *Ferguson v John Dawson & Partners Ltd* (see para 2.134) on the ground that in the latter case there was little evidence as to what the actual contract was.

2.118 In truth, before a clear and satisfactory answer can be given to the question 'Who is an employee?' we may well need to pose a second one, namely, 'For what purpose is the question being asked?' A part-time lecturer may well be a self-employed person for income tax purposes but an employee in relation to national insurance contributions, and he may well be an employed person (using the 'organisational test') if the issue was raised as to the vicarious liability of his employer for wrongful acts committed by him during the course of his work. The pragmatic approach adopted by the courts is to say that the matter is a question of fact, to be determined by the evidence in each case. For example, in *Maurice Graham Ltd v Brunswick* a company engaged self-employed bricklayers, who paid their own income tax and were responsible for their own national insurance contributions. The company was convicted of breaches of the Construction (Health and Welfare) Regulations 1966, and argued on appeal that those regulations only applied to 'employees', not independent contractors. It was held that though the outward arrangement gave the appearance of a worker being an independent contractor, this was not conclusive. The company controlled and supervised the men, and supplied them with the necessary equipment and materials, and the court refused to disturb the convictions.

2.119 An employment tribunal should therefore take the following factors into account, and make its determination accordingly:
a. the contractual provisions (*BSM (1257) Ltd v Secretary of State for Social Services*);
b. the degree of control exercised by the employer (*Global Plant Ltd v Secretary of State for Health and Social Security*);
c. the obligation of the employer to provide work (*Nethermere (St Neots) Ltd v Gardiner*);
d. the obligation on the employee to do the work (*Ahmet v Trusthouse Forte Catering Ltd*);
e. the duty of personal service (*Ready Mixed Concrete Ltd (South East) v Ministry of Pensions and National Insurance*);

f.   the provision of tools, equipment, instruments, etc (*Willy Scheiddgger Swiss Typewriting School (London) Ltd v Minister of Social Security*);
g.   the arrangements made for tax, national insurance, VAT, statutory sick pay (*Davis v New England College of Arundel*);
h.   The opportunity to work for other employers (*WHPT Housing Association Ltd v Secretary of State for Social Services*);
i.   other contractual provisions, including holiday pay, sick pay, notice, fees, expenses, etc (*Tyne and Clyde Warehouses Ltd v Hamerton*);
j.   the degree of financial risk and the responsibility for investment and management (*Market Investigations Ltd v Minister of Social Security*);
k.   whether the relationship of being self-employed is a genuine one, or whether there is an attempt to avoid modern protective legislation (*Young and Woods Ltd v West*);
l.   the number of assignments, the duration of the engagement, and the risk of running bad debts (*Hall v Lorimer*);
m.   the presence or absence of mutuality of the obligation to provide or do the work (*Carmichael v National Power plc*).

2.120   No single factor, by itself, is conclusive, and all the relevant circumstances must be considered. As long as the employment tribunals take these into account, their decision is a question of fact, not law, and their findings (either way) cannot normally be challenged (*O'Kelly v Trusthouse Forte plc* and see *Hall v Lorimer*) unless they took a view on the facts which would not reasonably be sustained (*Lee Ting Sang v Chung Chi-Keung*). However, if there is a written contract which determines the relationship between the parties, the interpretation of that contract is a question of law, which can be considered on appeal (*Davies v Presbyterian Church of Wales*).

2.121   The rule that no single factor can, by itself, be conclusive, is illustrated by the decision of the EAT in *City and East London FHS Authority v Durcan*. The claimant ran his own dental practice on a self-employed basis. Once each week, he worked on a rota at a local hospital, providing emergency services. He was paid a fixed fee, made his own arrangements for tax and national insurance, and, if he was unable to attend, he had to make arrangements for a replacement. When the hospital trust sought to reduce the number of hours worked, he claimed that he had been constructively and unfairly dismissed. The respondents resisted the claim, arguing that he was self-employed. The EAT noted that the claimant used the hospital's premises, equipment and medicines, but, on the other hand, he was not subject to any form of control as to how the work was to be done. The fact that he had to provide a replacement if he was unable to attend was not fatal to the existence of an employment contract, because the replacement had to be on an approved list, and this was not inconsistent with the modern trend towards job-sharing. It was true that the claimant did not enjoy the usual benefits of employment status, including sick pay, holiday pay, and notice rights, nor did he have the right to pursue any grievance procedure or take advantage of any disciplinary procedure. He had to treat any patient who attended for treatment, but his remuneration was not dependent on the number of patients who attended, and thus there was no risk or profit or loss from his working activities. The label attached to the relationship was not determinative of the worker's legal status, although it could tip the balance if all the relevant factors were evenly balanced. Mutuality of obligation is an important factor, but again not conclusive. Nor was it relevant that he worked only for a limited number of hours each week, because since the removal of the eight hour per week qualification, employment tribunals will increasingly be called upon to determine the legal status of workers who only work for a few hours each week. Taking into account all the considerations, the EAT refused to disturb the decision of the employment tribunal that the claimant was an employee, and was therefore entitled to pursue his claim.

2.122–2.130 A completely different approach was taken by the House of Lords in *Carmichael v National Power plc*, where the claimant was offered employment as a tour guide 'on a casual as required basis'. She performed work as and when it arose, but she was not obliged to take the work, and the company were not obliged to provide work and did not guarantee that work would be available. She was paid for the hours worked, and tax and national insurance contributions were deducted. She requested a statement of terms of employment under s 1 of ERA, and when this was refused, she complained to an employment tribunal. The House of Lords held that she was not an employee. There was no obligation for the company to provide the work, and the claimant was not obliged to take it when offered. Thus there was an absence of the irreducible minimum of mutual obligation necessary to create a contract of employment.

Distinction between employees and self-employed persons

2.131 There are a number of reasons for stressing the importance of this distinction between a contract of service and a contract for services, although recent decisions are tending to minimise this importance.

2.132 *a.* Under the Social Security Contributions and Benefits Act 1992 an employer must pay secondary Class 1 contributions in respect of employed earners (the primary contribution being made on an earnings related basis by the employed earner—which term includes an office holder). Self-employed earners pay a flat rate Class 2 contribution, and in addition a Class 4 contribution based on the gains or profits derived which are chargeable to income tax under Schedule D. The employer does not need to deduct PAYE income tax under Schedule E in respect of his self-employed independent contractors (who must make their own arrangements under Schedule D), and he need not pay a levy for industrial training purposes. An independent sub-contractor may have to charge VAT on services supplied, which would not be so if he were an employee. But it must be stressed that it is the substance of the relationship which will count, not the form. Thus if a person is an employee in the legal sense, the employer's obligations will arise despite any artificial attempt or arrangements made to avoid such duties (*Pennington v Minister of Social Security*). Nor does the fact that a person pays his own insurance stamps and is responsible for his own income tax payments necessarily mean that he is a self-employed person. In *Jennings v Westwood Engineering Ltd* the applicant was offered employment. He was told that he could work at a lower rate of remuneration on PAYE, or at a higher rate, paying his own tax and insurance, and he chose the latter option. It was held that he was employed under a contract of employment nonetheless. Conversely, in *President of the Methodist Conference v Parfitt*, the fact that the applicant paid Class 1 national insurance and was taxed under Schedule E did not *per se* make him an employee.

2.133 One of the more intractable industrial problems which caused concern some years ago was the existence of the 'lump', ie self-employed sub-contractors in the building industry. In *Construction Industry Training Board v Labour Force Ltd* when main contractors required labour they would contact Labour Force Ltd who would supply the men at agreed rates. The main contractor could dismiss the men but never paid them, and merely told Labour Force Ltd the number of hours each had worked. Labour Force Ltd paid the men on this basis, but the men agreed that they were self-employed, and agreed to be responsible for their own income tax, national insurance and holiday pay. It was held that there was no contract of any kind between the main contractors and the men, and further that there was no contract of service between Labour Force Ltd and the men, and consequently Labour Force Ltd were not liable to pay industrial training levy (which would be normally calculated on a percentage of the payroll).

2.134 The Court of Appeal has also indicated that it is concerned with the realities of the situation, rather than the form of the arrangement. In *Ferguson v John Dawson & Partners Ltd*, a builder's labourer agreed to work on the 'lump', or as the court found, as a 'self-employed labour only sub-contractor'. He was seriously injured as a result of the employers' failure to provide a guard rail on a roof, and he sued for this breach of statutory duty. He could only succeed if he could show that he was an employee, and, by a majority, the Court upheld this contention. Megaw LJ agreed that the 'lump' arrangement was a mere device, capable of being put to advantage by each side, but which did not affect the strict legal relationship between the parties. Dissenting, Lawton LJ thought that there was no reason in law why a man could not sell his labour without becoming the employee of the other party. Also, he thought that it was contrary to public policy to allow a man to claim that he was self-employed for the purposes of evading taxation, but an employee for the purpose of claiming compensation.

Certainly, where health and safety issues are being considered, there is a policy reason which leans towards holding that injured workmen are employees as opposed to self-employed specialist sub-contractors, and tax and other such considerations are less significant than those features which would lead to the conclusion that a contract of service exists. The responsibility for overall safety is an important factor to be taken into account (*Lane v Shire Roofing Co (Oxford) Ltd*).

2.135 The alleged problems caused by the 'lump' illustrate the difficulties in trying to squeeze 'the economic man' into tight legal compartments, for in the building industry there are large numbers of 'genuine' self-employed independent contractors who provide invaluable services, and no satisfactory way has been devised whereby the one can be distinguished from the other. Since one of the problems raised by the 'lump' was income tax avoidance, the Finance Act 1979 provided that an employer in the construction industry must deduct at source 25 per cent of the income price (excluding the cost of materials) of sub-contractors, which at least ensures that income tax liability is met by such persons. The 'genuine' sub-contractor may apply for a tax exemption certificate, provided he meets certain stringent requirements. But the problems of the industrial training levy, holiday stamps, safety, etc, remain to be resolved.

2.136 *b.* An employer will not normally be vicariously liable for the tortious acts (civil wrongs) committed by independent contractors (though there are certain exceptions to this rule) whereas he would be so liable for torts committed by his employees in the course of their employment which cause injury or damage to third parties (see Chapter 10). Two contrasting cases will illustrate this point. In *Hillyer v St Bartholomew's Hospital* the plaintiff selected a consultant who negligently performed an operation. It was held that the hospital was not liable, because the consultant was an independent contractor who was merely using the facilities of the hospital. On the other hand, in *Cassidy v Ministry of Health*, a resident surgeon operated negligently on the plaintiff, and it was held that the hospital board, as the employer, was liable.

2.137 *c.* An employer owes a duty at common law to his employees to take reasonable care for their safety, whereas these duties do not normally apply with respect to his independent contractors, although again, there are exceptions. Thus in *McArdle v Andmac Roofing Co* the claimant worked for one of several sub-contractors who were employed on converting a building at a holiday camp, who were all under the direction of Pontins (Contractors) Ltd. The latter had made no arrangements for safety precautions with the sub-contractors, and as a result, the claimant suffered severe injuries when he fell off a roof. It was held that the main contractors (Pontins) assumed the responsibility of co-ordinating the work, and were therefore under a duty to ensure that reasonable safety precautions were taken for all those who were working on the job, even though they were not the employers of those who were working. The duties owed by the employer to his employees under the Health and Safety at Work etc Act 1974 are more extensive than those owed to independent contractors (see Chapter 11). In practice this may mean that a self-employed person who is injured whilst at work may be unable to claim any compensation from the employer, and additionally will be unable to claim industrial injuries benefit and/or sick pay.

2.138–2.145 *d.* An employee is entitled to receive details of his terms of employment under ERA s 1 and to receive certain minimum periods of notice on his dismissal. He has protection against unfair dismissal under ERA, can claim redundancy payments in appropriate circumstances, and has various other rights under the Act. None of these benefits apply if the person is a self-employed independent contractor. On the other hand, a court may be able to make an attachment of earnings order whereby an employer is compelled to make certain deductions from the earnings of an employee; this is not possible in respect of a self-employed person.

Secondment of employees

2.146 Occasionally, an employer may second an employee to another employer for a certain purpose or a given period of time, and the question may then arise as to who is the employer of the loaned employee, particularly when the issue involves the responsibilities of the employer to third parties. For example, in *Mersey Docks and Harbour Board v Coggins & Griffiths (Liverpool) Ltd* the Harbour Board loaned a crane and driver to a firm of stevedores, the latter being responsible for the driver's wages. Because of the driver's negligence, there was an accident. It was held that the Harbour Board was the employer for the purpose of being held vicariously liable for the driver's negligence, for they had failed to discharge the burden of showing that the driver was no longer their employee. The courts will not readily accept that an employee has been transferred from one employer to another unless there is some evidence of his consent, and in general the first employer will still be responsible for ensuring a safe system of work (*Morris v Breaveglen Ltd (t/a Anzac Construction Co)*). But in *Arthur White*

(Contractors) Ltd v Tarmac Civil Engineering Ltd, a crane and a driver were hired out. Under the contract, which was the standard form used in the plant hire industry, the driver was stated to be under the direction and control of the hirer, and for all purposes was to be regarded as the employee of the hirer. It was held that as between the main employer and the hirer, the latter was liable for damages which resulted from an accident due to the driver's negligence. In other words, the two employers had, as between themselves, come to a contractual arrangement as to their respective liabilities, even though this did not necessarily affect the legal relationship which existed between the driver and his own employer.

2.147–2.155 But a person who is the temporary employer may incur liabilities in appropriate circumstances. In *Garrard v AE Southey & Co and Standard Telephones and Cables Ltd* the claimant was loaned by his employers (the first defendants) to the second defendants to carry out some electrical work. The foreman of the second defendants not only told the claimant what to do but also specifically controlled the way he was to do his work. The claimant was injured and sued both employers for common law negligence. It was held that the temporary employers were liable, as they were his employers for the purpose of ensuring his safety at work. The court drew a distinction between those cases where a complicated piece of equipment was loaned together with an employee, and where an unskilled or semi-skilled workman is loaned on his own. In the former case it may be easier to infer that the general employer does not intend to part with the control over a complex and valuable piece of machinery, but if labour only is loaned, it is easier to infer the transfer of the rights of the general employer to the temporary employer. Further, it will be noted that in the *Mersey Docks* case, the issue was the liability of the employer to third parties, and it will be rare that the courts will accept the transference of the employee in the absence of an express agreement to this effect (as in *Arthur White's* case). In *Garrard's* case the temporary employer was the one who could and should have been responsible for the safety of the employee, and a transfer of that burden was not unreasonable.

Agency workers

2.156 Occasionally an employer may turn to an agency to provide him with staff for a specific or indefinite period. An agency worker is not necessarily an employee of the employer to which he has been assigned, nor is he necessarily an employee of the agency. In principle, he is likely to be a self-employed person (*Serco Ltd v Blair*). Under the Conduct of Employment Agencies and Employment Business Regulations 1976, an employment agency (defined in s 13 of the Employment Agencies Act 1973) must, on entering into a contract with a worker, provide the worker with a written statement, which must include full details of the his terms and conditions of employment, stating, in particular, whether he is employed under a contract of service or a contract for services (ie as an employee or self-employed person), the kind of work which he may be expected to do, the minimum rate of pay, and details of any expenses payable. If there are changes in the terms and conditions of employment, a new statement must be provided immediately. If the worker who is engaged is under a personal obligation to do the work, then it is likely that the contract of employment may come into existence. On the other hand, if the duty of the agency is to provide workers, but there is no obligation to provide a specific person, then this would be a contract whereby the agency agrees to provide services, and the worker in question would not be an employee. Also if the employer pays the agency for the services provided, and the latter pays the employee, then again, no contract of employment exists. Some agencies act as employers by deducting all lawful stoppages (tax, insurance, etc) at source. Others merely act as a placing bureau. In *McMeechan v Secretary of State for Employment* the claimant worked for an employment agency under a series of temporary contracts. The terms of his engagement specifically stated that he was self-employed, but he was paid on a weekly basis when he worked, and tax and national insurance were deducted. The agency became insolvent, and the applicant sought to recover from the National Insurance Fund a payment in respect of wages owed to him from his last assignment. An employment tribunal dismissed his claim, the decision was reversed by the EAT, and that decision was upheld by the Court of Appeal, albeit on different grounds. The Court of Appeal drew a distinction between the general terms of engagement which exist with the employment agency, and the specific engagement the worker undertakes. In respect of the latter, a single task was capable of giving rise to a contract of employment, even though the worker might not be entitled to employee status under his general terms of engagement.

2.157   The Income and Corporation Taxes Act 1988 s 134 provided that if a worker is supplied to the client by an agency, and that worker is subject to supervision, direction or control as to the manner in which those services are rendered (or the client has the right to exercise such supervision, etc) then for the purpose of the Income Tax Acts, such services will be treated as if they were provided under a contract of employment, and any payments received by the worker, whether from the client or from the agency, shall be taxable under Schedule E. There are, however, a number of loop-holes in this provision. The terms of the contract between the worker and the agency may be relevant in determining the legal relationship which may exist in this tripartite situation (see *Construction Industry Training Board v Labour Force Ltd*).

2.158–2.165   A sponsored employee is the employee of the organisation he worked for, not the sponsor (*Secretary of State for Education and Employment v Bearman*).

Temporary employees

2.166   A temporary employee has all the rights of any other employee as long as he has the appropriate length of service. An exception here is to be found in ERA s 106, which states that if an employee is employed on a temporary basis in order to replace a woman who has been given maternity leave or to replace someone suspended on medical grounds, and the latter returns to work, the dismissal of the temporary employee will amount to some other substantial reason for the dismissal, but without prejudice to the rule that the employer must still show that he acted reasonably in dismissing the employee. It is essential that the employee has been informed in writing that the employment will be terminated when the absent employee returns to work. However, since it is unlikely that the temporary employee will have obtained the one-year qualifying period of employment, s 106 has little value. Also, in *Dean v Polytechnic of North London*, Sir John Donaldson thought that the temporary nature of the employment could well amount to 'some other substantial reason' so as to justify a dismissal, though the employment tribunal would have to be convinced that the employer had acted reasonably in the circumstances.

Part-time workers

2.167 The Part-Time Workers (Prevention of Less Favourable Treatment) Regulations 2000 are designed to implement EC Directive 97/81/EEC, and to ensure that part-time workers are to be treated no less favourably, in relation to terms and conditions of employment, than a comparable full-time worker. However, less favourable treatment will not be unlawful if it is objectively justified. The regulations came into force as from 1 July 2000.

2.168 Hitherto, any rights enjoyed by part-time workers were inextricably bound up with claims of sex discrimination, on the basis that since the majority of part-time workers were women, any less favourable treatment which occurred was because of their sex (eg *R v Secretary of State for Employment, ex p Equal Opportunities Commission*). The Part-Time Workers (Prevention of Less Favourable Treatment) Regulations 2000 will undoubtedly go some way towards the elimination of such claims. But the regulations only apply to direct discrimination, which is capable of being justified, whereas the Sex Discrimination Act applies to direct and indirect discrimination, and only the latter is capable of being justified. The part-time worker will always have to find a full-time comparator for the purpose of showing less favourable treatment, whereas under the Sex Discrimination Act, the search is for a person of the opposite sex.

2.169 The regulations apply to 'workers', not just employees. A worker is an individual who has entered into or works under (or worked under):
(a) a contract of employment
(b) any other contract, whether express or implied, whereby the individual undertakes to do or perform personally any work or services for another party to the contract whose status is not by virtue of the contract that of a client or customer of any profession or business undertaking carried on by the individual.

2.170 In other words, a worker is anyone who works for another person (not necessarily under a contract of employment) other than in a professional or business relationship. Only genuinely self-employed persons are excluded from the regulations.

2.171 A part-time worker is defined as one who is paid wholly or in part by reference to the time he works and, having regard to the custom and practice of the employer in relation to workers employed by the worker's employer under the same type of contract is not identifiable as a full-time worker. Conversely, a full-time worker is a worker who is paid wholly or in part by reference to the time he works and, having regard to the custom and practice of the employer in relation to workers employed by the worker's employer under the same type of contract, is identifiable as a full-time worker.

2.172 In order to avoid being subjected to less favourable treatment, the part-time worker must be able to compare his treatment with that given to a full-time worker. This involves finding the comparator. A full-time worker will be comparable if:
(a) both workers are employed by the same employer under the same type of contract, and engaged in the same or broadly similar work, having regard,

45

where relevant, to whether they have a similar level of qualifications, skills and experience, and

(b) the full-time worker works or is based at the same establishment as the part-time worker or, where there is no full-time worker working or based at that establishment, works or is based at a different establishment and satisfies the above requirements.

2.173 A full-time worker who becomes a part-time worker can compare his treatment with the way he was treated when he was full-time. A worker who has had a period of absence (which cannot exceed more than 12 months) and then returns to work at the same job or to a job at the same level but with fewer hours can compare his treatment with the way he was treated prior to his absence.

2.174 A part-time worker has the right not to be treated by his employer less favourably than a full-time worker is treated, as regards the terms of his contract, or be subjected to any detriment by any act, or deliberate failure to act, of his employer (reg 5). However, this right only applies if the treatment is on the ground that the worker is a part-time worker, and cannot be justified on objective grounds. A pro rata principle must be applied unless it is inappropriate to do so. Thus, where a comparable full-time worker is entitled to receive pay or any other benefit, a part-time worker is entitled to receive not less than the proportion of that pay or benefit that the number of his weekly working hours bears to the number of weekly working hours of the comparable full-time worker.

2.175 If a part-time worker considers that he is receiving less favourable treatment than a full-time worker (bearing in mind the pro rata principle) he may request from his employer a written statement giving particulars of the reasons for the treatment. The employer shall provide the statement within 21 days, but if, in subsequent tribunal proceedings, the tribunal finds that the employer deliberately and without reasonable excuse omitted to provide the statement or finds that the written statement is evasive or equivocal, the tribunal may draw any inference which it considers to be just and equitable to draw, including an inference that the employer has infringed the right in question (reg 6).

2.176 It is thus clear that as a matter of principle, part-time workers must be paid the same rate of pay as comparable full-time workers. Contractual sick pay, maternity pay, access to pension schemes, access to training, holiday entitlement, etc must all be no less favourable, on a pro rate basis. Statutory rights, such as time off work (see Chapter 7) apply. Any different treatment, eg on redundancy selection, or severance payments, must be capable of being justified (*Barry v Midland Bank plc*). But if a part-time worker works overtime, he will not be entitled to any overtime premium which a full-time worker receives until he works the normal standard working hours of the full-time worker. Also, since a part-time worker is not required to pay national insurance contributions if his or her wages are below the lower earning limit, this may result in the exclusion from the right to receive statutory maternity pay and statutory sick pay.

2.177 A worker has the right not to suffer a detriment because he brought proceedings under the regulations, or requested a written statement, or gave evidence or information in connection with such proceedings brought by any worker, or otherwise did anything under the regulations, or alleged that the employer had infringed the regulations, or refused to forgo a right conferred by the regulations, or because the employer believed that the worker has done or intends to do any of these things. It will also be an automatic unfair dismissal to dismiss an employee (but not a worker) on any of those grounds (reg 7).

2.178 A worker may lodge a complaint to an employment tribunal that his rights under the regulations have been violated (within the usual time limits: see Chapter 20). The burden will be on the employer to identify the grounds for any less favourable treatment or detriment. The tribunal can make the usual awards (declaration, compensation, and recommendation) but not compensation for injury to feelings. The claimant is under a duty to mitigate the loss, and the rules on contributory conduct apply.

2.179 The regulations provide that so far as the police are concerned, the holding of an office of constable or police cadet (otherwise than under a contract of employment) shall be treated as being employment under a contract of employment. The regulations also apply to Crown employment, members of the armed forces, staff of the House of Lords and House of Commons, but not, apparently, to an individual in his capacity as the holder of a judicial office if he is remunerated on a daily fee-paid basis (it is submitted that this latter exclusion is capable of being challenged, there being no such provision which permits such derogation in EC Directive 97/81/EEC).

2.180-2.185 A set of guidance notes has been issued to assist in compliance with the regulations. Basically, these suggest that, unless there is some objective justification, part-time workers should receive the same treatment as full-time comparable workers, when considering hourly rates of pay, contractual sick pay and maternity pay (applied pro rata), access to pensions schemes, training, holiday entitlement, contractual maternity and parental leave, career breaks, selection for redundancy, etc. Less favourable treatment may be objectively justified if he intended to achieve a legitimate objective, is necessary to achieve that objective, and it is an appropriate way of doing so,

Probationary employees

2.186 The essence of a probationary appointment is that the employer retains the right not to confirm the appointment after a specified period, particularly on the grounds of capability. The majority of the tribunal in *Donn v Greater London Council* thought that the tests which are applied to a probationary employee are not necessarily the same as those which apply to a confirmed appointment, and a decision not to retain a probationer may be justified even though a similar decision made with respect to a fully established employee may not be justified. This view has been followed on a number of occasions (eg *Hamblin v London Borough of Ealing*), for a probationary employee must know that he is on trial, and must therefore establish his suitability for the post. The employer, however, must give the employee a proper opportunity to prove himself, and give a warning if the required standards are not being met (*Post Office v Mughal*). A probationary employee is still an employee, and is therefore entitled to have appropriate guidance and advice (*Inner London Education Authority v Lloyd*).

2.187 Certainly, if the probationary period is less than one year, few problems will arise, but a longer probationary period could create difficulties. In *Weston v*

University College, Swansea the applicant was appointed as a lecturer for the probationary period of three years. At the end of this time he was not placed on the permanent staff. It was held that he was entitled to pursue his complaint in respect of his alleged unfair dismissal, for his contract was not for a fixed term. The employer must still show that he acted reasonably in dismissing a probationer, and that the reason was within the statutory requirements, and it is submitted that if a different test is to be applied, the employer must show a valid reason why a probationary period of such a length of time is required in order to establish the suitability of the employee for the post in question.

2.188–2.195 If an employee is told that his appointment is subject to a probationary period of a certain length of time, this does not give him a legal right to be employed for that length of time, and the employer may lawfully dismiss him before that period has expired (*Dalgleish v Kew House Farm Ltd*) as long as he is given his correct contractual notice (*Fosca Services (UK) Ltd v Birkett*).

Trainees

2.196 Section 230 of ERA defines a contract of employment as 'a contract of service or apprenticeship, whether express or implied, and (if it is express) whether it is oral or in writing'. It is clear, therefore, that a trainee can be employed under a contract of employment, and this includes, for example, an articled clerk employed by a solicitor (*Oliver v JP Malnick & Co*). However, not all such trainees are so employed. In *Wiltshire Police Authority v Wynn*, it was held that police cadets are not employees, but persons who are training to become policemen. During their training, even though they are being paid, they are not employed under a contract of employment. Similarly, in *Daley v Allied Suppliers Ltd* a young black girl was working on a Youth Opportunities scheme operated by the respondents. She alleged that she had been discriminated against on the ground of race, but it was held that the Race Relations Act was not applicable, as she was not a person employed within the meaning of s 4 and s 78 of the Act.

2.197–2.205 Indeed, the fact that young people on work experience courses are not employees has caused some concern, particularly in relation to their health and safety, for many of the duties owed by an employer are only owed to employees. Consequently the Health and Safety (Training for Employment) Regulations 1990 apply the provisions of the Health and Safety at Work etc Act 1974 to youth trainees as if they were employees.

Minors

2.206 A contract of employment entered into by a minor (ie a person under the age of 18) is a valid agreement provided that on the whole it is substantially for his benefit. Otherwise, it will be void. Even though the contract contains terms which are onerous or detrimental to his interests, one must look at the effect of the whole agreement. In *De Francesco v Barnum* a 14-year-old girl bound herself by an apprenticeship deed to the claimant in order to become a professional dancer. She agreed not to marry during this time, and to perform engagements only with the plaintiff's permission. The claimant was under no obligation to provide engagements, but when he did, the pay was somewhat ungenerous. It was held that the deed was void, for it was totally unreasonable, and was not in the interests of the girl. In contrast, we can consider *Clements v London and North-Western Rly Co*, where a boy entered into the defendants' employment on terms which excluded his right to sue under the Employers' Liability Act 1880, in respect of injuries suffered during his employment. Instead, he was covered by the company's own insurance scheme, which had a wider range of protection, though the benefits were somewhat lower than the State scheme. It was held that on the whole the contract was to his advantage and was therefore binding.

2.207–2.215 Cases on this subject illustrate somewhat graphically the changing social scene. In *Denmark Productions Ltd v Boscobel Productions Ltd* a contract by four infant members of a pop group to employ a manager was held to be binding, and in *Chaplin v Leslie Frewin (Publishers) Ltd* the son of a famous film star contracted to assign to a firm of publishers a book containing his life story. This too, was held to be binding, as it conferred a financial benefit on him.

Young persons

2.216 Special protection is given to young persons, ie persons over compulsory school leaving age but below the age of 18, by the Management of Health and Safety at Work Regulations 1999. Before employing a young person, the employer must make a risk assessment, taking into account his inexperience, lack of awareness of risks and immaturity, the fitting and layout of the workplace, exposure to physical, biological and chemical agents, the way work equipment is handled, the organisation of the processes, the extent to which health and safety training is provided, and the risks from certain dangerous processes. Employers must ensure that young persons are protected at work from any risks to their health and safety which are a consequence of their lack of experience, absence of awareness of risks and lack of maturity. Special provision has been made for young persons in the Working Time Regulations 1998 (see para 7.221).

Children

2.217 The Children (Protection at Work) Regulations 1998 deal with the employment of children below the minimum school leaving age. Hitherto, restrictions on the working hours of children were contained in local authority byelaws, but these are now to be standardised by virtue of provisions contained in the Children and Young Persons Act 1933 and the Children and Young Persons (Scotland) Act 1937. Children will have the right to have a two-week break from any work during school holidays, and local authorities will update their byelaws to include a list of jobs which a 13-year-old child may do. No child of that age may do a job unless it is on the list. The Children (Performances) Regulations 1968 will be amended so as to extend controls on the employment of children in performances to include sport, advertising and modelling. Further information about the new rules can be obtained from the education welfare office of a local education authority. Local authorities have the power to prohibit the employment of children who are employed in a manner which may be prejudicial to their health, or render them unfit to obtain the benefit of full-time education, and they may also impose restrictions on such employment (Education Act 1996 s 559). A child may not be employed in an industrial undertaking or on a sea-going boat, unless the undertaking or boat is one in which only members of the child's family are employed (Employment of Women, Young Persons, and Children Act 1920 ss 1–3). A child may not be employed in a factory (Education Act 1918 s 14) nor employed underground in a mine, except for the purpose of receiving prescribed instruction (Mines and Quarries Act 1954 s 124). A child may not be required to lift, carry or move anything so heavy as to be likely to cause injury.

2.218–2.225   School children may be employed for work experience from the beginning of the school term preceding the start of the school year in which they become entitled to leave school (Education (Work Experience) Act 1973 s 1, as amended).

Apprentices

2.226   A contract of apprenticeship is an agreement whereby the apprentice binds himself to his employer in order to learn a trade, and the employer on his part agrees to teach and instruct him. The contract must be in writing, signed by the parties, and cannot be terminated by the employer except for grave misconduct (such as theft) or a refusal to attend to his duties. However, it appears that there is no longer any need for a formal apprenticeship agreement to be entered into; to give a statement of terms and conditions which described a person as an 'apprentice sheet metal worker' was sufficient to create a contract of apprenticeship in *Wallace v C A Roofing Services Ltd*, and it was not possible to terminate that contract on grounds of redundancy. An apprentice who is wrongfully dismissed may claim by way of damages not only his immediate loss, but a sum representing the value of his loss of future prospects as a qualified person (*Dunk v George Waller & Son Ltd*). Also, since an employer is, in one sense, *in loco parentis* to an apprentice, a certain latitude must be shown in respect of minor lapses in conduct. For example, in *Shortland v Chantrill*, an apprentice was criticised by a managing director about his work, and he retorted 'You couldn't have done any fucking better'. For this, he was dismissed. It was held that the dismissal was unfair; one isolated step of impudence did not warrant the termination of an apprenticeship which had only ten months to run.

2.227   But although a contract of apprenticeship is essentially a common law concept, with the old (ie pre-1971) remedies still applying, an apprentice is also within the protection of the new laws. This could cause a certain conflict. For example, in *Finch v Betabake (Anglia) Ltd* the claimant was an apprentice motor mechanic. The employers received a report from an ophthalmic surgeon that the apprentice could not continue to work at that job without undue danger to himself and to other employees. Consequently, he was dismissed. It was held that the fairness of the dismissal had to be determined under ERA s 98(4) (see Chapter 17). The fact that the employers may have been in breach of the apprenticeship agreement did not mean that the dismissal was unfair. The circumstances which could justify the dismissal of an apprentice were very limited, but in the instant case, the employers acted fairly and reasonably.

2.228–2.235   If, on the expiry of an apprenticeship agreement, the apprentice is not re-employed, he has not been dismissed for reason of redundancy (*North East Coast Shiprepairers v Secretary of State for Employment*).

Domestic servants

2.236 A domestic servant is an employee, and provided she has the requisite periods of continuous employment, may claim appropriate statutory rights. She may claim redundancy payment, for employment in a private household is deemed to be a business like any other. However, this does not apply if she is a close relative of the employer (see para 18.101). Nor do the special rules relating to the transfer of a business apply, except where the head of the household dies, for here there may be a transfer to the new head of the household for redundancy purposes (see ERA s 175 and *Ranger v Brown*). The Race Relations Act 1976 does not apply to employment for the purpose of a private household, and under the Sex Discrimination Act 1975 (as amended in 1986) the sex of a person may be 'a genuine occupational qualification' (see para 4.132) if the employment is in a private home.

Foreign employees

2.237 A person who is not a national of a member state of the European Economic Area (ie European Union, Iceland, Liechtenstein and Norway), or who is not a Commonwealth citizen with the right of abode, must obtain the necessary permission to take up employment in Great Britain, otherwise the employment will be illegal. The Immigration Rules currently in force detail a number of different categories of workers who may be granted entry clearance to enter this country for specified periods of time, with or without work permits, and the conditions which will be attached thereto if they wish to take up employment. A consideration of these matters is outside the scope of this book, but information can be obtained from either the Home Office or the Overseas Labour Services section of the Department of Education and Employment.

2.238 The illegality of the employment has two consequences. In the first place, a person who is employed under an illegal contract cannot acquire any legal rights under that contract. Thus he will have no employment protection rights at all (*Sharma v Hindu Temple*). Additionally, if the contract was legal at one time, periods when the contract became illegal will not count towards continuity of employment, and will also break continuity (*Bamgbose v Royal Star and Garter Home*).

2.239 Second, s 8 of the Asylum and Immigration Act 1996, which came into force in January 1997, makes it a criminal offence to employ in the UK a person who is subject to immigration control, if that person has not been given leave to enter or remain in the UK, or his leave is not valid, or he is subject to a condition precluding him taking employment. An employer found guilty of this offence may be fined an amount not exceeding level 5 on the standard scale (currently £5,000) for each offence, and, where the offence is committed by a body corporate, any director, manager, secretary of similar officer will be jointly liable, if the offence was committed with his consent, connivance, or attributable to any neglect on his part. The above offence does not apply if the employee was an asylum seeker who has been given written permission to work, or an asylum seeker who had permission to work before appealing against a refusal to grant asylum. It will be a defence for the employer to show that before the employment began, he was shown a document which related to the employee, and which was of a description specified in an order made by the Secretary of State. The documents in question are set out in the Immigration (Restrictions on Employment) Order 1996, and include a passport, a document issued by a previous employer (P45 or P60) or the Inland Revenue or Benefits Agency etc, which contain a national insurance number, a birth certificate issued in the UK or a certificate of registration or naturalisation as a British citizen, etc. A copy of the document must be kept for the duration of the employment and for a further six months after it ends.

2.240   The purpose behind s 8 was to try to limit the number of foreign nationals working here illegally. However, the requirement that before permitting a person to commence employment, the employer must ask certain questions and seek confirmation of nationality or status raises issues of race discrimination (*Dhatt v McDonalds Hamburgers Ltd*). The CRE has issued provisional guidelines for employers which contain a number of 'good practice recommendations'.

2.241–2.250   If the employment of a foreign worker is perfectly legal, then he will have all the employment protection rights which are applicable to his case, in the same manner as a UK or EU national, apart from being able to obtain employment in certain official posts.

Offshore employment

2.251–2.260   Offshore employment is defined as employment for the purposes of activities:
(a)   in the territorial waters of the United Kingdom; or
(b)   connected with the exploration of the seabed or subsoil, or the exploration of their natural resources, in the United Kingdom sector of the continental shelf; or
(c)   connected with the exploration or exploitation, in a foreign sector of the continental shelf, of a cross-boundary petroleum field (ERA s 201; TULR(C)A s 287).

2.261–2.270   Orders have been made extending the provisions of various employment legislation to offshore employment, including the Employment Rights Act 1996 (except time off work for public duties), Sex Discrimination and Race Relations Acts, Equal Pay Act 1970, Wages Act 1986 and Trade Union and Labour Relations (Consolidation) Act 1992. Employment in the Grigg Gas Field comes within the scope of the various Acts if the employer is a British company, or has a place of business in Great Britain from which the activities are directed.

Retainers

2.271   A person who is retained for employment is not an employee merely because he is 'on call' even though he is paid during that time. Employment involves work or other activity carried out for the employer. In *Suffolk County Council v Secretary of State for the Environment* it was held that a retained fireman, who was permanently on call, was not an employee, for a contractual obligation to remain on call within a prescribed area did not constitute employment. His hours of work only began when he was on duty following a call.

National security (ERA s 193)

2.272 The provisions relating to protected disclosures (ss 43A–43L of ERA) do not apply in relation to employment for the purposes of the Security Service, the Secret Intelligence Service or the Government Communications Headquarters. If a complaint is made under s 146 of TULR(C)A (detriment for trade union membership, see para 21.58) or s 111 of ERA (unfair dismissal, see Chapter 17) and it is shown that the action complained of was taken for the purpose of safeguarding national security, the employment tribunal shall dismiss the complaint. The former power of a Minister of the Crown to issue a conclusive certificate that the act was done on the grounds of national security has been repealed, and staff in the security and intelligence services, as well as other Crown employees, may present claims to an employment tribunal in the normal way. However, in such cases, a specially constituted employment tribunal will be convened, with special powers and procedures to ensure that secrecy and confidentiality is maintained (see Employment Tribunals Act s 10 and regulations to be made thereunder).

Global contracts

2.273 There are some employees who work on short-term periodic contracts, with various breaks of employment in between. Attempts have been made to treat such employees as having been employed under one 'global contract', but so far with limited success (see *Boyd Line Ltd v Pitts*). For a global contract to exist, there must be mutual legally binding obligations on both sides, and it cannot be brought into existence merely by counting together a number of individual contracts which have subsisted over a period of time (see *Hellyer Bros Ltd v McLeod*). Thus if the employer is under no obligation to provide work under the contract, and equally the employee is not obliged to perform any work offered, then no global contract can exist. In *Clark v Oxfordshire Health Authority* the claimant was a nurse who was offered work as and when a temporary vacancy arose. The Court of Appeal refused to find that there was a global contract, in the absence of any mutuality of obligations. But the existence of a retainer during the periods when work was not offered would undoubtedly be strong evidence of a global contract.

In *Carmichael v National Power plc* the appellant was engaged as a guide at a power station. She was paid for the number of hours worked, and had tax and national insurance deducted. Her contract stated that she was employed 'on a casual and as required basis.' The Court of Appeal held that, on the facts of the case, there was an implied term that the employer would offer her a reasonable amount of work, and that if so offered, she would carry out a reasonable amount of work. Thus it was held that a contract of employment existed. However, the House of Lords disagreed, and held that she was not an employee. The absence of mutuality of obligation will frequently by determinative of the matter, for if a person is not obliged to offer work, and the other party is not obliged to accept the work when offered, there is an absence of the irreducible minimum of mutual obligation necessary to create a contract of employment. It would therefore appear that the fact that a contract is repeated does not create a global contract of employment.

Fixed-term contracts

2.274 A fixed-term contract is a contract of employment for a specified period of time, ie, with a defined beginning and a defined end (*Wiltshire County Council v National Association of Teachers in Further and Higher Education and Guy*). As a general rule, such a contract cannot be terminated before its expiry date except for gross misconduct or by mutual agreement (*Lyritzis v Inmarsat*). However, a contract can still be for a fixed term if it contains within it a provision enabling either side to terminate it on giving notice before the term expires (*Dixon v BBC*). A contract of apprenticeship is a classic example of a fixed-term contract (*Wallace v CA Roofing Services Ltd*).

2.275 Contracts 'to perform a specific task' (*Ryan v Shipboard Maintenance Ltd*), or which will come to an end on the happening of a certain event (eg the cessation of funding, see *Brown v Knowsley Borough Council*) are not fixed-term contracts, and they will be discharged automatically on the completion of the task or the occurrence of the event, as appropriate. As long as the minimum and maximum period of duration is uncertain, a contract cannot be for a fixed term. The mere fact that a date is stated will not make it a fixed term. For example, in *Weston v University College Swansea* the claimant was employed for a probationary period of three years, but this did not make it a fixed-term contract, because it could have been terminated any time before the end of the three years, and it was contemplated from the outset that it could continue for longer than that period. Similarly, if the contract specifies a minimum term, but no maximum, then it cannot be for a fixed term. Thus in *Cohen v London Borough of Barking*, the employee was employed under a contract which was for one year, but thereafter terminable on two months' notice. It was held that this was not a fixed-term contract, because there was no defined end.

2.276 Whether a contract of employment is for a fixed term, a specific task or purpose, or for an indefinite period, is a question of construction for the court or tribunal. The terms of the contract must be considered, as well as 'the matrix of surrounding circumstances' (*Wiltshire County Council v NATFHE and Guy*). Section 1(4)(g) of ERA states that if a contract is for a fixed term, the written particulars given should state the date when it is due to end, and it must therefore follow that a contract to perform a specific task, (eg to complete a sea voyage), or a contract terminable on some future event, the date of which is unknown (eg for the duration of the present Parliament) cannot be a fixed-term contract, as it will be of uncertain duration (*Wiltshire County Council v NATFHE and Guy*).

2.277–2.285 There are a number of significant points to bear in mind when dealing with a fixed-term contract.
(1) In respect of a fixed-term contract of short duration, the normal continuity rules apply on renewal (see Chapter 13), including the statutory presumption in favour of the presumption of continuity (ERA s 210(5)). This may enable an employee whose employment was intended to be temporary to obtain various employment protection rights in appropriate circumstances. The normal rules about giving statutory notice do not apply when the contract period expires, except where an employee has been employed under a fixed-term contract of one month or less, and has actually been employed for three months or more (ERA s 86(6)). Guarantee payments and medical suspension

payments are excluded if the employee is employed under a fixed-term contract of three months or less (ERA ss 29(1), 65(2)), as are consultation rights on redundancies (TULR(C)A s 282), unless the employee has worked more than three months.

(2) If a fixed-term contract is not renewed on expiry, that will not amount to a dismissal at common law, because the contract has been terminated automatically by effluxion of time. However, non-renewal under the same contract will be a dismissal for the purpose of ERA. Whether the dismissal was fair or unfair will be determined by whether or not the employer can show that he acted reasonably in not renewing the contract. If the contract is terminated prior to the expiry of the fixed term, the employee will have the normal rights in respect of breach of contract (see Chapter 15), and the employer will be liable to pay the employee for the rest of the term, subject to the employee's duty to mitigate against his loss. He will also have the right to claim unfair dismissal, provided he has been employed for the requisite period of continuous employment. However, if the contract is terminated by mutual agreement, no dismissal has taken place (*Lyritzis v Inmarsat*), although a mutual acknowledgement that the contract will terminate on the fixed date will be a dismissal nonetheless (*Thames Television v Wallis*). Nor will there be a dismissal for redundancy payment purposes if the employee is employed under a new contract which takes effect within four weeks of the expiry of the old (ERA s 138(1)). A dismissal will take place if the new contract is substantially different from the old (ERA s 138(2–6)), but the right to obtain a redundancy payment will be lost if the employee unreasonably refuses an offer on the same or different terms (ERA s 141).

(3) As a general rule (see para 20.66) any agreement which purports to exclude or limit an employee's rights under ERA is void, but an exception to this rule is made in respect of fixed-term contracts.

Section 197(3) provides that an employee can exclude his right to claim a statutory redundancy payment, by entering into a written agreement to that effect, although, in this case, the fixed-term contract must be for two years or more.

It will be noted that for a valid waiver clause to operate, there must be a written agreement, which can be either in the contract or a separate agreement entered into during the currency of the term.

(4) If there is a fixed-term contract of two years, containing a waiver clause, and the contract is renewed (including the waiver clause) for a further period which is less than two years, does the waiver clause still apply? In redundancy cases, where the original contract must be for two years or more, the rule appears to be clear. As long as the original contract was for two years or more, the length of the final contract is immaterial. In *Housing Services Agency v Cragg*, the employee was employed on a fixed-term contract for two years, which contained a waiver clause. The contract was renewed several times, so that in total, he was employed for over four years, although the last extension was for three months. When the contract was not renewed, he applied for a redundancy payment, which the employers refused to make, relying on the waiver clause. An employment tribunal held that as the final term was not for two years, the waiver clause did not apply, but the decision was reversed by the EAT. As long as the employee entered into a fresh waiver agreement during the currency of the extended term, he will not be able to claim a redundancy payment, irrespective of the length of the final contract.

Other flexible working arrangements

2.286 In recent years there appears to have been a greater interest in finding alternatives to conventional full-time and part-time employment, partly with a view to trying to avoid legal responsibilities (with very limited success), but mainly because of the genuine needs of employers and employees for new-style flexible working arrangements, which can, in certain circumstances, be commercially advantageous. Each arrangement will have its own legal pitfalls, and thus likely complications need to be foreseen. Because the statutory rules were not designed to deal with such arrangements, legal disputes arising out of them have to be resolved by the use of a certain amount of judicial creativity.

2.287–2.295 Flexitime has, of course, a long history, but job sharing, performance contracts, zero hours contracts, annualised hours contracts, home working etc are now being used with greater frequency. All that can be said at this stage is that the courts and employment tribunals will look with distaste on any arrangement which is designed to avoid statutory responsibilities, and even genuine arrangements, entered into freely and for the convenience of both parties can flounder on the rocks of judicial interpretation. For example, in *Catamaran Cruisers Ltd v Williams* the employers paid a gross 'fee' to a limited company in respect of services provided by the claimant, but it was held that he was an employee nonetheless.

Common law remedies

2.296 Although most of the cases involving employment law are brought in employment tribunals, there has been a small resurgence in recent years of claims seeking the old common law remedies. Thus actions may still be brought for wrongful dismissal (see para 16.11), and also for damages based on a failure by the employer to follow contractual disciplinary procedures, the measure of damages being the loss suffered by the employee as a result of that failure (*Boyo v Lambeth London Borough Council*). Also, an application may be made for an injunction to restrain an employer from purporting to act in breach of a contractual disciplinary procedure (*Jones v Lee and Guilding*) and, somewhat rare, an action seeking specific performance of the contract (*Powell v London Borough of Brent*). These matters will be explored in Chapter 10 (and see *Jones v Gwent County Council*).

Public law remedies

2.297 An application may be made for judicial review, seeking to ensure that a public body carries out its public duties in a manner consistent with the legal requirements. Generally speaking, there are three grounds on which judicial review may be granted: (1) where the public body has acted illegally, ie contrary to the legal rights and duties of the parties; (2) where the public body has acted irrationally, ie where the decision arrived at was so outrageous that no sensible body or person acting responsibly could have reached that decision; and (3) where there has been a procedural impropriety, ie a failure to act with procedural fairness (*Council of Civil Service Unions v Minister for the Civil Service*, per Lord Diplock).

2.298 Attempts have been made by employees in the public sector to establish legal rights based on such principles, but with mixed success. The claim must be brought within the procedure laid down in the Civil Procedure Rules (judicial review) and the remedy is not generally available if a remedy based on contractual principles would suffice. There must be a further element of a public right or the enforcement of a public duty (*R v East Berkshire Health Authority, ex p Walsh*). The public law remedies sought will be certiorari, prohibition and a declaration.

2.299 In *McLaren v Home Office*, Woolf LJ suggested that there are four general principles which apply when an employee of a public body is proposing to proceed by way of judicial review: (1) in relation to personal claims against an employer, an employee of a public body is in the same situation as other employees; (2) however, if there exists some disciplinary or other body established under the Royal prerogative or a statute to which disputes can be referred, judicial review may be the appropriate remedy; (3) if an employee of a public body is adversely affected by a decision of general application, judicial review of that decision may be sought (see *R v Secretary of State, ex p CCSU*); (4) if disciplinary procedures are of a domestic nature, judicial review will not be sought.

2.300 However, if a person is seeking to enforce a private right which has a public law element, he can pursue his claim through the normal procedure of issuing a writ, and is not required to seek redress by means of judicial review (*Roy v Kensington and Chelsea and Westminster Family Practitioner Committee*). This is of particular importance if the public law issue is raised after the time for applying for judicial review has lapsed (*Doyle v Northumbria Probation Committee*).

2.301 In Scotland, however, for historical reasons, the situation is slightly different. Scots law does not depend on a distinction between public and private law, but the court will accept jurisdiction by way of judicial review to regulate the process by which decisions are taken by a person or body to whom a power has been delegated by statute, agreement or other instrument, in order to ensure that the person or body does not exceed or abuse that power. But there must always be a tripartite relationship between the person or body to whom the power has been delegated, the person or body by whom it has been delegated, and the person for whose benefit the power is to be exercised. Strict contractual rights, such as those which exist between employer and employee, are not amenable to judicial review (*West v Secretary of State for Scotland*), whether they occur in the public or the private sector. Thus where a local authority suspended a senior employee, it was exercising a power derived from the contract of employment, rather from a statutory grant (*Blair v Lochaber District Council*).

CHAPTER 3

The formation of a contract of employment

3.1 A contract of employment can be entered into formally or informally. It can emerge as a result of interviews, negotiations, exchange of letters, or a casual conversation at the factory door. It can be made orally or in writing, although apprenticeship deeds and articles for merchant seamen by definition must be written. But essentially it is a contract like any other contract, and in principle subject to the general contractual rules of the common law. The normal canons of legal construction must be applied (*Hooper v British Railways Board*).

3.2 There must be an offer of employment, and an acceptance of that offer. In *Wishart v National Association of Citizens' Advice Bureaux Ltd*, the claimant was offered a job 'subject to the receipt of satisfactory references'. The defendants received references from the claimant's existing employer which indicated that he had been absent from work through illness for a considerable number of days, and consequently the offer was withdrawn. The claimant sought an interlocutory injunction to restrain the defendants from appointing anyone else to the post and requiring them to provide him with the job in question. The injunction was granted by a deputy High Court Judge, but on appeal the decision was reversed by the Court of Appeal. On the facts, there was a conditional offer of employment, and the only obligation on the defendants was to consider the references in good faith. Whether or not the references were satisfactory was a subjective matter. The Court of Appeal suggested that it was possible to make a conditional offer of employment subject to something which could be objectively determined, eg the passing of a medical examination, but that did not apply in this case.

3.3 If an employer makes an offer of employment, which is accepted, and before the date of performance the employer withdraws the offer, the disappointed employee is entitled to damages for breach of contract. These will usually be assessed according to the loss suffered, ie the lawful notice the putative employee would have been entitled to receive had he commenced the employment, less any mitigation of the loss, unless there is a collateral contract (see para 3.21). Further, such a claim for lawful notice may be brought in the employment tribunal under the provisions of the Employment Tribunals (Extension of Jurisdiction) Order (see para 1.55) which permits employment tribunals to hear claims arising or outstanding 'on the termination of the employee's employment', even though, as in this case, the employment had not commenced! The phrase has to be construed as meaning 'on the termination of the employee's contract of employment' (*Sarker v South Tees Acute Hospitals NHS Trust*).

3.4   Of interest in connection with 'job offers' is the new scheme arising from the Police Act 1997 ss 112–127, whereby the Secretary of State may issue certificates on application which will detail an individual's criminal record, or the absence of any such record (see para 4.356). Thus an employer would be able to discover certain relevant information prior to offering employment. Enhanced criminal records covering applicants who apply for certain sensitive posts (care of children or working with vulnerable adults) will be available from July 2001. Other certificates are expected to be available from July 2002. A code of practice will be issued before the scheme comes fully into force.

3.5   In addition, there must be an intention to create legal relations (see *R v Lord Chancellor's Department, ex p Nangle*), consideration (but this doctrine does not apply in Scotland) and the absence of vitiating elements (mistake, misrepresentation, illegality, etc). Thus if an employee is seeking to rely on, or enforce, or found a claim on a contract of employment, that contract must not be tainted with illegality, for it is contrary to public policy to claim statutory protection in respect of an illegal contract, eg when seeking compensation for unfair dismissal or a redundancy payment. But if the protection or remedy sought does not involve relying on or enforcing the contract of employment, the illegality of that contract is not a bar to a claim. Thus, a person may claim sex or race discrimination even though the contract is prima facie illegal (*Leighton v Michael* and see *Hall v Woolston Hall Leisure Ltd*, para 3.11), but if the contract is central to the claim, eg in unfair dismissal complaints, and is tainted with illegality, it will be unenforceable (*Johal v Adams*). In *Cole v Fred Stacey Ltd*, the employee was given an additional payment which was not taxed as income. He was subsequently made redundant, but it was held that he was not entitled to a redundancy payment, as the contract was illegal and unenforceable, being a contract to defraud the Revenue (see also *Tomlinson v Dick Evans U Drive Ltd*). In *Rastegarnia v Richmond Design* the applicant (who came from Iran) had been granted a work permit for a specific job. Without obtaining permission from the Department of Employment he changed his job and went to work for the respondents. He was subsequently dismissed, but his claim for unfair dismissal was rejected. His employment was unlawful, and he could not obtain any legal rights thereunder.

3.6   If the terms of the contract are designed to avoid or postpone the proper payment of income tax, then the contract is illegal, and it matters not that the parties are aware of the illegality. In *Salvesen v Simons* the employee was employed as a farm manager. He requested that his remuneration be paid in two parts— £10,000 as a salary, and £2,200 as a management fee to be paid into a firm which he owned. This enabled him to claim business expenses and defer payment of any income tax due on the management fee. A new owner took over the farm, and refused to continue the arrangement. The employee resigned, and claimed constructive dismissal. His claim succeeded before the employment tribunal, but the decision was reversed by the EAT. Ignorance of the illegal nature of the agreement did not prevent the application of the maxim *ex turpi causa non oritur actio* (no legal rights can arise out of wrongful dealings).

3.7   The fact that the employer makes an occasional tax-free payment to the employee does not render the contract illegal for this is not part of the remuneration as defined in the contract of employment (*Annandale Engineering v Samson*). Nor is a legitimate tax avoidance scheme unlawful, provided it is a proper method of reducing liability for tax and national insurance contributions, and has been (or would be) disclosed to the Inland Revenue (*Lightfoot v D & J Sporting Ltd*).

3.8   However, a fraud or dishonesty against an employer by an employee, whilst it may be grounds for dismissal, does not make the contract inherently illegal so as to make it void ab initio (*Broaders v Kalkare Property Maintenance Ltd*).

3.9   Nor will the contract be unenforceable for illegality if the employee does not receive any benefit from the illegality. In *Hewcastle Catering Ltd v Ahmed* the employers devised a scheme to avoid paying VAT, and gave certain instructions to the employees to facilitate the scheme. The employees did not receive any direct benefit. Following investigations by the Customs and Excise, the employers were prosecuted, and the employees were called as prosecution witnesses. They were subsequently dismissed, and claimed that the dismissals were unfair. The employers argued that the contracts of employment, being tainted with illegality, were unenforceable, but this claim was rejected by the employment tribunal, the EAT and the Court of Appeal. The employers had involved the employees in the fraud, but the employees did not benefit from it and were not essential parties to it. It would be contrary to public policy to deny the employees compensation when the employers had involved them in the fraud and dismissed them because they gave evidence in criminal proceedings taken against the employers.

3.10   For an employee to have certain statutory rights, he must be continuously employed under a legal contract of employment, and any period wherein the contract becomes illegal cannot be relied upon in counting towards that continuity. Thus a period of time prior to the illegality, when the contract was legal, is lost, and continuity can only be reckoned from the date when the contract became legal (*Hyland v J H Barker (North West) Ltd*). As already noted (see para 2.237), periods of employment when a foreign national is working in breach of immigration rules will render the contract unenforceable for illegality (*Bamgbose v Royal Star and Garter Home*).

3.11   If, on a complaint of unlawful discrimination, it is discovered that the contract of employment is tainted with illegality, it is possible for an employment tribunal to make an award for injury to feelings, but no compensation can be awarded for loss of earnings, for that would offend against the principle that the courts will not enforce an illegal contract (*Hall v Woolston Hall Leisure Ltd*).

3.12   If the alleged illegality lies in the performance of the contract, then a distinction must be drawn between the cases where the contractual obligation is to do an act which is unlawful, and those where the obligations are capable of being performed lawfully, but which were in fact performed by unlawful means. In *Coral Leisure Group Ltd v Barnett*, the claimant was dismissed from his post as a public relations executive. He alleged that part of his duties was to keep rich punters happy by obtaining for them, among other things, the services of prostitutes. It was held that the fact that an immoral or unlawful act was committed during the course of the employment did not render the contract void, unless it was entered into with the object of doing that unlawful or immoral act, or the contract itself (as opposed to the mode of performance) was prohibited by law.

3.13–3.20 But the contract will only be void if the party seeking to enforce it was aware of the illegality. If it can be shown that the employee was not a party to the illegality, or did not know about it, he can still rely on the contract as an innocent party (*Davidson v Pillay*). Thus if an employee is paid part of his wages in cash as a tax-free payment, the essential question to ask is, has the employee knowingly been a party to a deception on the Revenue (*Newland v Simons and Willer (Hairdressers) Ltd*)?

Collateral contracts

3.21 At common law, when an employer terminates the contract of employment, the only remedy for the employee is to claim money for the period of notice to which he is entitled (see para 15.11). However, if the employer promises that the contract will subsist for a certain period of time, this may be a collateral contract to the main contract, and the employee may be able to claim damages for a breach of that collateral contract. In *Gill v Cape Contracts Ltd* the claimant gave up his job in Belfast to go to work for the defendants in the Shetlands. He was told that the work would last for at least six months, but the defendants repudiated the contract before he could start work. It was held that the plaintiff was entitled to damages for a breach of contract by the defendants, who had made representations which had been acted on by the claimant to his detriment. These representations formed a collateral contract to the main contract of employment.

Terms and conditions

3.22 It is usual to speak of the 'terms and conditions of employment' which are part of every contract of employment, although no attempt ever appears to have been made to define or delineate this expression (but see *Cory Lighterage v T & GWU* and *Universe Tankships v ITWF*). It is submitted that the terms of the employment are bilateral, ie they are part of the agreement made between the employer and employee, whereas the conditions of employment are unilateral instructions which are laid down by the employer. The result is that a change in the terms can only be made by an express or implied agreement to that effect, whereas a condition can be changed by the employer unilaterally at any time (see *Cadoux v Central Regional Council*) on giving reasonable notice.

3.23 If an employer has a code of practice, or issues a policy statement, such documents do not necessarily constitute employment terms. In *Wandsworth London Borough Council v D'Silva* the local authority issued a code of practice on staff sickness, to which they proposed to make changes unilaterally. The employment tribunal and the EAT held that the relevant provisions of the code were contractually binding and the employers could not alter them unilaterally, but the decision was reversed by the Court of Appeal. The code merely set out good practice which management intended to follow, but did not constitute contractual requirements. Similarly, an equal opportunities policy was a mere statement of policy in generalised terms, and did not give rise to contractual obligations (*Grant v South-West Trains Ltd*). In *Pendragon plc v Jackson* the employer inserted a clause into a share option scheme which stated that the scheme was non-contractual. It was held that the employee had no legal entitlement to any benefits under the scheme. The employers had discharged the burden of proof to show that the scheme was not intended to create a legally binding contract.

3.24   But although a policy or practice set out in a staff manual may not be contractual, if it is relied upon by an employee, it cannot be changed unilaterally to his detriment, because that would be a breach of the implied term of trust and confidence (*French v Barclays Bank plc*).

3.25–3.35   Terms of employment can be found in express or implied agreements, collective agreements, and various statutory provisions; conditions of employment are usually contained in works rules, disciplinary and grievance procedures and job descriptions. Care should be taken not to place a term or condition in the wrong category. For example, it may be a term of a contract that an employee shall be entitled to four weeks holiday per year; it will be a condition that he shall take those holidays at particular times of the year. A term will specify the number of hours he shall work; a condition will instruct him as to when he shall work those hours. A term will specify his employment duties; a condition will lay down how he shall perform those duties. The fact of payment is a term; the mode of payment is a condition.

Interpretation of terms

3.36   Under the modern law of employment, contractual terms must be applied reasonably, not literally. In *United Bank Ltd v Akhtar*, the claimant was subject to a clause in his contract which required him to work anywhere in Great Britain. On 5 June he was informed that as from 8 June he would be required to transfer from Leeds to a branch in Birmingham. He requested that the transfer be delayed for three months, because of his wife's illness, and also the impending sale of his house. This request was refused. He then asked if he could take 24 days' leave due to him to enable him to sort out his affairs, and he offered to commence work in Birmingham on 10 July, but he received no reply to this request. His pay was then stopped as from 5 June, so he resigned, and claimed he had been constructively dismissed. His claim succeeded. There was an implied term in his contract that the employers would give reasonable notice if they wished to exercise their rights under the mobility clause.

3.37   Similarly, an employer may still be acting fairly even though he dismisses an employee in circumstances which amount to a breach of contract by the employer, for statutory rights and obligations exist concurrent with, but are sometimes different from, those which exist at common law (see *Hooper v British Railways Board*).

3.38–3.45   In *Farrant v Woodroffe School* the claimant was employed as a laboratory technician at a school. Following a reorganisation of technical support services he was required to transfer from the science department where he worked and divide his time between other departments. He refused to accept the new job description and was dismissed. The dismissal was held to be fair. The employers had given him ample warning of the proposed change, had fully consulted with him, and thus had acted reasonably in the circumstances in dismissing him. The lawfulness of the instruction is not by itself determinative of the fairness of a dismissal.

Express terms

3.46   At the conclusion of the negotiations the parties may have expressly stated the terms which form the basis of the contract. These terms may deal with wages, salaries, commissions, bonuses, hours of work, the nature of the duties, holidays, overtime, sick pay, pension schemes and so on. The task of the courts and tribunals is to interpret the meaning of such express terms in a manner consistent with industrial realism. Thus in *Cole v Midland Display Ltd* the employee was a manager employed on a 'staff' basis. He refused to do overtime without pay, and his subsequent dismissal was held to be fair. The essence of being employed as 'staff' meant that he was guaranteed his wages whether there was work or not, and during sickness. In return, 'staff' are apparently required to work reasonable overtime without pay if required to do so.

3.47   On the other hand, in *Redbridge London Borough Council v Fishman*, the employee was appointed as a teacher in charge of a resource centre. Gradually, she was asked to teach more and more, and eventually dismissed when she refused. Her dismissal was held to be unfair. A headteacher could require teachers to do work other than that for which they were engaged, provided that such requests were reasonable. In this case, the teaching was ancillary to her main job, which was as a director of the resource centre. Consequently, the headmaster's instructions went beyond the strict contractual obligations of the employee, and were therefore unreasonable.

3.48   Although it may be permissible to refer to statements made in a job advertisement to ascertain the terms of a contract (*Tayside Regional Council v McIntosh*), such statement cannot override the express terms. In *Deeley v British Rail Engineering Ltd*, the employers advertised for a 'Sales Engineer (Export)'. The claimant applied for the job and was appointed, but his contract was for a 'Sales Engineer'. It was held that there were no grounds for implying the word 'Export' into his contract.

3.49   If there is an express term in the contract which permits an employee to have short-term or long-term sickness benefits, or there is in force a permanent health insurance scheme, the employer cannot bring these to an end by dismissing the employee (*Adin v Sedco Forex International Resources Ltd*), and it is probable that there is also an implied term that the employer will not dismiss an employee who is off work sick while covered by such a scheme (*Aspden v Webbs Poultry and Meat Group (Holdings) Ltd*). If the employer has the right to terminate the scheme without prior notice, benefits under the scheme will continue until the employee is notified of the change (*Bainbridge v Circuit Foil UK Ltd*).

3.50   An express term may be used to negate a liability. In *Petrie v MacFisheries Ltd* the employers posted a notice stating that half pay for sickness would be paid as an act of grace by the company to all employees with over six months' service. All the employees knew of the position and the company acted on it consistently. It was held that the company was not bound to make payments when employees were off sick.

3.51   If an employer provides facilities for his employee's property (eg car parks, cloakrooms, etc) he cannot restrict his liability for death or personal injury resulting from negligence, and he may only be able to restrict or exclude his liability for damage to the employee's property by a term in the contract which is reasonable in the circumstances (Unfair Contract Terms Act 1977 s 2).

3.52   If the employee is in breach of a contractual term this will be ground for dismissal. Equally, if the employer is in breach, the employee may accept the breach and bring a claim for constructive dismissal (see Chapter 17). In either event, the fairness or unfairness of the dismissal has to be determined in accordance with established legal principles, though clearly the breach of a contractual term must be regarded with greater seriousness than the breach of a non-contractual term. In *Martin v Solus Schall*, the claimant signed a contract which included a clause stating 'you will be expected to work such overtime as is necessary to ensure continuity of service'. This was held to be a contractual obligation, and on the facts his dismissal for refusing to do overtime was fair.

3.53   Whether a breach by the employer of a term in a contract is so fundamental as to amount to a repudiatory breach will depend on the nature of the breach and the circumstances which gave rise to it. Thus, if there is a non-payment of agreed wages, or an interference by the employer with a salary package, a distinction must be drawn between the employer's failure to pay, or his delay in paying, and his deliberate refusal to do so. A unilateral reduction in pay diminishes the value of the employee's remuneration, and undermines the whole foundation of the contract of employment. But if the failure to pay is a result of temporary fault in the employer's technology, or a simple accounting error or mistake, or due to accident or illness etc, it would be open to the court to hold that the breach did not go to the root of the contract. A repeated or persistent failure or delay, or one which was unexplained, might lead the court to hold that the breach was indeed repudiatory (*Cantor Fitzgerald International v Callaghan*).

3.54   At one time it was thought that a breach of contract by an employee amounted to a 'constructive resignation', but this view is now regarded as being incorrect (see *London Transport Executive v Clarke* para 17.73). The legal position is that the employer may 'accept' the breach or not, as he wishes. If he does accept the breach, he dismisses the employee, and the fairness of the dismissal must be justified in accordance with the usual principles (see Chapter 17).

3.55–3.65   A strike by an employee is a breach of contract, as is a refusal to perform contractual duties. Either of these events gives rise to legal consequences, including the right of the employer to deduct a sum of money from the wages or salary of the employee, calculated on a proportional basis (*Sim v Rotherham Metropolitan Borough Council*).

Implied terms

3.66   Occasionally the courts and tribunals are prepared to imply a term into the contract in circumstances where the parties did not expressly insert a term to meet a particular contingency. The theory adopted was that the term in question was so obvious that the parties did not see the need to state it expressly. Clearly, a certain amount of judicial hindsight is required in order to imply a term after a dispute has arisen, and there is frequent room for disagreement on whether or not the court was correct in making its assumptions. However, in *Mears v Safecar Security Ltd*, the Court of Appeal held that the correct approach was to consider all the facts and circumstances before implying a term into the contract, including the way the parties had carried out the contract since it was formed. There is no presumption either way about an implied term. For example, in *O'Grady v M Saper Ltd* the employee claimed his wages for a period in which he had been off work through sickness. He had been away sick before, and had not received any wages. Indeed, he never asked for them nor expected them, until he saw an item in a newspaper which led him to believe that he might be able to claim. It was held that there was an implied term that he would not be paid.

3.67 The original justification for the implied term theory was the need to give business efficacy to the contract, but there is now a much wider approach, implying terms which are a necessary incident of a definable category of contractual relationship. In *Scally v Southern Health and Social Services Board*, the claimant was a doctor, whose terms and conditions of employment were to be found in a statutory scheme. This scheme gave doctors the right to purchase added years of pension entitlement, but this valuable right had to be exercised within certain time limits. The claimant was never informed about the scheme, and so he failed to exercise his option to purchase the added years pension. When he did discover the existence of the scheme, he was outside the time limits. He claimed that his employers had broken an implied term of the contract by failing to take reasonable steps to bring to his notice his right to enhance his pension entitlement by the purchase of added years. The House of Lords unanimously upheld his claim. It was noted that the terms of the contract had not been negotiated with the individual employee, but were negotiated with a representative body or otherwise incorporated by reference. The contract thus contained a valuable right for the employee, but this was contingent on him taking action to avail himself of the benefit. He could not be expected to do this unless the term was drawn to his attention. There was an implied term, therefore, that the employer could take reasonable steps to bring the provisions of the pension scheme to the employee's attention, so that he could enjoy its benefits if he so wished.

3.68 It is not possible to imply terms which are too vague or unpredictable to be given efficacy, or to which the parties would not have agreed had the matter been drawn to their attention (*Lake v Essex County Council*). Thus, in *Cresswell v Board of Inland Revenue*, staff employed by the Inland Revenue habitually carried out their tasks by dealing manually with files and records. The Inland Revenue introduced a programme of computerisation, and the claimant alleged that in so doing there was a breach of contract, arguing that there was an implied term that he could not be required to perform tasks or carry out functions in a manner other than that which they had habitually used by custom and practice. He sought a declaration that he could not be required to operate computerised systems. It was held that the employers were not in breach of the contract by requiring employees to use computer systems. An employee is expected to adapt himself to new methods and techniques introduced in the course of his employment. It is a question of fact whether the retraining involved the acquisition of such esoteric skills that it would not be reasonable to expect the employee to acquire them. Nowadays, it is not unusual to ask an employee to acquire basic skills such as retrieving information from a computer or feeding information into one. However, the employer must be expected to provide any necessary training for the acquisition of these skills.

3.69   Recent cases have established that there is an implied term that an employer will treat the employee with respect and trust, and will not treat an employee in an arbitrary or vindictive manner. Thus falsely to accuse an employee of theft (*Robinson v Crompton Parkinson Ltd*), unreasonably to deny an employee an increase in remuneration which had been granted to other employees (*FC Gardner Ltd v Beresford*) and, in the case of a large firm, to refuse to give an employee time off work to deal with a domestic emergency (*Warner v Barbers Stores*), have all been held to amount to conduct by the employer which could constitute a breach of the implied term that the employer should treat an employee fairly and reasonably.

3.70   It may be possible to imply a term by reference to the practices of the industry and/or the national agreements which are in force. For example, in *Stevenson v Teesside Bridge and Engineering Ltd* a steel erector's employment was governed by the national agreement for the time being in force in the industry. Although there was no express term in his contract stating that he was expected to work away from home, this was clearly envisaged, for the national agreement made provision for lodging allowances, travelling expenses, etc. The court held that there was an implied term in his contract that he could be sent anywhere to work, for it was recognised that in the construction steel industry, where sites are, by their very nature, scattered around the country, employees know that mobility is a feature of their employment.

3.71   There is an implied term that the employer will not prevent the employee from performing his contract of employment, or delay or hinder him so as to prevent him from earning his full remuneration, but the employer is entitled to take steps which may improve that performance, and to see that the work is done in a proper manner, for example, by engaging time and motion experts (*Davies v Richard Johnson & Nephew Ltd*). If an employee is contractually obliged to do overtime without pay, there is an implied term that the requirements of overtime will always be reasonable, and would not be excessive (*Gilbert v Goldstone Ltd*). On the other hand, if a contract of employment is silent on the actual place of work, it may be necessary to imply a term to give that contract business efficacy. In *Jones v Associated Tunnelling Co Ltd* it was held that there was an implied term that the employers were entitled to require the employee to work anywhere within a reasonable daily commuting distance from his home.

3.72   There is also an implied term that the employer will not conduct his business in a fraudulent and dishonest manner so as to cause damage to the employees' reputation and consequently place them at a disadvantage in the labour market (*Malik v BCCI SA*).

3.73   The basis for the implied term theory is that it is the courts' (or tribunals') view about a provision that was 'obvious' where the contract was silent. In *Shell UK Ltd v Lostock Garage Ltd*, Lord Denning suggested that if a contract of employment did not define the obligations of the parties, the courts (or tribunals) should ask what would be reasonable in the general run of such cases, and then say what the obligation shall be. This view was followed in *Pepper and Hope v Daish* (see para 17.47) but in view of the importance of the issues involved, a more authoritative ruling is needed. There is a fundamental difference between importing into a contract an implied term which is 'obvious' and one which is 'reasonable'. However, the contracts of employment of professional employees do not always detail the contractual obligations, and these may be defined by reference to the nature of the profession, and the obligations incumbent on those who follow that profession (*Sim v Rotherham Metropolitan District Council*).

3.74 There is no implied term that an employer will look after the employee's property (clothes, car, etc) which are left on the employer's premises (*Edwards v West Herts Group Hospital Management Committee*), though there is an obligation under the Workplace (Health, Safety and Welfare) Regulations 1992 for employers to provide suitable and sufficient accommodation for clothing which is not worn during working hours, and if there is a statutory obligation to do something, a failure to comply with that requirement will amount to a breach of an implied term (*W A Goold (Pearmak) Ltd v McConnell*: see para 3.174). Nor is there an implied term that an employee will be entitled to work overtime if the employer is not contractually obliged to provide overtime (*McClory v Post Office*).

3.75 There is no implied term that the employer will provide personal accident insurance for the benefit of an employee who is required to work abroad, or that the employer should give specific advice on special risks, and advise the employee to take out personal accident insurance (see *Reid v Rush & Tompkins Group plc*, para 10.31). Nor can a duty in tort be imposed to enlarge on contractual duties.

If there is no agreement on the matters which should be included in the written statement which has to be given to employees under the provisions of s 1 of the Employment Rights Act 1996, then it may not be possible to rely on an implied term concerning matters which ought to be, but are not, set out in the statement (eg whether an employee is entitled to accrued holiday pay on a pro-rata basis, see *Morley v Heritage plc*, but see now Working Time Regulations, para 7.221).

3.76 It is clear that if an employer breaks an express term of the contract, the employee may 'accept' the breach, resign from his employment, and claim that he had been 'constructively' dismissed (see para 17.35). This is equally true in the case of a breach of an implied term, and in particular when the conduct of the employer amounts to a breach of the implied term of mutual trust and confidence which must exist between the parties (*Post Office v Roberts*). These developments will be considered in detail in Chapter 17.

3.77–3.85 It is not possible to predict when the courts or tribunals will imply a term into a contract. Thus in *Ali v Christian Salvesen Food Services Ltd* individual contracts of employment were varied by a collective agreement. Certain topics had been omitted, and the employment tribunal refused to fill in the gaps. The decision was reversed by the EAT, using implied terms, but that decision was itself reversed by the Court of Appeal. If there were omissions in a collective agreement, the inference is that the topic was too complex or controversial for discussion or agreement, and it is not for the judiciary to speculate on what might have been agreed.

Express incorporation of the terms of a collective agreement

3.86   A collective agreement is an agreement made between an employers' association, or a single employer, on the one hand, and a trade union on the other, which, as well as laying down the procedure which will govern the relationship between the signatories will also provide for the terms and conditions of employment of those covered by the agreement. There are currently about 7,500,000 employees who are members of trade unions, and many of these, but not all, will doubtless be covered by such agreements, as well as an unknown number of non-trade unionists in respect of whom their employer will apply the terms of a relevant collective agreement. There are, however, a number of different situations to consider. There can be a national or federation agreement, made between an employers' association and a trade union, on the conclusion of which the individual employers who are members of the association will start to apply its provisions to their employees. There is no rule of law which requires this, only the practice of industrial relations. The terms of the agreement will be binding in law on the individual employer and the employee if, and only if, they are expressly or impliedly incorporated into the individual contract of employment. The same rule applies to a local or plant agreement, which is usually made between a single employer and a trade union. Also, there are some employers who, though not members of the employers' association, voluntarily undertake to observe the terms of a negotiated agreement.

3.87   Certain terms contained in a collective agreement govern the relationship between the trade union and the employer. Other terms are designed to benefit individual employees, and this becomes part of the contract of employment (*National Coal Board v National Union of Mineworkers*). These latter terms are said to have a 'normative' effect. In *Alexander v Standard Telephones and Cables plc*, the claimant was employed on the basis of the terms contained in a collective agreement. The agreement contained a redundancy procedure, which stated that LIFO would be the basis of selection in the event of compulsory redundancies. The company wished to select on the basis of skills and flexibility, and the claimant sought an injunction to prevent this. The application failed, but it was suggested that there was an arguable case that the terms of the collective agreement formed part of his contract of employment. Any remedy for breach of that contract would lie in an action for damages and the case was sent for trial on that basis (see para 3.90).

3.88   The 'normative' terms of a collective agreement may be incorporated into the individual contract of employment by an express provision to this effect. For example, employment may be undertaken on the basis of 'union rates of pay', or 'union conditions'. It is at least arguable that the former term refers solely to the wages rates clauses in the collective agreement, whilst the latter term may be somewhat wider, and may include other provisions. In *Jewell v Neptune Concrete Ltd*, the employee's written particulars stated that his rate of wages was to be based on the national agreement. It was held that this did not, by itself, incorporate the working rule agreement's lay-off provisions into his contract of employment. Employees who work for public bodies are normally engaged on the basis of the appropriate scale laid down by the negotiating bodies and the only scope for individual bargaining may be on the precise point of entry into the scale for salary purposes. Thus in *Knox v Down District Council* the Northern Ireland Court of Appeal were prepared to incorporate into the employee's contract of employment a car assisted purchase scheme which had been negotiated by the National Joint Council, the terms of which were expressly incorporated into his contract. In *National Coal Board v Galley*, the defendant was employed on the basis of 'the national agreements for the time being in force'. These agreements required him to do a certain amount of overtime, and when he refused to do a Saturday morning shift it was held that he was in breach of his contract.

3.89 Frequently the terms of a collective agreement will be expressly incorporated into the individual contract by means of the statement given to the employee under ERA s 1. In *Camden Exhibition and Display Ltd v Lynott* notices issued to the employees stated that their hours of work, wages, etc, would be in accordance with the working rule laid down by the National Joint Council for the industry. Rule 6 of this agreement stated that 'Overtime required to ensure the due and proper performance of contracts shall not be subject to restriction, but may be worked by mutual agreement and direct arrangement between the employer and operatives concerned.' Workmen who were dissatisfied with a wage award decided to cease overtime working. It was held that r 6 was a term of the contracts of employment of each employee. However, its effect was obscure. Lord Denning thought that it meant that the workmen would not collectively impose an overtime ban, but Russell LJ thought that the rule did not import into the contract of any individual an agreement not to limit overtime save for a reason special to himself.

3.90 To determine whether or not the terms of a collective agreement can be incorporated into an individual's contract of employment, regard must be had to the contractual intentions of the parties. In *Alexander v Standard Telephones and Cables plc*, the claimant was given a statement of written particulars, issued under s 1 of ERA. This stated that the basic terms and conditions of employment were in accordance with and subject to the provisions of a plant agreement negotiated by his employers and a trade union. One of the terms of the collective agreement provided that in the event of redundancy, selection will be on the basis of service with the employers. When the company wished to make a number of employees redundant, it was decided to retain employees whose skills and flexibility were best suited to the circumstances. The trade union insisted that selection should be on the basis of length of service. After negotiations broke down, the employers went ahead with their proposals, and the claimant was one of those dismissed. He sought an interlocutory injunction to restrain the employers from terminating his employment without applying the principles of collective agreement, but this was refused. He also claimed damages for breach of contract, arguing that he would have continued in his employment until retiring age.

His claim for damages was dismissed. The only relevant document applicable to the claimant's employment was the written statement issued under s 1 of ERA. This had to be construed in accordance with the relevant contractual principles. The statutory statement did not deal with redundancy matters, and therefore it did not incorporate the terms of the collective agreement into his contract of employment. The collective agreement itself, not being a contract, could be incorporated into the individual contract of employment if there was a cogent indication that this was intended. However, the clauses in question had to be considered in the context of a joint consultation scheme of a procedure agreement, and it was not sufficiently cogently worded to support the inference of incorporation into the individual contract of employment.

A contrary view was taken by the Court of Session in the recent case of *Anderson v Pringle of Scotland Ltd*, where the claimant's terms and conditions of employment were in accordance with the agreement made between the employer and a trade union. This agreement contained, inter alia, a redundancy procedure which provided that selection for redundancy was on the basis of last in first out (LIFO). When the employers decided to make a large number of employees redundant, they decided not to follow that procedure, but to use a selective scheme. The claimant would not have been selected under LIFO because of his long service, but he was to be chosen for redundancy under the selective scheme. He sought an injunction to prevent the employers from selecting for redundancy on any basis other than LIFO. The court granted the injunction. It was decided that the relevant terms of the collective agreement made between the employers and the trade union had been incorporated into the contracts of employment of the individual employees. Further, although the injunction would appear to have the effect of enforcing the performance of a contract of employment—which is not normally permissible, (see Chapter 10)—in this case there was no loss of trust or confidence in the employee, for the issues were the mechanics of dismissal rather than the principles of dismissal. While it might be difficult for the employer to abide by the LIFO selection system, it was not unfair to hold them to the agreement they had made (see also *Edinburgh Council v Brown*).

The terms of the collective agreement must be suitable for incorporation into the individual contract of employment. In *Griffiths v Buckinghamshire County Council* a redundancy procedure agreement negotiated between the employers and a trade union recommended that 12 months' notice should be given of impending redundancies. It was held that this was advisory in nature, and was a procedural, not a contractual obligation.

3.91 Once the terms of a collective agreement are incorporated into the individual contract of employment, they are part of that contract, and cannot be unilaterally altered. In *Robertson v British Gas Corpn*, the employee was appointed as a gas meter reader/collector, his letter of appointment stating that an incentive bonus scheme would apply. The terms of this scheme were negotiated between the employers and a trade union. Subsequently the employers gave notice to the trade union to terminate the scheme, and no new scheme was negotiated. The employee brought an action for arrears of pay. It was held that the letter of appointment was a binding contract, which gave the right to an incentive bonus scheme. Although the collective agreement had no legal force as between the signatories, it was incorporated into the employee's contract, and the employers could not terminate the scheme unilaterally.

3.92 A different result was reached in *Airlie v Edinburgh District Council*, where the employers entered into a collective agreement with trade unions representing workers in the direct labour organisation which contained, inter alia, a bonus scheme. The scheme was incorporated into the individual contract of employment, but a clause permitted the employers to alter it after consultation with the unions. When the department was making a loss, the employers wanted to alter the scheme. The unions agreed that alterations had to be made, but there was a failure to reach agreement. Nonetheless, the employers modified the scheme, which resulted in a reduction in the wages of the employees concerned. It was claimed that an unlawful deduction had been made from wages, but the claim was dismissed by an employment tribunal and the EAT. The employers had properly consulted the unions about the changes, but there was nothing in the scheme which required the agreement of either the employees or the trade unions concerned.

3.93–3.100 Indeed, the fact that the collective agreement contains a clause to the effect that its terms are binding in honour only does not affect the legal enforceability of those terms which are expressly or impliedly incorporated into the individual contract (*Marley v Forward Trust Group Ltd*). However, a distinction must always be made between contractual terms, which are bilateral in effect, and rules, which are unilateral. The latter do not have a legally binding effect (*Cadoux v Central Regional Council*).

Implied incorporation of the terms of a collective agreement

3.101 It is equally possible to incorporate the terms of a collective agreement into an individual contract of employment by implication. In certain types of employment it will be 'assumed' that employees are employed on the basis of union/management agreements. Thus, in *MacLea v Essex Line Ltd*, the plaintiff took a job as a seaman, and the court implied into his contract the contents of an agreement made by the National Maritime Board, which was the negotiating forum for the industry. In *Wilton Ltd v Peebles* employers had paid to their employees for 20 years the annual pay increases negotiated by a national agreement made between the trade unions and the employers' trade association, and the EAT confirmed that, despite the absence of any written terms of employment or oral agreement as to pay, there was an implied term that the wages of employees were to be those stipulated in the national agreement.

3.102–3.110 If the employers are not members of the employers' association, there is little scope for the implied incorporation of the terms of the collective agreement into the individual contract of employment. There would have to be strong evidence to indicate that the agreement had been so incorporated by way of custom and practice (*Hamilton v Futura Floors Ltd*).

Changing the terms of a collective agreement

3.111 Terms which are incorporated into the contract of employment as a result of a collective agreement remain part of that contract until or unless they are changed either by agreement with the employees concerned or under a specific right contained in the contract. The trade union is not, *per se*, an agent of its members with authority unilaterally to negotiate a variation. Thus, in *Lee v GEC Plessey Telecommunications*, the employers had reached an agreement with trade unions in 1985 which gave enhanced redundancy terms to its employees. In 1990 they purported to withdraw those terms, but, following objections from the unions, negotiations took place on revised terms. An agreement appeared to have been reached which enabled the employers to withdraw the enhanced redundancy payments and substitute less favourable terms, but this was on the basis that there would be no further redundancies in the future. However, redundancies were announced, and individual employees brought an action for a declaration that the attempt to vary the enhanced redundancy terms was ineffective. Their claim succeeded in the High Court. It was not necessary to give fresh consideration every time a new collective agreement was reached, for a continuation by the workforce in their employment was a value attributed to the employer. Although the employers could unilaterally determine the collective agreement, this would not be effective to change the terms contained in the individual contracts of employment. Nor were the trade unions acting as agents for their members when they attempted to negotiate the change. They were acting in a collective manner, not on behalf of each individual.

3.112   For example, in *Burke v Royal Liverpool University Hospital NHS Trust* the claimant was employed as a domestic worker. Her terms and conditions of employment were regulated by a Whitley Council agreement. In order to assist the trust in submitting a competitive tender, the two recognised trade unions agreed to less favourable terms and conditions than those previously enjoyed. The tender was successful, the lower wage rates were put into effect, but the claimant made a complaint under the protection of wages provisions of ERA, claiming that an unlawful deduction had been made to her wages. An employment tribunal held that the agreement made between the unions and the trust constituted a collective agreement which has the effect of incorporating the new terms and conditions into the claimant's contract of employment. An appeal against this decision was dismissed. The claimant had signed the new contract, the consideration for her agreement to accept a reduction in her wages was the greater sense of security of employment, and the agreement was capable of being incorporated into her contract of employment.

3.113–3.120   If an agreement states that its terms can be changed after consultation, that does not require the agreement of the parties, and provided the consultation is carried out in good faith, changes can be made unilaterally (*Airlie v Edinburgh District Council*, para 3.92).

Collective agreements and non-unionists

3.121   Just as the terms of a collective agreement may be binding on a non-federated employer who assents to it, so also will those terms apply to a non-unionist if his contract of employment states so expressly. In the absence of such express incorporation, the collective agreement will not apply. In *Singh v British Steel Corpn*, the employee's contract stated that he was to work a 15-shift system over a five-day week. He resigned from his trade union, and instructed his employers to cease paying the union subscription under a check-off agreement. The union then negotiated a new agreement with the employers which provided for a 21-shift system over a seven-day week, but the employee refused to agree to this, and was dismissed. It was held that there was nothing in his contract which permitted a change in the system of working, either by the employers unilaterally or by means of a collective agreement. The tribunal thought that while he was a member of the union he was bound by such agreements because it was his negotiating body, but when he left, he ceased to be bound. The union and the employers had no power to vary the terms of his agreement without his consent.

3.122–3.130   There is clearly less scope for the implied incorporation of the terms of a collective agreement into the contracts of employment of non-unionists. In *London Passenger Transport Board v Moscrop* a collective agreement provided that on a disciplinary charge, an employee could take with him a trade union official. The claimant was a member of another union which had not been a party to the agreement, and he wished to be accompanied by an official of his own union. It was held that the terms of the agreement were not necessarily applicable to employees who were not members of the signatory union. In *Singh v British Steel Corpn* (above) it was equally held that there was no implied term of his contract that as a non-union member he would be bound by union agreements.

Back dating agreements

3.131 A further problem can arise when the terms of a collective agreement are back-dated. As a general rule, it would seem that there is no implied term in a contract of employment that a wage award can be back-dated, although this may come about by an express agreement to that effect. However, an express agreement cannot override the statutory position. In *Leyland Vehicles Ltd v Reston* the claimant was made redundant in February, and received his redundancy payment calculated on the basis of the wages he was then receiving. In April a new wage agreement was negotiated with the union, and this was backdated to January. The claimant contended that his redundancy pay should be calculated so as to take account of the increase in his wage rate, but his claim was dismissed by the EAT. Section 225 of ERA refers to the amount of pay actually payable at the calculation date. It does not include increases made by agreement concluded after the employment has ended, even though the agreement provided for the back-dating of the increase. The payment of a back-dated wage increase to employees who have left the firm is usually a matter to be considered on an *ex gratia* basis.

Conflicting collective agreements

3.132 A difficulty sometimes arises when there is an overlap between the national agreement and a local agreement which covers the same or similar ground. In *Clift v West Riding County Council* the claimant was paid less by virtue of a local agreement than he would have received on the basis of a national agreement. It was held that since the local agreement was later in time, its terms prevailed. But 'the latest agreement prevails' doctrine is not a rule of law, as *Gascol Conversions Ltd v Mercer* demonstrates. Here, a national agreement provided that the working week should be 40 hours, and overtime worked as necessary. It also stated that if the national agreement was at variance with any local agreement, the national agreement was to prevail. A subsequent local agreement provided that the working week should be 54 hours. The employee was made redundant, and the question arose as to whether his redundancy payment was to be calculated on the basis of a normal working week of 40 hours or one of 54 hours. The Court of Appeal held that the employee was employed on the basis of the national agreement, and though it was at variance with the local agreement, its terms took precedence.

Which terms are employment terms?

3.133 Another difficulty is to determine which terms of a collective agreement are to be incorporated into the individual contract of employment. Clearly, there are many terms which are capable of such incorporation, such as wage rates, hours, overtime payments, travel allowances, and so on. Equally, there are other terms which govern the relationship which is to exist between the signatories, and have no relevance to the individual contract of employment. Since the law on collective bargaining is still in its infancy, we may well expect further developments in this field in the coming years. For example, in *Gallagher v Post Office*, the defendants recognised two trade unions for negotiating purposes, and informed their employees that they were entitled to join either union. Recognition was then withdrawn from one union, and the claimant alleged that this constituted a breach of contract. It was held that there was no term, express or implied, that the Post Office should continue to recognise the union to which the claimant belonged. Any statement about recognition was purely informative, and not part of the contract of employment of any individual employee.

3.134–3.140 Some difficulty has been experienced in the past with the 'no strike' clause, or the procedural aspects of settling disputes. In *Rookes v Barnard*, this clause was held to have been incorporated into the contracts of employment of the employees, but as the point was conceded rather than argued, the case adds little to our knowledge of the subject. A great deal may well turn on the precise wording of the agreement. Supposing this states 'the union will not call a strike until the procedure for settling the dispute is exhausted'. This is an obligation on the union, and is not part of the contracts of employment of the employees. Supposing the agreement states 'the employees will not go on strike until the procedure for settling the dispute is exhausted'. This term is clearly capable of being so incorporated. However, by TULR(C)A s 180 the incorporation of such a clause will not be binding unless:
a. the collective agreement is in writing;
b. it expressly states that the terms are to be incorporated into the individual contract;
c. a copy of the collective agreement is reasonably accessible to the employees concerned;
d. the agreement is made by an independent trade union; and
e. the individual contract of employment expressly or impliedly incorporates the terms of the collective agreement.
However, it must be borne in mind that a strike, whether in breach of a collective agreement or not, is always a breach of contract at common law, so that the effect of s 180 must be minimal.

Custom as a source of employment terms

3.141 It is sometimes argued that terms of employment can be found in those practices which are customary in a particular industry or local area, or even within a single firm. Support for this view can be gleaned from the case of *Sagar v Ridehalgh*, where a deduction from the wages of a cotton weaver for bad workmanship was upheld by virtue of the existence of a long-standing custom of the trade which, apparently, was well known. But a custom, to be upheld, must be long established, reasonable, certain, not contrary to law, and must be strictly proved. In *Hardwick v Leeds Area Health Authority* the claimant was dismissed after exhausting her period of sick pay, which was an entitlement of two months on full pay and two months on half pay. This was in accordance with the normal practice of the Health Service. It was held that such an automatic rule, whereby an employee could be dismissed irrespective of the circumstances, was totally outmoded and unreasonable, and the dismissal was held to be unfair. In *Singh v British Steel Corpn* (para 3.121) the fact that the claimant had considered himself in the past to be bound by trade union agreements was not sufficient evidence to establish a custom to that effect. Moreover, in *Gascol Conversions v Mercer* (para 3.132) the court stated that if the parties had reduced the contract to writing, it is not permissible to say that they intended something else, and thus it would appear that a custom cannot override a written statement of the terms of employment.

3.142 This point has considerable implications when, as sometimes happens, an appeal is made to 'custom and practice' as a basis of employment terms. It is true that in *Heaton's Transport Ltd v T & GWU* the House of Lords upheld custom and practice as being the basis of the authority of a shop steward to initiate action on behalf of a trade union, but this was a case where the union rule-book was silent on the point. However, it might be easier to argue that 'custom and practice' can override the terms of a collective agreement which has been incorporated into an employment contract (see *Parry v Holst & Co*, para 3.190). It is also arguable that a 'custom' is different from a 'practice'. The former has a legal significance which the latter does not possess. In *Spencer Jones v Timmens Freeman*, it was a 'common practice' in the hairdressing trade for shops to be open on Saturday afternoons, but this did not make it a custom.

3.143 Clear and compelling evidence is required to establish that a custom and practice exists. In *Samways v Swan Hunter Shipbuilders Ltd* the claimant, who was originally employed as a labourer, was appointed as a chargeman over a gang, and was given an additional £4 per week allowance. The company then informed him that owing to a reduction in production, it was necessary to withdraw the allowance, and he was offered employment as a labourer. It was held that this constituted a dismissal for reason of redundancy, as there was a reduction in the requirements of the company for chargemen. An argument by the company that by virtue of custom and practice chargemen's allowances were temporary payments for additional responsibility so long as this lasted was rejected by the tribunal, who thought that the 'allowance' was in fact remuneration. That other men had, in the past, reverted from the job of chargeman to their former positions was not sufficient to establish a custom, for their conduct could be explained on the ground that they wanted to keep their job with the firm, and it did not follow that they were contractually bound to do so.

3.144 It may be possible to claim sick pay if there is a local custom to this effect which can be proven to exist (*Scott v Pattison*).

3.145–3.155 It is submitted that with the increasing formalisation of contracts of employment, the scope for custom and practice as a source of employment terms has decreased, and indeed there is very little by way of modern legal authorities which could indicate that 'custom and practice' have any relevance in modern employment law. For example, in *Quinn v Calder Industrial Materials Ltd*, a policy document was issued to all member companies of a group holding company, which contained guidelines on additional redundancy payments. The document had not been formally communicated to the employees or their trade unions, although its terms were generally known. Indeed, enhanced redundancy payments based on the document had been made on four occasions, although a decision to do so had to be made by higher management on each such occasion. When the claimant was made redundant, he was not given any enhanced redundancy payment, and he contended that the employers were in breach of their contractual obligation. He argued that his entitlement to enhanced payments had been incorporated into his contract through custom and practice. His claim failed. Factors to be taken into account include whether management had drawn the attention of employees to the policy, whether it had been followed without exception for a substantial period, and whether employees had a genuine expectation that the terms of the policy would be applied to them. In the circumstances, it was not possible to infer that the policy document had achieved the status of a contractual obligation.

Works/Staff rules

3.156   Some employers issue booklets or post notices containing the rules of the workplace, and the legal significance of these is still being explored. Such rules can either be part of the contractual terms or unilaterally imposed instructions, a distinction which is important, because in the former case, they can only be changed by mutual assent and agreement, whereas in the latter case, the employer may, at any time and on reasonable notice, change them (see *Cadoux v Central Regional Council*) and substitute new instructions or impose new obligations, and a failure by the employee to obey would be a breach of his duty to follow all lawful and reasonable orders.

3.157   Thus a code of practice to be invoked in cases of long-term sickness (*Wandsworth London Borough Council v D'Silva*) and an equal opportunities policy (*Grant v South Western Trains Ltd*) were statements of policies in general terms, and not contractual documents (but see *French v Barclays Bank plc*, para 3.24).

3.158   The fact that the change bears hard on a particular individual does not justify an inference that the employer has acted in such a way as to repudiate the contract of employment. In *Dryden v Greater Glasgow Health Board*, the claimant was a heavy smoker, and was accustomed to smoking cigarettes in areas of the hospital where she worked set aside for this purpose. The employers decided to ban smoking throughout the hospital and, after extensive consultations, imposed a smoking ban. The claimant decided that she could not continue to work without smoking, and resigned her employment. She claimed that she had been constructively dismissed. It was held that 'the right to smoke' was not a customary term nor an implied term of the contract, and the employers had not acted in such a way as to frustrate the employee's ability to perform her contract. In *Secretary of State for Employment v ASLEF*, railwaymen proposed to engage in a work-to-rule campaign. If the rule book, by which they were working, was a part of their contracts of employment, then, by adhering to it, albeit strictly, they could hardly be said to be breaking their contracts. However, one of the rules stated that employees should 'make every effort to facilitate the working of trains and prevent unavoidable delay', which would clearly prohibit any deliberate attempt to interpret the rules in such a way as to achieve disruption of services, and to that extent there was clearly a breach of contract on either view of their legal significance. But Lord Denning held that the rules were 'in no way terms of his (ie the individual railwayman's) contract of employment. They were only instructions to a man on how he was to do his work.' It will clearly be an implied term of his contract of employment that he will interpret those rules reasonably.

3.159 In *Peake v Automotive Products* it was held that the contents of a rule book were non-contractual administrative arrangements for running the factory. If this view is correct, then works rules are non-negotiable instructions laid down by the employer. They may deal with all manner of subjects, including the method of performing the work, safety policy, disciplinary matters, concessions and privileges, and so on. A breach of the rules may lead to appropriate penalties. In *Blake v Berkel Auto Scales Co Ltd* an employee was summarily dismissed for a serious breach of the company's rules, and the dismissal was held to be fair. Indeed, a rule may be enforced even though the employee is in no way blameworthy. In *Jeffries v BP Tanker Co Ltd* the company had a rule that an employee with a history of cardiac disease should not be employed at sea as a radio officer, and an employee who had had two heart attacks was held to have been fairly dismissed, even though he had made an excellent recovery. The rule in this case was more in the nature of company policy.

3.160 But this does not mean that an employer can lay down rules and act on them in an autocratic manner, for the courts and tribunals will use the test of reasonableness to circumscribe management prerogatives. The rules must be clear and unambiguous; their contents must be made known to the employees, and reasonable in the circumstances. Thus in *Talbot v Hugh H Fulton Ltd* an employee was dismissed for having long hair, contrary to the works rules. It was held that this would only be reasonable if there was a safety hazard, and if the exact length which was acceptable was made known. Presumably the rule should have applied to female employees as well, otherwise it would have been an act of prejudice against modern styles worn by young persons.

3.161 There may be circumstances when some aspects of the works rules can be regarded as contractual terms, despite their unilateral nature. In *Briggs v Imperial Chemicals Industries Ltd* the claimant was employed as a process worker at a cyanide plant. The employers decided to pull the plant down and build another one, and consequently he was asked to work elsewhere in the firm as a process worker. He refused and claimed that he was entitled to a redundancy payment. The Divisional Court dismissed his appeal from an employment tribunal finding that he was not entitled. His terms of employment were governed by the statement given under ERA s 1 (see para 3.201), which stated that his pay would vary with the job he was performing, and clearly this contemplated that he could be transferred from one job to another. Also, he had been issued with a booklet containing the works rules of the factory, r 17 of which stated 'You must accept the right of management to transfer you to another job with a higher or lower rate of pay, whether day work, night work or shift work.' The court held that r 17 was a term of his employment, but this is probably because there was some implied (if obscure) reference to the works rules in his contract of employment. It would seem to follow that if the contract makes express reference to the works rules as being part of the contract of employment, they will more readily be regarded as part of the contractual terms. In *Singh v Lyons Maid Ltd* it was a requirement of the company that employees should not wear beards; this was in order to maintain the company's high standards of hygiene. The applicant knew of this rule, but none the less grew a beard in accordance with his religious beliefs. The dismissal was held to be fair. He had refused to obey a contractual term which the employers felt to be fundamental and which did not appear to be unreasonable.

3.162–3.170 At this stage it can only be said that the legal significance of the rules is a question of fact, to be determined by the circumstances of each case. For example, if the company's rule permits security guards to search employees before they leave the premises, will a refusal to be searched amount to a breach of an express term of the contract, or will it amount to a breach of the duty to obey a lawful (and reasonable) order? If a company does not have such a 'search' policy, but wishes to introduce one, can it be done unilaterally, or must the consent of each individual employee be obtained? Would a refusal to agree to be searched amount to 'some other substantial reason' for dismissal, by analogy with *R S Components Ltd v Irwin* (see Chapter 19)? It is clear that there are a number of possibilities in this field which require further exploration.

Disciplinary and grievance procedures

3.171 It is generally a condition of the contract that the employment is subject to the disciplinary and grievance procedures which are in force from time to time. These procedures are unilateral in the sense that it is the employer's responsibility to draw them up, with the co-operation of the employees and/or any relevant trade union if possible, without such assistance if necessary. Some form of incorporation into the individual contract of such conditions is also desirable, especially if these procedures are contained in a collective agreement, for this will then avoid the problems of incorporation so far as non-unionists are concerned.

3.172 But if a disciplinary procedure is incorporated into the contract, it must be adhered to, and a failure may attract the usual legal remedies. In *Jones v Lee and Guilding*, the claimant was dismissed from his post as headmaster of a Roman Catholic school after he had divorced his wife and remarried. His conditions of tenure stated that before any decision to dismiss a teacher was taken, the teacher had a right to be heard and to be represented before the local education authority. This procedure had not been followed, and the Court of Appeal granted an injunction restraining the school managers from purporting to dismiss the claimant without a hearing being held by the local education authority. In *Gunton v London Borough of Richmond* the claimant was given one month's notice of dismissal, though the disciplinary procedure, which was conceded to be part of his contract of employment, had not been fully implemented. The Court of Appeal held that his damages for wrongful dismissal should be limited to the loss he had suffered, which was assessed by reference to a reasonable period it would have taken the employer to implement the disciplinary procedure. (The decision was followed, albeit with some reluctance, by another division of the Court of Appeal: see *Boyo v Lambeth London Borough Council*).

3.173 Disciplinary procedures, discussed in Chapter 12, are designed to ensure that the employee is given every possible opportunity to put right any conduct which is likely to be the subject of critical appraisal; to this extent, the object of the procedure is corrective rather than punitive. Grievance procedures are designed to ensure that the individual employee has a proper outlet for such complaints that he may have, so as to prevent an employee from nursing a grievance. The importance of such procedures can be seen from the case of *Witham v Hills Shopfitters*, where a foreman swore at an employee, using somewhat foul language. The employee resigned, and claimed that this constituted constructive dismissal. It was held that the language used was fairly commonplace on the shop floor, and hence was not conduct which was destructive of the contract of employment. Moreover, the claimant should have gone through the company's grievance procedure before he made the hasty move to resign, for then the foreman could have been made to apologise to him. In other words, it is contrary to good industrial relations for an employee to go running to an employment tribunal with a claim without first exploring and exhausting such internal procedures as may exist. While there are circumstances where such action may be justified (eg if the employer has broken a term of the contract, see *Seligman & Latz Ltd v McHugh*), other grievances should first be resolved if possible within the internal machinery.

3.174–3.180 On the other hand, the absence of a proper and workable grievance procedure can be equally fatal for the employer. In *W A Goold (Pearmak) Ltd v McConnell* the employee was a salesman. Because of a change in sales methods he suffered a substantial drop in his take-home pay. He discussed this problem with his manager, but nothing was done. He then had discussions with the managing director, who said the matter would be seen to, but again nothing was done. He sought an interview with the company chairman, but was told that an application had to be made through the managing director. He therefore resigned his employment, and claimed he had been constructively dismissed. His claim was upheld by an employment tribunal, and, on appeal, by the EAT. The written statement which employers are required to give to their employees under s 1 of ERA (see para 3.201) should include a note specifying to whom and in what manner an employee may apply for the purpose of seeking redress of any grievance. A failure to provide and implement any such grievance procedure amounted to a breach of an implied term of the contract of employment, sufficiently serious to justify the employee resigning and claiming constructive dismissal.

Job description

3.181 A modern practice is to draw up and give to an employee a job description document, detailing the nature of his duties. Again, this should be a unilateral document, and should be specific enough to identify the employee's tasks, yet general enough to enable variations to take place within the context of the contract. The ambit of contractual obligations is not the same as the ambit of the duties which an employee in fact performs. This is especially true in small firms, where greater flexibility is needed, and thus the former may be wider than the latter (*Glitz v Watford Electric Co Ltd*). An employer may be able to change the job description provided the proposed work is still within the contractual obligations.

Variation of contractual terms

3.182 The terms of the contract of employment may only be varied with the consent of both parties, and there is no power which enables one side to act unilaterally. It follows that a unilateral variation which is not accepted amounts to the repudiation of the contract. Thus if an employee is demoted, this will be repudiatory conduct by the employer, and a consequent resignation by the employee will be an acceptance of the repudiation and hence is, in law, a dismissal by the employer (see *Marriott v Oxford and District Co-operative Society (No 2)*). But if, subsequent to the variation, the employee stays on with the firm for a considerable length of time, it is likely that he will be regarded as having accepted the change, and the modified contract will be in existence. Where an employee protests about the change, but continues with the employment, it is a question of fact in each case as to whether or not he has accepted it (albeit under protest).

3.183 The employer unilaterally varies the contract if he insists that the employee performs duties other than those contained in the contract, as in *Dwyer v Superguard Ltd*, where the applicant was engaged as a telephonist-typist. Typing work declined, and she was under-employed. She was asked to take on other work, splitting invoices, but she refused and was dismissed. This was held to be unfair, for her contract could only be varied with her consent. However, such a situation could be dealt with in future cases either by stating in the contract an obligation 'to perform such other duties as may be assigned from time to time', or by declaring a redundancy situation and making an offer of alternative employment.

3.184 An employer has no right unilaterally to vary the terms of a contract of employment, eg by reducing wages or salaries (*Miller v Hamworthy Engineering Ltd*), and if he does so, the employee is entitled to a common law remedy for the whole of the time the employer is in breach, and not merely for the period of notice which the employer could lawfully give to terminate the contract. In *Rigby v Ferodo Ltd* the claimant's wages were £192 per week, and his contract of employment terminable by 12 weeks' notice. As a result of a financial crisis, the employers tried to get the trade unions to agree to wage reductions, but the unions refused to agree. The employers then unilaterally reduced the plaintiff's wages by £30 per week. The claimant continued to work at the lower rate, but issued a writ claiming damages for breach of contract. The House of Lords upheld his claim. The employers had unilaterally repudiated the contract, but the employee had not accepted that repudiation, and thus the contract had not been terminated by the reduction in wages. Thus the employee was entitled to damages for the breach of contract for the whole of the period of the breach, and not for the period after 12 weeks when the employers could have lawfully terminated the contract.

3.185 An employee has been 'dismissed' for the purpose of s 95(1) of ERA even though he remains in employment! Thus in *Alcan Extrusions v Yates* the employers wished to impose a new working pattern system, which had the effect of reducing the employees' earnings. After negotiations with trade unions had failed, the new pattern was unilaterally imposed. Employees sent a pro forma reply to the employers, stating that they would work the new system under protest, reserving their rights to claim unfair dismissal and/or redundancy payments. They subsequently lodged claims with an employment tribunal, who held that they had been dismissed. The decision was upheld by the EAT. Where an employer unilaterally imposes radically different terms of employment, that could amount to a dismissal if the changes constitute a very substantial departure from the old contract. In this case, the old contract had been removed, and a new, substantially inferior, contract had been substituted.

3.186 But a contract of employment cannot remain static over the years, and some element of change is inevitable. In strict law, a variation must be mutually agreed by both sides, but if an employee refuses to accept such a change, this does not mean that he can exercise a power of veto over any new proposal. Ultimately, the employer retains an equal right lawfully to terminate the contract. In *Grix v Munford Ltd* the employee was dismissed when she refused to work a new shift system at a service station, which the employers had claimed was necessary on the grounds of efficiency and financial expediency. The employment tribunal, in holding that the dismissal was fair, gave some guidelines on the approach which employers should adopt in these circumstances. They should consult fully and properly with the employee, and they must give reasonable and due consideration to any objections or alternative suggestions. It is also necessary to prove that the change is necessary, and thus amounts to 'some other substantial reason' should a dismissal prove to be necessary. It is not necessarily unfair to dismiss an employee who refuses to obey an order which is outside the terms of his contract, for the test is focused on the reasonableness of the employer's actions, not whether the employer was in breach of the contract (*Farrant v Woodroffe School*). In *Bowater Containers Ltd v McCormack*, the claimant was a supervisor. After a reorganisation, it was decided that another small section should come under his supervision. He refused to take on these additional duties, as he maintained that he was not contractually obliged to do so. His dismissal was held to be unfair by the employment tribunal, but the decision was reversed by the EAT. The reason for the dismissal, ie consequent on the reorganisation, was some other substantial reason and, in the circumstances, the employers had acted reasonably.

3.187 Thus if the employer wishes to vary the contract, and the employee refuses to accept the variation, the employer must give notice to terminate the contract (*Rigby v Ferodo Ltd*). This will, of course, amount to a dismissal, and would normally give the employee a right to bring a claim for unfair dismissal. In such proceedings, the employment tribunal may make a finding as to the advantages to the employers of the proposed changes, and whether it was reasonable for them to implement them by terminating the contract and offering a new one. The question then becomes, have the employers acted reasonably in dismissing the employee for his refusal to enter into the new contract (*Chubb Fire Security Ltd v Harper*)? To answer this question, the nature of the new offer, the advantages to the employer, and the method of handling the situation, the incentives offered, etc all become relevant considerations (*Hollister v NFU*). The dismissal will be fair if the offer is one which a reasonable employer would make in the circumstances (*Richmond Precision Engineering Ltd v Pearce*). The employment tribunal should not look solely at the advantages and disadvantages of the new contract from the employee's point of view, but should also consider and take into account the benefits to the employer in seeking to impose the change (*Catamaran Cruisers v Williams*).

3.188 However, the express terms of the contract may permit substantial variations, and if this is so, the other party is bound to accept, whether he agrees in principle or not. The terms may expressly permit a change in the location of employment, or the duties of the employee, or any other relevant matter. In *Bex v Securicor Transport Ltd* it was a condition of the employee's contract that the nature of his work could be changed by the company. When they appointed him to another position, which he regarded as a demotion, he resigned. It was held that as the employers were expressly entitled to require the employee to serve the company in any capacity, there had been no breach of contract by the employer, and consequently his resignation did not amount to a dismissal. He had the choice of carrying out his contract, or resigning.

3.189 An implied variation, accepted by both sides. may be inferred from the parties' conduct. In *Armstrong Whitworth Rolls v Mustard*, when the employee was engaged, his hours were fixed by a national agreement, and he worked an eight-hour shift for five days per week. One of his workmates left, and he was asked to work twelve-hour shifts for five days per week. This arrangement continued for seven years, and when he was eventually made redundant, it was held that his redundancy payment was to be based on a normal working week of 60 hours. Although there was no express mutual agreement to vary his hours, such agreement could clearly be inferred from the conduct of the parties.

3.190 A contract may also be varied by virtue of the terms of a collective agreement. In *Parry v Holst* the claimant's employment was expressly governed by the terms of the Working Rule Agreement of the Civil Engineering Construction Conciliation Board, Clause XD (f) of which provided that 'At the discretion of the employer, an operative may be transferred at any time during the period of his employment from one job to another'. The employee's work in South Wales came to an end, and his employers asked him to work in Somerset. He refused, and claimed a redundancy payment. It was held that he was not entitled. His employment was subject to the Working Rule Agreement, which provided for travelling and shift allowances, and there was nothing unusual about the employers' request. However, if the proposed transfer had been so unreasonable that it could be said to be outside the contemplation of the parties to the contract, then the literal application of Clause XD (f) would be precluded. Also, it was suggested that the Clause would not apply if there was a custom and practice of a particular company which would have the effect of varying the way the rule operated. None of these considerations applied in this case, and the application for a redundancy payment was rejected.

3.191–3.200 Where a variation of an existing contract is based on a change brought about by a revised collective agreement, the change will only be binding on individual employees if it is accepted by them, or if they were collectively represented at the time the change was agreed (*Land and Wilson v West Yorkshire Metropolitan County Council*). Thus employees who are not union members, or who are members of another union, are not necessarily bound by the change. But if the collective agreement is expressly incorporated into the individual's contract, or if the union has authority to negotiate a change, the variation will bind (*Nelson and Woollett v Post Office*).

Written particulars of the contract of employment

3.201 Section 1 of the Employment Rights Act 1996 provides that no later than two months after the commencement of employment, the employer shall give to the employee a written statement containing the following information:
(1) (a) the names of the employer and employee;
   (b) the date when the employment began;
   (c) the date on which the employee's period of continuous employment began, taking into account any employment with a previous employer which counts towards continuity;

(2) as at a specified date, not more than seven days before the statement is given;
- (a) the scale or rate of remuneration, or the method of calculating remuneration;
- (b) the intervals at which remuneration is paid;
- (c) any terms and conditions relating to hours of work;
- (d) any terms and conditions relating to:
  - (i) entitlement to holidays, including public holidays, and holiday pay (being sufficient to calculate the entitlement, including accrued holiday pay on the termination of employment);
  - (ii) incapacity for work due to sickness or injury, including any provision for sick pay;
  - (iii) pensions and pension schemes;
- (e) the length of notice the employee is obliged to give, and entitled to receive to determine the employment;
- (f) the title of the employee's job;
- (g) if the employment is not intended to be permanent, the period for which it is expected to continue; if it is for a fixed term, the date when it is to end;
- (h) either the place of work or, where the employee is required or permitted to work at various places, an indication of that, and of the address of the employer;
- (j) any collective agreement which directly affects the terms and conditions of employment; where the employer is not a party to the agreement, the persons by whom they are made;
- (k) where the employee is required to work outside the United Kingdom for more than one month:
  - (i) the period for which he is to work outside the United Kingdom;
  - (ii) the currency in which remuneration is to be paid while so working;
  - (iii) any additional remuneration payable to him, and any benefits to be provided by reason of his working abroad; and
  - (iv) any terms and conditions relating to his return to the United Kingdom.

3.202 So far as the above matters are concerned, it should be noted that:
(1) if there are no particulars to be entered under any of these headings, that fact should be stated;
(2) the written statement may refer the employee to the provisions of some other document which he has a reasonable opportunity of reading in the course of his employment, or which is made reasonably accessible to him in some other way, in respect of sick pay and pension schemes;
(3) all the above particulars shall be given in one document (known as the principal statement) except terms and conditions relating to sickness, pensions, length of temporary or fixed term contracts, collective agreements and details given to employees who are to work outside the United Kingdom. These terms may be contained in a separate document or documents;
(4) the statement shall be given to the employee notwithstanding that his employment has ended before the end of two months from its commencement.

3.203 In addition to the matters required to be given under s 1, the statement shall include a note:
(a) specifying any disciplinary rules applicable to the employee, or referring him to the provisions of a document which he has reasonable opportunities

of reading in the course of his employment, or is made reasonably accessible to him in some other way, and which specifies such rules;

(b) specifying, by description or otherwise a person to whom the employee can apply if he is dissatisfied with any disciplinary decision relating to him, the person to whom he can apply for the purpose of seeking redress of any grievance relating to his employment, and explaining any further steps which may be taken, or referring to a document which the employee has a reasonable opportunity of reading or which is made accessible to him. However, the provisions relating to disciplinary procedures do not apply if, on the date when the employee's employment began, the relevant number of employees was less than 20 (including employees employed by an associated employer). Nor do the provisions relating to rules, disciplinary decisions, grievances or procedures apply if they are related to health and safety at work.

3.204   If there is any change in the matters specified in the written particulars, the employer shall give, within one month of the change, the relevant particulars.

3.205   It is not necessary to give written particulars to an employee if his employment continues for less than one month.

3.206   It must be borne in mind that the statement given by virtue of s 1 is not necessarily a contract, and is not conclusive evidence of that contract (*System Floors (UK) Ltd v Daniel*). But it certainly helps to establish what those contractual terms were, and a failure by an employer to provide such a statement may well lead an employment tribunal to draw adverse presumptions against that employer in subsequent litigation, should the terms of the contract be in dispute.

3.207   If an employer does not provide the written statement under s 1, or if it is incomplete, the employee can require a reference to be made to an employment tribunal to determine what particulars ought to be included in such a statement. But this power only extends to matters which should be in the statement in accordance with the above statutory requirements. The tribunal has no power to amend or rewrite a contract of employment merely because there is some misunderstanding about its meaning (*Construction Industry Trading Board v Leighton*).

3.208–3.215   An employment tribunal may only state those terms which have been agreed. They cannot remake the contract and insert terms which should have been agreed. 'Mandatory' terms can be determined by looking at all the evidence, including the express, implied and statutory terms. If there has been no agreement on the 'non-mandatory' terms, the employment tribunal should record this (*Eagland v British Telecommunications plc*). There is no power to invent terms which have not been agreed, except, perhaps, terms which are necessarily imposed by law, eg reasonable notice.

Itemised pay statement (Employment Rights Act 1996 ss 8–10)

3.216   Every employee has the right to be given by his employer an itemised pay statement, giving particulars of the gross amount of wages or salary, the amount of any variable or fixed deductions, and the purposes for which they are made, the net wages or salary payable and, where the net amount is paid in different ways, the amount and method of each part-payment. A pay statement need not contain separate particulars or fixed deductions as long as the aggregate amount of all deductions is stated, and the employer had given to the employee a standing statement of fixed deductions which contains all the relevant details. Such standing statement must be reissued every 12 months.

3.217–3.225 If an employer fails to give an itemised pay statement, the employee may require a reference to be made to an employment tribunal, to determine what particulars ought to be included in such a statement. But where the tribunal finds that the employer has failed to give an employee any itemised pay statement, or that it does not give the required particulars concerning deductions, the tribunal shall make a declaration to that effect (*Coales v John Wood & Co*) and, if there have been any unnotified deductions from the employee's pay within 13 weeks preceding the date of the application for the reference to the tribunal, then the tribunal may award that the employer shall pay to the employee the aggregate of the deductions made. However, no application for a tribunal reference can be made more than three months after the employment has ceased. The requirement to give an itemised pay statement does not apply to employees who work outside Great Britain, share fishermen or merchant seamen.

Holidays

3.226 Under the provisions of the Working Time Regulations 1998, in force from 1 October 1998 (see para 7.221), all workers are now entitled to four weeks' holiday each year. There is a qualifying period of employment of three months, and thereafter entitlement will be proportionate to the length of employment in the relevant year, which will run from the date specified in a workplace agreement, or, if there are no such provisions, 1 October (in respect of workers whose employment began on or before 1 October 1998), or, in respect of workers who became employed after 1 October 1998, on the date when the employment began and each subsequent anniversary of that date. Leave entitlement is only in respect of the holiday year in which it is due, and may not be replaced by a payment in lieu except on the termination of employment. The employer may require the holidays to be taken at particular times, provided he gives notice in writing specifying the dates when leave is or is not to be taken, which must be at least four weeks in advance of the earliest date specified in the notice. Otherwise, the worker may give notice in writing of the dates when he wishes to take his holidays, at least four weeks in advance of the date. Details of holiday dates should therefore be given in the written statement provided under s 1 of ERA, or contained in the works rules/staff handbook etc.

3.227 If an employee takes a contractual holiday, he will be entitled to be paid his normal week's pay, calculated in accordance with ss 221–224 of ERA. Entitlement to accrued holiday pay will be determined by the provisions of the workplace agreement, or, if there are no such provisions, by the application of the formula $(A \times B) - C$, where A is the period of leave to which he is entitled, B is the proportion of the worker's leave year which has expired before the termination date, and C is the period of leave already taken. It would thus appear that existing contractual provisions which enable an employer to refuse to pay accrued holiday pay to employees who are dismissed for gross misconduct, or who resign without giving contractual notice, are no longer valid.

3.228–3.235   It should be noted that the Regulations apply to workers, not just to employees. There are a number of exclusions from entitlement (see para 7.241). If an employer refuses to permit a worker to take his holiday entitlement, or refuses to pay holiday pay, the worker may bring a complaint before an employment tribunal within three months, or such further period as the tribunal considers reasonable. If the complaint is well founded, the tribunal shall make a declaration, may award compensation as it considers to be just and equitable, and/or order the employer to pay the appropriate holiday pay. A worker has the right not to suffer a detriment because he refused to comply with a requirement which the employer imposed in contravention of his obligations under the regulations, refused to forgo a right conferred on him by the regulations, failed to sign or enter into a workplace agreement, performed functions as a representative of the workforce, brought proceedings to enforce a right, or alleged that the employer had infringed a right conferred on him (ERA s 45A). It will also be an automatically unfair dismissal if an employee (not a worker) is dismissed for any of the above reasons (ERA s 101A), or selected for redundancy (ERA s 105(4), (4A)).

Occupational pension schemes

3.236   The Occupational Pension Schemes (Disclosure of Information) Regulations 1986 require an employer who runs an occupational pension scheme to disclose automatically certain information to members and beneficiaries, including details of the scheme, rights of leavers, amount of pension payable to a new pensioner, and options available to persons on the death of a member or beneficiary. Other information is to be disclosed on request, including trust deeds and rules, benefit statements, trustees' annual report and the actuarial valuation report.

3.237   The persons entitled to this information include current members and deferred pensioners, prospective members and their spouses, and recognised independent trade unions (except that the latter are not entitled to benefit statements).

CHAPTER 4

Discrimination in employment

Sex discrimination

4.1 Although it is generally considered that the Sex Discrimination Act 1975 (as amended by the Sex Discrimination Act 1986) was designed to prevent unlawful discrimination against women, the Act makes it equally unlawful to discriminate against men, or against a married person of either sex on the grounds of that person's marital status. But no account is to be taken of special treatment afforded to women because of pregnancy or childbirth. It is permissible, however, to discriminate against (but not in favour of) a single person of either sex. Thus if a firm wishes to offer cheap mortgage facilities to its staff, then if these facilities are made available to married men, they must be equally available to married women (*Sun Alliance and London Insurance Co v Dudman*). But it is permissible to exclude single persons of either sex from the scheme and it is permissible to discriminate between married and unmarried couples (*Bavin v NHS Trust Pensions Agency*).

4.2 The Act does not permit 'affirmative' or 'positive' action designed to give priority to persons of either sex (other than single sex training permitted under s 48: see para 4.134) and indeed such positive discrimination has been held to be contrary to the Equal Treatment Directive (76/207/EEC). In *Kalanke v Freie Hansestadt Bremen*, a man successfully claimed unlawful discrimination because he was passed over for promotion when an equally qualified woman was given the post, pursuant to a law which provided that women were to be preferred to a male candidate if their qualifications were equal.

4.3–4.10 However, this case was distinguished by the ECJ in *Marschall v Land Nordrhein-Westfalen*, where it was held that where there are fewer women than men in a particular post in public service, legislation can provide for preferential treatment for women, if there is a saving clause which guarantees that women are not to be given priority if there was a reason specific to an equally qualified male candidate which would tilt the balance in his favour. In other words, if a rule does not guarantee absolute and unconditional priority to women, it does not go beyond the limits of the Directive.

What constitutes discrimination?

4.11 The test for determining whether or not an act was discrimination is objective, not subjective. In other words, regard must be had to what was done, not the reasons or motives behind what was done. The question to be asked is 'would the complainant have received the same treatment from the defendant but for his or her sex'? In *James v Eastleigh Borough Council*, Mr and Mrs James were both aged 61. The local authority adopted a policy whereby children under three years of age, and members of the public over pensionable age, were permitted free entry into the local swimming pool, whereas everyone else had to pay 75p entrance fee. Mr James complained that he had been discriminated against because of his sex, as he was required to pay an admission fee, whereas his wife was not. The House of Lords upheld his contention. Lord Bridge stated that the purity of the discriminator's subjective motive, intention or reason for discriminating cannot save the criterion applied from the objective taint of discrimination on grounds of sex. Lord Ackner stated that the reason why the local authority adopted its particular policy (ie to benefit state pensioners) cannot affect the fact that men were treated less favourably than women.

4.12 So far as discrimination in employment is concerned, there are three types of circumstances to consider:

A. Direct discrimination (s 1(1)(a))

4.13 This arises when a person of one sex is treated less favourably than a person of another sex, and the sex of that person is the reason for the unfavourable treatment. To refuse to employ a woman because 'it is a man's job' is an example of direct discrimination (*Batisha v Say*). To discriminate against a transsexual who has undergone a sex change operation is contrary to EC Directive 76/207/EEC (see para 1.142) because that amounts to treating that person unfavourably by comparison with persons of the sex to which he or she was deemed to belong before undergoing gender reassignment, and amounts to a failure to respect the dignity and freedom to which that person is entitled (*P v S*, see below, para 4.102).

4.14 Discrimination against a married person of either sex is also covered (s 3(1)(a)).

4.15 Whether a person has been treated 'less favourably' on the ground of sex is an objective matter, for the employment tribunal to determine, and does not depend on whether the claimant subjectively thinks that the treatment is less favourable. For example, some employers may decide to lay down different rules relating to dress or appearance for men and women, and the question will then arise as to whether or not such rules constitute sex discrimination. Thus in *Schmidt v Austicks Bookshops Ltd*, the owner of a bookshop had a rule which forbade female employees wearing trousers, and obliged them to wear overalls. Male employees were forbidden to wear T-shirts. A female employee refused to comply with the rule forbidding trousers, and she was dismissed. It was held that as there were rules governing the appearance of both male and female employees, so that they were both restricted as to clothing, the appellant had not been unlawfully discriminated against. Further, the requirement that she should wear overalls was not sufficiently serious or important so as to constitute a detriment within the meaning of s 6(2)(b). In *Burrett v West Birmingham Health Authority* male and female nurses were required to wear a uniform. Female nurses wore a starched cap, which had no practical or hygienic purpose. The claimant found the wearing of this cap demeaning and undignified, and when she refused to wear one, she was transferred to another department where she had less opportunity to work overtime. She claimed that she had been unlawfully discriminated against, but her claim was dismissed. The fact that there was a different uniform for men and women did not constitute less favourable treatment. The fact that she thought she had been treated less favourably was irrelevant, for the test under s 1(1)(a) was not subjective, but was for the employment tribunal to decide (see also *Stewart v Cleveland Guest (Engineering) Ltd*).

4.16   The approach adopted in the above cases was confirmed by the Court of Appeal in *Smith v Safeway plc*, where a male assistant who worked in the delicatessen department was dismissed because his ponytail hairstyle breached the company's rule that hairstyles should not be unconventional, and should not be permitted to grow below collar length. His claim for sex discrimination was dismissed by an employment tribunal, who held that a retail store was entitled to have a dress and appearance code, and that such a code did not have to make identical provision in relation to men and women. A majority of the EAT allowed his appeal, but the decision of the employment tribunal was restored by the Court of Appeal. A code governing the appearance of male and female employees, which laid down conventional standards, and was even-handed in its approach, was not discriminatory on grounds of sex. There is a distinction between discrimination between the sexes (which may be permissible) and discrimination against one or another of the sexes, which is forbidden by the Act.

4.17   Discrimination can take place even though the act is done with the best of motives, and in the best interests of the person concerned. In *Grieg v Community Industry*, the claimant and another woman were appointed to two jobs, which involved working with men. The other woman failed to turn up for work, and so the claimant was not allowed to start work, as in the past there had been problems with one woman working with an all-male team. It was held that this constituted direct discrimination; the motive of the employers was irrelevant.

4.18   Section 5(3) provides that a comparison of the cases of persons of different sex or marital status under ss 1(1) and 3(1) must be such that the relevant circumstances in the one case are the same, or not materially different, in the other. Those 'relevant circumstances' must be judged objectively. In *Bullock v Alice Ottley School* the employers decided to establish a common retiring age for all members of their staff irrespective of sex. Teaching, administrative and domestic staff had to retire at 60, and gardeners and maintenance staff at 65. The higher retirement age of the latter group was necessary because of the difficulty in obtaining such personnel, and the need to keep them in employment as long as possible. The claimant was required to retire when she became 60, and she claimed she had been discriminated against on grounds of sex, because all the gardening and maintenance staff, who stayed on until 65, were men. An employment tribunal dismissed her complaint holding that it was not discriminatory to have differing retiring ages for persons in different groups provided it was applied irrespective of sex. The EAT reversed the decision, holding that the 'like for like' comparison had to be made in respect of all the staff, not separate groups. On a further appeal, the Court of Appeal restored the decision of the employment tribunal. The conclusion that everyone employed by the same employer had to have the same retiring age was one which could not be accepted. The comparison between the claimant (who was domestic staff) and the maintenance and gardening staff could not be made, since there were special difficulties in recruiting the latter which justified the later retiring age. The 'relevant circumstances' in s 5(3) had to be those circumstances which were relevant to the comparison.

4.19 Further, the claim based on indirect discrimination would also be dismissed. The employers had objectively justified the later retirement age for gardeners and maintenance staff, for reasons which had nothing to do with sex. There was a genuine need for the later retirement age for the latter group of employees, ie the difficulty in recruiting them, and the need to retain their services as long as possible.

4.20 If an employer has a rule which applies equally to men and women, no apparent discrimination exists, but this will not be so if the rule in question affects pregnant women. Thus in *Brown v Rentokil Ltd* the employers had a rule which stated that any employee who was absent from work because of sickness for more than 26 weeks would be dismissed. The claimant had a series of pregnancy-related illnesses, and was dismissed after 26 weeks' absence. The ECJ held that it was contrary to the Equal Treatment Directive to dismiss a woman at any time for absence owing to pregnancy-related illnesses even though a man absent for that period would also be dismissed.

B. Indirect discrimination (s 1(1)(b))

4.21 Indirect discrimination arises:
a. when a person applies a condition or requirement to another,
b. but which is such that the proportion of persons from one sex who can comply with that condition or requirement is considerably smaller than the other sex,
c. it cannot be shown that the condition or requirement is justified irrespective of the sex of the person to whom it is applied, and
d. which is to that person's detriment because he/she cannot comply.
   Indirect discrimination against a person on the ground of marital status is also covered (s 3(1)(b)).

4.22 Thus to advertise for a 'Male or female clerk, must have a large beard' would amount to an indirect discrimination, unless the whiskered requirement can be justified. There is a heavy burden of proof on the employer to satisfy the employment tribunal that the requirement or condition is necessary (*Steel v Union of Post Office Workers*). In *Home Office v Holmes*, it was held that an obligation on an employee to work full-time as opposed to part-time was a requirement or condition, which, on the facts, could not be justified.

4.23 Whether or not the requirement or condition is justified must also be assessed objectively, not subjectively. In other words, it matters not if the discriminator genuinely thought the requirement or condition to be justified, if, looking at the matter objectively, it is not. For example, an employer must be careful not to discriminate indirectly by making generalised assumptions based on sex or marital status. In *Hurley v Mustoe* the claimant, who was a married woman with four young children, applied for a job as a waitress. The manager decided to give her a trial, but on the first night at work the proprietor of the restaurant asked her to leave. It was against his policy to employ women with young children, as he thought they were unreliable. The EAT held that the claimant had been directly discriminated against on grounds of sex contrary to s 1(1)(a) and indirectly discriminated against on grounds of marital status contrary to s 3(1)(b). There were other ways of finding out whether or not a potential employee was reliable without imposing a blanket rule which excluded all women with children. Equally, it is wrong to 'assume' that a married woman will leave her job to be and live with her husband in another town (*Horsey v Dyfed County Council*) or that a man will be 'the breadwinner' of the family (*Skyrail Oceanic Ltd v Coleman*).

4.24   However, in *Briggs v North Eastern Education and Library Board*, the Northern Ireland Court of Appeal took the view that a contractual requirement imposed on a teacher that she should assist in the taking of school games outside school hours was a requirement which was justified irrespective of a person's sex or marital status. A balance must be made between the discriminatory effect of the requirement or condition and the reasonable needs of the employer, objectively determined (see also *Bilka-Kaufhaus v Weber von Hartz*).

4.25   In *London Underground Ltd v Edwards* the claimant was employed as a train driver, working generally from 8.00am till 4.00pm. As part of a cost savings plan, the employers introduced a new shift system, which required her to start work at 4.45am. As she was a single mother with a young child, she was not prepared to work the new system, and resigned, claiming sex discrimination. The EAT held that the employment tribunal had been entitled to take into account their common knowledge that proportionately a larger number of women have childcare responsibilities than men, and thus indirect discrimination had been made out. Having regard to her long service (10 years) and the fact that the demands for her family would be less in the future, the employers should have made arrangements to accommodate her personal requirements. Thus the defence of justification was not made out. An appeal to the Court of Appeal was dismissed.

4.26   It will be an act of indirect discrimination for an employer to insist that a woman who is returning to work from maternity leave shall work on a full-time basis, and to refuse a request from her to work part-time. The insistence on full-time working is a requirement or condition, and the proportion of women who can comply is self-evidently smaller than the proportion of men who can comply. However, the employer can defend the claim if he can show (a) that there is no special reason why the woman cannot comply with the requirement or condition or (b) that the requirement or condition is justified (*Eley v Huntley Diagnostics Ltd*) or the woman has not suffered a detriment because she cannot comply (*Stevens v Katherine Lady Berkley's School*).

4.27   The tribunals must consider not merely whether as a matter of theoretical exercise a woman can comply with the condition which has been imposed, but whether, as a matter of reality and practice, it is possible to do so. This was the reasoning of the EAT in *Price v Civil Service Commission*, where employers advertised for executive officers, a requirement being that candidates had to be over the age of 17$^{1}/_{2}$, but under the age of 28. The claimant, who was aged 36, contended that this amounted to indirect discrimination, because far fewer women than men could comply with this requirement in practice, as they were out of the labour market having or bringing up children. In theory, there is hardly any difference in the numbers of men and women in those age groups, but the EAT held that it was relevant to take into account the realities of the situation, which suggested that there were indeed fewer women available for employment in this age group. As the claimant could not comply, and as it was to her detriment that she could not comply, the EAT remitted the case to the employment tribunal for further consideration. The employment tribunal subsequently held that the respondents had failed to show that the requirement that direct entrants to the Executive Grade of the Civil Service had to be under the age of 28 was justified irrespective of sex. The test of 'justified' was that the requirement or condition should be necessary, not merely convenient. Consideration should be given to whether there is some other non-discriminatory manner of achieving the desired objective without imposing a discriminatory requirement or condition.

4.28 A claimant cannot select the appropriate 'pool' merely because it is convenient to do so, where, in fact, a non-discriminatory pool exists. Further, the objective balance which can justify discrimination must take into account the reasonable needs of the person applying the condition against its discriminatory effect, and if the discrimination affects only a small proportion of the total number of eligible persons adversely, the employment tribunal is not entitled to concentrate on the particular circumstances of the complainant (*University of Manchester v Jones*).

4.29 Whether or not a person 'can comply' with a condition or requirement depends on whether he/she is able to comply, not on whether he/she does not wish to comply. In *Turner v Labour Party* the claimant was a divorcee. She was required to join her employer's occupational pension scheme, which provided, inter alia, for a pension for a surviving spouse. Since she was not likely to have any such survivor, she claimed that the scheme was discriminatory. It was held that although the claimant may not wish to marry, it could not be said that she could not marry. Consequently, she was able to comply with the requirement.

4.30 In *Perera v Civil Service Commission* (a case decided under similar provisions contained in the Race Relations Act) it was decided that an inability to comply with the requirement or condition must be a bar to obtaining a post for it to be discriminatory, but the Scottish EAT in *Falkirk Council v Whyte* refused to follow that decision. In this case, managerial posts at a prison were advertised, it being stated that management experience and supervisory training was desirable. It was held that if there was a requirement or condition imposed which was desirable, but which in practice was decisive, this could be discriminatory.

4.31 It must be remembered that indirect discrimination is not unlawful if it can be objectively justified. Thus if, in a redundancy exercise, the size of an enhanced severance payment is dependent on final salary, and hence discriminatory against women who generally have less continuous service, the employer's desire to cushion employees against the effects of unemployment and to reward long service can amount to objective justification (*Barry v Midland Bank plc*).

C. Victimisation (s 4(1))

4.32 It is also unlawful to victimise a person because he/she has:
i. brought proceedings under the Act, or the Equal Pay Act 1970, or
ii. given evidence or information in connection with proceedings under either Act, or
iii. done anything (in relation to either Act) to the discriminator or any other person, or

iv. has made allegations of a contravention of either Act unless the allegation was false and not made in good faith.

4.33 In order to establish that a person was victimised, it must be shown that s/he did one of the protected acts (above), that s/he was treated less favourably, and that the reason for the less favourable treatment was the doing of the protected act (*Aziz v Trinity Street Taxis Ltd*). But if a person claims that s/he was victimised because s/he made a complaint in respect of something which took place outside working hours, this cannot be within s 4(1)(d), because it is not in respect of an act by the employer which was in contravention of the Act (*Waters v Metropolitan Police Comr*).

4.34–4.40 As a matter of construction, the employment provisions of the Sex Discrimination Act can only apply to existing employees, or to persons seeking employment, or to ex-employees in respect of an act committed during employment. It cannot apply to persons who are no longer in employment. But under European law, the situation is different, certainly with regard to the victimisation provisions. In *Coote v Granada Hospitality Ltd*, the claimant brought a claim of sex discrimination against her former employers, alleging she had been dismissed because of her pregnancy. The claim was settled, but she then alleged she was subsequently unable to obtain further employment, because her former employers had failed to provide an employment agent with a reference. The ECJ held that national laws should provide protection for workers whose ex-employers refuse to provide a reference as a reaction to legal proceedings which had been brought to enforce compliance with the principles of equal treatment, and substantial compensation was awarded by the employment tribunal when the case was remitted for a hearing on its merits. The Equal Treatment Directive would be undermined if an employer could take retaliatory action after the employment had ceased.

Discrimination in employment

4.41 Part II of the Act prohibits unlawful discrimination in employment, which is defined as 'employment under a contract of service or apprenticeship or a contract personally to execute any work or labour'. This definition is wider than the relationship of employer/employee, and can include self-employed persons (*Quinnen v Hovells*, see para 5.4), but there must be a personal obligation to perform that work or labour, and that performance must be the dominant purpose of the contract (*Mirror Group Newspapers Ltd v Gunning*).

4.42 There are five types of unlawful discriminatory acts which may be committed against a person in relation to employment at an establishment in Great Britain.

1. The arrangements a person makes for the purpose of determining who shall be employed (s 6(1)(a))

4.43 The arrangements must ensure that job opportunities are available to all, irrespective of sex. However, an advertisement which indicates an intention to discriminate is not, by itself, discriminatory against any particular person (see *Cardiff Women's Aid v Hartup*, para 4.232). Only the EOC can bring an action in respect of discriminatory advertisements, under s 38 of the Act (post, para 4.147) not an individual.

4.44 Even if an advertisement in itself is non-discriminatory, an unlawful act may be committed if subsequent events disclose an intention to discriminate. In *Brennan v JH Dewhurst Ltd*, a girl applied for a job as a butcher's assistant. She was interviewed by the branch manager, who made it clear that he had no intention of employing a woman in the job. However, the district manager, who had the responsibility for making the appointment, decided that the vacancy need not be filled. The EAT held that the interview by the branch manager, which was a 'first filter' arrangement, operated so as to discriminate against the girl, even though it was not made for that purpose.

4.45 Questions which are asked at interviews are also part of the employment arrangements, as can be seen from *Saunders v Richmond-upon-Thames Council*, where a woman applied for a job as a professional golfer. She was confronted with questions which were not put to male applicants, and which were concerned with the ability of a woman to do the job in question ('Are there any other woman golf professionals?', 'Are you blazing a trail?', etc). It was held that to put certain questions to women applicants which are not put to men does not necessarily make those questions an indication that the employer intends to discriminate. Clearly, an employer may wish to put certain questions to a woman which may be more pertinent in her case (eg 'do you intend to have children?' or 'who will look after the children if they are off school sick?' etc), and which are capable of indicating an intention to discriminate on ground of parenthood rather than sex.

4.46 A similar problem may arise at some future date over the use of application forms, for it could be argued that some of the questions which are directed to finding out factual information (eg sex, marital status, number of children, etc) are discriminatory in that they have no bearing on the employment situation. On this point there is no direct decision.

4.47 It may amount to sex discrimination to insist that a woman's job is not suitable for job sharing (*Cast v Croydon College*).

2. The terms on which a person offers employment to another (s 6(1)(b))

4.48 If an employer makes an offer of employment to a woman on terms which are less favourable than those offered to a man, then clearly an act of discrimination has occurred. This does not apply to any provision for the payment of money unless her contract is subject to an equality clause by virtue of the Equal Pay Act 1970 (see Chapter 5), in which case it is discriminatory. To make an offer of employment to a woman on terms which are different from those offered to a man will be *prima facie* discriminatory. But if the employer can show that the variation was due to a genuine material difference between the two applicants which had nothing to do with their sex, it will not be unlawful. For example, if a woman is offered employment commencing at 9 am because she has to take her children to school, a man must be offered the same facility if he is in a similar situation. A problem may arise if an offer is made which is more favourable than the terms enjoyed by existing employees, for the latter may well decide to make a subsequent complaint.

4.49 It is permissible to discriminate in the terms offered which relate to death or retirement (see para 4.121).

3. Refusing or deliberately omitting to offer employment because of a person's sex (s 6(1)(c))

4.50 In *Batisha v Say* a woman was turned down for a job as a cave guide because 'it is a man's job', and in *Munro v Allied Suppliers* a man was not taken on as a cook because women employees would not work with him. In both cases it was held that an act of discrimination had occurred. A more difficult situation arises if there is an act of discrimination, but in the final event no one is appointed to the post. Can it thus be argued that the person concerned has been treated less favourably? On this, there are tribunal decisions both ways; in *Roadburg v Lothian Regional Council*, the claimant was told that she was unsuitable because she was a woman. This was held to be unlawful discrimination even though no one was appointed to the post. In *Thorn v Meggitt Engineering*, the tribunal dismissed a claim of sex discrimination on its facts, but added that even if there had been discrimination, the claimant was treated no less favourably than a man, for no one was appointed to the job. It would appear that this decision is incorrect; once there has been a finding of unlawful discrimination, the remedy is a declaration, and an award may be made in respect of injury to feelings, even though no other pecuniary loss has been suffered (*Brennan v J H Dewhurst*, above).

4.51 An employer still retains his prerogative right to choose the person he believes will best do the job, and the fact that a rejected candidate has qualifications or experience which are better than the appointee will not be sufficient to found a claim of discrimination. As long as there is no evidence of discrimination on grounds of sex, the employer may select a candidate on the basis of any criteria he thinks fit. In refuting a claim, an employer may well point to the fact that women have been engaged in such positions before, and indicate that there were other reasons why the candidate was not offered employment. Thus in *Steere v Morris Bros* a woman applied for a job as a heavy goods vehicle driver. When she was rejected, she claimed she had been discriminated against. The employers were able to show that they had employed women drivers in the past, and the reason she was not appointed was because she lived too far away from the place of employment. The reasons for her non-appointment had nothing to do with her sex.

4. In the way a person offers access to opportunities for promotion, transfer or training, or to any other benefits, facilities or services, or by refusing or deliberately omitting to afford her/him access to them (s 6(2)(a))

4.52 To deny a woman an opportunity for promotion (eg by refusing to send her on a development course), or to restrict her training opportunities would be discriminatory, although it may be noted that a crash programme of single sexed training is permissible under s 47 in order to alter an imbalance of the sexes in a job which has become apparent within the previous 12 months. The words 'benefits, facilities or services' are capable of covering almost any discriminatory practice in employment. For example, in *Peake v Automotive Products*, the terms and conditions of employment of men and women were the same. However, it was an established practice of the firm, going back some 30 years, that women and disabled persons were allowed to leave work at 4.25 pm, whereas the men left at 4.30 pm. This arrangement was made for safety reasons, in order to prevent women and handicapped employees from being jostled in the rush to the gate. The male claimant complained that this amounted to an act of unlawful discrimination on grounds of his sex. His claim was rejected by the employment tribunal, but on appeal, the EAT held that he had been refused access to a benefit (of leaving early) and had been subjected to a detriment (of not being allowed to leave at 4.25 pm) on grounds of his sex. This decision was reversed by the Court of Appeal. Lord Denning held that the Act did not obliterate all the chivalry and courtesy which it was expected that men would give to women. Nor did the Act require that elemental differences of sex must be disregarded in the interpretation of an Act of Parliament. Arrangements which were made in the interests of safety or good administration were not infringements of the law. In the last analysis, Lord Denning was prepared to adopt the rule *de minimis non curat lex* (the law does not concern itself with trifling matters). This decision has been criticised on the ground that the interests of safety and good administration could be met without relying on a scheme which was fundamentally based on sex, and that some other equally efficacious manner of achieving these objects could be devised without perpetuating the myth of 'the weaker sex'. Indeed, the Court of Appeal subsequently held that the only sound reason for the decision in *Peake's* case is the *de minimis* rule, and in so far as the decision rested on chivalry and administrative convenience, it was no longer to be relied upon (*Jeremiah v Ministry of Defence*).

4.53   If the facts give rise to an inference that a person has been treated less favourably because of his or her sex, the burden is on the employer to show that there was a non-gender specific reason for the less favourable treatment (*King v Great Britain-China Centre*). Thus in *ACAS v Taylor* a man claimed that he had been denied the opportunity to apply for promotion because his employers had operated a policy of positive discrimination in favour of women, and as the employers failed to rebut the allegation, his claim for unlawful discrimination succeeded.

5. By dismissing a person, or subjecting her/him to any other detriment (s 6(2)(b))

4.54   The term 'dismissal' includes constructive dismissal (see para 17.35) and the non-renewal of a fixed term contract (ERA s 197).

4.55   A dismissal on grounds of sex is unlawful even though the employer acts under pressure from other employees. In *Munro v Allied Suppliers*, a man was offered a job as a cook. He was dismissed before he started work, as other women employees indicated that they would not work with him. This was held to violate the Act.

4.56 A 'detriment' can take many forms. Thus to dismiss a woman following a disciplinary hearing which she was unable to attend because of a pregnancy-related illness is to subject her to a detriment (*Abbey National plc v Formoso*). In *Day v T Pickles Farms Ltd* it was held that a failure to carry out a risk assessment when employing a woman of child-bearing age, as required by reg 16 of the Management of Health and Safety at Work Regulations (see para 11.94) was to subject her to a detriment, as was a failure to investigate an allegation of sexual harassment in *Coyne v Home Office*.

4.57 A detriment may exist even though the employee is compensated for it. In *Jeremiah v Ministry of Defence*, it was the practice of the respondents not to require women to do certain dirty work, as they did not wish to take showers afterwards. When men did the work, they received extra pay. It was held that the fact that the employee was compensated for the dirty work by an additional payment did not mean that he was not subjected to a detriment. An employer cannot buy the right to discriminate.

4.58 The employment tribunals have met with some difficulties in those cases where a woman has been dismissed, but sex, although relevant, has not been the primary consideration. In *Gubala v Crompton Parkinson*, the choice of a dismissal in a redundancy situation lay between a man and a woman. The woman had longer overall service, but the employers took into account the fact that the man was 58 years old, and had a family to support and a mortgage to keep up. The woman was young, married, with a husband who was working, and she was dismissed. It was held that this amounted to unlawful discrimination; the tribunal refused to accept the 'breadwinner' criterion as a basis of redundancy selection.

4.59 A somewhat different result was reached in *Goult v Reay Electrical*, where the claimant was dismissed when it was discovered that she had married a sales representative who was in the employ of a competitor. The employment tribunal held that she was not dismissed because of her sex, or her marital status, but because she had formed a relationship between an employee of her employer's principal competitor. The marriage was irrelevant except in so far as it indicated that there was a close relationship between her and her husband!

4.60 Further difficulties have been met in cases where a woman has been dismissed because she has announced an intention to get married. It will be recalled that discrimination on grounds of marital status is dealt with in s 3 of the Act. In *Bick v Royal West of England Residential School for the Deaf*, it was held that to dismiss a single woman who announced her intention to get married was not discrimination on grounds of her marital status, for she was not yet married! The tribunal did not appear to consider s 6(2)(b) (dismissal by way of discrimination) as there does not appear to have been any evidence that men were treated in a different manner if they made a similar announcement. On the other hand, in *McLean v Paris Travel Service*, it was contrary to the company's policy to employ married couples, and the claimant was dismissed when she announced her intention to marry the assistant manager. This was held to be contrary to s 6(2)(b), and she was awarded £200 for injury to her feelings, as well as compensation for unfair dismissal.

4.61 A case which illustrates some of the difficulties arising from dismissal on grounds of sex and marital status is *Skyrail Oceanic Ltd v Coleman*, where the claimant was employed as a booking clerk in a travel agency. She then became engaged to a man who worked for a rival firm. The two employers discussed the matter, as it appeared that there would be a possibility of leakage of confidential information. It was agreed that the claimant's husband-to-be would be the breadwinner of the marriage. After the marriage had taken place, she was dismissed. An employment tribunal awarded her £666 compensation for unfair dismissal and £1,000 for injury to feelings under the Sex Discrimination Act. The EAT allowed the employer's appeal under the Sex Discrimination Act, but this was reversed by a majority of the Court of Appeal, who held that an assumption that men are more likely to be the breadwinner of the family than women was an assumption based on sex. Therefore, the dismissal of a woman based on that assumption amounted to sex discrimination.

4.62 To dismiss a woman because she is pregnant, or for a reason connected with her pregnancy, is automatically unfair under the provisions of the Employment Rights Act 1996 (see post para 6.42). However, the question will sometimes be raised as to whether such dismissal is also an act of sex discrimination as well (this may be important because there is no limit to the level of compensation which may be awarded in sex discrimination cases, (see *Ministry of Defence v Cannock*)).

4.63 There are two schools of thought on this question, The first school argues that since men cannot become pregnant, there is no question of treating a woman less favourably because of her sex. Therefore, a 'like with like' approach must be used, ie the treatment of a woman must be compared with the treatment of an analogous man in a similar situation. Thus, if a woman is off work because of pregnancy, the question would be, how would a man have been treated if he was off work for a similar period because of a sickness?

4.64 This approach was approved by the House of Lords in *Webb v Emo Cargo (UK) Ltd*, so far as British domestic law is concerned. In this case, a female clerk informed her employer that she was pregnant, and would eventually be taking maternity leave of absence. The claimant was taken on as a temporary replacement, it being recognised that she would require several months' training in order to learn how to do the job. A few weeks after commencing her employment, she informed the employer that she too was pregnant. The employers dismissed her, and she therefore claimed that she had been unlawfully discriminated against on grounds of sex. Her claim failed. She was not dismissed because of her sex, or because of her pregnancy. A man who announced that he would be absent for a comparable period would, in the circumstances, have been treated in a like manner. The claimant's dismissal was therefore for a neutral reason.

4.65 The second school of thought stems from European law, and is based on an 'automatic approach' under the provisions of the Equal Treatment Directive (76/207/EEC). The approach here is to refuse to treat pregnancy as a pathological condition, and therefore the unavailability for work of a man, whether for medical or non-medical reasons, cannot be used for comparison purposes. Thus in *Dekker v Stichting Vormingscetrum voor Jong Volwassenen (VJV-Centrum) Plus*, the claimant applied for a job as a training instructor. In fact, all the applicants were women. The applicant told the selection committee that she was pregnant, but although she was the most suitable candidate, she was not offered the job. The reason was that the employers' insurers would not reimburse the employers for the sickness benefit they would have to pay her, because she was pregnant at the time of the application. Mrs Dekker claimed that the refusal to offer her employment was contrary to the Dutch equal treatment law, and also contrary to the Equal Treatment Directive EEC 76/207 (see para 1.142). The European Court upheld her claim. Whether a refusal to employ results in direct discrimination on grounds of sex depends on whether the reason for the refusal was a reason which applied without distinction to persons of both sexes, or whether it applied exclusively to one sex. Since she was refused employment because she was pregnant, and only women can be pregnant, the refusal was because of her sex. Further, the fact that there were no male applicants for the post was irrelevant, for if the reason for the refusal to employ her was a reason which exclusively applied to one sex, the reason is inherently discriminatory.

4.66 The House of Lords in *Webb v Emo Air Cargo Ltd* referred the appeal to the European Court of Justice for a ruling on these conflicting approaches. The ECJ confirmed the 'automatic' approach, and held that it was contrary to the Equal Treatment Directive to dismiss a woman who was employed for an unlimited term, and who was found to be pregnant shortly after her recruitment, notwithstanding that she was employed to replace a woman who was on maternity leave, and even though the employer would have dismissed a man who had been engaged in similar circumstances who required leave of absence for medical or other reasons. The ECJ seemed to think that if a woman risked dismissal because of pregnancy, there was a danger that she would be prompted voluntarily to terminate her pregnancy. Further, the Pregnant Workers Directive (92/85/EEC) prohibits the dismissal of a woman from the beginning of her pregnancy until the end of her maternity leave. Thus the protection offered by EC law during and after her pregnancy is not dependent on whether her presence at work is essential to the proper functioning of the undertaking in which she is employed.

When the appeal was returned to the House of Lords, it was noted that the ECJ considered it relevant that Mrs Webb was engaged for an indefinite period, and that her inability to carry out the task for which she was engaged affected only a limited period in relation to the total length of her contract. This leaves open the possibility of distinguishing this case when a woman's absence for pregnancy would make her unavailable throughout the whole of the period for which she was engaged, eg a seasonal contract, or one for a fixed term or specific event (eg a sporting fixture of limited duration). However, on the facts of the case, the appeal was allowed, and remitted to the employment tribunal for an assessment of compensation.

4.67 It thus appears that the comparative approach is correct under UK law, whereas the automatic approach is correct under EU law. But although it has been held (see *Marleasing SA v La Comercial Internacional de Alimentación SA*, para 1.139) that it is the duty of UK courts to interpret domestic legislation so as to give effect, as far as possible, to EC Directives, this rule can only apply when the purpose of domestic law was to implement the Directive (the decision in *Marleasing* appears to go further than this, *sed quare*). The problem is that a Directive can only be enforced against an organ of the state (see *Foster v British Gas*, para 1.138), and not against a private employer. Thus, in the absence of amending legislation, a woman who is seeking a remedy in 'like with like' cases against a private employer cannot use EU law (in so far as her claim is based on sex discrimination) although she might be able to bring an action against the state under the *Francovich* doctrine (see para 1.139). A woman who is employed by an organ of the state may rely on the rulings of the ECJ on the automatic approach, and thus is initially in a much more favourable position.

4.68 But if a woman is dismissed for a reason other than pregnancy, even if that reason flows from the pregnancy, this is not an act of sex discrimination. In *Berrisford v Woodard Schools* the claimant was employed as a matron at a Church of England girls' boarding school. She informed the headmaster that she was pregnant. Initially, he congratulated her, and made certain proposals regarding married accommodation, but his attitude changed when the applicant informed him that she had no intention of marrying the father of the child. She was subsequently dismissed, and claimed she had been discriminated against on grounds of sex and family status, contrary to the Sex Discrimination Act and the Equal Treatment Directive. Evidence was given that the school governors expected somewhat high moral standards from their staff, and it was argued that the claimant was dismissed because her pregnancy manifested extra-marital sexual activity. The employment tribunal dismissed her complaint, holding that the reason for the dismissal was the adverse example to the pupils at the school conveyed by the pregnancy, coupled with the continuing unmarried status. The decision was upheld by the EAT. It was the example given to the pupils at the school which was the objectionable conduct, and a man who displayed continuing evidence of extra-marital sexual activity would have been treated in a similar fashion. *Dekker's* case was distinguished because it concerned a woman who was pregnant, and nothing more, whereas in the present case the dismissal was not because of pregnancy, but because of the adverse effect, by way of example, of the pregnancy on the pupils at the school.

As the school was not an organ of the state, the Equal Treatment Directive could not be enforced directly, but in any event, the EAT were not convinced that the Directive had been infringed, because no discrimination on grounds of sex had been shown.

4.69 A different approach was taken by the EAT in *O'Neill v Governors of St Thomas More School*. In this case, the claimant, who was unmarried, was employed to teach religious education and personal relationships at a Catholic school, it being expected that she would make the ideologies and ethos of the Catholic faith clear to her pupils. She then announced that she was pregnant, as a result of a relationship with a Roman Catholic priest who used to visit the school, and who was well known locally. She was invited to resign her post, on terms, but she refused to do so, and instead took maternity leave, and announced her intention to return to work. The school governors refused to permit her to return, and so she claimed that she had been discriminated against on grounds of her sex and/or pregnancy. An employment tribunal dismissed her complaint, holding that her dismissal was not because of her pregnancy, but because she was pregnant as a result of a relationship with a locally well-known Roman Catholic priest. The decision was reversed by the EAT. There is no distinction between pregnancy *per se* and pregnancy in the circumstances, because there are always circumstances which surround pregnancy, whether before, during or afterwards. The Sex Discrimination Act requires the employment tribunal to decide whether the treatment complained of was on the ground of sex, and the subjective motives of the discriminator were irrelevant.

4.70 Two further cases, decided after the decision of the House of Lords in *Webb v Emo Air Cargo Ltd*, but before the ruling of the ECJ in that case, both upheld the comparative approach. In *Dixon v Rees* a pregnant woman was dismissed ostensibly for insubordination, but in reality because the employer had found an adequate replacement whom he did not want to lose. The employment tribunal held that a man in analogous circumstances would have been treated in the same way, for the employer was putting his business interests first. Gender did not enter into the matter. In *Hopkins v Shepherd & Partners*, a pregnant woman, who was employed as a veterinary nurse, was dismissed because the employers thought that the work, which involved exposure to X-rays, anaesthetics, lifting of heavy objects, and possible infection from animals, would make it unsafe for her to continue in employment. The employment tribunal held that in a comparable situation involving a man the employers would have acted the same way. Both these decisions were confirmed on appeal by the EAT.

Clearly, as these cases concerned non-state employers, the provisions of the Equal Treatment Directive cannot apply, and therefore there is no question of interpreting the Sex Discrimination Act accordingly. In reality, the question is one of causation. What was the effective and predominant cause of the action complained of? The intentions, subjective motives, beliefs or subjective purposes of the alleged discriminator may be relevant to remedies, but not to liability. If action is taken against a woman because she is pregnant, then since only women can become pregnant, there is direct discrimination (*P & O Ferries Ltd v Iverson*).

4.71 A dismissal on the ground of periodic absences from work due to an illness attributable to pregnancy or childbirth is not contrary to the Directive. In *Handels-og (acting on behalf of Larsson) v Dansk Handel & Service*), a woman took her statutory maternity leave following a pregnancy, but as she was still receiving treatment for an illness caused by her pregnancy, remained absent from work. She was dismissed because of her absence, and she claimed that her dismissal was contrary to the Directive, because her illness began during her pregnancy and continued afterwards. The ECJ dismissed her claim. Outside the period of maternity leave, laid down by national law, a woman has no more protection than a man would have in respect of absenteeism caused through illness.

4.72–4.80 To put women only on short-time working is to subject them to a detriment, and hence is unlawful (*Morris v Scott*).

Sexual harassment

4.81 Sexual harassment is defined in the Code of Practice issued by the European Commission (see Appendix J) as being '... unwanted conduct of a sexual nature, or other conduct based on sex affecting the dignity of men and women at work. This can include unwelcome physical, verbal or non-verbal conduct.' Thus to subject a person to unpleasant treatment of a sexual nature which amounts to sexual harassment can amount to treating a person less favourably on grounds of sex (s 1(1)(a)), and may amount to a detriment. In *Porcelli v Strathclyde Regional Council*, Mrs Porcelli was a science laboratory technician at a school. She alleged that two male laboratory technicians were sexually harassing her as part of a campaign to make her leave, by deliberately brushing against her and making suggestive remarks of a sexual nature. Accordingly, she felt obliged to apply for a transfer to another school, and complained that she had been unlawfully discriminated against, and subjected to a detriment contrary to s 6(2)(b) of the Act. It was held that as she had been subjected to treatment of a sexual nature to which a man would not have been vulnerable, unlawful discrimination had occurred. The Act is concerned with less favourable treatment, not with motive.

4.82 A single incident, provided it is sufficiently serious, can constitute a detriment within the meaning of s 6(2)(b) (*Bracebridge Engineering Ltd v Darby*). But if the same treatment had been meted out to a man, a woman is not treated less favourably, and therefore there is no detriment to her. In *Balgobin v Tower Hamlets London Borough Council*, the claimants were cleaners at a hostel run by the council. It was alleged that a male cook sexually harassed them, and a complaint was made to management. The cook was suspended pending an investigation, but management were unable to determine the truth of the allegations. The women were then required to continue to work with the man, and they therefore claimed that they had been discriminated against. An employment tribunal dismissed the claim, and the EAT upheld the decision. Although there may be a risk of sexual harassment, the reason they were exposed to that risk was because of the inconclusive nature of the investigation. Had the victim been a man to whom homosexual advances were made, the matter would have been dealt with in the same way.

4.83 Conduct is 'unwanted' within the meaning of the EC Code of Practice in the sense of being 'uninvited' or 'unwelcome'. In *Insitu Cleaning Co Ltd v Heads* it was alleged that the son of a director (who was also a manager) met the applicant (who was a supervisor, and twice the age of the director's son) at a meeting. and said 'Hiya big tits'. The claimant found the remark to be distressing, but when she complained, she was advised to pursue the matter further through the company's grievance procedure. She did not consider this to be satisfactory, and resigned her employment, claiming constructive dismissal. The employment tribunal upheld the claim based on sex discrimination, holding that the remark was sufficient to constitute a detriment. However, the employer's insistence that she should use the company's grievance procedure was not a breach of contract entitling her to claim that she had been constructively dismissed. An appeal and cross-appeal were both dismissed by the EAT. For the employer, it was argued that a single act cannot constitute 'unwanted conduct' because until it was done and rejected a man would not know if the conduct was indeed unwanted. The argument was dismissed by the EAT, for to hold otherwise would grant a licence for harassment, as the man would always argue that he was testing to see whether the act was unwanted or not!

4.84 Compensation for sexual harassment must reflect the degree of detriment. There must be an assessment of the injury to the woman's feelings, looked at both objectively, ie with reference to what any ordinary reasonable female employee would feel, and subjectively, with reference to the particular individual. In *Snowball v Gardner Merchant Ltd* a woman claimed that she had been sexually harassed by her manager. The allegations were denied, and when she gave evidence, she was cross-examined about her sexual attitudes, in an attempt to show that even if there was harassment, she did not suffer any injury to her feelings. Thus, it was alleged that she referred to her bed as a 'play pen', and that she slept between black satin sheets. When she denied these allegations, it was proposed to call evidence to establish the truth. On appeal, it was held that such evidence was admissible. If it could be established that she was unlikely to be upset by a degree of familiarity with a sexual connotation, then it could hardly be said that she had suffered a detriment or hurt feelings. And in *Wileman v*

Minilec Engineering Ltd the EAT refused to disturb an award of £50 made for injury to feelings, because the claimant had worn scant and provocative clothing, which made it inevitable that sexually orientated remarks would be made. However, in more recent cases, substantial sums have been awarded under the heading of injuries to feelings, in some cases running to many thousands of pounds!

4.85 If an employer has reason to believe that sexual harassment is taking place, it is incumbent upon him to investigate the matter, and to take some action if necessary, without waiting for a formal complaint to be made. A failure to do so could well amount to a breach of the implied term of trust and confidence (*Reed and Bull Information Systems Ltd v Stedman*).

4.86–4.95 It must also be borne in mind that an allegation of sexual harassment (as with allegations of other acts of sex discrimination) may be met with certain defences, in particular (a) that the act was not done within the course of employment (see *Tower Boot Co Ltd v Jones*, para 4.166), and that (b) the employer took such steps as were reasonably practicable to prevent an employee from doing the act complained of (see para 4.168). If an act of sexual harassment (or sexual assault) takes place outside working hours, the employer will not be vicariously liable, for the act was not committed in the course of employment (*Waters v Metropolitan Police Comr*) (but see *Chief Constable of Lincolnshire v Stubbs*, para 4.167).

Sexual orientation

4.96 It is clear from a reading of the Sex Discrimination Act that the intention of the legislature was to prohibit discrimination between the sexes, ie men and women. There is nothing in the Act which would prevent discrimination on the grounds of sexual orientation, ie, homosexuality, lesbianism or gender reassignment. But the law does not remain static, and has to deal with problems which arise, usually in a manner consistent with social policy. It appears that there are three general areas which need to be explored, namely (a) discrimination against a person because of his/her sexual orientation (homosexuality or lesbianism) (b) discrimination against a person because of his/her sexual relationship with another person of the same orientation, and (c) discrimination against a person on the ground of gender reassignment.

4.97 The problem is compounded by the fact that there are three jurisdictional bodies involved, namely the UK employment tribunals and appeal courts, the European Court of Justice, and the European Court of Human Rights. The law to be applied is also different in each case, for there is the Sex Discrimination Act, the Equal Treatment Directive, and the European Convention on Human Rights (now given partially effect to in UK courts by virtue of the Human Rights Act 1998 (see para 1.166).

(a) Discrimination because of sexual orientation

4.98 If a person is discriminated against purely because he is a homosexual, or she is a lesbian, then, at first sight, it is difficult to see how the Sex Discrimination

Act could apply. Thus in *Smith v Gardner Merchant* a homosexual employee complained to an employment tribunal that he had been sexually harassed and dismissed because of his sexual orientation. His complaint was dismissed by the employment tribunal and the EAT, it being held that neither the SDA nor the Equal Treatment Directive applied, but a further appeal to the Court of Appeal was allowed. It was accepted that discrimination on the ground of sexual orientation did not fall within the meaning of the SDA as such, but discrimination against a male homosexual based on his homosexuality could be discrimination against him as a man. Therefore, argued the Court of Appeal, the employment tribunal had to decide if he had received less favourable treatment than a woman with whom he fell to be compared, which, in his case, would be a homosexual woman (ie lesbian)! The Court of Appeal did not specify the sort of evidence which would be required to satisfy the tribunal that the employer would have treated a lesbian in the same way as the applicant was treated.

4.99 The issue was raised again in *R v Ministry of Defence, ex p Smith* where the claimant was dismissed from the armed forces because of the policy of the Ministry of Defence to dismiss known homosexuals and lesbians. On an application for judicial review, the Court of Appeal dismissed the case, holding that the Equal Treatment Directive did not apply, and it was not the appropriate forum to determine issues arising from the European Convention on Human Rights (the Human Rights Act not being in force at that time). However, the European Court of Human Rights held that the claimant's discharge from the armed forces solely on the ground of his sexual orientation constituted a direct interference with his right to have respect for his private life, contrary to art 8 of the Convention. It was not shown that that interference was necessary in a democratic society, and thus the UK Government were in breach of the Convention (see *Smith and Grady v United Kingdom*).

4.100 The Human Rights Act is now in force (see para 1.166) and it is the duty of the courts and tribunals not only to apply the Convention, but also to apply the jurisprudence of the European Court of Human Rights. The main problem is that the Convention only applies to the acts of public bodies, not to private employers. There can be little doubt that employment tribunals will apply the principles set out in *Smith and Grady* where they can do so, but this may not always be possible, Thus, if a man is dismissed (or sexually harassed so that he resigns and claims constructive dismissal) by a private employer because he is a homosexual, his dismissal will almost certainly be unfair under the Employment Rights Act 1996 s 94 (see para 17.96), but he will have to show that he had a sufficient period of continuous employment (ie one year) in order to bring such a claim. Such a claim cannot be brought under the provisions of SDA or Equal Treatment Directive.

(b) Discrimination because of homosexual relationships

4.101 The fact that two people of the same sex have a stable relationship cannot be equated with a heterosexual marriage or a stable relationship between two people of the opposite sex. Thus in *Grant v South-West Trains Ltd* it was the policy of the employers to permit their employees and their opposite sex partners (whether married or unmarried) to have favourable travel concessions. The claimant was a lesbian, and she wanted to have the travel concession for her female partner. When this was refused, she claimed that her employers were in breach of art 119 (now 141) of the Treaty of Rome and the Equal Treatment Directive. The ECJ dismissed her complaint. European law does not regard a stable relationship between two persons of the same sex as equivalent to marriage or a stable relationship outside marriage between two persons of the opposite sex. The employers treated the claimant in the same way they would have treated a male homosexual living with a male partner, and no unlawful discrimination existed.

(c) Gender reassignment

4.102 Discrimination against a person because of a gender reassignment is discrimination based on the sex of the person concerned, and hence falls to be considered under the Equal Treatment Directive. In *P v S* a male employee informed his manager that he was going to have a gender reassignment. After having the necessary operations, she was not permitted to return to work, and was dismissed. On a claim for sex discrimination the employment tribunal referred the issue to the European Court, who held that the Equal Treatment Directive cannot be confined to the fact that discrimination had to be between one sex and another. The Directive was an expression of the fundamental principle of equality, and its scope applied to discrimination based on the sex of person conceded. Thus, in this case, the claimant was treated unfavourably by comparison with persons of the sex to which he or she was deemed to belong before undergoing the gender reassignment. To tolerate such discrimination would be tantamount to failing to respect the dignity and freedom to which persons are entitled, and which the court felt it had a duty to safeguard.

4.103–4.110 The problem, of course, is that the Directive only applies to public bodies, and to bring the private sector within the scope of the decision in *P v S* required legislation. Consequently, the Sex Discrimination (Gender Reassignment) Regulations 1999 were passed, and amended the Sex Discrimination Act by inserting new sections 2A and 7B. The regulations define gender reassignment as being '…a process which is undertaken under medical supervision for the purpose of reassigning a person's sex by changing physiological or other characteristics of sex, and include any part of such process'. Section 2A now makes it unlawful directly to discriminate by treating a person less favourably on the ground that he intends to undergo a gender reassignment. If a person is absent from work as a result of undergoing treatment for gender reassignment, he is not to be treated less favourably than he would have been if the absence was due to sickness or injury, or some other cause, and, having regard to the circumstances of the case, it is reasonable for him to be treated no less favourably.

Discrimination in occupational pensions

4.111 Article 141 of the Treaty of Rome requires that men and women must receive equal pay for equal work. 'Pay' is defined as any basic wage or salary and '… any other consideration, whether in cash or kind, which the worker receives, directly or indirectly, in respect of his employment from his employer.' It will be recalled (see para 1.138) that the article has a direct effect, and can thus be enforced in national courts against both public and private employers.

4.112   In 1986 the European Court of Justice held that benefits paid under an occupational pension scheme are pay for the purpose of art 141 (*Bilka-Kaufhaus GmbH v Weber von Hartz*). In a series of judgments the ECJ has given further rulings on how this complex topic should be treated in member states, which may be summarised as follows:

(1)   The exclusion of part-time workers from access to an occupational pension scheme is in breach of art 141 if the effect of that exclusion is to discriminate against one sex (ie women), because a greater number of women than men were excluded. However, because such discrimination is indirect, it may be objectively justified on grounds unrelated to sex discrimination, eg in order to discourage part-time work. However, it must be shown that there is a genuine need on the part of the business, the means are appropriate to that need, and are necessary.

(2)   Dependants' benefits are also within the scope of art 141, and thus subject to the principle of equality. Thus, if a scheme offers benefits for the worker's surviving spouse, this must apply to both sexes (*Ten Oever v Stichting* etc).

(3)   It is not contrary to art 141 for a pension scheme to award a bridging pension, to take into account the fact that the worker has not received a state pension. Since men and women historically receive a state pension at different ages, the bridging pension is designed to remedy an inequality, and is not therefore discriminatory (*Roberts v Birds Eye Walls Ltd*).

(4)   The use of sex-based factors in calculating the actuarial value of pensions does not contravene art 141. Thus, although the employer has a commitment at a given moment in time to pay a periodic pension, the employer's contribution to the scheme is concerning with funding arrangements to meet that commitment (*Neath v Hugh Steeper Ltd*).

(5)   Trustees of an occupational pension fund, although not themselves party to the employment relationship, are bound to do everything in their power to ensure compliance with the principle of equal treatment under art 141 (*Coloroll Pension Trustees Ltd v Russell*). Further, the rules of the pension scheme or the trust deed cannot be used as a means of avoiding the principle of equality, and, if necessary, the trustees would have to apply to the national courts for permission to amend these in order so to comply.

(6)   Additional benefits which stem from additional voluntary contributions (AVCs) made by the employee are not covered by art 141. If a worker transfers from one scheme to another consequent on a change in employment, the receiving scheme is bound to pay any increase in benefits in order to comply with art 141 even though the transfer payment is not sufficient to meet this obligation (*Coloroll*).

(7)   Social security schemes, which stem from national legislation, including retirement pensions, do not fall within art 141, because these are determined by social policy, and do not arise out of the employment relationship (*Bestuur van het Algemeen v Beune*). But payments which flow from statutory provisions, such as statutory redundancy pay, are within art 141 (*Barber v Guardian Royal Exchange Assurance Group*).

(8)   Because of the potentially huge financial burden which would be imposed on pension funds if the decisions of the ECJ were to be applied retrospectively, it was ruled in *Barber* that art 141 may not be relied upon to claim entitlement to a pension in respect of service prior to 17 May 1990 (the date of the decision) except in those cases where legal proceedings had commenced before that date. This also applies to dependants' benefits, which are only equalised in respect of a worker's service after that date (*Ten Oever*

v Stichting BGS). However, access to pension schemes, ie the right to join, applies from 8 April 1976, the date when the ECJ held that art 141 was directly enforceable (*Defrenne v Sabena*). This point may be of particular importance to part-time workers who have previously been excluded (although the employers may still argue that the exclusion was justified, (*Fisscher v Voorhuis Hengelo*), but they would be required to pay arrears of their own contributions. The time limits for asserting the right to join are to be determined by national law, which, in the case of the UK, are believed to be the same as those which apply to equal pay claims generally (see para 5.94). Existing employees may bring a claim at any time during their employment, but ex-employees must apply to an employment tribunal within six months from the date when the employment ceased.

4.113 The Pensions Act 1995 (ss 62–66) provides that there shall be equal treatment in benefits in respect of pensionable service on or after 17 May 1990 (the date of the *Barber* decision), although it will be a defence if treatment is unequal due to actuarial factors. An equality clause on the lines of the Equal Pay Act is to be imported into all contracts of employment in relation to pension benefits. The legislation contains exceptions in relation to bridging pensions (due to the different ages at which men and women receive their State pension) and lists the circumstances in which sex related actuarial factors may be taken into account.

4.114–4.120 The major outstanding problems concerns the right of part-time employees who had previously been excluded from pension schemes, whether domestic time-limits are to be applied when lodging claims, and how far back claims can be backdated. In *Magorrian v Eastern Health and Social Services Board* the ECJ ruled that the limitation in time laid down in *Barber* did not apply to the right to join an occupational pension scheme, because the right of access to such a scheme, as opposed to entitlement under the scheme, dates from the decision of the ECJ in *Defrenne v Sabena*, and not from *Barber v Guardian Royal Exchange*. Further it was held that a national rule which limits the entitlement of a claimant to join an occupational scheme to a period which starts to run from two years prior to the date when proceedings were commenced is also prohibited. Such a rule would have amounted to the denial of an effective remedy under Community law. In *Preston v Wolverhampton Healthcare NHS Trust* the House of Lords referred two questions to the ECJ as to the compatibility of s 2(4) and s 2(5) of the Equal Pay Act with EC law, namely (a) the rule which requires a claim to be brought within six months from leaving employment, and (b) the rule which limits claims to a period not exceeding two years from the date of leaving employment. The court ruled that s 2(4) did not offend against the principle of effectiveness, and did not render it impossible or excessively difficult for a person to exercise rights conferred by EC law. However, the two-year time limit specified in s 2(5) was contrary to EC law, in so far as it prevented access to membership (*Lerez v TH Jennings (Harlow Pools) Ltd*, para 5.95),

Exceptions to the Act

4.121 Provisions relating to death or retirement are excluded from the Sex Discrimination Act (s 6(4)), but this does not permit discrimination against a person in provisions relating to retirement in the field of promotion, training, transfer, demotion or dismissal. But it is permissible to discriminate in relation to retirement in the provision of benefits, facilities or services. Thus, if there is an age at which men retire, or beyond which they cannot be promoted, trained, etc, it is not permissible to have a lower age limit for women.

4.122–4.130 The age at which the state retirement pension is payable is also permitted to be discriminatory (EC Directive 79/7, art 7).

Permissible discrimination

A. Health grounds (s 51(1))

4.131 Nothing in Part II of the Act (which deals with discrimination in employment) shall render unlawful any act done by a person in relation to a woman if it is necessary to comply with any existing statutory provision concerning the protection of women, or a relevant statutory provision within the meaning of the Health and Safety at Work etc Act 1974, and the act was done for the purpose of the protection of women. Thus it is permissible to discriminate against women in order to protect them against definable health risks, which are specific to women, including risks associated with pregnancy and childbirth (see *Page v Freight Hire (Tank Haulage) Ltd*).

B. Genuine occupational qualification (s 7)

4.132 It is permissible to make arrangements which will lead to a person being offered a job, or to refuse another person that post, if the sex of the person is a genuine occupational qualification (GOQ) for the job, and it follows that an employer does not unlawfully discriminate if he does not employ, or if he denies an opportunity for promotion or transfer to, or training for, such employment to a person of the other sex.

4.133 The sex of a person is a genuine occupational qualification for the job in the following circumstances:
a. The essential nature of the job calls for authentic male or female characteristics (excluding physical strength or stamina). Thus it is permissible to advertise for a man to play Hamlet, or for a woman to play Ophelia. It would be interesting to know if it is discriminatory to advertise for a man to play the role of a dame in a pantomime, or for a woman to take the role of principal boy! But if the job merely calls for an ability to haul around 25 kg parcels, it must be open to either sex.
b. The job needs to be held by a person of one sex in order to preserve decency or privacy, because:
   (i) it is likely to involve physical contact with a person in circumstances where that person may reasonably object to it being carried out by a person of the opposite sex. For example, it may be presumed that women would object to men assisting them whilst trying on underwear. In *Etam plc v Rowan* a man applied for a job as a sales assistant in a shop which sold women's and girls' clothing. He was refused employment because the employers considered that a major part of the work involved personal contact with women when they were in a state of undress, and in response to a claim of sex discrimination, pleaded the defence of genuine occupational qualification. However, his claim was upheld by an employment tribunal and, on appeal, by the EAT. On the facts of the

case, a man would have been able to carry out adequately the job of a sales assistant, and such functions as he could not perform could easily have been done by one of the other female sales assistants without causing any inconvenience or difficulty. Further, s 7(4) (see below), which negates the defence of genuine occupational qualification, was applied. In *Timex Corpn v Hodgson* the claimant was a supervisor who was dismissed for reason of redundancy. A female supervisor, who had less service, was retained. The employers sought to justify this on the grounds that all other female supervisors were leaving and they needed to retain one woman supervisor (a) to deal with the private problems of female shop-floor employees, (b) to take women to the first aid room (a man would have to be accompanied), (c) to ensure there was an adequate supply of sanitary towels and pills for period pains kept in the ladies' lavatory, and (d) to take urine samples from women engaged on work involving toxic materials. The EAT held that the male employee had not been discriminated against on grounds of sex. The employers had discriminated by selecting the female supervisor to do a revised job. They had failed to transfer a man to that job, and deliberately refused to offer a man employment in that job. But the sex of the person who was to do the job was relevant, and it amounted to a GOQ;

(ii) persons of one sex might reasonably object to the presence of the opposite sex because they are in a state of undress or using sanitary facilities. This might cover, for example, lavatory attendants, or swimming pool attendants (see *Sisley v Britannia Security Systems Ltd*);

(iii) the job is likely to involve the holder doing his work, or living, in a private home, and needs to be held by a person of one sex because objection might reasonably be taken to allowing a person of the other sex

    (a) the degree of physical or social contract with a person living in the home, or

    (b) the knowledge of intimate details of such a person's life, which would be allowed to, or available to, the holder of the job.

c. The employee is required to live in premises provided by the employer, and those which are available are not equipped with separate sleeping accommodation and sanitary facilities, and it is not reasonable to expect the employer so to equip those premises or to provide such facilities, or to provide other premises. Thus employment on a remote site, or a lighthouse, could be single-sex.

d. Where the job has to be done by a person in a hospital, prison, or other establishment for people who need special care, supervision or attention, and all the inmates thereof are persons of one sex (disregarding the presence of persons of the other sex whose presence is exceptional), and it is reasonable, having regard to the essential characteristics of the establishment that the job should be held by a person of a particular sex. This would cover, for example, a single-sex mental institution.

e. The holder of the job provides individuals with personal services promoting their welfare or education, which can be most effectively provided by one sex. A tough male youth club leader, for example, may be required for a boys' club.

f. The job needs to be held by a man because it is likely to involve performance of duties outside the United Kingdom in a country whose laws or customs are such that such duties could not effectively be performed by someone of

the opposite sex. There could be difficulties, for example, in sending a woman
to negotiate with an eastern potentate! In *O'Conner v Kontiki Travel*, a woman
was turned down as a coach driver because, it was argued, she would have to
drive through Muslim countries, where women drivers are unacceptable. If
true, this would have amounted to a GOQ, but it was found that the only
Muslim country to which the tour was going was Turkey, and as no evidence
had been produced that there would be such objections to women drivers in
that country, this amounted to unlawful discrimination.
g.   The job is one of two held by a married couple.

4.134   It is not permissible to use the 'decency' defence when filling a vacancy
if the employer already has employees of one sex capable of carrying out the
above duties (except g. above), whom it would be reasonable to employ on those
duties and whose numbers are sufficient to meet the employers' likely
requirements in respect of those duties without undue inconvenience (s 7(4)).
But this has to be considered as at the time the alleged discrimination took place.
Thus, if, at that time, the employer did not have sufficient female employees to
carry out duties which would otherwise be reserved to them, then it would be
permissible to refuse employment to a male applicant (*Lasertop Ltd v Webster*).
Also, s 48 permits an employer to train members of one sex only for a job which
has been previously performed exclusively, or nearly so, by members of the other
sex during the preceding 12 months but the anti-discrimination provisions in
selection and recruitment still apply. Thus positive action is encouraged, but
not positive discrimination. There are special exemption provisions for police,
prison officers, and ministers of religion.

4.135–4.145   Supplementary genuine occupational qualifications apply when
a person has had (or is proposing to have) a gender reassignment. Thus, it will
not be discriminatory if the employer can show that the treatment is reasonable,
having regard to the following factors:
(a)   the job involves the holder performing intimate physical searches pursuant
to statutory powers;
(b)   the job involves doing work in, or living in a private home, and objection
may be taken to allowing a person who has undergone gender reassignment
from
(i)   having physical or social contact with a person living in the home, or
(ii)   gaining knowledge of intimate details of such person's life;
(c)   reasonable objection could be taken to the holder of the job sharing
accommodation or facilities in living premises provided by the employer
whilst undergoing gender reassignment, and it is not reasonable to expect
the employer to provide separate premises;
(d)   the holder of the job provides vulnerable persons with personal services
promoting their welfare (ss 7A–B).

Employment outside Great Britain (s 10)

4.146   The provisions relating to discrimination in employment only apply to
employment in an establishment in Great Britain. If the work is to be performed
wholly outside Great Britain, the provisions of the Act do not apply (see *Haughton
v Olau Line (UK) Ltd*). This exclusion will not apply to employment on a ship,
aircraft or hovercraft registered in Great Britain unless the work is done wholly

outside Great Britain. Offshore installations are within the scope of the Act (see para 2.251).

Employment advertisements (s 38)

4.147 It is also unlawful to advertise in a manner which might be taken as indicating an intention to discriminate, and the use of job descriptions in advertisements with a sexual connotation, such as 'waiter', 'salesgirl', 'postman', 'stewardess' etc will be assumed to be discriminatory unless the advertisement contains an indication to the contrary. The EOC has issued a document called 'Guidance on Employment Advertising Practice' which contains some useful information and advice on this subject.

4.148–4.155 To determine whether an advertisement shows an intention to discriminate unlawfully, it must be read as a whole, according to what an ordinary reasonable person, without any special knowledge, would find to be the natural and ordinary meaning of the words used. In *Equal Opportunities Commission v Robertson*, the respondent placed an advertisement for 'a good bloke (or blokess to satisfy fool legislators)'. It was held that this might reasonably be understood to indicate that the job was not open to women, the word 'blokess' being inserted as a formality. On the other hand, an advertisement for a 'departmental manager' was not discriminatory, as in this context there was no sexist connotation.

As noted (*Cardiff Women's Aid v Hartup*, para 4.232) the placing of a discriminatory advertisement does not, *per se*, give rise to an individual complaint.

Unlawful acts (ss 39–40, 42)

4.156 It is unlawful:
a. for a person who has authority over another to instruct that other to do an unlawful act (s 39);
b. to induce another to do an unlawful act by offering a benefit or threatening a detriment (s 40); and
c. to aid another person to do an unlawful act (s 42) (see *A M v W C and SPV*).

4.157–4.165 It should be noted that ss 38, 39 and 40 may only be enforced by the Equal Opportunities Commission (see s 72).

Liability of employers (s 41)

4.166 Anything done by a person in the course of his employment shall be treated as done by his employer as well as by him, whether or not the act was done with the employer's knowledge or approval. At one time, the test to be applied was taken from the common law rules relating to vicarious liability (see para 10.161, and see *Irving v Post Office*), but this view is wrong. In *Jones v Tower Boot Co Ltd* an employee was racially harassed at work, by having to suffer physical and verbal abuse from his fellow employees. It was argued for the employers that the acts were not committed by their employees acting in the course of their employment, because it was no part of their work to do such acts, which were unauthorised and unconnected with anything the employees were employed to do. The Court of Appeal rejected the argument, and held that the employers were liable for racial discrimination. The words 'in the course of employment' were to be given a purposive construction, and were to be interpreted in the sense in which they are employed in everyday speech. The application of the phrase is a question of fact for each employment tribunal to resolve.

4.167   If an act of sex discrimination (or sexual harassment) takes place at a social gathering of work colleagues, it is for the employment tribunal to consider, as an industrial jury, whether the circumstances are an extension of the employment. Factors to consider include (a) whether the person was still on duty (b) whether the conduct took place on the employer's premises (c) whether the social gathering was organised by or on behalf of the employer, and (d) whether the incidents took place immediately after work (*Chief Constable of Lincolnshire v Stubbs*).

4.168–4.175   But an employer will not be liable for such acts if he can show that he took such steps as were reasonably practicable to prevent the employee from doing that act, or doing in the course of his employment acts of that description (s 41(3)). Thus, if an employer can show that he had a system of proper supervision, had published an equal opportunities policy, and was unaware of the acts in question, it may be that he can successfully raise this defence. Thus in *Balgobin v Tower Hamlets* (see para 4.82) the EAT commented that it was difficult to see what steps could have been taken by the employers in practical terms to prevent harassment from occurring.

Application to the Crown

4.176   The Act applies to the Crown as it applies to a private person, including to service in the armed forces, although nothing is rendered unlawful if it was done for the purpose of ensuring combat effectiveness.

Enforcement of the Act (s 63)

4.177   Any person may complain to the employment tribunal that another person has committed an act of discrimination. Initially, the conciliation officer will try to promote a settlement, but if this fails, the tribunal, if it finds the complaint well founded, may:

a.   make an order declaring the rights of the claimant;

b.   order the respondent to pay compensation, and may include an award for injured feelings, which is fundamental to a claim based on discrimination (*Murray v Powertech (Scotland) Ltd*). Since the Sex Discrimination and Equal Pay (Remedies) Regulations 1993, there is no limit on the amount of compensation which can be awarded, and the employment tribunal must assess the whole of the loss suffered (*Ministry of Defence v Cannock* and *Ministry of Defence v Wheeler*). Also, interest on the compensation element (but not on an award for injured feelings) may be awarded, both in respect of the period up to the date when the compensation is assessed and for the period following the promulgation of the award (but not if the full amount is paid within 14 days): see Employment Tribunals (Interest on Awards in Discrimination Cases) Regulations 1996 as amended; and/or

c.   make a recommendation that the respondent takes action to obviate or reduce the adverse effect on the claimant of any act of discrimination to which the complaint relates.

4.178   In the latter case, a failure to comply may lead to an increase in the amount of compensation awarded. However, the employment tribunal has no power to recommend that a certain wage shall be paid in the future, as this is covered by the provision which enables compensation for the loss suffered to be awarded (*Prestcold Ltd v Irvine*).

4.179   Damages may be awarded for unintentional indirect discrimination (ie falling within ss 1(1)(b) or 3(1)(b)) if the employment tribunal considers that it is just and equitable to make such an award and a declaration and/or a recommendation is insufficient (s 65(1)(b)).

4.180   An employer's motive for discriminating is irrelevant to liability, but may be relevant to the award of compensation, which is made on just and equitable grounds (*Chief Constable of Manchester v Hope*).

4.181   A complaint of discrimination in the field of employment must be laid before the employment tribunal within three months of the act complained of being done, unless it was not practicable to present it earlier (s 76). The 'act' of discrimination can be a single act, or a continuing one. In the latter case, the right to bring legal proceedings will continue until three months from the end of the period when the discrimination ceases. In *Calder v James Finlay Corpn Ltd*, the employers operated a mortgage subsidy scheme. In order to be eligible to join the scheme, employees had to be over the age of 25. Shortly after the claimant became 25, she applied for a mortgage subsidy, but this was refused, no reason being given. She continued in her employment for a further six months, she then left, and claimed that she had been discriminated against on grounds of sex. An employment tribunal concluded that the reason she was refused the mortgage subsidy was because of her sex, but also held that her application was out of time. On appeal, the EAT reversed the decision. Section 6(2)(a) of the Act makes it unlawful to refuse her access to benefits, facilities or services, and thus she was subjected to a continuing discrimination throughout her employment. Also, as long as the employment continued, she was being subjected to a detriment, contrary to s 6(2)(b). As her claim was brought within three months of her leaving her employment, she was entitled to succeed. Further, the EAT noted that s 76(6)(b) states that an act extending over a period shall be treated as done at the end of that period.

4.182   However, it is important to distinguish between an act of continuing discrimination and an act of discrimination which has continuing consequences. In the latter case, the time limit of three months will normally apply (see *Sougrin v Haringey Health Authority*, para 4.275). But if there is a deliberate omission to do something, time will run from the date when the discriminator is in a position to do that thing (*Swithland Motors plc v Clarke*).

4.183   The EOC may itself bring proceedings in respect of alleged violations of certain provisions in the Act (ie ss 38, 39 or 40, see above) within six months of the act complained of, and obtain an injunction from a county court or sheriff court to restrain a person from repeating the unlawful act at any time within five years of a non-discrimination notice (ss 71–72). The Commission may also bring a preliminary action in an employment tribunal on behalf of a person, even though that person has not made a complaint, and the employment tribunal can make an order of rights or a recommendation that appropriate action be taken to obviate or reduce the adverse effect of the discrimination (s 73).

4.184 The Commission may give help to persons who feel that they have been discriminated against, in order to assist them in obtaining the necessary information, and questionnaires have been approved which can be sent to the alleged discriminator. Assistance to an aggrieved person may also be given by means of advice, attempting to procure a settlement by conciliation, arranging for legal advice and assistance, and arranging and paying for legal representation. It may also undertake or assist in any research or other educational activities.

4.185 The Commission may carry out formal investigations, either on its own initiative or at the request of the Secretary of State, with specific terms of reference, and notice will be given to persons affected. Any person may be required to furnish information, or to attend a hearing and give oral information on specified matters, and to produce any relevant documents. If a person fails or refuses to comply, the Commission may apply to a county court (or sheriff's court) for an order requiring him to comply, and failure to do so may be punishable in like manner as neglecting a witness summons. To wilfully alter, suppress, conceal or destroy a document, or knowingly or recklessly to make a statement which is false in a material particular is an offence punishable on summary conviction by a fine not exceeding level 5 on the standard scale. In the light of their findings, the Commission may make recommendations with a view to promoting equality of opportunity between men and women (ss 57–61).

4.186–4.195 If, in the course of investigations, the Commission is satisfied that a person is committing an unlawful discriminatory act, or contravening an equality clause under the Equal Pay Act 1970, the Commission may issue a non-discriminatory notice. They must first inform the person of their intention, specifying the grounds, and give him an opportunity to make oral or written representations and take these into account. An appeal may be lodged to the employment tribunal within six weeks against any requirement, and the tribunal may quash the requirement if it thinks it is unreasonable. A register of non-discrimination notices shall be kept, and if at any time within five years of the notice becoming final it appears to the Commission that the discriminatory act is likely to be repeated, the Commission may apply to a county court for an injunction restraining that person from doing so (ss 67–71).

Racial discrimination

4.196 The Race Relations Act 1976 is intended to be a powerful influence in the fight to eliminate discrimination on racial grounds. The Act is modelled closely on the Sex Discrimination Act 1975, and an interpretive decision on one Act may be used when considering the meaning of the other.

Direct evidence of race discrimination is likely to consist of inferences raised from primary facts (*King v Great Britain-China Centre*), If these lead to a provisional conclusion that there has been discrimination, the employer will be required to give an explanation. If this is not forthcoming, or if it is unsatisfactory, the complaint will succeed (*North West Thames Regional Health Authority v Noone*). But the fact that an employer treats an employee unreasonably does not, by itself, lead to the conclusion that the employer has treated the employee less favourably on racial grounds (*Glasgow City Council v Zafar*).

4.197 Generally speaking, it is unlawful to discriminate against a person on grounds of race, and this could arise in any of three ways.

A. Direct discrimination (s 1(1)(a))

4.198 This occurs if on racial grounds a person treats another person less favourably than he would treat someone else. Thus if the grounds for the discrimination are racial, the race of the person discriminated against is irrelevant, for it is possible for A to discriminate against B on grounds of C's colour or race (*Race Relations Board v Applin*). In *Zarczynska v Levy* a barmaid alleged she was dismissed for refusing to obey an order not to serve coloured persons in a pub. The EAT held that even though she had not been personally discriminated against on grounds of her race, she had been treated less favourably on racial grounds, and was entitled to pursue a claim. (The case was remitted to the employment tribunal, which found that no such unlawful instruction had been given; see also *Showboat Entertainment Centre Ltd v Owens*.) In *Wilson v TB Steelworks* a white woman was on the point of being offered a job, but when she disclosed that her husband was black, the offer was withdrawn. It was held that this amounted to unlawful discrimination.

The fact that members of a racial group are treated differently does not, by itself, constitute unlawful discrimination. It must be shown that the treatment was less favourable on grounds of race (*Barclays Bank plc v Kapur* and *Weathersfield v Sargent*).

4.199 The Act specifically states (s 1(2)) that the segregation of a person on racial grounds is to be regarded as treating him less favourably, but this does not mean that congregation is unlawful. Thus to provide separate (but equal) toilet facilities for Asians and non-Asians would be discriminatory, and hence unlawful, but to allow an Asian night shift to develop in a factory because this is the wish of all concerned does not amount to unlawful conduct. The employer, however, would be acting unlawfully is he insisted that Asians went on the night shift (*Pel Ltd v Modgill*).

4.200 There can be unlawful discrimination under the Act even though it was done for a worthy motive. In *R v Commission for Racial Equality, ex p Westminster City Council*, a black person applied for a job as a refuse collector. He was given a temporary appointment, but this was later withdrawn, as it was feared that other workers would take industrial action. The High Court held that the CRE were entitled to issue a non-discrimination notice. For an employer to give in to such threats would frustrate the purpose of the Act.

B. Indirect discrimination (s 1(1)(b))

4.201 This occurs when:

a.   a person applies a requirement or condition,
b.   which is such that the proportion of persons from the same racial group who can comply is considerably smaller than persons who are not of that racial group, and
c.   it cannot be shown that the condition is justified irrespective of the racial origins of the person concerned, and
d.   it is to that person's detriment that he cannot comply.

4.202   The requirement or condition has to be one which the applicant 'must' comply with. If it is a factor which 'may' be taken into account, there is no indirect discrimination. In *Meer v London Borough of Tower Hamlets*, the respondents advertised a vacancy for a head of their legal department. There were 23 applicants, 12 of whom were put on a 'long list'. The council applied 10 criteria for drawing up the 'long list', one of which was experience with Tower Hamlets. Of those on the 'long list' four had such experience. The claimant, who was not placed on the long list, complained that he had been indirectly discriminated against on ground of race, arguing that the proportion of this racial group who could comply with the requirement was smaller than other groups. His claim was dismissed. The requirement was not one with which the successful applicants 'must' comply; it was a factor which the local authority were entitled to take into account. A different view appears to have been taken in *Falkirk Council v Whyte* (see para 4.30).

4.203   If a claim of indirect discrimination is made, it must be shown that the claimant has suffered a detriment. An unjustified sense of grievance does not constitute less favourable treatment, and an employee who, for sound reasons, is treated differently but no less generously than others in a different racial group cannot claim that he has suffered a detriment (*Barclays Bank plc v Kapur*).

4.204   Even though there is indirect discrimination, a complaint will not succeed if it can be shown that the requirement or condition is justified irrespective of race. In *Panesar v Nestlé & Co Ltd* a factory rule prohibited beards and long hair. This was indirect discrimination against the claimant, who was a Sikh, but the Court of Appeal held that the condition was justified in the interests of hygiene and safety.

4.205   To determine whether or not the requirement or condition was justified, the employment tribunal should consider (a) was the objective legitimate (b) were the means used to achieve that objective reasonable in themselves, and (c) were those means justified when balanced on the principles of proportionality between the discriminatory effect upon the claimant's racial group and the reasonable needs of those applying the requirement or condition (*St Matthias Church of England School (Board of Governors) v Crizzle*).

C. Victimisation (s 2)

4.206   It is unlawful to treat a person less favourably because he has:
i.   brought proceedings under the Act;
ii. given evidence or information connected with proceedings brought by another person;
iii. done anything under the Act in relation to the discriminator; or

iv. made allegations that a person has committed an unlawful act of racial discrimination.

However, it is not unlawful victimisation if a person is accorded less favourable treatment as a result of an allegation which is untrue and not made in good faith (*Aziz v Trinity Street Taxis*).

4.207–4.215 It is not necessary under s 2 to show that the alleged discriminator was consciously motivated because the person victimised had done one of the protected acts. Subconscious motivation will suffice to show victimisation. All the claimant has to show is that the reason (or principal reason) for the less favourable treatment was the fact that the person victimised had done the protected act (*Nagarajan v London Regional Transport*). Thus in *Chief Constable of West Yorkshire v Khan* a police officer made a complaint to an employment tribunal alleging that he had been the victim of racial discrimination, in that his application for promotion had not been supported. Before the claim was heard, he applied for promotion to another police authority, who wrote to his present employers seeking a reference. The latter's Chief Constable refused to provide a reference because he feared it would prejudice his own case before the impending employment tribunal hearing. It was held that the claimant was entitled to compensation for injury to his feelings as a result of the victimisation he suffered because he had brought proceedings under the Act.

Racial grounds (s 3)

4.216 The Act defines racial grounds as meaning colour, race, nationality or ethnic or national origins. This definition may give rise to a number of problems. The term 'nationality' was included to overrule the decision of the House of Lords in *Ealing London Borough Council v Race Relations Board*, where it was held that 'national origins' meant race rather than citizenship. Now, both meanings are included. Thus, it is now unlawful to discriminate against, eg nationals of EU countries. 'National origins' has a different meaning from 'nationality'. The latter term points to citizenship, whereas the former term refers to a historical and/or geographical feature which would have revealed at some point in time the existence of a nation. Thus, England and Scotland were once separate nations, and it would therefore be unlawful to discriminate against a person because of such national origins (*Northern Joint Police Board v Power*).

4.217 In *Mandla v Dowell Lee*, the House of Lords held that the term 'ethnic' was appreciably wider than 'race'. For a group to constitute an ethnic group for the purpose of the Act, it must regard itself as a distinct community by virtue of certain characteristics. These include:
1. a long shared history, of which the group is conscious as distinguishing it from other groups, and the memory of which keeps it alive, and
2. a cultural tradition, including social customs and manner.

4.218 In addition, some of the following factors may be relevant:
1. a common geographical origin or descent from common ancestors;
2. a common language (but not necessarily peculiar to the group);
3. a common literature;
4. a common religion different from that of neighbouring groups;

5.   being a minority or being an oppressed or a dominant group within a large community.

4.219   With these factors in mind, the House of Lords had no hesitation in holding that Sikhs were a racial group within the meaning of the Act.

4.220   The Act does not appear to cover religion as such, but this may be covered under the concepts of race, ethnic or national origins. And since reference to a person's racial group includes reference to any racial group into which a person falls (s 3(1)), converts are clearly within the definition. But if it is unlawful to advertise 'No Jews need apply', then why should it not be equally unlawful to state 'No Catholics need apply'? (In Northern Ireland, such discrimination is specifically declared to be unlawful.) Are all Muslims of the same racial, ethnic or national origins? If the legislation wished to include discrimination on religious grounds, it is submitted that a clear and specific statement to this effect would have been a simple matter.

4.221   In *Commission for Racial Equality v Dutton*, the Court of Appeal held that gypsies were a racial group within the meaning of the Act, defined by reference to their racial origins. In *Seide v Gillette Industries* the EAT held that although religion is not within the provisions of the Act, the term 'Jewish' can mean membership of a race or of an ethnic group as well as being a follower of a particular religious faith. If what happens to a person is for the former reason, not the latter, this can amount to racial discrimination.

4.222   An ability to speak a particular language is not, *per se* an essential factor in the definition of a racial group, and a requirement of such an ability may be justified irrespective of racial origins. Thus in *Gwynedd County Council v Jones*, it was accepted that Welshmen were a distinct ethnic group, but the EAT held that there was no distinction between Welsh-speaking Welsh and English-speaking Welsh. However, a requirement that applicants for a post should be able to speak Welsh was held, in the particular circumstances, to be justifiable. Rastafarians are a religious, not an ethnic, group. Consequently, to refuse employment to a man because he wore his hair in 'dreadlocks' is not discrimination on grounds of race (*Crown Suppliers (PSA) v Dawkins*).

4.223–4.230   When comparing the case of a person from a particular racial group with that of a person not of that group, the relevant circumstances must be such that they are the same, or not materially different. In *Wakeman v Quick Corpn*, Japanese managers, who were seconded from Japan, were paid more than locally recruited managers. It was held that the higher level of pay was attributed to their status as secondees. As such, their circumstances was materially different from those of the claimant, and so no proper comparison could be made, as required by s 3(4) of the Act.

Racial discrimination in employment (s 4)

4.231   It is unlawful to discriminate against a person on racial grounds:
a.   in the arrangements for determining who shall be offered employment;
b.   in the terms on which employment is offered;

c.   by refusing or deliberately omitting to offer him employment (s 4(1); *Johnson v Timber Tailors (Midlands) Ltd*).

4.232   Placing a discriminatory advertisement is not, by itself, part of the arrangements for determining who shall be employed. In *Cardiff Women's Aid v Hartup* a charity advertised for a black or Asian woman to fill the post of information centre worker. Mrs Hartup, who is white, did not apply for the job, but claimed that she had been discriminated against on grounds of race. It was held that the act of placing a discriminatory advertisement was not an act of discrimination within the meaning of s 4. It may have indicated an intention to discriminate, but this is actionable only at the instance of the CRE under s 29 of the Act (see para 4.268).

4.233   Once a person is employed, it is unlawful to discriminate against him on racial grounds:
a.   in the terms of employment which are afforded to him;
b.   in the way he is afforded access to opportunities for promotion, transfer or training, or any other benefit, facilities or services, or to refuse or omit to afford him access to them;
c.   by dismissing him, or subjecting him to any other detriment (s 4(2)). In *De Souza v Automobile Association* it was held that a racial insult, by itself, was capable of constituting a detriment if the employee felt disadvantaged thereby. If an employee is given an instruction to carry out a policy which is racially discriminatory, and would clearly contravene the Act, and resigns his employment because he feels unable to carry out the policy, he has suffered a detriment, and consequently has been unlawfully discriminated against. It is not necessary for the discriminatory act to be because of that person's race (*Weathersfield Ltd v Sargent*).

4.234   The above provisions do not apply to employment for the purpose of a private household, although the provisions relating to victimisation do so apply. Also s 75(5) allows discrimination on grounds of birth, nationality, descent or residence for Civil Service posts and employment with certain public bodies (see Race Relations (Prescribed Public Bodies) Regulations 1994).

4.235–4.245   Clearly, if a person is dismissed on racial grounds, a complaint under the Act may be made. If a contract of employment provides that, following a dismissal, an appeal may be made to an appropriate body or person, and that pending such appeal the employee is suspended, then it is permissible to argue that there was racial (or sexual) bias at the appeal hearing. But if the contract of employment makes it clear that the dismissal takes effect from the date it is made (see *J Sainsbury Ltd v Savage* para 12.20) although if the appeal is successful reinstatement is possible, then the dismissed person is not an employee at the date of the appeal hearing, and thus cannot pursue a claim on the ground that the reason the appeal was rejected was because of race (or sex) discrimination (*Post Office v Adekeye*).

Racial harassment

4.246   An employer may be liable for an act which constituted harassment on racial grounds. Although earlier cases appear to hold that a racial insult, by itself, does not constitute a detriment (eg *De Souza v Automobile Association*) it is submitted that these decisions are no longer good law. Liability may arise even though the employer neither knew nor could foresee that the act took place. It is sufficient if he causes or permits harassment in circumstances when he could control whether it happened or not. In *Burton v De Vere Hotels* a well-known comedian made racist and sexist remarks at a function held in an hotel. The claimant, who is black, and was a waitress at the function, felt humiliated and distressed, and although the hotel management subsequently apologised to her, she claimed race discrimination. The EAT held that the event was under the control of the hotel, and, if management assistants had been properly instructed, they could and should have withdrawn the applicant from the banqueting hall. By failing to do so, the employers had subjected the applicant to racial harassment.

Genuine occupational qualifications (s 5)

4.247 It is permissible to discriminate where being a member of a particular racial group is a genuine occupational qualification for the job. There are four racial GOQs, and hence the provisions are more restrictive than the corresponding provisions in the Sex Discrimination Act 1975. Racial GOQs are as follows:

a. the job involves participation in a dramatic performance or other entertainment in a capacity for which a person of that racial group is required for reasons of authenticity;

b. the job involves participation as an artist's or photographic model in the production of a work of art or of visual images, for which a person of that racial group is required for reasons of authenticity;

c. the job involves working in a place where food and drink is provided to, and consumed by, members of the public in a particular setting (eg a Chinese restaurant), for which a person of that racial group is required for reasons of authenticity;

d. the holder of the job provides persons of that racial group with personal services promoting their welfare, and those services can be most effectively provided by persons of that racial group.

4.248–4.255 In *Tottenham Green Under Fives' Centre v Marshall*, the EAT thought that the phrase 'promoting their welfare' was a wide expression, and the view was expressed that it was unnecessary to seek to limit the scope of the words. But in *Lambeth London Borough Council v Commission for Racial Equality*, the Court of Appeal refused to uphold the decision of a local authority to confine applications for vacant posts in their housing benefits department to applicants from Afro–Caribbean or Asian communities, because the jobs were essentially managerial in nature, and did not involve the provision of personal services promoting the welfare of a particular racial group.

Contract workers (s 7)

4.256 As well as giving protection to job applicants and employees, the Act also covers contract workers, and thus pre-empts any attempt to circumvent the anti-discrimination provisions. It is unlawful for a principal to discriminate against a person, even though the latter is employed by a third party (eg an employment agency). It is also unlawful for the principal to discriminate against a contract worker:

a. in the terms on which he is allowed to do the work
b. by not allowing him to do it
c. in the way he affords him access to benefits, facilities or services
d. by subjecting him to any other detriment.

4.257–4.265 Section 7 will also protect staff employed by one employer at premises controlled by another. Thus in *Harrods Ltd v Remick* the claimant was employed as a pen consultant for concessionaires who had a sales counter at Harrods store. Harrods withdrew her store approval because she failed to comply with their dress code. Consequently she was dismissed. It was held that she was entitled to pursue a claim for racial discrimination against Harrods, even though that firm was not her employer. The concessionaires were supplying employees to 'work for' Harrods within the meaning of s 7.

Application of the Act (s 8)

4.266 The Act only applies to employment at an establishment in Great Britain (*Deria v General Council of British Shipping*). There are some special provisions relating to seamen (see ss 8–9). But s 8 has to be read in conjunction with art 39 of the Treaty of Rome, which is designed to facilitate the free movement of workers within the European Community. Thus in *Bossa v Nordstress Ltd* the claimant, who was an Italian national, applied for a job which was to be performed in Italy. The employers declined to interview him, and he claimed that he had been discriminated against on grounds of nationality, contrary to s 4(1)(c) of the Race Relations Act. An employment tribunal dismissed his claim, on the ground that because the job was to be performed outside the UK, s 8 applied. But the EAT reversed the decision; article 39 of the Treaty of Rome had a direct effect (see para 1.137) and overrode s 8.

Other unlawful acts

A. Discriminatory practices (s 28)

4.267 It is unlawful to apply a discriminatory practice, ie conduct which, while not amounting to discrimination, in fact is designed to produce unlawful discrimination. For example, if it is well known that blacks need not even bother to apply for a job at a certain factory, because they stand no chance of being appointed, this can amount to a discriminatory practice even though no one applies and is discriminated against.

B. Discriminatory advertisements (s 29)

4.268 Other than the permitted exceptions (ie where race is a GOQ) it is unlawful to publish an advertisement which indicates an intention by a person to do an act of discrimination (see *Cardiff Women's Aid v Hartup*, para 4.232).

C. Instructions to discriminate (s 30)

4.269 It is unlawful for a person who has authority over another to instruct him to do an unlawful act, or to procure the doing by him of an unlawful act.

D. Pressure to discriminate (s 31)

4.270   It is unlawful to induce or attempt to induce a person to do any act which is unlawful. Thus to call (or threaten to call) a strike over the appointment of a black supervisor would be unlawful.

4.271   Proceedings in respect of the above four unlawful acts may only be brought by the Commission for Racial Equality.

E. Vicarious liability (s 32)

4.272   Anything done by a person in the course of his employment shall be treated as done by his employer, whether or not the act was done with the employer's knowledge of approval. However, the common law rules relating to vicarious liability, which used to be applied in such cases, are no longer applicable (see *Jones v Tower Boot Co Ltd*, para 4.166). It is a defence for an employer to show that he took such steps as were reasonably practicable to prevent an employee from doing the act in question, eg by proper supervision, having an equal opportunities policy, taking firm steps to bring to employees' notice that acts of discrimination or harassment will not be tolerated, etc. In *Marks & Spencer plc v Martins*, the Court of Appeal considered that, having regard to the arrangements made for interviewing the claimant, the firm's equal opportunities policy, their compliance with the CRE's Code of Practice on selection procedures, criteria and interviewing, and the selection of an interviewing panel to include a person with an interest in recruiting from ethnic minorities, the employers had made out a defence under s 32(3).

Enforcement by individuals (s 54)

4.273   Any claim in respect of discrimination in employment must be submitted to an employment tribunal within three months from the date of the alleged act, unless it is just and equitable to extend the time limit. However, by virtue of s 68(7)(b), any act extending over the period shall be treated as having been done at the end of that period. Thus where there is a continuing act of discrimination, the three months time limit does not run until the discrimination ceases (*Barclays Bank plc v Kapur*).

4.274   In determining the time limits, a distinction has to be drawn between an act of continuing discrimination and an act of discrimination which has continuing consequences. In *Clarke v Hampshire Electro-Plating Co Ltd* the claimant, who was black, saw an advertisement for a supervisory job with his present employers. On 25 April he saw his employer about the vacancy, but was told that he would not be considered. On 4 September a white man was appointed to the job, and the claimant then submitted a complaint, alleging he had been discriminated against on grounds of race. The employment tribunal held that his complaint was out of time, because the discrimination (if this was so) dated from 25 April, but on appeal the decision was reversed by the EAT. Time will start to run from the date the cause of action crystallised, not from when the claimant feels he has been discriminated against. In this case, the claimant's cause of action had not crystallised when his application for promotion was rejected, but from the date a white man was appointed, because this provided the comparison which enabled him to believe that he had been discriminated against.

4.275 A somewhat different approach was taken by the Court of Appeal in *Sougrin v Haringey Health Authority*, where the claimant, a black nurse, appealed internally against her employer's decision to place her in a certain salary grade. Her appeal was unsuccessful, although an appeal by a white colleague succeeded. Six months later she submitted her application to an employment tribunal, arguing that she had been discriminated against on grounds of race, and that the discrimination was a continuing act. The employment tribunal held that the claim had not been submitted within the statutory time limits, a decision which was upheld by the EAT and the Court of Appeal. The regrading decision was a one-off act with the continuing consequence that she was being paid less than a white colleague. There was no suggestion that the employers had a policy to pay black nurses less than white nurses; had there been such a policy, it is arguable that there was a continuing act of discrimination (*Barclays Bank plc v Kapur*).

4.276 A copy of the complaint will be sent to a conciliation officer, but if he fails to promote a settlement, the matter will go to an employment tribunal for hearing. If it is decided that the complaint is well-founded, the tribunal may make one of the following orders:
a. a declaration of the rights of the claimant,
b. an order that the respondent shall pay compensation. The former maximum award of £11,000 has been repealed (Race Relations (Remedies) Act 1994) and there is now no limit on the amount of compensation which can be awarded. If the act of discrimination has caused pecuniary loss, such as a refusal to offer employment, or dismissal from employment, the amount of damages is readily quantifiable. However, damages may also be awarded for injury to feelings, humiliation and insult. The award for these should not be minimal, but should be restrained. Injury to feelings will normally be of a relatively short duration, and the award should reflect this (*Sharifi v Strathclyde Regional Council*). But an award of £10,000 for injury and feelings (and £5,000 aggravated damages) was held not to be too high in *Racial Equality Council v Widlinski*.
c. a recommendation that the respondent shall take, within a specified period, such action as appears to the tribunal to be practicable for the purpose of obviating or reducing the adverse effect on the claimant of any act complained of (*North West Thames Regional Health Authority v Noone*). If the respondent fails to comply with any such recommendation, the tribunal may increase the compensation award, or make such an award if they have not already done so.

4.277 Although there are a number of conflicting decisions on the point, it has recently been confirmed that, as a matter of principle, aggravated damages ought to be available in what are in effect statutory torts of race and sex discrimination, and an award made by an employment tribunal cannot be challenged unless it is manifestly excessive (*HM Prison Service v Johnson*).

4.278 The fact that the employer already employs people of different racial groups is not conclusive (*Johnson v Timber Tailors (Midlands) Ltd*), but it is a relevant consideration of evidential value (*Piperdy v UEM Parker Glass*). If an employer's replies to a questionnaire sent by the CRE are evasive, it could lead to an inference that discrimination took place (*Virdee v EEC Quarries Ltd*). Evidence of events which took place subsequent to the alleged act of discrimination is admissible where it is logically probative of a relevant fact (*Chattopadhyay v Headmaster of Holloway School*).

4.279 If discrimination takes place in circumstances which are consistent with the treatment being meted out because of a person's race, an employment tribunal should be prepared to draw the inference that it was unlawful discrimination, unless the alleged discriminator can satisfy them that there was some other innocent explanation (*Baker v Cornwall County Council*). Otherwise, the general burden of proving the case lies upon the claimant. If, after hearing all the evidence, the employment tribunal finds primary facts which, in the absence of explanation, point to unlawful discrimination, and no such acceptable explanation is offered, then the tribunal may find, by inference, that discrimination existed (*British Gas plc v Sharma*).

4.280 A claimant may be able to obtain the discovery of existing statistics, showing the number of persons from the different racial groups who have applied for posts, been engaged, or promoted, for such evidence may have some probative value, from which inferences may be drawn that the employer has adopted racially discriminatory practice or policies (*West Midlands Passenger Transport Executive v Singh*). But an employment tribunal has no power to order a respondent to produce details of the ethnic or racial composition of the workforce, where such evidence does not exist, for this is not 'discovery' of documents, and not 'particulars' of the grounds on which the respondents seek to rely. Nor is there power to order interrogatories (*Carrington v Helix Lighting Ltd*).

4.281–4.290 A cause of action under the Act can be continued after the death of the claimant, by his personal representatives, under the provisions of the Law Reform (Miscellaneous Provisions) Act 1934 (*Lewisham and Guys Mental Health NHS Trust v Andrews*).

Statutory immunity (s 41)

4.291 A discriminatory act shall not be unlawful if it is done in pursuance of any enactment, or any instrument made under any enactment, or in order to comply with any condition or requirement imposed by a Minister by virtue of any enactment. However, in *Hampson v Department of Education and Science*, the House of Lords gave a very restricted meaning to this immunity, holding that a decision given on a matter where the statute gives a discretion was not within the section.

Enforcement by the Commission (s 58)

4.292 The Commission for Racial Equality has the power to carry out a formal investigation into any practice carried on by an individual or an organisation, either of its own volition or at the request of the Secretary of State, and has wide powers to obtain any necessary information. If the investigation is confined to the activities of named persons, an opportunity must be given for them to make oral or written representations (*Re Prestige Group plc*). A report may then be issued, with or without recommendations. If, in the course of such investigations, the Commission concludes that a person is committing an unlawful act, the Commission may serve a non-discriminatory notice on him requiring him not to commit any further such acts, to inform the Commission on what changes (if any) have been made in such practices, and to notify the other party concerned. Before issuing the notice, the Commission must inform the person, specifying the grounds, and offer him an opportunity of making oral or written representations.

4.293–4.300   If there is any repetition of the discriminatory act or practice within the five years following the issuing of a non-discriminatory notice, the Commission may obtain an injunction in the county court against that person, restraining him from committing further discriminatory practices. An appeal may be made against a non-discriminatory notice within six weeks to an employment tribunal, who may quash any requirement contained therein, or, if they so wish, substitute their own directions. On such an appeal, it is open to the person against whom the order has been made to challenge the findings of fact on which the order was made (*Commission for Racial Equality v Amari Plastics Ltd*). A public register will be maintained of all non-discriminatory notices.

Discrimination against disabled workers

4.301   Following an extensive period of consultation, the Disability Discrimination Act 1995 has been passed, with an avowed aim of eliminating discrimination against disabled persons. A code of practice has been issued (see Appendix H) and guidance notes are available. An employment tribunal should always make express reference to any relevant provision of the code or the guidance notes which has been taken into account when arriving at its decision (*Goodwin v Patent Office*).

4.302   In many ways, the provisions of the Disability Discrimination Act are similar to those found in the Sex Discrimination Act and the Race Relations Act, but there are some important differences. Thus, the Act contains no provision for indirect discrimination, because direct discrimination itself is capable of being justified (see s 5(3)), and regulations specify the circumstances in which discriminatory treatment is or is not justified. The Act requires employers to take steps to make adjustments to accommodate a disabled person (see s 6), and again, regulations spell out when a failure to comply with that duty is or is not justified. There are no like-for-like competitor principles, for the Act is dealing with how a disabled person is treated, not with the fact of his disability (*Clark v Novacold Ltd*).

4.303–4.310   There is nothing in the Act which prohibits an employer from requiring a job claimant to undergo a pre-recruitment medical examination and, indeed, if a person refuses such a request, there is no obligation to offer him employment (*X v EC Commission*).

A. Definition of 'disabled persons' (ss 1–2)

4.311   A person will be regarded as being disabled for the purposes of the Act if 'he has a physical or mental impairment which has a substantial and long-term adverse effect on his ability to carry out normal day-to-day activities.' A mental impairment, to come within the Act, must arise from a clinical well-recognised illness. Any impairment must have lasted for at least 12 months, or be reasonably expected to last for that period, or be reasonably expected to last for life. If the impairment ceases to have a substantial impact on a person's ability to carry out day-to-day activities, it will still be treated as having that effect if it is likely to recur (eg a mental illness) except in prescribed circumstances.

An impairment is to be taken as affecting normal day-to-day activities if it affects a person with regard to mobility, manual dexterity, physical co-ordination, continence, ability to lift, carry or move everyday objects, speech, hearing, eyesight, memory or ability to concentrate, learn or understand, or perception of risks of physical danger (see Sch 1). Registered disabled persons are deemed to be disabled for the purposes of the Act for an initial period of three years. But the fact that a person is disabled within the meaning of other legislation (eg for the purposes of the disability living allowance) does not mean that he comes within the definition of disability within the meaning of this Act. Past disabilities are within the scope of the Act (s 2).

B. Other disabilities

4.312   Addictions to alcohol, nicotine or other substances does not amount to an impairment for the purpose of the Act. Nor is a tendency to pyromania, kleptomania, physical or sexual abuse, exhibitionism or voyeurism. Seasonal allergic rhinitis (hay fever) is excluded (but not if it aggravates the effect of another condition), as are tattoos or the piercing of the body by objects for decorative or non-medical purposes (Disability Discrimination (Meaning of Disability) Regulations 1996). A severe disfigurement is to be treated as having a substantial effect on the ability of a person to carry out normal day-to-day activities.

C. Discrimination against disabled persons (s 4)

4.313   It is unlawful for an employer to discriminate against a disabled person:
(a)   in the arrangements which he makes for the purpose of determining to whom he should offer employment;
(b)   in the terms on which he offers that person employment; or
(c)   by refusing to offer, or deliberately not offering him employment.
    Further, it is unlawful to discriminate against a disabled employee:
(a)   in the terms of employment;
(b)   in the opportunities afforded him for promotion, transfer, training or any other benefit;
(c)   by refusing to afford him or deliberately not affording him, any such opportunity; or
(d)   by dismissing him, or subjecting him to any detriment.

D. Victimisation

4.314   It is also unlawful to victimise a person (whether disabled or not) because that person has brought proceedings under the Act, given evidence or information in connection with such proceedings, or made allegations that someone has contravened the Act. However, this does not apply in respect of any allegations not made in good faith.

E. Meaning of discrimination (s 5)

4.315   A person discriminates against a disabled person if:
(a) for a reason which relates to the person's disability, he treats him less favourably than he treats others to whom that reason does not apply; and
(b) he cannot show that the treatment is justified.

4.316   In *Clark v Novacold Ltd*, the Court of Appeal held that the less favourable treatment does not turn on a like-for-like comparison of the disabled person and of others in similar circumstances, and thus it was not appropriate to make comparisons of the cases in the same way as the Sex Discrimination Act and the Race Relations Act. The comparison is to be made with others to whom the reason for the treatment does not apply, even if their circumstances are different from the disabled person. Thus to dismiss a person who is absent from work for a long time because of sickness is less favourable treatment when compared with the non-dismissal of a worker who is still performing his work.

4.317   Discrimination also is committed if an employer:
(a) fails to comply with a s 6 duty (see below); and
(b) cannot show that his failure to do so is justified.

4.318   In order to show that the treatment of the disabled person was justified, an employer would have to show that it was both material to the circumstances of the particular case, and substantial. This includes taking into account the circumstances of the employer and those of the employee. Thus the employer should always seek an up-to-date medical report and warn the employee that he is at risk of dismissal (*Baynton v Saurus General Engineers Ltd*).

4.319   The Disability Discrimination (Employment) Regulations 1996 provide for certain circumstances when less favourable treatment of a disabled person is justified. These are:
(a) when pay is linked to performance;
(b) where there are uniform rates of contribution to an occupational pension scheme regardless of the benefits received, and the costs of providing for benefits on termination of service, retirement, old age or death, or accident, injury, sickness or invalidity, are likely to be substantially greater than they would be for a comparable person without a disability;
(c) where building works complied with the building regulations in relation to access and facilities for disabled persons at the time the work was carried out.

F. Duty of employer to make adjustments (s 6)

4.320   Where any arrangement made by or behalf of the employer (relating to employment offers or terms or conditions or other arrangements on which employment, promotion, transfer or training is offered), or any physical feature of premises occupied by the employer, places the disabled person at a substantial disadvantage in comparison with persons who are not disabled, it is the duty of the employer to take such steps as it is reasonable in all the circumstances of the case for him to take in order to prevent the arrangements or feature having that effect. The Act gives a list of steps which an employer may have to take in relation to a disabled person in order to comply with s 6, including making adjustments to the premises, allocating some of the disabled person's duties to another person, transferring him to fill an existing vacancy, altering his working hours, assigning him to a different place of work, allowing him to be absent during working hours for rehabilitation, assessment or treatment, giving him training, acquiring or modifying equipment, modifying procedures for assessment or testing, providing a reader or interpreter, and providing supervision.

4.321 To determine whether it would be reasonable for an employer to take a particular step, regard shall be had to the extent the taking of the step would prevent the discriminatory effect, whether it would be practicable to take that step, the financial and other costs which would be incurred, and the extent it would disrupt the employer's activities, the extent of the employer's financial and other resources, and the availability to the employer of financial or other assistance with respect to taking that step. Reasonable adjustments must be job-related. It is not the duty of the employer to provide personal carers or special facilities (eg assistance in going to the toilet) (*Kenny v Hampshire Constabulary*). The employer is not required to make reasonable adjustment if he does not know that the claimant for employment has a disability (*Ridout v TC Group*).

G. The 'purposive' approach

4.322 There is a danger of adopting a stereotype approach to disabled persons. Only a relatively small proportion of the disabled community are visibly disabled, ie in wheelchairs, or carrying white sticks or other aids. The vast majority of disabled persons will have a physical or mental disability which may not be immediately obvious, and will only come to light when they fail to do that which a non-disabled person can do. Thus in deciding whether a claimant's impairment is substantial, a purposive approach should be taken by the employment tribunal, having regard to the guidance notes and the code of practice issued by the Secretary of State. The focus of the Act is on the activities which the claimant cannot do (or can only do with difficulty), rather on the things he can do. 'Substantial' means 'more than minor or trivial' rather than 'very large' (*Goodwin v Patent Office*). But the list of examples in the guidance notes are illustrative, not exhaustive. In *Vicary v British Telecommunications*, the employers had relied largely on the opinion of their medical officer who was of the opinion that the claimant's disabilities were not substantial, and did not affect her normal day-to-day activities, a conclusion which the employment tribunal appeared to adopt. On appeal it was held that a medical expert is entitled to express an opinion based on observation and examination, but it was for the employment tribunal to make this finding of fact, based on their own assessment of the evidence.

4.323 Numerous cases have now been heard in the employment tribunals and the Employment Appeal Tribunal alleging disability discrimination, and generally a purposive approach is being taken. Thus whether a person is disabled within the meaning of the Act is an objective fact, and does not depend on the knowledge of the employer. The decision in *O'Neill v Symm & Co Ltd*, which held that an employer does not discriminate against a disabled person if he has no knowledge of the disability was disagreed with by another division of the EAT in *H J Heinz Co Ltd v Kenrick*. Section 5 of the Act does not require the employer to have knowledge of the disability, although the absence of knowledge may be highly relevant to the issue of justifiability under s 5, or as to the steps to make a reasonable adjustment under s 6. Similarly, whether there is a duty to make reasonable adjustments, and whether a failure to make adjustments can be justified are also objective facts, and the employment tribunal can substitute its own views for those of the employer (*Morse v Wiltshire County Council*).

4.324   It has been held that the failure to place a disabled person on a short list for interview did not, by itself, indicate that the employer had discriminated unlawfully, for frequently there are a large number of applicants for a particular job, and thus it is inevitable that only a limited number of applicants can be called for interview. In another case, an employee developed multiple sclerosis, and it was held that the employer acted unreasonably in dismissing him without taking heed of a report from a neurologist, who thought that the employee's prospect of working should be assessed on a 'try and see' basis. By and large, the employment tribunals appear to be applying the same tests under the new Act towards the dismissal of a disabled person as they did before the Act came into force, ie did the employer act reasonably in dismissing this employee for the reason put forward (see, eg *Pascoe v Hallen and Medway*). Thus, a consideration of alternatives, proper consultation, a review of attendance and performance, providing additional support facilities, obtaining a full and up-to-date medical report, are all steps which a reasonable employer would take.

H. Advertisements (s 11)

4.325   If a job advertisement indicates that a job is only open to persons not having a disability, or that the employer is unwilling to make any reasonable adjustments, and a disabled person applies for but is refused that job, there is a rebuttable presumption that the reason for the employer's refusal amounted to unlawful discrimination.

I. Other provisions

4.326   The Act prohibits discrimination against disabled contract workers (s 12), or by trade organisations (s 13), and makes provision for when the only way an employer can comply with the s 6 duty is by applying for permission to alter premises occupied under a lease (s 16). It is also unlawful to discriminate against a disabled person by way of victimisation (s 55).

J. Vicarious liability of employers (s 58)

4.327   Anything done by a person in the course of his employment shall be treated as also done by his employer, whether or not it was done with the employer's approval. However, in any proceedings brought under the Act, it will be a defence for the employer to prove that he took such steps as were reasonably practicable to prevent the employee from doing that act, or from doing acts of that description in the course of his employment.

K. Remedies (s 8)

4.328   A complaint may be made to an employment tribunal that a person has been discriminated against because of his disability, which, if well-founded, may lead to a declaration, award of compensation, or a recommendation that the employer takes action for the purpose of obviating or reducing the adverse effect on the claimant. Compensation may include an award for injured feelings, and if an employer fails to comply with any recommendation made by the employment tribunal may increase the compensation award.

In respect of any such proceedings, the Secretary of State made regulations making provision for restricted reporting orders to be made in cases where evidence of a personal nature is likely to be heard by the employment tribunal, if such evidence is likely to cause significant embarrassment to the complainant if reported. A similar power exists with regard to appeals before the EAT.

L. Disability Rights Commission

4.329   The DRC was created by the Disability Rights Commission Act 1999 (see para 1.96), and has power to carry out formal investigations, issue non-discrimination notices, give assistance in relation to proceedings, and prepare and issue codes of practice.

M. Exclusions for small employers (s 7)

4.330   The Act does not apply in relation to any employer who employs fewer than 15 employees (Disability Discrimination (Exemption for Small Employers) Order 1998).

N. Repeals

4.331   The requirement contained in the Disabled Persons (Employment) Act 1944 that an employer should employ at least 3 per cent of employees who are registered disabled persons (the quota system) has been repealed. Also repealed are the 'designated employment' provisions (car park and lift attendants).

The Act applies to Northern Ireland (with modifications) and to the Crown, but not to service in the armed forces, or to prison officers or firefighters (s 64).

O. Annual reports

4.332–4.340   In respect of companies which employ (on average throughout the year) more than 250 employees, the annual directors' report must contain a statement describing such policy as the company has applied during the preceding year as to the employment, training, career development and promotion of disabled persons (Companies Act 1985 Sch 7 para 9).

Rehabilitated persons

4.341   The Rehabilitation of Offenders Act 1974 seeks to ensure that if a person has made a genuine effort to rehabilitate into society after conviction for a serious criminal offence, he may be spared the indignity and embarrassment of subsequently having to disclose his unsavoury past. Provided he does not commit a serious offence within the rehabilitation period, he may, at the end of that time, be regarded as a rehabilitated person, and his conviction will be treated as having been 'wiped off the slate'. The Act is somewhat complex, but the general rule is that the length of the rehabilitation period will depend on the age of the offender at the time of conviction, and the sentence given for the offence. Thus the period will vary from six months in the case when an absolute discharge was granted up to ten years in respect of a sentence of imprisonment of 30 months. A sentence of imprisonment of more than 30 months will never become 'spent'. Once a person has become 'rehabilitated' evidence of his previous conviction is not generally admissible, and he may not be asked about it or, if he is asked, he need not tell the truth, and may deny his previous conviction. The rehabilitation period runs from the date of the conviction, not from the expiry of the sentence.

4.342 So far as the law of employment is concerned, s 4(3)(b) of the Act provides that (subject to certain exceptions) a 'spent' conviction, or failure to disclose such, shall not be grounds for dismissing or excluding a person from any office, profession, occupation or employment, or for prejudicing him in any way in any occupation or employment. However, the limits of the section need to be noted. At common law, an employer has the right to please himself whether or not to employ someone and although to refuse to employ a rehabilitated person may be to 'exclude' him, the section provides no remedy for a person who may feel that he has been discriminated against. Equally, a refusal to promote a rehabilitated person may amount to prejudicing him in that employment, but again no remedy is provided. On the other hand, if an employee who was a rehabilitated person was dismissed, and the sole ground was the discovery of his past convictions, this would undoubtedly amount to an unfair dismissal if he was otherwise within the protection of the Employment Rights Act (see Chapter 17). In *Hendry v Scottish Liberal Club*, one of the reasons why the claimant was dismissed was connected with the discovery that he had been convicted many years ago of possessing cannabis. This conviction was 'spent' within the meaning of the Act, and hence it was not a statutory reason for dismissal.

4.343 In *Property Guards Ltd v Taylor and Kershaw* the two claimants were employed as security guards. On commencing their employment they signed a statement to the effect that they had never been guilty of a criminal offence. When the employers discovered that they had both been convicted of minor offences of dishonesty, they were dismissed. The EAT upheld the finding of the employment tribunal that the dismissals were unfair. In both cases the convictions were 'spent' within the meaning of the Act. They were entitled not to disclose their previous convictions.

4.344 If an employer subsequently discovers that the employee has had a previous conviction, he must make all necessary enquiries to ascertain whether or not the conviction is spent before he starts taking action. In *Brooks v Ladbroke Lucky Seven Entertainment*, the claimant was dismissed when it was discovered that he had had a prior conviction. It was argued on behalf of the employer that the dismissal was necessary in view of the nature of their business (as a gambling club), and as they did not know that the conviction was spent, they were not acting unreasonably. It was held that the employer should have sought further information about the nature of the offence and the penalty imposed, and a failure to do so rendered the dismissal unfair.

4.345   The main rehabilitation periods are as follows:

Sentence	Rehabilitation period
Imprisonment or youth custody of more than 6 months and up to 2½ years	10 years
Imprisonment or youth custody not exceeding 6 months	7 years
Fine or community service order or probation order or detention and training order	5 years
Conditional discharge, bind over, care order, or supervision order	One year, or until the order expires, which ever is the longer
Absolute discharge	6 months

4.346   Other sentences which come within the Act include orders for custody in a remand home, an approved school, an attendance order, and a hospital order. In respect of persons under the age of 18 at the time of conviction, the rehabilitation period is generally reduced by half. In the case of imprisonment, it is the period of sentence imposed by the court which counts (including a suspended sentence) not the actual time spent in prison. The rehabilitation period runs from the date of the conviction. A prison sentence (or youth custody sentence) of more than 2½ years is never 'spent'.

4.347–4.355   The Act does not apply to questions which are asked of a person in order to assess the suitability of a person for admission to the professions of medical practitioner, barrister, accountant, solicitor, dentist, dental hygienist or auxiliary, veterinary surgeon, nurse, midwife, ophthalmic or dispensing optician, pharmaceutical chemist, or a Scottish registered teacher. Such people must still tell the truth about their previous convictions. Nor can a person tell a lie if the questions are asked for the purpose of assessing his suitability for the following employments, namely, certain legal appointments and offices, certain employment connected with the punishment of offenders, constables, traffic wardens, probation officers, further education teachers, proprietors of independent schools, certain local government social workers, hospital workers, persons who work for building societies or who provide financial services, youth club leaders and employment with cadet forces. Certain other occupations are also excluded from the provisions of the Act (see the Rehabilitation of Offenders Act 1974 (Exceptions) Orders 1975 and 1986), and see *Wood v Coverage Care Ltd*).

Access to criminal records

4.356   Employers who wish to know whether or not an applicant for employment has or has not got a criminal record may be able to use the new procedures set out in the Police Act 1997, which makes arrangements for access to criminal records for employment-related purposes. This Act enables a criminal record check to be made available by a new Criminal Records Agency from computerised national criminal records, in response to an application by a person who is the subject of the check. Three types of certificates are available.

A. Criminal conviction certificate (s 112)

4.357 This certificate gives prescribed details of every conviction which is recorded in central police records. A 'conviction' for this purpose means a conviction within the meaning of the Rehabilitation of Offenders Act, other than a conviction which is spent. Alternatively, the certificate will record that there is no conviction. An employer cannot apply direct to the Criminal Records Agency for this certificate, but can request that the job applicant provides one as a prerequisite for employment.

B. Criminal record certificate (s 113)

4.358 This is a more detailed certificate, which will record every matter recorded in central police records, including a conviction which is spent under the Rehabilitation of Offenders Act. This certificate can be asked for by a person seeking employment in one of the occupations where a conviction under the Rehabilitation of Offenders Act must be disclosed, even though it would otherwise be spent. An application for this type of certificate will be made by the subject of the check, countersigned by a person who is listed in a register to be kept by the Secretary of State as being likely to employ persons in occupations which are excluded from that Act. It is likely that this certificate will be sought by persons who wish to be employed in a large number of occupations which are exempt from the 1974 Act, including the judiciary, police, Crown employment, probation officers, prison staff, professional groups generally, banking and financial services, carers/social workers, etc.

C. Enhanced criminal record certificate (s 115)

4.359 This certificate, as well as containing the information found in the criminal record certificate, may contain additional information provided by local police forces, including cautions and relevant non-conviction information. This certificate will be used when seeking employment caring for or being in sole charge of persons under the age of 18 or vulnerable adults, or being involved in training or supervising them. Again, the application will be made by the job-applicant, and countersigned by the registered person. These certificates should be available from July 2001, in respect of applicants who apply for such posts.

4.360 It is an offence for members and staff of any registered body to make an unauthorised disclosure of any information provided in a criminal records check or enhanced criminal records check.

4.361–4.370 A code of practice on the operation of the above provisions of the Police Act is to be issued shortly.

Unfair recruitment (TULR(C)A s 137)

4.371 There are provisions in the Trade Union and Labour Relations (Consolidation) Act 1992 which protect a person from being refused employment on grounds of trade union membership or non-membership. These matters will be considered in Chapter 21.

Employment of women

4.372 Most of the statutory provisions passed for the protection of female employees have been repealed in so far as they enabled different treatment to be accorded to women. Thus women may now clean parts of machinery while in motion, they may work underground in mines, and perform a number of other tasks which were previously not open to them (see Employment Act 1989 s 9). This is in accordance with the Equal Treatment Directive (see para 1.142) and the desire of the Government to reduce the legislative and administrative burdens on industry.

4.373 However, a number of statutory provisions relating to the health and safety of women have been retained, particularly dealing with those risks associated with pregnancy, childbirth and other risks specifically affecting women. Thus a woman may not work in a factory within four weeks of childbirth, (Factories Act 1961 Sch 5, Public Health Act 1936 s 205), or in any employment within two weeks of childbirth (Maternity (Compulsory Leave) Regulations 1994). Women are prohibited from working in certain processes and activities involving lead products (including lead paint); there are limits on exposure to ionising radiations, and on working in an aircraft or at sea while pregnant (Employment Act 1989 s 4 and Sch 1). Indeed, it is lawful to discriminate against a woman in so far as it is necessary to comply with the above restrictions (see para 4.131).

4.374–4.380 Restrictions on hours of work (including overtime and night work) for women were abolished in the Sex Discrimination Act 1986 (s 7) but the position is now governed by the Employment Act 1989 (s 1) which effectively nullifies any statutory provision which produces a discrimination as regards access to employment and working conditions (see para 4.52).

Employment of young persons

4.381 All legislative provisions which dealt with the hours of work and holidays of young persons (defined as persons over school-leaving age) have been repealed (Employment Act 1989 s 10 and Sch 3). The health and safety of young persons is provided for in the Management of Health and Safety at Work Regulations 1999 (see Chapter 11).

Adult workers

4.382 The sole remaining legislation imposing restrictions on the hours of work of adult workers are (1) Mines and Quarries Act 1954 (underground miners), (2) Hours of Employment (Conventions) Act 1936 (sheet glass workers), (3) Shops (Early Closing Days) Act 1965 (shop assistants), and (4) Transport Act 1968 (vehicle drivers) and the Working Time Regulations (see para 7.221). It is not unlawful to discriminate against a person on grounds of his/her age (unless this also amounts to discrimination on some other grounds: see *Price v Civil Service*

Commission), but a new code of practice (with no statutory backing) has been drawn up with a view to promoting fair employment practices, with particular reference to the needs of older workers who are in work or looking for work. It would appear that legislation on this topic is not being considered for the foreseeable future.

Duty of local authorities

4.383 Section 71 of the Race Relations Act provides that it shall be the duty of every local authority to make appropriate arrangements with a view to securing that their various functions are carried out with due regard to the need:
a. to eliminate unlawful discrimination, and
b. to promote equality of opportunity and good relations between persons of different racial groups.

4.384–4.390 A local authority cannot use the powers conferred by this section to punish a person who has done no wrongful act (*Wheeler v Leicester City Council*).

Contract compliance

4.391 Section 17 of the Local Government Act 1988 provides that in exercising any function dealing with public supply or works contracts, a public authority must not take account of non-commercial considerations. These include such matters as a contractor's terms and conditions of employment, the composition of his workforce, arrangements for promotion, transfer or training of the workforce, or the country of origin of supplies to contractors, the location in any country of the business activities of contractors, etc.

4.392 Clearly, since race relations matters are non-commercial considerations, the 1988 Act imposes a limit on the operation of s 71 of the 1976 Act. However, s 18(2) of the 1988 Act permits a local authority to ask approved questions, in writing, seeking information or undertakings relating to workforce matters, and considering the responses to them, and may also include in draft contracts terms or provisions relating to workforce matters, if the information, the undertaking or the inclusion of the terms are reasonably necessary to secure compliance with s 71. A local authority may also request evidence in support of any answer given.

4.393 The Secretary of State will specify the approved questions and description of evidence which may be requested for the purpose of s 18(2).

4.394–4.400 Somewhat curiously, there are no corresponding statutory provisions relating to sex discrimination (*R v London Borough of Islington, ex p Building Employers' Confederation*).

Criminal harassment

4.401 Section 4A of the Public Order Act 1986 (as inserted by s 154 of the Criminal Justice and Public Order Act 1994) creates a new offence of harassment.

This is committed by a person if, with intent to cause another person alarm or distress,

(a) he uses threatening, abusive or insulting words or behaviour, or disorderly behaviour, or

(b) he displays any writing, sign, or other visible representation which is threatening, abusive or insulting,

thereby causing another person harassment, alarm or distress.

It appears that this offence may well be committed by an individual in an employment context, eg, by way of sexual harassment, using racial abuse, etc, and may even extend protection to classes of employees not currently protected in law, eg persons with disabilities or on grounds of sexual orientation. The new law may also be relevant to the law on picketing (see para 23.181). Any criminal liability will fall on the individual who committed the offence, not on his employer.

A person convicted of the offence of harassment faces a fine of up to £5,000, and/or a term of imprisonment of up to six months.

4.402 Further criminal offences, as well as civil remedies, are provided in the Protection from Harassment Act 1997.

CHAPTER 5

Equal pay

5.1 The Sex Discrimination Act 1975 is concerned with the elimination of discrimination in the recruitment, training, promotion and other aspects of the employment relationship. The Equal Pay Act 1970 is concerned with the establishment, where necessary, of equal terms and conditions of employment. This Act, as amended by the Sex Discrimination Act and by the Equal Pay (Amendment) Regulations 1983, has now been examined by the EAT and higher courts on a number of occasions as well as by the European Court of Justice, and the broad principle has emerged that as it is essentially a reforming statute, it must be interpreted accordingly. The employment tribunals must therefore apply its provisions in accordance with the statutory objective of eliminating discrimination in terms and conditions of employment which exist solely because of a person's sex.

5.2 It must be stressed that the application of the Equal Pay Act and the various relevant regulations (as well as the decisions of the UK courts and tribunals), are subject to the overriding views of the European Court of Justice, applying art 141 (formerly 119) of the Treaty, and the Equal Pay Directive. In the event of a conflict arising, or a disputed interpretation, it is European law which will be applied.

5.3 Article 141 provides that member states shall maintain the application of the principle that men and women should receive equal pay for equal work. As we have noted (see *Barber v Guardian Royal Exchange*, para 4.112), the term 'pay' is very wide, and means 'the ordinary basic or minimum wage or salary and any other consideration, whether in cash or kind, which a worker receives, directly or indirectly, in respect of his employment from his employer'. In *Worringham v Lloyd's Bank*, female clerical officers under the age of 25 were not required to contribute to a pension scheme. Male clerical officers under the age of 25 were required to contribute 5 per cent of their salary to the scheme, but to compensate them for the difference the men were paid 5 per cent more. The Equal Pay Act (s 6(1A)(b)) excluded terms relating to death or retirement or any provision made in relation to death or retirement. On a reference to the European Court of Justice it was held that art 141 had a direct effect so as to confer an enforceable Community right on all individuals within the EEC. Thus the scheme operated by the bank was in violation of art 141, which overrode s 6(1A)(b) of the Equal Pay Act.

5.4   The Act can apply to self-employed persons as well as employees, for it covers 'employment under a contract of service or apprenticeship, or a contract personally to execute any work or labour'. In *Quinnen v Hovells*, the claimant was a self-employed salesman engaged by the respondent to demonstrate goods for sale in a department store. He complained that two female demonstrators were receiving a higher rate of pay, and the EAT held that he was entitled to have his claim considered on its merits, for the definition of employment in the Act clearly covered self-employed persons.

5.5   Whereas under UK law, the burden of proof lies upon an applicant to show that, on the balance of probabilities, s/he is not receiving equal pay, the decision of the European Court in *Handels-og v Dansk Arbejdsgiverforening* (the '*Danfoss*' case) indicates that if a pay system manifestly produces inequalities of pay between the sexes, the burden lies upon the employer to show that the criteria used which produces those inequalities are not discriminatory.

5.6   Men and women are entitled to equal pay if they are employed 'in the same employment'. This means that they must be employed at the same establishments at which common terms and conditions of employment are observed (s 1(6)) ie the same terms and conditions (*British Coal Corpn v Smith*). In *Leverton v Clwyd County Council*, a nursery nurse was employed by a local authority, and she sought equal pay with male clerical staff employed by the same authority in different establishments. She and her comparators were covered by the same national collective agreement, but they were on different pay scales, with different hours and holiday entitlements. The employers contended that there were no common terms and conditions, and hence that the Act did not apply, but this view was rejected by the House of Lords. The terms and conditions, as laid down in the collective agreement, were applied generally, even though there were differences when applied to individual employees (nb, the claim failed under the defence of 'genuine material factor' see para 5.56).

5.7   The Act requires that the contract of employment of all women shall be deemed to include an equality clause. This will operate when a woman is employed either on:
a.   like work (ie work which is the same or broadly similar), or
b.   work which has been rated as being equivalent under a job evaluation scheme, or
c.   work which is of equal value to that performed by a man in the same employment.
   If any of these three situations exist, then any term in a woman's contract which is less favourable than a man's contract shall be modified so as to be not less favourable, and any benefit in a man's contract shall be included in the woman's contract.

5.8–5.15   If the same rules apply to men and women, and to both full-time and part-time workers, the fact that some workers are less well off in consequence is irrelevant. In *Barry v Midland Bank plc* a contractual redundancy scheme, which provided for severance pay to be based on final salary at the date of termination, did not breach the Act, even though part-time women workers received less under the scheme than full-time employees. Their final salary was less because they were working less, and they would have received severance pay on the same basis as male part-timers.

Like work (s 1(4))

5.16 To determine whether a woman is employed on like work, the Act states that the work must be the same or broadly similar, and any differences between the work done are not of practical importance. In *Capper Pass v Lawton*, a woman worked as a cook in a company directors' dining room, providing lunches for between 10 and 20 persons. She sought equal pay with two assistant chefs who worked in the factory canteen, and who prepared 350 meals each day. Other differences were that she worked 40 hours per week, and had no one supervising her, whereas the men worked 45 hours per week, and were under the supervision of a head chef. The EAT upheld a decision of the employment tribunal that she was entitled to equal pay. The work did not have to be the same; it was sufficient if it was broadly similar, and the differences were not of practical importance. It would have been wrong to take a too pedantic approach, or to find that there was no like work because of insubstantial differences.

5.17 If there are differences between the work done, the tribunals must ask if these are such that it is reasonable to expect to see them reflected in different wage settlements which contain no element of sex discrimination. Three such differences which may be of practical importance have been identified.

A. Different duties

5.18 In *Electrolux Ltd v Hutchinson* it was held that as well as there being a contractual obligation to perform different duties, those duties must be actually performed to an extent which was significant enough to warrant different pay treatment. In this case, men and women were performing broadly similar work, but the men were graded on a higher rate. The employers argued that the men had different contractual obligations, such as accepting transfer to different work, working compulsory overtime, and working nights. The EAT upheld a decision of the employment tribunal that the women were entitled to equal pay; the question had to be asked, what happens in practice? If and when the men performed these additional obligations, the situation could be dealt with by paying additional premiums. This, however, should not affect the basic grade which was applicable. In *Noble v David Gold & Son (Holdings) Ltd*, men worked in a warehouse loading and unloading, whereas women did lighter work such as sorting, packing and labelling. The Court of Appeal agreed with the finding of the employment tribunal that the women were not on like work. Nor was the work broadly similar, for the differences were of practical importance in relation to terms and conditions of employment.

5.19 Employees who have received different professional training, and thus could be called upon to perform different duties, are not employed in the same work (*Angestelltenbetriebsrat der Wiener v Wiener*).

B. Different hours

5.20 In *Dugdale v Kraft Foods Ltd* men and women worked on broadly similar work, but the men had to work a compulsory night shift, and a voluntary shift on Sunday mornings. It would have been unlawful by virtue of the Factories Act 1961 for women to have worked on these occasions. It was held that the hours at which the work is performed is by itself no bar to equal pay at the basic rate. The men could be compensated for these extra burdens by a night shift payment or premium. The equality clause does not have to produce equal pay if in fact the men were paid for something which the women did not do, eg work nights.

5.21 But this reasoning only applies when the difference in hours applies only to men. If in fact *men and women* work different hours to other employees (men and/or women), then because the difference has nothing to do with the sex of the person who is working those different hours, the difference in hours is a genuine material difference other than sex, and hence basic rates can vary between the employees concerned (*Kerr v Lister & Co Ltd*, see para 5.58).

5.22 If a contract (or collective agreement) provides that full-time employees who work in excess of their normal contractual hours are entitled to an overtime supplement, but part-time workers do not get this supplement if they work above their normal contractual hours, this is not unequal treatment of the part-timers, the majority of whom are women. The overall pay is the same for the same number of hours worked. A part-time worker whose contractual working hours are 18, and who works for 19 hours, receives the same pay as a full-time worker who works 19 hours. If the part-time worker works more than the normal contractual hours of the full-time worker, the overtime supplement would be payable. Thus this arrangement is not discrimination against part-time workers, and not incompatible with art 141 of the Treaty of Rome (*Stadt Lengerich v Helmig*).

C. Different responsibilities

5.23–5.30 In *Eaton Ltd v Nuttall*, a man and woman worked on like work, but the man received a higher rate of pay because his responsibilities were greater. He handled more expensive products, and consequently a mistake by him would have had far more serious financial consequences. The EAT held that it was proper to take into account the additional responsibilities which the job entailed.

Work rated as being equivalent (s 1(5))

5.31 A woman's work will be considered to have been rated equivalent to that of a man if it has been given equal value under a properly conducted job evaluation scheme, in terms of the different demands made upon an employee, eg effort, skill, decision, etc. In *Eaton Ltd v Nuttall* it was stated that such a scheme must be capable of satisfying the test of being thorough in analysis and impartial in application. Once it is established that it is a genuine scheme, it must be accepted by the parties and the employment tribunals, for the latter cannot act as an appeal court from a valid job evaluation scheme. In placing an employee in a particular grade, it is then proper to take into account such factors as merit, seniority, etc.

5.32 It is irrelevant that there is a difference between the actual points scored under the job evaluation scheme, if there is no difference in the allocation to a particular salary grade or scale at the end of the evaluation process. In *Springboard Sunderland Trust v Robson*, the claimant was awarded 400 points following a job evaluation, but on appeal this was increased to 410 points. She claimed equal pay with a male comparator who had been awarded 428 points. The relevant salary scales provided were Grade 3 for 360–409 points, and Grade 4 for 410–449 points.

Thus, although her job was not rated as being equivalent to the comparator, her claim succeeded, because what mattered was the grade to be allocated to her following the evaluation, rather than the values assigned to her under the evaluation.

5.33–5.40 A job evaluation scheme has to be carried out with a view to evaluating jobs in terms of the demands made of a worker under various headings (eg effort, skill, decision, etc) so as to lead to a fair comparison with the comparator's job. This is the so-called 'analytical' approach, which is to be preferred to the 'felt fair' or 'whole job' approach (*Bromley v H & J Quick Ltd*).

Equal value

5.41 In *EC Commission v United Kingdom*, the European Court held that the Equal Pay Act did not comply with art 141 of the Treaty of Rome, for although the Act provided for equal pay when a job evaluation scheme was in existence, there was no way a woman could compel her employer to undertake such a scheme. Consequently, the Equal Pay (Amendment) Regulations 1983 were passed, which are designed to enable a woman to claim equal pay on the ground that her work is of equal value to that of a man.

5.42 A claim for equal value may be made to an employment tribunal, which will first determine whether or not it can be dealt with under the headings of like work or job evaluation study. In the latter case, the claim may only proceed if it can be shown that the study discriminates on grounds of sex. If not, the tribunal may decide that there are no reasonable grounds for making the claim (eg if a nurse were to seek equal pay with a surgeon, see *Sheffield Metropolitan District Council v Siberry*), or decide the question of equal value themselves, or refer the claim to an expert (from a list of such persons held by ACAS) who will prepare a job evaluation study to see if the jobs are of equal value. If this latter course is adopted, the employment tribunal will not be able to decide the question of equal value until they have received the expert's report (Employment Tribunals (Constitution and Rules of Procedure) Regulations 1993 Sch 2). However, the report of the expert is not binding on the tribunal, for whether jobs are of equal value is a question of fact for the tribunal to decide (*Tennants Textile Colours Ltd v Todd*). If the tribunal decide not to commission a report from an expert (eg, because they regard the case as being hopeless) they must not determine the matter without giving the parties an opportunity to adduce their own evidence (*Wood v William Ball Ltd*).

5.43 The first major case under the new Regulations was *Hayward v Cammell Laird Shipbuilders Ltd*, where the claimant joined the company as a catering trainee. During the first three years of her employment, she was paid at the same rate as apprenticed painters, insulation engineers and joiners, but thereafter she was paid at a lower rate than these skilled workers. However, she enjoyed superior sickness benefits, paid meal breaks and extra holidays. Her claim for equal pay based on 'work of equal value' was referred to an independent expert, who evaluated the jobs under the headings of (a) physical demands, (b) environmental considerations, (c) skill and knowledge, (d) planning and decision making, and (e) responsibility. He concluded that the work of the claimant was of equal value with the three selected male comparators who were now earning higher rates.

When the case came back to the employment tribunal, it was held that the terms and conditions of employment *as a whole* must be not less favourable, and not just the actual cash pay received by her. Thus her claim for equal pay was dismissed, and the decision was upheld by the EAT and the Court of Appeal. The argument was based on art 141 of the Treaty of Rome, which provides that 'pay' means 'the ordinary basic or minimum wage or salary, and any other consideration, whether in cash or in kind, which a worker receives, directly or indirectly, in respect of his employment from his employer'. Thus it was thought that although her cash pay was less than her selected comparators, her other terms and conditions had to be taken into consideration.

However, on a further appeal, the House of Lords reversed the decision and upheld her claim. Lord MacKay, the Lord Chancellor thought that the word 'term' in s 1(2) of the Act meant a distinct provision or part of the contract, and, in this case, the basic salary of the appellant had to be compared with the basic salary in the men's contracts. Lord Goff stated that a simple question should be asked: is there, in each contract, a term of a similar kind, which makes comparable provision for the same subject matter? If so, then the term in the woman's contract and the men's contract can be compared, and if, on that comparison, the term in the woman's contract proves to be less favourable than the term in the men's, then the term in the woman's contract is to be treated as being modified so as to make it not less favourable. Their Lordships thought that the Equal Pay Act required the courts and employment tribunals to look at a particular term in a woman's contract which was less favourable, and did not require a holding that terms as a whole should not be less favourable.

Although the decision will inevitably result in a process of leap-frogging on contractual terms and conditions (doubtless the male joiners, insulation engineers and painters will be able to pursue a claim for better sickness benefits, paid meal breaks and extra holidays), the long-term impact of this decision will be to increase the momentum towards greater harmonisation of terms and conditions of employment, not only between the hourly-paid and staff employees, but also between those occupations which are traditionally regarded as being male or female preserves.

It should be noted that in *Hayward's* case the employers did not plead a possible defence they may have had under s 1(3) of the Act (genuine material factor, see para 5.56), and it is arguable that the additional perks which the appellant enjoyed could constitute a genuine material factor which would defeat a claim for equal pay.

5.44   An equal value claim may be brought by a woman even though she works with men doing the same work and who are paid the same as she, as long as there is another man with whom she wishes to be compared earning a higher wage. In *Pickstone v Freemans plc* the claimant was a warehouse operative, who worked alongside other male warehouse operatives, and who all received the same pay. She brought an equal value claim, naming as her comparator a male checker warehouse operative who was paid at a higher rate. It was held that she was entitled to succeed under s 2(1)(c) of the Act. To hold otherwise would enable an unscrupulous employer to defeat equal value claims by ensuring that one man worked alongside women. On the other hand, the House of Lords did not appear to consider the leap-frogging effect of the decision, for undoubtedly the other male warehouse operatives would subsequently be able to claim equal pay with the applicant, once she was given the higher rate.

5.45–5.55 The principle of equal pay applies even if it is discovered that the claimant is in fact doing work which is of greater value than the comparator (*Murphy v Bord Telecom Eireann*), as long as she is paid less.

Genuine material factor (s 1(3))

5.56 Even though a woman can show that she is employed on like work, or work rated as equivalent, or work of equal value, the employer may still be able to resist an equal pay claim on the ground that the variation in pay 'is genuinely due to a material factor which is not the difference of sex'. However, at this stage an important distinction must be made. If the claim is based on like work or work rated as being equivalent under a job evaluation study, the employer has to show that the material factor which causes the difference in pay *must* be a material difference between the woman's case and the man's, whereas in a claim based on equal value, the material factor *may* be such a material difference. The distinction between these two cases is as follows. In a claim based on like work or work rated as the same, any variation in pay can only be based on non-sex factors (eg long service, red-circling, etc, see below). Market forces are not such a factor, for this was one of the reasons the Act was passed (*Clay Cross (Quarry Services) Ltd v Fletcher*; but see *Rainey v Greater Glasgow Health Board*, para 5.63). In equal value claims, however, there may be other forces at work which account for the difference in pay. For example, it may be necessary to pay the men more because their skills are in short supply, or because in that area it is necessary to pay the going rate for men in order to attract them, or because their work is more profitable and hence they demand higher pay. In other words, where equal value claims are concerned, since like is not being compared with like, there are a number of material factors at work which *may* (but not must) be a material difference.

5.57 The defence of 'genuine material factor' cannot apply to any difference in the actual work done, for this must be considered when it is decided whether or not there is like work or work rated as being equivalent. Thus if a man is employed lifting heavy weights, this is relevant to the question of whether a woman is employed on like work; it should also be given an appropriate weighting in any job evaluation scheme. Further, once like work or work rated equivalent has been established, there is a burden of proof on those who seek to show that there is a difference in treatment which is 'genuinely due to a material factor' which has nothing to do with the sex of the person concerned. Thus if the underlying reason for a difference in treatment is sex based, even though this is of historical origin, it cannot amount to a material difference. In *Snoxell v Vauxhall Motors Ltd* men and women were doing like work as inspectors. The men were in a 'red circle' group, ie their pay was higher because many years ago they were part of a separate male group who received higher wages, but as a result of a revision in pay structure, they were regraded. By being placed in the 'red circle' (so-called because of the practice of putting a circle in red around the names of the affected employees on the tables of wages) their higher wage rates were protected until the group was phased out. The red circle group was clearly an historical anomaly, but the EAT held that the women inspectors were entitled to equal pay with them, for s 1(3) could never provide a defence when past discrimination had contributed to the variation.

5.58 Non-sex-based factors which could amount to genuine material factors include additional responsibility allowances (*Waddington v Leicester Council for Voluntary Services*), extra pay for academic qualifications (*Murray v East Lothian Regional Council*), long service increments (*Honeywell Ltd v Scott*) a genuine mistake in putting an employee in the wrong salary grade (*Yorkshire Blood Transfusion Service v Plaskitt*) and differences in the place where the work is done (*NAAFI v Varley*). As noted above, a difference in hours which is not sex based could be a material difference. In *Kerr v Lister & Co Ltd* men and women doing the same work on the night shift were paid the same rate, but this was higher than that paid to the women who worked on the day shift. Thus the differences in the rate had nothing to do with sex; it was paid in order to attract workers (of either sex) to the night shift. Since the difference was between that of day and night work and not due to a difference of sex, there was a genuine material factor which justified the employers' contention that a woman worker was not entitled to equal pay.

5.59 Similarly, a red circle treatment whereby employees can have their wages protected for reasons other than sex could also amount to a genuine material factor. Thus if an employee on a higher grade is made redundant, and given employment on work which is graded at a lower rate, it is permissible to give him red circle treatment without attracting a successful claim for equal pay on the part of the other employees in the lower grade (*Charles Early and Marriott (Witney) Ltd v Smith*). This also applies if a man is demoted or downgraded, but is permitted to retain his former (higher) rate of pay (*Forex Neptune (Overseas) Ltd v Miller*). But if a man's wages are protected on a transfer, the employment tribunal must be satisfied that the reason was not just that he was a man, or that the job to which he was appointed was not one which has been exclusively reserved for men (*Methven v Cow Industrial Polymers Ltd*).

5.60 If the defence under s 1(3) is being raised, the burden is on the employer to prove, on the balance of probabilities, that the differences are due to a genuine material factor other than sex. Thus a grading scheme which operates according to skill, experience or ability can be an integral part of good management. As long as it is a genuine scheme, and operates irrespective of sex, it is not rendered inoperative by the Act (*National Vulcan Engineering Insurance Group Ltd v Wade*).

5.61 If a premium is paid, partly for working a rotating shift, and partly for working unsocial hours, it is not necessary to quantify precisely how the premium is made up. The employment tribunal should only be concerned with whether the scheme is genuine, not that it is fair (*Calder v Rowntree Mackintosh Confectionery Ltd*).

If the differences are due to length of service, the employer must show the terms and conditions relating to service increments, or at least show some evidence as to how the differences have come about. It is not sufficient merely to state the fact, without some attempt to justify any variation (*Honeywell Ltd v Scott*). Similarly, the mere attaching of a label, such as 'red circle' will not, without further evidence, constitute a defence (*Outlook Supplies Ltd v Parry*). However, it is permissible to take into account experience and training (*De Brito v Standard Chartered Bank*).

5.62 The mere fact that a woman carried out the same duties as a man for a short period of time or as a deputy as a temporary measure does not entitle the woman to equal pay with that man, for basically their responsibilities are different (*Ford v R Weston (Chemists) Ltd*). Also, if a woman works substantially fewer hours than a man, eg as a part-timer, and men and women who work full-time are paid the same, the part-time nature of the employment is a relevant factor in concluding that the variation in her pay may be a genuine material factor (*Handley v H Mono Ltd*). However, in *Jenkins v Kingsgate (Clothing Productions) Ltd (No 2)* the EAT referred to the European Court the question as to whether a woman part-timer could claim the same hourly rate as a full-time man. The Court held that a difference in pay between full-time and part-time workers does not constitute discrimination prohibited by art 141 of the Treaty of Rome unless it is in reality an indirect way of reducing the pay of part-time workers who were wholly or predominantly women. When the case returned to the EAT it was held that it was not sufficient for an employer to show that he had no intention of discriminating on grounds of sex. Any variation in the pay of part-time women and full-time men had to be justified by reference to some non-discriminatory objective. The case was thus remitted to the employment tribunal to determine whether the lower rates for part-time workers were reasonably necessary in order to reduce absenteeism and obtain the maximum utilisation of plant.

5.63   In determining whether or not there is a genuine material factor between 'her case and his' in like work and work rated as equivalent claims the employment tribunal may have regard to the extrinsic forces which led to the man being paid more. In *Rainey v Greater Glasgow Health Board*, a health authority decided to set up its own prosthetic fitting service. The rates of pay for qualified prosthetists was to be on the same scale as medical physics technicians. However, in order to attract a sufficient number of qualified persons to get the service started, it was necessary to make a higher pay offer to those who came from the private sector. The claimant, who came into the service direct from her training, sought equal pay with a man on a higher salary who had come from the private sector. It was held that the difference in pay was due to a genuine material factor which had nothing to do with sex. The reason the man was paid more was because of the need to attract qualified persons (of either sex) from the private sector in order to form the nucleus of the new service. The House of Lords thought that the earlier decision of *Clay Cross (Quarry Services) v Fletcher* was unduly restrictive, for economic grounds, objectively justifiable, were capable of being a genuine material factor.

5.64   Thus, genuine economic considerations, such as a change in the volume of the work reflecting the profitability of the firm, may amount to a genuine material factor (*Albion Shipping Agency v Arnold*).

5.65   A disparity between other terms and conditions may constitute the defence of genuine material factor. In *Leverton v Clwyd County Council* (see para 5.6) the claimant was required to work $32^{1}/_{2}$ hours per week and had holidays which were coterminous with school holidays, whereas the male comparators worked for 37 hours per week, and only had 20 days annual holidays. Thus the notional hourly rate (taken over the year) did not reveal any significant difference, and the inequality in pay was thus justified by the criteria of reasonable necessity and objective justifiability.

5.66   Also, as has already been noted, market forces may be raised as a genuine material factor which justifies unequal pay if the claim is based on equal value.

5.67 In *Enderby v Frenchay Health Authority*, the ECJ held that if statistical evidence discloses an appreciable difference in the pay of two jobs which are of equal value, one of which is carried out almost exclusively by women and the other predominantly by men, it is for the national courts to assess whether the statistics are significant. If a *prima facie* case of sex discrimination is revealed, the employer must show that the difference in pay is objectively justified on grounds other than sex. The state of the employment market, which leads an employer to increase the pay of a particular job in order to attract appropriately qualified workers may constitute such justification. But the use of separate collective bargaining arrangements which bring about a discriminatory effect is not an objective justification.

If the genuine material factor is due to the difference of sex, because the particular labour market is almost exclusively female, the defence in s 1(3) cannot apply. Thus in *Radcliffe v North Yorkshire County Council* the claimant was employed as a dinner lady, her pay having been rated as equivalent to certain other manual jobs. Following the introduction of competitive tendering, the council set up a direct service organisation in order to compete with rival commercial firms who were bidding for school meals contracts. One contract was lost because the rival firm had lower labour costs, and so, in order to be able to compete for other contracts, the Council decided to reduce the pay of the dinner ladies. The claimant complained of a breach of the Equal Pay Act. It was held that although the need to reduce the pay of dinner ladies so as to compete in the open market was a material factor, the factor was due to the difference of sex, because the work was being done almost exclusively by women. The House of Lords stated that the Act must be interpreted without reference to 'direct or indirect discrimination'. As long as the work was rated as being equivalent to that done by male comparators, to reduce the pay of women amounted to a breach of the Act.

5.68 Once the genuine material factor has been identified, and it is established that it has nothing to do with the sex of the person concerned, does it have to be capable of being objectively justified, in the sense that it is significant and relevant, and enabling the employer to pursue measures to meet a real need? In *Rainey v Greater Glasgow Health Board* (see para 5.63) the House of Lords held that the employers had indeed objectively justified the difference in pay, but it appears that objective justification is only necessary when the factor relied upon affected a considerably higher proportion of women than men. In principle, if the factor is not a factor of sex, or tainted in any way with sex discrimination, it is not necessary to show that the factor can be objectively justified. Thus in *Tyldesley v TML Plastics Ltd*, two women were employed as inspection supervisors. One of them was transferred to other work, and the employers advertised for a replacement. A man was appointed, but he was paid more than the claimant, who thus brought a claim for equal pay. The employers argued that they paid the man more money because he had had previous training in total quality management, a skill in which the applicant had no experience. The employment tribunal allowed her claim, holding that the employers had failed to show that there was a real need for inspectors with the type of experience possessed by the man who was appointed to the job, but the decision was reversed by the EAT. Once a genuine material factor has been identified, which has nothing to do with sex, a defence under s 1(3) has been made out. Objective justification is not necessary. Thus, if a difference brought about by a careless mistake, which could not possibly be objectively justified, would be a valid defence under s 1(3), then *a fortiori* a genuine perception about the need to engage a person with particular skills and experience.

5.69 A point on which there has been some judicial observations, but no direct decision, concerns the 'anomalous' comparator. The question arises, must the woman compare herself with a representative man, or can she compare her position with any man, even though that man represents an anomaly? In *McPherson v Rathgael Centre for Children etc*, the claimant, a woman, worked alongside five men as an outdoor pursuits instructor. She, and all the men bar one, were on the same pay scale, which was appropriate to them as instructors without a teaching qualification. One man, however, was paid £1,500 more. This was because it had previously been assumed that certain qualifications he possessed entitled him to be paid as a qualified teacher. It was then discovered that this was not so, but it was decided to continue to pay him as a qualified teacher. The claimant brought a claim for equal pay with him. The employment tribunal dismissed her claim, holding that she was not being paid less than the norm, but rather the comparator was being paid more, due to an initial mistake which had never been rectified. There were men being paid the same rate as the applicant, and it was merely fortuitous that the person being paid more was a man. Thus it was held that the employers had established a defence under s 1(3). On appeal, the Northern Ireland Court of Appeal reversed the decision. It was not sufficient for the employer to show that he did not intend to discriminate on grounds of sex. There must be an objective justification for the variation which exists. An understandable error could not amount to the statutory defence.

However, the court queried whether the applicant was entitled to select the anomalous man as a comparator, rather than the other men who were paid at the same rate as she. Presumably, once the claimant succeeded in her claim, the other men would be entitled to claim equal pay with her, resulting in an escalation of all the salaries. Further, it cannot be right that the sex of the anomalous person gives a right to persons of the opposite sex, although not to a person of the same sex. However, as the matter had not been canvassed before the employment tribunal, the court reserved their opinion. Perhaps it should have been argued that the 'anomalous man' was analogous with a 'red circle' case.

5.70 If the employer seeks to rely on the defence in s 1(3) (genuine material factor), he can do so with the ordinary civil burden of proof on the balance of probabilities, and the burden is no heavier than this (*National Vulcan Engineering Insurance Group Ltd v Wade*). However, in deciding whether the differences in the work done by the relevant employees were of practical importance in relation to terms and conditions of employment, this can be done by looking at the observed activities of the employees, not their notional paper obligations. In *Shields v E Coomes (Holdings) Ltd* a woman counter clerk in a betting shop sought equal pay with a male clerk doing the same work. The employers argued that the man was paid more because he was needed to cope with trouble that could arise from customers. In fact, there was no evidence that this need ever arose. Nor was the man specially trained to tackle intruders. Thus the only reason for his higher rate of pay was because of his sex, and hence it was held that she was entitled to equal pay with the male counter-hand.

5.71–5.80 The matter was summed up by the House of Lords in *Strathclyde Regional Council v Wallace*. There must be a genuine factor, which is material, and not due to the difference of sex. In order to be genuine, it must not be a sham or pretence; to be material, it must be significant and causally related to the difference in pay, and the factor must not be connected with the sex of a person. Once the genuine material factor has been established, the employer is not required to justify it objectively by showing that there was no other way of avoiding disparity of treatment. Objective justification is only needed when the factor relied upon is itself sexually discriminatory.

Pay structures, etc

5.81   Any discrimination based on sex must be eliminated from an employer's pay structure, employment conditions, collective agreements, wage regulation orders, etc. Any term contained in a collective agreement, employers' rules, rules made by a trade union or an employers' association or professional or training body, which is discriminatory, is void. But this is without prejudice to the rights of the person discriminated against in respect of any lawful term of the contract (Sex Discrimination Act 1986 s 6).

5.82   An individual who considers that the terms of a collective agreement could affect him as being contrary to the principle of equal treatment may present a complaint to an employment tribunal. This applies to actual and potential employees. If the complaint is well-founded, the tribunal will declare the term to be void (Sex Discrimination Act 1986, s 6(4A)). Also, a collective agreement which indirectly discriminates against part-time employees (the majority of whom are women) is contrary to art 141 of the Treaty of Rome, unless the employers can objectively justify the discrimination (*Nimz v Freie und Hansestadt Hamburg*).

5.83–5.90   Article 141 cannot be invoked if the difference in pay is due to sexual orientation. In *Grant v South-West Trains Ltd* the employers permitted employees and their partners (whether married or unmarried) to benefit from free travel facilities (this being 'pay' for the purpose of art 141). However, they refused to grant this benefit to the applicant's lesbian partner. The ECJ held that there had been no violation of art 141. The employers' policy applied equally to homosexuals and lesbians, and did not constitute discrimination on grounds of sex (see para 4.101).

Remedies under the Act

5.91   A complaint by an aggrieved party of the contravention of the equality clause, including a claim for arrears of remuneration or damages, may be presented to an employment tribunal, and a dispute as to its effect may similarly be resolved on an application by the employer (s 2). On such a complaint, the employment tribunal should first consider the contract of employment and draw its appropriate conclusions, but if there is no such guide, it is permissible for the tribunal to visit the premises and actually observe the woman at work and the man with whom she wishes to be compared (*Dorothy Perkins Ltd v Dance*). Moreover, the claimant may choose the man with whom she wishes to be compared, and the employment tribunal cannot substitute another man whom it thinks would be more appropriate for the purpose of comparison. Thus if a woman is getting equal pay with some men, she can still seek equal pay with a man who is paid at a higher rate, if his work is the same or broadly similar, etc (*Ainsworth v Glass Tubes and Components*).

5.92   The claim can only be in respect of the salary the comparator was earning, ignoring any potential increments which could have been earned. In *Enderby v Frenchay Health Authority (No 2)* the claimant had worked for a health authority for six years. She successfully made an equal value claim, using as her comparator a man who had only been employed for one year. She argued that she was entitled to the pay her comparator would have received had he been employed as long as she, ie to include the potential increments he would have had. The Court of Appeal held that she was entitled to receive the same pay as her comparator was currently receiving (see also *Evesham v North Herts Health Authority*).

5.93   It is also possible to use a former employee as a comparator. In *Macarthys Ltd v Smith* a man was employed as a stockroom manager, and was paid £60 per week. He left the job, and four months later the woman claimant was appointed as stockroom manageress, and was paid £50 per week. She subsequently brought a claim for equal pay. This was upheld by the employment tribunal and EAT, but the Court of Appeal doubted that she could succeed under the Equal Pay Act. However, the matter was referred to the European Court to consider the effect of art 141 of the Treaty of Rome. This Court held that the principle that men and women should receive equal pay for equal work applied also to the situation where a woman received less pay than a male predecessor, provided they were both doing the same or broadly similar work. Since, under the European Communities Act 1972, the provisions of EU law take precedence whenever there is a conflict with British law, the interpretation of art 141 had to be applied in British courts, and the Court of Appeal subsequently upheld her claim.

5.94   A claim cannot be referred to an employment tribunal if the claimant has not been employed in the employment within the six months preceding the date of the reference (s 2(4)). The decision in *British Railways Board v Paul*, which appears to suggest that this does not apply to a 'claim' made by a claimant is generally thought to be incorrect and was disapproved in *Etherson v Strathclyde Regional Council*. However, if a claim is made based on the failure by the state to implement the terms of an EC Directive, time will only start to run against a claimant from the date when the state made good its obligations (*Cannon v Barnsley Metropolitan Borough Council*).

5.95   Any award in respect of an equal pay claim made by an employment tribunal can be in respect of the period of six years from the date of the commencement of proceedings. The two-year limitation period on arrears of pay, set out in s 2(5) of the Equal Pay Act, is in breach of the EC legal principle of equivalence, ie remedies for breach of art 141 (or a Directive) must be no less favourable than similar domestic claims. The nearest domestic legal claim would be in respect of an unlawful deduction of wages at common law, where a claim could be backdated for six years. Thus the two-year back pay limit is unenforceable, as being incompatible with Community law (*Levez v T H Jennings (Harlow Pools) Ltd*). An award of interest may also be made, calculated in accordance with the provisions of the Sex Discrimination and Equal Pay (Remedies) Regulations 1993.

CHAPTER 6

Maternity rights

6.1 Following the adoption of the EU Directive 92/85/EEC on 'the introduction of measures to encourage improvements in the safety and health of pregnant workers who have recently given birth or are breastfeeding' (the Pregnant Workers Directive) various changes have been made to UK law in so far as it affects workers who are pregnant or who have given birth to a child. In particular, a number of recent changes have been made by the Employment Relations Act 1999 in order to resolve various legal problems which had arisen.

6.2 For the purposes of the Employment Rights Act 1996, childbirth is defined as the birth of a living child or the birth of a child whether living or dead after 24 weeks of pregnancy.

Time off work for ante-natal care (ERA ss 55–57)

6.3 An employee who is pregnant, and who, on the advice of a registered medical practitioner, registered midwife or registered health visitor, has made an appointment to attend any place for the purpose of receiving ante-natal care, shall have the right not to be unreasonably refused time off work during her working hours to enable her to keep that appointment. This right arises from the moment the woman commences her employment, and is irrespective of the number of hours or days worked (but see below) or whether or not she is a permanent or temporary employee. The size of the employer's undertaking is also irrelevant. The only women who do not enjoy this right are those who are not employed under a contract of employment, or who ordinarily work outside Great Britain, or who are share fisherwomen, or women employed as members of any constabulary.

6.4 If requested to do so, she must produce a certificate stating that she is pregnant, and some documentary evidence of the appointment (but not the first appointment).

6.5 She is entitled to be paid for the period of her absence at the appropriate hourly rate (calculated in accordance with the provisions of s 56). If she is refused time off work, or if she is not paid for the time off taken, she may make a complaint to an employment tribunal (within three months of the date of the appointment in question, or within such further time as the employment tribunal considers to be reasonable) that her employer has unreasonably refused to permit her to have time off work, or has failed to pay her the whole or part of the amount to which she claims she was entitled. If the employment tribunal upholds her complaint, they will make a declaration to that effect, and also award her the amount of remuneration to which she is entitled (s 57).

6.6 It should be noted that the right is not to be unreasonably refused time off work. Thus it may be possible to argue that in particular circumstances it would be reasonable for the woman to make arrangements for ante-natal care outside working hours (eg in the case of a woman who works part-time, or less than five days each week). Ante-natal care is not defined in the Act, but undoubtedly includes ante-natal relaxation classes and (possibly) classes in parentcraft, provided she attends on the advice of a medical practitioner etc (see *Gregory v Tudsbury Ltd*).

6.7–6.15 An employer cannot defeat a woman's statutory rights by rearranging her working hours or requiring her to work additional hours to make up for time lost (*Edgar v Giorgine Inns Ltd*). On the other hand, if a woman abuses the time off provisions, and takes additional time off work for activities which are not ante-natal care, she will have no rights under the Act, and will be subject to the usual consequences which flow from disciplinary proceedings (*Gough v County Sports (Wales) Ltd*).

Risk assessment and suspension on maternity grounds

6.16 Under the Management of Health and Safety at Work Regulations 1999 (see Chapter 11) every employer is required to carry out a risk assessment, designed to ensure the health and safety at work of new or expectant mothers, defined as employees who are pregnant, who have given birth within the preceding six months, or who are breastfeeding.

6.17 The first requirement is that where the workforce includes women of childbearing age, *and* the work is of a kind which could involve risk to the health or safety (because of pregnancy or maternity) to a new or expectant mother, or to that of her baby, from any processes or working conditions, or from physical, biological or chemical agents (including those set out in Annexes I and II of Directive 92/85/EEC) the employer shall carry out a risk assessment; see reg 16. It should be noted that although the provisions of the Management of Health and Safety at Work Regulations are essentially criminal in nature, there is an exception in that reg 16 does confer a right of action in civil proceedings. Thus in *Day v T Pickles Farm Ltd* the EAT thought that the failure to carry out a risk assessment on a woman of child bearing age could amount to sex discrimination.

6.18 The physical agents referred to are those which are likely to cause foetal lesions or disrupt placental attachment, eg shocks, movement, ionising or non-ionising radiation, extremes of heat or cold, travel, mental or physical fatigue, etc. The biological agents include those set out in Directive 90/679/EEC (the Biological Agents Directive) in so far as it is known that these agents can endanger the health of a woman or her unborn child. The chemical agents include dangerous substances set out in Directive 90/393/EEC (Carcinogens at Work Directive),

Annex I. Also included are certain industrial processes, underground mining work, pressurised enclosures (eg underwater diving) work with certain viruses (unless immunised), lead and lead derivatives.

6.19 The next requirement arises when the employer cannot take action under any relevant statutory provision (eg by providing protective clothing or equipment etc) which would avoid the risk; then, if it is reasonable to do so, and would avoid such risk, he must alter her working conditions or working hours. However, if it is not reasonable to do so, or if the alteration would not avoid the risk, then the employer must suspend her from work for as long as is necessary to avoid such risk (see para 6.23 below). It should be noted that an employer is not obliged to alter her working conditions or working hours, or to suspend her from work, unless she has informed him in writing that she is pregnant, or has given birth within the previous six months, or is breastfeeding.

6.20 Next, if a new or expectant mother works at night, and a certificate from a registered medical practitioner or registered midwife shows that it is necessary for her health or safety that she should not be at work for any period identified in the certificate, then the employer shall suspend her from work (subject to ERA s 66 below).

6.21 The maternity provisions stated above stem from s 66 of ERA, because the Management of Health and Safety at Work Regulations are specified as being the 'relevant statutory provision' for the purpose of that section (see Suspension from Work (on Maternity Grounds) Order 1994). Additionally a woman is entitled to be suspended from work on maternity grounds due to any recommendation contained in an approved code of practice issued by the Health and Safety Commission under s 16 of the Health and Safety at Work etc Act 1974 (see Chapter 11).

Flowing from her right to be suspended on maternity grounds, a woman will have two further rights.

A. Alternative work (ERA s 67)

6.22 Before suspending a woman on maternity grounds, the employer, if he has available suitable alternative work, shall offer it to her. The alternative work must be of a kind which is suitable for her, and appropriate in the circumstances (see *Poke v P & O European Ferries (Dover) Ltd*). If the terms and conditions differ from her normal contract of employment, they must not be substantially less favourable (see *British Airways (European Operations at Gatwick) Ltd v Moore and Batterill*). A failure to make such an offer entitles the woman to bring a complaint to an employment tribunal, within the usual time limits, which may make an award of compensation as the employment tribunal considers to be just and equitable in all the circumstances.

However, she is not entitled to be paid if the employer offers her suitable alternative work which she unreasonably refuses to do.

B. Maternity suspension pay (ERA s 68)

6.23 A woman who is suspended from work on maternity grounds is entitled to be paid a week's pay in respect of each week of suspension, reduced proportionately if the suspension is for less than a week. She is entitled to be paid her normal hourly rate of pay (ie the week's pay will be divided by the number of normal working hours). If her working hours vary from week to week they are to be averaged over the previous 12 working weeks. If she has not completed 12 weeks' service, an average shall be estimated from the agreed terms and conditions and from the work pattern of others in comparable jobs. A failure by the employer to pay the whole or any part of the remuneration due entitles the woman to bring a complaint to an employment tribunal, which, if it finds the complaint well-founded, shall order the employer to pay the amount of remuneration due to her.

6.24–6.30 Finally, it should be noted that no period of continuous employment is required for a woman to have the above rights (in contrast to the general right to be suspended on medical grounds—scc para 7.21, where continuous employment of one month is required).

Maternity leave

6.31 Under provisions which were contained in the Employment Rights Act 1996, the law on a woman's right to maternity leave and her right to return to work was somewhat confusing and convoluted. These provisions have now been amended by the Employment Relations Act 1999 (which inserted new sections 71–75 into the ERA,) and by the Maternity and Parental Leave Regulations 1999, which came into force as from 30 April 2000. The new provisions have attempted to simplify the situation in a number of ways. First, there is an automatic entitlement for all pregnant women to 18 weeks' maternity leave of absence, thus corresponding with the provisions of the statutory maternity pay scheme set out in the Social Security Contributions and Benefits Act 1992 (see below). Second, there is an additional maternity leave period for women who satisfy the relevant conditions. Third, the former provisions whereby return to work could be postponed by up to four weeks no longer apply. Fourth, the provisions relating to returning to work have been simplified.

Ordinary maternity leave of absence (Maternity and Parental Leave Regulations 1999).

6.32 All women employees, irrespective of their length of service and hours worked, are entitled to 18 weeks maternity leave of absence. To qualify, a woman must notify her employer, at least 21 days before her leave is due to commence (or if that is not reasonably practicable, as soon as is reasonably practicable) of:
(a) the fact that she is pregnant,
(b) the expected week of confinement, and
(c) the date she intends her ordinary maternity leave to commence. This must be in writing if the employer so requests, and cannot be earlier than the eleventh week prior to the expected week of confinement.

6.33 Additionally, if the employer so requests, she must produce for his inspection a certificate from a registered medical practitioner or registered midwife, stating the expected week of confinement.

6.34 The commencement of the leave period can be triggered automatically if:

(a) the childbirth occurs before the maternity leave period would have otherwise commenced (eg if the birth was premature). In such circumstances she must notify the employer (in writing if he so requests) as soon as is reasonably practicable after the birth; or
(b) where the employee is absent from work wholly or mainly because of pregnancy or childbirth after the sixth week prior to the expected week of confinement. Again, she must notify the employer (in writing if he so requests) that she is absent for that reason.

6.35 So far as ordinary maternity leave is concerned, she is simply on statutory leave of absence, with all the consequences which flow therefrom. Thus she is entitled to the benefit of all terms and conditions of employment which would have applied had she not been absent, which includes matters which are connected with her employment whether or not they arise under her contract of employment. However, she is not entitled to terms and conditions related to remuneration, which means sums payable to her by way of wage or salary. For her part, she is bound by any obligation arising under the terms and conditions of her employment. She is entitled to return from leave to the job in which she was employed before her absence (ERA s 71(4)–(7)).

6.36 A woman who is on ordinary maternity leave returns to work by simply presenting herself at the end of the 18-week period of leave. If she wishes to return on an earlier date, she must give her employer 21 days' notice of the date on which she intends to return. If she does not do so, the employer is entitled to postpone her return to work until a date which will ensure that he has 21 days' notice, although he cannot postpone her return to work beyond the date of the expiry of the 18-week period. Indeed, if she does return to work prior to the date of the employer's postponement, she will not be entitled to receive remuneration for the work. Otherwise, she is entitled to return to the job in which she was employed before her absence (s 71(4)(c)), on terms and conditions no less favourable than those which she previously enjoyed.

Additional maternity leave

6.37 A woman who is entitled to ordinary maternity leave, and who has been employed for one year or more at the beginning of the expected week of confinement, is also entitled to an additional maternity leave period, which commences on the day after the last day of her ordinary maternity leave and which will last until the end of the period of 29 weeks beginning with the week of childbirth. During her period of leave, she is entitled to the benefits of her employer's obligation to her of trust and confidence. She is also entitled to the benefit of any terms and conditions of her employment relating to notice of termination, compensation in the event of redundancy, and any disciplinary or grievance procedures. For her part, she is bound by her implied obligation of good faith, and also to any terms and conditions of her employment relating to the giving of notice by her, the disclosure of confidential information, the acceptance by her of gifts or other benefits, or her participation in any other business (Maternity and Parental Leave Regulations, reg 17).

6.38 Not earlier than 21 days before the end of her ordinary leave period, her employer is entitled to request her to notify him, in writing, of:
(a) the date when the childbirth occurred, and

(b) whether she intends to return to work at the end of her additional maternity leave period.

6.39 The employer's request must be in writing, and must be accompanied by a written statement telling her when her additional leave expires, and warning her that if she fails to respond within 21 days, she will not have the statutory protection against a detriment or dismissal (reg 12). This does not mean that the employer may dismiss without fear of any consequences. Presumably, the employer would have to implement the normal procedures which would have been applied in a similar case, eg, if an employee failed to return to work after a period of extended holiday leave. A dismissal would still have to be fair under s 98(4) of ERA, although doubtless the burden on the employer to show this would not be too great. The point is that there is no automatic protection against detriment or dismissal if a woman fails to notify her employer in accordance with these provisions, but, on the other hand, the employer must still go through the normal disciplinary procedures before dismissing.

6.40 If she wishes to return to work at the end of her additional maternity leave period (assuming that she has notified her employer of her intention to do so), then she merely returns to work. If she wishes to return to work before the expiry of her additional maternity leave period, she must give 21 days' notice of her intention, and if she fails to do so, the employer may postpone her return by up to 21 days (but not to a date beyond the end of her additional maternity leave period). In fact, if she returns earlier than the postponed date, the employer is not under any contractual obligation to pay her remuneration for so working. She is entitled to return to the job in which she was employed before her absence, or, if it is not reasonably practicable for the employer to permit this, to another job which is both suitable for her and appropriate for her to do in the circumstances. She is entitled to terms and conditions as to remuneration which are no less favourable than those which would have been applicable had she not been absent, with seniority, pension rights (subject to Social Security Act 1989 Sch 5) and similar rights as if her employment had been continuous, and other terms and conditions not less favourable than those which would have been applicable had she not been absent (reg 18).

Protection from detriment (ERA s 47C)

6.41 An employee is entitled not to be subjected to any detriment because she is pregnant, gave birth to a child, was suspended from work on maternity grounds, took ordinary or additional maternity leave, parental leave or time off work to care for dependants (reg 19). However, as noted, this does not apply if she failed to notify her employer (after being requested to do so, see reg 12, above) that she intended to return to work after the end of her additional maternity leave period.

Unfair dismissal (ERA s 99; Maternity and Parental Leave Regulations 1999)

6.42 A woman will be deemed to have been unfairly dismissed if the reason for her dismissal was that she was pregnant, gave birth to a child, was suspended from work on maternity grounds, took ordinary maternity leave, additional maternity leave, parental leave, time off work to look after dependants, refused to sign a workforce agreement, or acted as a workforce representative. It will also be unfair to dismiss her for reason of redundancy unless the provisions of reg 10 (below) have been complied with.

6.43   However, it will not be an automatically unfair dismissal if immediately before the end of her additional maternity leave period the number of employees employed by the employer does not exceed five, and it was not reasonably practicable for the employer to permit her to return to a job which is both suitable for her and appropriate in the circumstances, or for an associated employer to offer her a job of that kind (reg 20(6)). Nor is the dismissal automatically unfair if it was not reasonably practicable for a reason other than redundancy for the employer to permit her to return to a job which is both suitable and appropriate, and an associated employer offers her a job of that kind which she accepts or unreasonably refuses (reg 20(7)). Finally, she will not be protected from an automatically unfair dismissal if the employee failed to notify her employer (after being requested to do so, see reg 12, above) that she intended to return to work after the end of her additional maternity leave period.

6.44   If it is not practicable by reason of redundancy for the employer to continue to employ her under her existing contract of employment, then if there is a suitable available vacancy she is entitled to be offered alternative employment with her employer (or an associated employer) on work which is suitable for her and appropriate for her to do in the circumstances, and the provisions as to capacity and place of her employment, and other terms and conditions of employment are not substantially less favourable to her than under her previous contract (reg 10). If she is dismissed for reason of redundancy, and the above requirements are not met, the dismissal is automatically unfair (reg 20).

6.45   According to the European Court of Justice it is not contrary to the Equal Treatment Directive to dismiss a woman after her maternity leave has come to an end because of absences due to a pregnancy-related illness, even when that illness first appeared during her pregnancy (*Handels-og v Dansk Handel*). But in *Caledonia Bureau Investment and Property v Caffrey* the Scottish EAT held that to dismiss a woman when she failed to return to work after the expiry of her maternity leave due to post-natal depression was unlawful sex discrimination. Such a dismissal, it was held, was for a reason 'connected with her pregnancy' within s 99(1)(a), as long as the contract of employment continued. However, it is submitted that the decision is of doubtful authority, and post-maternity leave absences should now be dealt with under the normal procedures for dealing with sickness absences.

6.46   Of course, if the employer did not know that she was pregnant, and dismisses her for a reason unconnected with her pregnancy, she will not be able to claim that her dismissal was contrary to s 99. Equally, if she is selected for redundancy, and the pregnancy or childbirth had nothing to do with her selection, then her right to a redundancy payment falls to be considered under s 135.

6.47   If an employer has engaged a temporary replacement to do the work of a woman who is absent on maternity leave, then, if he has informed him/her in writing that the employment will be terminated on the return to work of the latter, and the employer does in fact dismiss the temporary replacement in order to make room for the woman returning from maternity leave, the dismissal shall be regarded as being for some other substantial reason of a kind to justify the dismissal, but the employer must still show that he acted reasonably in treating that reason as a sufficient ground for dismissal (see Chapter 17). The same rule applies when a replacement is taken on when a woman is suspended on medical or maternity grounds (ERA s 106).

6.48–6.55 Finally, a woman who is dismissed at any time while she is pregnant or after childbirth when the maternity leave period ends by reason of the dismissal is entitled to be given written reasons for her dismissal, without any request being made (see para 17.256).

Compulsory maternity leave (ERA s 72)

6.56 The taking of ordinary or additional maternity leave of absence is an option for women who are pregnant. It is not compulsory. It is not unknown for some women to want to return to work as soon possible after giving birth. To prevent this, s 72 of ERA provides that an employer shall not permit a woman to work within two weeks of childbirth. A contravention of this provision can lead to a fine not exceeding Level 2 on the standard scale. Any prohibition arising under the Health and Safety at Work etc Act will also apply. Also, it is an offence (punishable by a fine of up to Level 1 on the standard scale) to permit a woman to work in a factory within four weeks of childbirth (Factories Act 1961 Sch 5, Public Health Act 1936 s 205).

Statutory Maternity Pay (SMP); Social Security Contributions and Benefits Act 1992 ss 164–171 (as amended)

6.57 The old maternity pay scheme administered by the Department of Employment was abolished in 1987, and replaced by statutory maternity pay, which is payable by employers, and recouped by them from the national insurance contributions they pay to the Inland Revenue. SMP is payable for a maximum of 18 weeks; of these, six may attract the higher rate of SMP and 12 weeks will attract the lower rate of SMP.

6.58 The first qualification for SMP is that the woman must be an 'employed earner', ie whose earnings attract a liability for employer's Class I national insurance contributions. This is a concept somewhat different from the definition of 'employee' generally used in employment law (see Chapter 2). The result could well be that a woman could be regarded as being self-employed for SMP purposes (eg because no Class I contributions are being made) but an employee for the purpose of employment protection rights, and thus able to benefit from the provisions relating to maternity leave and right to return to work. However, self-employed women may be entitled to maternity allowance (see below). A woman who is employed by a foreign organisation with no place of business in Great Britain will also not qualify for SMP, although women who work within the European Community are entitled.

6.59 Second, she must have been employed for the requisite period of continuous employment up to the qualifying week, which is the 15th week before the expected week of confinement. She must have worked for at least one day in that week. There is no minimum number of hours qualification, and there are a number of provisions which help to retain continuity where it would otherwise be broken. A woman who is unable to meet these requirements may be able to get maternity allowance (see below).

6.60 Third, she must satisfy the earnings rule, ie her average earnings (including bonuses and overtime) must be at or above the lower earnings limit at which national insurance contributions are payable. Average earnings are calculated over the period of eight weeks ending with the last pay day before the end of the qualifying week.

6.61 Fourth, she must produce a medical certificate stating the expected week of confinement (which cannot be given earlier than the fourteenth week prior to the expected week of confinement), and she must inform her employer (in writing if he so requests) at least 21 days before her absence from work is due to begin (or as soon as reasonably practicable) that she intends to stop work because of her pregnancy. If she has more than one employer, each should be notified, and each will be liable to pay SMP at the appropriate rate.

6.62 Finally, SMP is not payable for weeks when the woman is actually working, and there are additional exclusions in respect of women who are taken into legal custody, or who go outside the European Economic Area (which is the European Union plus Norway and Iceland—the Isle of Man and the Channel Islands are not included), on the death of her employer, and if she changes her employer after her baby is born. Maternity allowance may be payable in certain circumstances (see below).

6.63 The maternity pay period (MPP) lasts for 18 weeks, and may begin any time after the eleventh week prior to the expected week of confinement up to the week following the week in which she is confined. The MPP will commence when the woman ceases to work, so there is some flexibility as to the starting date of payment. The first six weeks' SMP are earnings related, and is calculated at 90 per cent of the average gross weekly earnings. Income tax, national insurance contributions, pension contributions and trade union subscriptions may be deducted by the employer. The remaining period (up to 12 weeks) are paid at the standard SMP rate. Pay rises which take effect between the start of the relevant calculation period and the end of the maternity leave are to be included when calculating earnings related SMP (*Alabaster v Woolwich plc*).

6.64 Once the woman returns to work for the employer who is paying SMP, she will not get SMP for weeks in which she works, although if there are any remaining weeks in the maternity pay period when she does not work, SMP will be payable. However, entitlement will cease altogether if she commences work for a different employer after the birth of her baby but before the end of the maternity pay period.

6.65 There are a number of other provisions which deal with special situations which may arise, and which may therefore affect entitlement to SMP, including when she is dismissed because of pregnancy, when the business is transferred from one employer to another, when the baby is born prematurely, employees who have two or more contracts with a health authority or National Health trust, and so on.

6.66 If the employer refuses to pay SMP, a woman is entitled to a written statement of the reasons, and can apply to an officer from the Board of Inland Revenue for a formal decision, with the right of appeal to the Inland Revenue Commissioners.

6.67–6.75 Employers who make SMP payments are entitled to be reimbursed 92 per cent of the payments made. A small employer, ie one whose total National Insurance liability for the previous year was less than £20,000, is entitled to 100 per cent reimbursement, and an additional handling charge of 5 per cent.

Maternity allowance

6.76 A woman who does not qualify for statutory maternity pay may be entitled to maternity allowance (MA) paid to her direct by the Benefits Agency, under the provisions of the Social Security Contributions and Benefits Act 1992. She must show
(a) she is pregnant, and has reached the start of the eleventh week prior to the expected week of confinement, and
(b) she was employed as an employed earner or self-employed earner for at least 26 weeks in the period of 66 weeks immediately prior to the expected week of confinement, and
(c) in respect of a woman whose baby is due on or after 20 August 2000, earns at least an average of £30 per week (earnings from more than one job will count if necessary).

6.77 If the average weekly earnings are at least equal to the lower earnings limit which applies to national insurance contributions, she will be entitled to the standard rate of maternity allowance for up to 18 weeks. If the average weekly earnings are less than the lower earnings limit, but are at least £30 per week, she will be entitled to 90 per cent of her average earnings up to the maximum standard rate of maternity allowance.

CHAPTER 7

Employment protection

7.1–7.5 In this chapter we will consider a number of miscellaneous legal rights given to employees in the Employment Rights Act 1996 and other legislation. These are minimum standards which can be exceeded by agreement or negotiation, but they cannot be denied to an employee.

Guarantee payments (ERA ss 28–35)

7.6 Provided an employee has been continuously employed for at least one month, and is not employed under a fixed term contract of three months or less, the employer is bound to pay him a guarantee payment in respect of any whole day in which the employee is not provided with work because
a. there is a diminution in the requirements of the employer's business for work of the kind which the employee is employed to do, or
b. any other occurrence affecting the normal working of the employer's business in relation to work of that kind.
In *North v Pavleigh Ltd* the owner of a company closed his factory for Jewish holidays. The employment tribunal held that no guarantee payment could be claimed. Section 28 only applies to a diminution of work, or an 'occurrence', such as a power failure or national disaster. It was not intended to cover the religious habits of the proprietor.

7.7 However, if the contract of employment is expected to last no more than three months, there is no right to a guarantee payment, ie seasonal workers are excluded. A guarantee payment is not payable if the workless day occurs in consequence of a trade dispute involving any employee of the employer or of any associated employer. In *Garvey v J & J Maybank (Oldham) Ltd* there was a national lorry drivers' strike, and pickets at the employer's entrance refused to let the firm's own lorries in or out. The employer ordered the firm's drivers (who were not involved in the strike) to cross picket lines, but they refused. As a result, there were insufficient supplies coming into the firm, and the claimant was laid off. It was held that he was not entitled to guarantee pay. The refusal of the drivers to cross the picket lines meant that the lay off occurred in consequence of a trade dispute. Nor is the employee entitled to the payment if the employer offers to provide alternative work which is suitable in all the circumstances (whether or not it is within the employee's contract) and he unreasonably refuses that offer.

The employee must also comply with reasonable requirements imposed by the employer with a view to ensuring that his services are available.

7.8   The employee is entitled to be paid at the guaranteed hourly rate (which is one week's pay divided by the number of normal working hours) for the number of normal working hours in respect of any whole day he is laid off. He is entitled to be paid for five working days in any period of three months, at a rate of a maximum of (currently) £16.10 per day (ERA s 31). In other words, the present position is that an employee will be entitled to no more than £16.10 per day for a maximum of 20 days in each year. If the employee already has a contractual right to remuneration in respect of a workless day (eg by means of a collective agreement, etc) then any payment made under that agreement will go towards discharging the employer's liability to make the statutory guarantee payment, and equally, the latter will go towards discharging the contractual liability. If there is a guaranteed week agreement in existence, then the contractual remuneration shall be apportioned rateably between the workless days, and the statutory minimum will be used to 'top up' as appropriate. However, workless days when a contractual payment is made are taken into account when calculating the number of days guarantee pay is payable in any period of three months (*Cartwright v G Clancey Ltd*). It should be noted that if a contractual or statutory guarantee payment is being made, the employee is not entitled to apply for Jobseekers Allowance.

7.9   If an employer fails or refuses to pay the whole or part of the guarantee payment, the employee may complain within three months to an employment tribunal. If they find the complaint well founded, they will order the employer to pay to the claimant the amount due to him.

7.10–7.20   If there is a collective agreement in force which already relates to guarantee payments, then all the parties thereto may apply to the appropriate Minister for an exemption order. This will be granted if he is satisfied that the statutory provisions should not apply to those employees, but the collective agreement must contain provisions for an aggrieved employee to take a dispute about non-payment of the guarantee payment either to arbitration (or other procedure) or to an employment tribunal. A number of such exemption orders have been granted.

Suspension on medical grounds (ERA ss 64–65)

7.21   Provided an employee has been employed for not less than one month, he will be entitled to be paid remuneration if he is suspended from work in consequence of a requirement imposed by certain statutory provisions or a recommendation made in a code of practice issued or approved under s 16 of the Health and Safety at Work etc Act 1974 (see Chapter 11). The statutory provisions in question are (a) Control of Lead at Work Regulations 1998, (b) Ionising Radiations Regulations 1999, and (c) Control of Substances Hazardous to Health Regulations 1999. However, an employee will not be entitled to medical suspension pay if he is employed under a fixed-term contract of three months or less, or under a contract to perform a specific task which will last for less than three months, unless in fact it exceeds three months. If a health risk occurs within the scope of these provisions, certain processes must be suspended, and the result now is that in these circumstances the affected employees will be entitled to be paid for a period of up to six months from the day when the suspension period begins. An employee is not entitled to be paid during the suspension period if he is incapable of work because of illness or injury, or if he unreasonably refuses alternative work offered to him by the employer (whether within the terms of his contract or not) or if he does not make himself available for work.

7.22 An employee who is thus suspended on medical grounds is entitled to a week's pay in respect of each week the suspension lasts, and though the contractual right to remuneration is unaffected, the contractual and statutory remuneration can be set off against each other as appropriate. If the employer fails to pay the whole or any part of the employee's remuneration, the latter may present a complaint to the employment tribunal within three months, and if it finds the complaint well-founded, it shall order the employer to pay to the employee the amount due to him.

7.23 It must be stressed that a medical suspension payment can only be claimed if the employee is fit for work. In *Stallite Batteries Co Ltd v Appleton*, the claimant became ill after falling into a skip containing lead paste. In consequence, his blood lead level exceeded the limit laid down in the Control of Lead at Work Regulations 1980 but no medical suspension certificate was issued by the employment medical adviser. Nonetheless, the applicant's own doctor considered that he was not fit for work. The EAT held that he was not entitled to a medical suspension payment. He was not available for work due to sickness, and his claim was excluded by s 65(3) of the Act.

7.24 If an employee is dismissed for a reason which would otherwise amount to a medical suspension, he is only required to have been employed for one month (instead of one year) in order to present a claim for unfair dismissal (s 65(1)).

7.25–7.35 If the employer wishes to engage a temporary employee to take the place of the suspended employee, then, as long as he has informed the temporary employee in writing that the employment will be terminated when the suspension has ended, a dismissal of the temporary employee in order to allow the suspended employee to return to work will amount to 'some other substantial reason' for the dismissal (see Chapter 17), although the employer will still have to show that he acted reasonably.

For medical suspension from work on maternity grounds, see Chapter 6.

Time off work for public duties (ERA s 50)

7.36 An employer shall permit an employee of his who is a justice of the peace to take time off during his working hours for the purpose of performing any of the duties of his office.

7.37 An employer shall also permit an employee who is a member of certain specified bodies to take time off work during his working hours for the purpose of attending at a meeting of the body or its committees or sub-committees, and to do any other thing approved by the body for the purpose of discharging its functions. The specified bodies are

(a) a local authority (including the Common Council of the City of London, a National Parks Authority and the Broads Authority)
(b) a statutory tribunal
(c) a police authority
(d) a board of prison visitors or prison visiting committee
(e) a relevant health body (including a National Health Service trust, a health authority or health board
(f) a relevant education body (managing or governing body of an educational establishment maintained by a local authority or (in Scotland) a school or college council or governing body of further education
(g) the Environment Agency or the Scottish Environment Protection Agency
(h) Service Authority for the National Criminal Intelligence Service or the National Crime Squad.

7.38 There is no requirement that the employee be paid for taking time off work under s 50. The amount of time off permitted for these purposes, the occasions on which and the conditions subject to which time off may be taken are those that are reasonable in all the circumstances, having regard in particular to
(a) how much time off is required for the performance of the duties,
(b) how much time off the employee has had already in respect of trade union duties and activities, and
(c) the circumstances of the employer's business and the effect of the employee's absence on the running of that business.

7.39 In *Walters v British Steel Corpn* the claimant was transferred to an essential job, and it was difficult to release him for certain public duties. When he took the job, he had agreed that his public duties would take second place. Consideration of safety required certain minimum manning levels, and his colleagues refused to cover for him. It was held that he was not entitled to time off work for public duties, as the circumstances of the employer's business had to be taken into account.

7.40 In considering the amount of time off to be given under s 50, the needs of the employee to perform his public duties adequately must be balanced carefully with the requirements of the employer to have the work done. In *Emmerson v IRC* the claimant was the leader of the opposition party on Portsmouth Council. He had been given 18 days' leave (paid) each year to perform his duties, but this was insufficient. His application for further unpaid leave of absence was refused by his employers, as it was argued that he could not be spared from his job. The employment tribunal thought that the problem could be overcome by appointing a deputy to give him some assistance, for in other areas there was more than one person doing the same job as the claimant, who should not be put at a disadvantage because he was extra-efficient. Since the claimant was prepared to use some of his own holidays for public duties, the tribunal thought that he should be given a further 12 days' leave of absence without pay. However, in *Corner v Buckinghamshire County Council*, the EAT held that the employment tribunal has no power to make any recommendations of this nature, or to impose conditions.

7.41 Section 50 requires the employer to give time off work to the employee. Rearranging hours of work, and swapping duties so that the same number of hours are worked is not giving time off (*Ratcliffe v Dorset County Council*).

7.42–7.50 It has been noted that there is no legal requirement that the employee be paid for time off work under s 50. But if he is refused time off, he may present a complaint to an employment tribunal within the usual period of three months from the date of refusal. The employment tribunal must take account of all the relevant considerations (*Borders Regional Council v Maule*) including the employee's efforts to reorganise his commitments so as to produce a reasonable pattern of work, and if the complaint is upheld, the tribunal shall make a declaration, and may award compensation of such amount as it considers just and equitable, having regard to the employer's default and any loss sustained by the employee.

Time off work for occupational pension scheme trustees (ERA s 58)

7.51 An employee who is a trustee of an occupational pension scheme is entitled to be given time off work, with pay during working hours for the purpose of
(a) performing any of his duties as such a trustee, or
(b) undergoing training relevant to the performance of those duties.

7.52 The amount of time off which the employee is to be permitted to take, the purpose for which, the occasions on which and any conditions subject to which time off may be taken are those that are reasonable in all the circumstances, having regard to
(a) how much time off is required for the performance of the duties as a trustee of the scheme and to undergo the relevant training, and
(b) the circumstances of the employer's business and the effect of the employee's absence on the running of that business.

7.53–7.60 The employee must be paid his normal remuneration, or his average hourly earnings, or a fair estimate of those earnings, for the time off work under these provisions. If the employer refuses to permit him to take time off work, or refuses to pay for time off work taken, a complaint may be made to an employment tribunal. If the complaint is upheld, the employment tribunal shall make a declaration to that effect, and make an award of compensation to the employee, as it thinks just and equitable.

Rights of employee representatives (ERA s 61)

7.61 An employee who is a representative of an independent trade union, or an elected employee representative (or candidate for election) has the right to be allowed reasonable time off work, with pay, for the purpose of performing his functions as such when the employer is required to consult on redundancies (see para 18.111) or on transfers of undertakings (see para 9.101). He is entitled to access to the affected employees, and such accommodation and facilities as may be appropriate.

7.62–7.70 An employee representative has the right not to suffer a detriment because he performed any function or activity as such, and it will be an automatic unfair dismissal to dismiss him for the same reason.

Time off to look for work (ERA s 52)

7.71   An employee who is dismissed for reason of redundancy shall be entitled, before the expiration of his notice, to be given reasonable time off during his working hours to look for new employment or to make arrangements for retraining. This right, however, only applies to employees who have been continuously employed for more than two years. The redundant employee is entitled to be paid at his appropriate hourly rate, and if the employer unreasonably refuses to allow him to have the time off, or fails to pay him for it, a complaint may be presented to an employment tribunal within three months. An award of up to two-fifths of a week's pay may then be made.

7.72–7.80   It is not a prerequisite for time off that the employee should provide the employer with details of interviews or appointments he has made, as he is entitled to go to look for a job without having made any such arrangements. But if an employer thinks that the request for time off is not bona fide, it may be that he does not unreasonably refuse to permit it (*Dutton v Hawker Siddeley Aviation Ltd*).

Time off work to care for dependants (ERA s 57A)

7.81   An employee is entitled to be permitted by his employer to take a reasonable amount of time off work during the employee's working hours in order to take action which is necessary:
(a) to provide assistance on an occasion when a dependant falls ill, gives birth, or is injured or assaulted
(b) to make arrangements for the provision of care for a dependant who is ill or injured
(c) in consequence of the death of a dependant
(d) because of an unexpected disruption or termination of arrangements for the care of a dependant, or
(e) to deal with an incident which involves the child of the employee and which occurs unexpectedly in a period during which an educational establishment which the child attends is responsible for him.

7.82   The employee must tell his employer the reason for the absence as soon as is reasonably practicable, and also inform him how long he expects to be absent.

7.83   A dependant is a spouse, child, parent, or person living in the same household as the employee, otherwise than by reason of his being an employee, tenant, lodger or boarder. Additionally, for the purpose of (a) and (b) above, a dependant can also be any person who reasonably relies on the employee for assistance on an occasion when he falls ill or is injured or assaulted, or to make arrangements for the provision of care in the event of illness or injury. For the purpose of (d) above, a dependant can also include any person who reasonably relies on the employee to make arrangements for the provision of care.

7.84   There is no service qualification for the enjoyment of the above rights, but equally there is no requirement on the employer to pay an employee who takes such time off work. Any such entitlement must depend on the terms of the contract of employment.

7.85 An employee may complain to an employment tribunal (within the usual time limits) that his employer has unreasonably refused to permit him to take time off work for any of the above purposes, and, if the complaint is well-founded, the tribunal will make a declaration, and may award compensation as it considers to be just and equitable. Also, an employee has the right not to suffer a detriment because he took such time off work, and it will be automatically unfair to dismiss an employee for taking time off work for the above purposes.

Right to time off work for young person for study or training (ERA s 63A)

7.86 An employee who:
(a) is aged 16 or 17
(b) is not in full time secondary or further education, and
(c) has not attained certain minimum standards or education as set out in the Right to Time Off Work for Study or Training Regulations 1999 (and/or the Right to Time Off Work for Study or Training (Scotland) Regulations 1999),

is entitled to be permitted by his employer to take time off during the employee's working hours in order to undertake study or training leading to the relevant qualification, which is an external qualification the attainment of which would contribute to the attainment of one of the prescribed standards set out in the above regulations, and would be likely to enhance the employee's employment prospects (whether with his employer or otherwise). If an employee is aged 18, but began such studies before attaining that age, he is entitled to continue until he ceases to be 18.

7.87 The amount of time off, the occasions on which, and any conditions subject to which time off may be taken are those that are reasonable in all the circumstances, having regard to:
(a) the requirements of the employee's study or training, and
(b) the circumstances of the employer's business and the effect of the employee's time off on the running of that business.

7.88 The employee is entitled to be paid whilst taking time off work for study or training purposes, at the appropriate hourly rate, calculated in accordance with the normal rules which define 'week's pay' and 'normal working hours' (see ERA ss 220–229, 234, para 14.1). A complaint may be made to an employment tribunal, within the usual time limits, that the employer has unreasonably refused to permit the employee to have time off work as required by s 63A, or has failed to pay the whole or part of the remuneration due to him. If the complaint is upheld, the tribunal will make a declaration and award the remuneration due.

Parental leave; Maternity and Parental Leave Regulations 1999

7.89 These regulations, which came into force as from 15 December 1999, implement the EU Parental Leave Directive (96/34), which itself stems from the Charter of Fundamental Social Rights.

7.90 An employee who has been employed for a period of not less than one year, and has responsibility for a child, is entitled to have parental leave for a period of 13 weeks in respect of each individual child, for the purpose of caring for that child. A person has responsibility for a child if he (or she) has parental responsibility within the meaning of s 3 of the Children Act 1989 (or s 1(3) of the Children (Scotland) Act 1995), or is named as the father on the child's birth certificate, or has adopted a child. The child must have been born or adopted on or after 15 December 1999, and be under the age of five, except that in respect of a child adopted on or after that date, be under the age of 18, and the right will exist for a period of five years from the date of the adoption, or until the child reaches the age of 18, whichever is the sooner. There is no requirement that such leave be with pay.

7.91   Parental leave may be taken as soon as the child is born, or adopted, and the right will last until the child reaches the age of five, or, in the case of an adopted child, until five years from the date of adoption. Both parents have an individual right to parental leave. If the child is in receipt of Disability Living Allowance (at whatever rate) the right to parental leave is extended until the child reaches the age of 18.

7.92   An employee who takes parental leave is entitled to the benefit of the employer's implied obligation of trust and confidence, and any terms and conditions relating to notice of termination, compensation in the event of redundancy, and disciplinary and grievance procedures. On his (or her) part, the employee is bound by the obligation of good faith, and any terms and conditions relating to the giving by him of notice of termination, the disclosure of confidential information, the acceptance of gifts or other benefits, and his participation in any other business.

7.93   If the employee takes parental leave of four weeks or less, s/he is entitled to return to the job s/he was doing before s/he was absent. If the parental leave was for a period of longer than four weeks, s/he is entitled to return to the job in which s/he was employed before the absence, or, if it is not reasonably practicable for the employer to permit this, to another job which is both suitable and appropriate in the circumstances, on remuneration no less favourable than would have been applicable at the commencement of the period of parental leave. Pension rights, seniority rights and similar rights are to be preserved as if employment was continuous and other terms and conditions shall be not less favourable than those applicable before s/he took parental leave.

7.94   Parental leave may be taken by a woman as an extension of her maternity leave period. In respect of employees whose weekly working pattern varies, a week's leave is the period of absence which is equal in duration to the period calculated by dividing the total of the normal working periods for the year by 52. In respect of part-time employees, a week's leave is the period of absence which is equal in duration to the period the employee is normally required to work under his/her contract.

7.95   The regulations give power to employers and employees to make their own agreements about how parental leave will apply in practice. This may be done by means of a collective agreement or a workforce agreement either of which must be incorporated into the individual contract of employment (see Sch 1 to the Regulations). In the absence of any such agreement, the default provisions of Sch 2 will apply. This states that leave can only be taken in blocks or multiples of one week (except in respect of disabled children), employees must give minimum notice of 21 days, and employees may only take four weeks' parental leave in each leave year. The employer is entitled to request the employee to provide proof of his entitlement, and may postpone the leave if the operation of his business would be seriously disrupted, for a period of no more than six months.

7.96–7.115 An employee has the right not to suffer a detriment because s/he took parental leave (ERA s 47C) and it will be an automatically unfair dismissal to dismiss an employee because s/he took or sought to take parental leave (ERA s 99).

Other employment rights

7.116 There are a number of further provisions giving employment protection rights which are contained in the Employment Rights Act and the Trade Union and Labour Relations (Consolidation) Act. These will be considered under the following headings:
(a) the right not to suffer a detriment or dismissal in health and safety cases (see Chapter 11);
(b) the right not to suffer a detriment or dismissal because of trade union membership or non-membership (see Chapter 21);
(c) the right to have time off work for trade union duties and activities (see Chapter 21);
(d) time off work for safety representatives (see Chapter 11);
(e) interim relief for dismissed trade unionists and non-unionists (see Chapter 21);
(f) interim relief in health and safety cases (see Chapter 11);
(g) the right not to be unfairly dismissed for asserting a statutory right (see Chapter 17);
(h) maternity rights generally (see Chapter 6).

7.117–7.125 Time off work for members of a European Works Council, as well as protection from detriment and dismissal is considered in Chapter 23.

Sunday trading

7.126 The Sunday Trading Act 1994 was passed to reform the law relating to the circumstances when shops may be open on Sundays, and, at the same time, gave certain protections to employees who did not wish to work on Sundays. Identical provisions apply to betting workers, who work at a track for a bookmaker, or who work in a licensed betting shop. The relevant law is now set out in ss 36–43 of ERA. It should be noted that these provisions only apply to England and Wales, not to Scotland.

7.127 If an employee is a 'protected shop worker' or an 'opted out shopworker' he may refuse to work on Sundays. Any agreement or provision in the contract of employment will be unenforceable in so far as it requires him to work on Sundays. Further, a dismissal because an employee refuses to do Sunday work will be automatically unfair.

7.128 An employee will be a protected shop worker if
- he was in employment as a shop worker on the day the Act came into force (26 August 1994),
- he was not employed to work only on Sunday,
- he has been continuously employed since the Act came into force and the date he complains of dismissal, detrimental treatment or attempts by the employer to require him to work on Sundays under his contract of employment, and
- he has been a shop worker throughout that period of continuous employment.

A person is also a protected shop worker if he cannot be required to work on Sundays under his contract of employment, whether this was entered into before or after the Act came into force.

7.129 An employee will be an opted-out shop worker if
- under his contract he may be required to work on Sundays,
- but he is not employed to work only on Sundays, and
- he has given his employer an opting out notice stating that he objects to working on Sundays.

In these circumstances, the opted-out shop worker will obtain the statutory protections after three months from when the opting-out notice was served. However, an employer has a duty to provide any employee who could potentially be an opted-out shop worker with a statement in the prescribed form explaining his rights to become an opted-out shop worker (within two months from the commencement of the employment) and if the employer fails to do this, the three-month period referred to is reduced to one month.

7.130 A protected shop worker and an opted-out shop worker may decide to give his employer an 'opting-in notice' indicating that he wishes to work on Sundays or does not object to working on Sundays, in which case he will lose his status, provided he expressly agrees to work on Sundays or a particular Sunday. It would seem that any such agreement can be verbal or in writing.

7.131 It will be an automatic unfair dismissal:
(a) to dismiss an employee who is a protected or opted-out shop worker for refusing or threatening to refuse to work on Sundays;
(b) to dismiss an employee for giving or proposing to give an opting-out notice;
(c) to select a person for redundancy because he refused to work on Sundays he is a protected or opted-out shopworker;
(d) to dismiss an employee because he has asserted his rights under the Act (ERA s 101).

However, it should be noted that an opted-out shopworker has no protection until the expiry of the three-month notice period (above).

7.132 An employer cannot subject a person to a detriment because he is a protected or opted-out shop worker on the ground that he refuses to work on Sundays or because he has given an opting-out notice. However, an employer can offer financial or other inducements to such worker if they are prepared to work on Sundays, and those who are not so prepared are not thereby deemed to be suffering from a detriment (ERA s 45).

7.133 An employee who has protected status will not lose that status by agreeing to work on a Sunday, provided he has not given an opting-in notice.

However, an opted out employee will lose his status once he gives an opting-in notice, although presumably he can regain that status by giving a further notice.

7.134–7.140 Finally, it should be noted that there is no requirement of a period of continuous employment, or a minimum number of hours worked, for a worker to obtain rights under the Act.

Jury service (Juries Act 1974)

7.141 An employee who is summoned to attend for jury service must be given time off work for that purpose, unless he is within one of the excused categories, or unless he has been excused service on application to the appropriate authority or the court. Failure to attend without reasonable cause may result in a fine being imposed of up to £200. A juror is entitled to claim travel and subsistence allowances, and payment for financial loss at prescribed rates.

Other time off work

7.142 An employee who wishes to take time off work for other purposes (eg Territorial Army, extended holidays, etc) may only do so with the agreement of the employer. An employee who persists in taking unauthorised time off may find that his subsequent dismissal is fair.

Armed Forces Reserves

7.143 Reservists who are called up to serve in the armed forces (including those who volunteer for such service) have their civil employment rights protected by the Reserve Force (Safeguard of Employment) Act 1985. When the military service comes to an end, an employer must re-employ the employee
a. in the occupation in which he was last employed before the full-time service, on terms and conditions not less favourable than those which would have been applicable had he not undertaken full time service, or
b. if reinstatement is not reasonable and practicable, the employee must be offered the most favourable occupation, and on the most favourable terms and conditions which are reasonable and practicable in his case.

7.144 The employee must apply for reinstatement in writing, before the end of the third Monday after the full-time service has ceased, unless he was prevented from making it within that time by illness or other reasonable cause. The employer must be notified of a date (not more than three weeks) when the employee will be available for employment.

7.145 If the employer has already filled the vacancy, he cannot claim that it was not reasonably practicable to reinstate the reservist because he would have to dismiss that other person, and in practice it should be made clear to the replacement that the appointment may be for a temporary period.

7.146 A person who claims that his rights under the Act have been infringed may make an application to a reinstatement committee (see *Slaven v Thermo*

Engineers Ltd). They may order the employer to reinstate the employee, or make an award of compensation of between 13 and 52 weeks' pay, depending on his length of service prior to being called up. A further appeal will lie to an umpire. It is a criminal offence to fail comply with an order of the reinstatement committee or the umpire.

7.147   If an employee is dismissed before the commencement of military service, and the reason is the call-up, then, in addition to a claim being made for unfair dismissal, the employer again faces the prospect of being prosecuted for a criminal offence.

7.148   Once the employee returns to his employment, his employment will be deemed to be continuous. The period of absence will not count towards continuity, but will not break it. However, if the employee received permission from the employer to go, he will be absent from work by arrangement or agreement, and the period of absence will count under the provisions of ERA s 212(3) (see para 13.51).

7.149–7.155   The Reserve Forces Act 1996 makes provisions which would enable a reservist to be called out for a period of up to nine months, with the consent of his employer, and for employees to enter into employee agreements with registered employers specifying the maximum liability to service of the employee as a special member, events which will terminate that liability, and other terms relating to the obligations of a special members.

Access to medical reports

7.156   The Access to Medical Reports Act 1988 gives an employee the right to refuse permission to his employer who is seeking a medical report on the employee, the right to see any such report before it is supplied to the employer, and the right to correct any errors contained in the report.

7.157   A medical report is defined as being a report relating to the physical or mental health of an individual which has been prepared by the medical practitioner who is responsible for the clinical care of the individual. This would normally be the employee's own doctor or specialist consultant. Thus the Act does not apply to examinations and reports made by a company's own medical advisers, or a specialist report made on an ad hoc basis.

7.158   If an employer wishes to obtain a medical report from the employee's own doctor (or specialist), he must inform the employee, in writing, that he intends to make such an application, inform the employee of his rights under the Act, and obtain the employee's consent. If the employee refuses to give his consent, that is the end of the matter, and the employer may take any other steps he deems necessary, having regard to the refusal. Alternatively, the employee may agree to the application being made, but may insist on seeing the report before it is sent to the employer. He may then refuse consent to it being sent to the employer, or request the doctor to make amendments to the report which the employee considers to be incorrect or misleading. If the doctor refuses to do this, the employee may request the doctor to attach to the report a written statement from the employee, setting out his views in respect of any part of the report which the doctor declines to amend.

7.159 A doctor is not obliged to show to an employee any part of a medical report if he is of the opinion that the disclosure would cause serious harm to the employee's physical or mental health, or would indicate the doctor's intentions with regard to another person. Also, the doctor would not give access to any part of a medical report if this would reveal information about another person (unless that person consents).

7.160–7.170 An employee is entitled to access to a medical report which has been supplied for employment purposes any time within the preceding six months.

Statutory Sick Pay (SSP)

7.171 Under the provisions of the Social Security Contributions and Benefits Act 1992 ss 151–163 and the Statutory Sick Pay Act 1994 employers will be responsible for paying to their employees statutory sick pay in respect of the first 28 weeks of absence through sickness.

7.172 Originally, the whole amount of SSP paid out by employers could be recovered by means of deductions from national insurance contributions sent to the Inland Revenue, and there was also in existence a small employer's relief. However, these regimes have now been abolished and replaced by a percentage threshold scheme (PTS) designed to help all employers if they have a large number of employees off sick at the same time.

7.173 An employer can now recover SSP paid in a tax month where it exceeds 13 per cent of the employer's national insurance contributions liability in the same tax month. The excess amount of SSP paid can be deducted from the national insurance contributions due in that month (Statutory Sick Pay Percentage Threshold Order 1995).

7.174 To understand the scheme, certain expressions must be defined
1. *A day of incapacity for work*
   This is any day when an employee is incapable, by reasons of some specific disease or mental or bodily disablement, of doing work of a kind he might reasonably be expected to do.
2. *A period of incapacity for work*
   This means any period of four or more consecutive days, each of which is a day of incapacity for work in relation to the employee's contract of employment.
3. *A period of entitlement*
   This period starts with the first day of incapacity for work, and ends when either
   a. the period of incapacity has ended, or
   b. the entitlement to SSP has been used up, or
   c. the contract of employment is terminated, or
   d. a woman who is pregnant becomes disqualified under the provisions of the Act.

4. *Qualifying days*
   These are days on which the employee is required by his contract of employment to be available for work.

7.175 To qualify for SSP, three conditions must be satisfied, namely
1. the employee's day of incapacity for work must form part of the period of incapacity for work (ie four or more consecutive days)
2. the day must be within the period of entitlement
3. the day must be a qualifying day.

If there are two periods of incapacity (for the same or different reasons) separated by not more than two weeks, they will be treated as a single period of incapacity. This means that an employee will not have to requalify with another three 'waiting days'. Moreover, if an employee leaves his job and starts another one, his period of incapacity with his previous employer counts with his new one.

7.176 The entitlement to SSP is a flat rate payment for a maximum period of 28 weeks in any one period of entitlement, or in any one tax year. Thereafter, the employee will be able to claim incapacity benefit. From April 1996 SSP is payable to all employees who meet the qualifying conditions and whose average weekly earnings are above the level at which national insurance contributions are payable.

7.177–7.185 The above provisions apply to part-time employees (provided they earn the requisite amounts) and there is no minimum service qualification. SSP will be deemed remuneration, and therefore subject to deductions in respect of tax and national insurance contributions. Married women and widows who pay reduced national insurance contributions will qualify for SSP even though they do not qualify for incapacity benefit.

Exclusions from entitlement

7.186 The following employees are excluded from entitlement:
a. employees who are incapacitated from work for less than four days;
b. employees who are over pensionable age (however, state incapacity benefit may be payable);
c. employees who are employees under contracts of employment for 12 weeks or less (incapacity benefit may be payable);
d. employees who earn less than the current specified amount;
e. pregnant women whose first day of sickness is within the disqualifying period (ie 18 weeks beginning with the eleventh week prior to the expected week of confinement), or who are receiving SMP or MA;
f. employees who would be workless on the day when the period of entitlement would begin because of trade dispute, unless they can prove that they did not take part in the strike or did not have a direct interest in it;
g. employees who are sick on the day they are due to start new employment (incapacity benefit may be payable);
h. employees whose first day of sickness is within eight weeks of a claim in respect of one of the following state benefits—incapacity benefit, severe disablement allowance, invalidity pension, maternity allowance, or job seekers allowance if there has been a previous entitlement to incapacity benefit;

i.   employees who are in legal custody or who are outside the European Economic Area.

Leavers statement

7.187   When an employee leaves his employment his employer must give him a 'leaver's statement' if the employee has a period of incapacity for work which is separated from the date the contract ends by 56 calendar days, and SSP was payable for one week or more. The new employer will take account of the weeks of SSP shown, which may reduce his maximum liability towards the new employee in his period of incapacity for work, by the amount shown on the statement.

Enforcement

7.188   If an employee has not been paid SSP, he may refer the matter to the local officer of the Inland Revenue, with an appeal to the local tax commissioners. A decision made in the employee's favour can be enforced in the county court, should this be necessary. Certain questions may be referred directly to the Secretary of State for Social Services for a decision, namely
a.   whether a person is, or was, the employee or employer of another person
b.   whether an employer is entitled to deduct SSP from his contribution payments
c.   whether two or more contracts of employment, or two or more employers, shall be treated as one for SSP purposes.

7.189–7.195   Any agreement which purports to exclude, limit or modify an employee's entitlement to SSP shall be void, but this does not prevent an employer from operating a sick pay scheme which is more favourable than the statutory scheme.

Self-certification of illness

7.196   Since June 1982, doctors are no longer required to issue sick notes until after seven days of absence from work (instead of three days). Employees now have to obtain incapacity benefit claims forms, which are widely distributed to trade unions, employers, doctors' surgeries, or is obtainable from the DSS. This must be completed and signed by the employee, which amounts to a self-certification of absence through illness. If the illness lasts for a period longer than seven days, a continuation claim form can be obtained from the doctor. The result will be that there will be a decline in some of the more dubious sick notes which hitherto have been difficult for an employer to challenge. It is generally felt that self-certification enables an employer to set up more efficient control procedures to monitor persistent absenteeism, and thus take effective action to deal with the problem.

Rights in insolvency (Insolvency Act 1986 Sch 6)

7.197   If an employer becomes insolvent (through bankruptcy or liquidation) certain debts are paid in priority to others. These include

a. up to four months' wages, up to £800 (Insolvency Act 1986 Sch 6),
b. accrued holiday pay,
c. any guarantee pay due under ERA s 28,
d. remuneration payable on medical suspension under ERA s 64, or suspension on maternity grounds under ERA s 66,
e. any payment due for time off work for trade union duties (TULR(C)A) s 168, or time off to look for work (ERA s 52) or time off for ante-natal care (ERA s 55),
f. remuneration due under a protective award (s 189, TULR(C)A),
g. holiday pay, contractual sick pay and statutory sick pay.

Payments from the National Insurance Fund (ERA ss 182–189)

7.198 Certain monies due to an employee as a result of the employer's insolvency may be paid by the Secretary of State out of the National Insurance Fund (see *Secretary of State for Employment v Forde*, para 2.28). He must be satisfied that the employer is insolvent (ie bankrupt, or, if a company, being wound up or in receivership, ERA s 183), that the employee was entitled to be paid the whole or part of the monies due, and that the employee has not received payment as a preferred creditor. The debts are:
a. any arrears of pay for a period not exceeding eight weeks. This also includes any guarantee pay, remuneration or suspension on medical grounds and maternity grounds, payment for time off work for trade union duties, and the protective award (TULR(C)A s 189);
b. any minimum period of notice as computed by ERA ss 86–90 (see Chapter 15). The rights of the employee to claim against the Secretary of State are no greater than those he has against the employer. In *Secretary of State for Employment v Wilson* the employee was dismissed without notice, but he obtained employment immediately. His former employers went into liquidation, and he claimed four weeks' notice from the Secretary of State. It was held that he was not entitled. He was under a duty as against his former employers to mitigate against his loss, and having done so, he would have had no claim against them. Consequently, he had no claim against the Minister. But the employee is not obliged to bring into account any social security benefits received (*Westwood v Secretary of State for Employment*);
c. any holiday pay due in the preceding 12 months (but not exceeding six weeks' pay);
d. any basic award compensation for unfair dismissal (but not a compensatory or higher award);
e. any reasonable sum by way of reimbursement of the whole or part of a premium paid by an apprentice or articled clerk;
f. any of the priority debts mentioned above (para 7.197) which have not been satisfied as preferential debts in bankruptcy or liquidation, for a period not exceeding in the aggregate eight weeks.

Section 183 of ERA specifies the circumstances when a company can be regarded as being insolvent, namely (a) a winding up or administration order (b) the appointment of a receiver or manager, or (c) a voluntary arrangement has been approved under the Insolvency Act. The burden is on the applicant to show that one of these events has taken place. The fact that a company has ceased trading, or that it is unable to pay its debts when due, or has been dissolved, does not necessarily mean that it is insolvent within the meaning of s 183 (*Secretary of State for Trade and Industry v Walden*).

There is a maximum liability on the National Insurance Fund of £230 per week in respect of any debt which is referable to a period of time (with a proportionate reduction for periods of less than a week). The Secretary of State is entitled to deduct tax and national insurance contributions (*Morris v Secretary of State for Employment*). The person who is in charge of the winding up must provide the Secretary of State with a statement of the amount of the debt which is owed to the employee, although this is not essential if more than six months have elapsed since an application by the employee was made, and there appears to be a further delay, in which case the Secretary of State has a discretion to make the payment. The Act also provides that the Secretary of State may make payment out of the Fund in respect of any unpaid contributions which an insolvent employer has failed to make to an occupational pension scheme.

7.199 By the Insolvency of Employer (Excluded Classes) Regulations 1983, the right to claim payments on insolvency is extended to employees who, under their contracts of employment, ordinarily work in a member state of the European Community.

7.200 If the Secretary of State fails to make any of these payments, a complaint may be made to an employment tribunal within three months from his refusal (or within such further time as is reasonable). If the tribunal thinks that the payment ought to be made, it shall make a declaration to that effect, and state the amounts which the Secretary of State ought to pay.

7.201–7.210 On making the payment, the Secretary of State becomes subrogated to the rights of the employee (or pension fund) as a preferential creditor in the insolvency.

Death of the employer or employee

7.211 Section 206 of ERA deals with the situation where the employer or the employee has died. Tribunal proceedings under any relevant provision may be instituted, continued or defended by the personal representatives of the parties or in the case of a deceased employee, by a person appointed by the tribunal for that purpose. The personal representatives will have to perform all the obligations of the deceased, and any rights which accrue after death shall continue to devolve, and any liability which has not so accrued prior to death shall be treated as if it was a liability of the deceased employer immediately before death. For example, if an employer dies before or during a tribunal hearing, at the time of the death, no liability has been incurred; once the tribunal makes an award, the liability shall be treated as if it had occurred prior to the death. If, on a claim of unfair dismissal, the employee dies, the reinstatement or re-engagement provisions obviously cannot apply, but the tribunal can nonetheless consider the question of compensation.

7.212–7.220 Proceedings in respect of claims for sex, race and disability discrimination can be continued after the death of the claimant, under the provisions of the Law Reform (Miscellaneous Provisions) Act 1934 (see *Lewisham and Guy's Mental Health Trust v Andrews*).

Working Time Regulations 1998–99

7.221   New regulations came into force in October 1998 (amended in 1999), designed to implement the provisions of the Working Time Directive (93/104/ EC), and the Young Workers Directive (94/33/EC). Technically, these Directives should have been implemented by 23 November 1996, and thus in theory those employers who are emanations of the State (see *Foster v British Gas*) and private employers were exposed to 'Francovich' type claims. In *Gibson v East Riding of Yorkshire Council* the EAT held that art 7 of the Directive, which provided for workers to have four weeks' holiday with pay, was directly enforceable against an emanation from the State, because it was clear and precise, and gave rise to no ambiguity or conditionality. But the decision was reversed by the Court of Appeal. It is true that the minimum holiday period was precise (ie four weeks) but there were a number of other concepts in the Directive which could only be resolved by reference to national laws and/or practice, including collective agreements.

7.222   Generally, the regulations give a series of new rights to 'workers', a term which is wider than 'employees', and applies additionally to a person working under a contract 'to do or perform personally any work or services for another party to the contract whose status is not by virtue of the contract that of a client or customer of any profession or business undertaking carried on by the individual' (reg 2(1)). This clearly covers casual, freelance and some self-employed workers, other than self-employed persons who are pursuing a professional or business activity on their own account. However, advantage has been taken of a number of derogations and exceptions permitted by the Directive, and potentially by means of workplace or collective agreements.

   The main provisions of the Working Time Regulations 1998–99 are as follows.

7.223   (a) *Regulation 4 (maximum weekly working time)*. A worker's average working time for each seven– day period, including overtime, must not exceed 48 hours in any period of 17 weeks, although in certain circumstances (reg 21, special cases) the reference period can be 26 weeks, or 52 weeks if permitted by a collective agreement or workforce agreement (reg 23(b). The regulation will not apply if the worker agrees in writing to working more than 48 hours each week (reg 5). The agreement may be for a specified or an indefinite period, but may be terminated by either side giving the appropriate notice of not less than seven days and not more than three months.

   To calculate the average hours in any reference period, the formula to be applied is

$$\frac{A+B}{C}$$

7.224   This requires some explanation. In any reference period, there will be days when the employee will not work, eg, because of annual holidays, sick leave, maternity leave, etc. Clearly, to exclude those days from the calculation would distort the average hours worked. Therefore, those 'excluded days' must be added back in to the calculation. 'A' is the total number of hours worked during the reference period; 'B' is the total number of hours worked immediately after the reference period during the number of days equivalent to the number of excluded days. 'C' will be the number of weeks in the reference period. Thus the formula

(A+B÷C) will give the average number of hours in the reference period, which will, in effect, be extended by the equivalent number of 'excluded' days.

7.225 If a relevant agreement provided for successive 17-week reference periods, then each reference period will be self-contained, for the purpose of calculating average working hours. In the absence of any such agreement, the reference period will be a 'rolling' 17-week period, ie each week will be the start of a new 17-week reference period.

7.226 (b) *Regulation 6 (length of night work)*. The normal hours of work for a night worker (defined in reg 2) shall not exceed eight in any 24-hour period, again, the average being assessed over a 17-week period (which can be fixed successive 17-week periods, as set out in a relevant agreement, or, failing such agreement, a 'rolling' 17-week period). In *R v A-G for Northern Ireland, ex p Burns* the claimant worked a cycle of 15 shifts of eight hours' duration. During five of these, at least three hours of her working time fell between 11pm and 6am. It was held that she was a night worker within the meaning of reg 6. It was noted that the Directive defined a night worker as a person who works at night 'as a normal course', and this phrase was to be construed as meaning 'as a regular feature'.

7.227 An employer shall ensure that no night worker whose work involves special hazards or heavy physical or mental strain works for more than eight hours in any 24-hour period. The work shall be regarded as involving special hazards or physical or mental strain if it is identified as such in a collective agreement or a workforce agreement, or in a risk assessment carried out under the Management of Health and Safety at Work Regulations 1999. Further, a night worker will be entitled to a free health assessment before he takes up the assignment, with further such assessments at regular intervals. A young worker (ie between the ages of 15–17) must not work between the hours of 10pm and 6am unless he has had a free health assessment before commencing the assignment, and thereafter at such regular intervals as may be appropriate in his case (reg 7). If a registered medical practitioner advises the employer that a worker employed by him is suffering from health problems connected with night work, then, if possible, the employer should transfer the worker to other work for which he is suited, and undertaken at times so that he ceases to be a night worker.

7.228 To calculate the average working hours of a night worker, the normal working hours during the reference period must be divided by the number of working days in that period. The formula is

$$A \div (B-C)$$

Again, an explanation is required.

7.229 From the number of 24-hour periods during the reference period ('B') must be deducted the number of hours (divided by 24 to equate days) which comprise or are included in the weekly rest periods, as provided for in reg 11 ('C'). The amount of the normal working hours during the reference period ('A') can thus be ascertained by dividing the normal working hours during the reference period by the number of working days in that period.

7.230 If a worker has worked for less than 17 weeks, the average will be calculated by reference to the period since the worker started to work for the employer.

7.231 (c) *Regulation 8 (pattern of work).* Where the pattern according to which the employer organises work is such as to put the health and safety of a worker employed by him at risk, in particular because the work is monotonous or the work-rate is predetermined, the employer shall ensure that the worker is given adequate rest breaks.

7.232 (d) *Regulation 9 (records).* An employer shall keep records of the maximum weekly working time, length of night working, and health assessments etc of night workers, in respect of each worker in relation to whom they apply, and keep such records for two years.

7.233 (e) *Regulation 10 (daily rest).* An adult worker is entitled to a rest period of not less than 11 consecutive hours in each 24-hour period during which he works for an employer, although a young worker is entitled to a rest period of 12 consecutive hours.

7.234 (f) *Regulation 11 (weekly rest periods).* An adult worker is entitled to an uninterrupted rest period of not less than 24 hours in each seven-day period during which he works for his employer, although this can be changed to two uninterrupted periods of 24 hours in each 14-day period, or one uninterrupted period of 48 hours in each 14-day period. A young worker is entitled to a rest period of not less than 48 hours in any seven-day period, although this can be altered in certain circumstances.

7.235 (g) *Regulation 12 (rest breaks).* Where an adult worker's daily working time is more than six hours, he is entitled to a rest break, which shall be for an uninterrupted period of 20 minutes (unless a collective agreement or workforce agreement specifies otherwise), to be spent away from the workstation. A young worker who works for more than four and a half hours shall be entitled to a rest break of at least 30 minutes, spent away from the workstation.

7.236 (h) *Regulation 13 (annual leave entitlement).* From November 1999 a worker is entitled to four weeks' annual holidays each year, and to receive his normal weekly pay during his holidays, calculated in accordance with ss 221–224 of ERA (reg 16). If the employment is terminated during the leave year, the worker will be entitled to proportionate pay in lieu. To qualify for the right, the worker must have been employed for 13 weeks; thereafter entitlement is proportionate to the length of employment in the relevant leave year. Leave entitlement is only in respect of the holiday year in which it is due, and may not be replaced by a payment in lieu except on termination of the worker's employment.

7.237 To ascertain how much leave is owed on termination, the formula to use is $(A \times B) - C$, where 'A' is the period of leave the worker is entitled to under the Regulations, 'B' is the portion of the leave year which has expired prior to the effective date of termination, and 'C' is the period of leave already taken by the worker. If a relevant agreement so permits, a worker who has already taken holiday entitlement in excess of his statutory entitlement can be required to compensate the employer, either by way of a payment, or doing additional work.

7.238 It goes without saying that clauses sometimes found in existing employment contracts which specify that an employee dismissed for reason of gross misconduct shall not be entitled to accrued holiday pay are no longer valid.

7.239 The worker may give notice to the employer of the dates when he wishes to take his holidays, subject to the employer requiring the worker to take his holidays on particular dates. The worker must give twice the number of days' notice as days' leave he wishes to take. The employer can prevent the employee taking leave on a particular day by giving notice equivalent to the same number of days as the employer wishes to prevent the leave occurring on. However, the notice provisions are capable of being overridden by a relevant agreement, which may provide for longer (or shorter) periods of notice.

7.240 The commencement of the leave year should be specified in a relevant agreement, or, if there is no such agreement, it will run from the date the worker commenced employment, or when the Regulations came into effect.

Exclusions

7.241 There are a number of excluded sectors of employment and specified activities to which specific regulations do not apply, as follows.

7.242 *Regulation 18.*
(a) Employment in the following sectors of activity—
    (i) air, rail, road, inland waterway and lake transport,
    (ii) sea fishing,
    (iii) other work at sea, or
(b) the activities of doctors in training, or
(c) where characteristics peculiar to certain specified services, such as the armed forces or the police, or to certain specific activities in the civil protection services, inevitably inflict with the Regulations.

7.243 The above workers are excluded from reg 4 (maximum weekly working time), reg 6 (length of night work), reg 7 (health assessment for night workers), reg 8 (safe pattern of work), reg 10 (daily rest periods), reg 11 (weekly rest periods), reg 12 (rest breaks) reg 13 (annual leave) and reg 16 (annual leave pay).

7.244 *Regulation 19.* Domestic servants in a private household are excluded from reg 4 (maximum weekly working time), reg 6 (length of night work), reg 7 (health assessment for night workers), reg 8 (safe pattern of work).

7.245 *Regulation 20.* Workers who, on account of the specific characteristics of the activities engaged in, or where the duration of the working time cannot be measured or predetermined, or which can be determined by the worker himself. In particular—
(a) managing executives or other persons with autonomous decision-making powers, or
(b) family workers, or

(c) workers officiating at religious ceremonies in churches and religious communities.

7.246 The above workers are excluded from reg 4 (maximum weekly working time), reg 6 (length of night work), reg 10 (daily rest), reg 11 (weekly rest period) and reg 12 (rest breaks).

7.247 Where such workers' working time is partly measured, predetermined, or determined by the worker, and partly not, the weekly working time and night work provisions will apply only in relation to that part of the worker's work which is measured, predetermined or determined by the worker himself.

7.248 *Regulation 21.* There is a limited exclusion for the following group of workers—
(a) workers whose activities are such that his place of work and place of residence are distant from one another, or whose different places of work are distant from one another;
(b) where a worker is engaged in security and surveillance activities requiring a permanent presence in order to protect property and persons, particularly security guards and caretakers or security firms;
(c) workers whose activities involve the need for continuity or service or production, particularly—
   (i) services relating to the reception, treatment or care provided by hospitals or similar establishments, residential institutions and prisons,
   (ii) work at docks or airports,
   (iii) press, radio, television, cinematographic production, postal and telecommunications services and civil protection services,
   (iv) gas, water and electricity production, transmission and distribution, household refuse collection and incineration,
   (v) industries in which work cannot be interrupted on technical grounds,
   (vi) research and development activities,
   (vii) agriculture.
(d) where there is a foreseeable surge of activity, particularly in—
   (i) agriculture,
   (ii) tourism, and
   (iii) postal services;
(e) where the worker's activities are affected by—
   (i) an occurrence due to unusual and unforeseeable circumstances, beyond the control of the worker's employer, or
   (ii) or to exceptional events, the consequences of which could not have been avoided despite the exercise of all due care, or
   (iii) an accident or the imminent risk of an accident.

7.249 In respect of the above group of workers, the following regulations do not apply, namely, reg 6 (length of night work), reg 10 (daily rest periods), reg 11 (weekly rest periods) and reg 12 (rest breaks). However, if a worker is required to work during what would normally be a rest period, the employer shall allow him to have a compensatory period of rest, or, if this is not possible, afford him appropriate protection (reg 24).

7.250 *Regulation 23* provides that a collective agreement or a workforce agreement may modify or exclude the following regulations in relation to particular workers, namely reg 6 (length of night work), reg 10 (daily rest), reg 11 (weekly rest period) and reg 12 (rest breaks). So far as reg 4 (maximum weekly working time) is concerned, such agreement can substitute a different period over which the average can be worked out, not exceeding 52 weeks (in place of 17 weeks).

7.251   There are also a number of other limited exclusions in respect of workers in the armed forces, young workers employed on ships, and young workers affected by *force majeure* (regs 25–27). There are also special rules for agricultural workers (Sch 2).

Enforcement

7.252   The regulations can be enforced in three ways. First, inspectors from the Health and Safety Executive (or, in appropriate circumstances, the enforcement officers of local authorities) are responsible for the enforcement of the following provisions (see reg 28):
(a)   the duty of the employer to take reasonable steps to ensure that the provisions relating to the 48-hour week have been complied with. The inspectors will also have the right to inspect the employer's records in relation to workers who are subject to an opting out agreement;
(b)   the duty of the employer to take reasonable steps to ensure compliance with the limit on average hours for night workers, and the absolute limit on length of night work for night workers whose work involves special hazards or heavy physical or mental strain;
(c)   the provision of free health assessments for adult workers who work at night, and also health and capacities assessments for young workers;
(d)   the duty of the employer to transfer night workers to day work if, in the opinion of a registered medical practitioner, night workers suffer from health problems as a result of working at night;
(e)   the duty of the employer to provide adequate rest breaks where the pattern of work is such as to put the health and safety of the worker at risk, particularly if the work is monotonous or repetitive;
(f)   the duty of the employer to keep records showing that the 48-hour week, the limits on night work, and the provisions relating to free health assessments or health and capability assessments is complied with;
(g)   the duty of the employer to provide equivalent compensatory rest, or to provide appropriate protection, when the hourly night work limits are modified or excluded by a collective or workforce agreement.

7.253   In respect of the above matters, an employer may be prosecuted in the magistrates' courts, where a fine of up to £5,000 may be imposed, or an unlimited fine imposed in the Crown Court. Enforcement officers may also issue an Improvement Notice, requiring the employer to rectify matters specified therein, in order to ensure compliance with the statutory requirements, and a failure to comply with such notice can lead to a fine of up to £20,000, and/or six months' imprisonment in the magistrates' court, or an unlimited fine and/or up to two years' imprisonment in the Crown court.

7.254   The second way in which the Regulations can be enforced is by way of a complaint by a worker to an employment tribunal, alleging that the employer has failed to comply with any of the following provisions:

(a) the daily rest periods for adult or young workers (reg 10);
(b) the weekly rest periods for adult or young workers (reg 11);
(c) rest break periods for adult or young workers (reg 12);
(d) entitlement to annual leave (reg 13):,
(e) entitlement to equivalent compensatory rest, where the provisions of regs 10, 11 and 12 have been excluded or modified;
(f) entitlement to compensatory rest where the provisions of regs 10 and 11 have been excluded in respect of young workers serving in the armed forces, or where the *force majeure* exemption applies;
(g) the duty of the employer to pay a worker's statutory annual leave pay, or pay for leave outstanding on the termination of employment (regs 14, 16).

7.255 A complaint to an employment tribunal must be brought within three months from the date on which it is alleged that the exercise of the right should have been permitted, or, in the case of holiday pay, from the date when the payment should have been made, although the employment tribunal may extend the period if it was not reasonably practicable to bring the complaint earlier. If the complaint is well founded, the employment tribunal may make a declaration, and may award compensation of such amount as the tribunal consider to be just and equitable, having regard to the employer's default in refusing to permit the worker to exercise the right in question, and any loss sustained by the worker attributable to that default. In the case of holiday pay, the amount due will be awarded.

7.256 A worker will also have the right (ERA s 45A) not to be subjected to any detriment because:
(a) he refused to comply with a requirement that the employer imposed which would be in contravention of the regulations
(b) he refused to forgo a right conferred by the regulations
(c) he failed to sign a workforce agreement or an individual agreement opting out of the regulations
(d) he performed any functions or activities as a workforce representative, or as a candidate in an election for workforce representatives
(e) he brought proceedings against the employer to enforce a right conferred by the regulations
(f) he alleged that the employer had infringed a right conferred by the regulations.

7.257 An employee (not a worker) also has the right not to be unfairly dismissed for any of the above reasons (ERA s 101A), and also the right not to be unfairly selected for redundancy (ERA s 105(4A)). Again, the complaint must be brought within three months from the date of the act complained of, with the usual extension of time if it was not reasonably practicable to bring the complaint earlier. If the complaint is upheld, the employment tribunal will make a declaration, and may make an award of compensation, on just and equitable principles. If the employee was unfairly dismissed, no qualifying period of employment is required, interim relief is available, and the minimum basic award, as well as an additional award (of between 26 and 52 weeks' pay), may be made as appropriate.

7.258 The third way of enforcing the regulations is to seek an appropriate remedy for breach of contract of employment. In *Barber v RJB Mining (UK) Ltd* pit deputies, although contractually obliged to work for 42 hours a week, regularly worked a considerable amount of overtime, in excess of 48 hours. They were asked to sign an agreement opting out of their rights under the regulations, but refused, and they sought from the court a declaration to the effect that they need not work at all until such time as their average working hours fell below the limit specified in reg 4(1). The High Court granted the declaration. It was held that it was clearly the intention of Parliament that their contract of employment should be read so as to provide that an employee should work no more than 48 hours a week during the relevant reference period. Thus reg 4(1) created a free-standing right which took effect as a contractual term in the contracts of employment of the pit deputies.

CHAPTER 8

Protection of wages

8.1 Under the provisions of the Truck Act 1831 the wages of manual workers had to be paid in current coin of the realm. That Act (together with a number of similar legislative provisions) was repealed by the Wages Act 1986, and now cashless pay is lawful for all employees. The actual mode of payment of wages is a matter for agreement between employer and employee.

8.2 A further object of the Wages Act was to prevent an employer from making a deduction from a worker's wages, or requiring the worker to make a payment to the employer (except in specifically defined circumstances), and to give added protection to workers employed in retail trade. In consequence, the provisions of the Truck Act 1896 relating to fines and deductions were also repealed.

8.3–8.10 The Wages Act itself was repealed and re-enacted in ss 13–27 of the Employment Rights Act 1996 (ERA) and it is to this Act that reference will be made. Some confusion sometimes arises because of the provisions of the Employment Tribunals Extention of Jurisdiction Order (ETEJO, see para 1.55) made under what is now s 3 of the Employment Tribunals Act 1996, which gives jurisdiction to employment tribunals to deal with breach of contract claims. However, there are several important differences which need to be noted, as follows;

(a) Claims under ETEJO can only be brought in respect of matters outstanding on the termination of employment, whereas ERA claims are made in respect of unlawful deductions and payments made during the existence of the contract of employment (*Capek v Lincolnshire County Council*).

(b) Claims under ETEJO can only be made by employees, whereas ERA claims can be made by 'workers', a category which is somewhat wider (see s 230 and para 2.3).

(c) Under ETEJO an employer can bring a counterclaim, but this not possible under ERA, and if an employer wishes to make some sort of 'set-off' claim, he must pursue it through the normal court machinery.

(d) A claim under ETEJO is essentially a common law claim for breach of contract, and is thus subject to the usual rules relating to mitigation of loss, whereas an ERA is a claim for a specific sum protected by statute, and the full sum must be awarded.

General restrictions on unauthorised deductions and payments (ERA ss 13, 15)

8.11 An employer must not make any deductions from the wages of any worker employed by him, nor receive any payment from him, unless:
(a) the deduction or payment is required to be made or is authorised by a statutory provision; or
(b) the deduction or payment is authorised by a relevant provision in a worker's contract of employment. This can be a written term in the contract of which the employer has given a copy prior to the making of the deduction, or a term of the contract (express or implied, and if express, orally or in writing), the existence and effect of which the employer has notified to the worker in writing. Thus in *Kerr v Sweater Shop (Scotland) Ltd* it was held that the display of a notice by the employer, changing the company's rules so that a person dismissed for gross misconduct would not be paid accrued holiday pay, did not comply with the Act. The Act requires that the term must be 'notified to the worker'; this means that there must be a written notification given individually to each worker, eg by a statement inserted in the wage packet. The display of a notice was not sufficient to discharge the employer's obligation;
(c) the worker has signified in advance in writing his agreement to the deduction or payment.
These three categories need to be explored further.

A. Statutory deduction

8.12 The most usual type of deductions to be made under this heading will be income tax and national insurance contributions. Other examples include a deduction from earnings order made under the Child Support Act 1991 (whether or not the worker was correctly liable under that order: see *Reynolds v Cornwall County Council*), and an attachment of earnings order made by an appropriate court to secure payments of a maintenance order, judgement debts, fines, costs, compensation, forfeiture of recognisances, and legal aid contribution order, under the Attachment of Earnings Act 1971. But the statutory provision in question must specifically authorise the deduction or require it to be made (see *McCree v Tower Hamlets London Borough Council*); an employer cannot seek to rely on a statute which does not confer a power on an employer to do an act in consequence of which the alleged deduction is made (see *Morgan v West Glamorgan County Council*).

B. Contractual authorisation

8.13 The relevant provision in a worker's contract of employment must be contained in a written document a copy of which has been given to the worker before the employer makes the deduction, or be a contractual term (whether express or implied, and, if express, whether oral or in writing) whose effect and existence has been notified to the employee in writing before the deduction is made.

8.14 It will be noted that the power to make the deduction need not be in the actual contract. It is sufficient if the employer has notified the worker in writing of the term. Thus an implied term, or an oral term, will suffice, provided written notification of it is given before the deduction is made, and provided also that the notification is given to the worker individually. The mere display of a notice on a notice board will not suffice (see *Kerr v Sweater Shop (Scotland) Ltd* above).

C. Written consent

8.15　A deduction is permissible if the worker gives his written consent in advance. This provision is designed to cover those circumstances where there is no contractual term as such, but which are collateral to that contract. For example, an agreement to repay a loan made to purchase a season travel ticket, or the forfeiture of a week's pay from an employee who leaves without giving proper notice (see *Pename Ltd v Paterson*) will be valid, provided the appropriate prior written notification is given, and the worker consents to it, either expressly or impliedly, ie by continuing to work once the term has been validly brought to his attention (see *Kerr v Sweater Shop (Scotland) Ltd*, above). But the agreement must indicate with sufficient clarity the source from which the deductions are to be made, ie the worker's wages, and that the worker authorises the deduction from that source. Otherwise, all that may exist is an agreement to repay a loan, not an agreement which authorises a deduction from wages. Thus in *Potter v Hunts Contracts Ltd* the employer agreed to pay for the cost of an HGV driving course, on the understanding that the employee would repay some or all of the cost on leaving his employment. An agreement was drawn up requiring the employee to repay the fee incurred on a diminishing basis if he left the employment within two years. In fact, he left after one month, when most of the loan was still outstanding, and as this amount was more than the wages due to him on departure, he was not given any final wages. It was held that the deduction was unlawful. The loan agreement did not indicate that the repayment of the loan was to be made by way of deduction from wages.

8.16　It must further be noted that the worker's authority for the making of the deduction must not relate to anything that has happened before that authority was given. In other words, deductions must not have a retrospective effect, even if they are made with the worker's agreement. Thus a variation of a contract, or a worker's written consent, can only relate to future happenings (s 13(5), (6)). This is to prevent pressure being placed on a worker to agree or consent to deduction (*Discount Tobacco and Confectionery Ltd v Williamson*).

8.17　The contractual provisions or written agreement which authorise the deductions must be clear and unambiguous, for the mere fact that the worker owes the employer money does not entitle the latter to make a deduction. Employment tribunals can be very astute in striking down terms and agreements which contain ambiguities, the benefit of the doubt being given to the worker (see *Potter v Hunt Contracts Ltd* above).

8.18–8.25　Even if the employer does have the right to make a deduction, he must still show that the deduction is in fact justified. Thus in *Fairfield Ltd v Skinner* a van driver was given a document indicating that the employer would charge the employee for private calls made from the van telephone, charge for private mileage, and that the employee would be liable for any excess insurance arising from damage caused to the vehicle. When the employee was dismissed, a sum of £305 was withheld from his final pay packet. The employee brought a claim under the Act, arguing that the deduction was unlawful. The employer responded by claiming that half of the amount deducted represented damage caused to the van whilst being used privately, and the remainder was a provisional deduction for private mileage and telephone calls made. An employment tribunal found that the employee had carried out repairs to the van at his own expense, and that there was no evidence as to how the deduction for private mileage and telephone calls had been calculated. Thus the deduction was unlawful. The decision was upheld by the EAT. The fact that an employer had the right to make a deduction did not mean that he can make a deduction, if in fact the deduction is not justified on the facts of the case, and, if there was a dispute on those facts, it was for the employment tribunal to resolve the matter.

What are 'wages'? (s 27(1))

8.26 The term 'wages' is defined as any sum payable to the worker by his employer in connection with his employment. These include:
(a) any fee, bonus, commission, holiday pay or other emolument referable to the employment, whether payable under his contract or otherwise;
(b) statutory sick pay, statutory maternity pay, guarantee pay, medical and maternity suspension pay, and payments for statutory time off work;
(c) payment made pursuant to a reinstatement or re-engagement order, interim relief order and protective award.

8.27 It will be noted that the definition is very wide. It includes overtime pay (*Bruce v Wiggins Teape (Stationery) Ltd*), shift payments (*Yemm v British Steel plc*) guaranteed monthly payments paid as a retainer (*Thompson v Tech Communications Ltd*), long service awards (*Clarke v Hays Distribution Services Ltd*), holiday pay (*Thames Water Utilities v Reynolds*) and accrued holiday pay (*Kerr v Sweater Shop (Scotland) Ltd*), commission not payable until after the employment has been terminated (*Robertson v Blackstone Franks Investment Management Ltd*) and so on. A service charge added to a customer's bill in a restaurant (see *Saaverdra v Aceground Ltd*), or a tip added to that bill when it is paid by cheque or credit card (see *Nerva v R L & G Ltd*) is part of an employee's wages, and while the actual distribution of these monies among different employees may be allocated by the employer on a specified or discretionary basis (in accordance with the contracts of employment of his staff) he cannot appropriate part of the charge to himself, for, in doing so, he is making an unlawful deduction within the meaning of the Act. In *Kent Management Services Ltd v Butterfield*, a discretionary bonus, expressed to be ex gratia, was held to be part of the employee's wages, although it was suggested *obiter* that if such payment was intended to be non-contractual and discretionary, and payable only on the employee achieving a satisfactory performance, words to that effect in the contract could well take the payment outside the Act.

8.28 Accrued holiday pay is 'wages' which an employee is entitled to receive unless there is an express term in the contract negating this right. For example, in *Greg May (Carpet Fitters and Contractors) Ltd v Dring*, the employee's contract stated that on the termination of his employment he would be entitled to accrued holiday pay. However, this would not be paid if he was dismissed through gross misconduct. The employers dismissed the employee for what they claimed to be gross misconduct, and refused to pay him the accrued holiday pay. The employee complained to an employment tribunal that the employers had made an unlawful deduction. It was held that whether or not the sum 'was properly payable' was for the employment tribunal to investigate. On the facts, the employee had not been guilty of 'gross misconduct', and hence the accrued holiday pay was properly payable.

8.29–8.35 However, a payment in lieu of notice is not 'wages' under the Act, because it constitutes 'damages' for breach of contract, and is paid not in connection with the employment but in connection with its termination. In *Delaney v Staples* the House of Lords held that payments made under a 'garden leave' dismissal (see para 19.26) constituted wages, but other situations where a payment in lieu of wages is made or promised were not within the Act, because the essential characteristic of wages was consideration for work done under a subsisting contract of employment. Thus a payment made in respect of a period after the contract has terminated cannot be wages. The matter now is perhaps academic, since the passing of the Employment Tribunals Extension of Jurisdiction Order (see para 1.55), except perhaps for a highly paid employee whose notice rights exceed the limits laid down in that Order.

What are not 'wages' (s 27(2))

8.36 The following payments are excluded from the provisions of the Act:
(a) a payment made by way of an advance under an agreement for a loan or by way of an advance of wages, although s 13 (above) will still apply to any deduction an employer may make from a worker's wages in order to recover that advance;
(b) any payment in respect of expenses incurred by the worker in carrying out his employment. It does not matter if there is an element of profit in those expenses, it is still excluded from the Act, for any such payment does not cease to be expenses merely because the employer is generous (*Southwark London Borough v O'Brien*);
(c) any payment by way of a pension, allowance or gratuity in connection with the worker's retirement or as compensation for loss of office. As noted above, a payment in lieu of notice is not within the Act (*Foster Wheeler (London) Ltd v Jackson*);
(d) any payment referable to a worker's redundancy, whether statutory or not;
(e) any payment made to a worker otherwise than in capacity as a worker;
(f) any benefits in kind are not wages, except a voucher, stamp or similar document which is capable of being exchanged for money, goods or services (whether on its own or together with any other such document). Thus luncheon vouchers are wages within the Act, but other benefits, such as free meals, accommodation, discounts, etc, are not.

What is a deduction (s 13(3))

8.37 Where the total amount of wages paid on any occasion by an employer to a worker employed by him is less than the total amount of the wages properly payable (after lawful deductions), the amount of the deficiency shall be treated as a deduction made by the employer from the worker's wages on that occasion.

Thus a reduction in wages amounts to a deduction. In *Bruce v Wiggins Teape* the employers agreed to pay enhanced overtime rates to employees who worked on a rolling night shift. It was subsequently decided (without the agreement of the employees or their trade union) to withdraw the enhanced payment. An employment tribunal held that the Act dealt with deductions from pay, not with reductions, but this was reversed by the EAT. The wages properly payable included the enhanced overtime rate, which the employers could not terminate unilaterally. Thus the deductions were unauthorised and therefore unlawful. But if the employer has lawful contractual authority to transfer an employee from one shift to another, with a resultant loss of a shift premium allowance, there is no unauthorised deduction from wages within the meaning of s 13 (*Hussman Manufacturing Ltd v Weir*).

8.38   If a collective agreement, the terms of which are incorporated into the individual contracts of employment of employees, expressly provides for a reduction in rates of pay (eg when there is short-time working) such a deduction would not constitute a breach of the Act, although there would be a breach if the deduction could only be made with the approval of the employees and the trade union, and such approval was not obtained. It follows that if rates of pay are contained in a collective agreement which has been incorporated into the individual contracts of employment, these can only be changed in accordance with the terms of that agreement, not unilaterally by the employer (*Davies v Hotpoint Ltd*).

8.39   If there is no power in the contract of employment to demote an employee, then to do so and consequently reduce his salary would be an unlawful deduction under the Act (*Morgan v West Glamorgan County Council*). It will be recalled (see para 8.27) that in *Kent Management Services Ltd v Butterfield* the EAT held that even discretionary bonuses could constitute wages properly payable, if it was in the contemplation of the parties that outstanding commissions would be paid on termination of employment.

8.40–8.50   However, s 13(4) provides that a deficiency in wages, attributable to an error affecting the computation by an employer of the gross wages due to the employee, is not an unlawful deduction for the purpose of s 13(3). In other words, an arithmetical mistake is not an unlawful deduction, although a mistaken belief that certain monies ought not to be paid is a deduction (*Morgan v West Glamorgan County Council*, above).

Excepted deductions and excepted payments (s 14, 16)

8.51   The following deductions and payments. whether lawfully or unlawfully made, are not within the scope of the protection of wages provisions, and the employee's remedy, if any, would be to sue for breach of contract in the county court (unless the employment tribunal has jurisdiction to deal with the case under the provisions of the Extension of Jurisdiction Order, see para 1.55).

(a)   A deduction or payment for the purpose of reimbursing the employer in respect of an overpayment of wages (s 14(1)(a)), or an overpayment of expenses incurred by the worker in carrying out his employment (s 14(1)(b)), made to the employee for any reason. In *SIP Industrial Products Ltd v Swinn* an employer withheld part of an employee's wages as a reimbursement in respect of expenses which had been fraudulently claimed. An employment tribunal took the view that this deduction was not permitted by s 14(1)(b), because what the employee had done amounted to theft, and therefore had nothing to do with expenses incurred in the course of his employment. However, the EAT held that overpaid expenses made 'for any reason' were recoverable by the employer without being in breach of the Act.

If the worker disputes that there has been an overpayment, or claims that he is not required to repay the overpayment, this matter must be resolved in the ordinary courts, under the general law relating to mistake. It is now settled that there is no difference between a mistake of law and a mistake of fact (*Kleinwort Benson Ltd v Lincoln City Council*). All such overpayments are recoverable by the employer, except that he may not be able so to recover if
(i)   he made a representation of fact which led the employee to believe that he was entitled to treat the money overpaid as his own, and
(ii) the employee, bone fide and without notice of the mistake, consequently changed his position (eg by spending the money), and
(iii) the overpayment was not caused by the fault of the employee.

The general principles to be applied in such circumstances stem from the law of restitution (see *Lipkin Gorman v Karpnale Ltd*).

(b) A deduction made in consequence of any disciplinary proceedings held by virtue of a statutory provision (s 14(2)). This provision probably refers to disciplinary proceedings held by the police or fire service (see *Chiltern House Ltd v Chambers*). Such proceedings, however, may be the subject of judicial review (*R v Leicestershire Fire Authority, ex p Thompson*).

(c) A deduction made in consequence of a requirement imposed on an employer by a statutory provision to pay the money over to a public body, if the deduction is made in accordance with the relevant determination of that body (s 14(3)). This is not quite the same as the lawful deductions which can be made under s 13 (above), and would cover a case where a public body (eg local authority) has power to require an employer to deduct a sum from the worker's wages and pay that sum to the authority in question.

(d) A deduction which is paid to a third party at the employee's request (s 14(4)). There must be a relevant provision in the contract, to which the employee has signified his consent in writing, or otherwise with the prior agreement or consent of the worker in writing. This exclusion would cover, for example, the check-off system, whereby an employer deducts trade union subscriptions from the worker's wages, and pays the money to the trade union (see Chapter 21).

(e) A deduction which is made by the employer because the worker has taken part in a strike or other industrial action (s 14(5), and see *Sim v Rotherham Metropolitan Borough Council*). Thus, if the employee is not performing any of his duties the employer may deduct an amount which represents a fair proportion of his salary (*Miles v Wakefield Metropolitan District Council*). If the employee alleges that the employer has deducted more than a fair proportion, his remedy is to bring an action in the county court, not in the employment tribunal. In *Sunderland Polytechnic v Evans* an employee took part in a half-day strike. The employer deducted a full day's salary from her monthly pay, and she complained that an unlawful deduction had been made from her wages. On her behalf, it was argued that s 14(5) only applied to a 'lawful' deduction, ie in respect of the half day she was on strike, and therefore the deduction of a full day's pay was not protected by s 14(5). The employment tribunal held that they had jurisdiction to determine if the deduction was indeed lawful, but this decision was reversed by the EAT. In an unusual move, the EAT decided to look at *Hansard*, and it was noted that in both the House of Commons and the House of Lords, Government ministers were quite clear in their views that if a worker believed that a deduction was not contractually authorised, the remedy would have to be an action in the county court, not in the employment tribunal. Thus, if the amount of the deduction is in dispute, the matter must be settled in the county court. A decision of the EAT to the contrary (*Home Office v Ayres*) was disapproved.

More difficult, perhaps, is the situation where the employee is taking part in 'other industrial action', eg by working his full contractual hours, but only performing part of his contractual duties during those hours (eg by way of protest). In such circumstances, the employer will be entitled to deduct part of the employee's wages, based on his assessment of the amount of time when the employee is not working properly (*Wiluszynski v London Borough of Tower Hamlets*).

(f) A deduction made with the prior agreement of the worker to satisfy an order made by a court or tribunal requiring the payment of any amount to the employer (s 14(6)).

Deductions and payments in retail employment (s 17–18)

8.52   Special rules apply for the protection of persons who are engaged in retail employment, which is defined as:

(a) the carrying out of retail transactions, ie the sale or supply of goods or services (including financial services); or

(b) the collection by the worker of amounts payable in connection with retail transactions carried out by other persons, or other individuals in their personal capacities.

8.53   The definition covers a wide range of activities, including shop assistants, bus drivers, bank cashiers, insurance agents, petrol pump attendants, credit collectors etc.

8.54   The Act permits an employer to make deductions or require payments from the wages of such retail workers in respect of cash shortages and/or stock deficiencies which arise in the course of retail employment. These include shortages or deficiencies arising from dishonest, negligent or other conduct by the employee, or any other event in respect of which he has a contractual liability. Nor is it relevant that the amount of the deduction or payment does not reflect the actual amount of the shortage or deficiency (s 17(4)). But an employer cannot evade the provisions of the Act by defining wages by reference to cash shortages or deficiencies, for in such circumstances the gross wages are to be treated as being the amount they would have been but for the shortage or deficiency (s 19).

8.55   Under ss 17–18 of the Act, it is permissible to make a deduction (or require a payment) in respect of cash shortages or stock deficiencies subject to two conditions. First, the requirements of s 13 (above) must be met, ie an appropriate contractual agreement enabling the deductions (or payments) to be made. This contractual arrangement must have been agreed to before the happening of the event which was the cause of the purported deduction, because, as we have seen (above, para 8.16) the Act is designed to prevent pressure being put on the employee to agree to the deduction (*Discount Tobacco and Confectionery v Williamson*). Second, the deduction (or demand for payment) must not exceed 10 per cent of the gross wages payable on the day in question (see s 18). If the shortage or deficiency is greater than the sum to be deducted or demanded the employer may continue to deduct or demand the balance on subsequent pay days, provided that on each occasion the deduction or demand does not exceed 10 per cent of the gross wages payable.

8.56 If the employer wishes to make a demand for payment, he must do so in writing (on one of the worker's pay days) and notify him (again in writing) of the total liability, prior to receiving any payment (s 20).

8.57 Generally, the deduction or demand must be made within 12 months from the date when the employer discovers the cash shortage or stock deficiency, except
(a) if the deduction is one of a series of deductions in respect of the same shortage or deficiency in which case the 12-month period applied from the first deduction or demand of the series, or
(b) if the employer ought reasonably to have discovered the cash shortage or stock deficiency earlier, the 12-month period will run from the date when he ought to have discovered it, not from when he actually did so.

8.58–8.65 However, once the employment comes to an end, there is no limit on the amount which the employer may deduct or demand.

Excluded workers

8.66 The following workers are excluded from bringing a claim under the above provisions of ERA:
(a) members of the armed forces (s 192);
(b) employees who work under a crew agreement in a form approved by the Secretary of State (s 199(1)).

Complaints to an employment tribunal (s 23)

8.67 A worker may complain to an employment tribunal that his employer has:
(a) made a deduction or demanded a payment in contravention of ss 13–17;
(b) made a deduction which is outside the limit of 12 months as required by s 20(3);
(c) received a payment in respect of a cash shortage or stock deficiency without notifying the worker in writing of his total liability, or without making the demand in the prescribed manner as required by s 20(1);
(d) made a deduction or received a payment in excess of the limit of 10 per cent of the gross pay on a particular day as permitted by s 21(1).

8.68–8.75 The complaint must be made within three months from the time when the deduction was made or the payment received by the employer, with the usual extension of time if the employment tribunal is satisfied that it was not reasonably practicable to present a claim earlier. The three-month period runs from the date when contractually the wages were due to be paid, not when they were actually paid (*Group 4 Nightspeed Ltd v Gilbert*). If the complaint is well founded, the employment tribunal shall make a declaration to that effect, and order the employer to reimburse the worker the amount of any unauthorised deductions made or payments received. It should be noted that there is no limit to the amount which the employment tribunal can order to be repaid. Further, if there is an unlawful deduction or payment, which the employment tribunal orders to be repaid, the employer will lose all rights to it, and may not seek to recover that which could lawfully be claimed from the employee by bringing an action at common law (*Potter v Hunt Contracts*).

National minimum wage

8.76 Under the provisions of the National Minimum Wage Act 1998 workers are entitled to be remunerated in any pay reference period at a rate which is not less than the national minimum wage (s 1). The actual hourly rate will be determined in regulations made by the Secretary of State after receiving a recommendation from the Low Pay Commission, but he may not differentiate between different areas of the country, different sectors of employment, undertakings of different sizes, persons of different ages (except, in certain circumstances those under the age of 26, see below) or persons of different occupations (s 2.) There is no qualifying period of employment required, and no exclusion for small businesses.

8.77 The Act applies to all 'workers', as defined (which, it will be recalled, is a term wider than 'employee', see para 2.3), including agency workers and homeworkers, although there are a number of persons excluded by the Act, and a further number of persons excluded by the regulations made under the Act. So far as the Act is concerned, its provisions do not apply to share fishermen, voluntary workers, certain resident workers in religious communities, and prisoners, and serving members of the armed forces. Under the regulations, the following persons are excluded from the national minimum wage:
(a) workers under the age of 18
(b) apprentices below the age of 18, and apprentices between 19–26 in the first 12 months of their apprenticeship
(c) certain workers in schemes funded by the European Social Fund, on government-funded training schemes, work experience or temporary work schemes or schemes to help the unemployed to find work (who are not employed by the employer for whom they work under the scheme)
(d) undergraduates on sandwich course placements, trainee teachers on placement
(e) homeless persons taking part in certain schemes under which they are provided with shelter and other benefits in return for work
(f) au pairs, nannies, and companions who are treated as a member of the employer's family
(g) members of the employer's family who live at home and participate in running the family business.

8.78 It has been held that pupil barristers are not engaged under a contract of apprenticeship, and therefore do not qualify for the national minimum wage (*Edmunds v Lawson*). Agricultural workers covered by agriculture wages councils are entitled at least to the amount of the national minimum wage. Offshore workers are covered by the regulations.

8.79 The Department of Trade and Industry has produced a 'Guidance' booklet (running to 112 pages!) which, although not legally binding, gives guidance to employers and workers, and will doubtless be used by the enforcing authorities as a powerful aid to understanding and implementing the regulations.

8.80 The National Minimum Wage Regulations 1999 and the National Minimum Wage Act 1998 (Amendment) Regulations 1999 deal with a number of substantive matters, including the relevant pay period, how pay is to be calculated, what is to be included and excluded if there is a non-monetary element in the pay received, and the method of calculating the hours (time work, salaried hours work, output work and umeasured work), extension to offshore employment, etc. Various items are included in the definition of pay, eg tips received via the employer (but not those obtained directly from the customer) and incentive payments (but these will only count in the pay period in which they are received). Other items, eg premium payments for overtime or shift work, benefits (company cars, health insurance etc) are to be excluded, but not the value of accommodation. The hourly rate shall be payable for any period during which the worker is at the employer's disposal and carrying out his duties or activities. It is also payable for all times when the worker is required to be at the place of work and available for work, even though no work is actually available.

8.81 Every employer will be obliged to keep records (s 9), and if a worker believed that he is being remunerated at a rate which is less than the national minimum wage, he may require his employer to produce those records, and the worker may inspect and examine them, accompanied by any other person he thinks fit. The worker must first give notice to his employer (a 'production notice'), and the employer must produce the records at the worker's place of work or any other place at which it is reasonable for the worker to attend and inspect the relevant records (s 10). If an employer fails to produce the relevant records, or fails to allow the worker to inspect them, or fails to allow the worker to be accompanied by someone, the worker may make a complaint to an employment tribunal, who, if they find the complaint to be well-founded, will make a declaration to that effect, and make an award to the worker of a sum equal to 80 times the hourly amount of the national minimum wage (s 11).

8.82 A worker who is not an employee will be entitled to a written statement containing the prescribed information for the purpose of assisting the worker to determine whether he has been remunerated at a rate which is at least equal to the national minimum wage (s 12).

A. Enforcement by the worker

8.83 A worker who believes that he is being paid less than the national minimum wage may bring a claim in an employment tribunal or a county court, seeking the additional remuneration, either as a claim for unlawful deduction from wages under the Employment Rights Act (see para 8.11), or as a claim for breach of contract. On such a claim, the burden of proof is reversed, ie it will be presumed that the worker was not getting the national minimum wage until the contrary is proved by the employer (s 28). Further, employees have the right not to suffer a detriment or be dismissed (no qualifying period of employment being required) or victimised because they brought or became involved in proceedings relating to the enforcement of the national minimum wage (ss 23 and 25).

B. Enforcement by the state

8.84 The Secretary of State will appoint enforcement officers from the Inland Revenue who will have powers to require employers or an employment agency used by the employer or a worker who qualifies for the national minimum wage to produce any records, and be furnished with any explanation and any other additional information which might reasonably be needed in order to establish whether the Act is being complied with. If the officer is of the opinion that a worker who qualifies for the national minimum wage is not being remunerated for any pay reference period at a rate at least equal to the national minimum wage, he may serve an enforcement notice on the employer, requiring him to remunerate the worker for the pay reference periods ending on or after the date of the notice at a rate at least equal to the national minimum wage. The enforcement notice may additionally require the employer to pay a sum due to the worker in respect of the employer's previous failure to pay that rate. The employer may appeal against the enforcement notice within four weeks to an employment tribunal. The employment tribunal will dismiss the appeal unless it is established that the facts were such that the officer had no reason to serve the notice, or that no sum was due to the worker, or that the amount specified as being due is incorrect. If the amount specified in the notice is incorrect, the employment tribunal will rectify it, and it will take effect accordingly.

8.85 If the employer does not comply with the enforcement notice, the officer may present a complaint to an employment tribunal or commence civil proceedings in a county court, on behalf of the worker. The officer may also serve a penalty notice on the employer requiring him to pay a financial penalty to the Secretary of State. The penalty will be twice the hourly rate of the national minimum wage (as in force at the time of the notice) in respect of each worker for each day during which there has been a failure to comply. The employer may appeal against the penalty notice to an employment tribunal, who shall dismiss the appeal unless it is established that the facts are such that the officer had no reason to serve the notice, or that the penalty notice is incorrect in some of the particulars, or that the calculation is incorrect. If some of the particulars are incorrect, or if the amount is incorrect, the employment tribunal shall rectify the penalty notice, and it will take effect accordingly.

C. Offences (ss 31–33)

8.86 It is an offence to:
(a) refuse or wilfully neglect to remunerate a worker for any pay period at a rate which is at least equal to the national minimum wage
(b) fail to keep or preserve records
(c) make false entries in records
(d) produce or furnish any record or information which he knows to be false
(e) intentionally delay or obstruct an inspector, or refuse or neglect to answer any question or produce any document when required to do so.

8.87 If the offence committed by a body corporate is proved to have been committed with the consent or connivance of an officer of that body, or attributable to any neglect on his behalf, then he, as well as the body corporate, shall be guilty of an offence and liable to be proceeded against and punished accordingly.

8.88 A person guilty of an offence shall be liable on summary conviction to a fine not exceeding level 5 on the standard scale (currently £5,000).

8.89 Currently, there are three applicable rates of the national minimum wage:
(a) adult workers (age 22 and over) are entitled to a minimum of £3.70 per hour gross;
(b) workers who have attained the age of 18 but not 22 are entitled to £3.20 per hour gross;
(c) workers who have attained the age of 22 but are within the first six months of employment with a new employer and are on accredited training are entitled to £3.20 per hour gross.

CHAPTER 9

Transfer of undertakings

9.1 At common law, a contract of employment was a personal contract between the employer and the employee; when that relationship ceased, the contract of employment came to an end. Thus if a business was sold, the purchaser had the right to choose whom to employ, and the employee had the right to choose who he would work for. Indeed, '... the right to choose for himself whom he would serve ... constituted the main difference between a servant and a serf' (*Nokes v Doncaster Amalgamated Collieries Ltd*). Thus the sale or transfer of any business resulted in the termination of any existing contract of employment because at common law an employee's contract of employment cannot be transferred to another employer without his consent (*Bolwell v Redcliffe Homes Ltd*).

9.2–9.10 The position has been altered by the Transfer of Undertakings (Protection of Employment) Regulations 1981 (TUPE), which generally try to put the transferee employer in the same position as the transferor, so that the rights and obligations contained in the contract of employment between the employee and the transferor are passed to the transferee. Further changes were made by the Collective Redundancies and Transfer of Undertakings (Protection of Employment) (Amendment) Regulations 1995–1999.

Origin of the Regulations

9.11 In 1977 the Acquired Rights Directive (77/187/EEC) was passed (see para 1.144). Briefly, its aims are:
a. to ensure that when an employer transfers his business (or part of it) to another employer, the transferor and the transferee shall inform the representatives of the employees who are affected by the transfer, and consult with them;
b. to ensure that when the transfer takes place, the contracts of employment of the employees of the transferor are transferred to the transferee;
c. that the terms and conditions laid down in any collective agreement made by the transferor with the representatives of the employees shall be observed by the transferee for at least one year;
d. that the transfer, by itself, shall not constitute a ground for dismissal by the transferor or transferee, although this does not prevent dismissals brought about by economic, technical or organisational reasons;

e. if, as a result of the transfer, the employee suffers a substantial change in his working conditions to his detriment, this may constitute a dismissal.

9.12 Once a transfer has taken place, the employees of the transferor automatically become the employees of the transferee. There is no need for the transferee formally to engage them. If the transferee does not wish to employ any particular employee, he will be responsible for any dismissal, which will have to be justified by an economic, technical or organisational reason (see para 9.86), otherwise there may be liability for the dismissals. There is a transfer even if the transferee refuses to comply with his obligations. Neither the transferor nor the transferee can choose the date from which the contracts of employment are transferred, other than the date when the actual transfer takes place (*Rotsart de Hertaing v J Benoidt SA*).

9.13–9.20 In order to implement the Directive, the Transfer of Undertakings (Protection of Employment) Regulations 1981 (TUPE) were introduced into Parliament, albeit 'with a distinct lack of enthusiasm'. There was always considerable doubt that the regulations met with the requirements of the Directive and, indeed, following infraction proceedings brought by the European Commission, the European Court held that this was so, with the consequence that the regulations have been amended accordingly.

Further, in *Litster v Forth Dry Dock and Engineering Co Ltd* the House of Lords decided that the regulations must be given a 'purposive' construction so as to achieve the objections sought by the Directive, and went so far as to engage in judicial legislation by adding words which were not in fact there.

When do the Regulations apply?

9.21 The Regulations apply to an employee, defined as 'any individual who works for another person, whether under a contract of service or apprenticeship or otherwise' (reg 2(1)). This definition is somewhat wider than the one used in the Employment Rights Act, and may, for example, include agency supplied workers, casual workers, and so on. In *Mikkelsen v Danmols Inventar A/S*, the European Court of Justice held that the meaning of the term 'employee' was a matter for the national courts to decide. However, the definition does not include persons who work under a contract for services (see *Cowell v Quilter Goodison Co Ltd*).

9.22 The Regulations will apply on the transfer of 'an undertaking', which is defined as including any trade or business. Originally, the Regulations did not apply to non-commercial undertakings (eg charities etc) but, following the decision in *Dr Sophie Redmond Stichting v Bartol* (which held that there was no such restriction in the Directive) this exception was removed. They also apply if only part of an undertaking is transferred, as long as that which is transferred is a separate and self-contained part of the original business, and the employee concerned is actually employed in the part of the undertaking which is being transferred (see reg 3).

9.23 Whether the employee is employed in the part of the undertaking which was transferred will basically be a question of fact, but problems will arise when an employee works partly for a holding company, and partly for a subsidiary company. In *Sunley Turriff Holdings Ltd v Thomson* the employee was the company secretary and chief accountant for Lilley Construction Ltd and also Lilley Construction (Scotland) Ltd. His contract of employment was with the first-named holding company, but he did work for both. Receivers were then appointed for both companies, and the employee continued to work, assisting the receivers. The Scottish company was sold to Sunley Turrif Holdings, but the employee's name was not on the list of those transferred. The receiver told him that he still worked for the holding company. He was then made redundant, and claimed that he had been unfairly dismissed, as he was employed by the part of the undertaking transferred. His claim was upheld. Realistically, the employee was employed in part of the undertaking transferred, and should have been transferred along with the other employees, notwithstanding that he continued to work for the receivers. Nothing had been done to prevent the application of TUPE. To prevent them from applying, there should have been an express agreement which regularised his position one way or the other.

9.24   A somewhat different result was arrived at in *Michael Peters Ltd v Farnfield*, where the employee was the chief executive of a holding company which had 25 subsidiary companies. The group encountered financial difficulties, and receivers were called in. The employee was dismissed, and a few days later four of the subsidiary companies were sold to another company. However, the parent company was not a party to the sale. An employment tribunal held that there was a single economic unit in the sense understood by competition law, but this view was disapproved of by the EAT, who refused to pierce the veil of corporate personality. The employee had not been assigned to the part of the undertaking which was transferred.

9.25   A further problem arises when part of an undertaking is transferred. What is the position of an employee who performs certain functions in that part, but also in part of the undertaking retained? For example, suppose a personnel officer employed by Company X provides services to its machine tool section, which is then transferred to Company Y. Does it make any difference if he spends the whole of his time, or part of his time, with the machine tool section? The European Court of Justice in *Botzen v RDM* stated that art 3 of the Directive protects those employees who are 'assigned' to the transferred part, but this is not very helpful. Two theories are currently suggested by UK commentators. The first is to ascertain if the employee spends most of his activities in that department, or for its benefit (the so-called 'location' theory). The second is to ascertain if the employee's post is a part of the staffing structure of the department (the so-called 'belonging' theory). The 'location' theory appears to have some support from the decision of the ECJ in *Botzen v RDM*, but the EAT in *Duncan Web Offset (Maidstone) Ltd v Cooper* appears to have adopted the 'belonging' approach. The question as to whether an employee has been 'assigned' to the part transferred and the proportion of work he did for that part was to be determined on the facts by the employment tribunal.

9.26–9.35   An employee does not have to work exclusively in the undertaking or part of the undertaking transferred, and thus whether or not he has been transferred is a question of fact to be determined by a consideration of all the circumstances (*Buchanan-Smith v Schleicher & Co International Ltd*).

What is a transfer?

9.36 A relevant transfer can take place by sale or other disposition or by operation of law. There is no transfer if there is a sale or transfer of shares, because the corporate personality of the company does not change (*Brookes v Borough Care Services*). But as long as there is a change in the identity of the employer, it does not matter if there is no formal legal transfer (*Landsorganisationen i Danmark v Ny Molle Kro*). Thus a transfer can take place on a grant, or the surrender and regranting of a lease (*Premier Motors (Medway) Ltd v Total Oil GB Ltd*). In *Young v Daniel Thwaites & Co Ltd*, it was held that there was a relevant transfer when a change took place in the tenancy of a public house.

9.37 A transfer may be affected by two or more transactions, and it is irrelevant whether or not any property passes from the transferor to the transferee. Thus a concession, a permit to operate a licence, etc, now come within the scope of the Regulations.

9.38 However, there must be the transfer of a business, not a mere transfer of the assets of a business (see *Premier Motors* (above) applying *Melon v Hector Powe Ltd*). The European Court has held that it is for the national court to consider all the factual circumstances and assess whether they are characteristic of a transfer of an undertaking within the meaning of the Directive. The decisive factor is whether the business retains its identity, but it is also necessary to take into account the type of undertaking concerned, whether tangible assets were transferred, the value of intangible assets at the time of the transfer, whether or not the majority of employees were taken on by the new owner, whether customers were transferred, the degree of similarity between the activities carried on before and after the transfer, and the period, if any, for which those activities were suspended (*Rask and Christensen v ISS Kantineservice A/S*). Thus if the essential business activity is carried on by the new owner, it is likely that there has been a transfer within the meaning of the regulations (*Kenny v South Manchester College*). The transfer of goodwill (as opposed to physical assets) has been used as a criteria in a number of cases (eg *Kenmir Ltd v Frizzell*), and the fact that there was no transfer of goodwill has been used to hold that a transfer was outside the scope of the Regulations (*Robert Seligman Corpn v Baker*).

9.39 The existence before the transfer of a draft contract of sale, a payment on account, and negotiations which take place prior to a sale do not constitute a series of transactions by which the transfer of the undertaking is effected. Thus, if an employee is dismissed during the currency of those negotiations, and a transfer subsequently takes place, he will not have been employed immediately before the transfer (*Longden v Ferrari Ltd*). Equally, dismissals by receivers or administrators in order to make a business more saleable are not automatically unfair under reg 8, particularly if the subsequent transfer was no more than a 'mere twinkle in the eye' at the time of the dismissal, for then the dismissals were only connected with a possible transfer (*Ibex Trading Co Ltd v Walton*).

9.40 A transfer takes effect 'by operation of law' if a company is dissolved but continues to operate. In *Charlton v Charlton Thermosystems (Romsey) Ltd* a company was struck off the register of companies for failing to file annual accounts. Nonetheless the business continued to function, and its two directors were held to be personally liable for compensation due on the subsequent dismissal of employees. There had been a transfer of an economic identifiable identity, and the fact that the directors may have acted unlawfully in continuing to use the company's name and assets was irrelevant.

9.41 It was generally believed that the Directive only applied to the transfer of an identifiable economic activity, and not to the transfer of a contract for pure services, eg cleaning, maintenance, security, etc. However, in *Rask v ISS* this view was dispelled by the ECJ. In this case, a company (Phillips) decided to contract out the running of their works canteen to another company (ISS). Phillips were to pay a monthly fee to ISS, and also supply electricity, equipment, etc. ISS undertook to employ the former canteen staff of Phillips at the same rates of pay. ISS then decided to change the date of payment for the canteen staff from the last Thursday in the month to the last day in the month. Rask complained that she was not employed on the same terms as those previously in force. The ECJ held that the transfer of the service (of running the canteen) was within the scope of the Directive, and the fact that those activities were ancillary to the main activities of Phillips was irrelevant. Further, even though the amount of pay received by the employee was the same, the Directive did not permit a variation in the date on which remuneration was to be paid. This constituted a change in the applicant's working conditions.

9.42 It appears that the fundamental question to be asked is, has the business which has been transferred retained its identity, in the sense that its operations have been continued or resumed (*Porter v Queen's Medical Centre*). However, problems were caused when competitive tendering was introduced, and new providers of services became involved. Thus in *Dines v Initial Healthcare Services Ltd*, the claimants were cleaners, employed by Initial Healthcare, to clean at a hospital. The local authority then went to competitive tendering, and awarded the cleaning contract to Pall Mall. The claimants were dismissed by Initial Healthcare by reason of redundancy, and were offered and accepted employment by Pall Mall, albeit on less favourable terms. They claimed they were unfairly dismissed by Initial Healthcare (under reg 8 of TUPE) and also claimed under reg 5(1) (below) against Pall Mall. The employment tribunal held that there was no transfer within the meaning of the Regulations. There was no contractual relationship between Initial Healthcare and Pall Mall, the latter did not purchase any equipment or materials, and no sale or transfer of goodwill. The decision was upheld by the EAT, but reversed by the Court of Appeal. The transfer took place in two stages, ie the handing back of the cleaning services from Initial Healthcare to the hospital, and the handing over by the hospital of the cleaning contract to Pall Mall. The cleaning services to be performed were essentially the same, on the same premises, for the same hospital, and by the same employees. This therefore constituted a transfer within the meaning of the Regulations.

9.43 The transfer of activities, by itself, is not sufficient to bring TUPE into play. The 'entity' itself must retain some form of identity, because the fact that the service provided by the transferor and the transferee is identical does not necessarily mean that the undertaking has been transferred. Thus, as well as the activity, there must be a transfer of significant tangible or intangible assets, or the taking over by the transferee of a major part of the workforce, in terms of their number and skills who had previously been assigned by the transferor to the activities concerned. Thus, where the workforce is largely unskilled, and only activities are transferred, what will be of crucial importance is whether a substantial proportion of the workforce are taken over by the transferee. This appears to be the effect of the ruling of the ECJ in *Süzen v Zehnacker*, a case which represents a significant change of emphasis. In this case, the seven claimants were employed by a firm as cleaners, working at a private school. The school terminated the cleaning contract, and awarded it to another firm. The ECJ held that there was no transfer of significant assets, the new employer had not taken over the major part of the workforce, and that there was no transfer of an economic entity. The mere loss of a service contract to a competitor does not indicate that there has been a transfer of an undertaking within the meaning of the Directive.

9.44 It must be queried whether certain earlier cases (eg *Cristal Schmidt v Spar*) can still be relied upon, and the decision in *Süzen* should lead to a relaxation of fears arising from competitive tendering. *Süzen* was quickly followed by the Court of Appeal in *Betts v Brintel Helicopters and KLM ERA Helicopters (UK) Ltd*, where Brintel provided, under three separate contracts, helicopter services for Shell UK Ltd covering various sectors of the North Sea. Shell then put the contracts out to tender, and awarded two of them to Brintel, the third, which used to operate out of Beccles, to KLM. None of the 66 people who were employed by Brintel at Beccles were taken on by KLM, who operated the service from Norwich. Seven employees sought a declaration that there was a relevant transfer of an undertaking, as a result of which they became employees of KLM. A High Court judge accepted that there had been no transfer of assets or employees between Brintel and KLM, but held that since the same service or activity was being performed by KLM as had been performed by Brintel, there was an economic identity which remained identifiable after the transfer, and granted the declaration. The Court of Appeal reversed the decision. Hardly any of the assets of Brintel had been transferred to KLM, nor had any of the workforce. The undertaking had not retained its identity, and thus TUPE did not apply.

9.45–9.55 But the Court of Appeal in *ECM (Vehicle Delivery Service) Ltd v Cox* took a different view, and held that the importance of *Süzen* has been overstated, that there was no real conflict between that case and *Schmidt*, and that it was still for the national courts to consider all the facts characterising the transaction in question. It is therefore not surprising that the EAT in *OCS Cleaning Scotland Ltd v Rudden* stated that the law on whether a transfer has occurred is in such a mess that, where a tribunal has sought to apply the law as best it can, its decision should be upheld unless there has been an obvious misdirection. Certainly, in subsequent decisions (*Magna Housing Association v Turner*, and *Lightways (Contractors) Ltd v Hood*) the EAT has indicated that it was prepared to move away from the strict interpretation of *Süzen*, although the ECJ itself in *Francisco Hernandez Vidal SA v Gómez Pérez* reiterated the 'economic entity' test set out in *Süzen*. The law is indeed a mess!

The effect of the transfer (reg 5)

9.56 Regulation 5(1) provides that a relevant transfer shall not operate so as to terminate the contract of employment of any person employed by the transferor in the undertaking transferred, but any such contract shall have effect after the transfer as if originally made between the employee concerned and the transferee.

9.57 This provision is the nub of the Regulations, and constitutes a form of statutory novation of the contract of employment. The transferee 'steps into the shoes' of the transferor, as from the date when the original contract of employment commenced. Rights and liabilities which existed under the original contract continue in favour or against the transferee (see below, para 9.71). Indeed, the fact that an employer proposes to transfer all or part of the business is not a repudiatory breach of contract by the employer, and there is no implied right under the contract of employment which would enable an employee to restrain the proposed transfer by means of an interlocutory injunction. Regulation 5 makes it quite clear that the transferee will become the employer in place of the transferor (*Newns v British Airways plc*). For example, in *Morris Angel & Son Ltd v Hollande*, the defendant was the managing director of a company called Altolight Ltd. His service agreement provided that within one year after leaving his employment he would not seek business from any person with whom the company had done business within one year of the end of his employment. The company was then sold to the claimants, who sought to enforce the restrictive covenant. The question was whether, in the light of reg 5(1), the covenant was transferred to the claimants in respect of their business or whether it remained enforceable only against the business of Altolight Ltd. It was held that the effect of reg 5(1) was to put the claimants in the place of the transferor company (Altolight Ltd), and thus the covenant could be enforced to prevent the defendant from seeking business with anyone who had done business with that company within the year. It did not refer to the business activities of the claimants. Any other construction would impose a much wider obligation on the defendant, because at the time he entered into the covenant there was no possibility of him contemplating accepting a restraint in respect of the claimants' business activities.

9.58 Of course, the employee may be opposed to the transfer of his contract from one employer to another. He is free to choose whom he will work for, and cannot be compelled to work for an employer against his will. But if he informs the transferor that he refuses to accept the transfer, the transfer shall have the effect of terminating the contract of employment with the transferor, but the employee will not be treated for any purpose as having been dismissed by the transferor (see reg 5(4)). Thus, by refusing to accept the transfer, he will lose his rights to any claim for unfair dismissal or redundancy pay (*Katsikas v Konstantinidis*).

9.59 Employment tribunals should be careful to distinguish between an objection to the transfer communicated to the relevant persons, and an expression of concern and unwillingness to be transferred, which may be consistent with acceptance of the inevitable. A protest in advance of a transfer will not by itself amount to an objection unless it is translated into an actual refusal to consent to the transfer (*Hay v George Hanson (Building Contractors) Ltd*). But if the employee refused to go along with the transfer because there would be substantial detrimental changes to his terms and conditions of employment, he will be able to claim that he has been constructively dismissed by the transferor (since no transfer has taken place, the liability cannot pass to the transferee), or, alternatively, bring a claim at common law for wrongful dismissal (*Oxford University v Humphreys*).

9.60 There is no requirement that prior to the transfer, the transferor must inform his employees of that fact, or indeed the identity of the transferee (*Secretary of*

State for Trade and Industry v Cook, where it was stated that a decision to the contrary in *Photostatic Copiers (Southern) Ltd v Okuda* was not to be followed). But the employee is entitled to claim that he has been constructively dismissed by the transferor as a result of the transfer if a substantial change is made to his working conditions to his detriment, or the change in his employer is a change which is significant and is to his detriment (see reg 5(5)). There appears to be no legal authority on this point; presumably the 'identity' of the employer would be significant if there was some form of personal animosity between them. A substantial change in working conditions could occur, eg, if the employee's travelling time was considerably increased.

9.61 What he cannot do is claim constructive dismissal against a transferee for whom he has never worked. Thus in *Siga (GB) Ltd v Burton* the claimant was employed by a local authority. Following competitive tendering it was proposed that he would be transferred to the successful tenderer. However, he was led to believe that the transferee proposed to change substantially his terms and conditions of employment. He therefore resigned from the local authority, and claimed constructive dismissal against the transferee, arguing that there had been a breach of the implied duty to maintain trust and confidence, and act in good faith towards him. An employment tribunal allowed his claim, but the decision was reversed by the EAT. As he had never become an employee of the transferee, the latter could not have acted in breach of contract with him. His fears about worsening terms and conditions were totally protected by the adequate remedies available under TUPE, and therefore the conduct of a potential transferee could not be regarded as sufficiently affecting the obligation of mutual trust and goodwill which must exist in employment relationships.

9.62 Regulation 5(3) provides that any reference to a person employed in an undertaking transferred by a relevant transfer is a reference to a person employed 'immediately before the transfer'. The meaning of this latter phrase has given rise to some difficulties. In *Alphafield Ltd v Barratt*, an employee was made redundant on a Friday, and the business was transferred on the following Monday. Was the employee employed 'immediately before the transfer'? The EAT held that the gap between his dismissal and the transfer was so small that he was employed immediately before the transfer, and he could therefore claim that he had been unfairly dismissed by the transferee. Although this decision was followed in a number of cases, doubts were also expressed.

9.63 The matter was taken further by the Court of Appeal in *Secretary of State for Employment v Spence*. In this case, employees were dismissed at 11 am and the business was sold at 2 pm the same day. The workforce were re-engaged by the transferee, but the employees sought a redundancy payment from the Secretary of State, as the transferor had gone into liquidation. They argued that they were not employed 'immediately before the transfer'. The Court of Appeal upheld their claims. Regulation 5 only operates to transfer the contracts of employment of those employees who were still in the employment of the transferor at the moment of the transfer. There was no room for a gap in time, and *Alphafield Ltd* and other similar cases were overruled.

9.64 However, the saga continued! In *Bork International A/S v Foreningen*, the European Court of Justice agreed that the Directive only applies to workers who were employed at the time of the transfer (as was held in *Spence*). However, the Court held further that in construing the Directive, regard must be had to art 4(1) (which has been enacted by reg 8(1) of the Regulations). This prohibits a dismissal because of a transfer, except where there are 'economic, technical or organisational reasons'. Thus, if the worker was dismissed before the transfer, at the behest of the transferee, then, if this was in breach of art 4(1), the worker is to be regarded as being employed at the time of the transfer.

9.65 The matter was finally resolved so far as the Regulations are concerned by the House of Lords in *Litster v Forth Dry Dock and Engineering Co Ltd*. In this case, the employee was dismissed an hour before the transfer. He claimed that he had been unfairly dismissed by the transferor, but this claim was ineffective, because the transferor had gone out of business. Nonetheless, the House of Lords held that he could proceed against the transferee. It is true that there was a gap in time between his dismissal and the transfer, but reg 5 had to be read in the light of reg 8(1). The result was that reg 5 has to be construed as if after the words '... immediately before the transfer ...' there were inserted the words '... or would have been so employed if he had not been dismissed in the circumstances described in reg 8(1)'.

9.66 The House of Lords were satisfied that the decision in *Spence* was correct, because the reason for the dismissal in that case was economic circumstances, and therefore the dismissal would not have been unfair within reg 8(1). But if a dismissal takes place before the transfer, which is unconnected with the transfer, then since this would be unfair by virtue of reg 8(1), the employee will be regarded as being employed 'immediately before the transfer'. On the other hand, a dismissal before the transfer which is brought about by economic, technical or organisational reasons will have the effect of depriving the employee of a remedy against the transferee.

9.67 Regulation 5(2) provides that on the completion of the relevant transfer,

'(a) all the transferor's rights, powers, duties and liabilities under or in connection with any such contract, shall be transferred by virtue of the regulation to the transferee; and

(b) anything done before the transfer is completed by or in relation to the transferor in respect of that contract or a person employed in that undertaking or part *shall be deemed to have been done* by or in relation to the transferee' (emphasis supplied).

9.68 The operation of reg 5(2) is not limited to the contract of employment which was affected by the transfer, but covers matters *done before the transfer* in respect of the person employed by the transferor who has been transferred to the transferee. Thus in *DJM International Ltd v Nicholas* the applicant worked for a company for many years, but was forced to retire in 1992 when she reached the age of 60. Ten days later she was re-engaged on a part-time basis, and two months after that, following a transfer of the undertaking, she continued to work for the respondent company. Five months later she was made redundant, and she brought a claim alleging sex discrimination against the transferee, in respect of the termination of her contract of employment by the transferor when she had reached the age of 60 (although her claim was outside the normal three-month time limit, the employment tribunal exercised its discretion to extend the time).

9.69 For the respondent it was argued that the contract of employment in respect of which she was alleging sex discrimination had been terminated before the transfer took place, and was not therefore transferred to the transferee. The EAT dismissed the argument and upheld the applicant's right to pursue her claim. Regulation 5(2)(b) was very wide, and applied not only to things done before the transfer in respect of the contract of employment, but also to anything done before the transfer in respect of a person employed in that undertaking.

9.70 Although all rights and liabilities are transferred, these only apply in respect of employees who were employed immediately before the transfer. In *Tsangacos v Amalgamated Chemicals Ltd*, the claimant lodged a complaint of unfair dismissal and race discrimination in March 1995. In July 1995 the employers ceased trading, and all staff etc were transferred to another company. The claimant sought to join the latter employers as respondents, but this application was refused by an employment tribunal chairman, and the decision was upheld on appeal. The rights and obligations of a transferor are only transferred in respect of those employees who were employed immediately before the transfer, and clearly this did not cover the applicant.

9.71 It is thus clear that statutory rights, such as equal pay, maternity rights, etc, are transferred, as well as liability for a protective award on a failure to consult (*Kerry Foods Ltd v Creber*). Restrictive covenants made by the employee with the transferor are transferred, but clearly these need to be looked at in the light of the new situation (*Morris Angel & Son Ltd v Hollande*, para 9.57) But a non-competition clause agreed by the employee transferred will not be enforced if it occurred by reason of the transfer (*Credit Suisse v Padiachy*) because an employee cannot waive his rights under the contract which he had with the transferor (*Credit Suisse First Boston (Europe) Ltd v Lister*).

9.72 Rights under a share option scheme and profits sharing schemes are transferred to the transferee (*Thompson v ASDA-MFI Group plc*), which can bring about the odd result that the transferee will have to pay profit-related pay based on the employee's performance with the transferor (*Unicorn Consultancy Services Ltd v Westbrook*).

9.73 The liability of the transferor for tortious acts committed against his employees will be transferred (*Bernadone v Pall Mall Services Group*), but it is not certain if the transferor's vicarious liability to third persons is transferred, because it does not arise under or in connection with the contract of employment.

9.74 The transferor's liability to be prosecuted, convicted and punished for a criminal offence is not transferred (reg 5(4)).

Although EC Directive 77/187 requires (see art 3) the safeguarding of employees' rights following a transfer, reg 7 of TUPE permits the exclusion of occupational pension schemes. In *Walden Engineering v Warrener* the EAT held that the Directive meant that accrued rights which existed at the time of the transfer were to be protected, but that there was no obligation on the transferee to provide equivalent pension rights to those formerly provided by the transferor. Enhanced benefits payable on a premature retirement on grounds of redundancy are not transferred, nor are occupational pension schemes (reg 7, and see *Frankling v BPS Public Sector Ltd*).

9.75 Once reg 5 has operated so as to give effect to the consequences of the transfer, the transferred employee cannot pursue a successful claim against the transferor in respect of any matter transferred by the Regulations (see *Allan v Stirling District Council* para 9.89).

9.76 It is clear that the terms and conditions of employment of the transferred employees cannot be unilaterally changed by the transferee, but the question does arise as to whether there can be a consensual variation of those terms and conditions. In *Wilson v St Helens Borough Council*, because of financial difficulties, Lancashire County Council transferred a community home to St Helens Borough Council. The day before the transfer took place, employees at the home were dismissed by reason of redundancy, and the following day they were offered, and accepted, new but less favourable terms and conditions with St Helens. They subsequently claimed that St Helens were in breach of TUPE, and brought claims for unlawful deductions from their wages (see para 8.11). An employment tribunal agreed that TUPE applied, but held that they had been dismissed by Lancashire County Council for an economic, technical or organisational reason (ETO), and that there had been an effective variation of their terms and conditions of employment when they agreed to the new terms following the transfer. The decision was reversed by the EAT, who held that if the operative reason for the variation was the transfer, the variation was ineffective, and the terms and conditions of the original contract remained in force. The Court of Appeal reversed that decision, and that decision was upheld by the House of Lords. A dismissal because of the transfer is legally effective, and is not a nullity. A dismissed employee cannot compel the transferee to employ him. A variation in the terms and conditions of employment which is due to the transfer and for no other reason is invalid, but there can be a valid variation of those terms for reasons which are not due to the transfer.

9.77–9.85 If, at the time of the transfer, there is a collective agreement made between the transferor and a recognised trade union in respect of any employee who is to be transferred, then its application in relation to that employee shall have effect as if made by the trade union and the transferee (reg 6). Further, if the transferor recognised a trade union in respect of employees who are transferred, then such recognition will be deemed to have been made by the transferee, although, after the transfer, the recognition agreement may be varied or rescinded (reg 9).

Dismissal on transfers

9.86 Regulation 8(1) provides that where, either before or after the transfer, an employee of the transferor or transferee is dismissed, this will amount to an automatically unfair dismissal, if the principal reason for the dismissal was the transfer, or a reason connected with it. However, reg 8(2) provides that if the employee was dismissed for an economic, technical or organisational reason (ETO) which entailed a change in the workforce, the dismissal will be for a substantial reason of the kind such as to justify the dismissal of the employee holding the position which that employee held (*Collins v John Ansell and Partners Ltd*). The employer must still be able to show that he acted reasonably in treating that reason as a sufficient reason for the dismissal. If he does, the dismissal will be fair under ERA s 98(4), and the employee will be able to claim a redundancy payment, for redundancy is the commonest of the economic, technical or organisational reasons (*Gorictree Ltd v Jenkinson*). The decision must be one made on the need to entail changes in the workforce. If something else is sought to be changed (eg the pay of the employees who are transferred) the resultant dismissal does not come within reg 8(2), and the dismissal will be unfair (*Berriman v Delabole Slate Ltd*).

9.87 Potentially, 'economic, technical or organisational reasons' is a wide phrase, but it has been given a restricted meaning. In *Wheeler v Patel*, the EAT held that an economic reason entailing a change in the workforce must relate to the conduct of the business concerned, so that the transferor's attempts to obtain a higher price for the sale by acceding to the demands of the transferee to dismiss the workforce did not constitute an economic reason. An earlier decision to the contrary (*Anderson v Dalkeith Engineering Ltd*) has been disapproved (see *Gateway Hotels Ltd v Stewart*). Equally, a redundancy dismissal brought about in order to obtain a contract is an ETO reason, and is not analogous to a dismissal brought about solely to obtain a best price for the business (*Whitehouse v Charles Blatchford & Sons Ltd*). But if the transferee does not need the transferor's workforce, so that a redundancy situation is produced, this is within reg 8(2) (*Meikle v McPhail*). If, on the transfer of the business, employees are dismissed for reason of redundancy without the transferor being contractually required to do so, this will be evidence of the unfairness of the dismissals (*Litster v Forth Dry Dock and Engineering Co Ltd*) because even when there is a valid ETO reason, the employer must still act reasonably in treating that reason as a sufficient ground for dismissal (*Gibson v Ciro Cittero*).

9.88 If, following a transfer, a dismissal is necessary for an economic, technical or organisational reason (eg redundancy) then a failure to consult with the employee (as required by the normal rules relating to the need for consultation, eg see *Polkey v A E Dayton Services Ltd*, see para 12.14) will mean that the dismissal is unfair, although compensation may be minimal if it could be shown that consultation would not have made any difference (*Trafford v Sharpe & Fisher (Building Supplies) Ltd*).

9.89 If an employee is dismissed unfairly in connection with the transfer, his rights lie against the transferee, not the transferor. Further, the fact that the dismissal took place before the transfer will still result in the liability being transferred to the transferee, if the reason was connected with the transfer. Thus in *Allan v Stirling District Council* the employee was employed by the council's direct services department. Following competitive tendering, the work was awarded to a firm called Brophy Ltd. The employee was dismissed on 31 December 1992, and the following day Brophy's assumed responsibility for the service. The employee brought a claim for unfair dismissal against the council, which failed. The Inner House of the Court of Session held that reg 5(2) was clear and unambiguous. All the transferor's duties and liabilities in connection with the contract of employment were transferred to the transferee. The court noted that art 3(1) of the Directive gave member states an option of conferring joint liability, but this was not provided for in the regulations. It was stated in *Wendelboe v LJ Music* that if a state did not make use of this power, the transfer will have the effect of discharging the transferor from his obligations.

9.90–9.100 If an employee wishes to bring a complaint of unfair dismissal for a reason connected within a transfer within the provisions of TUPE, he is still required to meet the normal qualifying period of continuous employment of one year before bringing his complaint (the decision in *Milligan v Securicor Cleaning Ltd* has been nullified by reg 8 of the 1995 Amendment Regulations); and see *MRS Environmental Services Ltd v Marsh*).

Consultation on transfers (reg 10)

9.101   On the transfer of an undertaking, it is clear that employees of the transferor or the transferee may be affected in some way. The Transfer of Undertakings (Protection of Employment) Regulations 1981, as amended by the Collective Redundancies and Transfer of Undertakings (Protection of Employment) (Amendment) Regulations 1995–1999 provides that long enough before a relevant transfer to enable the employer of any affected employees to consult all the persons who are appropriate representatives of any of those affected employees, the employer shall inform those representatives of:

a.   the fact that the relevant transfer is to take place, when (approximately) it will take place, and the reasons for the transfer;

b.   the legal, economic and social implications of the transfer for the affected employees;

c.   the measures (if any) which the employer envisages he will take in relation to the affected employees; and

d.   the measures which the transferor envisages the transferee will take (if any) in relation to the affected employees. For this purpose, the transferee shall give to the transferor such information as will enable the transferor to perform this duty.

9.102   The information must be delivered to or sent to the appropriate representatives and, if either employer envisages that he will take measures in respect of any employees affected by the transfer, he shall enter into such consultations with a view to seeking the agreement of the representatives, he will consider representations made, reply to them, and, if he rejects them, state his reasons. If it is not reasonably practicable for him to consult as required, he shall take all such steps as are reasonably practicable in the circumstances. The employer shall also allow the appropriate representatives access to the affected employees, and shall afford them such accommodation and other facilities as may be appropriate.

9.103   The appropriate representatives of any employees are those employee representatives elected by them, or, if the employees are of a description in respect of which an independent trade union is recognised by the employer, the representatives of the trade union. If the employer recognises a trade union, and also has employee elected representatives, the employer must consult with the representatives of the trade union, not with the elected representatives. If there is no recognised trade union, the employer must consult with the employee elected representatives, and there are now detailed requirements governing how such representatives are to be elected (reg 10A(1)). They can either be employees who have been elected for the specific purpose of being given the information and consulted by the employer, or elected otherwise than for that purpose (eg staff representatives in an non-unionised situation) and it is appropriate for the employer to inform and consult with them. They must, however, be employed by the employer at the time they were elected. Employee representatives have a right not to suffer any detriment because he performed any function or activity as such an employee representative (or as a candidate for election). They are also entitled to reasonable time off work in order to perform their functions as such. The employer must also give the elected representatives access to the affected employees, as well as appropriate accommodation and facilities. It will be an unfair dismissal to dismiss an employee because he was an employee representative or candidate, and proposed to perform any functions or activities as such.

9.104 If the employer has invited affected employees to elect representatives, and the invitation was issued long enough before the time when the employer was required to give the information to enable those elections to take place, the employer will have complied with the consultation provisions if he does consult as soon as is reasonably practicable after the election of the representatives. If the employees fail to elect employee representatives within a reasonable time, after being invited to do so, the employer must disclose the information to each affected employee (reg 10(8A)).

9.105 A complaint that there has been a failure to consult may be made before the transfer has taken effect, because the duty to inform employee representatives has to be carried out long enough before the transfer to enable meaningful consultation to take place. The fact that a complaint to an employment tribunal must be made within three months after the transfer does not prevent a complaint being made before the transfer is completed (*South Durham Health Authority v UNISON*). It further appears that a complaint may be presented by an employee that the employer has failed to invite potentially redundant employees to elect representatives, contrary to the requirement in reg 10.

9.106 If an employer fails to inform or consult as required, the union or employee representative or affected employee may present a complaint to an employment tribunal. If the employer intends to rely on the defence that it was not reasonably practicable for him to perform the duty, he will need to show that there were special circumstances which rendered it not reasonably practicable to do so, and that he took all steps which were reasonably practicable. If the transferor intends to rely on the defence that the transferee failed to give him the required information within the requisite time, he must give notice of that fact to the transferee, thus making him a party to the proceedings.

9.107 If the complaint is upheld, the employment tribunal shall make a declaration to that effect, and may award 'appropriate compensation', which means up to a maximum of 13 weeks' pay, as the tribunal considers just and equitable, having regard to the seriousness of the failure of the employer to comply with his duty (reg 11). If at the same time, there is a complaint that the employer has failed to comply with s 188 of TULR(C)A (see para 18.112), any amount payable under these Regulations will no longer go towards reducing any protective award made under that Act.

9.108 The consultation provisions on transfers mirror those in s 188 of TULR(C)A (see para 18.112) on collective redundancies, except that there is no limit on the number of employees affected by the relevant transfer before the duty to consult arises.

9.109 The Acquired Rights Directive has recently been amended, and it is expected that changes will be made to TUPE by 2001. The rules relating to contracting out will be amended, workers' representatives will be allowed to negotiate changes to terms and conditions of employment in order to save jobs when an insolvent undertaking is transferred, and a transferor must notify the transferee of all the rights and obligations which will be transferred. Liability for occupational pension schemes will pass to the transferee.

CHAPTER 10

Performance of the contract of employment

Personal nature of the contract

10.1 A contract of employment is essentially one of personal service, which gives rise to duties and obligations on both sides, but the courts will not compel either side to carry out that contract by means of an order for specific performance or an injunction. In *Warner Bros Pictures Inc v Nelson* a film actress agreed to work for the claimants, and not to work for any other film company. It was held that an injunction would be granted restraining her from breaking the negative stipulation, for while she could not work for a rival film company, there were presumably other ways in which she could earn her living. However, the injunction would not be granted if its effect would be to compel the performance of the contract. In *Whitwood Chemical Co v Hardman* a manager agreed to devote the whole of his time to the company's business. He intended to work part-time for a rival company, and his employers sued for specific performance. It was held that the agreement was not enforceable, for while they could have obtained an injunction to restrain him from working for a competitor, the court would not compel him to work for the claimants.

10.2 By the same rule, the courts will not normally order an employer to continue to employ an employee (*Measham v AEEU*), though there are cases where this had been done (see para 10.5) and in recent years the courts have been more willing to do so than hitherto (see the cases cited in *Wadcock v London Borough of Brent*). There are also pressures on employers to offer reinstatement or re-engagement following employment tribunal proceedings (see Chapter 17) and a contract of employment may transfer from one employer to another when the Transfer of Undertakings (Protection of Employment) Regulations apply (see para 9.13). But the rule generally remains. In *Chappell v Times Newspapers Ltd*, members of a trade union were carrying on a disruptive campaign in support of a wage demand. The employers' association sent a telegram to the union stating that unless the campaign was called off, the members would be regarded as having broken their contracts of employment and thereby terminated their engagements. Several employees brought an action for an injunction to restrain their employers from terminating their contracts. It was held that, even on the assumption that the employers were acting in breach of contract, an injunction would not be granted, for to do so would be to compel specific performance by the employers. In particular, an injunction will not be granted if damages would be an adequate remedy for the alleged breach of contract (*Alexander v Standard Telephones and Cables plc*).

10.3   An exceptional case was *Hill v CA Parsons & Co Ltd*, where, following the making of a closed shop agreement with a trade union, the employers wrote to the claimant giving him one month's notice of dismissal because of his failure to join the union. The court thought that the claimant, who was a senior engineer, was entitled to at least six months' notice, and granted an injunction restraining the employers from treating the notice as having terminated the contract. (The effect of this was to delay the dismissal until after the coming into effect of the Industrial Relations Act 1971, which would have protected the claimant from dismissal for non-membership of the union.) But the court conceded that there were special circumstances in the case which enabled them to grant the injunction. There was no loss of confidence between the employers and the claimant, for the employers were acting under union pressure, and therefore there was no difficulty in enforcing the continuance of the contract.

10.4   *Hill v CA Parsons & Co Ltd* was followed in *Irani v Southampton and South West Hampshire Health Authority*, where the claimant was employed by the defendants as a part-time ophthalmologist. The claimant quarrelled with the consultant in charge of the clinic, and he was thus dismissed, although the defendants failed to operate the disputes procedure laid down in the Whitley Council Conditions of Service. The claimant was granted an injunction preventing the defendants from implementing the decision without invoking the disputes procedure. The court advanced three reasons. First, there was no lack of confidence in the claimant, for his professional competence was not in issue. Second, the claimant was seeking the protection of the disputes procedure which was incorporated into his contract. Third, damages would not be an adequate remedy. The balance of convenience lay in the granting of the injunction.

10.5   Whether the employee retains the confidence of the employer must be judged on the circumstances of the case, including the nature of the work, the people with whom the work is to be done, and the effect on the employer's operations if the injunction is granted. In *Powell v London Borough of Brent*, the claimant was told that she had been selected for promotion. It was then thought that the selection may have been in breach of the council's equal opportunity code, and her promotion was rescinded and the post readvertised. The claimant brought an action for an injunction to restrain the council from treating her other than as being promoted. By the time the case came to court, she was able to show that she had worked in the senior post without any complaints about her work and there were no problems in her working relationships. It was held that the injunction would be granted. A bare assertion by her employers that there was a lack of confidence was not sufficient.

10.6   The normal remedy in such cases is for the employee who is being threatened with dismissal to seek an interlocutory injunction restraining the proposed dismissal until the trial of action. The court must then consider whether the balance of convenience requires such a course of action (see *American Cyanamid Co v Ethicon Ltd*), leaving the substantial merits of the case to be argued subsequently at a full hearing. However, in *Jones v Gwent County Council*, the court held that under the Rules of the Supreme Court a judge can give a final ruling on any question of law or construction of document without a full trial of action, and such ruling can finally determine the matter, subject to an appeal. In this case, the claimant had been subjected to two disciplinary hearings which ended in her favour. Nonetheless the council brought further disciplinary proceedings on the ground that her return to work would cause an irrevocable breakdown in relationships between management and staff. It was decided that she should be dismissed. It was held that a declaration could be made that her dismissal was not valid, and a permanent injunction was granted, restraining the council from dismissing her other than in accordance with the proper procedure as laid down in her terms of appointment, and unless proper grounds existed.

10.7–10.15 TULR(C)A s 236 provides that no court shall compel an employee to work or attend at a place of work through the making of an order for specific performance, or an injunction. Thus an order cannot be granted, for example, to call off a strike.

Implied duties of the employer

10.16 We have seen (in Chapter 3) that there are a number of different ways by which the terms of a contract of employment may come into existence. We must now consider a number of duties and obligations which are imposed by law on both parties during the continuance of the performance of the contract. Some of these arise by virtue of the common law, but others arise out of the implications of legislative policy.

10.17 The distinction between those duties which are imposed by law and those which operate as an implied term of the contract is not at all clear. In more recent years, the courts have veered away from construing tortious liabilities in circumstances where contractual relationships exist. Prior to the massive explosion in employment law, which began about 35 years ago, there were few legal authorities on the contractual aspect of the employment relationship, and hence tort obligations emerged. More recently there is no dearth of legal authority arising from the contractual aspect, and rights have developed accordingly. The problem was explored by the House of Lords in *Scally v Southern Health and Social Services Board* (see para 3.67). But since the implied term theory is no longer limited by the 'business efficacy' test, but can also be extended to include terms which can be implied as a necessary incident of a definable category of contractual relationship (see *Liverpool City Council v Irwin*), it is possible to see the employers' duties as arising out of implied terms of the contract, rather than obligations imposed by law. The obligations once identified have now become implied terms of the contract.

A. Implied duty of trust and confidence

10.18 Now that the age when management could 'hire and fire' at will has gone, it is possible to assert that the employer has a legal duty to treat his employees with due respect and consideration, mindful of their needs and problems, sympathetic to their difficulties. It is no longer possible to treat an employee as an expendable chattel, or as an object without feelings and emotions. This duty is implicit in a number of cases which will be considered in due course when dismissal or disciplinary policies are discussed, but it is particularly evident where the employer is alleged to have been carrying out provocative conduct. In *Donovan v Invicta Airways Ltd* the employee resigned after what he considered to be a number of incidents where he thought the employer was being unfair, and claimed damages for breach of contract. In the circumstances it was held that such conduct, though irritating, was not substantial enough to amount to a breach, but it was stated that there was an implied duty that each of the parties to a contract of employment should treat the other with such a degree of consideration and courtesy as would enable the contract to be carried on.

10.19   It will be recalled (see para 3.72) that in *Malik v BCCI SA* the House of Lords held that there was a duty on an employer to conduct his business so as not to damage an employee's future prospects in the labour market. While the *Malik* decision was probably decided on its own facts, it does raise a number of interesting possibilities, including, for example, the case of an employee who has been dismissed for misconduct alleging that his reputation has been damaged by a false accusation, and suing accordingly. In the words of Lord Nicholls: 'Employers must take care not to damage their employees' future employment prospects by harsh and oppressive behaviour or by any other form of conduct which is unacceptable today as falling below the standards set by the implied trust and confidence term.'

10.20   Although to carry on a business in a corrupt and dishonest manner is an example of a breach of the implied term of trust and confidence, if a former employee wishes to claim damages as a result, he must produce credible evidence that prospective employers rejected his applications for employment on such grounds (*Bank of Credit and Commerce International SA v Ali*).

10.21   This duty arises at the outset of the employment, and continues during its performance right up to its termination. Employers will have to examine very closely their personnel and recruitment policies, for a mistake in selection or a failure to handle a problem in a proper manner could lead to an expensive action being brought in the future. For if an employer selects someone for a particular job, and that person does not have the necessary experience or capability for doing it, it is likely that the employer must accept some of the blame (*Bradley v Opperman Gears Ltd*). As a result, many employers are now commencing employees on the basis of a probationary period in order to assess properly their capabilities. The employer also has an obligation to ensure that the employee is provided with an adequate job description, with objectives clearly mapped out, is provided with adequate facilities and support staff, and is properly trained and supervised where necessary. A failure by the employer to attend to these and allied matters may well mean that any shortcomings on the employee's part may not be entirely his own fault, and it could well be unfair to dismiss him in these circumstances (*Burrows v Ace Caravan Co (Hull) Ltd*).

10.22   However, there are limits to the duty of trust and confidence. For example, in *University of Nottingham v Eyett* it was held that the duty did not create a positive obligation on an employer to advise an employee that if he delayed taking retirement for another month, when he would have received a salary increase, his pension would have been correspondingly higher.

B. Duty to provide work

10.23   The whole question of 'the right to work' is a confused one, principally because of the different meanings which may be given to the phrase. It may mean the right to work without a trade union membership card, as in *Hill v CA Parsons & Co Ltd*, or the right not to be unreasonably discriminated against, as in *Nagle v Feilden*, where the claimant argued that she had a right to obtain a licence to train horses despite the existence of an unwritten rule of the Jockey Club not to grant such licences to women. It can even mean the right to call on the State to provide jobs. In *Langston v Chrysler United Kingdom* the claimant objected to being compelled to join a trade union. The other employees threatened a strike, and so Chrysler suspended him from work for an indefinite period. He claimed that he had been denied the right to work, and in the Court of Appeal it was suggested that the courts would protect a man's right to work in appropriate circumstances, particularly if he was being denied job satisfaction. However, when the case was remitted to the National Industrial Relations Court, it was held that such documents as the Universal Declaration of Human Rights, para 9 of the 1971 Code of Practice, and other poetic allusions were considerations of public policy, rather than statements of contractual rights, and it was the contract which is the determining factor.

10.24   As a general rule, the employer is not under an obligation to provide work for his employee. As Asquith J said in *Collier v Sunday Referee Publishing Co*: 'Provided I pay my cook her wages regularly, she cannot complain if I choose to take any or all of my meals out'. Indeed, there are many circumstances when the employer may find himself unable to provide work for his employees, for example, as a result of reorganisation, shortage of materials, lack of orders, due to a strike, etc, where the employer may prefer to keep his workforce together and pay them for doing nothing. However, there are certain special circumstances where the failure to provide work may result in the breach of a legal duty.

a.   If the failure to provide work can lead to a loss of reputation or publicity. In *Herbert Clayton and Jack Waller Ltd v Oliver*, an actor was given a leading role in a musical comedy. He was subsequently offered a lesser role, but at the same salary. It was held that the employer was in breach of contract, because the nature of the work was as important as the salary to be paid.

b.   If the failure to provide work leads to a reduction in the employee's actual or potential earnings. Thus an employee is entitled to be given an opportunity to earn his commission (*Turner v Goldsmith*) or to earn a reasonable sum if he is on piecework (*Devonald v Rosser & Sons*). In *Bauman v Hulton Press Ltd* it was held that the employers 'were bound to give the claimant a reasonable amount of work to enable him to earn that which the parties must be taken to have contemplated'. It was the lack of opportunity to earn premium payments for hours worked on night-shift and overtime which constituted the breach of contract by the employers in *Langston's* case (above).

c.   There are dicta in *Langston's* case which suggest that if an employee needs practice in order to maintain or develop his skills in employment, the employer is under a duty to provide a reasonable amount of work for this purpose. This view has received further support from the 'garden leave' cases (see *Provident Financial Group plc v Hayward*, para 9.26).

d.   Recent decisions seem to lean to the view that a failure to provide work may constitute a repudiation of the contract by the employer if it is possible to imply a term into the contract that the employer shall provide suitable work. This appears to be particularly true when the employee is appointed to a specific office. In *Breach v Epsylon Industries Ltd*, the EAT thought that some of the earlier decisions on this subject were somewhat out of date and perhaps old fashioned in their approach. Consequently, in modern cases there may be facts which more readily lead to the conclusion that there is an implied term to the effect that there is an obligation to provide work. In *William Hill Organisation Ltd v Tucker* it was stated in the Court of Appeal that times had moved on from the days when only musicians, actors etc were perceived as requiring regular exercise of their skills and public performances in order to keep up their reputation. All employees with specific skills are entitled to exercise those skills, even during notice periods, provided that there is work to be done (see para 19.29).

e. If the contract of employment provides for suspension with pay pending the outcome of disciplinary enquiries, or criminal proceedings, there is no obligation on the employer to provide the employee with work or an opportunity to work overtime (*McClory v Post Office*).

C. Duty to pay wages or other remuneration when there is no work

10.25 The express terms of the contract will normally determine the amount of remuneration to be paid to the employee, but we must consider the situation where, because there is no work to do, the employee cannot earn his money. The question is, to what extent, if at all, does the employer undertake to pay the employee wages if the employer cannot provide work for the employee to do? To seek the answer, we must state the general rule, and then seek any modification which may exist by virtue of any express or implied terms of the contract of employment.

10.26 The general rule at common law is that an employer must pay the wages of all employees if they are available for work but none is provided by the employer. Clearly, this is the position in respect of salaried staff (who are paid weekly or monthly: see *Miller v Hamworthy Engineering Ltd*, para 3.184), and there is no legal distinction between them and hourly-paid workers or piece-workers. An hourly-paid worker is entitled to be paid for the number of hours he makes himself available for work, not the number of hours the employers permit him to work, and a piece-worker, though paid for the work actually done, is entitled to expect that the employer will give him an opportunity to earn his wages. Because of this general common law rule, it was a comparatively simple matter to imply into the contract of an employee a term that he would be paid if there was no work. In *Devonald v Rosser & Sons* the plaintiff was a piece-worker. His employers closed down the factory, and gave him one month's notice. It was held that there was an implied term in his contract that the employer would find him work to do, and he recovered damages based on his prior average earnings. An argument by the employers that there was a trade custom to the contrary was rejected by the court, because a custom has to be reasonable, certain and notorious. But if the failure to provide work was due to circumstances outside the control of the employer, different considerations could apply. In *Browning v Crumlin Valley Collieries* a colliery had to close down because it was in a dangerous condition, through no fault of the employers. It was held that there was an implied term that the employers were not obliged to pay wages in these circumstances.

10.27 The common law rule, however, can be varied by an express or implied term to the contrary. Thus if the contract states that there shall be no payment during a lay-off or in respect of short-time working, the employers will incur no obligation to pay. In *Hulme v Ferranti Ltd* the claimant was employed on terms that if there was no work, he would not be paid. He was laid off as a result of a strike involving other workers in the plant, and it was held that he was not entitled to be paid during that time. But the modern practice of concluding guarantee payment agreements lends greater credence to the view that the present law is that in respect of hourly or piece-workers, there is an implied term that they will not be paid during a lay-off or short-time working. For example, if an employer agrees to pay a minimum guarantee week to employees who have been employed by him for a certain period, those who do not qualify can scarcely be in a better position. The very existence of the guarantee payments rights in the Employment Rights Act 1996 (see Chapter 7) supports this view, for such rights would virtually be unnecessary if the common law rule was of general application. Nonetheless, a lay-off without pay is either a temporary suspension or a dismissal with the prospect of re-engagement, and the employer may only treat it as a suspension if there is an expressed or implied term in the contract giving him that right (*Jewell v Neptune Concrete Ltd*). In the absence of such a term the employee is entitled to treat the suspension as repudiatory conduct by the employer, and hence a dismissal. In appropriate circumstances (see Chapter 18) he may claim redundancy pay. Indeed, since there must be few contracts of employment which made provision for such eventuality, the Redundancy Payments Act 1965 was apparently based on the assumption that there is a general existence of an implied term that employees who are laid off or who are on short time are not entitled to be paid (see now ERA s 147).

D. Duty of confidentiality

10.28 Just as there is a duty on employees not to disclose confidential information about the employer's business (see para 10.136) so there is a similar duty on an employer not to disclose to third persons confidential information about the employee. This duty does not depend on any express or implied term of the contract (*Lord Advocate v Scotsman Publications Ltd* per Lord Couldsfield). In *Dalgleish v Lothian and Borders Police Board*, the employers held the names and addresses of all their employees. They were asked to provide this information to a local authority, for the purpose of discovering the identity of persons who had not paid the poll tax. The claimants sought an interim injunction restraining the employers from disclosing this information, which was granted. The information was not in the public domain, and was given by the employees to the employers for the purpose of the employment relationship, and for no other purpose. Hence it retained a characteristic of being confidential information, which could not be disclosed without the consent of the employees.

E. Duty to indemnify

10.29 Any expenses reasonably incurred by the employee in the performance of his contract ought properly to be met by the employer. Normally, one would expect express agreement to this effect, for example, travelling or lodging allowances, but circumstances do arise when an employee spends his own money in pursuance of his employer's business, and it is submitted that he is entitled to be reimbursed. More difficult is the situation which arises when the employee commits a wrongful act. If this was done for the employer's business, and was authorised, or if the employee was acting under his employer's orders, then the employee is entitled to be indemnified for any personal loss he suffers.

10.30 For example, if an employer requires an employee to take out the firm's van, which has a defective tyre, and the employee is consequently fined, then it is reasonable to expect the employer to reimburse the amount, even though he may be prosecuted in addition. But if the work can be done in a lawful or unlawful manner, and the employee choose the latter option, the employer would not be required to reimburse such expenditure. For example, if the employee, in order to deliver some goods, parks illegally, then unless he was told to perform his work in this manner, he must bear any subsequent fine himself. In *Gregory v Ford*, the claimant was injured due to the negligent driving of the defendant, whose employer did not have a valid third-party insurance policy as required by the Road Traffic Act 1988. It was held that there was an implied term of the contract that the employer would not require the employee to do an unlawful act, and therefore the employer should indemnify the employee in respect of the damages which were awarded to the claimant. In *Re Famatina Development Corpn Ltd*, a consulting engineer employed by the company was asked to prepare a report on the conduct of the managing director. The latter brought an action for an alleged libel, which the engineer defended. It was held that he was entitled to be indemnified by the company for his costs in defending the action, for he had been requested by his directors to make the report, which was therefore in the course of his duties as an employee.

F. Duty to insure

10.31 In respect of work activities taking place within the United Kingdom, an employer is obliged to take out compulsory employers' liability insurance, for the benefit of his employees of at least £5 million (Employers' Liability (Compulsory Insurance) Regulations 1998). However, an employer owes no duty in tort to any employee who is working abroad to take out appropriate insurance cover against special risks, or to advise the employee to take out his own cover. In *Reid v Rush & Tompkins Group plc*, the claimant worked for the defendants in Ethiopia. He received severe injuries in a road accident, which was the fault of the other driver, for whom the defendants were not responsible. The claimant was unable to obtain compensation from the other driver, as there is no third-party insurance in Ethiopia, and so he claimed damages from his employers. His statement of claim was struck out. An employer does not owe a duty to inform or advise on the potential danger of suffering economic loss in the form of uncompensated injuries.

G. References

10.32 In the absence of any express contractual obligation, the general rule is that an employer is under no legal duty to provide an employee or an ex-employee with a reference (*Gallear v JF Watson & Son Ltd*) although in *Spring v Guardian Assurance plc* (see below) Lord Woolf suggested that there may be circumstances in which it is necessary to imply a term into a contract of employment that the employer would provide the employee with a reference, particularly in those areas of employment where it is normal practice to require a reference from a previous employer before employment is offered, eg in the financial services industry. An employer who does provide a reference about an existing employee who is seeking employment with another employer is under an obligation to ensure that it is fair and reasonable, and a failure to do so may amount to a breach of the implied duty of trust and confidence entitling the employee to resign and claim constructive dismissal. In *TSB Bank plc v Harris* the employers sent a reference to a prospective employer about the employee which was factually true, but potentially misleading. Thus it stated that there were a number of complaints against her which were outstanding, but these complaints had never been drawn to her attention, and she had never had an opportunity to comment on them or to give her explanation. Her claim for constructive dismissal was upheld, even though she was considering leaving in any case. There is difference between leaving without a job to go to and leaving in order to go to another job.

10.33 But although the duty is to provide a reference which is in substance fair, true and accurate, it does not have to be full and comprehensive in every case. In *Bartholomew v London Borough of Hackney* the local authority commenced disciplinary proceedings against the claimant, in connection with alleged irregularities. Eventually, a settlement was reached whereby the claimant took voluntary severance, and the disciplinary action was terminated. Subsequently, in response to a request for a reference, the employers stated that at the time of leaving their employment, the claimant was under suspension, disciplinary action had been commenced, but this lapsed on the claimant's departure from the employment. The claimant claimed that the employers were in breach of their legal duty of care, because the reference, although factually correct, was unfair. The Court of Appeal dismissed his claim. Although the form of the reference might have been improved upon in some respects it was not unfair, inaccurate or false. The employers also owed a duty to the recipients of the reference not to be unfair or to mislead.

10.34 So far as existing employees are concerned, the provisions of the Sex Discrimination Act and the Race Relations Act protect an employee from victimisation because s/he had brought proceedings under either Act against the employer. It will be recalled that in *Chief Constable of West Yorkshire Police v Khan* (see para 4.207) the employer refused to provide a reference for a police officer who was seeking promotion with another police authority, because the employer feared that it would prejudice his defence to a claim for race discrimination which was being pursued by that officer in the employment tribunal. This refusal constituted victimisation under the Race Relations Act.

10.35 Several pitfalls can occur when providing a reference about an ex-employee to a prospective employer. First, a derogatory reference may expose the giver of the reference to an action for defamation. This may be defended on the ground that the statements made were true, or, if untrue, were made on an occasion when the law confers qualified privilege, and the statements were made without malice, in the sense of an improper motive. Next, the employer owes a duty of care to the ex-employee to ensure that the reference is not prepared carelessly or negligently, and will be consequently liable for damages in respect of any economic loss which flows from the negligent misstatement (*Spring v Guardian Assurance plc*). In this case, Lord Slynn suggested that the employers could avoid any liability by making it clear to the ex-employee that they will only provide a reference if he accepts that there will be a disclaimer of liability to him and to the recipient.

10.36   We have seen that so far as ex-employees are concerned, there is no general duty to provide a reference. However, a different rule may arise out of European law. In *Coote v Granada Hospitality Ltd* (see para 4.34) it was held that the Equal Treatment Directive would be undermined unless national laws provided some protection against a person being victimised because s/he sought to enforce his/her rights under the Directive, and a failure to provide a reference for an ex-employee because she had previously brought proceedings against her former employer alleging unfair maternity dismissal was held to be an act of victimisation for which the employers were liable. It is doubtful if the same rule would apply in race discrimination cases, because (a) *Coote v Granada Hospitality Ltd* was decided under European law (which, at the present time, does not apply to race discrimination), and (b) the Race Relations Act only confers rights on employees, not ex-employees (see *Adekeye v Post Office*, para 4.235).

10.37   On the other hand, to give a commendatory reference about a prospective employee which is untrue, and which is relied upon by a subsequent employer to his detriment, may well lead to an action based on deceit or negligent misstatement, unless the reference is qualified by a disclaimer of responsibility (*Hedley Bryne & Co Ltd v Heller & Partners Ltd*).

10.38   A further problem associated with the provision of a reference can arise in dismissal cases. In *Castledine v Rothwell Engineering Ltd*, one of the reasons given by the employer for dismissing the firm's buyer was that he was incapable of performing his job adequately. The tribunal found this difficult to reconcile with the reference given by the employer, which stated that the employee 'had carried out his duties satisfactorily, often under difficult conditions'. Not surprisingly, the tribunal found that the employee had been unfairly dismissed! And in *Haspell v Restron and Johnson Ltd* the respondents gave a reference which was laudatory of the claimant. It was held that they were estopped from relying on criticisms of her performance as a reason for her dismissal. Faced with these problems, a prudent employer may well prefer to refuse to give a reference in doubtful cases.

H. The right to privacy

10.39   There are many occasions during the performance of the contract of employment when an employer will be monitoring the employee's performance, as a matter of routine. The problem arises when such actions become intrusive into an employee's private life. For example, an employer may wish to monitor the employee's telephone calls, in order to assess performance, ensure that quality standards are met, that customer satisfaction is achieved, and provide a valuable record in the event of a subsequent dispute with customers or suppliers, etc. But what happens when the employee's telephone call is of a personal nature? Does this amount to an unwarranted infringement of his right to privacy?

10.40   The routine use of e-mail and the internet by employees during working hours will exacerbate the problem. The temptation for employees to use these facilities for their own purposes is ever-increasing, whether it be for booking holidays, purchasing goods for private use, playing games, or downloading pornography! The questions must be thus posed: can the employer (a) implement surveillance, (b) listen in and/or record such activities and (c) take disciplinary action in the event of suspected misuse? Clearly, a balance must be drawn between the employee's right to privacy on the one hand, and the legitimate interests of the employer in ensuring that the employee is doing his work properly, and not abusing facilities provided.

10.41 So far as the law is concerned, art 8 of the European Convention of Human Rights provides
(1) Everyone has the right to respect for his private and family life, his home and his correspondence.
(2) There shall be no interference by a public authority with the exercise of this right except such as is in accordance with the law and is necessary in a democratic society in the interests of national security, public safety or the economic well-being of the country, for the prevention of disorder or crime, for the protection of health or morals, or for the protection of the rights and freedoms of others.

10.42 It will be recalled (see para 1.166) that the Human Rights Act 1998 is designed to give effect to the provisions of the European Convention, and although this only applies to public authorities, doubtless the courts and tribunals will use it as an aid in the decision-making process when dealing with the private employer.

10.43 The right to privacy was an issue in *Halford v United Kingdom*, where the claimant, who was a senior police officer, alleged that she had been turned down for promotion because of her sex, and brought a claim of sex discrimination. She also alleged that her telephone calls at work and at home was being intercepted for the purpose of obtaining information to be used against her in the tribunal proceedings. The sex discrimination case was settled, but she brought further proceedings in the European Court of Human Rights, claiming that the interception of her telephone calls was an infringement of her right to privacy. Her claim succeeded. The Court held that telephone calls made from business premises may be covered by the notion of private life and correspondence within the meaning of art 8 of the Convention. The Court refused to accept the notion that an employer could, without prior knowledge of the employee, monitor calls made by the employee on telephones provided by the employer.

10.44 The Interception of Communications Act 1985 makes it a criminal offence to intercept a communication in the course of its transmission by post or by a public telecommunication system (unless the interceptor has a warrant, or believes that the recipient consents to the interception), but this would not apply to an employer's internal telephone system at the workplace. Nonetheless, an employee can expect that personal telephone calls made or received by him at his place of work are private, and an interception by the employer could amount to a breach of the implied duty of trust and confidence, leading to a potential constructive dismissal claim. But there will be no such breach if the employer has the right, by virtue of the contractual provisions, to intercept, monitor or otherwise impose surveillance on such communications. Also, if the employer warns the employee that private telephone calls should not be made or received at work, or that computer use will be monitored, or that private mail received will be opened, no breach of the right to privacy will occur. Clearly, the grievance procedure could be used to deal with complaints etc, by the employee, and the disciplinary procedure invoked against employees who abuse the system. The telephone regulator Oftel, in giving guidance to employers following the ruling in *Halford's* case, has suggested that the provision of a telephone line at work, which may be used by employees for private communications would clearly remove a source of potential trouble. Otherwise, employees should be warned that their calls will be monitored or recorded. Further, external callers may need to be notified that there is a possibility that their calls may be monitored or recorded.

10.45 Clearly, similar principles apply to the use (or misuse) of computer facilities, e-mail, internet communications, and so on. It may be that personal log facilities can be provided to ensure privacy, or an itemised call record would be less intrusive. To impose a complete ban may well be excessive and cause resentment, but to do nothing until the matter becomes a serious issue is likely to lead to greater problems.

10.46 The Regulation of Investigatory Powers Bill has recently been introduced into Parliament, and would enable employees to sue their employer if they believed it had unlawfully intercepted a telephone call made to a third party on the employer's network. However, regulations would describe the kind of interception that it would be lawful to carry out in the course of business, eg the recording of incoming calls so as to keep a record of transactions.

I. Duty to ensure employee's safety

10.47 Undoubtedly the most important aspect of the employer's duty which is implied by law is the duty to take reasonable care to ensure the safety of his employees. There are a number of common law rules which determine the extent of that duty, and in addition there are certain statutory provisions designed to ensure the employee's safety which, if broken or not observed by the employer, may lead to an action for damages by an injured employee based on a breach of statutory duties. Frequently, the two actions are run together, so that an employee may succeed for breach of the common law duty and/or a breach of the statutory duty, though, of course, only one set of damages will be awarded. The purpose of the common law rules is to compensate for injuries incurred as a result of the employer's negligence; the object of the statute will be accident prevention enforced by criminal penalties, but with a potential liability for compensation as well. But as Goddard LJ said in *Hutchinson v London and North Eastern Rly Co*, 'The real incentive for the observance by employers of their statutory duties … is not their liability to substantial fines, but the possibility of heavy claims for damages'. The whole question of compensation for injuries at work was reviewed by the Royal Commission on Civil Liability (the Pearson Commission, see para 10.108), but no significant changes were recommended in its report.

10.48 The duty owed by the employer is in respect of the employee's physical and mental health, including ill-health caused by overwork (*Johnstone v Bloomsbury Health Authority*), psychiatric illness (*Frost v Chief Constable of South Yorkshire Police*) and stress and anxiety caused thereby (*Walker v Northumberland County Council*). But if the employers do not know of the risk, or if, having knowledge, they take such steps as are reasonable in the circumstances to minimise the risk, or provide appropriate healthcare, no liability arises (*Petch v Customs and Excise Comrs*). A difficult case was *White v Chief Constable of South Yorkshire Police*, where it was held that a policeman was not entitled to recover damages for psychiatric illness suffered as a result of assisting in the aftermath of the Hillsborough disaster, either as an employee or a rescuer.

10.49   The duty of the employer to take care is one aspect of the law of negligence which requires everyone to ensure that his activities do not cause injury or damage to another through an act of negligence. The standard of care which an employer must observe is, as Lord Oaksey pointed out in *Paris v Stepney Borough Council*, 'The care which an ordinary prudent employer would take in all the circumstances'. The employer does *not* guarantee that an employee will not be injured; he only undertakes to take reasonable care, and he will only be liable if there is some lack of care on his part in failing to prevent something which was reasonably foreseeable. The employee, on his part, must be prepared to look after himself, and not expect to be able to blame the employer for every incident which takes place. In *Vinnyey v Star Paper Mills*, the claimant was instructed by the foreman to clear and clean a floor area which had been made slippery by a viscous fluid. The foreman provided proper equipment and gave clear instructions. The claimant was injured when he slipped on the floor, and it was held that the employer was not liable, for there was no reasonably foreseeable risk in the performance of such a simple task. So too, in *Lazarus v Firestone Tyre and Rubber Co Ltd*, where the claimant was knocked down in the general rush to get to the canteen. The court held that this was not the sort of behaviour which grown persons could be protected against. Such cases are in line with a number of judicial statements made in recent years deprecating 'any tendency to treat the relationship between employer and skilled workman as equivalent to that of nurse and imbecile child' (per Lord Simmons in *Smith v Austin Lifts*), or that of 'schoolmaster and pupil' (per Devlin LJ in *Withers v Perry Chain Co Ltd*).

10.50   Equally, if an employer does not know of the danger, and could not be expected to know in the light of current knowledge, or did not foresee the danger and could not be expected to foresee it, he will not be liable. In *Down v Dudley, Coles Long Ltd* an employee was partially deafened by the noise from a cartridge-assisted hammer gun. At the then state of medical knowledge (ie in 1964), a reasonable employer would not have known of the potential danger of using this particular piece of equipment without providing safety precautions, and hence the employer was not liable for the injury. But once the danger is discovered, he must take all reasonable steps to protect his employees from the consequences of risks which have hitherto been unforeseeable. In *Wright v Dunlop Rubber Co*, the employers used an anti-oxidant known as Nonox S from 1940 onwards. The manufacturers then discovered that the substance was capable of causing bladder cancer, and informed the defendants that all employees who had been exposed to it should be screened and tested. This was not done for some time, and thus the employers, as well as the manufacturers, were held liable to the claimants.

10.51   The matter was summarised by Swanwick J in *Stokes v GKN Ltd*.
a.   The employer must take positive steps to ensure the safety of his employees in the light of the knowledge which he has or ought to have.
b.   The employer is entitled to follow current recognised practice unless in the light of common sense or new knowledge this is clearly unsound.

c. Where there is developing knowledge, he must keep reasonably abreast with it, and not be too slow in applying it.

d. If he has greater than average knowledge of the risk, he must take more than average precautions.

e. He must weigh up the risk (in terms of the likelihood of injury and possible consequences) against the effectiveness of the precautions needed to meet the risk, and the cost and inconvenience.

10.52–10.60 Applying these tests, if the employer falls below the standards of a reasonable and prudent employer, he will be negligent. On the other hand, if the employer takes all such steps as are reasonably practicable, he will not be liable at common law (*Darby v GKN Screws and Fasteners Ltd*).

Duty to unborn children

10.61 Under the Congenital Disabilities (Civil Liability) Act 1976, an employer may be liable to a child of an employee who is born disabled as a result of any breach of legal duty, whether imposed by statute or by common law, to the child's parent. The child may thus sue in respect of a pre-natal injury suffered, whether or not the parent suffered any injury, and whether or not the employer knew of the existence of the foetus. The Act was intended to be a stop-gap measure until the passing of legislation consequent on the Pearson Report (para 10.108). The right of the child to sue is contingent on the existence of a right for the parent to sue; in other words, the claim is as good as, but no better than, the claim of the parent. Any contributory negligence on the part of the parent may reduce the child's damages.

Personal nature of the duty

10.62 The duty of the employer is a personal one, in the sense that he cannot absolve himself by delegating the duty to someone else. In *Wilsons & Clyde Coal Co Ltd v English*, the employer was compelled by law to employ a colliery agent who was responsible for mine safety; nonetheless, it was held that the employer was liable for an unsafe system of work in the mine. Thus it can never be a defence to argue that the employer has assigned the task of securing and maintaining safety precautions to a safety officer or other person.

10.63 Equally, the duty is owed to each employee as an individual, not to them all collectively. This means that one must take greater precautions when dealing, for example, with inexperienced employees, or with new and untrained employees or with young persons, etc, than one might do with more responsible staff. In *Paris v Stepney Borough Council* the claimant worked chipping away at rust and other superfluous rubbish which had accumulated underneath buses. Goggles were not provided for this work, for it was not customary to do so. The claimant only had one eye, and he was totally blinded when a splinter entered his good eye. It was held that the employers were liable. They should have foreseen that there was a risk of greater injury to the employee, and provided goggles for him, even though they may not have been under such a duty with respect to other employees.

10.64 Clearly, a higher standard of care must be shown to employees who lack a sufficient or adequate command of the English language, to ensure that they are properly trained and clearly instructed, so as not to cause injuries to themselves and to others. In *James v Hepworth and Grandage Ltd* the employers put up large notices informing employees that they should wear spats for their personal protection. Unknown to them, the claimant could not read, and when he was injured he claimed damages from his employers. His claim failed. He had observed other workmen wearing spats, and the court concluded that his failure to make enquiries meant that even if he had been informed about the notice, he would not have worn them. But with the growth of foreign labour in our factories, the problem is likely to cause growing concern, particularly as such labour tends to concentrate in the initial stages in those industries which have serious safety hazards. The responsibility of the safety officer, as the 'agent' of the employer, to ensure that the work can be done in safety is likely to be very onerous in practice (see *Hawkins v Ian Ross (Castings) Ltd*).

10.65 An employer has a duty to warn an employee of risks to his health and safety where those risks are not common knowledge and cannot be guarded against by the taking of sensible precautions, and where that knowledge would affect the employee's decision to accept the work. But the employer does not guarantee absolutely the safety of the employee. In *White v Holbrook Precision Castings Ltd* the claimant was employed as a grinder. He developed Reynaud's Disease (vibration white finger) and sued for damages. His claim was dismissed. The claimant knew of the risk when he accepted the employment, and the employers were merely aware that the disease could cause minor discomfort. No precautions had ever been suggested or were viable. The claimant would still have taken the employment had he been specifically told of the risk. However, given the current state of medical and scientific knowledge, a different conclusion may well be reached nowadays (see *Shepherd v Firth Brown Ltd*).

10.66–10.75 Modern technologies and modern working methods inevitably bring about new and special problems, and legal decisions must be adapted from existing principles to meet the factual situations which arise. Thus claims have succeeded and failed in respect of repetitive strain injury or work related upper limb disorder (*Pickford v ICI plc, Alexander v Midland Bank plc*), vibration white finger (*Armstrong v British Coal Corpn*), work induced stress (*Petch v Customs and Excise Comrs, Walker v Northumberland County Council*), acts of violence (*Haughton v Hackney Borough Council*), breach of health and safety regulations (see para 11.79), and so on.

The three-fold nature of the duty

10.76 Although recent cases have stressed that there is only one single duty to take care, it is convenient to examine the nature of that duty under three sub-headings.

A. Safe plant and appliances

10.77 This means that all the equipment, tools, machinery, plant, etc, where the employee works shall be reasonably safe for work. In *Bradford v Robinson Rentals Ltd*, a driver was required to drive an unheated van on a 400-mile journey during a bitterly cold spell of weather. It was held that the employer was liable when the driver suffered frostbite as a consequence. In *Close v Steel Co of Wales Ltd*, it was suggested by Lord Goddard that if an employer knows that a machine has a tendency to throw out flying parts so as to constitute a danger to the operative, this could well amount to common law negligence on the part of the employer if he fails to take reasonable precautions.

10.78   However, if an employer purchased tools or equipment from a reputable supplier, and has no knowledge of any defect in them, he will have performed his duty to take care, and will not be liable for negligence (see *Davie v New Merton Board Mill*s). This would not be so if the equipment was bought second-hand from, say, a scrapyard. If a remedy existed in *Davie's* case, it would be for the injured employee to sue the person responsible for the defect under the general law of negligence as propounded in the leading case of *Donoghue v Stevenson*, but frequently this might prove to be difficult or impossible in practice. The employee might not be in a position to prove just who was negligent. It might be a firm of stevedores at the docks, a foreign manufacturer, and so on. In view of these problems, the law was changed with the passing of the Employers' Liability (Defective Equipment) Act 1969. This provides that if an employee suffers a personal injury in the course of his employment in consequence of a defect in equipment provided by his employers for the purpose of the employers' business, and the defect is attributable to the fault of a third party, the injury shall be deemed to be attributable to the negligence of the employer. Thus, should facts similar to *Davie's* case arise again, the employee would be able to sue his employer for the 'deemed' negligence, and the employer, for his part, would be able to recover the amount of damages paid from the third party whose fault it really was. At the same time, the Employers' Liability (Compulsory Insurance) Act 1969 was passed, to ensure that all employers had valid insurance cover to meet personal injuries claims from their employees.

10.79   If an employer is aware that there are defects in tools or equipment he has bought then he should withdraw them from circulation if he wishes to avoid liability. In *Taylor v Rover Co Ltd* a batch of chisels had been badly hardened by the manufacturers. One had, in fact, shattered, without causing any injury, but the batch was still in use when another chisel shattered, injuring the claimant in his eye. The employers were held liable.

B. Safe system of work

10.80   Here we must consider all the factors which concern the manner in which the work is to be done. The layout, the systems laid down, the training and supervision, the provision of warnings, protective clothing, special instructions, and so forth, are all relevant. In *Barcock v Brighton Corpn*, the claimant was employed at an electricity sub-station. A certain method of testing was in operation, which was unsafe, and in consequence the claimant was injured. The employers were held liable. But if the employer gives proper instructions which the employee fails to observe, the employer will not be liable for a subsequent injury. In *Charlton v Forrest Printing Ink Co Ltd* a senior employee was required to collect the firm's wages of £1,500 each Friday from the bank. Because, several years earlier, there had been a wage snatch of the firm's payroll, the managing director had given instructions that the collection arrangements should be varied each week, for example, by using taxis instead of private cars, by going at different times and by different routes. Contrary to these instructions, in the course of time, a collecting pattern set in, and the employee suffered severe injuries when he was robbed in an attack. In the High Court, the judge found for the claimant arguing that the employers had been negligent in not employing a professional security firm, but this decision was reversed on appeal. The vast majority of firms of that size in that area made their own payroll collection, and hence the employers could not be said to be negligent in carrying on with that practice. Although there was a risk, they had taken reasonable steps to minimise or eliminate it. The Court of Appeal thought that the claimant's remedy would be through an application to the Criminal Injuries Compensation Board, which has funds for such contingencies.

10.81 If there are safety precautions laid down, the employee must be told what they are; if safety equipment is provided, it must be available for use. In *Finch v Telegraph Construction and Maintenance Co Ltd* the claimant was employed as a grinder. Goggles had been provided, but he was not told where they were. The employers were held to be liable when he was injured by a flying piece of metal whilst doing his work.

10.82 But if the employer, though not providing the safety precautions, can show that even if he had provided them the employee would not have used them, he may escape liability. In *Cummings (or McWilliam) v Sir William Arroll Ltd*, a steel erector fell from a scaffolding and was killed. The employer had provided safety belts in the past, but these had not been used, and they had been taken away to be used on another site. It was held that even though the employer was negligent in not providing the safety belts, it was unlikely that the employee would have used them had they been available. Accordingly, the employer's negligence was not the cause of the death, since this would have occurred anyway.

10.83 The more dangerous the process, the greater the need for safety precautions. On the other hand, the employer cannot be expected to be held liable in respect of accidents which occur in simple situations, as *Vinnyey's* case (para 10.49 above) illustrates. A situation which gives rise to some legal difficulties is where the employer provides the safety precautions, but the employees fail or refuse to use them. Is the duty of the employer a merely passive one, to provide and do no more? Or is it an active one, to exhort, propagandise, instruct or even compel their use? It is submitted that the answer to these questions can be given in four propositions.

a. If the risk is an obvious one, and the injury resulting from the failure to use the precautions is not likely to be serious, then the employer's duty is a passive one of merely providing the precautions, informing the employees and leaving it to them to decide for themselves whether or not to use them. In *Qualcast (Wolverhampton) Ltd v Haynes*, an experienced workman was splashed by molten metal on his legs. Spats were available, but the employers did nothing to ensure that they were worn. The injury, though doubtless painful, was not of a serious nature, and the employers were held not liable.

b. If the risk is that of a serious injury, then the duty of the employer is a higher one of doing all he can to ensure that the workmen will use the safety precautions which are provided. In *Nolan v Dental Manufacturing Co Ltd* a toolsetter was injured when a chip flew off a grinding wheel. Because of the seriousness of the injury should such occur, it was held that the employer should have insisted that protective goggles were worn.

c.   If the risk is an insidious one, or one the seriousness of which the employee would not readily appreciate, then again, it is the duty of the employer to do all he can by way of propaganda, constant reminders, exhortations, etc, to try to get the employees to use the precautions. In *Berry v Stone Manganese and Marine Ltd*, the claimant was working in an environment where the noise levels were dangerously high. Ear muffs had been provided, but no effort was made to ensure their use. It was held that as the workmen would not readily appreciate the dangers of injury to their hearing if they did not use the ear muffs, the employers were liable, as they had failed to take steps to impress on them the need to use the protective equipment.

d.   When the employer has done all he can do, when he has not only provided the protection, but instructed on its use, advised on how to use it properly, pointed out the risks involved in a failure to use, and given constant reminders about its use, then he can do no more, and from that time he will be absolved from liability. Admittedly, this does not solve the problem, which is how to ensure that employees do their work safely. It is possible to make the use of safety equipment part of the contract of employment, or a provision in the works rules, and, it is submitted, a failure to observe these terms or instructions may, after due warning, enable the employer fairly to dismiss the employee. There appears to be no legal duty to do so in order to protect the employee from the physical consequences of his own folly.

C. Reasonably competent fellow employees

10.84–10.90   If an employer engages an incompetent person, whose actions injure another employee, the employer will be liable for failing to take reasonable care. In *Hudson v Ridge Manufacturing Co Ltd* an employee who was known to be prone to committing practical jokes, carried one of his pranks too far, and injured a fellow employee. The employer was liable. The answer in these circumstances, is, after due warning, to dispense firmly with the services of such a person, for he is a menace to himself and to others. On the other hand, in *Coddington v International Harvester Co of Great Britain Ltd*, for a joke, an employee, M, kicked a tin of burning thinners close to X, and another employee, Y, was scorched by the flames, and in the agony of the moment, kicked the tin away so that it enveloped the claimant in flames, causing him severe injuries. It was held that the defendants were not liable. There was nothing in M's previous conduct which suggested that he might endanger others, and his act was completely outside the scope of his employment.

Defences to an action based on common law negligence

10.91   Since the duty of the employer is to take reasonable care, and not an absolute duty to prevent accidents, it follows that there are certain defences available.

A. Denial of negligence

10.92   The employer may deny that he failed to take reasonable care, or claim that he did all that a reasonable employer would have done in the circumstances. In *Latimer v AEC Ltd* a factory floor was made slippery owing to the interaction of water from an unprecedented rainfall with the oily surface of the floor. The management ordered sand and sawdust to be spread around, but there was not enough to cover the whole factory. The employee slipped on an untreated part and was injured. It was held that the employer had done all that a reasonable employer could have done, having regard to the nature of the risk. The only other alternative would have been to close down the factory, which would have been unreasonable in the circumstances. In *Brown v Rolls-Royce (1971) Ltd* the claimant contracted dermatitis owing to the use of an industrial oil. The employers did not provide a barrier cream on the advice of their chief medical officer, who doubted its efficacy. It was again held that the employers were not liable, for they were entitled to rely on the skilled judgment of a competent adviser, and no more could be expected. Indeed, the medical officer had instituted his own preventative methods, as a result of which the incidence of dermatitis in the factory had decreased.

10.93 The duty of the non-specialist employer in these circumstances is somewhat different. After all, not every firm can be expected to employ their own medical officer. Nonetheless, they must pay attention to the current literature which is available to them, either through their employers' associations or other sources. In *Graham v CWS* the claimant worked in a furniture workshop where an electric sanding machine gave off a quantity of fine wood dust. This settled on his skin and caused dermatitis. No general precautions were taken against this, although the manager had received all the information which was commonly circulated in the trade. It was held that the employers had not been negligent. They did not know of the danger, nor ought they to have known. The had fulfilled their duty to take reasonable steps to keep their knowledge up to date.

B. The injury was the sole fault of the employee

10.94 If it can be shown that the accident or injury was solely due to the fault of the employee, the employer will not be liable. In *Jones v Lionite Specialities Ltd* a foreman was addicted to a chemical vapour from a tank. One weekend he was found dead, having fallen into the tank. The employers were not liable. In *Brophy v Bradfield & Co Ltd* a lorry driver was found dead inside a boiler house, having been overcome by the fumes. He had no reason to be there, and his employers had no reason to suspect his presence. Again, the employers were not liable. And in *Horne v Lec Refrigeration Ltd*, a tool-setter had been trained to operate a machine, but was killed because of his failure to operate a safety drill. The employers were not liable, even though they were in breach of their statutory duty to ensure secure fencing.

10.95 It is sometimes inferred that this defence is one of *volenti non fit injuria*, ie that a person consents to the risk of being injured. But the doctrine of consent rarely succeeds in employment cases. The fact that an employee knows that he runs the risk of being injured does not mean that he consents to that risk because of the employer's negligence (*Smith v Baker & Sons*). The payment of 'danger money' to specialised employees (eg stunt artistes) may indicate that there is a special risk which cannot be guarded against, and to that extent consent may be raised; but even so, the real question to be asked is: was the employer negligent in the circumstances.

10.96 Moreover, the Unfair Contract Terms Act 1977 applies to those employment situations where the employer seeks to exclude his liability for injury to the employee by means of a prominently displayed notice or even a contract term. Section 2 of the Act states that a person cannot by reference to a contract term or to a notice exclude or restrict his liability for death or personal injury resulting from negligence. Thus an employer cannot escape his legal responsibility if he has been negligent.

C. Contributory negligence

10.97–10.105 This defence is based on the Law Reform (Contributory Negligence) Act 1945, which provides that if a person is injured, partly because of his own fault and partly due to the fault of another, damages shall be reduced to the extent the court thinks fit, having regard to the claimant's share in the responsibility for the damage. The defence is successfully raised in a number of cases. The employer will argue that even though he was negligent, so too was the injured employee, and a reduction in the amount of damages awarded will be the result. The actual percentage reduction made is scarcely based on scientific principles, and appeal courts may take a different view of the share of the blame to be apportioned.

Limitation of actions (Limitation Act 1980)

10.106 Any action in respect of negligence, nuisance or breach of statutory duty which has resulted in personal injury must be brought within three years from the date when the cause of action accrued, or from the date when the claimant had knowledge of the injury. 'Knowledge' in this connection, means when the injured person had knowledge that
a. the injury was significant
b. the injury was attributable wholly or partly to the act or omission which gave rise to the legal liability
c. the defendant was responsible
d. any other fact supporting the bringing of an action against the defendant.
A person's knowledge includes knowledge which he might reasonably be expected to acquire from facts which are observable by him, or from facts ascertainable by him with the help of medical or other expert advice which it is reasonable for him to seek. The Act does not apply in Scotland.

The Royal Commission on Civil Liability

10.107 For a number of years, voices have been raised against the whole system of tort liability, and in particular against the unfair manner in which it appears to operate. The function of the law seems to be directed to apportioning blame and awarding compensation, rather than in acting as a catalyst to eliminate fault, and the requirements of the rules of evidence have all been joined together to produce a system which has been castigated as being capricious in operation and unjust in its results. Two employees may be injured; the one who can point the finger of blame successfully at his employer will be compensated, the other may be unable to do so and will get nothing. But their needs are probably just the same. Because all employers are now obliged to have appropriate insurance cover, it may well be a matter of indifference to them whether or not they are legally liable, and indeed, it is not unknown for an employer to lean over backwards in order to make himself liable (see *Hilton v Thomas Burton (Rhodes) Ltd*).

10.108 In 1973 the Royal Commission on Civil Liability and Compensation for Personal Injuries (the Pearson Commission) was appointed, to consider 'to what extent, in what circumstances, and by what means compensation should be payable in respect of death or personal injuries (including ante-natal injuries) suffered by any person (a) in the course of employment ... having regard to the cost and other implications of the arrangements for the recovery of compensation, whether by way of compulsory insurance or otherwise'.

10.109–10.120 In its report, the Commission thought that the present system of compensating employees for injuries received at work was fundamentally sound, and no substantial changes were recommended. It concluded that the industrial injuries scheme constituted a substantial 'no fault system of liability', which could be extended and improved, but did not require radical alteration. The common law action for damages on tort liability could not be improved on a scale which warranted abolition and only minor changes were proposed.

Implied obligations of the employee

A. Duty of faithful service

10.121 Since the relationship between the employer and employee is one of trust and confidence the law implies into the contract of employment the term that every employee shall serve his employer faithfully. This is a fundamental obligation, and any serious or persistent course of conduct which is inconsistent with that obligation may well amount to a breach of contract. Examples which readily spring to mind include persistent lateness, incompetence, wilful neglect and theft of the employer's property. A strike, a go-slow, a work-to-rule, a sit-in, being contrary to the fundamental nature of the contract—which is to work in return for a reward—are also within this category, and an employee may be dismissed for them (see Chapter 21). The employee undertakes to perform his duties carefully and competently, with due regard for the interests of the employer. In *Secretary of State for Employment v ASLEF* (see para 3.158) Roskill LJ thought that it was an implied term that each employee would not, in obeying lawful instructions, seek to carry them out in a manner which had the effect of disrupting the employer's business. Whether the 'implied term' theory can stand up to analysis is another matter; all members of the Court of Appeal were prepared to import some form of obligation of fidelity arising from the very nature of the contract of employment.

10.122 In *Sim v Rotherham Metropolitan Borough Council* (para 3.55) it was held that the contractual obligations of a person employed in a professional capacity were those defined by the nature of his profession and the obligations incumbent on those who follow that profession.

10.123 If an employee fails to perform part of his duties, but indicates that he is prepared to perform the remainder, the employer may make it clear that he is not prepared to accept such partial performance, and may lawfully refuse to pay the employee the whole of the remuneration due (*Wiluszynski v London Borough of Tower Hamlets*).

10.124   A wrongful act which does not necessarily benefit the employee may still be a breach of fidelity if it is harmful to the employer's business. In *Dalton v Burton's Gold Medal Biscuits Ltd* the employee was dismissed for falsifying the clock-card of a fellow employee, and this was held to be a fair dismissal. A more difficult situation arises if there is a conflict between the duty of fidelity on the one hand, and an obligation the employee owes by virtue of his membership of a professional organisation on the other. It is submitted that there is an implied term that the employer will not require an employee to act in a manner contrary to professional ethics, and that this would override the duty to the employer.

10.125   It is a breach of the employee's duty of faithful service to compete with the employer while he is still employed but it is not a breach if an employee indicates that he intends to take steps at some future date which will enable him to compete after the employment has ceased, in the absence of any restrictive covenant to that effect (see para 19.41). In other words, there is a distinction between an intention to set up in competition with the employer in the future, and competing with the employer while still employed. In *Adamson v B & L Cleaning Services Ltd*, the employee was a foreman employed by a firm of cleaning contractors. The firm had a cleaning contract worth £60,000 per year. Tenders were invited for renewal, and the employee indicated that he had requested that his name be placed on the tender list. When the employers were informed of this, they asked him to sign an undertaking not to seek to obtain any contract for industrial cleaning while still in the firm's employment, but he refused to do so, and was dismissed. The dismissal was held to be fair. He was in breach of his duty of faithful service, which justified the termination of his employment.

B. Duty to obey lawful and reasonable orders

10.126   The employee undertakes to obey all lawful and reasonable orders. In *United Kingdom Atomic Energy Authority v Claydon*, the employee's contract required him to work anywhere in the United Kingdom. He refused to transfer to another base, and was dismissed. The order was clearly lawful and reasonable, for it was within the express terms of the contract. In *Pepper v Webb*, a gardener used some choice expletives accompanied by words which indicted that he had no intention of obeying his employer's instructions, and it was this refusal, rather than the language which accompanied it, which was held to be the breach of contract.

10.127   But if the employee can show that the order was unlawful, he need not obey it. In *Morrish v Henlys (Folkestone) Ltd* the employee refused to falsify some records, and was dismissed. It was held that he was entitled to refuse to obey an unlawful order, and the dismissal was unfair. Whether an order is unreasonable may well be a question of fact in each case. In *Walmsley v UDEC Refrigeration Ltd* the claimant was dismissed after refusing to work in Wexford in Eire on the grounds that it was a hotbed of IRA activity. He could not substantiate these allegations, and it was held that he had refused to obey a reasonable order. Had he been told to go to Belfast, a refusal may well have been justified, for this might involve a serious risk which was not contemplated at the time of the formation of the contract (*Wicks v Charles A Smethurst Ltd*). An employee need not obey an order which would expose him to the risk of danger to life or liberty (*Ottoman Bank v Chakarian*).

10.128   To determine whether or not an order is reasonable, principles of good industrial relations may be taken into account. Thus in *Payne v Spook Erection Ltd*, a foreman was instructed to compile a merit table each week, listing the performance of 25 employees, and to send warning letters to those whose name appeared at the bottom of the list. As he did not see all the employees each week, he refused to operate the system, as he thought that it would be based largely on guesswork. He was told that unless he operated the system he would be dismissed, but he refused to comply. An employment tribunal, although they had little sympathy with the system, held the dismissal to be fair, but the decision was reversed by the EAT. In considering whether or not a decision of an employment tribunal was perverse, matters of good industrial relations could be considered. The weekly merit rating system was clearly unfair, and to dismiss the foreman for refusing to operate an unreasonable order was also unfair.

10.129   Difficulty is frequently caused by loose contractual expressions relating to overtime. If this is stated to be voluntary, then the employee is entitled to refuse. If it is stated to be worked by arrangement, then again, it becomes a matter for negotiation. But if it is clear that some overtime is to be worked, and the negotiations are merely about the details, the refusal may well be unreasonable, particularly if this is designed to bring improper pressure to bear on the employer (*Pengilly v North Devon Farmers Ltd*). As we have seen (in Chapter 3) a refusal to accept a demotion or a change in contractual terms is not necessarily unreasonable, but refusal to obey instructions which are within the contract may be unreasonable. In *Connor v Halfords Ltd* the employee was obliged to 'obey all orders and instructions received from the directors'. He was dismissed because he refused to go on a training course, and the dismissal was held to be fair.

10.130   An employee who refuses to obey a lawful and reasonable order, which was given in good faith and without any ulterior motive, is in repudiatory breach of contract, which the employer may accept by dismissing him without notice or pay in lieu of notice (*Macari v Celtic Football and Athletic Co Ltd*).

10.131   However, it does not follow that an employee who refuses to obey a lawful order may automatically be dismissed, any more than it can be said that an employee cannot be dismissed if he refuses to obey an order which is outside his contractual obligations, for the strict legal rights are only relevant in considering the 'lawfulness' of the dismissal, but not its fairness. Two employment tribunal decisions will illustrate this point. In *Wilson v IDR Construction Ltd* the claimant was contractually bound to move from site to site in accordance with management instructions. He was asked to move to a new site, but refused, as his wife was ill, and he was having difficulty with his car. Although his refusal to obey a lawful and reasonable order would have entitled the employers to dismiss him at common law, the tribunal held that this was not an invariable rule so far as unfair dismissal law was concerned. The employers should have given him a chance to explain his refusal, taken into account the genuineness of the reason, the fact that he had never refused to change sites before, and that his refusal related only to that one day. In the circumstances, the dismissal was held to be unfair. On the other hand, in *Robinson v Flitwick Frames Ltd* the claimant was dismissed following his refusal to work overtime, although he was not contractually bound to do so. All the other employees in his section worked the necessary overtime, and the claimant gave no satisfactory explanation for his refusal. The tribunal held that his dismissal was for 'some other substantial reason' and that the employers had acted reasonably in the circumstances, for it would have caused considerable problems if the claimant had to be employed on terms different from the other employees (see also *Farrant v Woodroffe School*).

10.132 If the employees are not prepared to give an undertaking that they will desist from future disruptive conduct, an employer may suspend them from work until they do so, and the employees, though willing to work, will not be entitled to remuneration for the period of suspension (*British Telecommunications plc v Ticehurst*).

C. Duty to use skill and care

10.133 The employee undertakes to perform his work competently, using reasonable skill and care. This, of course, must be combined with the employer's duty to provide all necessary assistance, etc (see above), but if the employer has done all he can, then a dismissal for incompetence will usually be fair. Also, the employee undertakes to take proper care of the employer's property. In *Superlux v Plaisted* the employee negligently allowed some of his employer's property to be stolen from a van, for which he was held responsible. On the other hand, a tribunal has held that an employee who negligently lost the company cat should receive some disciplinary action short of a dismissal! For a dismissal to be warranted, the act of negligence must be a serious one (*Comerford v Swel Foods Ltd*) or a series of minor acts of neglect (*Lowndes v Specialist Heavy Engineering Ltd*, para 17.114). It is an implied term of the contract of employment that an employee will exercise skill and care in the performance of his duties, and a breach of that term entitles the employer to claim damages in respect of the negligent performance of the contract. In *Janata Bank v Ahmed*, the employee worked as a bank manager. It was alleged that he had been negligent in the way he carried out his duties, and after his dismissal, the bank issued a writ claiming £34,640 damages. The Court of Appeal upheld the claim. He had failed to exercise proper skill and care, as implied by his contract. It is irrelevant that the cause of action arises in contract or in tort (see *Lister v Romford Ice and Cold Storage Co Ltd*).

D. Secret bribes and commissions

10.134 The employee undertakes not to accept any secret bribes or commissions or gifts, or any reward in respect of his work other than from his employer. This rule applies even though the employee is in no way influenced by the favours he has received, for there is always the possibility that there will be a suspicion that his conduct has been influenced, or that it might be affected in the future. Tips, however, are a recognised method of being paid, and do not constitute a bribe which must be disclosed. An employee can only serve one employer, and it will be inconsistent with his obligation of faithful service to accept anything from another person in respect of things done within the performance of his work. In *Boston Deep Sea Fishing and Ice Co v Ansell* the defendant was a managing director of the claimant company. He placed orders for supplies with other companies, from whom he received a commission. It was held that his dismissal was justified. It is a violation of the duty of honest and faithful service for an employee to have an interest in a firm which is transacting business with his employer without disclosing that interest, and on discovering the facts, the employer is entitled to dismiss the employee summarily (*Horcal Ltd v Gatland*).

10.135 The rule is easy to state, but in practice it may be hard to apply, for there is no simple line between acts which are part of social or business intercourse and bribery. No one is going to quibble if a salesman offers a cigarette to the firm's buyer, or if two people go for a working lunch at a modest cafeteria. A hundred cigarettes or a slap-up lunch at an expensive restaurant may fall into a different category. Some firms may anticipate this problem by laying down the standards of conduct expected from those in a position of authority who may be affected by the rule. Employees may be warned not to accept gifts from suppliers, not to accept hospitality which might have a significant value, or to allow others to pay travel or hotel bills on their behalf.

E. Confidential information

10.136 The employee must not disclose any confidential information about the employer's business to an unauthorised person. Such information may be as to its profitability, new designs or models, mode of operation, or anything relating to the business. In *Foster v Scaffolding (GB) Ltd* the employee gave confidential information to a rival company which was to the disadvantage of the employer, and he was held to have been fairly dismissed. The obligations of an employee who leaves (or is about to leave) his employment will be considered in Chapter 19.

10.137 The rule will not apply if the employee is obliged by law to disclose information. For example, an employee is under a legal duty to give any necessary information to an inspector carrying out an examination or investigation under the Health and Safety at Work etc Act 1974 (see Chapter 11), and to produce any necessary books or documents.

10.138 If an employer discovers that an unidentifiable employee is leaking information to the press, he may be able to obtain a court order which will lead him to identify the person concerned (generally known as a 'whistleblower'). Clearly, there is a conflict between the public interest which requires that the press shall protect the identity of its sources and the right of an employer to identify a disloyal employee, particularly when it is likely that that employee may disclose other sensitive information. In *Camelot Group plc v Centaur Communications Ltd* the Court of Appeal set out certain principles which should be applied in such cases, but stressed that the resolution of such conflicts will very much depend on the facts of each case, ie the nature of the information disclosed, whether there is an allegation of wrongdoing, whether the information would eventually be in the public domain, etc. The law does not enable the press to protect the identity of a whistleblower in all circumstances.

10.139 Under the provisions of the Public Interest Disclosure Act 1998 (inserted into ss 43A–43L of ERA), legal protection is given to workers (a definition which is somewhat wider than usual: see ERA s 43K) who make a 'protected disclosure' in certain specified circumstances. They will have the right not to suffer a detriment (s 47A), not to be dismissed (s 103A) and not to be selected for redundancy (s 105(6A)). Moreover, as with all automatically unfair dismissals,

no qualifying period of employment is required, the age limit of 65 does not apply and there is no limit on the amount of compensation which can be awarded. Interim relief will also be available (ss 128(1)(b), 129(1)). A protected disclosure is a disclosure made by a worker which tends to show that
(a) a criminal offence has been, is being or is likely to be committed
(b) a person has failed, is failing or is likely to fail to comply with a legal obligation
(c) a miscarriage of justice has occurred or is likely to occur
(d) the health or safety of any individual is being endangered
(e) the environment has been is being or is likely to be damaged
(f) information tending to show any of the above matters has been or is likely to be concealed.

10.140 A disclosure of information is not protected if the person making it commits an offence by making it (eg, under the Official Secrets Act). Nor is information in respect of which legal privilege (or confidentiality between client and professional legal adviser) could be claimed.

10.141 To be protected, the information must be disclosed in good faith to the employer or other person in respect of whose conduct any of the above matters relate. Disclosure is also protected if it is made in the course of obtaining legal advice, or to a person appointed by the Crown, or to a prescribed person as set out in the Public Interest Disclosure (Prescribed Persons) Order 1999. The Order lists the persons and organisations who are prescribed for the purpose of s 43F of ERA, and the description of matters which may properly be disclosed with respect to those persons or organisations. If a worker wishes to make a disclosure to some other person or body (eg the media, an MP or a trade union), he will be protected if
(a) it is made in good faith, and
(b) the worker believes the information is substantially true, and
(c) it is not made for the purpose of personal gain, and
(d) either
    (i) the worker believes he will be subjected to a detriment if he makes the disclosure to his employer or other prescribed person, or
    (ii) if there is no prescribed person, the worker believes that it is likely that evidence will be destroyed or concealed if the disclosure is made to the employer, or
    (iii) the worker has already disclosed the information to his employer, and
(e) in all the circumstances, it is reasonable for him to make the disclosure.

10.142 To determine whether it is reasonable to disclose, regard shall be had to the identity of the person to whom the disclosure is made, the seriousness of the matter, whether action was taken by the employer or other person as a result of the previous disclosure, and whether the worker complied with any procedure laid down by his employer.

10.143 A disclosure may also be made if the worker makes it in good faith, reasonably believes the information to be true, does not make the disclosure for personal gain, and the matters disclosed (referred to above) are of an exceptionally serious nature. Any provision in a contract of employment which seeks to preclude a worker from making a protected disclosure is void.

F. Patents, inventions and copyright

10.144   The law relating to inventions made and patents taken out by employees has been altered drastically as a result of the Patents Act 1977. According to s 39, an invention made by an employee shall belong to the employer if (a) it was made during the employee's normal duties, or if such duties were specifically assigned to him and in either case the circumstances were such that an invention might reasonably be expected to result from those duties, or (b) because of the employee's particular responsibilities, he has a special obligation to further the interests of the employer's undertaking. Any other invention made by an employee shall belong to him, notwithstanding any term to the contrary in the contract of employment (see *Reiss Engineering Co Ltd v Harris*). Even if the invention belongs to the employer, the employee may apply to the Comptroller General of Patents (or Patents Court) for an award of compensation, which may be awarded if the patent is of outstanding benefit to the employer (having regard to the size and nature of the employer's undertaking) and it is just that compensation should be awarded. The amount of compensation should be a fair share of the benefit which the employer has derived, taking into account a number of factors, including (a) the nature of the employee's duties, his remuneration, etc, (b) the effort and skill provided by others, including any advice and assistance received from other employees, (c) the contribution made by the employer, whether by way of assisting in the manufacture, marketing, or other contribution.

10.145   If the invention belongs to the employee, he is free to dispose of it as he wishes. If he assigns his interest to his employer (whether by way of an assignment in the right to a patent, or a licensing arrangement, etc), then he is still entitled to apply for an award of statutory compensation, if he can show that the financial return he has received is inadequate in relation to the benefit derived from the patent by the employer, and it is just that compensation should be paid in addition to the benefit received from the relevant contractual arrangement between the parties. Such compensation will amount to a fair share of the benefit which the employer has derived from the assignment or licence, taking into account, *inter alia*: (a) any condition granted in respect of the licence or the patent, (b) the extent to which the invention was made jointly by the employee and any other person, and (c) the contribution made by the employer in the making, developing, manufacturing and marketing of the invention.

10.146   However, an award of compensation cannot be made if there is in force a relevant collective agreement which provides for payment of compensation for inventions made by employees. The collective agreement is only relevant if it is made by a trade union to which the employee belongs and by the employer, or an employers' association to which the employer belongs, which is in force at the time of the making of the invention. Non-unionists, therefore, may apply for compensation under the Act.

10.147   By the Copyright, Designs and Patents Act 1988, if the maker of a written work is employed under a contract of employment, the employer becomes the first owner of the copyright (s 11). This rule extends to literary, dramatic, musical or artistic works, but it is subject to any agreement to the contrary. There are no provisions in this Act for employee compensation on the lines of the Patents Act 1977.

G. 'Moonlighting'

10.148   The employee is obliged not to act in any manner which is inconsistent with his duty of fidelity. In *Gibson v National Union of Dyers, Bleachers and Textile Workers* a full-time trade union official worked in a mill during his holidays. There was clearly a conflict of interests between his union position and his spare-time employment, and his dismissal was only held to be unfair because of the manner in which it was done. Indeed, the modern practice of 'moonlighting' whereby an employee undertakes spare-time work outside his employment hours can raise problems, particularly if the work is in competition with the employer's business. In *Gray v C & P Pembroke Ltd* the employee agreed not to be engaged in any other business without the written consent of his employer. Contrary to this agreement, he took a part-time job with a rival employer. As well as being in breach of an express term of his contract, it was also a breach of fidelity, and his dismissal was held to be fair. On the other hand in *Frame v McKean & Graham Ltd* the National Working Agreement for the Building Industry provided that no operative should undertake any jobbing work on his own account. This had never been enforced or referred to by the employer, and there was no mention of it in his contract of employment. The tribunal held that his dismissal for doing some work for a former customer of the firm was unfair, but the decision seems to rely heavily on the fact that the employer had, in the past, condoned his employees doing spare-time work, and even allowed them to purchase materials for this purpose.

10.149   In the absence of any contractual term, it appears that the employee may not work for a competitor in his spare time. In *Hivac Ltd v Park Royal Scientific Instruments Ltd* an injunction was granted against the competitor restraining him from employing the claimant's employees who were making valves for him in their spare time. On the other hand, an employee cannot be restrained from working in a different business in his spare time which does not compete with his employer's business, provided, of course, that this does not interfere with his normal work.

H. Duty of disclosure

10.150–10.160   An employee is under no duty to disclose to his employer facts which are inimical to the employer (except in response to a direct question), nor to disclose his own misconduct (*Bell v Lever Bros Ltd*). However, he is under a duty to disclose the misconduct of his subordinates even if, by doing so, he incriminates himself. In *Sybron Corpn v Rochem Ltd*, a man called Roques was the European manager for Gamblem Chemical Co (UK) Ltd. During his employment, payments were made on his behalf by the company into a pension scheme, and on his retirement he received a lump sum payment. It was then discovered that Roques, together with several subordinates, had been conspiring to set up in direct competition with Gamblem, and the company sought restitution of the pension payments, claiming that under the rules of the pension scheme, Roques could have been dismissed for gross misconduct, and the payments would not have been made. The Court of Appeal held that the company was entitled to have the money repaid. As a senior executive, Roques was under a duty to report the continuing misconduct of his subordinates, and for this breach of duty he could have been dismissed summarily. The money was therefore paid under a mistake of fact, since, had Gamblem known about the breach, they could have invoked the rules of the pension fund.

Employer's vicarious liability

10.161 If an employee commits a wrongful (ie tortious) act in the course of his employment which causes injury or damage to a third party, the employee will, of course, be personally liable. In addition, however, the employer may be vicariously liable to compensate that third party. Two reasons are usually adduced for this principle. The first is that the employer, having initiated or created the situation where the employee has been in a position to cause the harm, should properly bear the loss; the second is the more practical reason that the employee will usually be unable to meet any substantial claim for damages, whereas the employer will normally have the financial resources to do so, or, at least, will be insured against such contingencies.

10.162 There are also a number of exceptional circumstances where an employer will be liable for the tortious acts of his independent contractors; for example, if he authorises the wrongful act, or where he has a responsibility to take care which cannot be delegated by employing someone else to do the work, eg if there is a hazardous task to be undertaken (see *Holliday v National Telephone Co*). It is also true that in recent years the courts appear to be gradually extending this principle of legal liability, and to that extent the distinction between an independent contractor and an employee (discussed in Chapter 2) is becoming possibly less important than before. But the general rule remains as stated.

10.163 The major problem is to determine which acts are committed by the employee 'in the course of his employment', and there are a number of marginal situations which cause difficulty. It is clear that if the employer expressly authorises the wrongful act, he will be liable. Equally the employer will be liable if he authorises the act, and the employee performs it in a wrongful manner, for this is the very essence of the legal principle under discussion. If the employer expressly forbids the act, he may still be vicariously liable if it can be shown that nonetheless the act was done in the scope of the employment, or for the purposes of the employer's business. In *Conway v George Wimpey & Co Ltd* the employers issued instructions to their drivers that no person other than a fellow employee was permitted to ride as a passenger in their lorries. In breach of these instructions, a driver gave a lift to a non-employee, and the passenger was injured as a result of an accident. It was held that the employers were not liable, for the express prohibition had taken the act (of giving lifts) outside the scope of the employment. But in *Rose v Plenty* the employers had made it clear that children were not allowed to travel on milk floats. In breach of this instruction, a milkman engaged a young boy to help him deliver and collect milk bottles, and as a result of negligent driving the boy was injured. The Court of Appeal held that the employers were nonetheless liable vicariously. The Court distinguished cases like *Conway v George Wimpey & Co Ltd* on the ground that in the latter case, employees who disregarded instructions by giving lifts to unauthorised persons were acting outside the scope of their employment, because what they did was not for the purpose of the employers' business. In *Rose v Plenty*, the act (of giving a lift to an unauthorised person), although prohibited, was done for the purpose of the employers' business and hence was within the scope of the employment.

10.164   If the employers permit the act, they cannot escape liability by prohibiting it from being done in a wrongful manner. In *Canadian Pacific Rly Co v Lockhart*, the employers issued instructions that staff should not drive uninsured cars while on company business. One of their employees disregarded this prohibition, and through negligent driving, injured the claimant. The employers were held to be vicariously liable. It was not the driving which was prohibited, and the prohibition merely limited the way in which the employee was to do his work. The same principle applies if the employee negligently performs his duties. In *Century Insurance Co Ltd v Northern Ireland Road Transport Board*, a driver of a petrol lorry, whilst transferring petrol from his lorry to an underground storage tank at a garage, struck a match in order to light a cigarette. He then threw the match on the floor, and an explosion ensued. It was held that the employers were liable. He was doing that which he was employed to do namely, deliver petrol, although he was negligent in the manner in which he was performing his work.

10.165   If employees are acting in a manner which clearly indicates that they are in breach of their contracts of employment, they cannot be said to be acting in the course of their employment. In *General Engineering Services v Kingston and St Andrew Corpn* firemen adopted a 'go slow' policy. They were called out to deal with a fire at the claimant's premises, but travelled there slowly, frequently stopping, with the result that the claimant's building and its contents were destroyed. Had they responded with normal speed, little damage would have resulted. The claimant's claim for damages failed. The firemen were acting in a wrongful manner, which was not authorised, and were not acting in the course of their employment.

10.166   The course of the employment can be extended to acts which are outside the employee's working hours, and need not be on the employers' premises, provided the act is done for the purpose of the employers' business. In *Ruddiman & Co v Smith* a clerk used a washroom provided by his employers after he had finished work, and left a tap running. His employers were held liable for the ensuing flooding of the adjoining premises, even though the employee had finished his work, for the wrongful act was consequential to that work. In *Poland v John Parr & Sons,* while an employee was travelling home for his lunch, he saw a boy trying to steal some sugar from a lorry belonging to his employer. The employee struck him a blow which caused serious injury. The employer was held liable, for the employee was acting in what he believed to be the interests of his employer by protecting the employer's property, even if his methods were somewhat over-enthusiastic.

10.167   However, if an employee uses excessive zeal or violence, this may take the act outside the scope of his employment. In *Warren v Henlys Ltd* a garage attendant had a violent altercation with the claimant, who was a customer, and committed an assault on him. It was held such acts were no part of his duties as an employee, and the employer was not liable for what was, in fact, the pursuit of a personal vendetta. A case which illustrates the distinction between *Poland v*

John Parr & Sons and *Warren v Henlys Ltd* is *Daniels v Whetstone Entertainments Ltd*, where a steward at a dance hall assaulted the claimant. After being ordered to return to his duties, he committed a second assault on the claimant. The first assault was within the course of his employment, for he was doing work which he was employed to do, namely keep order at the dance hall, even though this method was unauthorised. The second assault was outside his employment, for it was in pursuance of his own personal grievance.

10.168 The fact that the employee is seeking to obtain a personal gain will not necessarily take his acts outside the course of his employment. In *Lloyd v Grace, Smith & Co* a managing clerk of a firm of solicitors induced the claimant, a client of the firm, to sign some documents, which transferred the claimant's properties to him. The firm was held liable, even though they stood to obtain no personal gain from the wrongful act. The clerk was merely performing the class of duties for which he was employed. This principle was taken further in *Morris v CW Martin & Sons Ltd* where the claimant took a fur to a furrier for cleaning. This was stolen by an employee whose duty it was to do the work, and the employers were held liable.

10.169 A more restrictive view was taken in *Heasmans v Clarity Cleaning Co Ltd*, where the defendants entered into a contract for the regular cleaning of the claimant's telephones. The defendants employed an employee to do this work, and the employee, while on the claimant's premises, made £1,400 worth of overseas telephone calls. The Court of Appeal held that the defendants were not liable. The fact that the employee had an opportunity to commit a crime or a tort was not sufficient. For the employer to be vicariously liable there had to be some nexus other than mere opportunity established between the wrongful act and the circumstances of the employment.

10.170 On the other hand, an employer will not be liable for an incident which does not arise from the employment, and is not for his benefit. In *Hilton v Thomas Burton (Rhodes) Ltd* a gang of demolition workers were driven in the firm's van to the site. After working for a short time, they made several journeys to a public house, which was some miles away. The claimant's husband was killed due to the negligent driving of the van driver, as they were returning from the pub. Despite valiant efforts by the employer to make himself liable, the court could not accept that the men, while driving to and from the pub, were acting in the course of their employment. Older cases have established that if an employee makes a detour, it is a question of degree whether or not he is still acting in the course of his employment, or acting 'on a frolic of his own'. And even more difficult are those cases where, having made a detour, the employee purports to resume his employment duties.

10.171 If an employee is travelling to or from work, whether or not he is acting in the course of his employment at the material time will depend on whether he was going about his employer's business. A distinction must be drawn between travelling to work, and being on duty while travelling to work. In *Smith v Stages* Lord Lowry laid down a number of propositions which would generally apply to hourly paid workers, though not necessarily to salaried employees. The reality in these cases is that they are usually fought between two insurance companies, one holding the employers' liability policy, the other holding the third party motor insurance policy.

10.172   It is also possible for an employer to be held liable under criminal law for an act committed by his employee. The main relevance of this rule today lies in the numerous statutory duties which create absolute offences, and thus the act of the employee is regarded as being the act of the employer. Each statute must be construed with reference to its objects, for there may be certain defences available in appropriate cases. Thus in *Portsea Island Mutual Co-operative Society Ltd v Leyland* the appellants employed a milk roundsman who, contrary to instructions, took a ten-year-old boy with him to assist him delivering milk and collecting empties. A conviction for employing the boy contrary to a local bye-law was quashed. Neither the employer nor his agent (eg a personnel manager) had taken on the boy, and as the milkman had no authority to take on staff, the employer had committed no offence.

CHAPTER 11

Health and safety at work

11.1 As a result of the recommendations of the Robens Committee, the Health and Safety at Work etc Act 1974 was passed. In considering the then existing laws and practices relating to health and safety, the Committee came to a number of interesting conclusions. It found that in fact there was too much law, that much of it was unsatisfactory and unintelligible, and there was overlapping jurisdiction between those bodies whose task it was to enforce the law. The result of this was that there was a general feeling of apathy in the day-to-day implementation of safety rules, and little interest was shown in the subject. The new Act thus lays down the general legal obligations of all concerned in a single enactment, with the enforcement under the control of a unified administration. The old law (Factories Act 1961, Offices, Shops and Railway Premises Act 1963, etc) has been progressively repealed and replaced by regulations and approved codes of practice which are designed to maintain and improve the standards of health, safety and welfare.

11.2 Several fundamental changes were brought about by the new legislation. In the first place, the Act applies to people, not to premises. It covers all employed persons (with the exception of domestic workers), wherever they work, thus bringing within the orbit of safety legislation an additional 7,000,000 employees who were hitherto outside the protection of statutory rules. In addition, the Health and Safety (Training for Employment) Regulations 1990 apply the provisions of the Act to trainees on government sponsored training schemes as if they were employees. The Act also applies to people who are not employees, in so far as they may be affected by activities which are being carried on in places of work.

11.3 The Act applies to all employment situations, including (with appropriate modifications) to offshore installations and pipe lines within British territorial waters and areas designated under the Continental Shelf Act 1964, including construction work and diving activities. The Police (Health and Safety) Act 1997 applies the provisions of the Act to holders of the office of constable, even though they are not technically employees (Police (Health and Safety) Regulations 1999).

11.4 Next, it will be noted that obligations are placed on employers in their different capacities as manufacturers, suppliers, and importers of articles and substances to be used at work, to ensure that these can be used in safety and without risk to health. Health and safety has to be built into the design and manufacturing stages.

11.5   The emphasis of the Act is on criminal sanctions and enforcement of the law by new techniques, for the Act itself does not give rise to questions of civil liability. The inspectorate appears to be using their powers of prosecution at the rate of 2,000 per year, which is small compared with the number of offences revealed by inspections, for the emphasis is on co-operation rather than compulsion. In addition, however, the new powers of issuing improvement and prohibition notices have been widely exercised, and these are proving to have very dramatic effects. Currently, about 12,000 such notices are issued each year.

11.6   Finally, there are a number of provisions designed to bring about a greater awareness by all concerned of the need to promote safety and health at work, and thus provide the impetus to the greater self-regulatory system which the Robens Committee thought to be desirable.

11.7   Some amendments to the Act have been made by the Consumer Protection Act 1987 (Sch 3). The Act now applies to fairground equipment and micro-organisms. Customs officers may detain articles and substances for the purpose of enabling enforcing officers to perform their duties, and s 6 of the Act (see para 11.67) was significantly improved.

11.8–11.15   We can examine the provisions of the Act under five headings.

Enforcement of the Act

11.16   The overall responsibility for supervising and administering the law on health and safety lies with the Health and Safety Commission (HSC), although the enforcement of the Act is the responsibility of the Health and Safety Executive (HSE) and enforcement officers (usually designated Environmental Health Officers) of local authorities, to whom there has been a transfer of authority in respect of certain specified types of premises (Health and Safety (Enforcing Authority) Regulations 1989). Neither the Secretary of State nor the HSC can instruct an enforcing authority to enforce any particular provision or institute proceedings in any particular case.

11.17   All enforcing authorities will appoint inspectors, who will have the following powers, for the purpose of giving effect to the relevant statutory provisions:
a.   at any reasonable time, or, if there is a dangerous situation at any time, to enter premises;
b.   to take with him a constable if he has reasonable cause to apprehend any serious obstruction in the execution of his duty;
c.   to take with him any other authorised person and any equipment or materials required for any purpose for which the power of entry is being exercised;
d.   to make such examination and investigation as may be necessary;
e.   to direct that any premises shall be left undisturbed so long as is reasonably necessary for the purpose of examination or investigation;
f.   to take such measures and photographs and make such recordings as he considers necessary;

g. to take samples of any articles or substances found in any premises and of the atmosphere in, or in the vicinity of, such premises. The Secretary of State may make regulations concerning the procedure to be adopted in such cases;

h. in the case of any article or substance likely to cause danger to health or safety, to cause it to be dismantled or subjected to any process or test, but not to damage or destroy it unless it is for the purpose of exercising his powers. If the person who has responsibilities in relation to those premises is present, and so requests, the inspector shall exercise this power in that person's presence, unless he considers that it would be prejudicial to the safety of the state to do so. In any case, before exercising these powers, he must consult with appropriate persons for the purpose of ascertaining what dangers, if any, there may be in doing what he proposes to do;

i. in the case of any article or substance likely to cause danger to health or safety, to take possession of it, and detain it for so long as is necessary in order to examine it, to ensure it is not tampered with before he has completed his examination, and to ensure that it is available for use as evidence in any proceedings for an offence, or in respect of matters arising out of the issuing of an improvement notice or a prohibition notice. He must leave a notice giving particulars of the article or substance, stating that he has taken possession of it, and, if practicable to do so, leave a sample with a responsible person;

j. if conducting an examination or investigation under d. above, to require any person whom he has reasonable cause to believe to be able to give any information to answer such questions as the inspector thinks fit to ask, and to sign a declaration of the truth of his answers;

k. to require the production of, inspect, and take copies of any entry in, any books or documents which are required to be kept, and any other book or document which it is necessary for him to see for the purpose of any examination or investigation under d., above;

l. to require any person to afford him such facilities and assistance within that person's control or responsibilities, as are necessary for him to exercise his powers;

m. any other power which is necessary for the purpose of exercising any of the above powers.

Improvement notices (s 21)

11.18   If an inspector is of the opinion that a person is contravening one or more relevant statutory provisions, or has done so and the contravention is likely to be continued or repeated, he may serve on him an improvement notice, stating that opinion, specifying the relevant statutory provision, giving reasons why he is of that opinion, and requiring that person to remedy the contravention within such period as may be specified in the notice, but not less than 21 days (ie the period in which an appeal may be made—see below). For a specimen of an improvement notice, see Appendix F.

Prohibition notices (s 22)

11.19   In respect of any activity covered by a relevant statutory provision, if the inspector thinks that those activities are carried on or are likely to be carried on so as to involve a risk of serious personal injury, the inspector may serve a prohibition notice. This will state his opinion, specify the provisions which give rise to that opinion, and direct that the activities to which the notice relates shall not be carried on by or under the control of that person on whom the notice was served unless the matters specified and any associated contravention are remedied. This direction takes effect at the end of the period specified in the notice or, if the notice so declares, immediately. Prohibition notices can be issued on persons, eg for a failure to wear protective eye shields. One notice was issued on a worker who failed to use protective spats.

11.20   In the case of an improvement notice or a prohibition notice, the notice may (but need not) include directions as to the measure to be taken to remedy the contravention, which may be by reference to any approved code of practice or afford a choice between different ways of remedying the contravention. However, in respect of an improvement notice relating to a building, this cannot impose more onerous requirements than those imposed by the building regulations unless there is a statutory provision to the contrary. Also, if the notice relates to the means of escape in the event of fire, the inspector must engage in prior consultations with the fire authorities. Any improvement notice or a deferred prohibition notice may be withdrawn by the inspector before the expiry of 21 days, and may also be extended by the inspector at any time when an appeal is not pending. For a specimen of a prohibition notice, see Appendix F.

Appeals against improvement or prohibition notices (s 24)

11.21   An appeal from the imposition of an improvement notice or a prohibition notice may be made to the employment tribunal, which can cancel or affirm it, or affirm it with such modifications as the tribunal thinks fit. For the purpose of hearing such appeals, the tribunal may include assessors specially appointed to sit with the regular members. Once an appeal has been lodged, this will suspend the operation of the improvement notice until such time as the appeal is disposed of or withdrawn; in the case of a prohibition notice, however, the lodging of an appeal will only suspend it if the tribunal so directs, and then only from the time it does so direct.

11.22   An appeal against an improvement notice or a prohibition notice can be made on a number of grounds.

11.23   First, it could be argued that there is no breach of a statutory duty. To determine this, a tribunal may refer to any relevant code of practice and guidance note. In *Sutton & Co Ltd v Davies* the employers were in breach of s 13 of the Factories Act 1961 in not guarding transmission machinery. They appealed against an improvement notice, arguing that they had operated for 27 years without an accident. The appeal was dismissed, for the requirements of the Act are absolute. But in *Brewer & Sons v Dunston* the inspector issued a prohibition notice on a machine. No accident had occurred in 18 years of use, and the tribunal held that there was no evidence to support the contention that there was risk of imminent danger. The distinction is that for an improvement notice, the sole issue is whether or not there has been a breach of a statutory provision, whereas a prohibition notice is concerned with whether there is a risk of serious personal injury.

11.24   Secondly, an appeal may be against the time limit imposed for remedying the defect, and there the tribunal may consider any serious embarrassment which may be caused to the company, and may take into account any history of recorded accidents at the firm. A company with a good record may well be given an extension of time so as to maintain production, so long as there is no immediate risk of danger or injury, and there is a willingness to make the appropriate modifications.

11.25 A third ground for appeal may be based on the absence of any risk or danger. In *South Surbiton Co-operative Society v Wilcox*, a cracked washbasin was made the subject of an improvement notice. It was argued that the breach was trivial, there was little risk to health, and that there must be many employers who are similarly in breach and who have not been served with improvement notices. Nonetheless, the notice was confirmed by the tribunal. The requirements of the Act were absolute.

11.26 But in *Associated Dairies Ltd v Hartley*, an improvement notice required the company to issue safety shoes free of charge to employees. In the previous year, one employee had been injured when the wheel of a truck ran over his foot. The company employed 1,000 employees, with a high turnover. Free footwear would have cost £20,000 in the first year. The tribunal held that the expense of providing protective footwear was disproportionate to the risk, and the notice was cancelled. In this case, the Act only required the employer to do that which was reasonably practicable.

11.27 A final ground for appeal may be based on the financial inability of the employer to comply with the order. Such an appeal is doomed from the start. In *TC Harrison (Newcastle-under-Lyme) Ltd v Ramsey*, the company appealed against an improvement notice which required them to paint and clean the walls of the factory, in accordance with s 1 of the Factories Act 1961. It was stated that their financial position was precarious due to difficult trading conditions, but the employment tribunal had no hesitation in confirming the notice. To do otherwise would be to allow a firm to keep its charges low so as to undercut competitors, thus obtaining an unfair advantage over those who complied with the legal requirements. An employer cannot be relieved of his statutory duties because of financial difficulties.

11.28 Unlike other proceedings before employment tribunals, appeals against improvement and prohibition notices may result in an order for costs being made against the unsuccessful party. Such an order is entirely at the discretion of the tribunal, who may take into account the conduct of the party in failing to remedy the breach, and the hopelessness or otherwise of the appeal (see Employment Tribunals (Constitution and Rules of Procedure) Regulations 1993 Sch 4). In *South Surbiton Co-operative Society v Wilcox* (above) no order for costs was made, as the tribunal considered that the breach was trivial.

A failure to observe the requirements of a prohibition or improvement notice is a criminal offence, and it is no defence in criminal proceedings to argue that the employer has done all that is reasonably practicable to comply. The proper forum in which to argue questions of practicability is the employment tribunal (*Deary v Mansion Hide Upholstery Ltd*).

11.29 An appeal against a decision of an employment tribunal relating to a prohibition or improvement notice must be made to the Divisional Court. The reason is that the failure to comply with such notices is a criminal offence and the EAT, which would normally hear appeals from employment tribunals, is only concerned with civil matters.

Crown notices

11.30 Because there is a rule of law that the Queen cannot be prosecuted in her own courts, it is not possible to enforce prohibition and improvement notices against Crown organisations, even though they employ large numbers of employees in various government departments. Consequently, the HSE devised the Crown Notice, which will be issued when a prohibition or improvement notice would be appropriate. Such notices have only a moral sanction, but are designed to draw attention to potential hazards, and, as copies are to be given to employees' representatives, will naturally attract publicity. About 40 such notices were issued annually. So far as the health service is concerned, a health authority is no longer to be regarded as a servant or agent of the Crown for the purpose of health and safety legislation (see National Health Service and Community Care Act 1990 s 60). Thus the normal prohibition and improvement notices can be served on these bodies, and they may also be prosecuted for offences.

Power to deal with imminent danger (s 25)

11.31 If the inspector finds on any premises any article or substance which he has reasonable cause to believe is a cause of imminent danger of serious personal injury, he may seize it and cause it to be rendered harmless whether by destruction or otherwise. Before doing so if it is practicable for him to do so, he will give a sample with an identifiable mark to a responsible person. Thereafter, he will prepare and sign a report giving particulars of the circumstances, and give a copy to a responsible person at those premises, and also to the owner.

Enforcement powers of the court (s 42)

11.32 Where a person is convicted of an offence under any relevant statutory provision, the court may, in addition to, or instead of, imposing any punishment, order him to take such steps as may be specified in the order to remedy the matters specified, within such time as may be fixed. Failure to do so may amount to contempt of court, but an application may be made for an extension of the time limit. During the period given to remedy matters, the person cannot be liable for a failure to observe the provisions. After that time, if he continues with the contravention, he can be sentenced to six months' imprisonment and/or fined up to £20,000 in the magistrates' courts, or up to two years' imprisonment and/or an unlimited fine in the Crown Court.

11.33 If a person is charged with an offence in connection with the acquisition of explosives, the court may order the article or substance in question to be forfeited and either destroyed or dealt with as the court so orders. However, such order cannot be made unless the court gives the owner or any other interested party an opportunity to be heard.

Other matters

11.34 By s 26, if an inspector exceeds his statutory powers the enforcing authority may nonetheless indemnify him against the costs, damages, or expenses incurred if it is satisfied that the inspector acted in the honest belief that the act complained of was within his powers.

11.35–11.40 By s 28(8) an inspector is empowered to give information to employed persons (or their representatives) if it is necessary to do so for the purpose of keeping them adequately informed about matters affecting their health, safety or welfare. This may be factual information about the premises or anything going on, or information about action he has taken or is proposing to take. If he does this, he must also give the like information to the employer.

New statutory duties on health, safety and welfare

11.41 In general, there are three sets of guiding rules which will govern the operation of the new law. The first of these is the general duties laid down in ss 2–9, and which must be observed by the specified persons. The second will be the new regulations, which will supplement the new law and have superseded the old. The third will be the Codes of Practice, issued and approved from time to time. It must be borne in mind that a breach of the general duties laid down in ss 2–9 of the Act is a criminal offence, and does not give rise to civil proceedings (s 47), whereas a breach of the regulations will be actionable civilly unless the regulations themselves provide otherwise. However, by s 11 of the Civil Evidence Act 1968 any conviction for a criminal offence is admissible in civil proceedings as evidence that the person so convicted committed the offence, and therefore, a claimant may point to the conviction as being relevant to the issue of civil liability.

11.42 Some of the general duties are absolute ones, which means that the person on whom the duty is placed must carry it out. Others are preceded by the words 'so far as is reasonably practicable'. This is a somewhat lesser standard. The employer must weigh, on the one hand, the time, trouble and expense, etc of meeting that duty against the risks involved and the nature of the obligation on the other hand. Also, the duty can only be performed against the background of current knowledge which the employer knows, or ought to know. However, in *Marshall v Gotham Co Ltd* it was suggested that a precaution which was practicable would not lightly be held to be unreasonable. In other words, a duty or obligation must be performed or carried out unless it would be unreasonable to do so. Further, s 40 of the Act states that in any proceedings for a failure to comply with a duty or requirement, it will be for the accused to prove that it was not reasonably practicable to do more than was in fact done.

Duties of the employer owed to his employees (s 2)

11.43 It shall be the duty of every employer to ensure, so far as is reasonably practicable, the health, safety and welfare at work of all his employees. In particular, the employer must:
a. provide and maintain plant and systems of work that are, so far as is reasonably practicable, safe and without risks to health;
b. make arrangements for ensuring, so far as is reasonably practicable, safety and absence of risks to health in connection with the use, handling, storage and transport of articles and substances (see *Page v Freight Hire (Tank Haulage) Ltd*);

c.   ensure the provision of such information, instruction, training and supervision as is necessary to ensure, so far as is reasonably practicable, the health, safety and welfare at work of his employees. The employer must give such information etc. to his employees and to persons who are not his employees (eg to sub-contractors and their employees) if this is necessary to ensure the health and safety of the employees of the employer (*R v Swan Hunter Shipbuilders Ltd*);

d.   so far as is reasonably practicable as regards any place of work under his control, ensure the maintenance of it in a condition that is safe and without risks to health, and the maintenance of means of access and egress from it that are safe and without such risks;

e.   ensure the provision and maintenance of a working environment for his employees that is, so far as is reasonably practicable, safe, without risks to health, and adequate as regards facilities and arrangements for their welfare at work.

11.44   So far as the above duties are concerned, it will be noted that they bear a strong resemblance to the common law duties of care (see Chapter 10), spelt out, perhaps, in greater detail. An employer is only responsible for premises over which he has actual control, but that does not absolve him from the duty of ensuring a safe system of work on the premises of another (*General Cleaning Contractors Ltd v Christmas*). The duty to provide a safe working environment would cover noise, fumes, heat, etc; welfare at work is not defined, but would presumably cover washing and toilet facilities, drinking water, and possibly eating arrangements.

Written safety policy (s 2(3))

11.45   Except for employers who employ less than five employees (see *Osborne v Bill Taylor of Huyton Ltd* and Employers' Health and Safety Policy Statements (Exception) Regulations 1975) it shall be the duty of every employer to prepare and revise as often as is appropriate a written statement of his general policy with respect to the health and safety at work of all his employees, and the organisation and arrangements for the time being in force for carrying out that policy, and to bring this statement to the notice of all his employees. The Act does not give any guidance on the contents of this written statement, for the object of the exercise is for each employer to sit down and think about his own safety problems and work out the necessary solutions. Clearly, this would prove to be without value if the employer merely copied out a draft scheme drawn up by someone else.

11.46   It is suggested, however, that the safety policy should at least deal with the responsibility of all employees, including the board of directors, all levels of management, supervisors and operatives, inspection procedures, arrangements for dealing with special hazards, emergency arrangements, including fire drill, the provision and use of safety precautions generally, supervision, training, research and consultative arrangements. In drawing up the safety policy, it may be sound procedure to seek advice from the Commission, the Executive, employers' associations, and to consult with trade union representatives, but it must be stressed that the statement is not a joint consultative document, but one for which the employer has ultimate responsibility. The Act requires the statement to be brought to the notice of all employees, but no guidance is given on how this is to be done. It would clearly not be sufficient to place the statement on the notice board, and hope that workpeople will read it as they go past, and so the more formal channels of written communication should be used. If it is known that a particular employee does not read English, presumably some other way must be found of bringing it to his notice. The employer is obliged to revise the written statement as often as may be appropriate; it is suggested that the statement should be looked at at least once a year, in the light of practical experience of operating the safety policy, and taking into account any suggestions which might be received.

Safety representatives and safety committee (s 2(4), (6), (7))

11.47 A trade union which is recognised by an employer may appoint safety representatives from among the employees in respect of whom the union is recognised (*Cleveland County Council v Springett*). The persons so appointed need not themselves be members of the union.

11.48 The legal requirements are contained in the Safety Representatives and Safety Committees Regulations 1977 (as amended) and a Code of Practice issued and approved by the Health and Safety Commission. An independent trade union shall notify the employer in writing of the name of the safety representative, who shall hold the appointment until the union terminates it, or he ceases to be employed at the workplace, or resigns. So far as is reasonably practicable, he shall have been employed by that employer for the preceding two years, or have had at least two years' experience in similar employment.

11.49 An employer has a duty to consult with safety representatives over a wide range of issues, with a view to making and maintaining arrangements which will enable him and his employees to co-operate effectively in promoting and developing measures to ensure the health and safety at work of employees, and checking the effectiveness of those measures (s 2(6)). In particular, there shall be consultation about the introduction of measures which may substantially affect the health and safety of employees, the arrangements for appointing or nominating the safety assistant, the provision of health and safety information, the planning and organisation of health and safety training, and the health and safety consequences of the introduction of new technologies (Management of Health and Safety at Work Regulations 1999).

Additionally, the safety representative has the following functions:

a. to investigate the potential hazards and dangerous occurrences at the workplace, and to examine the causes of accidents;
b. to investigate complaints by any employee he represents relating to that employee's health, safety, or welfare at work;
c. to make representations to the employer about the above matters;
d. to make representations to the employer on general matters affecting the health, safety and welfare at work of the employees at the workplace;
e. to carry out inspections (see below);
f. to represent employees in consultations with inspectors of the Health and Safety Executive;
g. to receive information from the inspectors; and
h. to attend meetings of safety committees in his capacity as safety representative.

11.50 In order to perform these functions adequately, the employer shall permit the safety representative to have time off work with pay during his working hours, and also for the purpose of undergoing training in aspects of those functions as may be reasonable in the circumstances (see *White v Pressed Steel Fisher*), having regard to the provisions of the Code of Practice approved by the Commission for this purpose. The safety representative is entitled to be paid his normal earnings or average hourly earnings. In *Davies v Neath Port Talbot County Borough Council* it was held that a part-time employee, who went on a full-time health and safety training course, was entitled to be paid on the same basis as a full-time male counterpart. The training course was 'work' within the meaning of art 141 of the Treaty of Rome, and therefore she was entitled to equal pay

11.51 Safety representatives are entitled to carry out an inspection of the workplace at least every three months (or more frequently with the employer's consent), and also further inspections if there has been some substantial change in the conditions of work (eg by the introduction of new working processes, or the coming to light of new information disclosing a potential hazard). Inspections may also be carried out after a notifiable accident has occurred or a notifiable disease contracted, for the purpose of determining the cause. The employer shall provide reasonable facilities and assistance, but he, or his representative, may be present during the inspection.

11.52 The employer shall establish a safety committee when at least two safety representatives make such a request. For this purpose, he shall consult with these representatives, and also those of any recognised trade unions. A notice must be posted stating the composition of the committee, which must be established within three months of the request being made.

11.53 A complaint may be made to an employment tribunal that the employer has failed to permit a safety representative to have time off work for these purposes, or has failed to pay for such time off. If the complaint is well-founded, the tribunal shall make a declaration, and may make an award of compensation.

11.54 There was some doubt as to whether the Safety Representative and Safety Committee Regulations met the requirements of the 'Framework Directive' (89/391/EEC) because there was no means whereby employees in non-unionist firms could have a legal right to play their role in health and safety matters. Consequently, the Health and Safety (Consultation with Employees) Regulations 1996 were introduced. Under these regulations, an employer has two choices with respect to those employees who have no safety representative by virtue of the 1977 regulations. He can either consult with employees directly, or he can consult with one or more persons of any group of employees who were elected for the purposes of consultation, and who are referred to as 'representatives of employee safety'. There is no provision in the regulations as to how an employer shall organise any such elections, but apparently it is not necessary to have a statutory framework for this purpose (*R v Secretary of State for Trade and Industry, ex p UNISON*).

11.55 Under the 1996 regulations, employers must consult with their employees, or their elected representatives of employee safety, in good time, on matters concerning their health and safety at work, and, in particular, with regard to

(a) the introduction of any measures at the workplace which will substantially affect the health and safety of those employees
(b) the employer's arrangements for appointing or nominating a competent person to assist him, as required by reg 6(1) and 7(1)(b) of the Management Regulations
(c) any health and safety information he is required to provide to the employees under any relevant statutory provision
(d) the planning and organisation of any health and safety training he is required to provide by virtue of any statutory provision, and
(e) the health and safety consequences for the employees of the introduction of new technologies into the workplace (including the planning thereof).

11.56 In such consultations, representatives of employee safety have the following functions:
(a) to make representations to the employer on potential hazards and dangerous occurrences at the workplace, which affect the employees represented;
(b) make representations to the employer on general matters affecting the health and safety of employees, in particular, on matters referred to in paras (a)-(e) above;
(c) represent the group of workers he represents in consultations at the workplace with health and safety inspectors.

11.57 If the employer consults with employees directly, he must make available to them such information as is necessary to enable the employees to participate fully and effectively in the consultation process. If the employer consults with representatives of employee safety, he must make available such information as is necessary to enable them to carry out their functions. But the rights and functions of employee representatives under the 1996 regulations are more limited than those which apply under the 1977 regulations. In particular, they have no right to carry out workplace inspections, attend meetings of a safety committee, inspect statutory health and safety documents, or investigate employees' complaints and notifiable accidents or dangerous occurrences. However, such matters are provided for in the guidance notes which have been issued. An employee safety representative has the right to be paid when carrying out his functions as such, or is being trained.

Right not to suffer a detriment in health and safety cases (ERA s 44)

11.58 An employee is entitled not to be subjected to any detriment by an act or a failure to act by his employer on any of the following grounds:
a. having been designated by the employer to carry out activities in connection with preventing or reducing risks to health and safety at work, he carried out (or proposed to carry out) those activities;
b. being a safety representative or member of a safety committee, he performed (or proposed to perform) any functions as such or took part in consultations or in an election as an employee safety representative;
c. if there is no safety representative or safety committee where he is, or, if there are, it is not reasonably practicable to raise such matters, he brought the employer's attention (by reasonable means) to circumstances connected with his work which he reasonably believed were harmful or potentially harmful to health or safety;

d. in circumstances of danger which he reasonably believed to be serious and imminent and which he could not reasonably be expected to avert, he left, or proposed to leave, or, while the danger persisted, he refused to return to, his place of work or any dangerous part of his place of work;
e. in circumstances of danger which he reasonably believed to be serious and imminent, he took, or proposed to take, appropriate steps to protect himself or other persons from the danger. This is to be judged by reference to all the circumstances, including his knowledge, and the facilities and advice available to him at the time. However, he will not have been subjected to a detriment if he was so negligent in the steps he took that the employer treated him as a reasonable employer would have done in those circumstances.

11.59   An employee who believes that he has suffered a detriment contrary to s 44 may bring a complaint before an employment tribunal within the usual time limits. If the complaint is upheld, the tribunal shall make a declaration to that effect, and also award compensation to the complainant, the amount being such as the tribunal considers to be just and equitable in all the circumstances. This will include any expenses incurred and take account of any benefits lost. The employee is expected to mitigate against his loss, and the compensation award can be reduced on the ground of contributory conduct (see para 17.291).

11.60   But if a safety representative acts in respect of matters which are not within the area of the workplace for which he is a representative, or acts outside the laid down procedure, or acts in bad faith, then it may be that he is not pursuing a genuine health and safety matter, but is pursuing a personal agenda in order to embarrass the employer. In such circumstances, he may be disciplined as appropriate (*Shillito v Van Leer (UK) Ltd*).

Dismissal in health and safety cases (ERA s 100)

11.61   It will be unfair to dismiss an employee because of any of the following circumstances arising out of health and safety matters:
a. having been designated by the employer to carry out activities in connection with preventing or reducing risks to health and safety at work, he carried out (or proposed to carry out) those activities. In *Healey v Excel Logistics Ltd* a safety representative went to the site of another company in order to inspect an entry in that company's accident book concerning an accident which involved one of the employees he represented. His subsequent dismissal for doing so was held to be unfair, because his duties as a safety representative were not confined to incidents which took place on his employer's premises;
b. being a safety representative or member of a safety committee he performed (or proposed to perform) any functions as such, or took part in consultations as an employee safety representative, or in an election of representatives of employee safety;
c. if there is no safety representative or safety committee where he is, or, if there are, it is not reasonably practicable to raise such matters, he brought the employer's attention (by reasonable means) to circumstances connected with his work which he reasonably believed were harmful or potentially harmful to health or safety;
d. in circumstances of danger which he reasonably believed to be serious and imminent and which he could not reasonably be expected to avert, he left, or proposed to leave, or, while the danger persisted, he refused to return to, his

place of work or any dangerous part of his place of work. In *Harvest Press Ltd v McCaffrey* an employee left work because he felt he was in danger of being injured due to the behaviour of another employee towards him, who had been abusive and aggressive. His dismissal for leaving work was held to be unfair, for s 100(1)(d) was not confined to circumstances of danger which arose from working methods or equipment;

e. in circumstances of danger which he reasonably believed to be serious and imminent, he took, or proposed to take, appropriate steps to protect himself or other persons from the danger. This is to be judged by reference to all the circumstances, including his knowledge, and the facilities and advice available to him at the time. The term 'other persons' includes members of the public, as well as fellow employees, so that a chef who was dismissed because he refused to cook food which he believed to be unfit for human consumption succeeded in a claim for unfair dismissal under s 100 (*Masiak v City Restaurants (UK) Ltd*). However, his dismissal shall not be regarded as being unfair if he was so negligent in the steps he took that the employer treated him as a reasonable employer would have treated him in those circumstances.

11.62 It should be noted that if a dismissal is unfair by virtue of a. or b. above, and the employer refuses to reinstate or re-engage the employee following a tribunal order, an additional award (see para 17.303) can be made. The test to be applied is not only whether the employee genuinely feared for his safety, but whether that fear was based on reasonable grounds. This is a question of fact, to be determined not only by the nature of the potential danger, but the steps which the employee could have taken to follow any procedures laid down by the employer which would militate against the danger (*Kerr v Nathan's Wastesavers Ltd*). Otherwise, there is no limit on the amount of the compensation award if the dismissal (or selection for redundancy) was contrary to s 100.

11.63 However, when it comes to a dismissal on other grounds, the protection afforded to a safety representative is neutral. Like a shop steward, he has no specially privileged position, and thus may be selected for redundancy in accordance with the appropriate selection criteria (*Smiths Industries Aerospace and Defence Systems v Rawlings*).

Interim relief in health and safety cases (ERA ss 128–130)

11.64 If an employee is dismissed for an inadmissible reason because he has been designated to carry out health and safety activities, or is a safety representative or member of a safety committee (see para 11.61) and he proposed to carry out activities as such, he may apply for interim relief, within seven days following the effective date of termination of his employment. The procedure and remedies are similar to the interim relief provisions contained in TULR(C)A ss 161–166 (see para 21.126).

Duty owed to non–employees (s 3)

11.65 It shall be the duty of every employer, and every self-employed person, to conduct his undertakings in such a way as to ensure, so far as is reasonably practicable, that persons who are not his employees who may be affected thereby are not exposed to risks to their health or safety. This duty applies not only to persons who are lawfully on the employer's premises, for example, students in an educational establishment, but also persons who are outside those premises, but who may be affected by the activities in question. Thus if there is a potential hazard on the employer's premises, he must provide information not only to his own employees, but to visitors and the employees of a sub-contractor who may be working there (*R v Swan Hunter Shipbuilders Ltd*). The employer also has a duty to specialist contractors who come on to the employer's site for the purpose of carrying on activities in respect of the employer's undertaking (*R v Associated Octel*).

Duties of controllers of premises (s 4)

11.66 Every person who has control of premises (not being domestic premises) must ensure, as far as it is reasonable for a person in his position to ensure, that so far as is reasonably practicable, all means of access thereto or egress therefrom, and plant and substance, in the premises, shall be safe and without risks to health in respect of persons who use those premises as a place of work (*Westminster City Council v Select Managements Ltd*). A person who has, by virtue of a contract of tenancy, the obligation to maintain or repair those premises, or be responsible for the safety or absence of risks therein, shall be the person to be regarded as being in control.

Duties of manufacturers, etc (s 6 as amended)

11.67 A duty is imposed on any person who designs, manufacturers, imports or supplies any article for use at work or any article of fairground equipment:
a.   to ensure, as far as reasonably practicable, that the article is so designed and constructed that it will be safe and without risks to health at all times when it is being set, used, cleaned or maintained by a person at work. However, sub-s (8) provides that where a person designs, manufactures, imports or supplies an article for use at work or an article of fairground equipment and does so for or to another on the basis of a written undertaking by that other that he will take specified steps to ensure, so far as is reasonably practicable, that the article will be safe and without risks to health at all the above mentioned times, the undertaking will release the designer, manufacturer, importer or supplier (as the case may be) from this duty, to such an extent as is reasonable having regard to the terms of the undertaking. For example, if a person wishes to sell second-hand machinery, it might be advisable to extract a written undertaking from the purchaser to ensure its complete overhaul before putting it to use;
b.   to carry out or arrange for the carrying out of such testing and examination as may be necessary for the performance of the above duty. However, this does not require the repeating of any tests or examinations which may have been carried out by others, in so far as it is reasonable to rely on the results of those others' work;
c.   to take such steps as are necessary to secure that persons supplied by that person with the article are provided with adequate information about the use for which the article has been designed or has been tested, and about any conditions necessary to ensure that it will be safe and without risks to health at all times as are mentioned above, and also when it is being dismantled or disposed of;
d.   to take all such steps as are necessary to secure, so far as is reasonably practicable, that persons so supplied are provided with any revision of the

above information by reason of it becoming known that anything gives rise to a serious risk to health or safety.

11.68 Similar obligations are placed upon persons who design, manufacture, import or supply articles of fairground equipment used for or in connection with the entertainment of members of the public.

11.69 There is also a duty on designers and manufacturers (but not importers or suppliers) to carry out or arrange for the carrying out of any necessary research with a view to the discovery and, so far as is reasonably practicable, the elimination or minimisation of any risks to health or safety to which the design or article may give rise, but again, this does not require the repeating of any research already carried out, if it was reasonable to rely on the results.

11.70 It is the duty of any person who erects or installs any article for use at work, or any article of fairground equipment, to ensure, so far as is reasonably practicable, that nothing about the way in which the article is erected, or installed makes it unsafe or a risk to health, when it is being set, used, cleaned or maintained by a person at work.

11.71 A duty is imposed on any person who manufactures, imports or supplies any substance:
a.   to ensure, so far as is reasonably practicable, that the substance will be safe and without risks to health at all times when it is being used, handled, processed, stored or transported by a person at work or in premises to which s 4 (above) applies;
b.   to carry out or arrange for the carrying out of such testing and examination as may be necessary for the performance of the above duty, but again this does not require the repeating of any tests or examinations which have been carried out by others, in so far as it is reasonable to rely on the results of those others' work;
c.   to take such steps as are necessary to secure that persons supplied by that person with the substance are provided with adequate information about any risks to health or safety to which the inherent properties of the substance may give rise, about the results of any relevant tests which have been carried out on or in connection with the substances, and about any conditions necessary to ensure that the substance will be safe and without risks to health at all such times as are mentioned above, and when it is being disposed of;
d.   to take such steps as are necessary to secure, so far as is reasonably practicable, that persons so supplied are provided with all such revisions of information as are necessary by reason of its becoming known that anything gives rise to a serious risk to health or safety.

11.72 A manufacturer of any substance is under a duty to carry out (or arrange for the carrying out of) any necessary research with a view to the discovery and, so far as is reasonably practicable, the elimination or minimisation of any risks to health or safety to which the substance may give rise, but he need not repeat any test, examination or research done by others in so far as it was reasonable for him to rely on the results thereof.

11.73 For the purposes of s 6, an absence of safety or a risk to health is to be disregarded in so far as it has arisen by an occurrence which could not be reasonably foreseen, and so far as the obligations placed on designers, manufacturers, importers and suppliers of articles and substances are concerned, regard may be had to any relevant information which has been provided by them to any person.

11.74 Section 6(7) provides that the above duties only extend to things done in the course of a trade, business or undertaking (whether for profit or not), and to matters within a person's control. The definition of 'article for use at work' (see s 53) is 'any plant designed for use or operation (whether exclusively or not) by persons at work, and any articles designed for use as a component in any such plant', a definition which may be somewhat restrictive. A substance is defined as being 'any natural or artificial substance (including micro-organisms) whether in a solid or liquid form or in the form of gas or vapour'.

11.75 An interesting point arises concerning the effect on civil contracts of the above provisions. Supposing, for example, an employer purchases a machine from a manufacturer, and this is delivered without safety instructions, or in an unguarded state. Could the employer reject the machine on the grounds that it was not fit for its purpose or not of satisfactory quality, contrary to the Sale of Goods Act 1979?

Duties of employees at work (s 7)

11.76 Every employee is under a duty while at work:
a. to take reasonable care for the health and safety of himself and of others who may be affected by his acts or omissions at work; this could mean that an employee who failed or refused to wear or use safety precautions which are provided would be in breach of his legal duty;
b. as regards any duty imposed on his employer or any other person, to co-operate with him so far as is necessary to enable that duty to be performed or complied with.

Duty not to interfere with safety provisions (s 8)

11.77 No persons shall intentionally or recklessly interfere with or misuse anything provided in the interest of health, safety or welfare in pursuance of any relevant statutory provisions. This duty is wider than the old law, which was directed against 'wilful' conduct, defined as perverse or deliberate action. Intentional or reckless conduct does not need to be wilful.

Duty not to charge (s 9)

11.78 An employer shall not charge any employee in respect of anything done or provided in pursuance of any relevant statutory provision (see Personal Protective Equipment at Work Regulations 1992, para 11.97).

Health and safety regulations (s 15 and Sch 3)

11.79 As has already been indicated, one of the main purposes of the Act was to replace the existing statutory provisions by regulations, and over a period of time, the 'old' law contained in the Factories Act 1961, Offices, Shops and Railway Premises Act 1963, and so forth (for a complete list, see column 3 in Sch 1 of the Act), has been phased out, and replaced with a system of regulations and Codes of Practice which, in combination with the other provisions of the Act, are designed to maintain and improve the standards of health, safety and welfare. Regulations are of three general types; first, there are those which lay down standards to be applied in most or all employment situations, second, there are those which are designed to control a particular hazard which may exist in a particular industry, and third, there are those which refer to particular hazards or risks but which may be found in a number of different industries. The view appears to be held that the use of regulations as a device for laying down legal standards is a superior method to legislation, for regulations are simpler and more flexible; they can be altered more readily in accordance with experience and technological progress, and will be more manageable to those who have to implement them.

11.80 Regulations are to be made by the Secretary of State either as a result of proposals made to him by the Commission, or on his own initiative, but in the latter case he must consult with the Commission and any other appropriate bodies. If the Commission makes the proposals, it, too, must consult with the appropriate government departments and other bodies (s 50). Regulations may:

a. repeal or modify any existing statutory provision;
b. exclude or modify in relation to any specific class of case any of the provisions of ss 2–9 (above) or any existing statutory provision;
c. make a specific authority responsible for the enforcement of any relevant statutory provision;
d. impose requirements by reference to the approval of the Commission or other specified body or person;
e. provide that any reference in a regulation to a specific document shall include a reference to a revised version of that document;
f. provide for exemptions from any requirement or prohibition;
g. enable exemptions to be granted by a specified person or authority;
h. specify the persons or class of persons who may be guilty of an offence;
i. provide for specified defences either generally or in specified circumstances;
j. exclude proceedings on indictment in relation to certain offences;
k. restrict the punishment which may be imposed in respect of certain offences.

11.81 Additionally, the Deregulation and Contracting Out Act 1994 s 37 empowers the Secretary of State to repeal or revoke pre-1974 legislation without replacement, and some 100 regulations and seven statutes are currently being considered under this deregulation initiative.

11.82 Schedule 3 of the Act contains detailed provisions about the content of regulations, wide enough to enable the Secretary of State and the Commission actively to pursue all avenues in the interests of health and safety. In particular, however, we may note two further important provisions. The first is the power to prohibit the carrying on of any specified activity or the doing of any specified thing without a licence granted for that purpose, which may be subject to conditions. The second is contained in s 235 of the Companies Act 1985, so as to enable the Secretary of State to prescribe cases whereby directors' reports will contain such information about the arrangements in force for that year for securing the health, safety and welfare at work of the employees of that company (and any subsidiary company), and for protecting other persons against risks to health resulting from the activities at work of the employees. To date, no such regulations have been made.

11.83   A breach of duty imposed by regulations is, of course, punishable as a criminal offence. Additionally, a breach may give rise to civil liability, except in so far as the regulations provide otherwise.

11.84–11.90   A number of regulations have been passed since 1974 dealing with all aspects of health and safety law. Reference should be made to an established textbook on this topic.

The impact of European law

11.91   Article 137 of the Treaty of Rome provides that member states shall pay particular attention to encouraging improvements, especially to the working environment, as regards the health and safety of workers. Under this article, Directives may be adopted by the qualified majority voting system, and a considerable number of such Directives have been adopted, and others are currently under discussion. In particular, the 'Framework Directive' (98/391/EEC) and five 'Daughter Directives' have recently been given effect to by the so-called 'six-pack' regulations (see below). The general view taken by the HSC is that the European Directives do not involve any significant change in UK law, although they do require UK law to make explicit that which is generally regarded as being implicit. Legal standards on health and safety in the UK are very high, and it is not expected that the following of EU Directives will impose any onerous burdens on UK employers.

11.92   In particular, six regulations (the so-called 'six pack' regulations) came into force on 1 January 1993. These are (a) Management of Health and Safety at Work Regulations, (b) Personal Protective Equipment at Work Regulations, (c) Provision and Use of Work Equipment Regulations, (d) Workplace (Health, Safety and Welfare) Regulations, (e) Manual Handling Operations Regulations, and (f) Health and Safety (Display Screen Equipment) Regulations. Many 'old' regulations have been revoked, and most of the existing protective legislation, found in the Factories Act 1961, Offices, Shops and Railway Premises Act 1963 etc, has now been repealed.

11.93   Fundamental to the new law is the need to take proactive steps to ensure health and safety at work of employees and others. These will include risk assessment in certain specified situations, provision of information to all those who may be at risk, health surveillance, the use of safety advisers, co-operation between employers, the provision of approved equipment and personal protection equipment and so on. Employees have a duty to use the equipment etc provided in a proper manner, to report shortcomings in the employer's protection arrangements or which represent a serious and immediate danger to health and safety.

A. Management of Health and Safety at Work Regulations 1999

11.94   These regulations set out the principles of prevention which should be applied, require employers to make risk assessments (in particular when women of child-bearing age are employed (see para 6.16) and in respect of young persons, see para 2.216), provide employees with appropriate health surveillance, appoint safety advisers, establish emergency procedures provide training and information to employees, and cooperate with other employers where the workplace is shared. Employees are required to use all machinery, equipment substances etc in accordance with any relevant training and instructions, and to inform the employer of any dangerous work situation or shortcomings in the health and safety arrangements.

B. Workplace (Health, Safety and Welfare) Regulations 1992

11.95 These regulations apply to all workplaces as from January 1996. Workplaces are to be maintained in an efficient state, repaired and cleaned. There must be a sufficient fresh or purified air, reasonable temperature, and heating must not produce injurious fumes. Lighting must be suitable and sufficient, there must be sufficient floor area, suitable seats provided if the work can be done seated, floors and traffic routes must be suitable, and windows, skylights and ventilators must be safe. Doors, gates, traffic routes and escalators must be constructed with safety in mind. There must be suitable and sufficient sanitary conveniences, washing facilities, and drinking water, and accommodation for clothes not worn during working hours and for changing clothes where necessary. Rest facilities must be provided, with suitable arrangements to protect non-smokers from discomfort from tobacco smoke, and suitable facilities for eating meals.

C. Provision and Use of Work Equipment Regulations 1998

11.96 Work equipment must be suitable, efficiently maintained, kept in good repair and conform to any legislation which implements any relevant EC Directive. Employees must be given adequate health and safety information, written instructions where appropriate, and be properly trained. Effective measures must be taken to prevent access to any dangerous parts of machinery, and measures must be taken to prevent or adequately control certain specified hazards. Starting and stopping controls (including emergency stop controls) must be provided and clearly marked. Work equipment must be stable, capable of being isolated from all its sources of energy, maintenance operations must be carried out while work equipment is shut down, and warning devices clearly visible, unambiguous, easily perceived and understood.

D. Personal Protective Equipment at Work Regulations 1992

11.97 Personal protective equipment (PPE) is all equipment intended to be worn or held by a person at work which protects him from risks to health or safety. PPE is not suitable unless it conforms to applicable EC standards.

11.98 Employers must provide suitable PPE, which must be compatible with other such equipment worn. There must be an assessment of the suitability, and PPE must be maintained in an efficient state, kept in good repair, and cleaned or replaced as appropriate. Employers must provide employees with information, instruction and training about risks PPE will avoid or limit, and ensure that it is properly used. Employees must use PPE in accordance with instructions and training given, and report any defect or loss.

E. Manual Handling Operations Regulations 1992

11.99   Every employer must, so far as is reasonably practicable, avoid the need for his employees to undertake manual handling operations which involve the risk of injury. If such operations cannot be avoided, the employer must carry out an assessment of the operations, and take appropriate steps to reduce the risk of injury, and provide employees with indications of the risk and the weight of the load. Schedule 1 to the Regulations sets out a comprehensive list of questions to be asked and factors taken into account in order to avoid or minimise the risks from manual handling. Employees shall make proper use of any system of work provided.

F. Health and Safety (Display Screen Equipment) Regulations 1992

11.100–11.110   Employers are required to make an analysis of workstations for the purpose of assessing health and safety risks so as to reduce these to the lowest extent reasonably practicable. The activities of users must be planned, so as to ensure they have periodic breaks or changes in activities. If a user so requests, the employer must provide eye and eyesight testing, and provide special corrective appliances when needed. Adequate health and safety training must be given in the use of workstations, and information given about all aspects of health and safety relating to workstations.

Codes of practice (s 16)

11.111   For the purpose of providing practical guidance with respect to the general duties imposed by ss 2–7 (above), or by any regulation or any existing statutory provisions, the Commission may approve and issue codes of practice which are suitable for that purpose. The Commission may also approve other such suitable codes which are drawn up by other persons or organisations, and thus there is no reason why a private firm or employers' organisation should not draw up its own code and submit it for approval, should this be thought desirable. One might also expect approval to be given to the existing British Standards Institution's own codes. The Commission cannot approve a code without the consent of the Secretary of State, and prior to obtaining this, must consult with government departments and other appropriate bodies. The codes may be revised from time to time, and the Commission may, if necessary, withdraw its approval from a particular code.

11.112   A failure on the part of any person to observe the provisions contained in an approved code of practice shall not of itself render that person liable to any civil or criminal proceedings, but in any such criminal proceedings, if a person is alleged to have committed an offence concerning a matter in respect of which an approved code is in force, the provisions of that code shall be admissible in evidence, and a failure to observe it shall constitute proof of the breach of duty, or contravention of the regulation or statutory provision, unless the accused can satisfy the court that he complied with the requirements of the law in some other equally efficacious manner. The codes, therefore, will be the guides to good safety practice, and if a person follows the provisions of the codes, he cannot be successfully prosecuted for an offence. If he fails to follow the relevant code, he may be guilty of an offence unless he can show that he observed the specific legal requirement some other way.

11.113–11.120 The Act contains no guidance on the use of the codes in civil proceedings, but it is likely that a failure to observe any such provision as is contained therein may well constitute prima facie evidence of negligence, which can be rebutted by evidence to the contrary.

Penalties (s 33)

11.121 Any person or body corporate (eg a company) may be charged with and convicted of an offence under the Act, and punished accordingly. In addition, if an offence committed by a body corporate is proved to have been committed with the consent of, connivance of, or attributable to any neglect on the part of, any director, manager, secretary or other similar officer, then he, as well as the body corporate may be guilty of an offence, and liable to be proceeded against and punished accordingly (s 37) (see *Huckerby v Elliott*).

11.122 In *Armour v Skeen*, a senior local government official was prosecuted for failing to prepare and carry out a safety policy, for this neglect of duty ultimately led to breaches of safety provisions which resulted in the death of an employee. It was held that the official was guilty of an offence under s 37. He was in a senior position in his organisation, and was therefore responsible for the general safety policy in his department. But in *R v Boal* the accused was an assistant manager in a bookshop. Following a visit by inspectors, he was prosecuted and convicted in respect of a number of offences. On appeal, it was held that criminal liability was to be imposed on persons in authority in the company who were the 'decision makers', with the power and responsibility to decide corporate policy. As the accused was an 'underling', his conviction was quashed.

11.123 Where the commission of an offence by a person is due to the default of another person, that other person may be proceeded against, whether or not proceedings are taken against the first mentioned person (s 36). No proceedings under the Act may be brought except by an inspector, or with the consent of the Director of Public Prosecutions (in Scotland, the Procurator Fiscal).

11.124 There is an anomaly, however, in that although Crown bodies (excluding health authorities) have the same obligations under the Act as other employers, they cannot be prosecuted, and it is not possible to issue improvement or prohibition notices against the Crown. However, this rule does not prevent the prosecution of individual Crown employees.

11.125 If a person is found guilty of an offence on summary conviction in the magistrates' court, the maximum punishment is a fine of up to £5,000 or £20,000, depending on the nature of the offence, and/or six months' imprisonment. If proceedings are brought on indictment (ie in the Crown Court before a jury), there is the possibility of an unlimited fine, and in certain specified cases, up to two years' imprisonment. The full list of offences and punishments can be found in Appendix A. In *R v Howe & Son (Engineers) Ltd* the Court of Appeal gave guidance on how sentencing policies should be applied to convictions for health and safety offences.

CHAPTER 12

Disciplinary powers of management

12.1 During the performance of the employment contract the employer may find it necessary, through his appropriate manager, foreman, supervisor or committee charged with the necessary responsibility, to exercise some form of disciplinary authority over the employee, which may take one of a number of forms. It will be recalled (Chapter 3) that the employer must give a note to each employee specifying any disciplinary rules which are applicable to him (or referring him to a reasonably accessible document which contains those rules) and any appeal procedure.

12.2–12.10 Further guidance can be found in the Code of Practice on Disciplinary and Grievance Procedures and in the ACAS Advisory Handbook, which should be studied in detail by all levels of management. Basically, we are concerned with the procedures required for the exercise of disciplinary powers, the matters which will give rise to those procedures being implemented, and the exercise of the actual disciplinary powers.

Disciplinary procedures

12.11 The responsibility for drawing up a disciplinary procedure is on the employer. Clearly, if he can obtain the co-operation and assistance of any relevant trade union, or of his employees, so much the better, but in the absence of such co-operation, the employer must draw up a procedure. The advantages of having trade union involvement either in the drawing up stages or having the unions accepting the procedures which have been laid down, are numerous. For example, in *East Hertfordshire District Council v Boyten*, the claimant was dismissed for fighting in the street with another employee. He appealed through the internal machinery, which had been accepted by all the unions in the industry. The procedure permitted either side to call witnesses and have them cross-examined, but none was called at the appeal hearing, and the dismissal was confirmed. The employment tribunal thought that the appeal committee should, of its own volition, have called as witnesses the other employee involved in the fight as well as other employees who witnessed the incident. On appeal, the EAT held that the employer, by acting in accordance with the disciplinary machinery which had been drawn up with the approval of the unions could not be said to have acted unreasonably. It was not for the employment tribunals to rewrite that machinery. It is the duty of the employment tribunal to consider the employer's investigations and procedures on the basis of facts which were known to the employer at the time, and it is not for them to consider the employer's actions on the basis of facts which were placed for the first time before the employment tribunal (*Dick v Glasgow University*).

12.12   There is a distinction between disciplinary proceedings which are brought for misconduct, and those which are used in cases of capability, and indeed, the two things should ideally be dealt with under different procedures altogether. It has been held that misconduct procedures should be strictly construed, and hence pursued with all due formality, whereas the same strictness is not essential if the matter concerns the capability of the employee (*Littlewoods Organisation Ltd v Egenti*). Indeed, disciplinary procedures should only be used for matters which are truly issues of discipline.

12.13   On the other hand, the absence of a disciplinary procedure (except in very small establishments, see *MacKellar v Bolton*), or the existence of an unfair procedure, makes it very difficult for an employer to argue that he has acted fairly. This also applies to the unfair operation of a fair procedure, unless it can be shown nonetheless that the employer acted reasonably in the circumstances (*Earl v Slater & Wheeler (Airlyne) Ltd*). For example, in *Pritchett and Dyjasek v J McIntyre Ltd*, the employers received confidential information which implicated the appellants in a series of thefts. It was not possible to disclose to the employees the source of the information, and so they were dismissed without being given a chance to say anything in their defence. In the special circumstances of the case, the dismissals were held to be fair. The employers had acted on a genuine belief that the employees were guilty of theft, that belief was held on reasonable grounds, and there had been a full investigation into the whole matter. Had the employees been invited to comment on the allegations, there would have been merely a series of general denials. Thus a disciplinary hearing would have been a meaningless formality.

12.14   If the employer did not follow a fair procedure, it was long thought that the employment tribunal could engage in a hypothetical exercise and ask themselves whether, if a fair procedure had been followed, the employee would have been fairly dismissed. If this was so, it was argued, then the unfair procedure did not make any difference to the end result (*British Labour Pump Co Ltd v Byrne*). However, the House of Lords have recently confirmed that this view is incorrect. Whether or not a dismissal is fair is to be judged by what the employer did, not on what he might have done. In *Polkey v A E Dayton Services Ltd*, the appellant was one of four van drivers. It was decided to reorganise the work, and the four van drivers were to be replaced by two van salesmen and one representative. Only one of the four drivers was considered suitable for the new reorganised system, and hence the other three were made redundant. The appellant was called into the manager's office and was told that he was being made redundant with immediate effect. An employment tribunal held that there had been a complete disregard for the provisions of the Code of Practice in not consulting with or warning the appellant, but also held that had there been such consultation and warning, the result (ie the dismissal) would have been the same, and therefore the dismissal was fair. This finding was upheld by the EAT and the Court of Appeal, but the House of Lords reversed the decision, and remitted the case to another employment tribunal. If an employer could reasonably conclude in the light of circumstances known to him at the time that consultation and/or warnings would be utterly useless, then he might well act reasonably even if he did not observe the provisions of the Code of Practice. But an employment tribunal was not entitled to consider whether, if the employer had acted differently, he might have dismissed fairly. In other words, it is necessary to concentrate on what the employer did, not upon what he might have done. Thus, unless the employer has reasonable grounds for believing that consultation would be useless, the lack of a fair procedure will inevitably lead to a finding of unfair dismissal. The line of cases conveniently known as the *British Labour Pump* principle was consequently overruled.

12.15 However, it will still be necessary to look at the effect of the failure to follow a fair procedure for the purpose of assessing the amount of compensation to be awarded, for this is awarded on the basis of it being just and equitable to do so. Thus, if a dismissal is unfair because of a procedural defect, compensation may be reduced by a percentage, representing the chance that the employee would still have lost his employment (*Spink v Express Foods Group Ltd*). And even if no compensation is awarded, an employee may still be entitled to a basic award, for it can rarely be said that it would be useless to follow a fair disciplinary procedure (eg by failing to interview an employee prior to making a decision to dismiss, see *Charles Robertson Developments Ltd v White*). The basic award is not to be reduced under the *Polkey* principle (*Chamberlain Vinyl Products Ltd v Patel*).

12.16 A failure to follow the Code of Practice does not mean automatically that a dismissal will be unfair (*Lewis Shops Group v Wiggins*), but employers will ignore the Code at their peril. Further, if a disciplinary procedure is incorporated into the contract of employment, a failure to follow that procedure may constitute a breach of contract by the employer.

12.17 In some circumstances, an employee may be able to obtain an injunction to restrain the employer from taking disciplinary action in breach of the agreed procedure as set out in the employee's contract of employment (*Peace v City of Edinburgh Council*). Alternatively, an employee may be able to resign and claim that he was 'constructively dismissed' (see Chapter 17), although the employer would still be able to argue that the 'dismissal' was fair in the circumstances.

12.18 Further, the employee may also be entitled to bring a claim for damages at common law, based on the additional length of time he would have been employed had the procedure been followed (*Gunton v London Borough of Richmond upon Thames*).

12.19 If an employee is dismissed, but is given a right to make an appeal in accordance with the company's disciplinary procedure, what is his legal position up to the time the appeal is heard? There are two possibilities.

12.20 First, if he is dismissed (with or without notice) the dismissal takes effect from the effective date of termination, and the fact that an appeal is pending does not alter that date. In *J Sainsbury Ltd v Savage* the applicant was dismissed for gross misconduct. On the effective date of termination he did not have the requisite period of continuous employment (26 weeks, as the law then was), but by the time the appeal was heard, more than 28 weeks had elapsed since the commencement of his employment. It was held that he could not pursue a claim for unfair dismissal. Thus using domestic appeal machinery merely suspends the dismissal; if the appeal is rejected, the original decision is confirmed (*Natt v Hillingdon Area Health Authority*). It follows that if a person alleges that s/he has been discriminated against at the appeal hearing, in that a person of another sex or race would not have had an appeal against dismissal rejected, this will not constitute a breach of the Sex Discrimination Act or the Race Relations Act, (see Chapter 4), because that person is not 'an employee' at the date of the appeal hearing (*Post Office v Adekeye*, para 4.235, and see *Drage v Governers of Greenford High School*, para 20.38).

12.21   Second, if he is dismissed, and placed on full pay pending an internal appeal, there is a suspension which does not terminate the contract, and hence he is still an employee up to the time of the appeal hearing (*Duffy v Northampton Area Health Authority*). But if an employee is qualified to bring a claim for unfair dismissal, and delays in presenting it to an employment tribunal because an internal appeal is pending so that he is outside the normal time limits, he would not normally be able to argue that it was not reasonably practicable to present his claim earlier, and is unlikely to be able to benefit from the escape clause (*Palmer v Southend-on-Sea Borough Council*).

12.22   On the other hand, if a person is dismissed, and then his appeal against dismissal is allowed, his period of employment is to be regarded as being continuous, for it is implicit in the contract that the period between the dismissal and appeal is one of suspension, and the result of the ultimate decision of the appeal process relates back to the date of the purported dismissal (*Howgate v Fane Acoustics*).

12.23   The composition of any disciplinary body will doubtless be determined by each employer in accordance with the size of the firm and the circumstances of each case. The procedure will lay down who can exercise authority, the extent of the authority, and the circumstances when it is exercised. For example, informal warnings may be given at a certain level by supervisors, formal warnings should be given in writing, and signed by someone who has power to issue and act on them, and so on. If an appeal may be made to a disciplinary board, its composition should be specified, with due regard to providing substitutes as appropriate. Otherwise a failure to do this may result in a dismissal being rendered unfair when it may have been fair. Thus in *Westminster City Council v Cabaj*, the employee was dismissed. He was entitled to appeal to an appeal tribunal consisting of three council members. At the actual hearing, only two council members turned up, and they proceeded to hear the appeal, and dismissed it. The employee was not asked if he agreed to the appeal being heard by two members. The Court of Appeal held that where there is a failure to comply with a contractually enforceable disciplinary procedure, it was for the employment tribunal to determine whether a consequent dismissal is fair or unfair, and there is no automatic assumption of unfairness. The employment tribunal must decide the issue in accordance with the matters set out in s 98 of ERA. But where public institutions are concerned, the persons sitting on the appeal body must have been validly appointed, and there is no power to ratify an invalid appointment (*R v Secretary of State for Education, ex p Prior*).

Once a fair procedure has been laid down, an employee must follow it through even though he has little confidence in it (*Murray v British Railways Board*), for it will form part of his conditions of employment.

12.24 The actual operation of the procedure should be flexible enough to deal with all the likely occurrences. Thus, in a serious case, it should be possible to by-pass the early stages of procedure and go right to the final stage; if an employee committed an act of serious neglect or gross misconduct, it would be idiotic if this had to be dealt with by an informal warning, on the ground that this is the first stage!

12.25 In *Clark v Civil Aviation Authority*, the EAT gave some broad guidance on how disciplinary proceedings should be conducted. The purpose of the meeting should be explained, those present identified, representation should be arranged, the employee should be informed of the allegations being made, the evidence should be presented in statement form or through witnesses, the employee or his representative should be permitted to ask questions, the employee should be permitted to call witnesses, he or his representative will then explain or argue his case, both sides can then argue on the allegations and any possible consequences, including mitigation, and the employee will finally be asked if there is any further evidence or enquiry which will help his case. The decision will then be reduced to writing (whether or not an earlier oral decision has been given).

12.26 Particular care should be taken when it is proposed to take disciplinary action against shop stewards, and the Code of Practice recommends that it is advisable to discuss the circumstances of the case with a full-time official of the union concerned. However, being a shop steward is not a passport to disciplinary immunity (*Fowler v Cammell Laird (Shipbuilders) Ltd*).

12.27 A disciplinary hearing must be conducted fairly. To achieve this, a number of rules should be observed.
a. The employee is entitled to know the nature of the charge against him, in sufficient detail to enable him to prepare his case (*Hutchins v British Railways Board*). It is no bad thing to put this in writing, particularly if the employee's command of English is weak, so that he can get someone else to explain to him the nature of the allegations he has to meet (*Sharma v West Yorkshire Passenger Transport Executive*). Witness statements should be shown to him (*Louies v Coventry Hood and Seating Co Ltd*) although it is acknowledged that there may be occasions when it is necessary to preserve anonymity (*Linfood Cash and Carry Ltd v Thomson*, see para 12.46). But in *Fuller v Lloyds Bank plc* an employee of the respondents was in a public house on Christmas Eve, and received severe facial injuries from a glass which the applicant held in his hand. The employers took statements from a number of witnesses, but these were not disclosed to the applicant, as a matter of policy. Following a disciplinary hearing, he was dismissed, and claimed his dismissal was unfair. An employment tribunal dismissed his claim, arguing that the applicant knew the nature of the allegations. An appeal to the EAT failed. The procedure adopted was not so defective as to make the overall result unfair. Thus there is no universal requirement of natural justice or general principles of law that in all cases a witness statement must be shown to an employee who has been accused of misconduct. It is only a failure of natural

justice if the essence of the case against the employee is contained in the statements, and he has not been otherwise informed of the nature of the case against him (*Hussain v Elonex plc*).

b. An employee should always be given an opportunity to state his case (*Tesco (Holdings Ltd) v Hill*) no matter what the circumstances are. He is entitled to plead that he did not do the alleged act, or that he did not intend the construction which has been put on it, or that mitigating circumstances relating to his case should be taken into consideration (*Budgen & Co v Thomas*, below). To dismiss a woman who, because of a pregnancy-related illness, is unable to attend a disciplinary hearing is to cause her to suffer a detriment on grounds of pregnancy, and is therefore direct sex discrimination (*Abbey National plc v Formosa*). However, it is not essential that he should be present in person throughout the hearing, when all the evidence is being given, if his representative is there (*Pirelli General Cable Works v Murray*). The opportunity given to an employee to 'state his case' cannot be underestimated or undervalued. The reason is perhaps obvious; as Sir Robert Megarry said in *John v Rees*: '... the path of the law is strewn with examples of open and shut cases which, somehow, were not; of unanswerable charges which, in the event, were completely answered; of inexplicable conduct which was fully explained; of fixed and unalterable determinations that, by discussion, suffered a change. Nor are those with any knowledge of human nature who pause to think for a moment likely to underestimate the feelings of resentment of those who find that a decision against them has been made without their being afforded any opportunity to influence the course of events.'

However, in rare cases, where there is no possibility of any explanation of the conduct alleged, or where misconduct is admitted by the employee, it is legally permissible (although possibly in practice undesirable) to dispense with disciplinary formalities (*Clarke v Trimoco Motor Group Ltd*). Thus in *Sutherland v Sonat Offshore (UK) Inc* the employers had a strict rule forbidding alcohol or drugs while employees were on a drilling unit. The appellant was given a routine drug test, which showed the presence of cannabis in his urine, and the result was confirmed in further tests. He was dismissed without being given a proper chance to state his case, but the EAT upheld a finding of an employment tribunal that his dismissal was nonetheless fair. The requirement for investigation was met by the testing procedures, there was no possibility of an error and there was no way the substance could have been ingested by some other means, eg 'passive smoking'. Thus the employers were entitled to act on the evidence before them without involving the full disciplinary procedure.

c. He should be permitted the right to be represented or accompanied in accordance with the procedure (*Rank Xerox (UK) Ltd v Goodchild*). There is now a statutory right to be accompanied (see below).

d. He should be informed of his right to appeal to a higher level of management, who have not previously been involved in the decision (*S C Brown Communications Ltd v Walker*), or to an independent arbitrator. If he fails or refuses to exercise that right, then he does not contribute to the unfair dismissal, nor does he fail to mitigate his loss (*William Muir (Bond 9) Ltd v Lamb*) but he may find that his compensation will be reduced by an amount considered to be just and equitable, not exceeding two weeks' pay (ERA s 127A(1)).

Right to be accompanied: Employment Relations Act ss 10–15

12.28 Section 10 of the Employment Relations Act 1999 creates a new right for a worker, when invited by his employer to attend a disciplinary or grievance hearing, to make a reasonable request to be accompanied by a single companion, who can be either

(a) an official of an independent trade union (not necessarily one recognised by the employer), or

(b) a trade union official who has been certified by the trade union as having had experience or having received training in acting as a worker's companion in such hearings (eg a shop steward), or

(c) another of the employer's workers.

12.29 A disciplinary hearing is defined as being a hearing which could result in the administration of a formal warning by the employer, or the taking of some other action in respect of the worker, or the confirmation of a warning issued or action taken (eg at an appeal hearing). A grievance hearing is a hearing which concerns the performance of a duty by an employer in relation to the worker.

12.30 The companion is entitled to address the hearing, and confer with the worker during the hearing but he is not entitled to answer questions on behalf of the worker. However, there is no obligation on any person, whether he is or is not a trade union official, to accompany another worker.

12.31 If the worker makes a request to be accompanied, but the chosen companion is not available at the time proposed for the hearing, the employer must postpone the hearing to a time proposed by the worker. The alternative time must be reasonable, and within five working days after the date proposed by the employer.

12.32 The employer shall permit a worker to have time off work for the purpose of accompanying another worker, and, when acting in the capacity of a trade union official, this will count as trade union duties for the purpose of ss 168–173 of TULR(C)A, and thus the time off work will be with pay.

12.33 The right to be accompanied applies to workers as defined, including agency workers, homeworkers, persons in Crown employment and members of the staff of the House of Lords and House of Commons (s 13). However, persons employed by the Security Services, Secret Intelligence Service and Government Communications Headquarters are excluded from the above provisions (s 15).

12.34 A complaint may be made to an employment tribunal (within the usual time limits) that the employer has failed to permit the worker to exercise his rights under s 10, which, if it finds the complaint to be well-founded, shall make a compensation award of up to two weeks' pay (s 11).

12.35 A worker has the right not to suffer a detriment because he sought to be accompanied or to accompany another, and any dismissal because of the exercise of the above rights will be automatically unfair. The qualifying periods of employment and the age limits do not apply, and interim relief will be available, as appropriate (s 12).

Conducting a disciplinary procedure

12.36   If a disciplinary procedure has been incorporated into the employee's contract of employment, it should be strictly complied with. But if there is a defect in, for example, the constitution of an appeal body, it is still open to an employment tribunal to decide that a failure to follow a contractually enforceable disciplinary procedure did not render a decision to dismiss unfair (*Westminster City Council v Cabaj*). Thus, if the procedure is cumbersome, it must be followed unless the employee agrees to a variation (*Stocker v Lancashire County Council*). The proper way to proceed is to alter the procedure subsequently to avoid future problems, rather than to depart from it when a problem first presents itself.

12.37   If the initial procedure is flawed in some way a refusal by the employer to permit an employee to exercise the right of appeal to which he is contractually entitled will render a dismissal unfair (*West Midlands Co-operative Society v Tipton*) and may also result in an increase in the compensatory award of up to two weeks' pay (ERA s 127A(2)). If an employer's decision to dismiss would be fair at the time when the appeal machinery is exhausted, that decision does not become unfair because further information comes to light after the appeal has been dismissed (*Greenall Whitley plc v Carr*).

12.38   Whether an appeal hearing should be a rehearing of all the evidence *de novo*, or a review of all the evidence with an opportunity to make further representations, is a matter of style. However, if there is a substantial unfairness at the original hearing, this is unlikely to be corrected on review, and the appeal should then be a rehearing, when the unfairness can be rectified (*Whitbread & Co plc v Mills* and *Sartor v P and O European Ferries (Felixstowe) Ltd*). Thus if an initial decision to dismiss was unfair, the defect can be cured by a rehearing of the case by way of appeal (*Adwihalli v Export Guarantee Department*) provided there is a complete rehearing of all the evidence, and not merely a review of the original decision (*Lloyd v Taylor Woodrow Construction Ltd*).

12.39   However, it is very important that internal appeals procedures operated by commercial concerns should not be cramped by legal requirements which impose impossible burdens on the way they conduct their affairs. In *Rowe v Radio Rentals* the claimant was alleged to have been guilty of gross misconduct, and was dismissed by the area manager. An appeal was made to the regional manager and at the hearing the area manager outlined the facts of the case and remained present throughout the hearing. It was held that the appeals procedure was perfectly fair, even though it may appear to have offended against the rules of natural justice. It was inevitable that those who take the original decision to dismiss must be in daily contact with their superiors who would be hearing the appeal. Rules about lack of contact cannot be applied in the majority of cases. The EAT quoted with approval Lord Denning in *Ward v Bradford Corpn*: 'We must not force these disciplinary bodies to become entrammelled in the nets of legal procedure. So long as they act fairly and justly, their decision should be supported'.

12.40   Attempts to treat disciplinary and investigatory hearings with the same standards of strict legal proceedings have been resisted in a number of cases (eg *Longley v National Union of Journalists*), and the courts have insisted that they will only interfere in the most exceptional circumstances. Thus in *Ali v London*

Borough of Southwark, a local authority received allegations of mistreatment at an old persons' home, and set up an independent panel to investigate. The report of the panel contained detailed allegations of mistreatment by named members of staff, but the source of allegations was not disclosed, as the persons concerned had been promised confidentiality. The local authority then set up a disciplinary hearing, and the only evidence produced was the report. The claimant sought an injunction restraining the local authority from hearing the disciplinary charges without adducing evidence from witnesses to support the allegations, as required by the disciplinary procedure. The application was refused. A domestic tribunal would not be restrained unless it was acting improperly, or proposing to do so. The local authority could not substantiate the charges by direct evidence (indeed, they did not know the names of the witnesses who gave evidence before the panel of enquiry), but it was open to them to consider the report, and to weigh the evidence, along with all other matters. Further, although the report of the panel of enquiry was hearsay evidence which might not be admissible in a court of law, it was properly admissible before a domestic disciplinary hearing.

Investigations by the employer

12.41 There are certain limits to the extent an employer may properly make enquiries into an incident, particularly if the charge is a serious one, such as theft, for there may well be an improper interference with the processes of justice (*Tesco (Holdings) Ltd v Hill*). The important thing is that the employer does not have to prove that an offence took place, or even satisfy himself beyond all reasonable doubt that the employee committed the act in question. The function of the employer is to act reasonably in coming to a decision. Thus in *Ferodo Ltd v Barnes*, an employee was dismissed for vandalism. The employment tribunal was not satisfied that the employee was guilty, and therefore held that the dismissal was unfair. This finding was reversed by the EAT. The question was not whether or not the employment tribunal was satisfied that the employee was guilty, but whether they were satisfied that the employer had reasonable grounds for believing that the employee had committed the offence, and had acted reasonably in dismissing for that offence. The employer is not concerned to apply standards of proof which may be relevant in a criminal court. In *Docherty v Reddy*, the employee was dismissed for stealing 50p from the till. The employers took into account that they had suspected him of stealing similar sums on previous occasions, and it was held that they were entitled to have regard to their past suspicions. Clearly, a suspicion of previous theft is hardly evidence which would be admitted in a criminal court, but the issues are different. The employer is having to decide whether or not he wishes to retain the employee, not whether or not he was guilty of a particular offence. Thus the test is, what would a reasonable employer have done on the facts which he knew, taking into account the Code of Practice and current industrial relations practice (*Parkers Bakeries Ltd v Palmer*). The employment tribunal must not act as a court of appeal, nor retry a case, and the fact that in subsequent criminal proceedings an employee is acquitted of a charge against him is irrelevant to the issue of whether or not the employer has acted reasonably (*Davies v GKN Birwelco (Uskside) Ltd*).

12.42 Evidence which is not admissible in criminal proceedings may fairly be considered by an employer in disciplinary proceedings (*Dhaliwal v British Airways Board*) and a confession which would be inadmissible in a criminal court is also properly admissible before a disciplinary board (*Morley's of Brixton Ltd v Minott*).

12.43 If an employee pleaded guilty to a criminal offence in a court of law, or has been found guilty by the court, it is reasonable for an employer to believe that the offence has been committed by the employee. Any other conclusion 'would be ridiculous' (*P v Nottinghamshire County Council*). The fact of conviction might well form an adequate basis for dismissal, although the nature of the offence would be a relevant factor. Thus to dismiss for a trivial offence would not be reasonable (*Secretary of State for Scotland v Campbell*).

12.44 Whether an employer should carry out his own investigations after being informed that criminal charges are to be brought against an employee in respect of matters arising out of his employment is a question of circumstances. On the one hand, it is incumbent on an employer to embark on some form of investigation involving at least an interview with the employee, to give him an opportunity to state his position. On the other hand, if the circumstances are so blatant and sufficient to warrant a belief as to the employee's guilt, no further investigation is necessary. Within this spectrum there are many situations where a further consideration of the position, including an interview with the employee, should be considered before disciplinary action is taken (*Lovie Ltd v Anderson*).

12.45 The employer is not obliged to hold a full scale trial, but there must be a careful examination of all the relevant matters. An investigation should not be conducted with such haste that important evidence is overlooked (*Johnson Matthey Metals v Harding*), neither should it be delayed so long that issues become stale and hazy in the minds of witnesses (*Marley Homecare v Dutton*). There is no particular form of procedure to be adopted, as long as the employee is given a fair hearing (*Bentley Engineering Co v Mistry*). If it is necessary to consider disciplinary action in advance of criminal proceedings, it is still possible to discuss the matter without prejudicing a fair trial (*Harris (Ipswich) Ltd v Harrison*), and a decision may be made on the basis of known facts, even though the employee has been advised to remain silent. If the evidence produced is sufficiently indicative of guilt (in the absence of any explanation) the employer is entitled to take some action. If, however, there are doubts, fairness may require the employer to wait until the criminal proceedings have been concluded (*Harris and Shepherd v Courage (Eastern) Ltd*). The object in holding a full investigation is to confirm suspicions or clear up doubts as to whether or not a particular act of misconduct has occurred (see *British Home Stores v Burchell*). If an employee admits the offence, there is no need for a full investigation, unless some useful information could come to light (*Royal Society for the Protection of Birds v Croucher*).

12.46 When an allegation of an employee's misconduct has been made by an informant, a balance must be maintained between the need to protect the informant and respect his anonymity, and providing a fair hearing to the accused employee. In *Linfood Cash and Carry Ltd v Thomson*, the EAT laid down the following guidelines which could usefully be followed:
1. the information should be reduced into writing, although it may be necessary to 'doctor' the statement in order to prevent identification,
2. the statement should contain all the relevant facts, including dates, times, places, etc, the opportunity of the informant to observe clearly and with

accuracy, circumstantial evidence, and whether the informant had any reason to fabricate the evidence, whether from a personal grudge or any other reason,

3. further investigation should then take place to confirm, corroborate or challenge the information,
4. tactful enquiries should be made about the background of the informant, and to find any other information which would add to or detract from the value of the information given,
5. if the informant is not prepared to attend the disciplinary hearing, a decision will have to be taken on whether to continue or not,
6. if it is decided to continue, the person responsible for conducting the hearing should interview the informant, and assess the weight to be given to the information,
7. the written statement of the informant should be made available to the employee and his representatives,
8. if there are matters to be put to the informant, the person conducting the hearing should adjourn to make further enquiries,
9. full and careful notes of the disciplinary hearing should be taken,
10. evidence from the investigation officer should be prepared in a written form.

12.47 However, such tactics may not always result in the protection of the anonymity of the informant, as an employee who has been dismissed in consequence of information provided in this manner may be able to obtain from the High Court an order compelling his former employer to disclose the identity of the informant, so as to pursue an appropriate remedy, eg defamation and/or malicious falsehood (*P v T Ltd*).

12.48 A distinction must be drawn between the investigatory function and the disciplinary function. If the same person undertakes both, there is usually no problem, but when they are separate and distinct, there is an obligation to give an employee a hearing at both stages. In *Budgen & Co v Thomas*, an employee was dismissed after she had signed a written confession that she had stolen a small sum of money. The matter had been investigated by the security officer, and on the basis of his report, which was sent to the company's head office, the decision to dismiss was taken. This was held to be unfair. She was an 18-year-old girl, diabetic, and subsequently claimed that she was confused at the time she signed the confession, and that it was not true. It could not be said that in view of her personal circumstances the management would have dismissed her had she been given the opportunity to present her case; the person who took the decision to dismiss should at least have given her a hearing.

12.49 A person who is a witness in disciplinary proceedings should not act as a judge in those proceedings, otherwise this could be regarded as a breach of the principles of natural justice. However, there may be occasions when the person who has to take the decision to dismiss is also the person who witnessed the incident, and while this can be acceptable (and indeed inevitable) it is preferable for this dual role to be avoided (*Moyes v Hylton Castle Working Men's Social Club*).

12.50 In those cases where witnesses are not part of the employer's organisation, it is not necessary for the employer to carry out a quasi-judicial hearing, with a confrontation and cross-examination of those witnesses (*Ulsterbus Ltd v Henderson*).

12.51   A person who is involved in the investigatory stage should not, if possible, be involved in the appeal stage, as this would put him in a situation of being a judge in his own cause, and justice would not be done, as well as not appear to be done (*Byrne v BOC Ltd*). However, in the case of small employers, this counsel of perfection may not be possible.

12.52   At the end of the day, the employment tribunal must be satisfied that the employer's decision to dismiss fell within the range of reasonable responses of a reasonable employer. Tests laid down in earlier cases (eg *British Home Stores v Burchell*) and which were decided before the burden of proof was made neutral by the Employment Act 1980 should be regarded as laying down guidelines, not tramlines. For example, the fact that an employer fails to satisfy one of the tests laid down in *Burchell* does not, by itself, indicate that he has acted unreasonably, for the range of reasonable responses test must still be applied (*Boys and Girls Welfare Society v McDonald*).

Precautionary suspension

12.53   If an employee is suspended as a precautionary measure, and not for disciplinary purposes, the position is somewhat different. In *Jones v British Rail Hovercraft Ltd* the employee was suspended from duty without pay pending the outcome of investigations and proceedings against him which were brought by the police. He claimed that this amounted to a dismissal, but this argument was rejected. The rule book, which was part of his employment conditions, mentioned the distinction between precautionary and punitive suspension, and it was reasonable for the employer to take precautionary steps to protect his interest and his property. That the suspension was without pay could be dealt with by making up his back pay if the proceedings ended in his favour.

12.54   The Code of Practice states that precautionary suspension pending investigation should be with full pay, and this is probably correct in the absence of any contrary term in the contract. This could give rise to difficulties if the investigation is outside the control of management, for this could possibly go on for weeks or months. It is submitted therefore that precautionary suspension should be with pay if there is to be an internal investigation, but this may not be the rule in the case of external investigations. If this were not so, then the only alternatives available to the employer would be to retain an employee on full pay, or to dismiss him, and it is submitted that suspension without pay may turn out to be a better practice in some cases. In *Conway v Matthew, Wright & Nephew*, the claimant was a nightwatchman, and he was charged by the police with maliciously causing damage to the company's property. The company investigated the matter, and dismissed him. Subsequently, all criminal charges against him were dropped. It was argued that the company should have suspended him pending the outcome of criminal proceedings, but it was held that there was no legal obligation to do so, as it could have been many months before such charges were disposed of. The employers were under no obligation to refrain from dismissing him until the guilty conduct was established beyond reasonable doubt in a criminal court.

12.55   If there is an express contractual right to suspend with or without pay pending an investigation, this is subject to an implied term that the imposition of the suspension and its continuance would be on reasonable grounds. In *McClory v Post Office* three postmen were involved in a fight with employees from another office, and they were arrested and charged by the police with various offences. The Post Office suspended them on full pay, but without any payment for overtime which they would otherwise have worked. After making various enquiries, they were permitted to return to work some seven months later, and subsequently were acquitted of all the criminal charges. They brought an action for a declaration that their suspension had been in breach of their contracts of employment and they also sought damages for loss of overtime pay which they would have earned but for the suspension.

It was held that there was no breach of the employment contract. There was no duty on an employer to give reasons for the suspension or to give the employee an opportunity to be heard before it was imposed. The court refused to import the rules of natural justice into what is essentially a contractual arrangement between employer and employee. There was an implied term that the employer would exercise the express contractual right to suspend and to continue to suspend, only on reasonable grounds. To hold otherwise would enable an employer to suspend indefinitely. On the facts of the case, the employer had acted reasonably, and that aspect of the claim was dismissed.

The court also dismissed the claim for loss of overtime pay. The employees could not show that they had a right to overtime pay, only an obligation to work overtime when required. There was no duty on the employer to provide overtime on a regular basis, and thus the loss of a chance to work extra hours could not constitute the basis of a legal claim.

12.56–12.65 There is no legal requirement to suspend an employee prior to the undertaking of a full investigation, and a failure to do so does not weaken an allegation of gross misconduct. As a general rule, it is unwise to draw any conclusion from the act of or absence of suspension (*East Berkshire Health Authority v Matadeen*). If an employee is absent from work because he is suspended, there is no obligation for him to return to work until the suspension is lifted (*Hassan v Odeon Cinemas*).

Disciplinary rules

12.66 The actual rules which an employee is expected to observe can be found either in the disciplinary procedure itself, or in the works or staff rules (see Chapter 3) or even a combination of both. At one time it was customary to write them on a prominently displayed notice posted somewhere in the works, but this is not particularly satisfactory nowadays. The important thing is that they must be brought to the employee's attention, whether on an induction course, or in a specially prepared handbook or other suitable method. In *Pitts v Revertex* the employer posted a notice near the canteen on a notice board stating that any employee who absented himself without authority would be guilty of gross misconduct. The applicant was found to be absent, and was dismissed. It was held that if a rule was so important, posting a notice was not sufficient. It should have been communicated individually to each employee. The need to communicate the relevant rules to the employees concerned was stressed once again in *Brooks (W) & Son v Skinner*, where the employers agreed with a trade union that employees who over-indulged themselves at a Christmas party so that they were unable to attend work would be instantly dismissed. This agreement was not communicated to the employees. The applicant was dismissed for failing to turn up for work on the nightshift after a Christmas party, and his dismissal was held to be unfair. He would not have realised that this conduct would attract instant dismissal, and his lack of knowledge of the rule meant that the employers had acted unreasonably.

12.67 The rules should be clear and readily understandable by all affected employers, and should not be confused with extraneous matters. In *Rigden-Murphy v Securicor Ltd*, the claimant was dismissed after being seen to be breaking a company rule concerning the transfer of money from a bank to his vehicle. The rule in question was contained in a manual, which had 'Ten golden rules'. At the end, there was a statement that a failure to comply may lead to instant dismissal. Some of the 'rules' were in fact mere exhortations, such as 'Beware of complacency. Build up the habit of self-discipline'. Other rules had in the past been dealt with by a warning. It was held that the dismissal was unfair. The rules were somewhat ambiguous, in that they contained matters which were unconnected with discipline, and there was no clear line between those rules which attracted dismissal as a punishment, and those which were dealt with (if at all) with lesser severity.

12.68 Employment tribunals had, in the past, been most inconsistent in dealing with rules which contain automatic as opposed to discretionary sanctions. For example, in *Jones v London Co-operative Society* the staff code in a departmental store stated that an incorrect recording of a customer's purchase was a serious offence, 'and the employee *will be* summarily dismissed'. It was held that such a rule was too rigid, for it failed to distinguish between a genuine error and a calculated act. On the other, in *Lindsay v Fife Forge*, the works rules stated that employees who left the premises without permission '*may be* subject to instant dismissal' and the employment tribunal held that this did not amount to a clear and specific warning!

12.69 The problems caused by such sophistry can be illustrated by comparing *Dalton v Burton's Gold Medal Biscuits Ltd* and *Meridian Ltd v Gomersall*. In the former case, a man of 22 years' service was dismissed for a clocking offence, the works rules stating that such action 'will result in instant dismissal'. The National Industrial Relations Court held the dismissal to be fair. In the latter case, it was stated in the works rules that anyone guilty of a clocking offence 'will render themselves liable to instant dismissal'. The EAT upheld a tribunal decision that a dismissal was unfair, because the employee might take the view that to be caught once, even suspected of doing it previously, would not necessarily lead to an instant dismissal!

12.70 The question, in reality, is not the mandatory nature of the sanction, but whether the employer acts reasonably in imposing that sanction, or whether some other equally efficacious sanction could be imposed. It must be wrong to dismiss an employee for minor misconduct no matter how strongly worded is the rule, for the mandatory nature of a disciplinary rule does not exclude the jurisdiction of the employment tribunal to decide whether or not the employer has acted reasonably *(Ladbroke Racing Ltd v Arnott)*. On the other hand, automatic penalties fail to permit an employer to take account of mitigating circumstances, the employee's record, general conduct and so forth. The employer should be able to tailor the punishment to the offence, and then to the offender. He should be consistent in his procedures, but can be flexible in his punishments. In *Elliott Bros Ltd v Colverd* the EAT resolved doubts by stating that there is no legal requirement that a rule must indicate that a breach would inevitably lead to a dismissal, and a rule book did not need to indicate a distinction between the possibility and inevitability of dismissal. However the rule is worded, the employer is entitled to look at all the circumstances.

12.71 An employer must be prepared to justify any alleged disparity of treatment between different employees. In *Hadjioannou v Coral Casinos Ltd* the claimant was dismissed for breaking a rule which forbade socialising with members or guests at a gambling club. He argued that in the past other employees had broken the rule and had not been dismissed. In upholding a decision of the employment tribunal that the dismissal was fair, the EAT commented that action taken by the employers in previous cases was only relevant in three circumstances (a) to show that there may be certain categories of misconduct which may be overlooked (or at least not dealt with by the sanction of dismissal), (b) if it leads to the conclusion that the purported reason for the dismissal was not the real or genuine reason, and (c) to show that some lesser penalty would have been more appropriate. The EAT went on to comment that it was of the highest importance that flexibility should be retained, and employers should not be encouraged to think that there was a 'tariff' approach to industrial misconduct (see *Paul v East Surrey District Health Authority*, para 17.156).

12.72 Disparity of treatment is acceptable if culpability is not the same. In *Securicor Ltd v Smith*, the claimant and another employee were security guards, collecting and delivering cash. The employers had strict rules about the way they did their work. Following an incident when the rules were breached, the employers held a disciplinary hearing, and both employees were dismissed. An appeal was made to the area manager, who affirmed the dismissals. Both employees then lodged a further appeal to a special panel set up by the company, and at this level it was decided that as the other employee was less blameworthy, he would not be dismissed, but the dismissal of the claimant was confirmed. An employment tribunal held that his dismissal was unfair. They held that the original decision to dismiss both men was reasonable, but the final appeal body acted unreasonably in dismissing one employee but not the other on the ground that the other employee was less blameworthy. The decision was confirmed by the EAT. However, the Court of Appeal reversed the decision. The real question was whether the final appeal panel's decision was so unreasonable that no reasonable employer would have accepted it. Indeed, had the employers refused to accept the decision of the appeal panel not to dismiss the other employee, he would have had an unanswerable case for unfair dismissal in an employment tribunal. The appeal panel, having thoroughly investigated the matter, had distinguished the culpability of the two employees, and their decision was not unreasonable.

12.73 Similarly, disparity of treatment is permitted if disciplinary records are not the same. In *Harrow London Borough v Cunningham*, the claimant and a fellow worker were found to be doing unauthorised work in circumstances which amounted to gross misconduct. The claimant was dismissed, but his fellow worker was given a final warning. The reason for this was that the claimant had already been in receipt of a final warning, whereas his fellow worker had a clean disciplinary record. An employment tribunal held that the dismissal of the claimant was unfair, on the ground that both of them should have been treated equally, but the decision was reversed by the EAT. An employer is entitled to take into account aggravating factors, including an employee's previously poor disciplinary record as compared with the other employee concerned, as well as mitigating circumstances which affect one employee when compared with the other.

12.74 Once an employer lays down a particular rule, a failure to enforce it consistently may weaken any subsequent attempt to do so. In *Frame v McKean & Graham Ltd*, the claimant was dismissed for doing work on his own account contrary to the working rules for the industry. His dismissal was held to be unfair. The rule had never been enforced in the past, and indeed, such conduct had been condoned. Moreover, he had not taken any work away from the employer, for the customer for whom he worked had severed the relationship with the employer.

12.75 Rules may be of a general nature, eg defining conduct which, by the generality of the law of employment, cannot be tolerated; they may be specific, defining the sort of conduct which *this* employer will not tolerate, and they may be special, dealing with instant circumstances which have not arisen hitherto.

A. General rules

12.76 These are rules which govern conduct which is such that by common consent, disciplinary sanctions will be imposed. Examples which readily spring to mind include theft of the employer's property, theft from fellow employees, serious neglect, wilful damage, dangerous practices, and so on. It is not generally advisable to list all the matters which come under the heading of gross misconduct, for this could mean that an employee would be saved from dismissal who committed an act which was so outrageous that no-one thought it would ever happen (*Gardiner v Newport County Borough Council*). In *Clarkson v Brown, Muff & Co Ltd*, 'gross misconduct' was defined as being 'dishonesty, arson, violence, obscenity, neglect and insubordination'. It was held that this definition did not cover an employee who had been telling lies. Some firms make it clear that the definitions of gross misconduct contained in their rules are examples only, and any list of misdeeds is not intended to be exhaustive!

B. Specific rules

12.77 These rules cover the sort of misconduct which *this employer* will not tolerate under any circumstances. Thus each employer must judge for himself the standards which are to apply, based on his own circumstances. Thus fighting, swearing, lateness, absenteeism, drunkenness, trading, betting, and so forth, may all amount to industrial misconduct which, in the individual case, attracts disciplinary sanctions. Such rules must be fair and reasonable. In *Turner v Pleasurama Casinos Ltd*, the claimant was an inspector who was employed to observe gaming tables, to ensure that there was no dishonesty by croupiers. He was dismissed for 'neglect of duty' after a complaint that a croupier and a member of the public had been cheating under his nose. The allegation was denied by him, but after a full and proper investigation, the employer found against him. It was held that the dismissal was fair; the gaming world is a hard world, and even the smallest of mistakes could not be tolerated.

12.78 Provided such rules meet the standards of reasonableness, they can generally be enforced. In *Higham v International Stores*, the claimant was given to wearing sandals and clogs, and other casual clothes. He was told that he must comply with the company's requirement to wear proper shoes and socks, and to wear a tie and overall when serving customers. After failing to heed due warnings, he was dismissed for not complying with the rules. It was held that an employer is entitled to insist on a reasonable standard of dress. What was reasonable is always a question of fact, to be determined in each case by all the circumstances. Different standards apply in Bond Street and in Petticoat Lane. In this case, the shop had a middle class clientele in a conventional town, and the dismissal was thus fair.

C. Special rules

12.79 Since the rules cannot conceivably cover every possible situation, an employer must be free to lay down a rule specifically to deal with a matter which has not hitherto arisen. In *Spiller v Wallis Ltd* a company rule stated that employees should not have deep emotional relationships with other members of the staff which might impair their marital status. This rule had been promulgated after an incident where the spouse of an employee had come on to the premises and created an unpleasant scene. The claimant was in fact having a love affair with a senior employee, and she refused to discontinue the relationship. Her dismissal was held to be fair. She was told of the rule, but chose not to comply. NB: Whether such a rule contravenes art 8 of the European Convention on Human Rights (see para 1.166) is a matter upon which no doubt the tribunals will shortly adjudicate!)

12.80–12.85 Finally, the interpretation of the rules, and their reasonableness, is a matter for the employment tribunal to determine. In *Palmer v Vauxhall Motors Ltd*, the claimant was dismissed for spending 15 minutes in the club bar after her lunch break. It was alleged that this constituted gross misconduct in accordance with the works rules. It was held that even though the rules were somewhat ambiguous, the employment tribunal was entitled to find that the dismissal was fair. The EAT would only reverse that finding if it could be said that no person instructed in the relevant law could have come to that decision.

Disciplinary powers

12.86 The exercise of disciplinary powers is a corrective function, not punitive. The object is to improve an employee's performance, so that he can remain a valued and useful employee, not to give vent to management frustrations. The choice of the disciplinary sanction must therefore reflect this objective, and should, so far as is possible, be tailored to the individual case, bearing in mind the need to show some form of consistency in like cases. The Code of Practice should be borne in mind at all times.

A. Fines and deductions

12.87 It is possible to impose a fine or make a deduction for bad or negligent work, but the new principles laid down to prevent unlawful deductions (see para 8.11) must be observed. There must be a specific contractual power, and in respect of persons employed in retail employment the restrictions in s 18 of ERA must be observed. Deductions or payments made in consequence of disciplinary proceedings held under a statutory provision are excluded from the Act (eg police and fire service).

12.88 The Act specifically states that the only remedy for a breach is by way of a complaint to an employment tribunal under s 23, but it is submitted that an unauthorised deduction or payment may still give rise to a complaint of constructive dismissal. Thus, in *Lethaby v Horsman Andrew & Knill Ltd* the employer made a deduction from the employee's wages to cover the loss of the firm's property. This was done in the absence of any contractual authority to make such a deduction, and the employee, who refused to agree to it, resigned. It was held that this constituted repudiatory conduct by the employer of the contract, and as such constituted a dismissal (see Chapter 17). It is submitted that this decision is unaffected by the relevant provisions of Employment Rights Act.

12.89 The employer's power to fine or make deductions must be contained in the express terms of the contract, and it is now no longer possible to rely on an implied term, or (more likely) a customary term to this effect. This makes a number of current employment practices of dubious validity. For example, some firms make a practice of deducting 15 minutes from the pay of an hourly worker when he is a few minutes late (known as quartering); it is doubtful if the unilateral imposition of such a practice would be upheld in law.

B. Suspension without pay for misconduct

12.90 If there is an express term in the contract which permits the employer to suspend an employee for a specific reason, such as misconduct, the courts will uphold such a term provided the suspension is carried out in strict conformity with the laid down procedure. Sometimes the grounds for suspension, and the procedure to be adopted, will be laid down in the works rules, and the extent to which those rules will form part of the individual contract of employment will be a question of fact in each case. Even so, if an employee is, or ought to be, aware of the practice of a firm, or if there is a custom in the trade or industry or locality, then he will be bound by it. In *Bird v British Celanese Ltd* an employee was suspended for two days in accordance with the firm's practice, and this was held to be a valid exercise of disciplinary power by the employer.

12.91 Alternatively, the grounds for suspension and procedure to be adopted may be contained in a collective agreement, in which case there may be an express or implied incorporation of those terms into the individual contract of employment. In *Tomlinson v London, Midland and Scottish Rly Co* a trade union negotiated with the defendant company an agreement which, *inter alia*, laid down the procedure for dealing with breaches of discipline, and this was held to have been incorporated into an employee's contract of employment.

12.92 It is clear that the right of suspensory lay-off must be based on a contractual power, which will be either expressed, or implied, or based on custom and practice. The courts and tribunals are quite willing to discover such a power when minor disciplinary matters are concerned, though they appear to require strict proof if there is a major disciplinary matter which can lead to a dismissal. Recently, the EAT held that it may not be difficult to draw an inference that a contract contains an implied power to suspend as a disciplinary matter, or to enable an investigation to take place (*Pirie and Hunter v Crawford*). But in the total absence of such a power, it is clear that the employer may not purport to exercise it, for this would virtually enable him to assess unilaterally the damages for an employee's misconduct. It further follows that if an employee is wrongfully suspended without pay, he may recover any lost pay by way of damages. In *Hanley v Pease & Partners*, an employee was suspended for one day without pay, and it was held that he was entitled to the money which had been withheld.

12.93 If an employer lawfully suspends an employee, the legal position at common law appears to be that the employment has been temporarily put in abeyance, with a right for the employee to apply for reinstatement at the end of the suspension period (*Marshall v English Electric Co Ltd*). Presumably there is no break in continuity of employment in these circumstances. If the suspension is wrongful, the employee will be entitled to treat this breach as repudiatory conduct by the employer, and he will be entitled to resign and sue for wrongful or unfair dismissal. In *Davies v Anglo Great Lakes Corpn* an employee was suspended without pay after allowing his trade union membership to lapse, and this was held to be repudiatory conduct by the employer.

12.94 But if an employee decides to resign as a result of wrongful suspension he may find the tribunal somewhat unsympathetic, for he would have to argue that he was entitled to resign by reason of the employer's (wrongful) conduct, which the tribunal may not accept as a valid reason, particularly if the employer had reasonable cause to suspend, and the employee's conduct would otherwise have to be dealt with by a dismissal which would have been fair. It can hardly be right for an employer to be saddled with the burden of compensation if he exercises a lesser disciplinary power than he might have done. Another view which may be taken is that the employee's conduct was such that it 'contributed' to the repudiation by the employer, and hence reduced compensation may be awarded. Thus if the employee's conduct is such as to warrant a dismissal, but the employer suspends him without having the contractual power to do so, an action for unfair dismissal would probably fail because the constructive dismissal would be justified because of the misconduct, while an action for wrongful dismissal is unlikely to meet with any greater success. There have been a number of cases where the tribunals have held that an employee should not have been dismissed for misconduct, but the offence warranted some lesser disciplinary measure, such as suspension, even though the employer had no contractual right to do so. Thus in *Unkles v Milanda Bread Co Ltd* an employee was dismissed for smoking in breach of the company's rules. The tribunal thought that an appropriate penalty might have been a suspension for one month without pay, but there is no evidence in the report to suggest that the employer had the power to do this by virtue of the contract of employment. In seeking to encourage employers to exercise this lesser power, it would be inconsistent for the tribunals to penalise them for doing so.

C. Warnings

12.95 An employer does not need contractual power to issue warnings, but frequently this will be the subject of a disciplinary code or part of the works rules. These may state the procedural steps (for example, first oral warning, first written warning, final written warning), before further disciplinary action is taken. Strict adherence to these steps is necessary and a failure by the employer to observe them may lead to difficulties in unfair dismissal proceedings. Thus a failure to give a warning in writing as required by the agreed procedure resulted in a dismissal being held to be unfair in *Raymond v Sir Lindsay Parkinson Ltd.*

12.96 Nonetheless, the warning system must be operated sensibly, not merely as a form of mechanical procedure. It is possible to give an employee a final warning for a serious misdemeanour without having first to go through the processes of informal warning, first written warning, etc; equally, the fact that an employee has received a final warning does not mean that the next occasion on which he commits an 'offence' will be visited with an automatic sanction. Either course could lead to ludicrous results. There is no substitute for a full and fair investigation of all the facts. In *Newalls Insulation Co Ltd v Blakeman*, the claimant was dismissed for being absent on two occasions within 14 days, following a final warning for absenteeism. Prior to this, he had had two verbal warnings. The EAT held that the employment tribunal should look at all the circumstances of the case, and not simply whether it was reasonable to dismiss for two days' absence after the final warning. The issues were, what happened before the final warning was given, how many absences were there, why was he absent, and how did the absences fit in as part of the general picture?

12.97 A warning can deal with specific conduct which is the subject of complaint, and it should also deal with general matters, so that the totality of the employee's conduct can eventually be taken into account. This solves the problem, sometimes raised by management, as to whether or not, having given three warnings for one type of misconduct, it is necessary to give a further three warnings in respect of a different series of offences! Thus in *Donald Cook v Carter*, the claimant received a number of warnings; one for using bad language, and a year later, another one for the same offence. Two months later he was given a final warning for inefficiency, with a threat to demote or dismiss. Three months later, he was given another final warning for leaving work before the normal finishing time and he was suspended for five days. He was then guilty of inefficiency, and was dismissed. The employment tribunal held that the dismissal was unfair, in that he should have been given a further final warning, but this was reversed by the EAT. As long as the matter leading to the dismissal was properly investigated and the proper procedure followed, it was not open to the employment tribunal to find that fairness required a further warning being given, or that the employers should have suspended the employee, as they had done so previously.

12.98 This approach was recently confirmed by the EAT in *Auguste Noel Ltd v Curtis*, where an employee was dismissed for mishandling company property. He had previously received two final written warnings for different offences. An employment tribunal held that the previous warnings were not relevant, but the decision was reversed on appeal. The existence of previous warnings, the dates, numbers, and substance of the complaints were all relevant matters which an employer was entitled to take into account.

12.99 It is for the employer to determine the nature of the disciplinary sanction, and, generally speaking, an employment tribunal should not attempt to assess whether or not a final warning should or should not have been given. However, if there is something to suggest that a final warning was 'manifestly inappropriate' or given without *prima facie* grounds, then the employment tribunal will scrutinise carefully the employer's decision. In *Co-operative Retail Services Ltd v Lucas*, the employee was given a final warning for failing to carry out certain instructions. She did not appeal against this within the internal procedure. Two months later she was dismissed following three further incidents. It was accepted by the employer that the three incidents which led to the dismissal were of a minor nature, and did not warrant dismissal by themselves. An employment tribunal decided that the events which led to the final warning being given did not justify such a serious disciplinary sanction, and thus decided to ignore it. Since the other incidents did not warrant dismissal, her dismissal was unfair. On appeal, the EAT confirmed the decision. The employment tribunal was entitled to look at the background against which the final warning was given, and consider whether it was a reasonable response of a reasonable employer. This was a judgment of fact which the employment tribunal was entitled to make.

12.100 If a warning is stated to last for a certain length of time, then clearly it will lapse at the end of that time. In *Bevan Ashford v Malin* a letter was handed to the employee on 29 January 1992, stating that a final written warning would remain on his personal file for a period of 12 months from the date of the letter. He was dismissed following his involvement in an incident at work on 29 January 1993. The employment tribunal held that the final written warning had expired at midnight on 28 January 1993, and ought not to have been taken into account when considering the disciplinary action to be taken following the incident which occurred the following day, and the decision was confirmed by the EAT. The general rule is that penal documents should be construed strictly, and also any ambiguity has to be construed against the maker. Thus the final warning had expired the day before the conduct which led to the dismissal occurred, and could not be relied upon as a ground for dismissal.

12.101 The warning should refer to the past conduct which is the subject of complaint, and to future conduct. It should, where possible, state the remedial action to be taken, and should specify the period of time in which such action should be taken. Frequently, a disciplinary procedure will specify the length of time the warning will last, but perhaps a better approach is for the warning itself to state the operative period, for mechanical and automatic approaches to disciplinary problems are not sound policy. A warning can also be suspensive, when it will stay on the employee's record until such time as it is removed, or can be ignored, or resolutive, which will lapse on compliance. The latter can therefore be ignored when its objective has been achieved. In *Duncan v GEC Telecommunications Ltd* an employee failed to send in a medical certificate as required by the company's rules. After being warned, she sent in an appropriate certificate. A few months later she again failed to send in a medical certificate. It was held that the earlier warning had lapsed on her compliance, and therefore her dismissal was unfair.

12.102 A warning may lapse after a certain period of time, but an employer is not to be criticised because he is over-generous and extends the warning period, instead of acting on it. Being over-generous is not the same as being unreasonable (*Kraft Foods Ltd v Fox*). Further, a warning which is itself the subject of a pending appeal may be taken into account by an employer when considering dismissal for subsequent misconduct (*Tower Hamlets Health Authority v Anthony*).

12.103 Tribunals have frequently stressed the need to issue warnings before the power of dismissal is exercised. The warnings should be given by a person in authority, should be clear, incisive and firm. They should make clear the nature of the conduct which will not be tolerated, and spell out in no uncertain terms that the consequence of a failure to heed the warning will be a dismissal. Formal warnings should be given in writing and this is of particular importance when there are language or communication problems.

12.104 Failure to follow these rules may lead to the tribunal making a finding adverse to the employer. In *Wells v West Ltd* the employers gave a warning to an employee that his 'employment might be in jeopardy'. In holding that this was not a sufficient warning, the tribunal held that those who use circumlocutions will have to bear the burden which they subsequently impose. In *Bendall v Paine and Betteridge* the employee was given a verbal warning that smoking would not be tolerated on the premises. It was held that a failure to give a written, final warning meant that the dismissal was unfair. And in *Rosenthal v Louis Butler Ltd* the employee used some offensive language to her manager. It was held that she ought to have been warned about future conduct, and been given an opportunity to apologise before dismissal was warranted.

12.105 It must be stressed that there is no rule of law which requires warnings to be given in all cases; it is merely a rule of good industrial relations practice. Warnings are matters of substance, not procedure (*James v Waltham Holy Cross UDC*). Whether a warning should have been given will depend on all the circumstances of the case, including its effectiveness, and the alternative course which may have been available or adopted. If a tribunal considers that had a clear warning been given, a dismissal would not have been necessary, then it will conclude that a dismissal without such a warning will be unfair (*Jones v GEC Elliott Automation Ltd*). Conversely, if a warning would have had no effect, then a failure to give one will not by itself render a dismissal unfair (*AJ Dunning & Sons (Shopfitters) Ltd v Jacomb*). There should be no need to give a warning to a highly paid and qualified employee that he will be dismissed if there is dissatisfaction with his work, for he should know this. Nor is there a need to give an educated person in a responsible position a warning that he must co-operate with his head of Department (*Farnborough v Governors of Edinburgh College of Art*). Each case must be determined on its own merits.

12.106 If an employee is given a final warning against which he has appealed, there is no rule of law which requires the employer to await the outcome of the appeal before dismissing for another disciplinary offence (*Stein v Associated Dairies*).

D. Reprimand

12.107 The same is probably true about a reprimand, which is a mark of displeasure about past conduct and a warning about the future. Tribunals have held that misconduct which is not 'gross' should in some circumstances be punished by a reprimand rather than a dismissal, though to what extent a reprimand constitutes a punishment is somewhat difficult to see. Further, employers could be forgiven for thinking that this area of tribunal law is full of hazardous speculation, for when 'misconduct' becomes 'gross' is a somewhat subjective concept. In *King v Motorway Tyres and Accessories Ltd* a manager told his superior to 'fuck off' in the course of an argument. It was held that this did not amount to gross misconduct sufficient to warrant dismissal, and that in view of his long service and satisfactory record, he should have been 'severely' reprimanded! The precise distinction between a reprimand and a severe reprimand, and whether the latter is equivalent to a final warning, has yet to be decided. It is submitted that a reprimand is an appropriate sanction to be used when taking disciplinary action against management, or staff employees.

E. Demotion

12.108 An employee whose conduct is such that the employer has lost all confidence in his ability to do the job in question may be demoted, with or without review, and at a lower earning rate if this is appropriate. If there is an express power to do this in the contract or rules, then provided the sanction has been fairly exercised, there should not be any legal problem. In the absence of such a power, a demotion imposed following a disciplinary hearing is not a breach of contract when it is a lesser penalty than the dismissal which could otherwise have been imposed (*MacKay Decorators (Perth) Ltd v Millar*). If the employee refuses to accept the demotion, he can either resign and claim constructive dismissal, or leave it to the employer to dismiss him. If the employer has acted fairly, and with the interests of the employee at heart, such dismissal will be fair. In *Hall v Lodge*, the claimant was promoted from a supervisory post to manage a shop. Following serious stock deficiencies, her appointment was terminated, and she was offered re-engagement as a supervisor at another branch, at a lower salary. This offer was refused, so she was dismissed. It was held that her dismissal was fair. The company had made a mistake in promoting her too soon to a job which was too big for her. Having realised this, they then acted fairly by considering the alternatives which were available, by offering her a post which was within her competence. However, there is no legal requirement that an employer should demote a person who is incompetent (*Bevan Harris Ltd v Gair*).

12.109 But if a demotion on disciplinary grounds is out of all proportion to the offence, the employee may regard the employer as having repudiated the contract, and claim constructive dismissal. In *BBC v Beckett*, the claimant was employed for 14 years as a scenic carpenter. He was negligent in his work on one occasion, and was demoted to the position of building maintenance carpenter, at a lower salary. He resigned and claimed constructive dismissal, a claim which was upheld by the employment tribunal and by the EAT. The punishment was out of all proportion to the offence, given his long period of satisfactory service.

F. Transfer

12.110 Similar considerations apply to the transfer of an employee from one department to another, or one job to another. This power, however, would be used in different circumstances. Merely to transfer an incompetent employee from one department to another is to export one's problems from one manager to another. Transfer is best used as a means of overcoming personality clashes, so as to minimise the likelihood of future problems arising, or to place an employee in a job which he can do, rather than leaving him doing work which is beyond his competence. In *High v British Railways Board*, it was held that a disciplinary transfer which resulted in the employee suffering a drop in his earnings did not give rise to a claim for constructive dismissal.

G. Alternative employment

12.111 In appropriate cases, it may be unfair to dismiss an employee without considering whether there was any alternative work he could do, notwithstanding that he cannot be permitted to continue in his old job. However, there is no requirement that this should be investigated before the decision to dismiss is taken, as opposed to after the decision has been taken but before the expiry of any period of notice which may be given. To hold otherwise would mean that an employee would be unfairly dismissed notwithstanding that during his notice period alternative employment was found for him and the notice never took effect (*P v Nottinghamshire County Council*).

H. Other sanctions

12.112 There are a number of other disciplinary powers which may be used on appropriate occasions, and provided these are exercised in accordance with the relevant rules and procedures, these should cause few problems. For example, it may be possible to withdraw privileges for a certain period of time so as to deny to an employee certain non-contractual benefits, or to provide for the loss of so many years' seniority for certain purposes (but this does not affect the operation of the legal rules relating to continuity of employment). An employee who is persistently late in starting work may have flexi-time withdrawn, as an alternative to, or a precondition of, the implementation of other disciplinary action.

I. Non–employment situations

12.113 The above instances of disciplinary powers can only apply to acts of employees committed in the course of employment. An employer has no inherent power to discipline for acts which have occurred outside the employment, though if such acts adversely affect the employer's business, he may be justified in dismissing the employee (see Chapter 17). But if an employee is convicted of an offence outside his employment which may have an effect on his job, the employer should consider the employee's long and blameless record, and consider, for example, if some other means of dealing with the situation can be found. In *Jones v R M Douglas Construction Ltd* the employee, who was a plant engineer, was dismissed after being convicted of handling a stolen engine. The tribunal thought that the employer should have given some consideration to demoting him to his original trade of mechanic/fitter. Clearly, such a power cannot be found in the contract of employment, and amounts to a unilateral assessment by the employer of the necessary steps to be taken to protect his interests. A demotion is, as we have seen, equivalent to a dismissal, and one can only assume that if such steps are taken in serious disciplinary cases, the exercise of a lesser disciplinary power short of dismissal will, in cases of grave misconduct outside the employment, also be looked upon more favourably by the tribunals.

12.114 If the employee is convicted of an offence in connection with matters outside his employment, he is still entitled to present his side of the story to his employers, and the latter should not treat the fact of conviction *per se* as being conclusive without at least giving a chance to the employee to state his version (*Parsons v LCC*).

CHAPTER 13
Continuous employment

13.1 In order to obtain certain statutory rights, it is necessary to show that an employee has been continuously employed for a certain length of time, depending on the right in question. The statutory provisions which provide for continuity of employment are contained in ss 210–219 of the Employment Rights Act 1996, which provide 'a complete definition of what is meant by "continuously employed" ' (*Wood v York City Council*), and the Employment Protection (Continuity of Employment) Regulations 1996. Continuity of employment is a statutory concept (*Colinson v BBC*), generally used for two statutory purposes, namely (a) to determine whether an employee has been employed for a particular length of time so as to qualify for a specific statutory right, and (b) to ascertain the employee's length of employment for the purpose of obtaining certain financial benefits (ie a basic award (see para 17.268) and a redundancy payment (see para 18.103). However, for some statutory rights, no period of continuous employment is required.

13.2 There is nothing to prevent an employer from so arranging employment contracts so as to prevent continuity, and thus avoiding liability for unfair dismissal and redundancy payments. If there are legitimate breaks in employment, and re-employment does not become an arrangement by virtue of s 212(3)(c) (see below), continuity can be defeated (*Booth v USA*).

13.3–13.10 Continuity of employment is a concept which is only of importance in a statutory context. Thus, if an employer and employee make a private agreement to treat a particular period of employment as being continuous, this may create a private right, but cannot be used to enforce any statutory right, unless the statutory rules are also met. In *Secretary of State for Employment v Globe Elastic Thread Co Ltd*, an employee worked for a company for 22 years. He was then transferred to another company, after receiving assurances that his employment would be treated as being continuous. Five years later, he was made redundant, and he sought a redundancy payment based on the combined service. The House of Lords held that he was only entitled to a statutory redundancy pay in respect of the latter five years' employment. The private agreement may have given him a contractual right against the employers, but could not be used for the purpose of enforcing a statutory right. Similarly, in *Hanson v Fashion Industries (Hartlepool) Ltd*, an employee went on strike. Nine weeks later, she was re-engaged under a contract which stated that her continuous employment was to start afresh. In subsequent litigation to enforce a claim for maternity pay, it was held that her continuous employment had not been broken by the strike, for the statutory provisions (see below) came into play which preserved her continuity, and a private agreement cannot override those provisions.

Counting and computing continuity (ERA, ss 210–219)

13.11 The counting of a period of continuous employment is done in weeks, but the computation is done in months and years (s 210(3)). This requires some explanation. The rule is that to determine if an employee's employment, whether continuous or successive or broken, can be counted as being continuous is done on a week-by-week basis, because there is a general rule that continuity is broken by a complete week which does not count towards continuity (s 210(4)), unless continuity is preserved by one of the special rules (see below). A week will count, for the purpose of establishing continuity, if it is governed by a contract of employment, irrespective of the number of hours or days worked during the week. But a 'week', for the purpose of determining whether there has been a break in employment, means a complete week from Sunday ending with a Saturday (*Jennings v Salford Community Service Agency*).

13.12 Continuity is not broken unless there is a complete week in which there is no contract of employment. If there is one day in any week which is governed by a contract of employment, it matters not how or why a gap occurred, or what the employee did during that gap. Thus if an employee leaves one employer to work for another employer, but returns within a week of so leaving, continuity is preserved (*Sweeney v J S Henderson (Concessionaires) Ltd*).

13.13 However, the computation of the length of continuous employment is done in months and years. Thus, if an employee commences work on (say) 21 January 1996, he will complete two years' employment on 20 January 1998, assuming there is no break in his employment of a whole week. Similarly, if he commences employment on (say) 19 August 1996, he will have been continuously employed for three months on 18 November 1996. The terms 'months' and 'years' are to be treated as calendar months and years respectively.

13.14 Thus, in order to establish a period of continuous employment, it is necessary to ascertain the day when the employment commenced, the day when it ceased, whether there were any weeks which break continuity, and whether there were any weeks which do not break continuity, but which do not count towards continuity. Formerly, there were special rules to be observed in respect of part-time workers, who worked less than 16 hours per week, but these restrictions were abolished in 1995, and now part-time workers are to be treated in the same way as full-time workers, irrespective of the number of hours worked each week. Indeed, service prior to the change in 1995 is to be counted (ERA Sch 2 para 14(1)).

13.15 The first rule to note is that there is a presumption that continuity of employment exists. Thus, once an employee can show the date on which he commenced work, his employment will be presumed to be continuous until the effective date of termination (s 210(5), and see *Nicoll v Nocorrode Ltd*). Thus an employee can change his place of work, his terms of employment, or even his contract of employment, without his continuity being affected, provided he remains employed by the same employer (*Wood v York City Council*) or an associated employer.

13.16 Continuity begins on the day the employee starts work under the contract of employment, although if the starting day is in fact a non-working day (eg a holiday or a Sunday) the employment will be continuous from that date, even though he does not actually commence working until a day or two later (*Salvation Army v Dewsbury*). However, for redundancy pay purposes only, continuity does not start until an employee's eighteenth birthday (s 211(2)), and any period of employment prior to that date cannot be counted. If there are periods which do not count towards continuity, but do not break continuity (see below) the commencement of the period of employment is advanced by the period in question (s 211(3)). If a written statement of terms and conditions of employment given under s 1 of ERA contains a starting date, that will not be conclusive, if in fact the true starting date was different (*System Floors (UK) Ltd v Daniel*).

13.17 When a period of continuous employment ends will depend on the statutory right which is being claimed by the employee. For employment rights generally, and unfair dismissal claims in particular, it will be 'the effective date of termination' (see para 20.36). If the claim is for a statutory redundancy payment, the period will end on 'the relevant date', which will normally be the effective date of termination, although there are some variations on this (ss 136(3), 145(3)(b), 145(5), 145(7), 153). There are also provisions dealing with the termination of employment on the death of the employer and employee (ss 133(1) and 176(1)).

13.18 The employment must be legal for it to be continuous. Thus any period when the employment is illegal cannot count towards continuity, and will break continuity. Thus, if a person has no legal right to work in the UK (see para 2.237) any time spent so working cannot count towards continuity. If a legal contract becomes tainted with illegality (see para 3.6), continuity will be broken, and will have to start again from when it becomes legal. In *Hyland v J H Barker (North West) Ltd*, the employee was employed from 1967. For four weeks in 1982 he arranged with his employer that he would receive a tax-free lodging allowance, whereas in fact he returned home every night. Clearly, this arrangement was illegal, being an attempt to defraud the Inland Revenue. Thus, when he was dismissed a year later, it was held that the four-week period had broken the continuity, and that therefore he lacked the necessary qualifying period of employment to bring a claim for unfair dismissal.

13.19–13.30 Continuity of employment exists if an employee commences to work for a subsidiary or associated employer of the original employer, or if there is a takeover of the business (not just its assets) or on the transfer of an undertaking. Nor is it relevant that the employee's job changed. In *Lord Advocate v De Rosa* the employee was employed by Isaac Barrie (Transport) Ltd for 17 years, when the business was transferred to Isaac Barrie (Contractors) Ltd. There was no interruption in his employment, but he changed his job from transport manager to docks manager. It was held that his redundancy payment was to be calculated by reference to both periods of employment, and the fact that there had been a change in his employer and in his terms and conditions of employment was irrelevant.

Preserving continuity (s 212)

13.31   There is a general principle that if an employee is dismissed, or resigns, or his contract of employment comes to an end in some other lawful manner (frustration, project termination etc), then, if he is subsequently re-engaged, continuity will have been broken if there is a gap of more than one week between the two employments, and he will have to start again so far as computation is concerned. However, there are a number of rules which enable an employee to preserve continuity, despite the existence of a break between the two periods. Sometimes, the weeks in question may be added into the counting of continuity, although sometimes they are not to be counted, even though they do not break continuity.

13.32   Any week during the whole or part of which an employee's relations with his employer are governed by a contract of employment will count when computing the employee's period of employment (s 212(1)). Thus, if an employee is off work sick, away on a holiday, or otherwise absent with permission, the weeks in question will still count, are long as the contract of employment is still in existence. The whole of the period when a woman is on ordinary maternity leave of absence will count towards continuity.

13.33   Continuity will also be preserved in the following three circumstances (s 212(2) below), provided two conditions are met. First, there must be no contract of employment subsisting (because otherwise there would be no need to rely on these provisions to preserve continuity). Second, the employee must be re-employed during the relevant period. In other words, s 212(2) does not guarantee continuity; it merely preserves it in circumstances when it would otherwise be lost.

A. Incapable of work because of sickness or injury (s 212(3)(a))

13.34   For this rule to apply, the contract of employment must have been terminated (whether by dismissal or frustration or resignation etc). If so, then if the employee is re-employed within 26 weeks, his employment will be deemed to be continuous. In other words, he is entitled to be absent from work for up to 26 weeks after his contract of employment has ended without suffering a break in continuity should he be re-employed. He must, however, have been incapable of work, not merely absent from work (*Scarlett v Godfrey Abbott Group Ltd*). In *Donnelly v Kelvin International Services* the employee resigned from his employment with the respondent because his doctor advised him to obtain lighter work. He obtained employment with another employer, but five weeks later resumed his employment with the respondent. He was subsequently dismissed, and his claim for unfair dismissal could only proceed if he could link the two periods of employment in order to establish the necessary continuity. An employment tribunal dismissed his claim, holding that although he had resigned his employment because of sickness, he was not incapable of work because of that sickness, because he had demonstrated his fitness for work by obtaining other employment. The EAT allowed the employee's appeal, and remitted the claim for reconsideration by another tribunal. The phrase 'incapable of work' did not mean incapable of work of any kind. It referred to the work which the employee was doing prior to the period which interrupted the continuity of employment, and the fact that the employee had taken up other work during the period of interruption did not mean that he had ceased to be capable of the work he was doing by reason of sickness, within the meaning of s 212(3)(a). The proper approach was to look at what happened in the intervening period between the two employments in question. If, for example, the employee took employment of light work, in the hope that he may be able to return to his previous employment in time, this may not interrupt the period of continuity. But if the intervening employment was undertaken as full time permanent employment, then it was possible to conclude that his absence from the first employment was not because of incapacity for work.

13.35 A different result was reached in *Pearson v Kent County Council*, where the employee decided to resign his employment on 31 May on health grounds. He was offered, and accepted, a less demanding job with his employers, and commenced his new position on 11 June. Four years later he was made redundant, and sought to link the two periods of employment for the purpose of enhancing his claim for statutory redundancy pay. His claim failed. There was no medical reason why he could not have commenced his new job immediately after he left his former position. Thus, he was not incapable of work because of sickness or injury, and because there was a break of more than one week, the two periods of employment could not be linked to form one period of continuous employment.

B. Absent from work on account of a temporary cessation of work (s 212(3)(b))

13.36 Weeks will count when an employee is absent from work (again, without a contract of employment) on account of a temporary cessation of work. This provision was probably designed to deal with those industries where there may be lay-offs, eg the construction industry, but the practical effect has been much wider (see *Fitzgerald v Hall, Russell & Co Ltd*). In particular, it should be noted that a lay-off and a temporary cessation of work are the same thing (*Murray v Murray (t/a Newholme Decorators)*).

13.37 The term 'cessation of work' means that the work which the employee was employed to do must have ceased (*Fitzgerald v Hall Russell & Co Ltd*) or the quantum of work no longer exists. If an employee is 'laid off' because existing work has been redistributed, there has been no cessation of work (*Bryne v Birmingham City Council*). Further, the work which has ceased must be paid work, not voluntary work (*University of Aston in Birmingham v Malik*). Nor is the reason for the cessation relevant; it may be due to shortage of orders, shortage of supplies, cash flow problems etc (*Hunter v Smith's Docks Co Ltd*). There must be an interruption in the availability of work which, but for that interruption, would have been performed by the employee.

13.38 The absence from work must be 'temporary'. This is a question of fact, to be looked at with hindsight, not foresight. Although there is dicta in *Ford v Warwickshire County Council* (see below) to suggest that 'temporary' means 'lasting only for a relatively short time', this guidance has not always been followed (eg see *Bentley Engineering Co Ltd v Crown*, where a period of absence of two years was held to be temporary!). The whole of the employment history must be examined, and evidence may be adduced as to the expectations of the parties. In *Ford v Warwickshire County Council* the claimant was a teacher who was employed on a sessional basis. Each year she taught for three terms, and when the July term ended, her contract came to an end. Each year she was re-employed in September. This arrangement continued for eight years, and when she was not re-engaged at the commencement of a new session, she sought compensation for unfair dismissal and redundancy. The House of Lords held that the word 'temporary' was used in the sense of being 'transient' so that the absence was for a relatively short time. This was a question of fact to be determined by the employment tribunal. Thus, successive periods of employment with the same employer will be continuous under s 212(3)(b) if the length of time between those periods is short compared with the length of time the employment has lasted. In such circumstances, the intervals in between can truly be regarded as being temporary.

13.39   There have been a number of cases where employees have been employed on 'intermittent' contracts, each of varying lengths, and being separated by varying periods of non-employment. The correct approach in such cases is to consider all the relevant circumstances, and in particular to consider the lengths of the periods of absence from work in the context of the employment as a whole (*Sillars v Charrington Fuels Ltd*). Sometimes employment tribunals try to circumvent this enquiry by finding that 'a global contract' exists (see para 2.273), but with mixed success. So far as seasonal workers are concerned, if a greater time is spent out of employment than in, the period of non-employment cannot be regarded as being an absence because of a temporary cessation of work (*Berwick Salmon Fisheries Co Ltd v Rutherford*).

13.40–13.50   It will be clear that if an employee resigns, or is dismissed, and subsequently re-employed by the employer (or an associated employer, see para 13.87) he cannot be regarded as being absent from work because of a temporary cessation (*Wessex National Ltd v Long*). If, during the period of absence, the employee takes what he regards as being other permanent employment, then the absence ceases to be because of the temporary cessation of work. But if he takes temporary employment, making it clear that he was seeking to be re-employed by his former employers, continuity will be preserved (*Thompson v Bristol Channel Ship Repairer and Engineers Ltd*).

C. Absent by arrangement or custom (s 212(3)(c))

13.51   Continuity is preserved if the employee's absence from work such that, by arrangement or custom, he is regarded as continuing in the employment of his employer for any purpose. Clearly, if an employee's contract enables such absence, eg sabbatical leave, s 212(3)(c) has no relevance. The section only applies if the contract does not exist, and would cover, for example, an employee who has been seconded from one employer to another, or someone who has been given leave of absence for personal reasons. Indeed, the 'arrangement' need not have been made between the employer and the employee, but can arise from an agreement between the employer and a trade union (*Taylor v Triumph Motors Ltd*). Keeping an employee 'on the books' can be an arrangement for the purpose of continuity within s 212(3)(c), especially if the contract of employment has previously been frustrated (*G F Sharp & Co Ltd v McMillan*).

13.52   The arrangement must have been to preserve continuity for any purpose. In *Lloyds Bank Ltd v Secretary of State for Employment* an employee worked one week on and one week off for five years. She became pregnant, the employers paid her statutory maternity pay, and sought to recover the amount from the Maternity Fund. It was held that her employment was continuous for five years, her absence was by arrangement, and, having rightfully paid her the money, they were entitled to a rebate from the Fund. But in *Letheby & Christopher Ltd v Bond* a casual barmaid took leave over a Christmas period. Although this was by arrangement, there was no arrangement that the absence would preserve continuity, for she worked under a number of separate contracts, and it was not possible to say that any contract of employment would have continued after the cessation of the previous contract. Thus the absence broke her continuity.

13.53   However, the arrangement must have been made before the period of absence ceases (*Murphy v A Birrell & Sons Ltd*). One made after the absence has ceased may give rise to private contractual rights, but cannot affect the statutory position. Thus in *Morris v Walsh Western Electric UK Ltd* the appellant was summarily dismissed. Two months later he was re-employed, and was told by the company's general manager that the intervening period would be treated as being a period of unpaid leave. He subsequently terminated his own employment, and claimed that the two combined periods of employment gave him sufficient continuity to bring a case of constructive dismissal. His claim was dismissed by an employment tribunal and the EAT. The statutory provisions envisage that the arrangement exists when the employee is absent from work, not when he returns to work. A contrary view, expressed in *Ingram v Foxon*, that a retrospective arrangement could preserve continuity, was disapproved.

13.54–13.60   There are few cases dealing with 'custom' in modern employment law generally, let alone with reference to s 212(3)(c). Industry-wide customs (of the kind which would be upheld at law) rarely exist nowadays, as the greater formalisation of contracts of employment and collective agreements takes place. Older cases (eg *Sagar v Ridehalgh*) are no longer particularly relevant. But in *Gray v Burntisland Shipbuilding Co* a recognised custom in the shipbuilding industry whereby workers laid off when work ran out were recalled when more work became available was used to establish continuity under the statutory provision. In *Ford v Warwickshire County Council* (above) the EAT commented that detailed evidence about customs in certain industries could be usefully given, and, if there was an appropriate custom in the teaching profession, it should be brought to the attention of the employment tribunal for consideration.

Re-employment after unfair dismissal (s 219)

13.61   The Employment Protection (Continuity of Employment) Regulations 1996 (made under s 219 of ERA) deal with the situation where a person is reinstated or re-engaged in consequence of any of the following events, namely
(a)   a claim made under an approved dismissal agreement (s 110, — only one such agreement is known to exist, see para 17.11(g))
(b)   the presentation by the employee of a complaint of dismissal, ie under ERA, or in respect of sex, race or disability discrimination
(c)   action taken by a conciliation officer of ACAS under s 18 of the Employment Tribunals Act 1996 (see para 20.53)
(d)   the making of a compromise agreement authorised by s 203(3) of ERA
(e)   as a result of an arbitration award made under an approved ACAS arbitration scheme (see para 1.13).

13.62 In any of these circumstances, the employee's continuity of employment is deemed to be preserved, and the period beginning with the date on which the dismissal took effect, and the date when the re-engagement or reinstatement took place, will count in the computation of the employee's period of continuous employment.

13.63–13.70 The re-engagement or reinstatement must be 'in consequence of' any of the above actions. The mere fact of re-engagement or reinstatement, by itself, for some other reason, will not ensure continuity (*Gardener v National Coal Board*), unless the provisions of ERA s 212(3)(c) applies, it being recalled that this cannot apply to an arrangement which purports to be retrospective (*Morris v Walsh Western UK Ltd*).

Weeks which do not count towards continuity (ss 215–217)

13.71 There are certain circumstances when weeks of absence do not count towards continuity, but do not break continuity. The non-counting weeks are used to advance the starting date of the employment, by seven days for each non-counting week (s 215(2)) (except weeks spent abroad in redundancy cases: see below). The non-counting weeks arise in the following circumstances.

A. Periods spent working abroad (s 215(1))

13.72 A person who works outside Great Britain is generally excluded from employment rights and weeks of employment abroad will not normally count. However, there are circumstances when a period of employment spent outside Great Britain will count in computing continuous employment as if it were employment in Great Britain. Thus, if an employee works outside Great Britain, and his contract is then varied so that he works inside Great Britain, the whole of his period of employment will be continuous for the purpose of establishing a qualifying period of employment rights generally. However, for the purpose of calculating statutory redundancy pay, a week of employment abroad will not count towards continuity (but will not break continuity) if the employee spent the whole or part of the week working abroad, and he was not an employed earner for the purpose of national insurance contributions.

B. Strikes and lock-outs (s 216)

13.73 Any week during which, or during part of which, an employee takes part in a strike will not count towards continuity, but will not break continuity. This rule applies whether the strike is official or unofficial. However, the strike must be connected with terms and conditions of employment, and not, for example, a 'political' strike. If an employee is dismissed while on strike, and subsequently re-engaged, the weeks on strike will be deducted from his continuous employment, but continuity is preserved (*Hanson v Fashion Industries (Hartlepool) Ltd*). The total number of days deducted will be the actual number of days (not the number of working days) falling in the period between the last day when the employee worked and the day when he resumed work (s 216(2)). Thus, non-working days, eg Saturday and Sunday, can be deducted. If, during a strike, an employee takes another job, and is subsequently re-engaged then, if that job was a temporary one, his continuity will be preserved; but if it was a permanent job (eg there is evidence that he so regarded it) he will be treated as if he left his original employment, and continuity will be broken (*Bloomfield v Springfield Hosiery Finishing Co Ltd*).

13.74   Issues sometimes arise as to whether or not the employee is 'taking part' in a strike, or is absent from work during an industrial dispute for some other reason (see *Coates v Modern Methods & Material Ltd*). It is not relevant that the employer 'knows' that the employee took part in the strike, for the test is an objective one (see *Manifold Industries Ltd v Sim*). Indeed, off-duty employees, and employees who are away from work sick may be regarded as taking part in strike action in appropriate circumstances (see *Bolton Roadways Ltd v Edwards*).

13.75   Similarly, continuity of employment is not lost if the employee is absent from work because of a lock-out (s 216(3)), but there does appear to be a difference, in that if the contract of employment still subsists, s 212(1) (above) applies, and days when an employee is locked out will still count towards continuity. This is because s 216(1) only refers to strikes, not to lock-outs. It is only when there is no contract of employment in existence that s 216(3) provides that the number of days falling within the period between the employee's last working day and the day he resumes work are to be deducted from the start of the employee's period of continuous employment.

C. Military service (s 217)

13.76–13.85   An employee who is obliged to serve as an armed forces reservist may apply under the Reserve Forces (Safeguard of Employment) Act 1985 to be reinstated in his former employment within six months of the termination of the period for which he was called up. Weeks when the employee was called up will not count towards continuity, but continuity will not be broken.

Change of employer

13.86   As has been noted, if there has been a transfer of an undertaking within the meaning of the TUPE regulations (see Chapter 9) there is an automatic transfer of the contract of employment from the transferor to the transferee. Curiously enough, the regulations make no mention of continuity of employment being preserved in such circumstances, although there can be little doubt that this will happen, for otherwise the UK would be in serious breach of its obligations to transpose the Acquired Rights Directive into domestic law. It would seem that the provisions of s 218 of ERA are sufficient for this purpose, even though many of the legal decisions on this section were decided prior to the introduction of TUPE.

13.87   There are a number of circumstances to consider.
(a)   There is a transfer to which TUPE applies. Regulation 5(1) states that the contract shall have effect as if originally made between the person so employed and the transferee. This clearly preserves the continuity of the employee so transferred (*Royal Ordnance plc v Pilkington*).
(b)   There is a transfer to which s 218(2) of ERA applies. This section provides for continuity to be preserved when there is a transfer of a trade, business or undertaking from one employer to another. There must be a recognised and

identifiable part of the business transferred, not merely a collection of assets (*Melon v Hector Powe Ltd*).

(c) Statutory change of employer: here s 218(3) of ERA applies when an Act of Parliament substitutes one employer for another (see *Gale v Northern General Hospital NHS Trust*), where the rule was held not to apply.

(d) Although at common law the death of an employer would normally terminate the contract, s 218(4) of ERA provides that if the employee is kept on by the personal representative or trustee of the deceased employer, continuity will not be broken.

(e) A person who is employed by a partnership is employed by the individual partners jointly. Thus, if there is a change in the composition of the partnership, continuity is preserved. However, this may not necessarily be so if the partnership is dissolved, and the employee is taken on by one of the partners (compare *Harold Fielding Ltd v Mansi* and *Allen & Son v Coventry*).

(f) If an employee is transferred from an employer to an associated employer, the transfer does not break continuity (s 218(6)). However, the two employers must be 'associated' in the legal sense, in accordance with the definition contained in s 231 of EP(C)A. This states that any two employers are to be treated as being associated if one is a company of which the other (directly or indirectly) has control, or if both companies are controlled by a third person. 'Control' is a legal, not a factual concept (*Washington Arts Association Ltd v Forster*), to be determined by the number of votes attached to shares which can exercise control of a company in general meeting (*Secretary of State for Employment v Newbold*). Further, by the Interpretation Act 1978 s 6, the singular includes the plural; thus, if one or more people own 51 per cent or more of the shares of X Company, and the same person(s) hold a simple majority of the shares in Z Company, the two companies will be associated, since they are both controlled by a third person (*Umar v Pliastar Ltd*). But if the 'third person' who has control of the two companies is in fact two or more persons, they must be the same individuals with respect to both companies. Thus, if a man and his wife control X Company, and he and his sister control Z Company, the two companies are not associated (*Poparm Ltd v Weekes*).

　　The word 'company' in s 231 is not confined to companies incorporated under British law. In *Hancill v Marcon Engineering Ltd*, the claimant was employed by a company incorporated under American law. He then returned to the United Kingdom and worked for a British company. Both companies were wholly owned subsidiaries of a Dutch company. It was held that he could combine his service with the American and British companies for the purposes of computing his period of continuous employment. The definition of control does not extend to 'negative' control, so as to mean that a person who has exactly 50 per cent of the shareholding of a company has control, merely because he can thwart the wishes of those who hold the remaining 50 per cent (*South West Launderettes Ltd v Laidler*).

(g) If an employee transfers from employment by the governors of a school maintained by a local education authority to employment by that authority, continuity is preserved (ERA s 218(7)). Employees who transfer from one hospital to another, or from an NHS hospital to one with trust status, will generally have continuity preserved by s 218(8) of ERA (see also National Health Service and Community Care Act 1990 s 6), and certain senior hospital appointees whilst undergoing training, which involves being successively employed by different health authorities, have continuity for a number of employment protection rights specified in ERA (Employment Protection (Continuity of Employment of National Health Service Employees) (Modification) Order 1996). For redundancy payment purposes, if an employee transfers from one local authority to another, or to or from certain specified bodies, continuity is preserved (Redundancy Payments (Continuity of Employment in Local Government etc) (Modification) Order 1999). But a transfer to or from a body not included in Sch 1 to the Order will not give rise to continuity (*Liversidge v London Residuary Body*). Similarly, continuity is preserved on a transfer from one NHS body to another (Redundancy Payments (National Health Service) (Modification) Order 1993).

13.88–13.95 In particular, it should be noted that artificial breaks in employment consequent on a transfer are not generally favoured, and s 218, combined with TUPE, are to be given a broad interpretation so as to preserve continuity where possible (*Macer v Abafast Ltd*).

The effect of the continuity rules

13.96 The purpose of establishing continuity of employment is to enable an employee to qualify, by virtue of the length of his employment, for certain statutory rights. In particular, however, additional years of employment which can be saved by the continuity rules are of great value to an employee whose employment ultimately comes to an end for reason of redundancy, for he can then obtain a larger redundancy payment (or an increased basic award if he was unfairly dismissed). Thus, when there is a transfer of a business from one employer to another, if there is no continuity, he can apply for his redundancy payment, and then start again with his new employer; on the other hand, if there is continuity, the new employer takes over the obligations to make a redundancy payment should this prove necessary in the future. But if an employee is given a statutory redundancy payment and his contract of employment is renewed, or he is re-engaged (whether by the same employer or another employer), his continuity of employment is broken for redundancy payment purposes (s 214), unless he agrees to repay the redundancy payment (Employment Protection (Continuity of Employment) Regs 1996 reg 4).

CHAPTER 14

Normal working hours and a week's pay

Employment Rights Act ss 221–229

14.1 In order to quantify part of the amount of money payable to an employee in respect of the violation of certain specific statutory rights, it is necessary to ascertain the employee's weekly pay, which is done by reference to the employee's 'normal working hours'. The Employment Rights Act sets out precise formulae for determining how a week's pay is thus to be calculated and, in certain specific cases, puts a cap on that amount.

Contractual provisions

14.2 The Act envisages that there are a number of different possibilities when trying to assess an employee's 'normal working hours', and it is therefore necessary to choose the one which is most appropriate in the circumstances, so as to calculate the week's pay. To do this, one must start with a consideration of the contract of employment. Thus, if the contract specifies normal working hours, that will generally be conclusive, and it is immaterial that the employee works more or less than those hours, unless it can be shown that there has been a variation (express or implied) of the contract (*ITT Components (Europe) v Kolah*). If the contract is silent on this matter, the employment tribunal must infer the relevant term from what happens in practice (*Larkin v Cambos Enterprises (Stretford) Ltd*). Thus in *Armstrong Whitworth Rolls Ltd v Mustard* the contract of employment required the employee to work 40 hours per week. He was then asked to work for 60 hours per week, in order to ensure 24-hour coverage of the plant. He did this for seven years and, when made redundant, it was held that his contract of employment had been varied, so that he was entitled to a redundancy payment on the basis of a 60-hour week.

14.3 Overtime is generally excluded from normal working hours, unless it is included in the minimum number of hours fixed by the contract. In other words, it must be guaranteed by the employer and obligatory for the employee (*Tarmac Roadstone Holdings Ltd v Peacock*). If the employer is entitled, but not obliged, to call for overtime working, such hours as are worked will not count towards normal working hours, even though the employee is bound to work overtime under the terms of his contract (*Lotus Cars Ltd v Sutcliffe*).

14.4 It is then necessary to establish how much the employee was paid for those hours. Remuneration, for this purpose, can be quite wide. Clearly, wages or salaries will be included, but also contractual bonuses paid on a regular basis, eg per shift, or per site, or for undertaking additional duties (*A & B Marcusfield v Melhuish*). Commission payments are also included, although a commission paid annually has to be apportioned over the period when the employee actually worked (*J & S Bickley Ltd v Washer*), and consequently averaged over a period of 12 weeks (see below). Expenses do not count as remuneration if they are a reimbursement of an employee's expenditure, but will count if they represent a profit in the employee's hands (*S and U Stores Ltd v Wilkes*). However, expenses which represent a profit must have been declared to the Inland Revenue, otherwise there is a danger that the contract may be illegal (*Tomlinson v Dick Evans U Drive Ltd*). Payments in kind (car, accommodation, food etc) will not count (*Skillen v Eastwoods Froy Ltd*), although it should be noted that such benefits may be taken into account when determining any relevant compensation award. Tips and gratuities do not count if they are paid by the customer, not the employer (*Palmanor Ltd v Cedron*), but a service charge which is distributed among employees in a fixed proportion will count as part of a week's pay (*Tsoukka v Potomac Restaurants Ltd*). A lodging allowance is not part of a week's pay, although a deduction from pay in respect of lodging clearly would be. Overtime premiums also do not count (*British Coal Corpn v Cheesbrough*).

14.5 When calculating 'a week's pay' for statutory purposes, it is the gross pay which counts, not net pay (*Secretary of State for Employment v John Woodrow & Sons (Builders) Ltd*). Moreover, the amount must be calculated on the basis that the employer is complying with his legal obligations. Thus, in *Cooner v P S Doal & Sons*, an employee was paid less than that to which he was entitled under a Wages Council order, and it was held that it was pay under the order which counted, not the lower wage actually paid. Although the Wages Councils orders have now ceased to exist, the principle will no doubt apply to the new minimum wage legislation (see para 8.76).

14.6 Having ascertained an employee's normal weekly hours, and how much he is paid for those hours, we can now work out his week's pay for statutory purposes. The following four circumstances should cover all situations.

A. Remuneration does not vary (ERA s 221(2))

14.7 If an employee's remuneration does not vary in normal working hours (whether he be an hourly or weekly paid employee, or is paid for any other period) then the amount of a week's pay is the amount which is payable under the contract of employment. If the employee is paid by the hour, then the week's pay is to be determined as if he worked his full contractual hours in that week.

B. Remuneration varies with the amount of work (ERA s 221(3))

14.8 If the amount of remuneration does vary with the amount of work done in the period (eg piece workers) the week's pay is ascertained by finding the average hourly remuneration payable in the 12 weeks ending with the calculation date. If, in any of those 12 weeks, no remuneration was payable for hours when the employee was actually at work, earlier weeks can be taken into account, so as to bring the number up to 12 (s 223). Only weeks when the employee actually works will count (*Adams v John Wright & Sons (Blackwall) Ltd*). Thus if an employee is paid for work actually done in a week, even if those earnings were abnormally low, the week will count. If an employee is a recent recruit, so that he does not have 12 weeks' employment to take into account, an employment tribunal can determine an amount which fairly represents a week's pay, taking into account the amount already received, the remuneration offered in the contract, the remuneration of comparable employees of the same employer, and remuneration received by comparable employees of other employers (ERA s 228). Weeks with a previous employer which count towards continuity (see Chapter 13) may be taken into account (ERA s 229).

C. Remuneration varies according to the time of work (ERA s 222)

14.9   If an employee is a shift worker, or works on a rota, so that the hours when he is required to work differ according to the time of the day or the day of the week, with the consequence that his remuneration will correspondingly be different, the week's pay will be the average hourly rate multiplied by the average weekly hours in the period of 12 weeks prior to the calculation date. Again, earlier weeks can be counted, if necessary (see above).

D. No normal working hours (ERA s 224)

14.10–14.20   If the employee had no normal working hours, the week's pay is determined by taking the employee's average weekly earnings for the period of 12 weeks prior to the calculation date. If the employee was not paid during any of those weeks, earlier weeks can be included, if necessary, to make up the 12-week period, even if the employee agreed to waive an entitlement to be paid, which otherwise was legally required to be paid (*Secretary of State for Employment v Crane*).

Capping a week's pay (ERA s 227)

14.21   In respect of the following claims, there is a limit to the amount of a week's pay which can be calculated, which currently is £230 per week. These claims are
(a) basic award for unfair dismissal,
(b) additional award of compensation for unfair dismissal,
(c) statutory redundancy pay,
(d) arrears of pay (up to eight weeks), statutory notice, and holiday pay (up to six weeks) and a basic award, payable on an employer's insolvency (ERA s 186),
(e) right not to be unjustifiably disciplined by a trade union (TULR(C)A s 67),
(f) unreasonable exclusion from a trade union (TULR(C)A s 176).

14.22–14.30   It will be noted that guarantee pay (see para 7.2) is limited to £16.10 per day (ERA s 31) with a maximum of £80.50 is any period of three months. Pay for time off work to look for another job (see para 7.71) is limited to two-fifths of a week's pay, not capped (ERA s 54). In all other instances where a week's pay is used for calculation purposes, it is the actual gross pay which has to be taken into account.

The calculation date (ERA ss 225–226)

14.31   The date on which the above calculations are to be made will differ, depending on the nature of the employee's claim. Each statutory right has its own formula. For guarantee pay (s 30), it will generally be the day on which the guarantee payment is payable (unless a new contract or variation has been entered into, in which case it will be the last day when the old contract was in force). The calculation date in respect of a claim for remuneration for time off with pay to look for work (s 52) is the day the employer gave notice of termination for reason of redundancy. For time off work for ante-natal care (s 55) the calculation date is the date of the appointment, and for time off work for employee representatives (p 62) and time off work for study or training (s 63A) the calculation date is the date on which time off was taken or should have been permitted. For suspension on medical grounds (s 64) or maternity suspension (s 66), the calculation date is generally the day before the suspension begins.

14.32   For redundancy payment claims, if contractual notice was given which was greater than the statutory notice which could have been given, the calculation date will be the day on which, counting backwards from the effective date of termination, the statutory notice could have been given. If less than statutory notice was given, the calculation date will be the date that notice expires, and if no notice is given, the date the contract terminated. For payments due to an employee on the employer's insolvency, the calculation date becomes the 'appropriate date', ie the date on which the employer became insolvent (for holiday pay and arrears of pay). For the basic award, it will be the later of the date when the employer became insolvent, or the employment was terminated, or the basic award was made, as the case may be. For other payments (ie statutory notice, statutory redundancy pay), the calculation date will be the later of the date when the employer became insolvent or the employment was terminated (ERA s 186).

CHAPTER 15

Rights in notice

15.1–15.10 One of the features which distinguishes a contract of employment from other contractual situations is that a contract of employment is one of continuous obligation, with, generally speaking no specified time for its ending. Thus, apart from certain exceptions (eg fixed-term contracts, summary dismissal, retirement age, project termination) if either the employer or employee wishes to terminate the contract, notice of such termination must be given. Whether or not there is a termination is a factual and legal question (see para 17.23), but to be operative, the notice must give a clear indication of the actual date of termination (*Morton Sundour Fabrics Ltd v Shaw* para 18.24). This chapter will explore the rights and duties of the parties to give and receive lawful notice in the event of a termination, ie if there is a dismissal or resignation.

Notice to be given by the employer

15.11 The period of notice to be given by the employer will first be determined by having regard to the contract of employment, as required by s 1(4)(e) of ERA. In theory, this is a matter of negotiation between the employer and employee, although in practice it is the employer who will usually dictate the terms, depending on factors such as the need to harmonise terms with those of other employees in similar positions, the nature of the employment, the seniority of the employee's position, and so on.

15.12 If the contract of employment is silent on this matter, at common law, reasonable notice must be given. Again, what is reasonable will depend on the employee's position, the industry, nature of the work, etc. For example, in *Hill v C A Parsons & Co Ltd*, the Court of Appeal expressed the view that a senior engineer would have been entitled to between six months' to one year's notice, and there are a number of decisions (dating from the nineteenth century and the earlier part of the twentieth century) which deal with what would be reasonable notice for employees such as head gardeners, domestic servants, journalists, commercial travellers, chorus girls, hairdressers' assistants, and so on.

15.13 However, irrespective of the contractual terms, by statute, certain minimum periods of notice must be given (see s 86(1) of ERA). These periods are to be determined by the length of the employee's period of employment. Thus, after one month's employment, the employee is entitled to one week's notice, and this will apply until he has been employed for two years. Thereafter, he will be entitled to a week's notice in respect of each year's continual employment, ie two weeks' notice after two year's employment, up to a statutory maximum of 12 weeks' notice in respect of employment which has lasted for 12 years or more. But if contractual notice is for a period which is longer than that to be given by statute, the contractual notice will prevail.

15.14   If a contract of employment come to an end because of the operation of the doctrine of frustration (see para 17.76) no statutory or contractual notice can be or need be given (*G F Sharp & Co Ltd v McMillan*).

15.15–15.25   Notice to terminate a contract of employment may be given at any time, even before the employment has commenced. Thus in *Sarker v South Tees Acute Hospitals NHS Trust*, the claimant was offered a post in July, and was due to start work in October. However, the offer was withdrawn in September. The claimant brought a claim for her contractual notice, under the provisions of the Employment Tribunals Extension of Jurisdiction Order (see para 1.55). The EAT held that her contract had been terminated, and she was entitled to her contractual notice.

Giving notice

15.26   Notice may be given by either side either orally or in writing. In either case, apart from summary dismissal, it will run from the day after it is given (*West v Kneels*), unless a later date is specified, but it cannot operate unless the recipient has had an opportunity to know of it. Thus, if a letter giving notice to an employee is not received on a particular day (because the employee is not at home, or because of a postal strike etc), it will only operate when the employee has had a reasonable opportunity to read it (see *Brown v Southall and Knight*, para 17.21). If there is a collateral contract (see para 3.21) to the main contract, notice must be given in respect of both of them.

15.27   The general common law rule is that once notice has been given, it cannot be unilaterally withdrawn either by the employer (*Riordan v War Office*) or the employee (*Brennan v C Lindley & Co Ltd*) although it can be withdrawn by mutual agreement between the parties (*Harris & Russell Ltd v Slingsby*). The notice period may also be extended by mutual agreement (*Mowlem Northern Ltd v Watson*). However, modern cases draw a distinction between the deliberate giving of notice (by either party) and a resignation or dismissal given 'in the heat of the moment.' In such circumstances (usually following some form of argument) it is incumbent on the recipient to ascertain whether the other party really meant what he said (*Kwik-Fit (GB) Ltd v Lineham*, and see para 17.68).

15.28–15.35   If the employer gives notice to terminate the contract of employment, and during the period of that notice the employee gives a counter-notice that he intends to leave at an earlier date, the employee has still been dismissed for the reason for which the employer's notice was given (ERA s 95(2); see *Ready Case Ltd v Jackson*). However, if the employee resigns during the notice period, rather than giving a counter-notice, he will regarded as not having been dismissed but as having resigned (*Walker v Cotswold Chine Home School*), unless the employer agrees to him leaving, before the expiry of their notice, in which case it is treated as being a variation of the employer's notice of dismissal (*McAlwane v Boughton Estates*). There are special provisions dealing with the counter-notice to be given by an employee when he is dismissed for reason of redundancy (see para 18.35). Further, it should be noted that during the notice period, an employee retains those statutory rights relating to time off work (see ERA ss 50–63 and TULR(C)A ss 186–190, and see below, para 15.52).

Pay in lieu of notice

15.36 In *Delaney v Staples*, Lord Browne-Wilkinson listed four circumstances when a payment in lieu of notice may be made, with different consequences in each case. These are:

(a) the employer gives the appropriate notice of termination to the employee, but does not require him to work during the notice period. In effect, the employee is on 'garden leave'. Generally, there is no breach of contract in not requiring the employee to work until the termination date (but see para 15.71). Tax and national insurance contributions must be deducted, and restrictive covenants will normally be enforceable. If, during the 'garden leave' period, the employee works for another employer without permission, then he will be in breach of his contract, and the appropriate consequences will follow;

(b) the contract provides that the employer may terminate the contract, either with notice or summarily on the payment of a sum on money in lieu of notice. Here, two alternative ways are set out whereby the contract may be lawfully terminated. If the employer fails to make the payment, the employee can sue for the money as a debt. If the employer makes the payment, income tax should be deducted;

(c) the employer and employee agree that the employment is to be terminated immediately on payment of a sum of money in lieu of notice. (This could be an agreed termination, or employer terminating with a waiver of notice.) A statement of practice issued by the Inland Revenue indicates that an employee will not be taxed in full on a job termination payment which is made 'in full and final settlement' of all outstanding claims against the employer, at least up to the first £30,000;

(d) the employer summarily dismisses the employee and makes a payment of money in lieu of notice. This is the most common category of payment in lieu of notice. Since the employer is seeking to extinguish a claim for damages (for breach of contract) the payment is free from tax up to £30,000 (see below).

15.37 However, the categorisation was severely criticised by the EAT in *Cerberus Software Ltd v Rowley*, it being suggested that termination without notice or with the payment of a sum in lieu of notice would infringe the statutory protection contained in s 86 of ERA. The difficulty in these cases arises from the consequences when (a) the employer is acting within the terms of the contract and (b) when he is acting outside those terms. In the former case lawful obligations (restrictive covenants etc) may still be enforced, whereas in the latter case they may not be.

15.38 Either party may waive his right to receive contractual or statutory notice (ERA s 86(4)) and, in particular, an employer may decide to give a payment in lieu of the employee working during the notice period. Indeed, if the contract of employment gives the employer an option to make a payment in lieu of notice, the employee has no right to work out his notice, or to be compensated for non-contractual benefits he would have obtained had he worked his notice (*Marshall (Cambridge) Ltd v Hamblin*). But an employer cannot use the device of making a payment in lieu of notice to prevent an employee from achieving his contractual earnings, eg commissions, etc. An employee who is on piecework must be given enough work to enable him to earn his usual earnings, and this rule applies equally during the notice period (*Devonald v Rosser & Sons*).

15.39 There are, however, certain important tax consequences of making such a payment. If the employer does not have the contractual right to make a payment in lieu of notice, then, by making it, he is in effect paying damages for breach of contract. As such, the payment does not attract tax and national insurance contributions, and up to £30,000 may be paid tax free (Income and Corporation Taxes Act 1988 s 188) although, technically, the employee is only entitled to the net pay he would have received had tax and national insurance contributions been deducted by the employer. However, if the contract permits the employer to make a payment in lieu of notice, then there is no breach of contract, and tax and national insurance contributions should be deducted (*EMI Group Electronics Ltd v Coldicott*), because it is an emolument from employment (Income and Corporation Taxes Act 1988 s 19).

15.40–15.50 Additionally, as well as his salary, the employee is entitled to be compensated for the loss of other contractual benefits (car, health insurance, accrued holiday pay etc) for the period had the notice been worked out. Further, it has been held by the Court of Appeal (*Abrahams v Performing Right Society*) that if the contract gives the employer an option of terminating the contract with notice, or to make a payment in lieu of notice, the employee is not under a duty to mitigate against his loss, because the claim is for liquidated damages (ie a genuine pre-estimate of the loss suffered by the employee) which does not involve any duty to mitigate. This duty will only arise therefore if the contract does not enable the employer to make a payment in lieu of notice. In *Cerberus Software Ltd v Rowley* the contract of employment provided that the employer could either give six months' notice of termination or make a payment in lieu of notice on termination. The claimant was dismissed without notice and without a payment in lieu. After five weeks, he obtained employment at a higher salary, but nonetheless he claimed damages for wrongful dismissal. It was held that he was entitled to his six months' salary without any deduction in respect of his duty to mitigate his loss. The monies in lieu were claimable either as monies due under the contract or as damages for breach of contract. In neither event was the employer entitled to receive the benefit of the employee's mitigation.

Rights during the notice period; ERA ss 88–91

15.51 During the period of notice, the employee will still have certain statutory rights, contained in ERA ss 88–91. If the employer gives notice, the employee must have been employed for one month or more to obtain the statutory rights, but he will not have any of these rights if the notice to be given by the employer is at least one week more than the statutory notice laid down in ERA s 86(1).

Thus, if an employee, who has been employed for two years, is entitled to and is given four weeks notice, ss 88–91 do not apply, because the notice given is for a longer period than required by the statute. If an employee has been employed for five years, and is given four weeks contractual notice, or five weeks' statutory notice, the provisions of ss 88–91 apply. However, if the employee gives notice (after being employed for one month or more) he will be able to enjoy these statutory rights only for the statutory notice period required of an employee, ie one week (s 86(1)), even though he gives a longer period of notice.

15.52 The statutory rights in question are as follows:
(a) Where the employee has normal working hours, he is entitled to be paid for those hours when he is ready and willing to work, but
   (i)   the employer does not provide work (s 88(1)(a)), or
   (ii) he is incapable of work because of sickness or injury (s 88(1)(b)), or
   (iii) the employee is absent from work because of pregnancy or childbirth or parental leave (s 88(1)(c)), or
   (iv) he is absent from work in accordance with the terms of the contract relating to holidays (s 88(1)(d)).
      S/he is entitled to be paid at the average hourly rate, produced by dividing a week's pay by the number of normal working hours. It should be noted that, for the purpose of ss 88–91, a 'week's pay' is not subject to the statutory limit which is applied in unfair dismissal and redundancy claims. Any payment made by the employer by way of sick pay, statutory sick pay, statutory maternity pay, holiday pay etc, can be offset.
(b) If the employee does not have normal working hours, the employer shall pay a week's pay (or average weekly remuneration – calculated over a period of 12 weeks), for each week of the notice period, provided the employee is ready and willing to do work of a reasonable nature and amount in order to earn a week's pay (s 89(1), (2)). S/he is also entitled to be paid for periods when s/he is off work because of sickness or injury, absent through pregnancy or childbirth, or parental leave, or absent because of contractual holidays (s 89(3)). Any payments made by the employer can be offset (see above).
(c) Section 91 of ERA provides that an employer is not required to make payments under ss 88–89 in respect of any period during which the employee is absent from work with leave from the employer granted at the request of the employee, including any period of time off work taken for the purpose of public duties, looking for work or making arrangements for retraining, ante-natal care, acting as an occupational pension scheme trustee, or taking part in trade union duties and activities. At first sight this would appear to be strange, but in fact there is no problem. Sections 50–63 of ERA and ss 168–170 of TULR(C)A contain their own remedies for such absences from work, and thus the employee must pursue them under the appropriate section, without reference to ss 89–90 of ERA.

15.53 Section 91 further provides that no payment is due to an employee under ss 88–89 in the following circumstances;
(a) if the employee gives notice, and then takes part in a strike
(b) if the employer gives notice, and the employee then takes part in a strike (because he cannot be said to be ready and willing to perform some work)
(c) if, during the notice period, the employee commits an act which amounts to a breach of contract, eg something which amounts to gross misconduct, and the employer dismisses the employee forthwith (s 91).

15.54–15.60 The above rights contained in ss 88–90 apply when either the employer or employee give notice of termination of the contract. If the employer terminates the contract without notice, then the rights conferred by ss 88–90 shall be taken into account when assessing his liability for breach of contract.

Contractual rights during notice

15.61 If, during the notice period, there is a wage increase (eg as a result of negotiations with a trade union) the employee is entitled to be paid that increase. However, if, subsequent to leaving the employment, a wage increase is negotiated which is backdated to a period when the employee was working, it would appear that he has no legal entitlement to that increase (*Leyland Vehicles Ltd v Reston*). In legal reasoning, the employee has not given 'consideration' for the increase, because he has already worked under his contract, and 'past consideration is no consideration'.

Dispensing with notice

15.62 If an employee commits a 'fundamental breach of contract' which warrants summary dismissal (see para 16.21), the employer need not give notice of termination. If the employer commits a fundamental breach of contract entitling the employee to resign and claim constructive dismissal (see para 17.35) the employee need not give notice of termination. Nor need an employer give notice if the contract had already been frustrated, and the fact that the employer keeps an employee 'on the books' when he is unlikely to return to work may be the sort of arrangement contemplated by s 213(3)(c) of ERA (see para 13.51), but no contract of employment will be in existence (*GF Sharp & Co Ltd v McMillan*). If an employee is on a fixed-term contract (ie one with a fixed date of expiry) no notice of termination need be given, and a letter sent to the employee confirming that the contract will expire on a certain date is not a letter of dismissal (*London Underground Ltd v Fitzgerald*). However, notice will be required if the employer wishes to terminate the contract prior to the expiry of the fixed term (*Dixon & Constanti v BBC*), or if the employee wishes to resign before the end of that term, particularly if there is a restrictive covenant in force (*Thomas Marshall (Exports) Ltd v Guinle*).

15.63 If an employee is on a probationary period for a certain length of time, the successful completion of which will result in him being confirmed in his position, this is not a fixed-term contract, and he may be given lawful notice prior to the expiry of the probationary period. The employer is not obliged to employ the employee for the whole of the probationary period (*Dalgleish v Kew House Farm Ltd*). A training contract may or may not be a fixed-term contract, depending on how it is worded. If it is, it cannot be brought to an end until the period of training has expired, except for gross misconduct.

15.64–15.70 A project contract will expire when the project has been completed, and thus no notice need be given (*Ironmonger v Movefield Ltd*, see para 17.88). If an employee's contract comes to an end by virtue of a contractual provision relating to retirement age, again, no notice of termination need be given.

Garden leave clauses

15.71 It is always open to the employer to give notice to terminate the contract, and require the employee to work out his notice. If the employee fails or refuses to do so, he will lose his rights to pay (see s 88 above), because he is not able or willing to work. As an alternative, the employer may give lawful notice, but not require the employee to work. In effect, the employee will be on 'garden leave' (see para 19.26), and he is entitled to all his contractual benefits. During this time, the employee could be restrained by an injunction from working for a competitor, if by doing so the employer would suffer serious harm (*Evening Standard Co Ltd v Henderson*). The fact that an employee is forced to remain idle during the garden leave period is not a decisive factor against the enforcement of the employee's notice period (*Euro Brokers Ltd v Rabey*), although there may be special circumstances when an employee is entitled to be provided with actual work, if this is needed to protect his valuable reputation, or if a failure to do so leads to a reduction in actual or potential earnings (see para 10.24). But if an employee is given notice, and is not required to work during his notice period, the fact that he takes another job during the notice period is not repudiatory conduct by him. The notice money he receives is contractually due to him, and therefore there is no requirement for him to mitigate against his loss (*Hutchings v Coinseed Ltd*).

15.72–15.80 But a garden leave clause will only operate if there is an express power in the contract permitting this. Thus in *William Hill Organisation Ltd v Tucker*, the employee gave one month's notice of termination of his contract, although under the terms of his contract he was required to give six months' notice. The employers responded by requiring him to give six months' notice, although he would not be required to work during that period, and would receive all his contractual benefits. He refused to comply with that request, and the employers sought an injunction to restrain him from working for a competitor until the expiry of the six months. The application was refused. There was no power in the contract to insist that the employee took garden leave, and the courts would be reluctant to imply a term to that effect. An employee has a right to work, as well as a right to receive remuneration. Further, it was stated that the courts would be reluctant to enforce a garden leave clause to any greater extent than would be covered by a justifiable covenant in restraint of trade.

Notice and time limits

15.81 Once notice (by either side) is given, the effective date of termination, for unfair dismissal and redundancy pay purposes, is the date the notice expires, and the time for bringing a complaint before an employment tribunal will run from that date. However, an employer cannot 'short notice' an employee (ie give less notice than the statute requires) so as to prevent the employee from satisfying the qualifying period of employment. Thus if an employee has been employed for 51 weeks, and is dismissed without notice, his effective date of termination is the day he leaves, and, not having a requisite period of one year's continuous employment, he would appear to be unable to lodge a claim for unfair dismissal. However, ERA s 97(2) provides that the effective date of termination is the date on which his statutory notice would have expired. In other words, he is entitled to add to the period of employment the week's notice to which is entitled by statute. On the other hand, the dismissal will only operate for computation purposes from the date when the statutory notice expires, not from the date when his contractual notice (had it have been given) would have expired. Thus, if the employee has been employed for 50 weeks, and is entitled to four weeks' notice, but dismissed immediately with pay in lieu of notice, his period of continuous employment is two weeks short of the qualifying period. He is only entitled to add on the period of statutory notice, not his potential contractual notice (see *Fox Maintenance Ltd v Jackson*, para 17.11(c)). This provision also applies to constructive dismissal claims (ERA s 97(4)). However, s 97(2)-(4) only apply for the purpose of determining the qualifying period of employment (s 108(1)), the calculation of the basic award (s 19(1)), and the calculation of a week's pay where this has been increased by the Secretary of State during the statutory notice period (s 227(3)). A similar extension of the period of continuous employment is contained in s 92(7), with respect to written reasons for dismissal.

15.82–15.90 The continuous period of employment is not extended for the purpose of extending the time limit within which a claim for unfair dismissal may be brought. In other words, an unfair dismissal claim must be brought within three months of the effective date of termination, not from when the statutory notice period would have expired. Finally, it may be noted that an employee who has been given notice may commence proceedings for unfair dismissal without waiting for the notice period to expire, or within three months from the effective date of termination (ERA s 111(3)).

Notice to be given by the employee

15.91 An employee is required to give due notice of termination, as laid down in his contract of employment. If there is no such term, then, in theory, he should give reasonable notice, depending on his position, the industry, etc. There does not appear to be any legal authority on this point. We are therefore left with the statutory notice period, set out in ERA s 86(2), which provides that an employee who has been continuously employed for one month or more has to give at least one week's notice.

Employer's remedies

15.92 If the employee fails to give the required notice of termination of his contract, technically the employer has two remedies. The first arises where there is a restrictive covenant prohibiting the employee from working for a competitor etc (see Chapter 19). The employer may be able to obtain an injunction to prevent a breach of this term. However, he will not be able to obtain an order for specific performance of the contract (TULR(C)A s 236).

15.93 Second, in theory, the employer may sue for damages for breach of contract, although such actions are virtually unknown this century, and the most an employee stands to lose if he fails to give the requisite notice is his reputation, if any, as a responsible employee. But if, for example, in anticipation of an employee commencing work, the employer incurs considerable expenses (eg purchases equipment or machinery, or hires premises, or enters into an abortive advertising campaign), an action for damages against an employee who fails to meet his contractual obligations could well succeed (*Batty v Melillo*).

15.94–15.100 An employer may attempt to pre-empt this problem by providing, in the contract of employment, that he may withhold arrears of wages and/or accrued holiday pay if an employee fails to give proper notice or work out that notice in accordance with the contract. This would appear to be perfectly legal, to the extent that the employer can quantify the loss, and while the deduction from wages would not contravene the legal rules designed to prevent deductions from wages (because the deduction will have been authorised by a contractual provision, see ERA s 13(1)), a refusal to pay accrued holiday pay would certainly be in breach of the relevant provisions of the Working Time Regulations. Clearly, in the absence of any such contractual power, the employer would fall foul of both legal provisions (see Chapter 8).

Employee's remedies

15.101 If an employer fails to give notice to the employee, or gives notice which is less than the contractual or statutory notice (whichever is the longer) the employee's remedy is to bring an action either in the ordinary courts or in the employment tribunal, under the Employment Tribunals Extension of Jurisdiction Order (see para 1.55). A court action would be appropriate if the amount claimed by way of damages is in excess of £25,000, because that is the maximum sum which could be awarded by an employment tribunal. Further, an action for breach of contract may be brought in the ordinary courts any time within six years from the breach, whereas a claim in an employment tribunal must be brought within three months beginning with the effective date of termination, or, if there was no such date, within three months from when the employee last worked, or, if it was not reasonably practicable to present the claim in either of those periods, within such further period as the employment tribunal thinks reasonable.

15.102 The claim by the employee is one for breach of contract, the measure of damages being the monies he would have earned had he been given proper notice. If there was an element of discretion in certain payments (eg annual salary increases, bonuses) it must be assumed that the employer would have exercised that discretion in good faith, and thus they form part of the loss suffered (*Clark v BET plc*). The claim is subject to the common law rule that the innocent party to a breach of contract must take reasonable steps to mitigate against his loss. Thus, if the employee is dismissed without notice, and the following day he obtained fresh employment on equivalent or improved terms and conditions, then, since he has lost nothing, he is not entitled to anything (*Secretary of State for Employment v Wilson*). Further, credit must be given by the employee for any payment received by way of jobseekers allowance (*Westwood v Secretary of State for Employment*). In order words, the object of the exercise is to place the employee in the same position financially as he would have been had lawful notice been given.

15.103 In certain special circumstances, an employee may be able to obtain an injunction to restrain an employer from terminating the contract of employment without proper notice. Generally speaking, it has to be shown that the trust and confidence which should exist between employer and employee remains (*Hill v C A Parsons Ltd*), but an injunction may also be obtained where it can be shown that the employer has failed to operate a contractual disciplinary procedure, particularly where damages would not be an adequate remedy for the manner in which a dismissal without notice was carried out. The modern test to be applied is 'the workability' of the situation (*Robb v London Borough of Hammersmith and Fulham*).

15.104–15.110 It should be noted that there is no implied term that an employee will not be unfairly dismissed (eg without going through proper procedures), and thus the only damages which can be awarded are those which relate to contractual notice (*Fosca Services (UK) Ltd v Birkett*).

Notice pay on insolvency (ERA ss 182–186)

15.111 If an employer becomes insolvent (eg bankrupt or wound up; see s 183), so that the contract of employment is no longer capable of being performed, then clearly that contract has terminated. In such circumstances, the employee may make an application for his statutory notice to be paid from the National Insurance Fund. If the Secretary of State is satisfied that the employee is so entitled, he will pay out of that Fund the amount of statutory notice set out in s 86 (above) (as well as certain other payments, see para 7.198), although the 'week's pay' for the purpose of this provision, is limited to the statutory maximum as laid down (currently £230 per week). Other contractual benefits cannot be recovered from the Fund. The employee will be under a duty to mitigate against his loss (*Westwood v Secretary of State for Employment*), and an employee who obtains fresh employment immediately or during what would have been his notice period can only recover in respect of the period of loss, if any (*Secretary of State for Employment v Wilson*). Any award made by the Secretary of State from the Fund will be based on pay net of income tax.

Time off to look for work (ERA s 52)

15.112 An employee whose employment has been terminated because of redundancy has the right to have time off work (with pay) to look for work or make arrangements for retraining during his notice period. This topic has been dealt with in Chapter 7.

CHAPTER 16

Wrongful dismissal

16.1   Under the law which existed prior to 1971 an employer was entitled to dismiss an employee for any reason or no reason at all; the only issues which arose related to whether or not the employee was entitled to a certain period of notice, or whether his conduct was such as to warrant instant (summary) dismissal without notice. There were certain special cases where the right not to be dismissed was enshrined into an employee's contract by virtue of a special 'status' (see para 2.71), and there were other cases where when a dismissal could not be carried out unless the rules of 'natural justice' were observed (see *Ridge v Baldwin*), or because the approval of some other person or body had to be obtained (eg *Cory Lighterage v T & GWU*). These matters were dealt with in Chapter 2.

16.2   In 1971 the Industrial Relations Act created the right for many employees not to be unfairly dismissed, and though that Act was repealed, the relevant provisions were substantially re-enacted (with some minor amendments) in the Trade Union and Labour Relations Act 1974, and further changes were made by the Employment Protection Act 1975. All the relevant law was brought together in the Employment Protection (Consolidation) Act 1978, and further amendments were made in subsequent legislation. The Employment Rights Act 1996 (as amended) is the latest consolidation statute.

16.3   But although the new legal right has largely subsumed the old common law learning, it is still necessary to examine the old law relating to wrongful and summary dismissal, because there may be situations when the common law remedy is more advantageous, or indeed, the only remedy available. In particular, we may note the following circumstances:
(a)   the maximum compensation award for unfair dismissal is currently £50,000 plus an appropriate basic award. A highly paid employee who is entitled to a long period of notice may be able to obtain substantially higher damages at common law, (see *O'Laoire v Jackel International Ltd*, para 16.45);
(b)   an employee who lacks the relevant period of continuous employment to qualify for unfair dismissal rights may nonetheless sue for wrongful dismissal, and may also be able to sue for the loss of his right to bring a claim for unfair dismissal (*Robert Cort & Sons v Charman*), although this may not be possible if the employee is dismissed summarily for gross misconduct, or if the employer exercises a contractual right to make a payment in lieu of notice (*Morran v Glasgow Council of Tenants' Association*);

(c)   an employee who is past the normal retiring age, or who is over the age of 65, or who worked abroad, may be able to bring a claim for breach of contract based on wrongful dismissal (*Age Concern Scotland v Hines*);

(d)   a fair dismissal may nonetheless be a wrongful dismissal if proper notice has not been given (*Treganowan v Robert Knee & Co Ltd*);

(e)   an application for unfair dismissal is likely to be time barred if it is not brought within three months from the effective date of termination, whereas a common law action for wrongful dismissal may be brought within six years of the breach;

(f)   the rules relating to damages are different. In particular, a common law action does not permit a reduction for contributory conduct, and the mitigation rules are not the same;

(g)   the dispute may contain a public law element, and not be concerned with strict contractual rights (*R v Secretary of State for the Home Department, ex p Benwell*);

(h)   a dismissal which is in breach of a contractual or statutory dismissal procedure may enable an employee to bring a common law action for breach of contract (*Shook v London Borough of Ealing*) or to seek an injunction to restrain the breach (*Irani v Southampton and South West Hampshire Health Authority*), or seek a declaration as to his legal rights. But the employee's remedies in such circumstances may be limited to damages for the period up to which he would have been employed had the correct procedure been followed (*Gunton v London Borough of Richmond*). There is no implied term in a contract that an employee has the right not to be unfairly dismissed (*Fosca Services (UK) Ltd v Birkett*).

16.4–16.10   Since the jurisdiction of the employment tribunals is concurrent in many respects with that possessed by the ordinary courts, an employee will thus opt for whichever cause of action will produce the most advantageous results (see para 1.52).

Wrongful dismissal

16.11   There are a number of ways in which wrongful dismissal may occur:

(a)   the employer terminates the employment without notice, or with less notice than the employee is entitled to receive under the terms of his contract or the statutory provisions (see Chapter 15);

(b)   a fixed-term contract is terminated by the employer before the date it was due to expire;

(c)   a contract for the completion of a specific task is terminated by the employer before the task has ended;

(d)   the employer terminates the employment without carrying out the disciplinary procedure which has been incorporated into the employee's contract (*Gunton v London Borough of Richmond*);

(e)   the employee is selected for redundancy in breach of a selection procedure which has been incorporated into his contract (*Alexander v Standard Telephones and Cables plc*);

(f)   the employer wrongfully repudiates the contract, his actions indicating that he no longer intends to be bound by the contract (*General Billposting Co Ltd v Atkinson*). The employee 'accepts' the repudiation by resigning, or, if appropriate, keeps the contract alive and sues for whatever remedy is available (*Rigby v Ferodo*, see para 3.184). For example, if the employer has unilaterally reduced the employee's wages, a claim may be made under the appropriate provisions of the Employment Rights Act (see Chapter 8). On the other hand, if the employee delays action, he may be taken to have affirmed the contract, unless the employer has given him time to make a decision (*Bliss v South East Thames Regional Health Authority*). Whether the employer has in fact repudiated the contract is a matter to be determined in the particular circumstances of the case (*General Billposting Co Ltd v Atkinson*). Thus, if the employer fails or refuses to provide work for the employee (see para 10.24) or makes it impossible for the employee to do his work (*Collier v Sunday Referee Publishing Co Ltd*), or unilaterally attempts to vary the contract of employment, such actions can amount to a breach of contract by the employer which enables the employee to accept by resigning, and claiming wrongful dismissal. This is the common law counterpart of the statutory concept of 'constructive' dismissal, which will be dealt with in Chapter 17;

(g) the contract specifies that a dismissal may only take place in certain specified circumstances, or on specified grounds, and the employer dismisses for some other reason not stated in the contract (*McClelland v Northern Ireland General Health Services Board*).

16.12–16.20 However, if the contract expressly permits the employer to terminate the employment without notice on the payment of a sum of money in lieu of notice, and the employer summarily dismisses the employee, the dismissal is not wrongful, whether or not the employer pays the money in lieu of notice, because he is acting within the strict terms of the contract. In such circumstances, the employee may sue for the sum due under the contract, as liquidated damages, and the employee is under no duty to mitigate against his loss (*Abrahams v Performing Right Society*, and see below).

Summary dismissal

16.21 In *Jupiter General Insurance Co v Shroff* the Privy Council stated that summary dismissal was a strong measure, to be justified only in the most exceptional circumstances. Nonetheless, there are a number of well-recognised grounds on which an employer may dismiss an employee summarily; these include gross misconduct, wilful refusal to obey a lawful and reasonable order, gross neglect, dishonesty, and so forth (see, eg *Blyth v Scottish Liberal Club*). Whether the conduct in question is serious enough to warrant dismissal is always a question of fact in each case, and the standards to be applied are those of the current *mores*, not those which may have become somewhat outdated. In *Wilson v Racher*, Edmund-Davies LJ said 'Many of the decisions which are customarily cited in these cases date from the last century and may be wholly out of accord with current social conditions. What would today be regarded as almost an attitude of Czar–serf, which is to be found in some of the older cases where a dismissed employee failed to recover damages, would, I venture to think, be decided differently today. We have by now come to realise that a contract of service imposes upon the parties a duty of mutual respect'. It is thus clear that many of the older decisions on this subject lack authority today, and must be treated with reserve, if not disdain.

16.22   But certain principles remain constant. In *Sinclair v Neighbour* a manager took £15 from a till and left an IOU in its place. He intended to replace the money a few days later. His conduct was regarded as being dishonest and his summary dismissal was upheld. In *Ross v Aquascutum Ltd* the employee was a nightwatchman. He was observed to be absent from the building he was guarding for two hours of each night, and it was held that his conduct constituted a breach of contract so serious as to justify summary dismissal. When considering conduct which results from the interaction of human personalities, it is necessary to apply the standards of ordinary people, not those of the angels. In *Pepper v Webb* a gardener was asked to do certain work, but he refused to do so in language which was somewhat vulgar. His summary dismissal was held to be justified, for by refusing to obey a lawful and reasonable order he had broken his contract. Indeed, his conduct had been such as to give rise to a history of complaints for insolence, and the incident which gave rise to his dismissal was merely the last straw. On the other hand, in *Wilson v Racher* a gardener swore at his employer using some even choicer obscenities. Although this could have amounted to gross misconduct, the court held that '... it requires very special circumstances to entitle a servant who expresses his feelings in such a grossly improper way to succeed in an action for wrongful dismissal'. On the facts of the case, the special circumstance existed, and these lay in the employer's own conduct which had provoked the outburst.

16.23   The breach of an express term of the contract or of a provision in the works rules may justify summary dismissal, provided it has been brought expressly to the attention of the employee that there is certain conduct which the employer will on no account tolerate. Certain airlines, for example, have a rule that any pilot who takes drugs (other than on medical prescription) or is discovered drunk whether on or off duty will be instantly dismissed. Other employers may specify other conduct which is detrimental to the business and which may warrant summary dismissal. For example, smoking in prohibited areas, unhygienic practices in food premises, breach of safety rules which may lead to hazards or risk of injury to others, all constitute conduct which may, in the special circumstances, warrant dismissal. The importance of having a consistent and well-defined policy on this subject will be stressed when the cases dealing with unfair dismissal are discussed.

16.24   An employee is not in breach of his contract of employment merely because he indicates his intention to open a business in competition with his employer. In *Laughton and Hawley v Bapp Industrial Supplies Ltd* the two claimants, who were employed by the respondents, wrote to the company's suppliers stating that they intended to commence trading in the near future, and asked for product lists, prices and terms. When the employers discovered this, the employees were dismissed instantly without notice. The dismissals were held to be unfair. There was no abuse of their positions as employees, no breach of any covenant in restraint of trade, and no disclosure of trade secrets or confidential information. The employees had not failed to devote their efforts to their employer's business during working hours, and thus their activities did not constitute gross misconduct. But where a managing director formed a new business entity, sought to persuade his employer's major client to transfer business to it, and induced two senior employees to join him in the new venture which was in direct competition with the employer, it was held that this amounted to gross misconduct warranting summary dismissal (*Marshall v Industrial Systems and Control Ltd*).

16.25   A more difficult problem arises if conduct of the employee is in the nature of neglect, which causes damage to the employer. Should one consider the act itself, which may be of a minor or major nature, or should one consider the consequences, which may be insignificant or serious? In *Savage v British India Steam Navigation Co* it was stated that it was the nature of the act, not the consequences, which was relevant. A failure to observe instructions which resulted in damage was held to be of sufficient seriousness to warrant summary dismissal in *Howe v Gloucester and Severnside Co-operative Society*, but excessive zeal which caused damage did not warrant such drastic measures in *Newlands v Howard & Co Ltd*. Neglect by senior employees who hold responsible positions appears to amount to a greater dereliction of duty than junior staff, and hence more likely to attract instant dismissal. As a general rule, for an employee to be summarily dismissed on the grounds of neglect, the neglect should be something approaching habitual conduct, but a single act of neglect could justify instant dismissal if its consequences are likely to be serious enough (*Taylor v Alidair Ltd*).

16.26   A strike is a breach of contract by the employee, and is thus an act of such a nature as to justify summary dismissal. So too is any other conduct designed to disrupt the employer's business, such as go-slow tactics, work-to-rule, etc. Persistent lateness, drunkenness, fighting, swearing, immorality, skylarking, are all examples of conduct which could attract summary dismissal in particular circumstances. But it must be stressed that although dismissal would not be wrongful at common law, in most cases, the test of 'fairness' will have to be considered additionally, and this will be explored later in Chapter 17.

16.27–16.35   A summary dismissal takes effect immediately. Any rights an employee may have, eg for pay in lieu of notice, expenses, etc may be claimed by an action for damages for breach of contract in the ordinary courts (*Octavius Atkinson & Sons Ltd v Morris*) or the employment tribunal (see para 1.45).

Remedies for wrongful dismissal

16.36   It must be stressed that an action for wrongful dismissal is different from a claim for unfair dismissal, although there may well be some overlap in certain instances. But, in particular, it should be noted that the sole issue in a wrongful dismissal action is whether or not the employer has broken the contract of employment. The 'reasonableness' of the employer's conduct is not in issue, nor does 'contributory conduct' by the employee come into the equation. Also, care must be taken to distinguish between payments made by the employer, and awards against an employer made by a court or tribunal. It is with the latter that this chapter is concerned.

16.37   The normal remedy for wrongful dismissal is for the innocent party to bring an action for damages, although sometimes an application for an injunction or a declaration will be made. Also, if the breach of contract consists not in a dismissal, but an alteration in the terms of the contract which is not permitted by the contract, the employee can, at his option, either accept the breach and resign (claiming wrongful constructive dismissal) or refuse to accept the breach, and sue on the contract as it stands, thus seeking to insist that the employer performs the contract (see *Dietman v London Borough of Brent*). The majority of wrongful dismissal claims are brought in the county court or the High Court, although, with the new concurrent jurisdiction conferred on employment tribunals by the Extension of Jurisdiction Order, more and more claims are now being brought under a procedure which is cheaper and comparatively expeditious.

16.38 In rare cases, an employee may seek a public law remedy, by way of judicial review, generally when a private law remedy either does not exist, or would be inadequate in the circumstances (*R v Chief Constable of Merseyside Police, ex p Calverley*).

A. Damages

16.39 The general principle in contract law (and it must be remembered that employment law is basically concerned with a contract of employment) is that the purpose of damages is to put the innocent party in the position in which he would have been had the contractual obligations been performed, insofar as it is possible to do this by a monetary award. Thus, since an employer may always give notice to terminate the contract, then this will become the starting point for any claim. If the employer terminates the contract without notice, or gives less notice than the contract or the statutory provisions require, then damages will be initially limited to the period of notice that should have been given (*Fosca Services (UK) Ltd v Birkett*, and see Chapter 15). Similarly, if the contract was for a fixed term, and is prematurely terminated, damages will be the loss suffered by the employee as the result of the employer's action. However, if a fixed-term contract gives the employer the right to terminate before the end of that term, then damages will be limited to the notice period (*British Guiana Credit Corpn v Da Silva*). If the employer is in breach because he has failed to follow a disciplinary procedure which has been incorporated into the contract, damages will be limited to the period of time it would have taken the employer to put the contractual procedure into effect (*Dietman v Brent London Borough Council*). An apprentice who has been wrongfully dismissed may recover damages for the loss of training and work experience he would have gained had the contract not been broken or the diminution of his future prospects (*Dunk v George Waller & Son Ltd*). Artistes may be able to recover for loss of publicity (*Withers v General Theatre Corpn*), or the loss of enhancing their reputation (*Herbert Clayton & Jack Waller Ltd v Oliver*, see para 10.24).

16.40 Because there may be certain complications arising out of income tax liability and national insurance contributions, the actual computation of the financial loss may present problems. In principle, an employee is entitled to the net loss suffered (ie after the deduction of tax and national insurance), and whether one should start with the gross salary, less deductions, or the net figure grossed up, will frequently depend on the amounts at stake. It would appear that the latter course is more advantageous if the amount is comparatively large, whereas the former method appears to be appropriate when the length of the notice period is relatively short (*Shove v Downs Surgical plc*).

16.41 Also to be taken into account are commissions, bonuses, gratuities etc, which were contractually due to the employee (*Addis v Gramophone Co Ltd*), including an enhanced contractual redundancy payment (*Basnett v J & A Jackson Ltd*) but not discretionary payments (*Lavarack v Woods of Colchester Ltd*). Fringe benefits, eg company car (in so far as it was permitted for private use), subsidised mortgages, free lunches, the loss of the right to obtain share options (if there was a contractual right) or options already granted (*Chapman v Aberdeen Construction Group Ltd*), private medical insurance, rent-free accommodation etc, can be quantified and their value claimed. Expenses are not normally allowable, as they represent a reimbursement for expenditure incurred by the employee on behalf of the employer. Indeed, if it can be shown that the expenses were in fact a device to boost the employee's income, and were not genuinely incurred, it may be argued that this was an attempt to avoid paying income tax on the employee's salary, and, as such, the contract was illegal, and did not give rise at all to any cause of action (see para 3.6, and see Income Tax (Employments) (Amendment) Regulations 1999).

16.42   Also included in the compensation which may be awarded will be the loss of other actual or potential benefits, such as pension rights and/or the employers potential pension contributions, profit sharing schemes, the lost value of share options (*Micklefield v SAC Technology*), outstanding holiday pay, loss of statutory protection rights (*Stapp v Shaftesbury Society*), loss of the opportunity to claim a redundancy payment (*Basnett v J & A Jackson Ltd*), and so on.

16.43   At common law, no damages may be awarded for the manner of dismissal, or for injured feelings, or for the fact that the manner of dismissal makes it more difficult for the employee to obtain other employment (*Addis v Gramophone Co Ltd*). The decision of the House of Lords in *Malik v BCCI* (see para 3.72) is concerned with a complaint relating to a breach of trust and confidence owed by the employer to his employees during the period they were employed, and is not concerned with the actual manner of dismissal (*Johnson v Unisys Ltd*).

16.44   Damages for breach of contract at common law are always subject to the rule that the innocent party must take reasonable steps to mitigate against his loss, which, in this context, involves looking for other suitable employment. Any earnings from such employment (or from self-employment) can be deducted from the loss suffered (*Shove v Downs Surgical plc*). Thus if an employee is dismissed without notice, and obtains other employment, he must give credit for any earning from his new employment in respect of any payment for the period of notice he should have received (*Gregory v Wallace*). The problem here, however, is that the burden of proof is on the employer to show that the employee has failed to take reasonable steps to mitigate his loss (*London and South of England Building Society v Stone*). This he may be able to do, either by reference to matters known to him, or by obtaining some form of discovery from the employee concerning his attempts to seek alternative employment. Whether an employee has taken reasonable steps to mitigate against his loss is a question of fact to be determined by the court, bearing in mind all the circumstances, including the employee's age, mobility, personal commitments, qualifications, experience, and so on. For example, in *Brace v Calder*, the claimant was dismissed from a partnership as a result of a change in the partners, but offered his old job back by the new partners. He refused this offer, and it was held that he had failed to mitigate his loss, and was therefore only entitled to nominal damages. On the other hand, in *Yetton v Eastwoods Froy Ltd*, a managing director was dismissed from his post, but was offered the job of assistant managing director. It was held that his refusal of this job, which was a significant step down, was not unreasonable.

16.45   It is unusual, but not impossible, to bring a claim for unfair dismissal as well as an action for wrongful dismissal, although either the court or tribunal can stay one action, pending the outcome of the other (*Carter v Credit Change Ltd*). If one claim does not fully resolve the whole matter, the second action may then be resorted to. One would expect there to be a general rule that any award made in one jurisdiction would be deducted from an award stemming from the second claim. Thus, an award made by an employment tribunal will normally identify the various headings of loss in respect of which compensation is to be awarded, and double recovery of any particular loss would not be permitted in subsequent High Court proceedings. However, where the loss is in excess of the statutory compensation award, it may not always be possible to identify the particular heading awarded by the employment tribunal, and therefore there may not be an element of double recovery. Thus, in *O'Laoire v Jackel International*, an employment tribunal held that the claimant had been unfairly dismissed, and assessed his loss at £100,000. However, they could only award compensation of £8,000, which was the maximum compensation award at that time. The claimant then brought an action in the High Court, and the judge held that the sum of £8,000 had to be deducted from the damages of £100,000. However, the Court of Appeal held that this was wrong. It was clearly not possible for the employment tribunal to assess the maximum compensation award with reference to any particular head of loss, and thus the rule against double recovery did not apply.

16.46   The general principle relating to any award of damages by a court is that they should be paid net of tax (*British Transport Commission v Gourley*). However, the Finance Act 1988 provides that damages for wrongful dismissal are not taxable in the hands of the recipient unless they exceed £30,000. Thereafter, tax must be deducted at the employee's highest marginal rate. Thus a court must award a gross sum which, after tax, would leave the employee with a net sum which represents his loss.

B. Injunction and/or declaration

16.47   An employee who feels that he has been wrongfully dismissed may be able to bring an action for an injunction to restrain a breach of contract, or seek a declaration as to what are his rights under the contract. These are equitable remedies, and therefore will only be granted at the court's discretion. If an application is made for an interlocutory injunction pending the trial of the action, the principles laid down in *American Cyanamid Co v Ethicon* will apply, ie (a) has the claimant shown that there is a triable issue, and (b) does the balance of convenience favour the granting of the injunction? In particular, as we have seen (para 10.1), the courts will rarely grant an injunction if the effect is to compel specific performance of the contract. Exceptionally the court will do so in perhaps two circumstances, ie (a) if there is no loss of trust and confidence in the employee (*Powell v London Borough of Brent*) or (b) where the dismissal was in breach of natural justice or of a contractual disciplinary procedure (*Gunton v London Borough of Richmond*). It must be shown that damages would not be an adequate remedy (*Wadcock v London Borough of Brent*). A person seeking an injunction must first of all have pursued all internal remedies in so far as they are available (*R v BBC, ex p Lavelle*).

16.48   Similarly, an employee may seek a declaration as to his contractual rights. This remedy will usually be sought when an employee refuses to accept a decision by an employer which is outside the terms of the contract. For example, in *Stevenson v United Road Transport Union* an employee was dismissed without being given reasons (in breach of the contractual procedure), and a declaration was granted that the dismissal, in breach of natural justice, was void. A declaration may be sought if an employer unilaterally reduces an employee's wages, or otherwise purports to act in breach of the contract (*Rigby v Ferodo Ltd*). As with all equitable remedies, the employee must act expeditiously, (*Dietman v London Borough of Brent*).

C. Suing for breach of contract

16.49   An employee is not bound to accept a breach of contract which falls short of a wrongful constructive dismissal, and may, instead of suffering the breach in silence, sue for the loss suffered, while not accepting the alleged employer repudiation. Thus in *Rigby v Ferodo Ltd*, the employee recovered damages for loss of wages when the employer unilaterally reduced his earnings; in *Miller v Hamworthy Engineering Ltd* an employee recovered lost pay when put on short-time working without contractual authority; and in *Keir and Williams v Hereford and Worcester County Council*, damages were awarded to employees when an employer withdrew their car allowance. The correct procedure in such cases is for the employer to give lawful termination of the contract (ie by giving the requisite period of notice) and then to offer the employees new contracts with new terms before the notice period expires. A unilateral variation of the contract, by itself, is not a termination and offer of re-engagement under a new contract (*Burdett-Coutts v Hertfordshire County Council*). Thus by lawfully terminating the contract, the employer avoids any liability for wrongful dismissal, although it must be borne in mind that an employee's rights to claim unfair dismissal will be unaffected. Whether the dismissal is in fact fair or unfair will depend on all the circumstances of the case (see Chapter 17).

D. Public law remedies

16.50   The circumstances in which public law remedies (by way of judicial review) can be used to resolve private employment disputes, and the grounds on which decisions of public bodies can be challenged, have already been discussed (see para 2.297). But despite the attempt by Woolf LJ in *McLaren v Home Office* to lay down the principles which should be adopted when dealing with such applications, no coherent set of rules has ever been finally laid down, and the courts have developed the law on this subject on a case by case basis (*R v Derbyshire County Council, ex p Noble*). The actions brought generally seek an injunction and/or a declaration.

CHAPTER 17

Unfair dismissal

17.1 The statutory provisions relating to unfair dismissal are to be found in ss 94–107 of ERA. The interpretation of those provisions by the courts and tribunals has led to thousands of reported decisions which have laid down guidelines varying from legal ingenuity, through sound common sense, and ending up, on occasions, with cabalistic mystery! But many decisions can only be explained on their own special facts and on a consideration of the actual evidence presented to the tribunal, and it must be borne in mind that employment tribunal decisions are not, in themselves, binding precedents. Sometimes the successful claimant will be awarded a reduced compensation because of his own contributory conduct, and there have been cases where a dismissal though unfair, has resulted in a nil award.

17.2 Nonetheless, the decisions of the reported cases repay detailed study. In the first place, they give guidance to a generalised stream of thought which is rapidly becoming dominant thinking in employment law; guidance on how an employer should act so as to be regarded as being reasonable and fair, guidance on how disciplinary procedures should be operated, and on when an employer may adopt standards which are less than those expected by a perfectionist. Secondly, the decided cases point out the pitfalls into which other employers have fallen, and thus enable a conscientious personnel manager so to direct his policies as to avoid those very traps. Finally, they provide interpretation of the legislative provisions which have a persuasive effect until a higher court has had an opportunity to pronounce on their validity.

17.3–17.10 Every employee to whom the Act applies has the right not to be unfairly dismissed, and the remedy for the infringement of that right is by way of a complaint to the employment tribunal, and not otherwise. This means that unfair dismissal cases must go to the employment tribunals, whereas a person who wishes to sue in respect of *wrongful dismissal* must bring the action in the ordinary courts in the normal way, or in the employment tribunal as appropriate (see para 16.3).

Exclusions

17.11 The following categories of employees are not protected by the provisions of ERA:

a. any employment as a master or member of the crew of a fishing vessel where the employee is remunerated by a share of the profits;

b. merchant seamen may pursue claims for unfair dismissal provided they are employed to work on ships registered in Great Britain (ie excluding Northern Ireland, the Isle of Man and the Channel Islands) unless their employment is wholly outside Great Britain, or they are not ordinarily resident in Great Britain (ERA s 199(7), (8)). In *Wood v Cunard Line Ltd*, the claimant was engaged in Southampton, and then joined a ship which cruised around the Caribbean. It was held that his employment was wholly outside Great Britain.

Under the Employment Protection (Offshore Employment) Order 1976, employees who work in oil rigs and off-shore installations in British territorial waters or areas designated under the Continental Shelf Act 1964 are not excluded from the provisions of the Employment Rights Act 1996;

c. any employment where the employee has been continuously employed for less than one year. The period of continuous employment begins with the day on which he is due to start work under the contract (*Salvation Army v Dewsbury*). As has been noted (see para 15.81), an employee who had been employed for one week less than the qualifying period of one year, and is dismissed, is entitled to add to his computation the week's statutory notice to which he is entitled (s 97(2)), but not his contractual notice (see *Fox Maintenance Ltd v Jackson*, para 15.81). But if he is dismissed without notice for gross misconduct, he cannot rely on s 97(2) 'To pull him past the post' (*Ahmed v National Car Parks Ltd*)!

The fact that the reason for the dismissal is designated as 'gross misconduct' does not preclude the operation of s 97(2), for the employment tribunal can enquire into the facts on their merits, and decide whether in the circumstances the employer was entitled to terminate the contract without notice. If they decide that the employer was not so entitled, s 97(2) comes into operation (*Lanton Leisure Ltd v White and Gibson*).

If there is no adequate reason which would justify the summary dismissal, and if the consequence is to deprive an employee of his right to bring a claim for unfair dismissal by depriving him of the relevant period of continuous employment, the employee may have a remedy at common law for damages for wrongful dismissal. The measure of damages will include the loss of his right to claim unfair dismissal (*Stapp v Shaftesbury Society*).

For the general rules relating to continuous employment, see Chapter 13;

d. an employee who has reached the normal retiring age as laid down in his contract of employment (*Howard v Department of National Savings*).

The normal retiring age is not the same thing as the normal pensionable age, for the latter may merely be the age at which the employee is entitled to retire on a pension, without being obliged to do so. Thus to retire someone compulsorily short of the normal retiring age may be unfair, even though he has passed the pensionable age (*Ord v Maidstone and District Hospital Management Committee*). In *Wood v Louis C Edwards & Sons (Manchester)* a tribunal went even further, and awarded compensation to a 62-year-old manager on the basis that he would not have retired until he was 70, for although the exclusion prevents a person over 65 from claiming, it does not apparently prevent compensation being based on the assumption that a person below that age may continue to work after 65.

The starting point for the normal retiring age is the contractual retiring age. However, this may be displaced by evidence that the contractual retiring age is departed from in practice, or that there is some other age at which employees of that description in the relevant group can reasonably expect to be compelled to retire (*Age Concern Scotland v Hines*). Where there is a contractual retiring age applicable to all, or nearly all, of the relevant employees, there is a presumption that the contractual retiring age is the normal retiring age. But that presumption can be rebutted by evidence that there is in practice some higher age which those employees have reasonably come to regard as their normal retiring age (*Secretary of State for Scotland v Meikle*). If the contractual retiring age has been abandoned, so that employees retire at a variety of ages (eg between the ages of 60 to 63, see *Swaine v Health and Safety Executive*), then there is no normal retiring age (*Waite v Government Communications Headquarters*), and the exclusion at the age of 65 operates. If an employer wishes to introduce a new retirement age which will then constitute the normal retirement age then, so long as there is no breach of the employee's contract, and there is no suggestion that it is a sham policy, and it has been properly communicated to the employee, it will take immediate effect, even though it destroys a previous expectation of being retained in employment until a higher age (*Brooks v British Telecommunications plc*).

If members of a particular group are permitted (exceptionally) to retire at different ages, the question is whether there is a norm for the retiring age and whether the fact that it is not always applied destroys that norm. Thus, an exception to the normal retiring age which only affects a limited group of employees, which is limited in time, and which is made in response to representations made on their behalf on grounds of hardship is a special reason which does not destroy the norm (*Barclays Bank plc v O'Brien*). But the contractual age at which an employee in a relevant position is expected to retire cannot be changed to the disadvantage of the employee without a consensual variation of the contract or a termination by lawful notice followed by an offer to renew on new terms (*Bratko v Beloit Walmsley Ltd*);

e. if there is no normal retiring age, or if the contractual retiring age discriminated between men and women, the age limit of 65 applies to all employees. Formerly women over the age of 60 could not bring claims for unfair dismissal, but as a result of the decision of the European Court in *Marshall v Southampton Area Health Authority*, the law was changed by the Sex Discrimination Act 1986 to equalise the position of men and women;

f. any employment covered by a dismissals procedure agreement which has been designated and approved by the Secretary of State. This enables an employer and an independent trade union to create their own dismissals procedure which, provided it conforms with the laid down criteria, may be approved by the Minister, and those employees covered by it are excluded from the provisions of the Act. Very little use has been made of this procedure (see Dismissals Procedure Agreement made between the Electrical Contractors Association and the EEPTU);

g. an agreement to submit the dispute to arbitration under a scheme prepared by ACAS (see s 212A of TULR(C)A inserted by s 7 of the Employment Rights (Dispute Resolution) Act 1998). To date no such scheme has been prepared;

h. employees who work for foreign governments and other international organisations which enjoy diplomatic immunity (eg see *Gadhok v Commonwealth Secretariat*) can only bring appropriate claims if that diplomatic immunity is waived; otherwise the employment tribunals have no jurisdiction (*Mukoro v European Bank for Reconstruction and Development*). However, by the State Immunity Act 1978, a state is not immune in respect of proceedings relating to a contract of employment if (a) the contract was made in the United Kingdom, or (b) the work is to be wholly or partly performed in the United Kingdom. The Act does not apply if at the time of the claim the applicant was a national of the state concerned, or at the time when the contract was made he was neither a national of the United Kingdom nor habitually resident here, or if the parties have agreed to exclude the provisions of the Act.

17.12 No qualifying period of employment is required in respect of a dismissal alleged to be unfair if the reason was
(a) connected with pregnancy or childbirth, or the employee took ordinary or additional maternity leave, or parental leave, or time off to look after dependants, declined to sign a workforce agreement for maternity and parental leave purposes, or performed functions as a workforce representative (ERA s 99 and Maternity and Parental Leave Regulations 1999, reg 20);
(b) to do with health and safety (ERA s 100, see para 11.61);
(c) a shop or betting worker refused to work Sundays (ERA s 101, see para 7.131);
(d) the exercise of a right under the Working Time Regulations (ERA s 101A, see para 7.257);
(e) the performance of functions as a trustee of occupational pensions scheme (ERA s 102);
(f) the performance of a function as an employee representative (ERA s 103, see para 18.113);
(g) the employee made a protected disclosure (ERA s 103A, see para 10.139);
(h) the assertion of a statutory right (ERA s 104, see para 17.221);
(i) the exercise of a right under the National Minimum Wage Act (ERA s 104A, see para 8.83);
(j) the taking of action in connection with a tax credit (ERA s 104B);
(k) selection for redundancy for any of the above reasons (ERA s 195);
(l) membership or non-membership of a trade union (TULR(C)A s 154, see para 21.89);
(m) the employee took protected industrial action (TULR(C)A s 238A, see para 21.116);
(n) the employee did a wide range of actions in connection with the statutory procedure for recognition or derecognition (TULR(C)A Sch A1 (see para 21.70);
(o) he did acts in connection with his rights under the Part-time Workers (Prevention of Less Favourable Treatment) Regulations 2000;
(p) he did acts in connection with his rights under the Transnational Information and Consultation of Employees Regulations 1999 (see para 23.267).

17.13 If a person is over the normal retiring age, or over the age of 65, he is not excluded from bringing a claim for unfair dismissal if the reason for the dismissal was for any of the above reasons.

17.14–17.20 If a person is dismissed as a result of being suspended from work on medical grounds, s/he is only required to have one month's continuous employment (see para 7.21).

329

What is a dismissal? (ERA ss 95–96)

17.21   As a general rule, a dismissal will not operate until it has been received by the employee (*Widdicombe v Longcombe Software Ltd*). Thus if it is sent by post, it will be effective from the time when the employee has actually read the letter, or had a reasonable opportunity to do so. In *Brown v Southall and Knight* the employers sent a letter of dismissal to the claimant who, at that date, did not have the requisite period of continuous employment. He was away on holiday when the letter arrived, and thus did not read it until he returned a week later, by which time he had the necessary qualifying period. It was held that he was entitled to pursue his claim for unfair dismissal. Of course, if he deliberately did not open the letter, or went away in order to avoid reading it, he would have been debarred from saying that the notification of the dismissal was not given to him (see also *McMaster v Manchester Airport plc*).

17.22   There are three ways in which a dismissal may take place.

A. Employer termination

17.23   Where the contract of employment is terminated by the employer, with or without notice. It follows that (subject to the doctrine of constructive dismissal, discussed below) if an employee resigns of his own volition, there is no dismissal. In *Elliott v Waldair (Construction) Ltd* the claimant was engaged as a driver, and mainly drove a heavy lorry. It was decided that this work was too hard for him, and he was instructed to drive a smaller van. This he refused to do because it would reduce his opportunity of overtime earnings, and he resigned. It was held that the order to drive a different vehicle at the same hourly rate but with less opportunity to earn overtime could not be said to constitute a dismissal by the employer.

17.24   Equally, a mutually agreed termination does not amount to a dismissal. In *Harvey v Yankee Traveller Restaurant*, the claimant became pregnant, and although her employer made various arrangements to accommodate her, these were not satisfactory. After a discussion with her employer, she agreed to resign. It was held that this could not amount to a dismissal. A warning that a dismissal is being contemplated in the future (eg for reason of impending redundancy etc) is not a dismissal (*Doble v Firestone Tyre and Rubber Co Ltd*).

17.25   The fact that the employer invited the employee to resign may, however, constitute a dismissal, for the alternative may be expressed or implicit in the request. In *Robertson v Securicor Transport Ltd* the claimant had broken a company rule by signing for a container which had not been received. When this was discovered, he was given the alternative of resigning or being dismissed, and he chose the respectable course. It was held that he had been dismissed nonetheless. But although a resignation under duress may be a dismissal (*East Sussex County Council v Walker*), an invitation to resign as an alternative to facing a disciplinary hearing which may result in a dismissal is not, by itself, a dismissal (*Martin v Glynwed Distribution Ltd*). If the choice is put to the employee 'perform your contract or resign' this is not a dismissal, for the employee is making a decision not to carry out the terms of the contract which the employer is legally entitled to expect.

17.26 To falsely inveigle an employee to resign may also amount to a dismissal (*Caledonian Mining Co Ltd v Bassett and Steel*).

17.27 A dismissal can take place even though the employee invites this course of action. In *Thomas v General Industrial Cleaners Ltd* the claimant was in poor health, but did not wish to resign because of fears that he might lose certain benefits. He left the decision to the employers, who accepted the initiative and terminated his employment. The tribunal held that there was a dismissal by the employers.

17.28 A dismissal takes place if an employer unilaterally imposes radically different terms of employment, which are so substantially different as to have the effect of destroying the basis of the old contract. In *Alcan Extrusions v Yates* the employers unilaterally made changes in working hours, shift systems, weekend and bank holiday workings, shift premiums etc. The employees agreed to work the new system under protest, reserving their rights to claim unfair dismissal and/or redundancy payments, which they subsequently did. An employment tribunal chairman held that they had been dismissed, and the decision was upheld by the EAT. It was not correct to argue that the imposition of contractual changes can only be characterised as a potentially repudiatory breach, giving the employee an option to resign and claim constructive dismissal. Substantial departures from the original contract constitutes a dismissal in its own right.

17.29 Traditionally, the words used by the employer to denote that a dismissal has taken place are usually quite clear and explicit, but the niceties of social intercourse are not always observed in real life. In *Kendrick v Aerduct Productions*, the employer told an employee to 'fuck off'! Could this be construed as being equivalent to 'you're fired'? Or was it an expression of abuse with no other ulterior implication? If the words used are ambiguous, the employment tribunal must ask themselves, what would a reasonable man understand by the expression in the context of the industry and the surrounding circumstances. In *Futty v D and D Brekkes Ltd* the employee was a fish filleter. During an altercation with the foreman he was told 'if you do not like the job, you can fuck off'. He took this as a dismissal, found another job and claimed compensation. It was held that in the context of the particular trade, the words meant no more than 'if you do not like the work you are doing, you can clock off'. Indeed, had the applicant not received a promise of another job, he would have gone back to work the following day, and hence he had resigned, and had not been dismissed. But there is little doubt that there can be circumstances where telling an employee to 'fuck off' will amount to a dismissal (*a fortiori*, telling him to 'fuck off and piss off', see *King v Webb's Poultry Products (Bradford) Ltd*).

17.30 Equally, if the words used are unambiguous, the employment tribunal must give them their natural and ordinary meaning (*Sothern v Franks Charlesly & Co*).

17.31 A further refinement on this theme was pursued in *Davy v Collins (Builders) Ltd*. During an argument, the employer said to the employee 'if you are not satisfied, you can fuck off'. The employee left and brought a claim for unfair dismissal, which failed. With dialectic ingenuity the tribunal drew a distinction between an employer saying 'I am not satisfied, so you can fuck off', and 'if you are not satisfied, you can fuck off'. In the former case there is likely to be a dismissal; in the latter case, the employer is saying to the employee, 'If you don't like it, you can lump it' and the claimant, not liking it, lumped it!

17.32 It is thus not the actual words which are used which are significant, but the intention behind them, and this must be ascertained from all the surrounding circumstances and the accompanying words as well as the industry, the relationships between the parties, and so on (*J & J Stern v Simpson*). If an employer or his manager, speaking in anger, behaves in a way which he might not do ordinarily, and utters abusive words, the employment tribunal should consider very carefully whether the words amount to a dismissal, or whether they were little more than abuse (*Chesham Shipping Ltd v Rowe*). Events which followed the utterance of the offensive words and preceding the departure of the employee may be taken into account in so far as they throw light on the employer's intentions (*Tanner v DT Kean Ltd*).

17.33 Once a dismissal (or resignation) has taken place, it cannot be withdrawn unilaterally (*Harris and Russell Ltd v Slingsby*), but words used in the heat of the moment, and withdrawn almost immediately may be ignored, for it is vital to good industrial relations that either the employer or the employee should be given the opportunity to recant (*Martin v Yeoman Aggregates Ltd*).

B. Fixed-term contract expires

17.34 Where the employee is employed for a fixed term, a dismissal takes place if that term expires without being renewed under the same contract. But a dismissal which takes place in this manner must still be tested for fairness in terms of the reasonableness of the employer's action in not renewing the contract. Thus if there is a genuine need for an employee to have a fixed-term contract (eg of a temporary nature, or for a specific purpose, etc) then it may be reasonable not to renew this after expiry. It is important that employees should not be deprived of their statutory rights by dressing up an ordinary job as a fixed-term contract (*Terry v East Sussex County Council*). Further, when a fixed-term contract expires, an employer may be acting unreasonably if he fails genuinely to consider the employee for employment in some other suitable post (*Labour Party v Oakley*).

C. Constructive dismissal

17.35 Where the employee himself terminates the contract, with or without notice, in circumstances that he is entitled to terminate it without notice by reason of the employer's conduct: this is known as 'constructive dismissal', for although the employee resigns, it is the employer's conduct which constitutes a repudiation of the contract, and the employee accepts that repudiation by resigning. The employee must clearly indicate that he is treating the contract as having been repudiated by the employer (*Logabax Ltd v Titherley*), and if he fails to do so, by word or by conduct, he is not entitled to claim that he has been constructively dismissed (*Holland v Glendale Industries Ltd*).

17.36 The doctrine of constructive dismissal has had a somewhat chequered history. The real problem was to determine the nature of the conduct of the employer which entitles the employee to resign. Did such conduct have to amount to an actual breach of contract by the employer, or could any unreasonable conduct by the employer be sufficient to entitle an employee to resign? For a long time the latter theory held sway, leading to some of the most bizarre and eccentric decisions in the whole of employment law. This view was firmly disposed of by the Court of Appeal in *Western Excavating (ECC) Ltd v Sharp*, and all previous decisions must be read subject to this case. The facts were that the employee was dismissed for taking unauthorised time off work. He appealed to the internal disciplinary board, which substituted a penalty of five days' suspension without pay. This he accepted, but being short of money, he asked his employers if he could have an advance on his accrued holiday pay. This was refused. He then asked if he could have a loan of £40, but this too was refused. Consequently he resigned (in order to get his holiday pay) and brought a claim for unfair dismissal, alleging that he was forced to resign by virtue of the employer's conduct. His claim was upheld by the employment tribunal; the conduct of the employers was so unreasonable that the employee could not fairly be expected to put up with it, and justified him leaving. On appeal, the EAT was not sure that they would have come to the same decision had they heard the case, but held that the employment tribunal were entitled to come to that decision. This was reversed by the Court of Appeal. The test for constructive dismissal was to be determined by the contract test, ie did the employer's conduct amount to a breach of contract which entitled the employee to resign. The 'unreasonable conduct' theory was dismissed as leading to a finding of constructive dismissal on the most whimsical grounds. Since there had been no breach of contract by the employers in *Sharp's* case (for the employers were under no contractual obligation to make the payments which were requested) there was no dismissal, constructive or otherwise.

17.37   It follows, therefore, that only those cases where the employer's conduct amounts to a significant breach, going to the root of the contract, can now be regarded as being authoritative. Thus, if the employer tries to impose a unilateral change in employment terms, such as a change in the job, a significant change in hours (*Simmonds v Dowty Seals Ltd*), a lowering in earnings (*RF Hill Ltd v Mooney*), a significant change in the location of employment (*Courtaulds Northern Spinning Ltd v Sibson*), a demotion, then provided there is no contractual right to do so, such conduct will entitle an employee to resign. But a failure to pay salary on the due date was held not to have been so serious a breach in *Adams v Charles Zub Associates Ltd*. The employer's action did not show an intention not to be bound by the contract.

17.38   It must be borne in mind that although a constructive dismissal may amount to a dismissal in law, whether the dismissal is fair or unfair has still to be determined by the facts of the case, and whether or not the employer has acted reasonably (*Industrial Rubber Products v Gillon*).

17.39   If there is a genuine dispute concerning the nature of the parties' contractual obligations, this does not indicate an intention on the part of the employer to break the contract, and hence this will not be grounds for claiming constructive dismissal. In *Frank Wright & Co Ltd v Punch* the claimant claimed that he was entitled to receive cost of living increases in his salary. The employers disputed that they were contractually obliged to pay, and so he resigned, claiming constructive dismissal. The EAT held that where there was a genuine dispute as to the construction of a contract, or a genuine mistake as to fact or law, the courts would be unwilling to hold that an expression of intent by a party to carry out the contract in accordance with his (possibly erroneous) interpretation amounts to a repudiation of that contract. In *Bridgen v Lancashire County Council* the Master of the Rolls (Sir John Donaldson) expressed the view that the mere fact that a party to the contract takes a view of construction which is ultimately shown to be wrong does not, of itself, constitute repudiatory conduct. It has to be shown that he did not intend to be bound by the contract as properly construed. If the reasoning in these two decisions is correct, a number of previous decisions on constructive dismissal must be regarded as being of doubtful authority.

17.40 More difficult are those cases where the employee claims he is entitled to resign because the employer has broken an implied term of the contract (see para 3.66) because the nature of these terms may sometimes be a matter for speculation and conjecture. In *British Aircraft Corpn v Austin* a failure to investigate a complaint about the inadequacy of protective spectacles was held to be a breach of the employer's implied duty to take reasonable care for the employee's safety, and in *Graham Oxley Tool Steels Ltd v Firth* it was held that there was an implied term that the employer will provide a proper working environment. If no reasonable employer would have expected the employee to work in those conditions, then there is a fundamental breach of the contract of employment (*Dutton & Clark Ltd v Daly*). It will be recalled (para 10.18) that there is an implied duty of mutual respect, and therefore any action by or on behalf of the employer which runs contrary to that duty may amount to constructive dismissal. This could be the use of foul and abusive language (*Palmanor Ltd v Cedron*), making unjustifiable complaints or giving unjustified warnings (*Walker v Josiah Wedgwood*), making statements which destroy or seriously damage the relationship of trust and confidence which must exist between the parties (*Courtaulds Northern Textiles Ltd v Andrew*), such as ill-founded allegations of theft (*Robinson v Crompton Parkinson Ltd*), offensive and insensitive conduct by a supervisor (*Hilton International Hotels (UK) Ltd v Protopapa*), and so on.

17.41 There is no implied term in a contract which entitles an employee to facilities for smoking, and if an employer introduces a general rule which has the effect of banning smoking on the premises, this does not operate so as to frustrate the employee's attempt to perform the contract because he cannot comply with the rule. Such a rule has a legitimate purpose, and the fact that it bears hard on a particular individual does not warrant an inference that the employer had repudiated the contract so as to enable the employee to claim he has been constructively dismissed (*Dryden v Greater Glasgow Health Board*, see para 3.158). Indeed, it is more likely that there is an implied term that the employer will provide a safe working environment, and a non-smoker who is forced to work in areas where he would be affected by the smoking habits of other employees can claim constructive dismissal for a breach of that term (*Waltons & Morse v Dorrington*).

17.42 Even if there is an express term in the contract enabling an employer to transfer the employee to another location, there is an implied term that the employer will give reasonable notice of the transfer and, where appropriate, relocation and other allowances will be made, so as to make it feasible for the employee to comply with the contractual obligation to transfer (*United Bank Ltd v Akhtar*).

17.43 A further problem arises when the employer makes life as difficult or as uncomfortable as possible, in the hope (or expectation) that the hint will be taken, and the employee will resign. No doubt a great deal will depend on the extent of the evidence which shows whether or not the employer is in breach of an express or implied term of the contract. Situations do occur when the parties wish to part company, but the employer is scared to take the initiative for fear of having a claim being brought against him, and the employee is reluctant to resign without at least having an opportunity to collect some financial reward which is available under modern legislative provisions. It is here that the vagaries of the doctrine of constructive dismissal present the greatest menace, for the uncertainties are enormous.

17.44 In *Haseltine Lake & Co v Dowler* the claimant was told that there was no future with the firm for him and that he should seek another job elsewhere. Eventually he found another job, resigned his employment and claimed he had been constructively dismissed. The EAT rejected his claim. No date had been fixed by the employers for his resignation, and before a contract of employment can terminate, there must be an ascertainable date on which it came to an end. This was not a case of 'resign or you will be dismissed', and therefore there was no repudiation of the contract by the employers.

17.45 Although the 'implied term' theory has effectively replaced the unreasonable conduct test, it can be just as capricious and whimsical in its results. In *FC Gardner Ltd v Beresford* an employee resigned because she had not had a pay increase for two years, whereas other employees had. It was held that although there was no express term of the contract relating to pay increases, in most cases it was possible to imply a term that an employer would not treat an employee capriciously, arbitrarily or inequitably in matters of remuneration. The EAT remitted the case to the employment tribunal to ascertain whether or not in fact the employer had thus treated the employee, and if so, there would be a good claim for constructive dismissal under the new test in *Western Excavating (ECC) Ltd v Sharp*.

17.46 But this does not mean that a failure to give an annual pay rise to an employee is a breach of contract, for it is impossible to say that there is an implied term to that effect. The test is whether such failure is arbitrary and capricious. Thus, if the employer can show a good reason, such as inadequate performance by the employee, there is no breach of the duty of mutual trust and confidence (*Murco Petroleum Ltd v Forge*).

17.47 Occasionally, the 'unreasonable conduct' test makes a re-appearance in a new disguise. It will be recalled that in constructive dismissal cases, one must look for the breach of contract. There is generally no difficulty in ascertaining the express terms, but legal authorities are clear that the implied terms are discovered by looking at what was 'obvious', so obvious in fact that the parties omitted to insert them (para 3.66). However, in *Pepper and Hope v Daish* the EAT took the view that it was possible to imply a term into a contract if it was 'reasonable' to do so! In this case the applicant negotiated a personal hourly wage rate for himself in December 1978. In January 1979 there was a general increase for all hourly workers of 5 per cent, but this was not given to the claimant. He resigned and claimed constructive dismissal. It was held that he could succeed, on the basis that it was reasonable to imply a term into his contract that he would also be given general wage increases. It will be noted that the reasoning in this case is inconsistent with the later decision in *Frank Wright & Co (Holdings) Ltd* *v Punch* (para 17.39) for there appeared to be a genuine dispute as to the interpretation of the contract.

17.48 The EAT returned to orthodoxy in *White v Reflecting Roadstuds Ltd.* Here, the employee was working in the employer's despatch department but, at his own request, he was transferred to the mixing department, which involved higher pay, but also harder work. After about a year, he requested a move to lighter work, which was not then possible. From then on, his attendance deteriorated, and, after being given a formal warning, he was transferred to the pressing department, which involved a considerable drop in his pay. He then resigned, claiming that the decision to move him to another department constituted a fundamental breach of his contract of employment. In their defence, the company pointed to a flexibility clause in the contract which gave them the right to transfer employees to alternative work if the requirements of operational efficiency so dictate, and also that a willingness of employees to do so was a condition of the contract. An employment tribunal held that the express right to transfer from one department to another was subject to two implied terms, namely (a) that it would be exercised in a reasonable manner, and (b) that the transfer would not result in a unilateral reduction in the employee's pay. On appeal, the EAT reversed the decision on both grounds. On the first point, the EAT stated that to imply a term that a flexibility or mobility clause should be handled reasonably would be to introduce the 'reasonableness' test into constructive dismissal cases by the back door and would fly in the face of the authority of *Western Excavating (ECC) Ltd v Sharp*. Although a 'capricious' decision would not create any difficulty (*United Bank Ltd v Akhtar*), if there are reasonable and sufficient grounds for operating the clause, the employers are entitled to reach such decisions. On the second point, it was held that if an employer acts within the contract, the fact that the change results in a unilateral reduction in the employee's pay does not constitute a fundamental breach of the contract (see *Spafax Ltd v Harrison*).

17.49 Also, if the employer is in breach, but the employee does not resign, and subsequently alleges a further breach, the employment tribunal should take into account the whole of the employer's conduct, and not merely the latest incident which led to the resignation (*Lewis v Motorworld Garages Ltd*).

17.50 Lawful conduct by an employer is not capable of constituting a repudiation (*Spafax Ltd v Harrison*). Thus a disciplinary transfer, carried out in accordance with a proper procedure, which results in an employee suffering a drop in his earnings, is not a constructive dismissal (*High v British Railways Board*). Nor can an employee claim constructive dismissal merely because he is moved away from that part of his job which he enjoys the most on to less interesting work, if he is contractually obliged to do that work (*Peter Carnie & Son Ltd v Paton*). However, a disciplinary sanction which is disproportionate to the offence, even though carried out in accordance with the terms of the contract, can be a constructive dismissal (*BBC v Beckett*, para 12.109).

17.51 Since the employee is claiming that the employer has broken the contract, he must resign as a result of that breach (*Holland v Glendale Industries*). If he continues to report to work, he may be deemed to have waived the breach, and can hardly bring a claim subsequently based on the employer's repudiation, for 'the law does not allow him to have his cake and eat it' (*Hunt v British Railways Board*). But if he protests about the breach, but stays on until he finds himself another job, he may not necessarily be deemed to have accepted the employer's breach (*Miller v Shanks & McEwan*) provided that he acts reasonably expeditiously (*WE Cox Toner (International) Ltd v Crook*). But a distinction must be drawn between the waiver of a breach and the non-waiver of a continuing breach.

17.52 If there is a series of breaches which lead the employee to look for another job before handing in his notice, the employment tribunal must consider whether those breaches were the effective cause of a resignation. They do not have to be the sole cause. If the taking of other employment was the consequence of the breaches, then the employee can claim he has been constructively dismissed (*Jones v Sirl & Son (Furnishers) Ltd*).

17.53 If the employer announces an intention to break the contract at a future date, and the employee does not accept the breach, it is open to the employer to inform the employee that the contract will be performed. The employee will thus lose the right to claim constructive dismissal (*Norwest Holst Group Administration Ltd v Harrison*). On the other hand, if the employee accepts the contructive dismissal, and gives notice to terminate the contract, conduct between the resignation and termination can be taken into account when assessing compensation (*Peterborough Regional College v Gidney*).

17.54–17.65 It must be stressed that the fact that there is constructive dismissal does not necessarily mean that the dismissal is unfair (*Milthorn Toleman Ltd v Ford*), and there have been a number of cases where a constructive dismissal has been held to be a fair dismissal (eg *Savoia v Chiltern Herb Farms Ltd*). Even if it is unfair, compensation may still be reduced for contributory conduct. An employer faced with a constructive dismissal claim should be prepared to fight it on two fronts: (a) he may argue that there was no dismissal, and (b) in the alternative, if there was a dismissal, it was fair because ... etc. A failure to adopt this course may result in a finding that there was a (constructive) dismissal, and, if no reason for the dismissal is advanced, it must automatically be unfair (*Derby City Council v Marshall*). Whether an employer's conduct amounts to a constructive dismissal is a question of fact for the employment tribunal to determine (*Woods v W M Car Services (Peterborough) Ltd*).

Termination of the contract

17.66 There are a number of ways in which a contract may come to an end, but which do not amount to a dismissal in law.

A. Resignation

17.67 If an employee resigns, then (unless it is a constructive dismissal) he has not been dismissed. If the words used by the employee are clear and unambiguous (eg 'I am leaving, I want my cards') then there are no grounds for the employment tribunal to find that the words have a significance other than their plain meaning (*BG Gale Ltd v Gilbert*). If the words are ambiguous, then the test is, what would a reasonable employer have understood by those words in that context (*Tanner v Kean Ltd*)? If an employee is threatened that if he does not resign he will be dismissed, a consequent resignation will amount to a dismissal, but if his resignation is brought about by other factors, such as an offer of a financial inducement, this is not a dismissal (*Sheffield v Oxford Controls Co Ltd*).

17.68 Words spoken or action taken by an employee in the heat of the moment or under extreme pressure should not necessarily be taken at face value. The employer should allow a reasonable time to elapse before accepting such an apparent resignation to see whether this was what was really intended. If the employer fails to make a proper investigation, he runs the risk that an employment tribunal may hold that there are special circumstances where the apparent resignation was not really intended by the employee (*Kwik Fit (GB) Ltd v Lineham*).

17.69 For a resignation to be effective to terminate the contract there must be an ascertainable date (express or implied) on which it will take effect. To say 'I am resigning at some future point in time' is a statement of intention, not a resignation, but to say 'I am resigning' is not ambiguous, for it indicates a present intention (*Sothern v Frank Charlesly & Co*). An employment tribunal is entitled to conclude on the evidence that the words of apparent resignation used by the employee 'in the heat of the moment' should not be accepted at their face value (*Sovereign House Security Services Ltd v Savage*).

17.70 If the employee indicates an intention to resign, but in terms which are somewhat equivocal, so that the position is mistakenly construed by the employer as a resignation, although the employee has not in fact resigned, this can be relied upon by the employer for the purpose of supplying an employment tribunal a potentially fair reason for the dismissal (for some other substantial reason, see below) even though, in error, the employer is seeking to hold the employee to the alleged resignation. What matters are the facts which led to the dismissal/ resignation, not the precise label put on it by the employer (*Ely v YKK Fasteners (UK) Ltd*).

17.71 If an employee resigns, giving lawful notice, the employer may bring the employment to an end at an earlier date than that on which the employee's notice expires, provided he is entitled to exercise the option of making a payment in lieu of notice. If the employer does this, he does not dismiss the employee, for the resignation is still effective (*Marshall (Cambridge) Ltd v Hamblin*).

17.72 Whether an employee has resigned or was dismissed is a question of fact for the employment tribunal to determine, and their findings cannot be challenged unless their conclusions were such that no reasonable employment tribunal could have reached them (*Martin v Glynwed Distribution Ltd*).

B. Constructive resignation

17.73 If a breach of contract by the employer entitles the employee to resign and claim constructive dismissal, then why should not a breach of contract by the employee entitle the employer to claim that the contract has been terminated by 'constructive resignation'? This view was supported by a number of decisions by the EAT and employment tribunals, but must be discounted in the light of the decision of the Court of Appeal in *London Transport Executive v Clarke*, and all earlier decisions must be read in the light of this case. The facts were that Clarke wanted to go to Jamaica on extended unpaid leave, but permission was refused by the employers as he had already exhausted his entitlement under the rules. When he asked what would happen if he went without permission he was told that his name would be removed from the books. Nonetheless he went to Jamaica, stayed for seven weeks, and on his return he submitted a medical note, which the employment tribunal viewed 'with some surprise'. While he was away, the employers wrote to his home address, stating that if no reply was received within 14 days, it would be assumed that he did not wish to continue his employment, and eventually his name was removed from the books. When he returned from Jamaica, he applied for his job back, and when this was refused, he claimed he had been unfairly dismissed. For the employers, it was argued that the applicant had 'resigned' but this view was rejected. It is trite law that if a person breaks a contract, the other party has two options; he can either accept the breach, and treat the contract as being at an end, or refuse to do so, and treat the contract as still subsisting. If he accepts the breach, he terminates the contract. Thus Clarke had been dismissed, and had not resigned. However, the Court of Appeal then went on to find that the dismissal, in the circumstances, was fair.

17.74   There is no doubt that this analysis is correct. The reason for the doctrine of constructive dismissal is because there is a statutory provision for it (ERA s 95(1)(c)). There is no statutory doctrine of constructive resignation. Thus if an employee walks out of his job, or commits any other breach of contract, but nonetheless claims that he is entitled to resume his work, the employer must expressly or impliedly accept the repudiation, and this will constitute a dismissal. He must then satisfy the employment tribunal that in the circumstances, having regard to the equity and substantial merits of the case, he acted reasonably in treating the repudiatory conduct as sufficient reason for dismissing the employee.

C. Implied resignation

17.75   However, it is submitted that there may be circumstances of implied resignation or resignation by conduct. Thus, if an employee disappears, and does not respond to the employer's communications, or if it is discovered that the employee is working for another employer, it may not be difficult to infer that he has resigned his employment. The point was made by Sir John Donaldson in *Harrison v George Wimpey & Co Ltd*. 'Where an employee so conducts himself as to lead a reasonable employer to believe that the employee has terminated the contract, the contract is then terminated'.

D. Frustration of the contract

17.76   If the performance of the contract of employment is rendered impossible by some intervening event, then it will be terminated by frustration, not by dismissal. Frustration can only arise where there is no fault by either party, eg where accident or illness prevents the employee (or employer) from performing the contract. Where there is fault by one party, this is repudiatory conduct, not frustration. It is thus up to the other party to accept the repudiation and terminate the contract, or keep the contract open, as he chooses (*London Transport Executive v Clarke*, above). Clearly, if the repudiatory conduct was serious (eg being sent to prison) it would be rare for the dismissal to be categorised as being unfair (*Norris v Southampton City Council*).

17.77   There are two situations which commonly occur, and which may give rise to the doctrine of frustration. The first is long-term absence through accident or illness (*Notcutt v Universal Equipment Co (London) Ltd*), the second is imprisonment (*FC Shepherd & Co Ltd v Jerrom*).

17.78   To decide whether or not a contract will terminate by frustration, regard must be had to the length of time the employee is likely to be away from his work, and thus be unable to perform his contract, the need for the employer to obtain a replacement, the length of time he has been employed, his position, and so forth. In cases where the employee is absent for a long time through sickness, all these factors are relevant, and in addition the employer must consider the nature of the illness (or injury), how long it has continued and the prospects for recovery, as well as the terms of the contract, including the provision of sick pay (see *Marshall v Harland and Wolff Ltd*). The mere absence from work, even for a long time, will not automatically constitute frustration. Thus in *Maxwell v Walter Howard Designs Ltd* the claimant was away sick for nearly two years, during which time he sent in regular sick notes. His job, as a cabinet maker, was one which did not need to be filled by a permanent replacement, and so, despite the passage of time, it was held that the contract had not been frustrated.

17.79   But if it is clear that on the medical evidence, the employee is unlikely to return to work for a considerable time, then there must come a point at which the employer is entitled to decide that the employee will not be returning to work, and consequently treat the contract as being frustrated. The problem is, when, exactly, does that point in time come about, and to this question there is no easy answer (see *Scarr v FW Goodyear & Sons Ltd*). In employment cases, the courts and tribunals must guard against too easy an application of the doctrine of frustration, especially when redundancy occurs, or where the true reason for the dismissal is disability (*Williams v Watsons Luxury Coaches Ltd*).

17.80   In *Egg Stores (Stamford Hill) Ltd v Leibovici*, the EAT stated that there may be a long process before it can be said that illness has brought about a frustration of the contract. But if the time arrives when one can say that matters have gone on for so long, and the prospects for future employment are so poor, that it is no longer practical to consider the contract as still subsisting, then frustration will occur. Among the matters to be taken into account to reach this conclusion are (1) the length of the employment (2) how long it would have been expected to continue (3) the nature of the job (4) the nature, length and effect of the illness (5) the need to appoint a permanent replacement (6) the risk to the employer of acquiring further obligations in respect of redundancy payments or unfair dismissals (7) whether wages are still being paid (8) the acts and statements of the employer in relation to the employee, including his failure to dismiss, and (9) whether in all the circumstances a reasonable employer could be expected to wait for the employee any longer. To this we may add (a) the terms of the contract as to sick pay, and (b) a consideration of the prospects of recovery (*Williams v Watsons Luxury Coaches Ltd*).

17.81   That none of these tests, by themselves, can be conclusive can be seen from the decision in *Hart v AR Marshall & Sons (Bulwell) Ltd* where the claimant became sick in April 1974. In August of that year, the employers engaged a permanent replacement but the claimant continued to send in sick notes. In January 1976 he presented himself for work, but was told there was no job for him, and he was given his cards. He claimed that this constituted unfair dismissal, but the EAT upheld a tribunal finding that the contract had been frustrated. The failure by the employers to act on the absence by dismissing the claimant was not, by itself, evidence that they will continue to regard him as an employee. Otherwise an employer would be in a difficult situation with regard to a sick employee; if he dismissed him prematurely, this might be unfair, if he engaged a temporary replacement, he might have to pay compensation at the end of that contract in order to permit the sick employee to return to work. Nor was the fact that the employee continued to send in sick notes indicative of anything other than the employee was keeping in touch in case there was a prospect of future employment. The crucial factor appears to be the finding that the claimant occupied a key position, which had to be filled, and thus the contract was frustrated.

17.82 Imprisonment, though self-induced, is not strictly speaking repudiatory conduct, for it does not amount to a breach of the contract of employment. But there is an inherent contradiction, because the doctrine of frustration arises when an event occurs without the fault of either party, and a person who had been given a custodial sentence will invariably be at fault. The answer appears to be that the person asserting the frustration (ie the employer) must show that there was no fault on his part, and the person against whom frustration is being asserted (ie the employee) cannot rely on his own misconduct by way of an answer (*FC Shepherd & Co Ltd v Jerrom*).

17.83 If it is clear that the employee is permanently unfit to do his job, the contract will be frustrated. The fact that the employer keeps the employee 'on the books' may be an arrangement which falls short of contract of employment, of the sort expressly recognised in s 212(3)(c) of ERA (see para 13.51) as being relevant to the question of continuity of employment when no contract is actually in existence. But if the contract is frustrated the statutory or contractual rights to notice on termination do not apply (*G F SharpCo Ltd v McMillan*).

17.84 Frustration arises by operation of law, not a conscious decision by the parties, and whilst it is not necessary to be able to point to the exact moment in time when the relationship between the parties is dissolved, the burden of proving that the contract has been frustrated lies on the employer. Thus, if an employee is sent to prison, this can be an instantaneously frustrating event or a potentially frustrating event. Accordingly, regard has to be paid to:
a.   when it was commercially necessary for the employer to make a decision about the employee's future;
b.   what a reasonable employer would consider to be the likely length of the employee's absence; and
c.   whether it was reasonable to engage a permanent rather than a temporary replacement (*Chakki v United Yeast Co Ltd*).

E. Consensual termination

17.85 A consensual termination arises when the employment is terminated by mutual agreement, and the reason for that agreement is generally irrelevant (*Birch v Liverpool University*). Since there is no dismissal, no statutory rights ensue. However, a person who volunteers for redundancy has volunteered to be dismissed, and is entitled to a redundancy payment (*Burton Allton and Johnson Ltd v Peck*).

17.86   A mutual agreement whereby the employment will come to an end on the happening of a future event is not a consensual termination. In *Igbo v Johnson Matthey Chemicals Ltd* the claimant wished to take extended leave. She signed a document which stated that she agreed to return to work by a certain date, and that if she failed to do so the contract of employment would automatically terminate. She failed to return to work on the due date, and her employers treated the contract as being at an end. She claimed that she had been unfairly dismissed. The Court of Appeal applied s 203 of ERA which stipulates that any provision in an agreement shall be void in so far as it purports to limit the operation of any provision in the Act. The document she signed purported to take away her right to claim that she was unfairly dismissed, and it was therefore void. The Court of Appeal overruled earlier authorities on this topic (including the case of *British Leyland (UK) Ltd v Ashraf*) and remitted the case to the employment tribunal to determine whether her dismissal was fair or unfair.

17.87   However, a mutual agreement to bring a contract of employment to an end, made for good consideration, after the employee had received proper advice, and made without duress, is effective. In *Logan Salton v Durham County Council*, the claimant was due to attend a disciplinary hearing which was to consider a recommendation that he be dismissed. An agreement was then reached whereby, on terms, his employment would come to an end by mutual agreement. He subsequently claimed he had been unfairly dismissed, but his claim failed. The agreement was not void by virtue of s 203 of ERA, because it was not a contract of employment, or the variation of a contract of employment. The EAT distinguished this type of situation from that which occurred in *Igbo v Johnson Matthey Chemicals* (above).

F. Project termination

17.88–17.95   If a person is employed for a specific project, then on its completion, the employment will come to an end, and there is no dismissal (*Ironmonger v Movefield Ltd*). The contract is discharged by performance. For example, a contract to build a house, or to complete a sea voyage, will terminate when the object has been achieved (*Wiltshire County Council v NATHFE and Guy*). In *Ryan v Shipboard Maintenance Ltd* the claimant worked for the employers on 31 jobs over a five-year period. Each job varied in time from one to eleven weeks, and at the end of each job, he would draw unemployment benefit until the next lot of work was available. After waiting eight weeks for a job, he decided to make a claim for a redundancy payment. It was held that his employment was on a job-to-job basis, at the end of which there was a discharge by performance. Thus he had not been dismissed.

Fair and unfair dismissal (ERA s 98)

17.96   Once it has been established that a dismissal has taken place, it must then be determined whether or not the dismissal was unfair. Section 98 of the Employment Rights Act 1996 lays down five grounds on which a dismissal is capable of being fair, as follows:
a.   a reason relating to the capability or qualifications of the employee for performing the work of the kind which he was employed by the employer to

do. 'Capability' includes any assessment by reference to skill, aptitude, health or other physical or mental quality, and 'qualifications' means any degree, diploma or other academic, technical or professional qualification relevant to the position which the employee holds;

b. a reason which relates to the conduct of the employee;
c. the redundancy of the employee;
d. because the employee could not continue to work in the position which he held without contravention (either on his part or on the part of the employer) of a restriction or a duty imposed by or under a statute;
e. some other substantial reason such as to justify the dismissal of an employee holding the position which he held.

17.97   Whether a particular dismissal based on one or more of these five reasons will be fair or unfair will depend on whether in the circumstances of the case (including the size and administrative resources of the employer's undertaking) the employer acted reasonably or unreasonably in treating the reason as a sufficient reason for dismissing the employee, and the question will be determined in accordance with equity and the substantial merits of the case (ERA s 98(4)). Further, whereas it is for the employee to prove that he was dismissed, it is for the employer to show the reason for the dismissal, and that it was one of the above five reasons. It will then be for the employment tribunal to find, on the basis of the evidence presented, whether or not the employer had acted reasonably in treating that reason as a sufficient ground for dismissal. Thus if he fails to show the reason, or fails to show a reason which is one of the above five, the dismissal is automatically unfair. In *Raynor v Remploy Ltd* a group general manager was dismissed for alleged lack of business judgment and general inefficiency. He had been employed for five years, and the tribunal rejected the company's allegations as spurious. Since there was no evidence of incapability, the dismissal was unfair. In *Castledine v Rothwell Engineering Ltd* (see para 10.38) the tribunal refused to accept the general allegations of incompetence, pointing to the favourable reference given to an employee subsequent to his dismissal. The employer cannot expect to win his case if he fails to give or call evidence on which the tribunal can reach its conclusion on the reason for the dismissal or its reasonableness, and general allegations without such evidence will normally be insufficient. In *Whitaker v Milk Marketing Board*, an artificial inseminator was dismissed for incompetence and misconduct. Although the Board mentioned various farmers who were supposed to be dissatisfied with the service they had received, none was called to give evidence, and the dismissal was held unfair.

17.98   Broadly speaking, there are two stages in the process of determining whether or not a dismissal was fair. The first is the means whereby the decision is reached. This involves going through proper procedures (see Chapter 12) bearing in mind especially the provisions of the Code of Practice (*Lock v Cardiff Railway Co Ltd*), so that there is a full investigation, a proper hearing, a right to appeal, etc. If the employer fails to follow a fair procedure, he must show that nonetheless he acted reasonably on the basis of the information at his disposal (*Polkey v A E Dayton Services Ltd*, see para 12.14), otherwise the unfair procedure will result in a dismissal being unfair, with compensation being reduced, if necessary (*Whitbread & Co plc v Mills*). The second stage is the actual decision taken, bearing in mind the reason for the dismissal, the need to consider mitigating circumstances, consistency and/or flexibility as appropriate, the terms of the contract, the size and nature of the employer's undertaking, and so on. No single factor, by itself, can be conclusive, and each case will turn on its own peculiar facts.

17.99 Further, the test is 'did the employer act reasonably?' not 'did the employment tribunal agree with what the employer did?' (*Grundy (Teddington) Ltd v Willis*). A decision on whether the employer acted reasonably is a question of fact for the employment tribunal to decide (*Iceland Frozen Foods Ltd v Jones*), which can only be challenged if the decision was perverse or based on an incorrect perception of the law.

17.100 In *Anandarajah v Lord Chancellor's Department*, the President of the EAT, Waite J, made a major policy statement about the use of precedents in employment tribunal hearings. Although these are of great practical assistance, they must not be relied upon as being of binding authority, but rather treated as guidelines. He continued:

> 'Sometimes the judgment in a particular case will be found to express, in helpful and concise language, some concept which is regularly found in this field of enquiry and it becomes of great illustrative value. But reference to such a case can never be a substitute for taking the explicit directions of the statute as a guiding principle.'

17.101 To determine whether or not the employer has acted reasonably in dismissing the employee, the current test is 'What would a reasonable employer have done'? There is a band of reasonableness within which one employer might decide to dismiss, whilst another might decide not to do so. If the circumstances of the case are such that a reasonable employer might dismiss, the dismissal will be fair even though not all the employers would take that view (*British Leyland (UK) Ltd v Swift*). However, the 'band of reasonableness' test has been challenged (somewhat belatedly) by the EAT in *Haddon v Van Den Burgh Foods Ltd*, but the Court of Appeal in *HSBC plc v Madden* disagreed, and reaffirmed the correctness of the 'range of reasonable responses' test as laid down in *Iceland Frozen Foods Ltd v Jones*. Further, the Burchell test (para 17.151) applied to the assessment of the fairness of the dismissal under s 98(4), not to establishing the reason for the dismissal under s 98(1)-(3).

17.102 In *Kent County Council v Gilham* the Court of Appeal stressed once again that whether or not an employer acts reasonably is a question of fact for the employment tribunal. That two employment tribunals, considering the same broad issues, had reached opposite conclusions did not indicate that either had misdirected themselves in law. It is endemic in the system that different answers will be given to broadly similar situations, and the decision cannot be challenged just for that reason. But on rare occasions higher courts will interfere if the decision of the employment tribunal is thought to be perverse (*British Railways Board v Jackson*).

17.103 The point in time at which the reasonableness of the employer's decision to dismiss is to be tested is when the employment comes to an end, not when the decision is taken, nor when the notice to terminate is given (*Stacey v Babcock Power Ltd*). Thus if an initial decision to dismiss was unfair because of a defect in the disciplinary proceedings, it may be cured if an appeal hearing is properly conducted (see *Clark v Civil Aviation Authority*, para 12.25). The reason for the dismissal is to be assessed both at the time notice of termination was given right through to the actual date of the termination of the contract (*West Kent College v Richardson*). Matters which come to light after the employment has ended are generally irrelevant (*Greenall Whitley plc v Carr*).

17.104–17.110 Certain dismissals are automatically unfair, and no question arises as to whether or not the employer has acted reasonably. These are dismissals connected with

(a) pregnancy or childbirth, the taking of ordinary or additional maternity leave or parental leave or time off to look after dependants, declining to sign a workforce agreement for maternity or parental leave purposes, the performance of functions as a workforce representative (ERA s 99, and Maternity and Parental Leave Regulations 1999);

(b) a health and safety case (ERA s 100);

(c) a shop or betting worker who refuses to work on Sundays (ERA s 101);

(d) the exercise of a right under the Working Time Regulations (ERA s 101A);

(e) performing a function as trustee of an occupational pension fund (ERA s 102);

(f) performing a function of an employee representative (ERA s 103);

(g) the making of a protected disclosure (ERA s 103A);

(h) the assertion of a statutory right (ERA s 104);

(i) the exercise of a right under the National Minimum Wage Act (ERA s 104A);

(j) taking action with regard to a tax credit (ERA s 104B);

(k) selection for redundancy for any of the above reasons (ERA s 105);

(1) membership or non-membership of a trade union (TULR(C)A s 154);

(m) the taking of protected industrial action (TULR(C)A s 238A);

(n) doing a wide range of actions in connection with the statutory procedure for recognition or derecognition (TULR(C)A Sch A1, see para 21.70);

(o) doing acts in connection with rights under the Transnational Information and Consultation of Employees Regulations 1999 (see para 23.267);

(p) doing acts in connection with an employee's rights under the Part-time Workers (Prevention of Less Favourable Treatment) Regulations 2000 (see para 2.167).

Reasons for the dismissal

17.111 Although the Act lays down five potentially fair reasons for dismissal, it will be convenient to make further sub-divisions, so that in practice a number of potential reasons for fair dismissal appear. This enables a more practical analysis to be made. Bearing this in mind, we can examine the general approach of the courts and tribunals to the problems of dismissals.

A. Inherent inability

17.112 To dismiss an employee who is not capable of performing his job properly will be fair provided the employer acts reasonably in the circumstances. Thus, faced with the problem of an incompetent worker, what does the reasonable employer do? He enquires into the matter, to find out why the employee cannot do the job adequately. Has he been trained properly, so that he knows how the job should be done? Has he been properly supervised, been given an adequate job description? Does he have proper equipment, sufficient support staff and facilities? In other words, the employer's first task is to find out the reason for the alleged incompetence, and so far as it is possible, do something about it from the employer's point of view.

17.113 For example, in *Davison v Kent Meters Ltd* the claimant was dismissed for assembling nearly 500 components in the wrong sequence. She claimed that she had followed the pattern of work in accordance with the instructions received from her chargehand, but the latter denied having shown her how to assemble the parts, and maintained that she was entirely to blame for the errors. The employment tribunal thought that if the chargehand had not shown her what to do, he should have done so, and the mistakes were therefore hardly her fault! Further, he should have checked on her performance, and supervised her properly. Not surprisingly, the dismissal was held to be unfair.

17.114 A warning should not be given merely for the sake of conforming with a laid down procedure, for this is to treat it as a mechanical system with no real significance. A warning is designed to do a job of work; it should have as its purpose the object of bringing an employee away from the brink of dismissal. It follows, therefore, that if the employee is suffering from an irredeemable incompetence, no amount of warnings will make any difference, and therefore there cannot be a need to issue them (*Sutton & Gates Ltd v Boxall*). In *Littlewoods Organisation Ltd v Egenti* the EAT pointed out that there is a distinction between disciplinary procedures and capability procedures. The former should be applied strictly, whereas this does not need to be so with regard to the latter. To give a warning in capability cases is not a matter of procedure; it is a matter of substance (*AJ Dunning & Sons (Shopfitters) Ltd v Jacomb*). In other words, the question is, would a warning have done any good? Would it have rendered this dismissal unnecessary? If the answer is yes, then the warning should have been given. If the answer is no, then, since no amount of warnings would make any difference, there is no need to give them. Thus in *Lowndes v Specialist Heavy Engineering Ltd* the claimant was dismissed after five serious and costly errors. No written warnings were given, and he was not allowed an opportunity to state his case. The dismissal was held to be fair; it would have made no difference had a different procedure been adopted. But if the employment tribunal finds that a fair procedure might have rendered the dismissal unnecessary, then a failure to follow that procedure would make the dismissal unfair (*Charles Letts & Co Ltd v Howard*).

17.115 Finally, the reasonable employer will consider alternatives before he dismisses the employee. Is there some other work which can be offered within the level of competence of the employee? Would he accept it if it was offered? Would he make a success of it? Clearly, much will depend on the circumstances of the case. In *Bevan Harris Ltd v Gair*, the claimant, who had been employed as a foreman, was dismissed after 11 years' service for poor performance, about which he had been warned on four occasions. The employment tribunal held the dismissal to be unfair, because a reasonable employer would have demoted him rather than resort to dismissal. The decision was reversed by the EAT. The employer had given serious consideration to offering the claimant another job, but had decided against it. The small scale of the business, and the loss of confidence in the employee's abilities, meant that the decision to dismiss fell within the band of reasonableness and, in the circumstances, the dismissal was fair.

B. Neglectful incompetence

17.116 Here we must consider the employee who could do the job, but is not achieving his potential. The object of the exercise is to bring him up to the standards which he is capable of reaching, and for this purpose, the disciplinary procedure should be invoked, in accordance with the gravity of the matter.

17.117 If an employee is not working as well as he could, then a warning is appropriate; if he is refusing to obey instructions or is being generally unco-operative, then he should be told, firmly and by someone in authority, of the consequences which are likely to ensue. If the tribunal considers that had a clear warning been given a dismissal would not have been necessary (*Winterhalter Gastronom Ltd v Webb*), then it will conclude that a dismissal without such warning being given will be unfair (*Jones v GEC Elliott Automation Ltd*). An employee with long service is entitled to more consideration, if only because the employers can hardly be heard to say that it took them many years to discover his incompetence, but the fact that the employer has tolerated poor performance in the past is not conclusive, if the employee fails to respond to proper warnings (*Gozdzik v Chlidema Carpet Co*). A newly appointed employee should be given a chance to prove himself, and not judged on short-term results. Senior staff should have a greater appreciation of what is expected from them, whereas employees not in the managerial range should have greater attention paid to their requirements. If possible, the employer may consider giving the employee further training, should suitable facilities be available, assuming, that is, that the employee would be likely to benefit from such training. If the employee refuses to take advantage of this offer, at least the employer has acted in a reasonable manner, and a consequent dismissal may well be fair (*Coward v John Menzies (Holdings) Ltd*).

17.118 If there is a minor act of neglect, a warning is appropriate, to be followed, as necessary, with a further or final warning. A serious act of neglect might lead to an immediate final warning. But there are some acts of neglect which dare not be repeated, and hence dismissal is not inappropriate. In *Taylor v Alidair Ltd*, an airline pilot landed his aeroplane in a manner which caused some concern among the passengers and crew. After a proper investigation, it was decided that he had been negligent, and was dismissed. This was held to be fair: there are some activities where the degree of skill required is so high, or where the potential consequences of a departure from the highest standards are so serious, that one failure is sufficient to justify dismissal. A warning in such cases is totally inappropriate.

17.119 The law which prevents unfair dismissal must not be used to impede the efficient management of business by compelling employers to retain incompetent employees (*Cook v Thomas Linnell & Sons Ltd*), and once an employer has lost confidence in the employee's ability to do the job, then it is reasonable to dismiss and offer other employment should this be available. But the employer is not bound to create a vacancy if none exists; he should at least consider the possibility, and consider if the employee would make a success of it (*Brush Electrical Machines v Guest*).

17.120 If an employee is dismissed because of his incapability, the correct test to apply is whether the employer honestly and reasonably held the belief that the employee was not competent, and whether there are reasonable grounds for that belief. It is not necessary for the employer to *prove* that the employee was incompetent (*Alidair Ltd v Taylor*). In other words, the test under s 98(4) is a subjective one. The employment tribunal must consider the employer's state of mind as well as his reasons. But it is sufficient if the employer honestly believes on reasonable grounds that the employee is incompetent.

C. Long-term sickness

17.121 An employee who is absent from work for a long time because of sickness or ill-health is entitled to sympathetic consideration by the employer, but the employer can only be expected to act within sensible limits. The questions to be asked are (a) how long has the employment lasted (b) how long had it been expected the employment would continue (c) what is the nature of the job (d) what was the nature, effect and length of the illness (e) what is the need of the employer for the work to be done, and to engage a replacement to do it (f) are wages continuing to be paid (g) why had the employer dismissed (or failed to do so) and (h) in all the circumstances, could a reasonable employer have been expected to wait any longer (*Egg Stores (Stamford-Hill) Ltd v Leibovici*)? In other words, the employer is entitled to consider his business needs, as well as the employee's situation. An important point to consider is 'has the time arrived when the employer can no longer reasonably be expected to keep the absent employee's post open for him?' (*Hart v AR Marshall & Sons (Bulwell) Ltd*). Thus if an employee is away for a long time, the employer should not dismiss as an automatic matter, but consider whether it is necessary to dismiss. The employer should make all necessary enquiries, from the employee, from his doctor, and if possible obtain an opinion from the firm's medical advisers (*East Lindsey District Council v Daubney*).

17.122 In all cases where dismissal on the grounds of ill-health is being considered, there is a need for enquiry, consultation, warnings, a search for alternatives etc, before the decision is taken (*A Links & Co Ltd v Rose*). But while in the normal case consultation is necessary, in wholly exceptional circumstances the absence of consultation does not render a dismissal unfair (*Eclipse Blinds Ltd v Wright*).

17.123 The purpose of consulting with the employee about his health is to weigh up the situation, balancing the need of the employer to get the work done against the employee's need for time in order to recover his health. Without such consultation, the employer may act precipitously, with unfair consequences. But consultation is not demanded by law; if it is clear that the consultation would not have made any difference to the result, a failure to consult does not make a dismissal unfair (*Taylorplan Catering (Scotland) Ltd v McInally*).

17.124 Earlier cases had stated that an employer should warn an employee that unless he returns to work he will be dismissed, but this view is erroneous, for an employee cannot be warned that he has got to be in good health. However, the employer should make all proper and necessary enquiries from the employee, and not act in a precipitous manner. Perhaps the best way to express the employer's obligation is to say that he should treat the employee with sympathetic consideration, and that he should hold the job open for as long as is possible. In *Coulson v Felixstowe Dock & Rly Co Ltd* the claimant was away from work due to ill-health for considerable periods of time. He could no longer perform his duties, and was put on light clerical work. He was told that if he could not return to his old job, he would be regraded, and was given six months in which to prove his fitness. However, he fell ill again and was dismissed. It was held that the employer had treated the employee with every consideration, but there must come a time when the employer cannot be expected to keep someone on who is not doing his work. The tribunal had to consider fairness to the business as well as to the employee.

17.125 On the other hand, in *Converform (Darwen) Ltd v Bell*, the claimant was a works director who was off work because of a heart attack. He recovered, but the employers refused to permit him to return to work, as they thought there was the risk of another attack. His subsequent dismissal was held to be unfair. A risk of future illness cannot be used as a ground for fair dismissal unless the nature of the employment is such that the risk made it unsafe for the employee to continue in the job.

17.126 A good employer will try to fix a date by which time he must know when the employee expects to be able to give information about the likely date of return to work (*Marder v ITT Distributors Ltd*), but once having explained and discussed the situation with the employee, the employer is entitled to make a decision in the light of the information available (*Spencer v Paragon Wallpapers Ltd*).

17.127 In *Merseyside and North Wales Electricity Board v Taylor* the Divisional Court held that there is no rule of law which requires the employer to create a special job for an employee who is off sick. Nor is there a rule that an employer is obliged to find alternative employment for an employee plagued by ill-health. Each case must be judged on its own facts in the light of the employer's circumstances. It may be that the employer has some light work available of the kind which is within the employee's capacity to do, and the employee should be encouraged to take such a post, even at reduced rates of pay, before dismissal is considered.

17.128 In larger firms it may be possible for the company to place a sick employee in some form of holding department, so that he can recommence employment when fit, but there are certain legal problems about such a course which require further consideration. In *Burton v Boneham & Turner Ltd*, the management placed an employee in such a holding department after several spells of absence through illness. It was held that such conduct amounted in law to a dismissal, although in the circumstances, it was held to be fair. On the other hand, in *Parker v Westland Helicopters Ltd* a sick employee was transferred from the department concerned with sick employees to a holding department, where she had to wait for a suitable vacancy before being employed again. As this was done with her agreement, on the facts it was held that no dismissal had taken place.

17.129 The legal significance of placing employees in a holding department has yet to be fully explored. In *Marshall v Harland and Wolff Ltd* the NIRC held that such a transfer meant that the employee ceased to be employed in a legal sense, but the employers merely undertook some obligation to provide work if and when possible. If this is so, then the act of placing in the holding department could well be as the result of a frustrating event, and should not amount to a dismissal (*G F Sharp Ltd v McMillan*). On the other hand, it has been suggested (*O'Reilly v Hotpoint Ltd*) that such transfer suspends the contract of employment. If this view is correct, then continuity will doubtless be preserved for redundancy and other purposes for 26 weeks (ERA s 212(3)(a)), and presumably there is a legal (as opposed to moral) obligation to find an employee work when he recovers. It is clear that the matter should be subject to a defined policy which can be stated in the works/staff rules, so that the legal situation will be determined by the contractual obligations which can be laid down by the parties in accordance with the objective which they seek.

17.130   If an employee is retired (or dismissed) on ill-health grounds, the employment tribunal should not be concerned with whether or not the illness was caused or contributed to by the employer, but should consider whether the employer acted reasonably in dismissing the employee for that illness (*London Fire and Civil Defence Authority v Betty*).

17.131   Employers cannot be expected to go to unreasonable lengths in seeking to accommodate a sick employee, and what is reasonable is largely a question of fact and degree in each case (*Garricks (Caterers) Ltd v Nolan*). There is no absolute rule that an employer must consult with the employee's general practitioner (and indeed, since this could result in a breach of professional confidence, it may not be a profitable exercise), although it may be desirable to do so if the employee gives his consent (see *Tower Hamlets London Borough v Bull*). In the last analysis, the employer must act within the range of reasonable responses, depending on the circumstances (*Rolls Royce Ltd v Walpole*).

17.132   When dismissing on ill-health grounds, an employer must bear in mind the provisions of the Disability Discrimination Act 1995 (see para 4.301), for many sickness/ill-health absences may well come within the definition of a long-term disability. The employer has a duty to make reasonable adjustments, and in some circumstances, the dismissal of a disabled person can be justified. Thus a full, fair and comprehensive review is required.

17.133   An employee who is away from work through illness etc is still within the pool of selection for redundancy, but the usual criteria of consultation etc must be applied (*Hill v General Accident Fire and Life Insurance Co*).

D. Persistent absenteeism

17.134   The employee who is persistently away from work (whether because of illness or other reasons) for short periods at a time presents a different problem. This employee can be cautioned about his absences; he can be confronted with his record, told that it must improve, and be given a period of time in which an improvement can be monitored. Indeed, the employer should not ignore the powerful medicinal effect of a final warning, and a failure to give one may mean that the employee is unaware that the situation is causing the employer great concern. The effect of such a warning might be to stimulate the employee into seeking proper medical advice in case there is an underlying cause of the continuous minor ailments, it may deter the employee from taking time off when not truly warranted, and it may even lead the employee to look for other work where such absences could be tolerated (*Smith v Royal Alfred Merchant Seamen's Society*).

17.135 The employer should approach the situation with 'sympathy, understanding and compassion'. Factors to be taken into account include: (a) the nature of the illness, (b) the likelihood of it recurring, (c) the length of the various absences and the spells of good health in between, (d) the need of the employer to have that work done by that employee, (e) the impact of the absences on other employees, (f) the adoption and carrying out of the policy, (g) a personal assessment of the ultimate decision, and (h) the fact that the employee is fully aware that his employment will be terminated unless there is an improvement (*Lynock v Cereal Packaging Ltd*).

17.136 At the same time, the employer can hold out a helping hand; he can enquire from the employee the nature of all these minor ailments, offer such medical help as the firm can provide, provide counselling, etc, in those cases where the employment is itself a major contributing factor to the illness, and so on.

17.137 In practice, it is essential to establish the reason for the absences, as this may well determine the appropriate procedural steps to be taken. For example, the employer may have issued a policy statement on alcohol or drug abuse, which may override standard procedures. In most cases, it will be necessary to interview the employee on his return to work, which will assist in establishing the reasons for the absence, assess the likelihood of recurrence, and determine whether the appropriate 'trigger' has been reached under any attendance procedure. If an underlying medical condition is suspected, advice may be given on the need to seek further treatment. The implications of the Disability Discrimination Act will need to be considered, so that reasonable adjustments can be made where possible. Alternative employment may be considered, or flexibility introduced into attendance improvement schemes. In other words, a great deal can be done to resolve the problem, rather than merely consider dismissal as a solution (*Kerrigan v Rover Group Ltd*).

17.138 In *International Sports Ltd v Thomson* the claimant was away from work for about 25 per cent of the time, with a variety of complaints (all of which were covered by medical certificates) including dizzy spells, anxiety and nerves, bronchitis, virus infection, cystitis, althrugia of the left knee, dyspepsia and flatulence. She was given a series of warnings, including a final warning, and before deciding to dismiss her, the company consulted their medical adviser. He saw no useful purpose in examining her, as none of the previous illnesses could be verified, there was no common link between them and she was not suffering from any chronic illness. She was then dismissed, and the EAT held that the dismissal was fair. The company had undertaken a fair review of her attendance record, she had been duly warned and given the opportunity to make representations. A further medical investigation would have produced no worthwhile results. There must come a point in time when a reasonable employer is entitled to say 'Enough is enough'.

17.139 It is normal for many firms to have contractual entitlement to a certain amount of sick leave, some of which may be regarded as 'certified' or covered by sick notes. Certainly, an employee should keep his employer informed by the proper means, and a failure to do so may mean that the employee contributes to his own dismissal and receives reduced compensation. But sick notes, by themselves, can never be conclusive, for there are serious doubts about their factual validity. Thus, if an employer believes that a sick note is phoney, or may not be accurate, then he is entitled to disregard it (*Hutchinson v Enfield Rolling Mills Ltd*).

17.140   In *Wilkes v Fortes (Sussex) Ltd* the EAT placed particular emphasis on a consideration of the size of the firm in determining whether or not it would be fair to dismiss an employee who is off work intermittently for sickness reasons. In a large firm, the disruption caused by such illnesses may be minimal; it is easy to have a float of overmanning to cover for absent employees. But in a small business, such absences may be extremely serious or even disastrous.

17.141   If a person's health is such that continued employment may well constitute a hazard, either to himself, to other employees, or is likely to cause damage to property, then provided the employer undertakes full consultation with the employee, and obtains expert medical opinion, this is capable of being a fair dismissal (*Spalding v Port of London Authority*), and it is not necessary for the employer to wait until an accident occurs before taking steps to dismiss (*Parsons v Fisons Ltd*). In *Finch v Betabake (Anglia) Ltd* the claimant was an apprentice motor mechanic. The employers received a report from an ophthalmic surgeon that the boy could not continue to work without undue danger to himself and to others. He was therefore dismissed. It was held that the circumstances in which an apprentice could be dismissed were limited, but in the circumstances, the dismissal was fair.

17.142   If the persistent absenteeism is due to factors other than ill-health, then warnings, as appropriate, should be given. It has been suggested that a dismissal because of an unacceptable level of short-term persistent absenteeism should properly be considered under the heading of 'some other substantial reason' rather than capability or conduct (*Post Office v Wilson*).

E. Lack of qualifications

17.143   There have been very few cases concerning the lack of qualifications for the job as a reason for dismissal. In *Blackman v Post Office* a telegraph officer was required to pass an aptitude test, but he failed after a maximum number of attempts. It was held that his dismissal was fair on the ground of lack of qualifications. But there must be a contractual obligation (express or implied) to hold the relevant qualification. In *Litster v M Thom & Sons Ltd* the applicant was employed as a foreman fitter/driver. Government regulations required that special driving licences had to be obtained for drivers of heavy goods vehicles, and the claimant failed the necessary test. Nonetheless he was continued in employment as a fitter. His contract of employment contained no reference to the necessity of having an HGV licence. Following a dispute, he was told that unless he obtained such a licence, he would be dismissed. It was held that since his contract did not require him to hold that particular licence, a dismissal based on his lack of qualifications would be unfair.

17.144   However, it may be permissible to go outside the formal requirements of the contract. In *Tayside Regional Council v McIntosh*, the employers advertised for a vehicle mechanic, an essential requirement being that the successful applicant should have a driving licence. The claimant was appointed to the job, but his contract of employment made no mention of the need to hold a driving licence. He was subsequently disqualified from driving, and as there was no other suitable employment for him, he was dismissed. The EAT held that he had been fairly dismissed. The nature of the job clearly required the holding of a valid driving licence.

17.145 But even though it can be shown that the employee lacks the necessary qualification for the job, the employer must still act reasonably in treating that reason as a sufficient ground for dismissal. Thus in *Sutcliffe and Eaton Ltd v Pinney* the claimant was dismissed from his job as a trainee hearing aid dispenser after he failed to pass the necessary examinations. It was held that the employers should have applied for an extension of his training period so that he could take the examination again. In other words, as always, the reasonable employer will look around for alternatives to dismissal.

F. Conduct inside the employment

17.146 Under this heading we can consider all those acts of the employee which occur during the performance of the contract, and which are alleged to have an adverse effect on that contract. Such acts may be sub-divided in accordance with their gravity, ie acts of trivial nature (minor misconduct), serious matters (major misconduct) and extremely serious matters (gross misconduct). The importance of such a classification lies in the methods which are required to be adopted to solve the problem in question. For acts of minor misconduct, these can usually be dealt with by a warning (informal, then perhaps formal), but it would be wrong to utilise the full weight of a disciplinary sanction in order to deal with a trivial matter. Thus to give an employee a final warning 'if you come in late again you will be dismissed' is bound to lead to trouble at some later stage, for the sanction is out of all proportion to the offence. Such a person could be dealt with, for example, by a short period of suspension. Further, for some acts a single repetition would suffice to warrant dismissal (eg theft) and hence the warning would spell this out. But other acts may have to be monitored over a period of time, (eg lateness, absenteeism), and hence the warning will indicate the period, spell out the improvement required, and state the ultimate sanction. An act of major misconduct could be handled by an immediate final warning, without the need to go through stages in a procedure (ie informal warning, first written warning, etc), for the seriousness of the matter is sufficient to leap over other stages. And acts of gross misconduct, once proven, can lead to instant dismissal without notice, for this amounts to a breach by the employee which in effect repudiates the contract.

17.147 For all acts of misconduct, the employer must show that he gave the matter a prompt and thorough investigation, that he gave the employee an opportunity to state his case, interviewed witnesses and collected evidence so far as it was possible to do so, but there are limits to the power of an employer to investigate, and indeed, it may well be improper for him to do so on occasions. This is particularly true when the matter is to be the subject of criminal charges or investigation by the police. Thus in *Carr v Alexander Russell Ltd*, the claimant was dismissed when it was learned that the police had found some company property in his possession, and that he was to be charged with theft. It was held that the employers had no duty to carry out any detailed form of enquiry, for it would have been improper of them to do so, and a subsequent trial might have been seriously prejudiced.

17.148   There is no absolute prescription that an employee must be given an opportunity to explain his conduct before he is dismissed, though this course is clearly desirable. In *Parker v Clifford Dunn Ltd* the employers received information from the police that the claimant had admitted stealing from the company. He was therefore dismissed in accordance with the works rules. He did not appeal through the procedure, and made no protestation of innocence. His dismissal was held to be fair; it was reasonable for the employers to rely on the police investigations rather than carry out their own. But the mere fact that the police intend to charge an employee with theft is not conclusive, as they may decide not to proceed with the charge, or the evidence may be too weak to secure a conviction, and so on. Some enquiry may therefore be necessary (*Scottish Special Housing Association v Cooke*).

17.149   The acts which can constitute misconduct inside the employment are too numerous to categorise. Fighting, swearing, trading, drunkenness, betting, horseplay, incompetence, theft, neglect, dangerous or obstructive conduct, clocking offences, breach of safety rules, immorality, refusal to obey orders, breach of hygiene rules, insubordination, unauthorised absenteeism, disloyalty, breach of confidence, taking unlawful drugs, sleeping while on duty, computer hacking or seeking unauthorised access to a computer program, telling lies, unsuitable clothing, dishonesty, taking property without authorisation and lateness, have all, in their turn, been the subject of employment tribunal proceedings. To deal with such conduct, the employer must consider the gravity of the offence, its effect on the employment generally, and the previous history of the employee. In other words, the employer, it is submitted, must take into account the offence, and the offender.

17.150   It is not the function of the employment tribunal to substitute its views and opinions for those of management, but merely to decide if management has acted reasonably. For example, if an employee has committed an act of theft, it is for management to decide what should be done in the circumstances of the case, and provided a fair procedure is adopted, the eventual decision is that of management. In *Trusthouse Forte Hotels Ltd v Murphy*, the claimant was a night porter. He kept a small supply of liquor for hotel guests, but when his stock was checked, there was a deficiency of £10. He admitted taking some of this for his own use, and was dismissed. The employment tribunal found this to be unfair, but the decision was reversed on appeal by the EAT. It would place an unreasonable burden on employers if they could not fairly dismiss employees who had stolen property which had been entrusted to their care. Although management might have been influenced by compassionate grounds, and might have decided not to dismiss an employee who had stolen a small amount of property, a reasonable management may have taken either view. Hence it was not possible to argue that this employer had acted unreasonably.

17.151   Nor need the employers prove that an offence has been committed beyond reasonable doubt, for this would impose on them a higher commitment than would ever be possible to fulfil, and impose a duty which rightfully belongs to a court of trial. The employers must genuinely believe that the employee has been guilty of the misconduct in question, they must have reasonable grounds for that belief, and they must have carried out such investigation into the matter as is reasonable in the circumstances (*British Home Stores v Burchell*). In *Laurie v Fairburn* the claimant was dismissed because the employers believed that she was stealing from them. The employment tribunal was not convinced that this was so, and held the dismissal to be unfair. This was reversed on appeal; the question is not whether or not the employee was guilty, or would have been found guilty if tried, but whether it was reasonable for the employers to dismiss her, taking into account all the circumstances and facts known to the employers at the time of the dismissal.

17.152 If an employee makes a confession, this is a fact which the employer is entitled to take into consideration when forming his views, and the rules about the non-admissibility of confessions made involuntarily (the Judge's Rules) have no application in such circumstances (*Morley's of Brixton Ltd v Minott*).

17.153 Where an employee has pleaded guilty to a criminal offence, or been found guilty by the decision of a court or the verdict of a jury, it is reasonable for an employer to believe that the employee committed the offence. Any other conclusion would be ridiculous (*P v Nottinghamshire County Council*). This is so even if the employee alleges that he pleaded guilty on the advice of his lawyers, in order to avoid a prison sentence (*British Gas plc v McCarrick*).

17.154 The fact that an employee faces criminal charges subsequently, and is acquitted on those charges, is also irrelevant to the issue of the fairness of the dismissal. In *Da Costa v Optolis* the claimant was dismissed from his job as a book-keeper for not keeping proper accounts, and he subsequently faced criminal charges, though these ended in his favour. It was held that the fact the Crown Court had acquitted him did not preclude a finding by the employment tribunal that the dismissal was fair. The issues involved were different. In the Crown Court, it had to be decided whether he was guilty of the charge beyond reasonable doubt, whereas in the employment tribunal, it had to be shown whether the employer had reasonable grounds for dismissing him.

17.155 It must surely be sound policy for the employer to be consistent in his procedure, flexible in his decisions. Thus an employer may take into account the fact that the employee has had a long record of exemplary conduct (*City of Edinburgh District Council v Stephens*), but the importance of such mitigating factors is a matter for the employer's discretion (*AEI Cables Ltd v McLay*). In *Taylor v Parsons Peebles Ltd* the claimant, who had been employed for 20 years without complaint, was dismissed for fighting. The EAT held the dismissal to be unfair. The company's policy had to be considered in the light of a reasonable employer's reaction to the incident. Given that the applicant had 20 years' good conduct, a reasonable employer would not have applied a rigid sanction of automatic dismissal. In failing to take account of mitigating circumstances, the employers had acted unreasonably. In *Hadjioannou v Coral Casinos Ltd* (see para 12.71) it will be recalled that the EAT stressed the need for flexibility in dealing with industrial misconduct, saying that a tariff approach was not correct.

17.156 An employee who admits that his conduct is unacceptable, and accepts advice and help to avoid any repetition may be treated differently from an employee who refuses to accept responsibility for his actions, argues with management, or makes unfounded allegations that his colleagues have conspired to make false accusations against him (*Paul v East Surrey District Health Authority*).

17.157   If the conduct in question amounts to gross misconduct, then this should be acted upon immediately by management, for a delay may lead the employment tribunal to conclude that the conduct was not so wrongful as to warrant the drastic punishment of instant dismissal, although in rare cases it is proper to dismiss summarily a long time after the event (*Refund Rentals Ltd v McDermott*). Normally, it would be reasonable to suspend pending an investigation, but again, this counsel of perfection cannot always be followed (*Conway v Matthew Wright & Nephew Ltd*).

17.158   If the conduct falls under the heading of breach of works rules (eg smoking in prohibited areas, fighting, failing to observe safety precautions, etc) then provided the rule is a reasonable one, has been duly promulgated and brought to the attention of the employees, then the tribunals will usually uphold management action (*Richards v Bulpitt & Sons Ltd*), particularly if there has been an act of dishonesty (*British Railways Board v Jackson*). But a minor breach should not be treated as an excuse for dismissal, no matter how strongly worded the rule may be (*Ladbroke Racing Ltd v Arnott*).

17.159   Before dismissing for gross misconduct, the employer should consider any alternative course of action, for it is not inconsistent with a finding of gross misconduct to offer the employee alternative employment in a different capacity (*Hamilton v Argyll and Clyde Health Board*). Each case must be considered on its merits, taking into account the special facts and mitigating circumstances. If, in the past, an employee has not been dismissed for a similar offence, management should enquire into those circumstances. The dangers of a tariff or consistent approach in cases where there is no true comparability should be avoided (*Procter v British Gypsum Ltd*).

17.160   Equally difficult is conduct by the employee which is strictly within his contractual rights, but which is obstructive in nature. In *Pengilly v North Devon Farmers Ltd* it was held that a refusal to work overtime, even though not compulsory within the terms of the employee's contract, warranted a dismissal, as the refusal was contrary to the normal practice, and the employee was trying to put improper pressure on the employer. But in *Burns v Ideal Timber Products* it was held that a refusal to work overtime in order to get the employer to improve working conditions did not amount to improper pressure.

17.161   The conduct of the employee must in some way reflect on the employment relationship. In *Thomson v Alloa Motor Co Ltd*, the applicant was employed as a petrol pump attendant. One day she finished work, and drove off in her car, but collided with a petrol pump, causing substantial damage. She was summarily dismissed, because of the seriousness of the damage and the fact that her employers would have to sue her for compensation. The dismissal was held to be unfair. The accident had no bearing on her ability to do her work, it was an incident unlikely to be repeated, and her employers were undoubtedly covered by insurance.

17.162   While it may not generally be possible to dismiss an employee who is acting within the terms of the contract, it should be possible to call for a variation of that contract, or to terminate it and offer a new one (see Chapter 3). Provided the proper procedure is adopted, a subsequent dismissal may well be for 'some other substantial reason' (see below).

17.163 Other types of conduct which have been held to warrant dismissal include a refusal to wear the appropriate clothing required for the job (*Atkin v Enfield Hospital Management Committee*), wearing provocative badges contrary to instructions and warnings (*Boychuk v Symons Holdings Ltd*), carrying on sexual relations during business hours (*Newman v Alarmco*), passing on information to a former employee of the firm who is working for a competitor (*Smith v Du Pont (UK) Ltd*), refusing to cut exceptionally long hair after being warned of a safety hazard (*Marsh v Judge International*), breach of works rules (*Palmer v Vauxhall Motors Ltd*), suspected dishonesty (*Parkers Bakeries Ltd v Palmer*), breach of safety instructions (*Wilcox v HGS*), fighting (*Parsons & Co Ltd v McLoughlin*), being a drug addict (*Walton v TAC Construction Materials Ltd*), refusal to go on a training course (*Minter v Wellingborough Foundries Ltd*), unauthorised access to a computer (*Denco Ltd v Joinson*), and so on.

17.164 Every employer is strongly urged to observe the provisions of the Code of Practice on Disciplinary Practice and Procedures, and although a breach of the Code will not automatically make a dismissal unfair (*Lewis Shops Group v Wiggins*), in practice it can be said that the provisions of the Code matter most when the decision to dismiss is at its weakest. Thus it is still possible to dismiss summarily for gross misconduct (*Retarded Children's Aid Society v Day*), but procedural fairness should always be observed, and a failure to follow the Code's recommendations may lead to a finding that the dismissal was unfair, even though the compensation may be reduced because of the employee's contributory conduct.

G. Conduct outside the employment

17.165 The problem which arises here is, what has it got to do with the employer what an employee does outside his working hours? The answer may well depend on a number of factors, including the nature of the employment, the position held by the employee, the nature of the incident and its effect on the employer, on customers, on fellow employees, and so on. If it can be said that the conduct in question has an adverse effect on the employer's business, then a dismissal may be fair. For example, the conduct may be a conviction by a court of law for a criminal offence unconnected with the employment. In *Richardson v City of Bradford Metropolitan Council* the claimant was a senior meat inspector, who was convicted of theft of money from his local rugby club on several occasions. When his employers were informed, he was suspended, but as there were no other suitable vacancies which could be offered to him, he was dismissed. This was held to be fair. The integrity of a public servant who was in a position of trust was of prime importance. In *Bradshaw v Rugby Portland Cement Co Ltd* the claimant was dismissed following a conviction for incest with his own daughter, for which he was placed on probation by the Crown Court. The dismissal was held to be unfair. The offence had no bearing on his work as a quarryman, the firm's customers would not have objected to his continued employment, and his relationship with his fellow-employees had not deteriorated to the extent that they objected to working with him. There must have been strong mitigating circumstances for the court to deal with the matter so leniently, and the tribunal did not see any reason to impose a further punishment. Clearly, different considerations would have applied had the applicant been (say) a schoolmaster. In *Gardiner v Newport County Borough Council* the claimant was a lecturer at an art college, in charge of a foundation course on which were pupils who were between the ages of 16–18. He was convicted of gross indecency with another man in a public lavatory, and his dismissal by the college was held to be fair. The tribunal held that *Bradshaw*'s case was no authority for saying that a person who receives a moderate punishment from the court is immune from dismissal, for the courts are frequently being reminded in mitigation that whatever punishment they impose is only part of the misfortune which will befall the accused. The employers could not be expected to waive the consequences which the courts had anticipated and possibly allowed for in fixing the penalty. Nor is it relevant that the employer never told the employee of the kind of conduct outside his employment which would warrant dismissal, for an employer cannot possibly specify or anticipate all the possible circumstances which may lead to a dismissal. To hold otherwise would mean that an employee would be safest from dismissal if he committed some act which was more outrageous than anyone ever envisaged.

17.166 If the employee is charged with a criminal offence, then clearly the employer will need to make a decision about whether the employment can continue, in advance of a hearing in the criminal courts. The employee should be interviewed (strictly, this is not part of the disciplinary procedure, because no breach of internal discipline has occurred), and invited to explain the position. If he intends to plead guilty, the employer can then make a decision, depending on the circumstances, nature of employment, position held etc. If the employer considers that valuable customers would be lost if the employment continued, he should first attempt to ascertain the views of those customers, and not just make bland assumptions. If the employee states that he intends to plead not guilty, then ideally he should be suspended until the outcome of the criminal proceedings. Whether this suspension should be with pay or without pay is a matter of style and agreement, taking into account the length of time it will be before the hearing takes place, the circumstances of the employer's business, the seriousness or otherwise of the offence, and so on. If there is a collective agreement or a disciplinary procedure which provides that suspension on full pay will be appropriate where investigations cannot be completed, then that agreement or procedure must be followed (*Securicor Guarding Ltd v R*).

17.167 Thus an employer is entitled to make a judgment based on the criminal conduct of the employee, as to whether or not the conviction has impaired the employee's ability to do the job, and whether there has been a loss of confidence in the employee (*Robson v Brian Mills*). In *Moore v C & A Modes* the claimant was a section leader in a store, where she had been employed for 20 years. It was alleged that she had been caught shoplifting at another store. Her consequent dismissal was held to be fair. No-one should be more alive to the damage caused by shoplifters than such an employee, and it was unreal to expect an employer in the retail trade not to dismiss an employee whom he believed to be stealing from another store. In *Mathewson v R B Wilson Dental Laboratory Ltd*, the claimant was arrested during his lunch break for purchasing a small amount of cannabis. His subsequent dismissal was held to be within the range of reasonable responses which a reasonable employer might take.

17.168 'Moonlighting', ie the taking of additional employment outside normal working hours, may be grounds for dismissal if this has an adverse effect on the employer's business. It will be recalled (para 10.149) that in *Hivac Ltd v Park Royal Scientific Instruments Ltd* the employees were in breach of their contracts for which they could have been dismissed, although this was prevented at the time by the operation of the Essential Works Order. The court stated that it would be reluctant to impose on the employees a restriction which would hamper their ability to increase their earnings in their spare time, but on the facts they were inflicting great harm on the employer's business. In *Gray v C & P Pembroke Ltd* the claimant agreed to not engage in any other business without the written consent of the employer. Contrary to this agreement he took a part-time job with a rival company, and this was held to be a breach of faith for which he could be fairly dismissed. However, in *Nova Plastics Ltd v Froggatt* the claimant was employed as an odd-job man. He was dismissed when it was discovered that he was working for a rival firm. The dismissal was held to be unfair. Having regard to the nature of his work as an odd-job man, he could hardly be contributing very seriously to the competition from the rival firm, and in the circumstances there was no breach of duty towards his own employer merely because he worked for a competitor in his spare time.

17.169   In some circumstances, it may be relevant to consider whether or not the outside activity is compatible with the dignity of the employee holding a particular post; in other circumstances an employer may be entitled to forbid an employee engaging in certain leisure pursuits or additional employment if the result is that the employee is too exhausted to follow his normal occupation. If an employee wishes to stand at a parliamentary or local election, this is of concern to the employer only if the activity spills over into the employment scene. For example, supposing a supervisor, who controls a labour force made up largely of coloured immigrant workers, announces his intention of standing for election as a National Front candidate. It could be argued that the potential disruption likely to be caused to a contented workforce may well justify an employer dismissing the employee concerned.

17.170   The conduct in question must be such as to cause a loss of confidence in the employee. Thus in *Whitlow v Alkanet Construction Ltd* the claimant was asked by the company's executive to do some work on the latter's house. There he met the executive's wife, and love play took place between them in the house, and they had sexual intercourse elsewhere. Although the tribunal recognised that the claimant had been subjected to a temptation which few men would have resisted, his dismissal was held to be fair.

H. Redundancy

17.171   Although a redundancy situation may be grounds for dismissal, in respect of which the employee may be able to obtain a redundancy payment (see Chapter 18), it does not follow that such a dismissal will automatically be fair, or that the employer acts reasonably in treating that reason as a sufficient ground for dismissal. In *Williams v Compair Maxam Ltd* the EAT laid down five principles for good current industrial relations practice which should be adopted in appropriate circumstances:
1.   the employer will give as much warning as possible of impending redundancies so as to enable trade unions and employees to consider alternative solutions and seek alternative employment;
2.   the employer will consult with the unions as to the best means by which the desired object can be achieved with as little hardship as possible. In particular,

the criterion for selection should be agreed, and the actual selection should be made in accordance with that criterion;

3. the criterion for selection should not depend solely on the opinion of the person making the selection, but should be one which can be objectively checked;

4. the employer must ensure that the selection is made in accordance with that criterion, and will consider any representations made;

5. the employer will ascertain whether there is any alternative employment which can be offered.

17.172 However, the principles laid down in *Williams v Compair Maxam Ltd* are guidelines, not rules of law. They refer primarily to the situation found in large companies when a significant number of redundancies are being contemplated. They should be applied with caution in small firms (*Meikle v McPhail*) or where there is no trade union involved. The principles should not be regarded as a shopping list with a finding of unfairness if one or more points have not been followed (*A Simpson & Son (Motors) v Reid*).

17.173 Bearing this in mind, there are three ways in which redundancies should be handled.

17.174 (a) *Consideration of alternatives*. Faced with a redundancy situation, the reasonable employer considers whether it is necessary to act on it, or whether there is some other way of dealing with the problem. For example, it may be possible to restrict recruitment, cut down on overtime, introduce work-sharing, introduce short-time working. In *Allwood v William Hill Ltd* the employers closed down 12 betting shops and declared the managers redundant. No warning was given and no alternative employment within the company was offered. It was held that merely because a redundancy situation existed, it did not follow that the employees had to be made redundant. There was a high wastage in the industry, and more effort should have been made to transfer them to other establishments, even on a temporary basis. The employers should also have considered retraining the employees until vacancies arose through wastage or expansion. It may be possible to offer a redundant employee another job which amounts to a demotion, and leave it to him to decide whether or not to accept (*Avonmouth Construction Co Ltd v Shipway*).

17.175 The reasonable employer also takes steps to see if the employee can be absorbed elsewhere in the concern, or with associated companies (*Vokes Ltd v Bear*), but the employer need only take such reasonable steps as are available for this purpose, and though an employment tribunal must scrutinise critically a complaint of unfair redundancy, it should also guard against adopting a standard which is unrealistic, and it should not find a dismissal unfair merely as a means of topping up an inadequate redundancy payment (*British United Shoe Machinery Co Ltd v Clarke*). If an employer merely states that he decided not to offer a redundant employee alternative work, without advancing any reasons for the decision, he does not discharge the burden of showing that he has acted reasonably (*Thomas and Betts Manufacturing Ltd v Harding*). If the employer has failed to act reasonably in searching round for alternative employment, the employment tribunal must consider whether in fact any loss has accrued to the employee as a result of that failure, or whether in fact it made no difference. In the latter case, there could be a finding that the dismissal was consequently not unfair, or that even if it was unfair, no loss was suffered by the employee, and therefore he is not entitled to any compensation.

17.176 (b) *Lack of consultation.* To dismiss without warning or proper consultations, or without considering the recommendations of the Code of Practice relating to redundancies, may also result in a finding that a dismissal is unfair. But a failure to consult with the unions as provided by s 188 of TULR(C)A (see Chapter 18) does not by itself mean that a dismissal is unfair (*Forman Construction Ltd v Kelly*). At the same time, consultation with trade unions does not preclude consultation with individuals (*Walls Meat Co Ltd v Selby*). If the employer fails to consult with the affected individuals, he must supply a cogent reason why it was not possible to do so (*Holden v Bradville Ltd*).

17.177 The fact that the employer has established a policy not to consult in the event of redundancies being imminent, based on previous experience and the wishes of the workforce in the past, is not, *per se*, sufficient reason not to consult (*Ferguson v Prestwick Circuits Ltd*), particularly when the criteria for selection is vague and subjective (*Graham v ABF Ltd*). Even a small company is expected to act reasonably. Thus, if redundancy is being proposed, the size of the undertaking may affect the nature or formality of the consultation process, but it does not excuse the lack of consultation (*De Grasse v Stockwell Tools Ltd*).

17.178 In *Mugford v Midland Bank plc* the EAT suggested three propositions for the guidance of employment tribunals. (1) If there is no consultation with trade unions or individuals when redundancies are contemplated, a dismissal will normally be unfair, unless a reasonable employer would have concluded that consultation would have been an utterly futile exercise. (2) Consultation with a trade union does not of itself release the employer from an obligation to consult with individuals concerned. (3) It will be a question of fact and degree for the employment tribunal to consider whether such consultations as had taken place were so inadequate as to render a dismissal unfair. The lack of consultation by itself does not automatically lead to a finding of unfairness.

17.179 The effect of a failure by the employer to consult or warn an employee of an impending redundancy was examined by the House of Lords in *Polkey v A E Dayton Services Ltd* (see para 12.14). The test of fairness is to be judged by what the employer did, and not by what he might have done. Thus if, on the basis of information which he has available at the time of the dismissal, or circumstances which are known to him, he can be said to have acted reasonably despite the absence of a warning or consultation, then the dismissal may still be fair even though the provisions of the Code of Practice were not followed. However, if he acted unreasonably (even though the decision would have been fair had he followed the correct procedure) the dismissal must be regarded as being unfair. It does not follow that in these circumstances the employee will receive additional compensation on top of his statutory redundancy pay (*Lifeguard Assurance Ltd v Zadrozny*), for the consequence of the unfairness can be reflected by reducing the amount of the compensatory award by a percentage reflecting the chance that the employee would still have lost his employment (*Campbell v Dunoon and Cowal Housing Association Ltd*). Further, if the dismissal is thus held to be unfair, an employment tribunal may exercise the option of awarding reinstatement or re-engagement under s 113 ERA, should there be altered circumstances which justify this course (per Lord Bridges in *Polkey v A E Dayton Services Ltd*). In thus overruling the line of cases which supported the so-called *British Labour Pump* principle, the House of Lords re-emphasised the importance for employers of following fair procedures before taking a decision to dismiss, on whatever ground the decision is taken.

17.180 A warning that redundancies are being contemplated, coupled with an indication of the selection procedure, does not satisfy the requirements of a fair procedure. Consultation must be fair and genuine. An opportunity must be given to the affected employees to express their views (*Rowell v Hubbard Group Services*) Thus in *Heron v Citilink-Nottingham* the employers found it necessary to make significant economies, and dismissed the claimant without any warning. The EAT held that his dismissal was unfair. For there to be exceptional circumstances which obviates the need for consultation, it had to be shown that it was necessary to dismiss the applicant when they did, and at no later date. It may well be that had he been consulted, he may have been able to make suggestions as to how the situation could be ameliorated. He may have agreed to accept a more junior post, or work for a lower salary. Unless the employer consults the employee in such circumstances, the latter will have no opportunity to put forward any suggestions.

17.181 It had been suggested that a redundancy dismissal without consultation can only be fair if the employer took a deliberate decision not to consult (see *Robertson v Magnet Ltd (Retail Division)*) but this view was rejected by the Court of Appeal in *Duffy v Yeomans and Partners Ltd*. What matters is whether consultation would have been useless, taking into account the circumstances known to the employer at the time.

17.182 If a dismissal is unfair because of a failure to consult, the employment tribunal must consider whether consultation would have made any difference, or whether the employee would have had a chance of being retained in his employment. If the answer is uncertain, then a percentage assessment should be made to reflect the probability that he would have been retained (*Dunlop Ltd v Farrell*), because the claimant must still show that a loss has resulted from the unfairness, and the employment tribunal must not speculate, guess, or indulge in conjecture. The claimant must show a sensible and coherent suggestion as to what was the result of the failure to consult or warn, and what would have happened had there been no such failure. The employer must then refute such suggestions (*Barley v Amey Roadstone Corpn Ltd*). The employment tribunal may then decide that the failure made little or no difference, and reduce compensation to an amount they deem appropriate, to reflect the additional period of time by which the employee's employment would have been extended had consultations taken place (*Mining Supplies (Longwall) Ltd v Baker*).

17.183 (c) *Proper selection procedures.* It is the duty of the employment tribunal to examine the employer's procedures for selecting redundancies to ensure that these are fair. Even a selection system which is based on custom and practice in the industry can be challenged if it is unreasonable (*Watling & Co v Richardson*). The tribunal is entitled to know (a) who made the decision to select, (b) what information was taken into account, and (c) upon what criteria the information was assessed (*Bristol Channel Ship Repairers Ltd v O'Keefe*). Otherwise unfair selection for redundancy may also amount to an unfair dismissal. Faced with the decision of choosing which employee(s) shall be made redundant, the employer must engage in a genuine exercise in reaching his choice. If there is an established procedure in existence, he should follow it; in the absence of such pre-arranged procedure, the general rule in industry for redundancy selection is based on the principle of last in, first out (LIFO), and this principle should always be considered as an important feature of any redundancy agreement (*Brook v London Borough of Haringey*). LIFO is always subject to any reasonable and proper modification, particularly if this has been considered by shop stewards and management acting in concert (*Crump v Chubb & Sons Lock and Safe Co Ltd*). In *International Paint Co Ltd v Cameron* it was held that the customary arrangements of LIFO, without further specification, had to be based on continuous service, not cumulative service, so that an employee with longer continuous service ought to be retained in preference to an employee with a longer overall service, but less continuous service.

17.184 If there is no agreed procedure or customary arrangement, the employer may take into account long services, superior abilities and experience, and the respective hardship caused. In *Selby and Tesse v Plessey Co Ltd*, it was held that a selection based on an effective evaluation system, which was customary in the company, was fair. Adherence to a redundancy agreement made with a trade union is generally sufficient evidence to rebut unfairness (*Taylor v Conveyancer Ltd*) though a failure to consult that union as provided by the agreement may be unfair. Also, if the redundancy agreement is discriminatory on grounds of sex and race, it would be unfair to follow it (*Clarke v Eley (IMI) Kynoch Ltd*). However, if the decision has to be made in a hurry for sound reasons, and consultations with the union or employees would result in serious delay, the employer does not act unfairly in failing to consult (*Guy v Delanair (Car Heater) Ltd*).

17.185 Although the actual selection criteria is for management to determine, it is sound practice to agree this in advance with trade unions. The more vague and subjective the criteria, the greater is the need to consult with affected employees (*Graham v ABF Ltd*). It is the employer's responsibility to set up a fair system of selection, and to administer it fairly. If selection for redundancy is based on proper assessments, it is not for the employment tribunal to engage in a re-assessment exercise (*Eaton Ltd v King*).

17.186 In *Clyde Pipeworks v Foster*, selection for redundancy was based on a points system, which took into account bad time-keeping, workmanship, absenteeism, and merit on conduct. This procedure had been agreed with the unions, but they were not consulted about its implementation. It was held that there was no need to involve the unions in the detailed arrangements for selection for redundancy, provided the method was fair in general terms. But if management were to take into account improper factors (such as a disciplinary warning which should have been expunged from his record) there could be an unfair selection (*Pyle v Cleeson Civil Engineering Ltd*). If jobs are interchangeable between departments, then the basis for selection is between employees of the same description within the whole concern, not on a departmental basis (*Wailes Dove Bitumastic v Woolcocks*).

17.187 If a dismissal for redundancy is generally fair in terms of the procedure adopted and the selection criteria, it does not become unfair because of a failure by the employer to give the affected employees a right of appeal against their dismissal, even though an employee dismissed for gross misconduct would have that right. There is no suggestion in the Code of Practice that there should be a right of appeal against a dismissal for redundancy (*Robinson v Ulster Carpet Mills Ltd*). The advantage of having an appeal machinery is that an original decision to dismiss for redundancy which is unfair can be cured if there is a complete rehearing on appeal (*Lloyd v Taylor Woodrow plc*).

17.188 But if there is an appeal procedure, it must be operated fairly, and not be a mere sham. Thus, if selection for redundancy is based on a points system which had been agreed with union representatives, an employee is still entitled to know how his own marks had been calculated, otherwise he will have no material with which to present his case on appeal (*John Brown Engineering Ltd v Brown*).

17.189 To select a woman for dismissal because she is pregnant, or on maternity leave of absence, would be unfair under s 99 (see para 6.42), but if a woman is made redundant because of the operation of a fair selection procedure (eg based on LIFO), then the fact that she is or was pregnant is coincidental, and has nothing to do with her selection., Her dismissal would be fair in accordance with the usual criteria (*Brown v Stockton-on-Tees Borough Council*). Equally, a long-term sick employee may still be selected for redundancy, even though this terminates his entitlement to sickness pay under the employer's scheme (*Hill v General Accident Fire and Life Assurance Corpn plc*).

17.190 In the last analysis, the test is not whether the employment tribunal agrees with the actual selection made by the employer, but whether the employer acted reasonably. Thus it is not the duty of the employment tribunal to decide who they would have made redundant had they had to make the choice, but to ensure that management acts from genuine motives. In *Grundy (Teddington) Ltd v Willis*, the choice for making an employee redundant lay between two persons. Management chose one, but the employment tribunal held that this was unfair, in that the other should have been chosen. The EAT reversed this finding; the ultimate decision must remain with management, provided it acts fairly.

17.191 If an employee is given notice of dismissal, for reason of redundancy, and during that notice period new work becomes available, it may be unfair not to rescind the notice and offer further employment to him (*Stacey v Babcock Power Ltd*). However, if the alternative employment becomes available after the employee's contract of employment has ended, an employer does not act unreasonably in failing to offer that employment to him (*Octavius Atkinson & Sons Ltd v Morris*).

17.192 It will be automatically unfair to select a person for redundancy if the reason was a reason specified in ERA ss 99–105 (see para 17.104), or TULR(C)A ss 152–153 (see para 21.89).

I. Statutory restriction

17.193 An employer cannot be expected to continue to employ an employee if such employment would be contrary to the law. For example, if an employee is employed as a driver, and it is a term (express or implied) of his contract that he should hold a valid driving licence, then clearly, if he loses that licence, the employee is barred from pursuing that occupation by statute (Road Traffic Act

1974 s 84). Additionally, the employer may be guilty of an offence if he permits a disqualified driver to drive. But this does not mean that a dismissal will always be fair in such circumstances. The test is, as always, the reasonableness of the employer's action (*Sutcliffe and Eaton Ltd v Pinney*). He must consider the length of the disqualification, the needs of the business, whether the employee can do his job without driving a motor vehicle, whether alternative arrangements can be made, whether the employee could be given some other work to do until his licence is restored, and so on. In *Mathieson v WJ Noble* the claimant was a salesman who was disqualified from driving. He made arrangements to engage a chauffeuse at his own expense to drive him around during the period of disqualification, but his employers decided to dismiss him. It was held that the employers had acted unreasonably in not giving him a chance to see if the new arrangements were satisfactory. This may be contrasted with *Appleyard v FM Smith (Hull) Ltd* where it was an essential requirement for the mechanics that they should hold valid driving licences so that they could test vehicles which they had repaired. When the claimant lost his licence, the company had given some thought to placing him elsewhere in the business, but this was not practicable in such a small firm, and his dismissal was held to be fair.

17.194   There are a number of other legal restrictions on the employment of certain employees in special circumstances. In *Gills v Wall's Meat Co Ltd* the claimant, who was a Sikh, was involved with dealing with open meat. When he commenced employment he was clean shaven, and did not observe his religion by growing a beard, but after a while he was 'converted back to the paths of righteousness' and grew a beard. To have continued to employ him in this capacity would have involved a breach of the Food Regulations 1970, and so the employers, after offering him alternative employment which he refused, dismissed him. This was held to be fair. (It may be noted that a refusal by a Sikh to wear a safety helmet on a construction site as required by regulations made under the Health and Safety at Work etc Act does not entitle an employer to dismiss him as long as he is wearing his turban, see Employment Act 1989 s 11).

J. Some other substantial reason

17.195   It was never intended that the above reasons for fair dismissal could constitute an exhaustive catalogue of the circumstances in which the employer would be justified in terminating the services of an employee, and there have been a number of cases where 'some other substantial reason' for the dismissal has been held to be fair. In *Wilson v Underhill House School Ltd* the claimant was a schoolteacher in a school which was in financial difficulties, and which could not pay in full a pay award. All the other teachers except her agreed to take less, but she refused and was dismissed. Her dismissal was held to be fair for some other substantial reason. In *Foot v Eastern Counties Timber Co Ltd* the claimant, who was a valued employee, was dismissed when it was discovered that her husband had started a business which was in competition with the employers. It was held that the company had acted reasonably in dismissing an employee who had access to confidential information at a time when her husband was running a rival business. In *Farr v Hoveringham Gravels Ltd* the company had a rule that employees must live within reasonable travelling distance of the firm, and they dismissed a manager who had moved to live 44 miles away. A person in his position may have to be called out in an emergency, and this would prove to be difficult in view of the distance involved. Hence the dismissal was fair.

17.196   It has to be recognised that frequently the legitimate interests of the employer in making a change in employment terms are irreconcilable with the equally legitimate interests of the employee. Thus a sound good business reason for a particular reorganisation has to be looked at in that context (*St John of God (Care Services) Ltd v Brooks*).

17.197   An employer need not wait until a problem arises before he takes action to protect his commercial interests. In *O'Brien v Prudential Assurance Co*, the claimant applied for a job as a district insurance inspector, but deliberately concealed that he had a history of mental illness. When this came to light, the company obtained further medical reports, on the basis of which he was dismissed. Again, this was to be for some other substantial reason, and in the circumstances fair. As an inspector, he would have to go into people's homes, and the company could not risk the possibility that an unsavoury incident might occur.

17.198   Although an employee is not legally obliged to accept a variation in the terms of his contract, a refusal to do so may amount to a substantial reason for dismissal if it is in the commercial interests of the firm that a variation should be made, and it is a reasonable request to make in the circumstances. In *Muggridge and Slade v East Anglia Plastics Ltd* the employers found it necessary to change the working hours, and fairly dismissed two ladies who refused to accept the change, and in *RS Components v Irwin* (see para 19.41) the company fairly dismissed a salesman who refused to sign a restrictive covenant. However, a dismissal for refusing new contractual terms may be unfair if there is no immediate need for the variation (*Evans v Elemeta Holdings Ltd*).

17.199   A change in employment terms may well be necessary even though these are to the detriment of the employee, if commercial necessity so dictates, for a contract of employment cannot remain static throughout the whole of its existence. In *Sycamore v H Myer & Co Ltd* the claimant refused to accept a new payment system which would have resulted in his wages being reduced from £130 per week to about £90 per week. The new system was negotiated with the trade union because the old method of payment was clearly defective. All the other employees accepted the change, and it was held that the claimant's dismissal was for some other substantial reason, and fair in the circumstances. The new terms were not ungenerous, and had been negotiated with the trade union concerned. In *Storey v Allied Brewery*, the respondents introduced a rota system of working due to the changing pattern of their trade. The claimant refused to work on Sundays, as she wished to go to church. Her dismissal was held to be fair. The change was necessary in the interests of economy, and to balance and share the workload with all the relevant employees. In *Oliver v Sperry Vickers*, the claimant was dismissed for refusing to accept a change in his job title and job content following a reorganisation of the supervisory structure. He was the only one of 22 employees affected who refused. Although this involved minor additions in his duties, he would have received a higher rate of pay. The dismissal was held to be for some substantial reason, and in the circumstances, fair, for he had no reasonable objection to the change.

17.200   A change in working hours does not give rise to a redundancy, but a dismissal due to a refusal to accept such a change consequent on a reorganisation may be for some other substantial reason (*Barnes v Gilmartin Associates*).

17.201 The test in these cases is whether the offer of new terms is within the range of offers which a reasonable employer would make in the circumstances. The task of weighing the advantages to the employer against the disadvantages to the employee is merely one factor to be taken into account (*Richmond Precision Engineering Ltd v Pearce*). Whether or not other employees have accepted the proposed changes, and whether a trade union have recommended acceptance of the changes are relevant factors to be taken into account. The imposition of the new terms and conditions does not have to be solely on the ground that the changes are vital for the survival of the business, and other valid reasons may be equally acceptable (*Catamaran Cruisers Ltd v Williams*).

17.202 If an employee is dismissed because he refuses to carry out an order which is not within his contractual obligations, this may be a factor in deciding whether or not he has been unfairly dismissed, but it is not determinative of the issue. There may be sound organisational reasons for the employer seeking to change working conditions or altering the terms of the contract. If the employee has been given ample warnings of the changes, and ample time to discuss his concerns a dismissal for refusing to accept the changes could well be fair (*Farrant v Woodroffe School*).

17.203 A difficult situation arises when an employer knows that a disciplinary offence (eg theft) has been committed, but is unable to identify the actual person responsible. Can he then dismiss all the suspects? In *Parr v Whitbread & Co plc* the claimant was a branch manager of an off-licence. There were three other employees working in the shop. It was discovered that the sum of £4,600 was missing, but the circumstances were such that each of the four employees had an equal opportunity of committing the theft. After carrying out a thorough investigation, all four were dismissed. An employment tribunal held that the dismissal was for some other substantial reason, and fair in the circumstances, and the decision was upheld by the EAT. The following guidance was offered: (1) the act must be one which would justify dismissal if committed by an individual; (2) the employer must carry out a reasonable and thorough investigation; (3) as a result of the investigation, the employer must reasonably believe that one of the employees committed the act; (4) the employers must have acted reasonably in identifying the group of employees one of whom could have committed the act; and (5) as between the members of that group, the employer could not reasonably have identified the actual perpetrator.

17.204 But the employer does not have to dismiss all of the group, if he can show solid and sensible grounds for differentiating between members of the group. In *Frames Snooker Centre v Boyce*, three managers had access to a safe in the employers' premises. After several burglaries had occurred, the police formed the view that each burglary was an inside job. There was no evidence against any of the managers, but the employer decided to dismiss two of them. He did not dismiss the third, because she was his daughter, and he had faith in her honesty and integrity. An employment tribunal held that the dismissal of the two managers was unfair because of the failure to dismiss all the suspects, but the decision was reversed on appeal. There is no 'all or none' principle in dismissing a group when it is not possible to identify the culprit.

17.205 To dismiss one of two incompatible employees in order to restore harmony among the workforce (*Gorfin v Distressed Gentlefolk's Aid Association*)

367

may be fair provided that steps are taken to investigate the conflict and attempts are made to see whether or not an improvement in the relationship can be effected (*Turner v Vesteric Ltd*). Equally, to dismiss an employee who is unable to obtain a fidelity bond (*Moody v Telefusion Ltd*), can be a substantial reason for dismissal. If an appointment is expressed to be of a temporary nature, pending the return to work of an absent employee, this could also constitute grounds which a tribunal may feel justified a dismissal. In particular, the Employment Rights Act 1996 s 106 provides that in two specific instances the dismissal of a temporary employee will be regarded as a substantial reason. These are where a temporary replacement is taken in because there has been a suspension on medical grounds, or a temporary appointment has been made to replace a woman who is absent on maternity leave. In both these cases the replacement must be informed in writing of the temporary nature of the appointment, and that he/she may be dismissed when the absent employee returns to work. However, although such dismissal amounts to a substantial reason, it will be without prejudice to the application of the rule that the tribunal must find that the employer has acted reasonably in treating the reason as sufficient ground for dismissal.

17.206 If an employee indicates that he intends to resign his employment, with the result that the employer engages a replacement in anticipation, the employer is entitled to refuse to accept a late notification that the employee has changed his mind, and his dismissal may be fair for some other substantial reason (*Ely v YKK Fasteners Ltd*).

17.207 An employment tribunal will not accept any reason advanced by the employer as coming within the definition of another substantial reason. In *Hedger v Davy & Co Ltd* the employer received a request from an employment agency for a reference in respect of the applicant. This was held not to be another substantial reason for the dismissal. And in *Wadley v Eager Electrical Ltd* the claimant was a valued worker who had been employed for 17 years. His wife, who worked at the same firm, was summarily dismissed for theft, and the employers felt that they has lost confidence and trust in the applicant. They also felt that his continued employment would have an adverse effect on customers. His dismissal was held not to be for some other substantial reason. It was unfair to dismiss an employee because some other person in the household was fairly dismissed. But a dismissal because of third party pressure may amount to some other substantial reason (*Davenport v Taptonholme for the Elderly*).

17.208 It must be remembered that even though a reason is capable of being another substantial reason for the dismissal, the employer must still act reasonably in treating that reason as a sufficient reason for dismissal. To do this, he should have a full investigation of the problem, and explore any alternatives which may be available (*Scott Packing and Warehousing Co v Paterson*). There is no absolute requirement that consultation with the employee should take place, but this is one of the factors to be taken into account in determining if the employer has acted reasonably (*Hollister v National Farmers' Union*). In *Johnson v Tesco Stores Ltd* the claimant made a false statement on his job application form. He was subsequently employed for 18 months before the falsity came to light, during which time he was perfectly satisfactory. Nonetheless he was dismissed, and this was held to be unfair. In *Debaughn v Star Cinemas (London) Ltd* it was contrary to the company's policy to employ people who had had previous criminal convictions, particularly for violence, and they dismissed a doorman who had been employed satisfactorily for 12 months when it was discovered that he had failed to disclose a previous conviction for assault. This was held to be fair. The distinction between these cases lies in the fact that in the former case, there was no real need to act on the information which had come to light, whereas in the latter case the firm's policy could not admit of exceptions for very sound reasons.

17.209–17.220 It is frequently useful for an employer to plead or argue 'some other substantial reason' in addition to another reason advanced, for this enables him to have two bites at the cherry! Thus, to dismiss an employee who has been sent to prison may be regarded as conduct or frustration or some other substantial reason. But whatever the 'label', the employer must always be prepared to show that he had acted reasonably in treating the reason as a sufficient reason for dismissing the employee (*Bouchaala v Trusthouse Forte Hotels Ltd*).

Dismissal for asserting a statutory right (ERA s 104)

17.221 It will be unfair to dismiss an employee because:
(a) he has brought proceedings against an employer to enforce a relevant statutory right; or
(b) he has alleged that the employer has infringed a right of his which is a relevant statutory right.

17.222 The relevant statutory rights for the purposes of s 104 are as follows:
(a) all the rights contained in ERA for which the remedy for infringement is to make a complaint or reference to an employment tribunal;
(b) the following rights made under TULR(C)A—the right not to have the deduction of unauthorised or excessive trade union subscriptions, or unauthorised payment to the union's political fund, right not to have action taken short of dismissal on the ground of union membership or non-membership, right to have time off work for trade union duties or activities, and rights conferred by the Working Time Regulations, Part-Time Workers (Prevention of less Favourable Treatment) Regulations 2000, and Transnational Information and Consultation of Employees Regulations 1999.

17.223 It will also be unfair to select a person for redundancy on any of the above grounds.

17.224 The right will apply irrespective of the employee's length of service, because no qualifying period of continuous employment is required.

17.225 It is immaterial whether or not the employee in fact has the right, or whether or not it has been infringed, as long as the employee makes the claim in good faith. Nor need the employee specify the right, as long as it is made reasonably clear to the employer what the right claimed to have been infringed was. Thus, for example, if an employee were to bring a claim before an employment tribunal alleging that he is entitled to a right contained in the Working Time Regulations, and he is dismissed in consequence, the dismissal would be in breach of s 104, irrespective of whether his claim was justified.

17.226 But the employee must be able to identify the right alleged to have been infringed by the employer, and if he cannot show that he ever made an allegation that the employer had been in breach of a statutory duty, then the allegation could not be the cause of his dismissal (*Mennell v Newell & Wright (Transport Contractors) Ltd*).

17.227–17.235 The interesting thing about this new right is that the 'dismissal' referred to in s 104 must inevitably include a constructive dismissal. Hence, if an employee feels that he is being deprived of his statutory rights, he can resign and make a claim accordingly.

Other dismissals

17.236 For dismissals on grounds of trade union membership or non-membership, in closed shop situations, lockouts, strikes, and industrial pressure, see Chapter 21. Dismissal on grounds of sex or race or disability are dealt with in Chapter 4, maternity dismissals in Chapter 6, and dismissals in health and safety cases in Chapter 11.

National security

17.237 As already noted, there is a special procedure to be adopted by employment tribunals when dealing with complaints made by members of the security service which involve issues of national security (see para 2.272).

Written reasons for dismissal (ERA s 92)

17.238 When an employee is dismissed, either with or without notice, or by the expiry of a fixed-term contract, he is entitled to receive, on request, a written statement of the reasons for his dismissal within 14 days. This statement shall be admissible in any proceedings before a tribunal or a court. He will not be so entitled unless he has been continuously employed for one year.

17.239 A complaint may be presented to an employment tribunal by an employee that the employer has unreasonably failed to provide a written statement, or that the statement which has been given is inadequate or untrue. If the tribunal finds the complaint well founded, it may make a declaration as to what it finds were the employer's reasons, and shall make an award of two weeks' pay.

17.240 To be adequate under s 92, the written statement must be such that anyone reading it can know the essential reasons for the dismissal. No particular technicalities are involved, and no particular form is required (*Horsley Smith and Sherry Ltd v Dutton*). If the employer denies that the employee has been dismissed, the employment tribunal must make a finding on that issue before it can consider whether or not there was an unreasonable refusal to provide a written reason. But if the employer reasonably and conscientiously believes that there was no dismissal, the employment tribunal is unlikely to find that there was an unreasonable refusal to give a reason for a dismissal which the employer genuinely believed did not occur (*Brown v Stuart Scott & Co Ltd*).

17.241 The reason given by the employer must be the true reason for the dismissal, but it does not have to be an adequate reason. That is a matter for subsequent investigation should the employee pursue his claim for unfair dismissal (*Harvard Securities plc v Younghusband*).

17.242 It is not sufficient compliance to refer to other documents, for to be adequate, the written reasons should make it quite clear to anyone reading them why the applicant was dismissed. But if, in reply to a request for written reasons, the employer *sends* a copy of an earlier document which contains those reasons, this is sufficient compliance with s 92 (*Kent County Council v Gilham*).

17.243 But s 92 has to be strictly construed; in *Keen v Dymo Ltd* the employers sent written reasons by second class post, so that it arrived a day outside the 14-day period; this was held to be an unreasonable refusal to supply written reasons. The written reasons must be in a distinct document. Filling in a reply on Form IT3 (respondent's reply to an application to an employment tribunal) is not a sufficient compliance with s 92.

17.244 If an employee does not make a request for written reasons, he cannot complain that the reasons which were given were untrue, and an employment tribunal has no power to make an award under s 92 in the absence of any such request (*Catherine Haigh Harlequin Hair Design v Seed*).

17.245–17.255 It should be noted that the employment tribunal has a discretion whether or not to make a declaration as to the reasons, whereas the award of two weeks' pay is mandatory. This award is *not* subject to the statutory maximum limit of £230 per week.

Dismissal on maternity grounds (ERA s 92(4))

17.256 A woman is entitled to written reasons for her dismissal if she is dismissed at any time while she is pregnant, or after her childbirth in circumstances in which her ordinary or additional maternity leave period ends by reason of her dismissal. She does not need to have the requisite period of continuous employment, and she must be given the written statement irrespective of whether or not she makes a request for it.

Interim relief; ERA ss 128–132

17.257 If an employee complains that the reason for his dismissal was because he was exercising his rights under s 100(1)(a), (b) (protected shop worker), s 101A(d) (representative of the workforce for the purpose of the Working Time Regulations), s 102(1) (trustee of occupational pension schemes), s 103 (employee representative under TULR(C)A or Transfer of Undertakings Regulations), or s 103A (protected disclosure) he may make an application for interim relief. A similar application may be made under the provisions of TULR(C)A ss 161–166 (dismissal for trade union membership and activities, etc) and para 161 Sch A1 to TULR(C)A (playing a role in proposing or opposing trade union recognition). The procedure and remedies are outlined at para 21.126.

Remedies for unfair dismissal

A. Reinstatement and re-engagement orders (ERA s 113)

17.258 If an employment tribunal finds that the employee has been unfairly dismissed, it shall explain to him that it has the power to make an order that he be reinstated or re-engaged, and shall ask him if he wishes the tribunal to make such an order. If he expresses such a wish, the tribunal may make the necessary order.

17.259 The requirement for the employment tribunal to explain its powers to award reinstatement or re-engagement is mandatory. However, if there is a failure to do so (and in practice many tribunals do so fail) this will not render any other award made a nullity. The order made without compliance with s 113 will only be set aside if the employee has been prejudiced, or if he has suffered an injustice, in consequence of the failure (*Cowley v Manson Timber Ltd*).

17.260 If the order is for reinstatement, the employer shall treat the employee in all respects as if he had not been dismissed, and the tribunal may specify the amount of arrears in pay payable to the employee, and rights and privileges, including seniority and pension rights, which must be restored to him, and the date by which the order must be complied with. If the employee would have benefited from an improvement in his terms and conditions of employment had he not been dismissed, the order shall require him to have those improvements. If the tribunal orders re-engagement, this is an order that the employee be re-engaged by the employer or by his successor, or an associated employer, in employment comparable to that from which he was dismissed, or other suitable employment. The tribunal will specify the terms on which the re-engagement will take place, stating the identity of the employer, the nature of the employment, the remuneration, any arrears of pay, any rights or privileges which must be restored to him (including seniority and pension rights) and the date by which the order must be complied with. If in either case the tribunal makes an order in respect of arrears of pay it will take into account (for the purpose of reducing the employer's liability) any sums received by the applicant between the date of dismissal and the date of reinstatement or re-engagement, by way of wages in lieu of notice, *ex gratia* payments, remuneration received from another employer, social security benefits, and any other benefits as the tribunal thinks appropriate.

17.261 It must be stressed that the tribunal has a discretion in making either of these orders. It must first consider whether to make an order for reinstatement, and in doing so, it must take into account three considerations:
a. whether the claimant wishes to be reinstated;
b. whether it is practicable for the employer to comply with an order for reinstatement;
c. where the claimant caused or contributed to some extent to the dismissal, whether it would be just to order his reinstatement.

If the tribunal decides not to make an order, it shall then consider whether to make an order for re-engagement, and if so, on what terms. Again, there are three considerations to take into account:
a. any wish expressed by the claimant as to the nature of the order;
b. whether it is practicable for the employer or his successor or an associated employer to comply with the order;

c.   where the claimant has caused or contributed to some extent to the dismissal, whether it would be just to order his re-engagement, and if so, on what terms (see *Boots Co plc v Lees-Collier*).

If a re–engagement order is made, it shall, so far as is reasonably practicable, be on terms which are as favourable as an order for reinstatement, unless the tribunal takes into account the contributory fault of the claimant.

17.262   The main restriction on making reinstatement or re-engagement orders appears to be the practicability of doing so. If a permanent replacement has been engaged in place of the dismissed employee, the tribunal shall not take this into account for the purpose of deciding whether it was practicable for the employer to comply with the order unless the employer shows:

a.   that it was not practicable for him to arrange for the dismissed employee's work to be done without engaging a permanent replacement; or

b.   that he engaged the replacement after the lapse of a reasonable time without having heard from the dismissed employee that he wished to be reinstated or re-engaged, and that when the employer engaged the replacement, it was no longer reasonable for him to arrange for the dismissed employee's work to be done except by a permanent replacement.

17.263   It is also submitted that earlier tribunal decisions on the impracticability of making reinstatement or re-engagement recommendations are still valid. For it should be noted that 'practicable' does not mean 'possible'. Thus the orders are unlikely to be made:

a.   if the dismissal was in a redundancy situation, or if reinstatement would result in redundancies (*Cold Drawn Tubes Ltd v Middleton*);

b.   the claimant is unfit for work (see *Rao v Civil Aviation Authority*); or

c.   if there is some friction or personal animosity either with the employer or with fellow-employees (*Coleman v Magnet Joinery Ltd*); or

d.   if the employer is a small firm, with few staff, reinstatement or re-engagement should only be ordered in exceptional circumstances, as there is a close personal relationship between the parties which may make such an order impracticable (*Enessy Co SA v Minoprio*); or

e.   if there is mistrust between the parties (*Nothman v London Borough of Barnet*); or

f.   if the order is likely to be ineffective (*ILEA v Gravett*); or

g.   if there has been a breakdown in trust or confidence between the employer and employee, eg if the dismissal was for alleged misconduct (*Wood Group Heavy Industrial Turbines Ltd v Crossan*); or

h.   if the employee's job has disappeared following a reorganisation (*Thamesdown Borough Council v Turrell*).

17.264   In other words, the practicability of ordering reinstatement or re-engagement must be looked at in a subjective and pragmatic sense, bearing in mind the particular circumstances of the case. The employer is entitled to give a logical and reasonable explanation why there are no vacancies, and to make a commercial judgment about the best interests of the business. An employment tribunal is not entitled to substitute its own views for those of management, provided the decision not to re-engage is in the bracket of reasonableness, for the test is whether it is practicable, not whether it is possible (*Port of London v Payne*). In practice, very few reinstatement or re-engagement orders are made, as very few applicants request this remedy.

17.265   If an employee is reinstated or re-engaged following an order to that effect from the employment tribunal, his continuity of employment is preserved, and the period between his dismissal and reinstatement or re-engagement counts towards his continuity (Employment Protection (Continuity of Employment) Regulations 1996). This also applies if reinstatement or re-engagement follows a compromise agreement, or action taken by a conciliation officer, or a claim based on a designated dismissal procedure or following an ACAS sponsored arbitration award.

B. Compensation awards (ss 117–125)

17.266   If the order for reinstatement or re-engagement is made, but its terms are not fully complied with, the tribunal may make an award of compensation of such an amount as it thinks fit having regard to the loss sustained by the claimant in consequence of the employer's failure to comply with those terms. If the order is made, but the applicant is not reinstated or re-engaged at all, then the tribunal will make an award of compensation. This will be under three headings:
a.   the basic award
b.   the compensatory award
c.   the additional award
If a reinstatement or re-engagement order is not made, then the tribunal shall make an award of compensation consisting of the basic award, the compensatory award and supplementary award, where appropriate.

17.267   *Basic award (i).* In two instances this will amount to two weeks' pay with a maximum of £230 per week. These are:
a.   Where the employee is dismissed for reason of redundancy, but is not entitled to a redundancy payment because of the operation of ERA s 138. This section states that an employee shall not be entitled to a redundancy payment if he unreasonably refuses the offer of alternative employment, or unreasonably terminates his new contract during the trial period of four weeks. Nonetheless, he is entitled to his basic award of two weeks' pay.
b.   If the employee is not entitled to be treated as having been dismissed by virtue of s 141 of ERA. This provides that an employee will not be regarded as being dismissed if there is a renewal of his contract or he is re-engaged under a new contract. Thus if a contract expires, and there is an offer of renewal or re-engagement, this can still amount to a dismissal (if for reason of redundancy) and if the employee chooses to so treat it, he is entitled to two weeks' pay.

17.268   *Basic award (ii).* In all other cases the amount of the basic award will depend on the number of years in respect of which the employee has been continuously employed (see Chapter 13), his normal week's pay (see Chapter 14) and his age. For those years of employment when the employee was 41 years old or more, he will be entitled to one and a half week's pay; in respect of employment when he was below the age of 41 but not below the age of 22, he will be entitled to one week's pay, and in respect of employment below the age of 22 (with no lower age limit) he will be entitled to a half of a week's pay. There is a maximum of 20 years' employment to be counted, and the amount of the week's pay to be calculated shall not exceed £230. Thus, the current maximum basic award is £6,900. If the employee is over the age of 64, there will be a reduction of one-twelfth in respect of each month over that age, and the entitlement to a basic award (but not the compensatory award) ceases altogether at the age of 65 (see Appendix B).

17.269 Where a dismissal has been held to be unfair on the grounds of trade union membership or non-membership (TULR(C)A s 156), or is a dismissal of a designated safety representative or member of a safety committee, or a trustee of an occupational pension scheme, or an employee representative for consultation purposes, the minimum basic award to be made shall be £3,100 (ERA s 120).

17.270 The amount of the basic award can be reduced in three circumstances (ERA s 122).

(a) If the employer has made an offer to reinstate the employee, so that in all respects he would be treated as if he had not been dismissed, and the employee unreasonably refuses that offer, the employment tribunal may reduce the basic award by an amount it thinks to be just and equitable. (Note that if the offer is made with different terms and conditions, an unreasonable refusal will not justify reducing the basic award, although it may be relevant to reduce the compensation award, because the employee has failed to mitigate his loss.)

(b) If the employee's conduct prior to the dismissal (or, where notice was given, before notice of dismissal) was such that it would be just and equitable to reduce (or further reduce) the basic award, the employment tribunal may do so. Normally, the conduct in question would have caused or contributed towards the dismissal, but this is not essential so far as the employment tribunal's powers under this section are concerned. Indeed, conduct which only comes to light after the dismissal (which occurred before the dismissal) may be grounds for reducing the basic award, eg if it is subsequently discovered that the employee had set up a rival business during his employment, or had been stealing from his employer. But misconduct during the notice period is not a ground for reducing the basic award, even though it would not be just and equitable to make that award, although it may be grounds for reducing the compensation award.

It is not permissible to make a reduction of the basic award on grounds of contributory conduct if the reason for the dismissal was redundancy, except in those cases where the dismissal was for an inadmissible reason (trade union membership or activities (TULR(C)A s 157), designated safety representatives (s 100), occupational pension scheme trustee (s 102), and employee representative (ss 101(A) and 103)), when the minimum basic award of £3,100 applies (s 120). In such cases, if the employee caused or contributed to the dismissal, there may be a reduction in the amount by which the minimum basic award exceeds the normal basic award (s 122(3)). Thus, assume that the employee's contribution towards the dismissal is assessed at 50 per cent, and his normal basic award would have been £920 (4 × £230). Since he is entitled to £3,100 by virtue of ERA s 120, the 50 per cent reduction is applied so as to reduce that amount by £1,090 (ie 50 per cent of £2,180). But if the conduct led to a selection for redundancy for trade union reasons (membership, non-membership or activities) no reduction can be made for contributory conduct (TULR(C)A s 155), eg if an employee was selected for redundancy because he refused to join a particular trade union.

(c) If an employee was dismissed for reason of redundancy, and was given a redundancy payment, the amount paid by the employer or awarded by a tribunal is to be deducted from the basic award. Normally, this would extinguish the basic award altogether, although if the employee commenced work before the age of 18, there could be a further award. But the fact that a redundancy payment was made will not extinguish the basic award if the real reason for the dismissal was not in fact redundancy (*Boorman v Allmakes Ltd*).

17.271   The entitlement to a basic award is automatic once a dismissal is held to be unfair, and cannot be reduced on the ground that there has been no financial loss to the claimant (*Cadbury Ltd v Doddington*). It is payable even if no compensation award is made (*British United Shoe Machinery Co Ltd v Clarke*). It cannot be reduced on the ground that the claimant has failed to mitigate against his loss, because there is no provision to this effect (*Lock v Connell Estate Agents*). Nor can it be reduced on the *Polkey* principle, ie on the ground that the employee would still have been dismissed had there been a proper investigation (*Taylor v John Webster Buildings Civil Engineering*). And it cannot be reduced when an *ex gratia* payment or a severance payment is made, unless it is made clear that the payment is in respect of all compensation an employee is entitled to should the employee subsequently bring a claim in an employment tribunal (*Chelsea Football Club and Athletic Co Ltd v Heath*). There is no requirement to make the same reduction in the basic and compensatory awards on the grounds of contributory conduct (*Optikinetics Ltd v Whooley*).

C. Compensatory award (ERA s 123)

17.272   This award will be such amount as the employment tribunal considers just and equitable in all the circumstances, having regard to the loss sustained by the claimant in consequence of the dismissal, in so far as that loss is attributable to action taken by the employer, including any expenses reasonably incurred by him, and the loss of any benefits which he might reasonably have expected to have had (ERA s 123(1)). Once an employment tribunal finds blameworthy conduct on the part of the employee which brought about his dismissal, it must reduce the compensation award by some proportion, under the just and equitable rule (*Optikinetics Ltd v Whooley*).

17.273   Under the 'just and equitable rule' the employment tribunal has a wide discretion, even so far as awarding nil compensation in appropriate cases (*W Devies & Sons Ltd v Atkins*). For example, in *Courage Take Home Trade Ltd v Keys*, the claimant accepted in sum in settlement of his claim, but then continued with proceedings for unfair dismissal, because, as the settlement did not involve ACAS, it was not binding. The employment tribunal did not think it was just and equitable to make a compensatory award, and declined to do so. If, after the dismissal, it is discovered that the employee had been guilty of conduct before the dismissal which would have merited dismissal, then it may not be just and equitable to award full or any compensation (*W Devies & Sons Ltd v Atkins*), but post-termination conduct should not be taken into account (*Soros v Davison*). Similarly, if a dismissal was unfair because of the failure to follow a correct procedure, but would have been fair had that procedure been followed, then it cannot be just and equitable to award compensation to an employee who has in practice suffered no injustice (*Polkey v A E Dayton Services Ltd*). If a redundancy dismissal is unfair because of the lack of consultation, the employment tribunal should assess the likelihood of there being a fair dismissal had there been proper consultation, and make an appropriate award on that basis (*Mining Supplies (Longwall) Ltd v Baker*).

17.274 There is no limit on the amount of a week's pay for the purpose of calculating the financial loss, although there is a statutory maximum limit on the compensatory award of £50,000 (which can be exceeded if an additional award is made: see below). If the reason for the dismissal was because the employee acted as a health and safety representative (ERA s 100) or because he made a protected disclosure (ERA s 103A), or if he was selected for redundancy for either of those reasons, there is no limit on the amount of the compensatory award. The employment tribunal must assess the compensatory award judicially, and specify how it is made up, but they can, and do, use a 'broad brush' approach (*Norton Tool Co Ltd v Tewson*). Only financial loss may be taken into account, for the object is to compensate the claimant, not to punish the employer for his wrong behaviour. The manner of dismissal cannot be the subject of a compensatory award, unless there is evidence that this has caused financial loss, eg if it affected the claimant's reputation, making him less attractive to future employers. Thus, unlike awards made in discrimination cases, no award can be made for injured feelings. It follows that if the claimant has lost nothing, eg if he has obtained other employment immediately, no award under this head can be made. The assessment of past losses should not be too difficult, but, when assessing future losses, the employment tribunal must inevitably indulge in a form of speculation. The burden of proof is on the employee to show the past and/or future loss, but this should not prove to be an onerous task in practice (*Adda International Ltd v Curcio*).

17.275 Generally speaking, there are six headings to consider.

17.276 *(a) Immediate loss of earnings.* The immediate loss is the loss incurred between the date the employment was terminated and the date when the employment tribunal assess the loss. In some cases, a considerable time may have elapsed between these two dates, while issues of procedure and/or liability are being argued. Nonetheless, if the employment tribunal feel that the claimant has taken reasonable steps to mitigate his loss, the length of time which may have elapsed is irrelevant (*Gilham v Kent County Council (No 3)*). The claimant's loss is assessed by reference to the net pay he would have received, although bonuses, overtime pay and pay increases can be taken into account, had these been likely (*Mullet v Brush Electrical Machines Ltd*). Tips which form part of normal remuneration (*Palmanor Ltd v Cedron*), expenses, to the extent they represent a profit in the hands of the employee (*S and U Stores v Wilkes*), and the loss of the opportunity to obtain an enhanced redundancy payment (*Lee v IPC Business Press Ltd*) are all part of the loss suffered. The loss of private use of a company car can be valued either by using the annual tables produced by the AA or RAC, or using the Inland Revenue calculations. Free or subsidised accommodation, private medical insurance, subsidised mortgage schemes (*UBAF Bank Ltd v Davis*), luncheon vouchers, are all benefits the value of which can be calculated.

17.277 If, at the time when the employment tribunal assess the loss, the employee has obtained fresh employment with the same or a lower earnings, those earnings can be offset when assessing the net loss. A problem may arise if the employee obtains employment which is better paid, because then compensation will be based on his loss during the period of unemployment, but the excess between his old and new salary also falls to be deducted (*Ging v Ellward Lancs Ltd*). However, because this can lead to an unfair result on occasions, the employment tribunal may fall back on the 'just and equitable' principle, and ignore this rule, particularly when there has been a long period of time between the dismissal and the date when compensation is assessed (*Fentiman v Fluid Engineering Products Ltd*). The principles to be adopted in these circumstances were set out by the EAT in *Whelan v Richardson*, where it was held that loss of earnings should be calculated from the date of dismissal up to the date when the applicant obtains higher paid permanent employment. Similarly, credit must be given in respect of earnings from self-employment (*Justfern Ltd v D'Ingerthorpe*).

17.278 Income support and/or jobseekers' allowance is not deducted at this stage, but are subject to the recoupment provisions (see para 17.321). There are conflicting authorities on how invalidity benefit received should be treated (compare *Rubenstein v McGloughlin* and *Puglia v C James & Sons*), but the better view appears to be that it is correct to deduct the amount of invalidity benefit received from the compensation award (*Chan v London Borough of Hackney*). Housing benefit is differently treated, and should not be deducted (*Savage v Saxena*). Money received under an early retirement scheme or ill-health retirement scheme is not to be deducted (*Smoker v London Fire & Civil Defence Authority*).

17.279 If an employee is dismissed without notice and without pay in lieu of notice, but nonetheless finds work within what would have been the statutory notice period, he is still entitled to receive compensation for that period, because that is a legal entitlement, not to be deducted from the compensatory award (*TBA Industrial Products Ltd v Locke*). But if the employee's notice period would have been particularly long (eg on the premature termination of a fixed-term contract), the additional notice period will not be added to the compensatory award, on the ground that the employee should have mitigated against his loss (*Vaughan v Weighpack Ltd*). If the employee is dismissed without notice but given his proper entitlement in lieu of notice, credit for this sum must be given (*Addison v Babcock FATA Ltd*), although the EAT in Scotland appear to have come to a different conclusion on this point (*Finnie v Top Hat Frozen Foods*).

17.280 *Ex gratia* payments should always be offset, to the extent that these exceed the basic award (*Horizon Holidays Ltd v Grassi*), as should severance payments (*Darr v LRC Products Ltd*). Income tax rebates received by the employee during his period of unemployment should be ignored unless there are substantial sums involved (*MBS Ltd v Calo*).

17.281 *(b) Future loss.* The employment tribunal must estimate the likely future loss, inevitably by indulging in speculation. They can take into account all the relevant circumstances, eg the age of the applicant and his general employability, his personal circumstances, his health (*Fougère v Phoenix Motors*), local employment conditions, the scarcity of jobs in a particular trade, industry, the current economic climate (*MacNeilgae v Arthur Roye Ltd*) and so on. They must form a judgment as to how long it will be before the claimant obtains comparable employment (*Courtaulds Northern Spinning Ltd v Moosa*). There is no objection, in theory, to consider making an award for the rest of the claimant's working life (see *Morganite Electrical Carbon Ltd v Donne*) although the existence of a maximum award of £50,000 will inevitably come into play at some point. If a claimant has become self-employed, future loss can be estimated to a point when he establishes an income comparable with that he has lost. As a general rule, the more senior the employee, the longer it may take him to obtain fresh employment, but the whole exercise is speculative. Compensation may also be awarded to take account of the fact that the claimant may have continued working beyond normal retiring age or the age of 65, as long as his dismissal took place before those dates (*Barrel Plating and Phosphating Co Ltd v Danks*). Of course, when assessing future loss, the employment tribunal will already have at its disposal much of the information needed on past losses, and will merely be projecting those losses forward for a period of time. Thus if the employee obtained new employment after the date of dismissal at a higher rate of pay, the employment tribunal should calculate the compensatory award from the date of the dismissal up to the date when the new employment commenced, and not up to the date when the tribunal makes the award (*Whelan v Richardson*, but see *Dench v Flynn & Partners*, below).

17.282 If the employment tribunal has evidence which would lead to the conclusion that the claimant would have lost his job anyway at some point in time, eg because of the redundancy situation, then that is a factor which should be taken into account when assessing the past and future loss of earnings (*Young's of Gosport Ltd v Kendell*). Equally, a supervening event, eg illness, which arises after the dismissal, and which causes the claimant to be out of work for a long time, is not a loss which is attributable to the action taken by the employer. But if the illness was brought on to some extent by the employer's action, that is a matter which an employment tribunal can take into account, for a certain period of time, at least (*Devine v Designer Flowers Wholesale Florist Sundries Ltd*). Also, if a claimant decides to take himself out of the labour market altogether and change his career by going on a retraining course (*Simrad Ltd v Scott* distinguished in *Khanum v IBC Vehicles*), the period in question cannot be the subject of compensation. Nor can losses which arise after the completion of the course be taken into account (*Holroyd v Gravure Cylinders Ltd*).

17.283 Since the employment tribunal is projecting the claimant's loss into the future, there is authority for the proposition that the employer should receive a discount for accelerated payment, of between 5–10 per cent (*York Trailer Co Ltd v Sparkes*), although it has been suggested that this brings into the calculations a complication which should not be introduced (*Les Ambassadeurs Club v Bainda*). Losses which are too remote from the employer's actions should also be excluded. For example, if the claimant obtained permanent employment, that is a fact which will normally break the chain of causation, so that if he has lost that employment at the time when the employment tribunal is assessing compensation, the subsequent period of unemployment is not a future loss which could have been contemplated (*Courtaulds Northern Spinning Ltd v Moosa*). But this rule is not one of universal application, for the ultimate duty of the employment tribunal is to make an award which is just and equitable (see *Dench v Flynn & Partners*, below). There is also an overlap between the question of remoteness and the claimant's duty to mitigate against his loss, which can usually be resolved by the application of the 'just and equitable' principle (*Simrad Ltd v Scott*).

17.284 *(c) Expenses.* The employment tribunal may award to the claimant any expenses reasonably incurred by him in consequence of the unfair dismissal. This could include money spent seeking fresh employment, eg on travelling to interviews, on buying-selling a home into order to obtain employment in a different area, or on setting up a new business (*Gardener-Hill v Roland Berger Technics Ltd*). However, legal expenses incurred in the bringing of the employment tribunal proceedings cannot be awarded under this heading, although there is a residue power for the employment tribunal to make an award of costs in appropriate cases (see para 20.126).

17.285 *(d) Loss of statutory rights.* Since it will take some time before a claimant is employed in a new job long enough to obtain the benefit of a number of statutory rights, (in particular, he will have to wait for a further year before he is protected against a future unfair dismissal), the employment tribunals will usually award a modest sum of £200 by way of compensation for this loss (*S H Muffett Ltd v Head*). Also, in the case of a claimant who had a long period of service with his former employer, it is possible to make an award in respect of the loss of the right to have a long period of statutory notice (*Arthur Guinness Son & Co (Great Britain) Ltd v Green*).

17.286 *(e) Loss of pension rights.* The loss suffered by a claimant under this heading will sometimes depend on the type of pension scheme, ie final salary scheme or money purchase scheme. The former scheme does not depend on contributions to the fund by the employer and/or employee, whereas the latter schemes are so dependent. So far as the compensatory award is concerned, a claimant may have lost (a) pension rights accruing to him since the dismissal (b) future pension rights, and (c) the loss of enhancement of accrued pension rights. To assist in resolving and quantifying the loss, reference may be made to the Government's Actuary's Guidelines *Industrial Tribunals–Compensation for loss of pension rights*. Obviously, if his pension is 'portable' his loss will be minimal.

17.287 *(f) Preventing the operation of an appeal procedure.* If the employment tribunal finds that the employer had a procedure for appealing against dismissal, but he prevented the employee from using it, a supplementary award may be made, of such amount as the employment tribunal considers to be just and equitable, not exceeding two weeks' pay (ERA s 127A).

D. Reducing the compensatory award (ERA s 123(4), (6))

(a) Mitigation of loss
17.288 A dismissed employee is under a duty to mitigate against his loss so far as possible (*Scottish and Newcastle Breweries plc v Halliday*). This means that he should take reasonable steps to obtain other employment, taking into account his skills, personal circumstances, health, etc (*Fourgère v Phoenix Motor Co Ltd*). Whether a claimant has taken such reasonable steps is a question of fact in each case (*Gardener-Hill v Rolands Berger Technics Ltd*). Thus, if an employer changes his mind about a dismissal, or recognises that it is unfair, and offers reinstatement or re-engagement on suitable terms which the employee unreasonably refuses, this may indicate that he has not taken reasonable steps to mitigate against his loss, and compensation may be reduced accordingly (*Hepworths Ltd v Comerford*). A failure by an employee to invoke an internal appeals machinery is not a failure to mitigate against the loss (*William Muir (Bond 9) Ltd v Lamb*), for the rules relating to mitigation apply to conduct after the dismissal

(*McAndrew v Prestwick Circuits Ltd*). However, that failure may now fall to be considered under the provisions contained in ERA s 127A (see below).

17.289 The burden of proof lies on the employer to show that the claimant has failed to mitigate against his loss (*Fyfe v Scientific Furnishing Ltd*). An employment tribunal is not bound to consider this heading unless it is raised by the employer, along with some supporting evidence. The employment tribunal should identify the steps taken to mitigate the loss, find the date by which such steps would have produced an alternative income, and then reduce the amount of compensation by the amount of income which would have been earned (*Savage v Saxena*).

17.290 If the employer provides a procedure for appealing against dismissal, and the claimant was given (at the time of the dismissal or within a reasonable time afterwards) written notice of its existence and details of it, but the claimant chose not to utilise it, the employment tribunal may reduce the compensatory award by such amount as it considers to be just and equitable, up to a maximum of two weeks' pay (ERA s 127A).

(b) Contributory conduct

17.291 Where an employment tribunal finds that the dismissal was to any extent caused or contributed to by any action of the claimant, it shall reduce the amount of the compensatory award by such proportion as it thinks just and equitable, having regard to that finding (ERA s 123(6)). In *Nelson v BBC (No 2)*, the Court of Appeal stated that there are three matters which must be taken into account under this heading. First, the action of the employee must be culpable or blameworthy; second, that action must have caused or contributed towards the dismissal; and, third, it must be just and equitable to reduce the compensatory award by the specified proportion. For example, in *Scottish CWS v Lloyd* a dismissal was held to be unfair because no specific warnings had been given to the claimant. But he had failed to reply to complaints which had been made against him, failed to obey certain instructions, and failed to achieve a modest sales target. All these factors were held to be conduct which contributed towards the dismissal and were therefore grounds for reducing the compensatory award. A failure to follow works rules, using company property for private purposes, unco-operative conduct, failure to apologise for wrongful acts (eg swearing at a manager), failure to explain unauthorised absences, a refusal to give an explanation for certain conduct, failing to return to work on time after holidays, and so on, have all been held to be grounds for reducing the compensatory award.

17.292 Since the conduct must in some way be blameworthy or culpable, matters which are beyond the employee's control, eg ill health (*Slaughter v C Brewer & Sons Ltd*) ought not to be taken into account. Similarly, an employee who is incompetent or incapable does not contribute to his dismissal, provided he is trying his best (*Kraft Food Ltd v Fox*), although if an employee is lazy, indolent, or does not make an effort to improve or avoid errors, he does so contribute. Further, the conduct in question does not have to be the main reason for the dismissal; it is sufficient (for the purpose of reducing the compensatory award) for it to have played a material part in the dismissal (*Robert Whiting Designs Ltd v Lamb*). A senior employee who is dismissed for serious misconduct must expect to have his compensatory award reduced substantially, for a higher standard of conduct is expected from him (*McPhail v Gibson*).

17.293 It is unlikely that the employment tribunal would reduce the compensatory award in cases of constructive dismissal, but there is no reason in principle why this cannot be done, because the employee's conduct may have played a material part in the events which led to his resignation (*Morrison v Amalgamated Transport and General Workers' Union*). For example, in *Polentarutti v Autokraft Ltd*, the employee machined a number of defective hub-caps. Subsequently, the employer refused to pay him for working overtime, and he resigned, claiming constructive dismissal. Although his dismissal was held to be unfair, the employment tribunal reduced the compensatory award by two-thirds on the ground that his poor workmanship contributed to the dismissal. The EAT dismissed an appeal by the employee, holding that there was a sufficient link between the events in question which justified a reduction in the award.

17.294 If a claimant was dismissed on the ground of his non-membership of a trade union, no reduction can be made in the compensatory award because he refused to join a trade union (see *T & GWU v Howard*). Nor can a reduction be made if the dismissal was because of his trade union membership or activities (TULR(C)A s 155). If an employee is dismissed because he took part in a strike, and it is subsequently held that that dismissal was unfair on ground of selective re-engagement (see para 21.105), a reduction for contributory conduct should not be made merely because he took part in the strike. It is only where there was some individual blameworthy conduct additional to or separate from the participation in industrial action that the employment tribunal should consider reducing the compensatory award (*Crosville Wales Ltd v Tracey*).

17.295 Contributory conduct has resulted in some cases with a reduction as high as 80–90 per cent, and for some time there was doubt as to whether it was a proper reduction to make, because there appears to be a logical inconsistency in saying that an employee was treated unfairly, and yet contributed to that extent towards his dismissal. However, in *Maris v Rotherham Corpn* the House of Lords thought that there was no particular problem in finding a dismissal unfair, yet reducing the compensatory award by 100 per cent. Compensation should only be awarded when it is just and equitable to do so, and it cannot be just to award compensation when the employee was totally responsible for his dismissal. Nor is there an inconsistency in finding a dismissal unfair yet not awarding compensation; a nil award or nominal compensation may be appropriate when the only reason a dismissal was unfair was a failure to follow the correct procedure, as laid down in the code of practice.

17.296 The assessment of the percentage reduction to be taken into account because of contributory conduct is essentially a question of fact, to be determined by the employment tribunal (*Hollier v Plysu Ltd*).

(c) Remoteness of loss

17.297 The tribunal must compensate the employee for the loss caused by the employer's wrongful conduct. That loss does not cease when the employee finds new alternative employment, because it is quite possible for the loss to continue. Thus, if the new employment is at a lower rate of pay, or is of a temporary nature, or entails additional expense by way of travel, relocation etc, these factors can be taken into account when assessing the compensation. In *Dench v Flynn & Partners*, the claimant was unfairly dismissed. She obtained employment with another firm but this only lasted for two months. The Court of Appeal held that the tribunal was wrong to limit the compensation award up to the time when she had obtained the new employment. The question was whether her losses were attributable to her unfair dismissal.

17.298 If an employee decides not to seek other employment, but to make a career change by going on a training course a tribunal may take the view that this is a reasonable course to take, having regard to the employee's age, the state of the employment market, the level of remuneration, the viability of the course, etc. However, there may well come a point in time when the loss suffered by the employee is too remote from the employer's wrongful action. Thus in *Simrad Ltd v Scott* an electronics technician was unfairly dismissed. She decided to change career and took a course in nursing. Although the tribunal thought that she had acted reasonably in taking up a new career, the EAT held that compensation was not payable from the time she commenced the nursing course, because this was too remote to be attributed to the actions of the employer.

17.299 In some cases, it may well be reasonable for the employee to become self-employed, and this should not be held against him, when weighed against his employment prospects generally. In *Gardiner-Hill v Roland Berger Technics* a 55 year-old managing director acted reasonably in setting up his own specialised business. Clearly, his initial loss was greater than if he had attempted to obtain immediate employment, but the loss was not too remote, although it could not be expected to go on indefinitely! Expenses reasonably incurred in setting up a new business are not too remote, but again, a sensible limit should be imposed.

E. Order of deductions

17.300 In order to arrive at the final compensatory award, the employment tribunal must arrange any deductions in the correct order, bearing in mind the principle that an employer must be given full credit for any payments made by him which are in excess of the basic award. Thus, in *Digital Equipment Co Ltd v Clements*, the employee was dismissed for reason of redundancy, and given a severance payment which exceeded his statutory redundancy entitlement by £20,500. An employment tribunal found that his dismissal was unfair because of the lack of consultation, but went on to hold that had there been a fair procedure, there was a 50 per cent chance that he would have still been made redundant. His total loss of earnings was assessed at £43,000.

The employment tribunal calculated the award as follows:

	£
Total loss of earnings	43,126
Deduct payment made	20,685
Loss	22,451
Less 50%	11,225
Net loss	11,250

Applying the then statutory limit, the employment tribunal made an award of £11,000. On appeal, that figure was reduced by the EAT, using a different method of calculation, but on review, the award was restored. However, the Court of Appeal reversed the decision, holding that full credit had to be given to an employer for any payments made. The correct order of calculation was as follows:

	£
Total loss of earnings	43,136
Less 50%	21,568
Loss	21,568
Less payment made	20,685
Net loss	£883

Thus, the total loss is to be assessed, the percentage reduction applied (whether under the *Polkey* principle or on grounds of contributory conduct or failure to mitigate), ex gratia payments are then deducted, and the balance will be awarded to the applicant, subject to the statutory maximum.

17.301 A payment in lieu of notice should be deducted before compensation is proportionately reduced on the ground of contributory conduct (*Heggie v Uniroyal Englebert Tyres Ltd*).

17.302 It is now clear that although a severance payment cannot be used to reduce the basic award, it must be used to reduce the employer's liability in respect of the compensatory award. Otherwise, those employers who made *ex gratia* payments would suffer further financial loss, and thus be deterred from following good industrial relations practice in making such payments.

17.303 *Additional award.* It will be recalled that if an employer totally ignores a tribunal order to reinstate or re-engage the employee, an additional award can be made. This order should not be made if the employer satisfied the tribunal that it was not practicable to comply with the order, but since the tribunal will have already considered this point when making the order (see above) it will presumably be open to the employer to adduce new evidence as to why it is not practicable to do so. Otherwise, if re-engagement or reinstatement is ordered and not complied with, and the reason for the dismissal was because of race, sex or disability discrimination, or victimisation for trade union membership, employee representation, pension scheme trustee, breach of working time provisions, or health and safety reasons, there will be an additional award of between 26 and 52 weeks' pay. A week's pay for the purpose of the additional award shall not exceed £230.

17.304 However, in the case of a highly-paid employee, or where proceedings have been considerably delayed, the total of the maximum of the basic, compensatory and additional awards may not be adequate to meet the loss actually suffered and it may be cheaper not to comply with the reinstatement order. In such cases, s 124(3) of ERA enables an employment tribunal to make a compensation award which is at least equal to the amount of pay lost between the date of dismissal and what should have been the date of reinstatement or re-engagement, to show their disapproval of the employer's decision (see *George v Beecham Group*), at the same time taking into account the employee's conduct and failure to mitigate against his loss (*Mabirizi v National Hospital for Nervous Diseases*).

17.305–17.310 Severence payments made may be deducted from the additional award to the extent that the basic and compensatory awards are exceeded (*Darr v LRC Products Ltd*).

Interest on awards

17.311   By the Employment Tribunals (Interest) Order 1990, interest is payable on all tribunal awards (but not the recoupment element) after 42 days from the date the decision is recorded and sent to the parties. Interest is also payable on awards made by the EAT. Any award by way of costs or expenses is excluded. If on a review or appeal the award is varied, interest accrues on the amount as varied. However, by the Employment Tribunals (Interest on Awards in Discrimination Cases) Regulations 1996, interest on awards made in respect of injury to feelings may be made from the date of the act of discrimination to which the complaint relates.

17.312–17.320   The rate of interest is the rate currently prescribed under the Court Funds Rules 1987 and the Act of Sederunt (Interest in Sheriff Court Decrees or Extracts) 1975.

Recoupment of unemployment benefit

17.321   Under the heading of the compensation award, a sum of money is ascertained as the loss suffered, and the tribunal will then deduct from that sum the amount of job seekers' allowance which the claimant has received. In fact, this amounts to the Government providing a subsidy to the employers, and thus regulations have been passed enabling the Government to recoup this money from the employer (see Employment Protection (Recoupment of Jobseekers' Allowance and Income Support) Regulations 1996). The consequence is that the tribunal must ascertain the prescribed element (which is the gross loss of earnings from the date of dismissal until the date of the hearing), and this may be withheld from the claimant until the Secretary of State has served a notice on the respondent to pay the whole or part of the prescribed element to the Department. When this has been received, the Secretary of State will pay to the claimant the sum due less the job seekers' allowance he has received. Recoupment only applies in respect of the period for which compensation is assessed (*Hosnan v Al Baca Ltd*).

17.322   Recoupment does not apply when a settlement is reached without a tribunal hearing, because private settlements (with or without the assistance of the conciliation officer) are not within the scope of the regulations.

CHAPTER 18

Redundancy

18.1 The basic purpose of the Redundancy Payments Act 1965 was to compensate a long-serving employee for the loss of a right which he has in a job. There may be other benefits or advantages, such as the need to encourage mobility of labour, redistribute economic skills, and assist in the process of rationalisation of resources, but whether such objects are being achieved must be a matter for the economist rather than the lawyer. The compensation paid is in respect of the loss suffered, and is not intended as a benefit to tide the redundant employee over a period of difficulty. Thus if a person is made redundant, he is entitled to his payment even if he obtains employment elsewhere immediately; similarly, he is entitled to job seekers' allowance in addition to his redundancy money.

18.2–18.10 The Act has been repealed and replaced by corresponding provisions in the Employment Rights Act 1996, and in this chapter appropriate references will be made to the latter Act. The provisions relating to collective redundancies are to be found in the Trade Union and Labour Relations (Consolidation) Act 1992 as amended.

Persons covered by the Act

18.11 The Act applies to 'employees', ie persons who have entered into a contract of service or apprenticeship. In order to qualify generally, the employee must have at least two years' continuous employment with that employer (but see Redundancy Payments (Continuity of Employment in Local Government, etc) (Modification) Order 1999, and Redundancy Payments (National Health Service) (Modification) Order 1993, which make provisions for continuity of employment for certain local government and health service employees who move from one employer to another).

18.12–18.20 The usual problem arises with the definition of the term 'employee', illustrated, perhaps, by *Challinor v Taylor* (see para 2.81), which shows one of the disadvantages of being self-employed. A partner is not an employee for redundancy purposes (*Burgess v O'Brien*), nor is a clergyman working at a Mission (*Parker v Orr*). A managing director or director of a company who has executive responsibilities may claim if he has a service contract, but in *Buchan v Secretary of State for Employment* it was held that a person who is a controlling shareholder of a company is always able to block his dismissal, and therefore he cannot be an employee for redundancy payment purposes. Nor does the appointment of a receiver alter the position, because if he was not an employee before that appointment, he cannot be one by reason of the appointment. It follows that the Secretary of State was not obliged to make a redundancy payment out of the National Insurance Fund to the controlling director of a company which went into receivership. The EAT further suggested that *Lee v Lee's Air Farming Ltd* (see para 2.14) could not be relied on in the context of employment protection legislation to support the view that a controlling shareholder of a company could also be an employee of that company. A person may pay a self-employed insurance stamp, and yet be regarded as an employee, for, as we have already seen, this fact is not conclusive evidence as to the true status. The matter is one to be decided in each case on its own special facts.

What is dismissal? (s 136)

18.21 A dismissal takes place if:
a. the employer terminates the contract (with or without notice);
b. a fixed term contract expires without being renewed;
c. the employee terminates the contract with or without notice in circumstances which are such that he is entitled to do so by reason of the employer's conduct (*Millbrook Furnishing Industries Ltd v McIntosh*); and
d. the employment is terminated by the death, dissolution, liquidation of the employer, or the appointment of a receiver.

18.22 We have seen in Chapter 3 that a variation of a contract may amount to a new agreement. If the variation is accepted by both sides, then there is no dismissal, and continuity of employment is preserved. But a variation unilaterally imposed by the employer may amount to a dismissal. In *Marriott v Oxford and District Co-operative Society (No 2)*, a foreman was told that he would be employed at a lower status and at a reduced rate of pay. This was held to be a dismissal. If the employee accepts the changed situation for a short time under protest there will still be a dismissal, though clearly there will come a point when he will be deemed to have accepted the change if he continues in employment. If the express or implied terms of the contract permit a variation, then no dismissal takes place if the employer exercises his rights thereunder. In *McCaffrey v EE Jeavons & Co Ltd* an express term of the contract stated that the employee should work anywhere in the United Kingdom. He was asked to move from Bristol to Reading, but he refused. His subsequent resignation was held not to amount to a dismissal.

18.23 If the employer and employee mutually agree to 'part company' this will not be a dismissal, unless there is a clear intention to this effect. But the fact that a contract specifically states that it can only be determined by mutual consent or with appropriate notice does not mean that if appropriate notice has not been given it must have been determined by mutual consent (*Hellyer Bros v Atkinson*). For example, some employers may call for 'volunteers' to be made redundant, and they will qualify for payments despite their willingness to be dismissed (*Burton, Allton and Johnson Ltd v Peck*) but a mutual agreement whereby the employee accepts terms for early retirement does not constitute a dismissal (*Birch and Humber v University of Liverpool*).

18.24 If an employee is told that there may be possible redundancies in the future, he may be penalised if he acts precipitously. In *Morton Sundour Fabrics Ltd v Shaw* a foreman was warned of impending redundancies, and he left the firm to take other employment. His initiative went unrewarded, for it was held that as he had not been dismissed, he was not entitled to a redundancy payment (see also *International Computers v Kennedy*).

18.25 As long as the employee is on the books of the firm, he is still employed, even though he is not working or not being paid. In *Marshall v Harland and Wolff Ltd* the employee was absent from work for 18 months because of illness. The company then decided to close down the works, and gave him four weeks' notice of dismissal. It was held that he was nonetheless entitled to a redundancy payment, for the employers had not discharged the burden of showing that the contract had come to an end by virtue of frustration through illness.

18.26–18.30 An employer may dismiss an employee with appropriate notice. If, during the period of that notice, the employee gives a written counter-notice, stating that he intends to leave before the notice expires, the employee is still regarded as having been dismissed. However, the employer is not bound to accept the counter-notice, and may (again in writing) inform the employee before the end of the counter-notice that he does not accept it, and require him to work until the expiry of the original period of notice. The sanction is that the employer may contest the redundancy payment, and the tribunal has power to reduce it either in whole or in part, as it thinks just and equitable. On the other hand, if there is a mutual agreement that the employee may leave early, this constitutes a variation of the employer's notice, not a consensual termination of the contract (see para 18.22). The employee, therefore, will still be regarded as having been dismissed. (*McAlwane v Boughton Estates Ltd*).

Dismissal for reason of redundancy (s 139)

18.31 For a claim to be made, the employee must be dismissed for reason of redundancy. In *Sanders v Ernest A Neale Ltd* employees went on a work-to-rule campaign in protest against management actions. The employers sacked them, and eventually the factory closed down. It was held that they were not entitled to redundancy payments. They were dismissed because they would not give an undertaking to work normally, and the dismissals caused the redundancy, rather than the redundancy bringing about the dismissals (see *Baxter v Limb Group of Companies*, para 21.107). There is a statutory presumption (s 163(2)) that if an employee is dismissed, it is presumed to have been for the reason of redundancy unless the contrary is proved. The burden of proof is on the employer to show the reason, and if none is forthcoming, or if the tribunal does not accept the reason as a genuine one, the statutory presumption will arise. However, if the employer does show a reason other than redundancy, the question may arise as to whether the dismissal was fair or unfair, but there will be no liability to redundancy payments.

18.32 A dismissal shall be for reason of redundancy if it is wholly or mainly attributable to:
a. the fact that the employer has ceased, or intends to cease, to carry on that business for the purposes for which the employee was employed; or

b. the employer has ceased or intends to cease to carry on that business in the place where the employee was employed; or

c. the fact that the requirements of that business for employees to carry out work of a particular kind, or for them to carry out that work in the place where they were so employed, have ceased or diminished or are expected to cease or diminish.

A. Cessation of business

18.33 This is a recognisable situation which produces a few legal problems. In *Gemmell v Darngavil Brickworks Ltd* the firm closed down temporarily for a period of 13 weeks so that repairs could be carried out, and the dismissed employees were held to be redundant, as a temporary cessation is within the meaning of the Act. If the part of the business where the employee works is closed down, but the rest of the business (in its corporate sense) carries on, there is still a cessation of the business.

B. The employer moving his place of business

18.34 Section 139(1)(a)(ii) provides that a dismissal shall be for reason of redundancy if it is due to the fact that the employer has ceased to carry on business in the place where the employee was employed. According to a recent decision of the EAT, this is a factual matter, not a contractual one. In other words, the test to be applied is where, in fact, the employee worked, not where, under his contract, he was required to work. Thus in *Bass Leisure Ltd v Thomas*, the employee worked from the company's depot in Coventry. It was then decided to close the depot, and transfer it to a suburb of Birmingham, some 20 miles away. Her contract stated that the employer reserved the right to transfer her to any other alternative place of work in order to meet the needs of the business. After working from the new depot for a short while, she found that it involved too much travelling, and she resigned, claiming a redundancy payment. The EAT held that the place where she was employed was at Coventry, and that her contractual terms were evidential in defining the place of her employment. However, it was not permissible to take into account those terms which permitted a variation of the place of employment. The EAT also held that earlier decisions, which take into account mobility clauses (eg *UKAEA v Claydon*) were not to be followed. This view has been given the approval of the Court of Appeal in *High Table Ltd v Horst*, where it was stated that the true test is a factual one, to be determined by the circumstances, and the fact that there was a mobility clause in the contract did not mean that 'the place where the employee was employed' extended to every place where he could be employed. If an employee only worked at one location for the purpose of his employer's business, the place where he was employed cannot be extended merely because there was a mobility clause. However, if an employee worked in different places, the contract would be helpful in determining the extent of the place where he was employed.

However, the test of the suitability of alternative work (see below) would still need to be met.

18.35 If the employer moves his place of work, whether the move is sufficient to constitute a redundancy situation will be a question of fact, depending on the distance between the old and the new premises, and the resultant inconvenience caused to the employees affected. In *Managers (Holborn) Ltd v Hohne*, the claimant was the manageress of premises in Holborn. The company decided to move its premises to Regent Street, a short distance away. It was held that it could not be said that there was an implied term in her contract that she would only work in Holborn. Both premises were in Central London, and easily accessible. To hold that the employers had broken the contract would mean that it would have been a breach had the employers moved just around the corner, even though the claimant's work or her travel had been completely unaffected.

C. Surplus labour

18.36   In this situation the employer requires fewer employees for existing work (*Carry All Motors Ltd v Pennington*), or there is less work for existing employees (*Chapman v Goonvean and Rostowrack China Clay Co*), and consequently some are redundant. The redundancy can arise because the work has been re-organised, thus requiring fewer employees to do the same work, or because of the introduction of labour-saving devices, or a change in the work pattern which requires the same number of employees but a different kind of skill, or one to whom different terms and conditions of employment will apply. But the time of day in which the work is to be performed does not make it 'work of a particular kind' so that if there is a reduction in the need for night workers, who are thus transferred to day working, this does not amount to a redundancy. In *Johnson v Nottinghamshire Combined Police Authority*, clerks were employed from 9.30 am to 5.30 pm. It was decided to introduce a shift system whereby they would work from 8.00 am to 3.00 pm and from 1.00 pm to 8.00 pm in alternate weeks. The clerks refused to do the shift work, and were dismissed. It was held that the change in the hours was to promote greater efficiency, and they were not entitled to redundancy payments (see also *Barnes v Gilmartin Associates*).

18.37   This reasoning was confirmed by the Court of Appeal in *Lesney Products & Co Ltd v Nolan*, where the company reorganised its working hours so that instead of the employees working one long day shift plus overtime, they were required to work two day shifts. Employees were offered work on the double day shift, and those who refused were dismissed. It was held that they were not entitled to redundancy payments. A redundancy only arises if there is a change in the terms and conditions of employment due to the fact that the employer's need for work of a particular kind is ceasing or diminishing. A reorganisation of work which results in reduced earning does not produce a redundancy situation if there is still the need for the same number of employees doing the same overall work, and the only change is that they earn less wages. The law should not inhibit the ability of the employer to reorganise the workforce so as to improve efficiency. The fact that overtime is reduced does not create a redundancy, if the employer's requirements for the work to be done, and the employees to do the work, are the same as before. But if an employee is on a temporary contract, which is not renewed, this can be a redundancy, even though it is known at the time of his appointment that there would be no work for him at the end of the period. Section 136(2)(b) of EPCA 1978 clearly provides that a failure to renew a fixed term contract is a dismissal for redundancy purposes, and this would be unnecessary if there was no entitlement to a redundancy payment on the expiry of such a contract (*Lee v Nottinghamshire County Council*).

18.38 In *Hindle v Percival Boats Ltd* the claimant was engaged in repairing wooden boats. The amount of work was declining because of the introduction of fibreglass, and it was uneconomical to retain his services, so he was dismissed because 'he was too good and too slow'. Although he was not replaced (a fact which is sometimes used to determine whether or not a redundancy exists) his work was carried out by other employees working overtime. A majority of the Court of Appeal thought that the employers had rebutted the presumption of redundancy. In another leading case (*North Riding Garages Ltd v Butterwick*) the employee was the manager of a repair workshop. New employers took over the business, and introduced new working methods to which the employee could not adapt. He was dismissed for incompetence and inefficiency, and applied for a redundancy payment. It was held that if the new methods had so altered the nature of the work that there was a lessening of the work of a kind he was formerly employed to do, this would amount to redundancy. On the facts, however, the overall requirements of the firm had not changed. It was the inability of the employee to change and adapt to new methods which brought about his dismissal.

18.39 In considering the definition of redundancy, earlier cases appear to have concentrated on the work which the employee actually did (the function test) and the work which the employee was obliged to do under his contract (the contract test); but in the recent case of *Safeways Stores plc v Burrell* it was stated that both these approaches were wrong, and that it is the statutory definition which must be considered. The true test requires employment tribunals to consider whether there was a diminution or cessation in the employer's requirement for *employees* to carry out work of a particular kind, and not to focus on the work of the individual employee.

18.40–18.50 The issue was finally resolved by the House of Lords in *Murray v Foyle Meats Ltd* where it was held that the key word on which tribunals should concentrate is 'attributable'. Thus if a dismissal of an employee was 'attributable' to a diminution of the employer's need for employees, then it is irrelevant to consider either the contractual obligations or the functions which the employee performed.

Transferred redundancy

18.51 If an employee is redundant, but, in accordance with a redundancy procedure he is retained in another post because he has seniority, and the holder of that other post is consequently dismissed, can the latter claim that he was redundant? Such transferred or 'bumping redundancy' has been considered in a number of cases, the prevalent view being that such a claim is valid and statutorily correct. Thus in *Elliott Turbomachinery v Bates*, a redundant employee was transferred to the claimant's department, 'bumping' the applicant out of a job. It was held that he was redundant. This line of cases was supported by the EAT in *Safeway Stores Ltd v Burrell*, but more recently another division of the EAT has expressed disagreement (*Church v West Lancashire NHS Trust*), where it was stated that a bumped employee was not dismissed for reason of redundancy, but rather because of the application of a procedure which required the dismissal of that employee to complete a reorganisation.

18.52–18.60   However, in *Murray v Foyle Meats Ltd* (above) the House of Lords approved *Safeway Stores Ltd v Burrell*, and thus a transferred redundancy is still a redundancy under the Act.

Presumption of redundancy

18.61   Section 163(2) of ERA provides that if there is a dismissal, it is presumed to be by reason of redundancy, unless the contrary is proved. Thus if two employees are dismissed, although only one is redundant, they are both entitled to rely on the statutory presumption (*Willcox v Hastings*) in the absence of evidence to the contrary.

Offer of suitable alternative employment (s 138)

18.62   If the employer makes an offer (whether in writing or not) to the employee to renew the contract of employment, or to re-engage him under a new contract, which is to take effect on the expiry of the old contract or within four weeks thereafter, then:
a. if the provisions of that new contract as to capacity, place at which employed, and other terms and conditions of employment would not differ from the corresponding terms of the previous contract; or
b. these terms and conditions do differ, but the offer constitutes an offer of suitable employment, and in either case the employee unreasonably refuses that offer, then he will not be entitled to a redundancy payment.

18.63   An offer, to be of suitable employment, must take into account all the relevant details, including the nature of the work, the hours, pay, conditions, qualifications and experience of the employee. It is a question of fact and degree in each case. In *Sheppard v National Coal Board* a redundant carpenter was offered a similar job which would have involved more travelling, less overtime, and the loss of certain fringe benefits. It was held that the additional travel was not excessive, and the loss of overtime did not, by itself, render the employment less suitable. The loss of the fringe benefits was more important, and it was held that the offer was not of suitable employment.

18.64   The suitability of the offer of alternative work must be assessed objectively, whereas to assess whether or not the employee's refusal is unreasonable (whether in relation to the offer to renew the old contract on the same terms or the offer of suitable alternative employment) it is permissible to take into account subjective considerations (*Cambridge & District Co-operative Society Ltd v Ruse*). Thus the employee's own personal problems which may arise through taking up the offer are relevant factors. Domestic difficulties, inadequate or inconvenient travel facilities, lack of suitable educational facilities for children, loss of friends, have all been matters which have been held to constitute reasonable grounds for refusal of the offer (*Paton Calvert & Co Ltd v Westerside*). An employee does not act unreasonably in refusing to accept alternative employment if he feels he cannot achieve a satisfactory standard in the new post (*Spencer v Gloucestershire County Council*).

18.65–18.70   But a personal whim or fad cannot constitute a reasonable refusal. In *Fuller v Stephanie Bowman (Sales) Ltd* the claimant was a secretary working in Mayfair. The employers decided to move the office to Soho. The claimant rejected the offer of employment at the new premises, for these were above a sex shop, and as she was opposed to 'money for sex' activities, she found the move too distasteful. Her application for a redundancy payment failed. The tribunal pointed out that the commercial exploitation of sex was no less in Mayfair than in Soho (except, perhaps a little more discreet), and if this was the basis of her reasoning, she should move away from London altogether. Her dislike of working near a sex shop was based on a personal fad, and thus is was held that she had unreasonably refused alternative employment.

Redundancy following transfers

18.71   As has been noted, redundancy is the commonest reason for a dismissal following the transfer of an undertaking. This topic is dealt with in Chapter 9.

Trial period in new employment (s 138(3))

18.72   If the contract is renewed on the basis of new terms and conditions of employment, then the employee is entitled to have a trial period of four weeks, or such longer period as may be agreed between the parties for the purpose of retraining the employee under that new contract. In the latter case the new agreement must be made before the employee starts to work under the new contract. It must be in writing, specifying the length of the trial period, and the terms and conditions of employment which will apply after the trial period. If before or during the trial period the employee terminates the contract, or the employer does so for a reason connected with the new contract, the employee shall be treated as being dismissed on the date on which his previous contract ended, and for the reason he was dismissed under that contract (*McKindley v William Hill (Scotland) Ltd*). However, in *Hempell v W H Smith & Sons Ltd* the EAT stated that this did not preclude an enquiry under s 98(4) to ascertain whether the dismissal during the trial period was fair or unfair. In other words, even if the employee accepts the job after a trial period, s 138(3) only provides that he has not been dismissed for reason of redundancy; he may (or may not) have been unfairly dismissed from his old job, and he is entitled to have that issue resolved by an employment tribunal (*Jones v Burdett Coutts School*). If before or during the trial period the employee unreasonably terminates the contract, he shall not be entitled to a redundancy payment by reason of his dismissal from the previous contract.

18.73   The statutory right to a trial period applies to those employees who are dismissed by the employer, or whose fixed term contract has expired. However, on several occasions the EAT have decided that an employee who is constructively dismissed has a reasonable period within which to decide whether or not to accept the repudiation by the employer or to carry on with the new contract offered. The statutory trial period of four weeks does not commence until after the expiry of that reasonable period (*Turvey v CW Cheyney & Son Ltd*). In *Air Canada v Lee* the applicant worked as a telephonist. The employers moved their premises and she was asked to work in a basement office, with no natural light. She objected, but worked there for three months, when she left. It was held that she had been made redundant when she was asked to move: it was reasonable that she should try the new premises for three months, even though the statutory period had expired.

18.74–18.80 Since an employee has a statutory right to a trial period, a refusal to offer him one may lead to a finding that his dismissal was unfair (*Elliot v Richard Stump Ltd*). The statutory trial period of four weeks is four calendar weeks, not four working weeks (*Benton v Sanderson Kayser Ltd*).

Laying off and short-time working (s 147)

18.81 An employer may find himself in a difficult economic situation which may be envisaged to be of a temporary nature, and he may decide, instead of dismissing his employees, to lay them off temporarily, or to put them on short time. A lay-off is where there is no work for the employees and no remuneration provided; short-time working is defined as being where less than half the normal week's pay is earned. If the lay-off or short-time has lasted for more than four consecutive weeks, or more than six weeks in any 13, then the employee may give written notice (not more than four weeks after the lay-off or short-time has finished) that he intends to claim a redundancy payment. He must then give the requisite notice to terminate his contract, and will be entitled to be considered redundant. The employer may agree to meet the claim, or refuse to do so and serve a counter-notice within seven days on the ground that he reasonably expects to be able to provide at least 13 weeks' continuous employment without further resort to lay-offs or short-time working. If the claim or counter-notice is not withdrawn, the matter will be determined by the employment tribunal, which will consider whether or not there was a reasonable prospect of full employment for 13 weeks. If the counter-notice is withdrawn by the employer, or the 13 weeks' continuous employment fails to materialise, the employee is entitled to be paid redundancy money.

18.82 If the employer offers work, but the employee refuses the offer because the rate of pay is too low, the employer has still offered to provide the work, and if, had he accepted the work the employee would have earned more than half a week's pay, there is no short-time working (*Spinpress Ltd v Turner*).

18.83 But an employer has no inherent right to lay off workers as he chooses. In the absence of an express right to do so in the contract, such unilateral action can be regarded as a repudiation of the contract, and hence a dismissal. Thus (in theory) at least one week's notice should be given of such intended lay-off (*Johnson v Cross*). But if the employer reserves the right to resort to a lay-off in the contract, the employee cannot treat this as a termination.

18.84–18.90 If the employer has a contractual right to lay off for an indefinite period (eg in the building industry) the employee's remedy is under s 148, and he cannot claim that the lay-off was for such an unreasonable length of time as to constitute a constructive dismissal (*Kenneth MacRae & Co Ltd v Dawson*).

Fair redundancy dismissals

18.91 If a dismissal for reason of redundancy is to be fair, the employer generally must show (a) that there was adequate consultation with the employee(s) and their trade union or other representatives (b) that the system for selection was fair and (c) that there was no other alternative employment which could be offered. In a sense, these matters are linked, because proper consultation will sometimes avoid an unfair selection system, and may result in alternative employment being offered. The need to consult with an employee prior to dismissing for reason of redundancy has been stressed many times (see *Polkey v A E Dayton Services Ltd*, para 12.14), otherwise a dismissal is almost bound to be unfair. The exception to the rule laid down in *Polkey* only applies if the failure led to a procedural unfairness, ie consultation would have made no difference (*Robertson v Magnet Ltd*). But if the failure to consult could lead to a substantive unfairness, eg a possible defect in the selection system, then the exception does not apply, and a dismissal will be unfair (*Steel Stockholders (Birmingham) Ltd v Kirkwood*). In the absence of proper consultation, a dismissal is almost bound to be unfair, although the amount of compensation to be awarded would depend on the extent to which the employer can show that consultation would not have produced a different result (see *Robertson v Magnet Ltd*). Consultation is also required when considering dismissal following the expiry of a fixed-term contract, or where external funding for a post has been exhausted, for it can only be on extremely rare occasions that consultation would be a futile exercise (*University of Glasgow v Donaldson*). But a failure to consult on a redundancy brought about by a transfer of an undertaking is not necessarily unfair if the circumstances are exceptional and urgent (*Warner v Adnet Ltd*).

Unfair selection for redundancy (ERA s 105)

18.92 It is unfair to dismiss a person for redundancy if the reason for his/her selection for dismissal was (a) health and safety reason (s 100) (b) protected or opted out shop worker (s 101) (c) refusal to comply with a requirement in contravention of the Working Time Regulations (s 101A) (d) acting as a trustee of an occupational pension fund (s 102) (e) acting as an employee representative (s 103) (f) making a protected disclosure (s 103A) (g) asserting a statutory right (s 104) (h) asserting a right under the National Minimum Wage Act (s 104A) (i) taking action to obtain a tax credit (s 104B) (j) taking action under the Transnational Information and Consultation of Employees Regulations 1999 (k) taking action under the Part-time Workers (Prevention of Less Favourable Treatment) Regulations 2000. Unfair selection for trade union membership and activities etc is covered by TULR(C)A s 153 (see para 21.92). Unfair selection for redundancy by reason of pregnancy, maternity leave, parental leave, time off to care for dependants, and workforce agreement cases is dealt with in the Maternity and Parental Leave etc Regulations 1999 (see para 17.155). Such dismissals will be automatically unfair, and no continuous period of continuous employment is required. Nor do the age limits apply.

Dismissal during the period of notice (s 140)

18.93 If an employee has been given due notice that he will be dismissed for reason of redundancy, and whilst he is working out that notice, he commits an act of misconduct which is sufficiently serious to warrant his instant dismissal without notice, and he is summarily dismissed, the question will arise as to whether or not he is entitled to his redundancy payment. On the assumption that the dismissal was justified (eg because the employee refused to obey a lawful order (*Cairns v Burnside Shoe Repairs Ltd*), or because the employee stole from the employer (*Jarmain v E Pollard & Co Ltd*)), then the employment tribunal shall determine whether it is just and equitable that the employee should receive the whole or part of the redundancy payment, as it thinks fit. In *Lignacite Products Ltd v Krollman* the claimant was given notice of redundancy. He was then found stealing from his employers and summarily dismissed. The employment tribunal reduced his redundancy pay by 40 per cent, and the EAT upheld the decision. It is difficult to reconcile this decision with the more recent case of *Bonner v H Gilbert Ltd*.

18.94–18.100   If an employee is given notice of dismissal by reason of redundancy, and during his notice period he takes part in a strike, then although this is conduct which entitles the employer to terminate the contract without notice, the employee is not barred from getting the whole of his redundancy payment (s 143). However, if an employee is on strike, and then is dismissed for reasons of redundancy, his claim will fail. The reason is that s 140 of the Act provides that the employee will not be entitled to a redundancy payment if the employer, being entitled to terminate the contract of employment, terminates it, with or without notice. Since an employee who is on strike is in breach of his contract, the employer is entitled to terminate it. In other words, s 143 deals with the situation when an employee is dismissed for reason of redundancy, and then goes on strike. In *Simmons v Hoover Ltd* employees who were actually on strike were dismissed for reason of redundancy, and it was held that s 140 operated, and s 143 did not operate to save their claim.

Excluded classes of employees

18.101   The following employees are not eligible for, or will not be entitled to, a redundancy payment:

a.   a person employed under a fixed term contract for two years or more, if before that term expires, he agrees in writing to exclude his rights to make a claim (s 197(3)). This is one of the very few circumstances when an employee can forgo his legal rights (see para 20.66);

b.   a miscellaneous class of employees, ie share fishermen, and men and women over the age of 65 or normal retiring age. Domestic servants employed in a private household *are* within the scope of the Act, unless the servant is a close relative of the employer (s 161);

c.   an agreement made between an employers' organisation and a trade union may provide exemption from the Act by a ministerial order on an application by both parties thereto, provided the conditions in s 157 are satisfied;

d.   if, on the termination of his employment, the employee is entitled to an occupational pension or a periodic payment or a lump sum, the employer may serve a notice on the employee that his right to a redundancy payment is excluded or reduced. If the annual value of the pension is equal to one third of the employee's leaving salary, and is payable immediately (even though the employee decides to accept a deferred pension) the employer may exclude altogether the right to receive a redundancy payment. If the pension is less than one third of the employee's leaving salary, or if it is not payable immediately but within 90 weeks, the redundancy payment is reduced proportionately (see *Royal Ordnance plc v Pilkington*). The annual leaving salary is subject to the statutory maximum of £230 per week, times 52 weeks, ie £11,960 (Redundancy Payments Pensions Regulations 1965).

Claims for redundancy payments

18.102 A claim must be made to the employment tribunal within six months from the relevant date, which is the date of the expiry of the notice to terminate the employment, or the date when the contract expires, or the date on which a fixed term contract comes to an end. The tribunal has a discretion to admit a claim which is outside the time limit if it thinks it would be just and equitable to do so, but no claim can be entertained after 12 months have elapsed. The claim, if admitted or successful, must be met by the employer. The amount of the claim will be determined by the length of time the employee has been employed, his normal week's pay, and his age.

18.103–18.110 The calculation of the amount of redundancy payment will be determined in accordance with the rules on continuous employment (see Chapter 13), normal working hours and week's pay (see Chapter 14), length of time he has been employed, and his age at the date of dismissal. For each year's continuous employment between the ages of 18 and 21, he is entitled to one half of a week's pay, between the ages of 22 and 40 he is entitled to one week's pay, and between the ages of 41 and 64 he is entitled to one and a half weeks' pay. In respect of employees over the age of 64, there is a reduction of one-twelfth in the total entitlement in respect of each month over the age of 65. All this is subject to a maximum of 20 years' reckonable employment, and a maximum week's pay of £230. Thus the maximum payment possible for an employee over the age of 60 with 20 years' continuous employment is 20 x $1\frac{1}{2}$ x £230, ie £6,900. When making the payment, the employer shall give to the employee a written statement showing how the amount of payment is calculated and it is an offence, punishable on summary conviction by a fine not exceeding level 1 on the standard scale, not to do so (s 165). If an employer gives a lump sum to a redundant employee without so indicating how it is made up, this may be regarded as an *ex gratia* payment, not intended to be by way of redundancy payment (*Galloway v Export Packing Services Ltd*).

Consultation on redundancies (TULR(C)A ss 188–192)

18.111 Article 2 of the EC Directive on Collective Redundancies (75/129/EEC) lays down the principle that when an employer is contemplating collective redundancies, he shall consult with employee representatives. Although a Directive is generally enforceable against a state body (see *Foster v British Gas*, para 1.138) this Directive is not so unconditional or sufficiently precise as to be capable of direct enforcement (*Griffin v South West Water Services Ltd*). Requirements for such consultations were provided for in the Employment Protection Act 1975 s 99, and repeated in the Trade Union and Labour Relations (Consolidation) Act 1992 s 188 (as amended by the Trade Union Reform and Employment Rights Act 1993). However, in *EC Commission v United Kingdom* infringement proceedings were brought alleging that neither the Transfer of Undertakings Regulations 1981 (see Chapter 9) nor the provisions of TULR(C)A correctly transposed the Directive, because there were no provisions which would require an employer to consult with employee representatives when the employer did not recognise a trade union. The UK Government argued that employee representation was traditionally based on the voluntary recognition by employers of trade unions, and therefore if an employer did not recognise a trade union, there were no 'employee representatives' with whom to consult. Nonetheless, the European Court held that the UK Government was in breach of the Directive. Legislation had to ensure that there was a mechanism whereby employee representatives were designated so as to enable employers to consult with them.

18.112 Section 188 of TULR(C)A was thus amended by the Collective Redundancies and Transfer of Undertakings (Protection of Employment) (Amendment) Regulations 1995, although it was not certain whether these regulations fully implemented the Directive, because although there arose a duty to consult with either trade unions or employee representatives, there was no mechanism by which those representatives could be elected. Thus the Collective Redundancies and Transfer of Undertakings (Protection of Employment) (Amendment) Regulations 1999 were passed to regularise the position. These latter Regulations make provision for the election of employee representatives (by inserting s 188A into TULR(C)A), and other changes).

18.113 Where an employer is proposing to dismiss as redundant 20 or more employees at one establishment within a period of 90 days or less, he shall consult with the appropriate representatives of any of the employees affected by the dismissal, or the measures taken in connection with those dismissals. The appropriate representatives are
(a) if the employees are of a description in respect of which an independent trade union is recognised (whether or not the affected employees are members of the trade union concerned, see *Northern Ireland Hotel and Catering College v NATFHE*), representatives of that union. Whether a trade union is recognised for the purpose of the consultation provisions is a question of fact (see Chapter 23). In any other case,
(b) either employee representatives who have been appointed or elected by the affected employees for some other purpose, who have authority to receive information or be consulted about proposed dismissals, or employee representatives who have been elected by the affected employees for consultation purposes, in an election which satisfies the requirements set out in s 188A. If the employees fail to elect representatives within a reasonable time after being invited to do so, the employer must consult with each affected employee, giving them the information he would have to give to their representatives.

18.114 The employer shall allow the appropriate representatives access to the employees affected, and shall afford those representatives such accommodation and facilities as may be appropriate, and time off work for training (ERA s 61). An employee who is an employee representative, or a candidate for election as such, has the right not to suffer a detriment on the ground that he has performed any function or activity as such, the right to have time off with pay to perform his functions, and the right not to be unfairly dismissed because he performed any function or activity as such.

18.115–18.125 The consultation shall begin in good time, and, in any event, if the employer is proposing to dismiss 100 or more within 90 days or less, consultation shall begin at least 90 days before the dismissals take effect. If less than 100 (but 20 or more) are to be dismissed within the 90-day period, consultation must begin at least 30 days before the dismissals take effect.

What is an establishment?

18.126 The term 'establishment' is not defined in the Act, and has thus been the subject of interpretation by the tribunals. In *Clarks of Hove Ltd v Bakers Union* it was held that separate premises can amount to one establishment, if there is no separate accounting, management or trading. In *Barratt Developments (Bradford) Ltd v UCATT* the company, which had its headquarters in Bradford, operated 14 building sites in Lancashire. On each site there was a temporary shed, with a telephone link to the headquarters. It was decided to reduce the labour force, and 24 employees were made redundant, being selected from eight different sites. It was held that all 14 sites were part of one establishment, and as there had been a failure to consult with the trade union, a protective award would be made.

18.127–18.135 However, in *Rockfon A/S v Specialarbejderforbundet i Danmark* the European Court of Justice noted that member states used different terms to describe an 'establishment', including undertaking, work centre, local unit, place of work, and so on. Since the term is one of European law, a uniform interpretation must be given. The ECJ held that the term 'establishment' must be understood as meaning the unit to which the workers who are made redundant are assigned to carry out their duties (see para 9.25). It is not necessary for the unit in question to have its own management structure which can carry out a redundancy programme independently. The irony is that in an attempt to extend the coverage of the Directive so as to protect as many employees as possible, this definition is probably a narrow one, for UK law triggers the consultation provisions only when more than 20 from one establishment are to be dismissed.

The consultation provisions

18.136 An employer is 'proposing to dismiss' employees as redundant (thus triggering the consultation provisions of the Act) when, 'following a diagnosis of the problem, specific proposals are formulated, with redundancies as one of the available options' (*Hough v Leyland DAF Ltd*).

18.137 The actual notice of dismissals can be issued during the consultation period, provided that the dismissals do not take effect until after the consultation period has elapsed. But if an employer issues dismissal notices the day after consultations begin, it may be thought that he does not intend meaningful consultations to take place (*NUT v Avon County Council*). Similarly, if the employer does not give the appropriate representatives sufficient time to consider the proposals before they are implemented, meaningful consultation is being denied (*T & GWU v Ledbury Preserves (1928) Ltd*).

18.138 The purpose of consultation is to consult about ways of
(a) avoiding the dismissals
(b) reducing the numbers of employees to be dismissed, and
(c) mitigating the consequences of the redundancies.

18.139 Consultation with employee representatives does not mean reaching an agreement, but should be undertaken by the employer with a view to reaching agreement. Thus, the consultation process must be genuine. If a redundancy situation is presented as a *fait accompli*, subsequent consultations may not be a genuine and open-minded review of the decision (*GMB and AEEU v Campbell's UK Ltd*).

18.140 True consultation involves:
a. consulting with employee representatives when the proposals are still at a formulative stage;
b. giving adequate information to which those representatives can respond;
c. giving adequate time for the response; and
d. a conscientious consideration by the employer of the response (*Rowell v Hubbard Group Services Ltd*).

18.141 But consultation does not imply agreement with those representatives, nor the adoption of any proposals made by them (*R v British Coal Corpn, ex p Price*).

18.142 In such consultations, the employer must disclose (in writing to the appropriate representative):
a. the reasons for his proposals;
b. the numbers and descriptions of employees whom it is proposed to dismiss as being redundant;
c. the total number of employees of that description employed by the employer at that establishment;
d. the proposed method of selecting the employees who are to be dismissed;
e. the proposed method of carrying out the dismissals, with due regard to agreed procedure, including the period over which dismissals are to take effect; and
f. the proposed method for calculating any redundancy payments to be made, other than statutory redundancy pay (s 188(4)).

18.143 Having provided the above information, the employer must consider any representations made by the appropriate representatives and reply to them. If he rejects any of those representations, he must state his reasons. It must be stressed that the employer's duty is to consult with the representatives. He does not have to reach any agreement, and the final decision is his. In *Perez v Mercury Display Ltd* the employer consulted with a trade union about a redundancy. The employer wanted selection to take place on the basis of LIFO, but the union wanted volunteers to be selected. The employer gave to the union his reasons for rejecting the representations, and dismissed the employees on the basis of LIFO. It was held that the employer had complied with his statutory obligations.

18.144 If there are special circumstances which render it not reasonably practicable for the employer to comply with any of the above provisions relating to consultation or considering representations, he shall take all such steps as are reasonably practicable in the circumstances. Special circumstances may exist if a company becomes insolvent but insolvency *per se* is not a special circumstance, for reasonable and prudent management may well foresee such a possibility (*Clarks of Hove Ltd v Bakers' Union*). The sudden appointment of a receiver would be a special circumstance (*FTATU v Lawrence Cabinet*). The loss of a key order (*AUEW v Cooper Plastics*) and the unexpected failure to obtain a renewal of an important contract (*NUPE v General Cleaning Contractors*) have also come within this defence. But the fact that the employer genuinely believes that he has not recognised a trade union for the purpose of collective bargaining does not constitute a special circumstance which would render it not reasonably practicable to comply with the obligation to consult (*Joshua Wilson & Bros Ltd v USDAW*). Special circumstances may also be said to exist if delicate negotiations are taking place which may be prejudiced if consultations are carried on with the union (*APAC v Kirvin Ltd*). A circumstance is likely to be special if it is sudden, as opposed to being gradual or foreseeable with reasonable prudence (*USDAW v Leancut Bacon Ltd*).

18.145 The dismissal of employees in order to make the sale of a business more attractive to buyers, or the absence of orders, are not special circumstances within the meaning of the Act (*GMB v Rankin and Harrison*). A failure on the part of a person who controls the employer (eg a multinational corporation in control of a subsidiary) to provide information to the employer also does not constitute a special circumstance (s 193(7)).

18.146–18.155 An employer does not fail to consult if he deals only with an accredited shop steward, for there is no requirement that the information should be conveyed to a full-time union official (*GMWU v Wailes Dove Bitumastic*).

Protective award

18.156 If the employer fails to consult as required by s 186, a trade union or an employee representative or an employee who has been or may be dismissed as redundant may present a complaint to an industrial tribunal (s 189). It further appears that an employee who has been dismissed for reason of redundancy may be able to bring a complaint that the employer has failed to invite potentially redundant employees to elect appropriate employee representatives as required by s 188. If the employer wishes to plead that it was not reasonably practicable for him to comply with these provisions, he must show that this was so, and that he took all reasonably practicable steps in the circumstances. Otherwise, if the tribunal finds the complaint to be well-founded, it will make a declaration to that effect, and may also make a protective award, which is remuneration for a protected period for those employees who were dismissed (or whose dismissal was being proposed) and in respect of whom the employer has failed to comply with the legal requirements. The protected period is such time as the tribunal considers to be just and equitable, having regard to the seriousness of the employer's default, but shall not exceed 90 days.

18.157 If a protective award is made, every employee to whom it relates shall be entitled to one week's pay for each week of the protected period, with proportionate reductions in respect of a period which is less than one week. If the employer has already made any payment to the employee in respect of any period falling within the protected period, or by way of damages for breach of contract, this will not reduce the employer's liability to pay remuneration under the protective award, and conversely, any payment made under a protective award will not reduce any liability to pay any sum due in respect of a breach of contract by the employer for that period.

18.158 If an employment tribunal finds that the employer is in default of the consultation provisions, then the making of a declaration to that effect is mandatory, but the amount of the protective award is discretionary (*UCATT v*

Rooke & Sons Ltd), and it should not be such as to register the tribunal's disapproval of the employer's conduct. Rather it should reflect the loss suffered by the employees. To use the protective award as a method of imposing a penalty for bad behaviour is inconsistent with modern legislation (*Talke Fashions Ltd v ASTWKT*). Subject to that, the award is a matter for the discretion of the employment tribunal (*Sovereign Distribution Services Ltd v T & GWU*) which can, if necessary, make a nil award if appropriate (*Spillers-French Ltd v USDAW*).

18.159 As a result of consultations with the appropriate employee representatives, there may well be an agreement that employees will leave the firm before the appropriate period of 90 or 30 days has expired Whether the agreement has been reached with the employee representatives or employees on an individual basis, it is probably void by virtue of s 288 of TULR(C)A which prevents the contracting out of the various statutory rights. It is clear therefore that the dismissals will take effect before the end of the consultation period, and there will be a breach of the Act. However, on a complaint that the employer has failed to consult within the statutory period, the employment tribunal will make the mandatory declaration, but not a protective award (*ASTMS v Hawker Siddeley Aviation*).

18.160 If, during the protected period, the employee is fairly dismissed for some reason other than redundancy, or if he unreasonably resigns, then his entitlement to the protective award shall cease from the time his contract is terminated. If the employer makes an offer to renew the contract, or to re-engage under a new contract, so that the renewal or re-engagement would take effect before or during the protected period, or the offer constitutes an offer of suitable employment, and the employee unreasonably refuses that offer, then he shall not be entitled to any payment under the protective award in respect of any period during which but for the refusal he would have been employed.

18.161 Once a protective award has been granted, then any individual employee may present a complaint to a tribunal that the employer has failed, in whole or in part, to pay him the remuneration under that award. If the complaint is well-founded, the tribunal shall order the employer to make that payment.

18.162 The fact that the employer has failed to consult in accordance with the above provisions is irrelevant to the issue as to whether a particular employee's redundancy is fair or unfair (*Forman Construction Ltd v Kelly*).

18.163–18.170 It should be noted that, for the purpose of the consultation provisions only, the definition of redundancy is not the same as the one laid down in s 139 of ERA. Under TULR(C)A s 195, when considering the consultation provisions, references to dismissals for reason of redundancy are references to a dismissal not related to the individual concerned (or for a number of reasons not so related). This wider definition throws out some interesting possibilities. For example, suppose an employer decides to give lawful notice to all his employees, coupled with an offer to re-engage them all on changed terms of employment. Since this 'dismissal' is not related to an individual, it is submitted that prior consultations with employee representatives are required under s 195 of TULR(C)A.

Notification of mass redundancies to the minister (TULR(C)A s 193)

18.171 If an employer is proposing to make redundant 100 or more employees at one establishment within 90 days, or 20 or more employees within 30 days, he must notify the Secretary of State of his proposals within 90 or 30 days respectively, and also give a copy of this notification to the representatives of any recognised independent trade union and/or to any elected representatives. If there are special circumstances which make compliance not reasonably practicable, he shall take all such steps as are reasonably practicable. But a failure on the part of a person who controls the employer to provide information to the employer does not constitute a special circumstance (s 193(7)).

18.172 An employer who fails to give the required notification to the Secretary of State may be prosecuted in the magistrates' court, and is liable on conviction to a fine not exceeding level 5 on the standard scale (TULR(C)A s 194(1)).

Duties of ex-employees

19.1   Since, as we have seen, the relationship between employer and employee is one of trust, confidence and faith, it must follow that an ex-employee does not escape entirely from those obligations merely by leaving the employment. How the law tries to achieve a balance between the conflicting interests of the individual, the employer and the state will be the subject of this chapter.

19.2   A distinction must be drawn between the duty of fidelity owed by an employee during the currency of the contract of employment (see *Marshall v Industrial Systems and Controls Ltd*, and *Laughton and Hawley v Bapp Industrial Supplies Ltd*, para 16.24) and the duty owed after the employment has ended. In *Faccenda Chicken Ltd v Fowler* (see below) the Court of Appeal made it clear that in the former case, the duty is contractual, whether as an express or implied term of the contract of employment as being part of the obligation of trust, confidence and faithfulness which must exist between employer and employee. This means that an employee cannot properly disclose information or give assistance to a competitor, even in his own time. On the other hand, in the absence of a restrictive covenant, the obligations of an ex-employee are more limited; he may be under a duty not to disclose information which has been imparted to him in confidence, such as secret processes, trade secrets, etc, but this does not cover all information given or acquired by the employee during his employment, and does not cover information which is confidential in the sense that it would have been a breach of the employee's duty of fidelity for him to have disclosed it to a third party during the course of the employment.

19.3   To determine whether particular information falls into the category of information which ought not to be disclosed after the employment has ceased, regard must be had to all the circumstances, and in particular to:
a.   the nature of the employment;
b.   the nature of the information;
c.   whether the employer regarded the information as being confidential and informed the employee of this;
d.   whether the information could be easily isolated from other information which the employee is free to use.

19.4   In *Faccenda Chicken Ltd v Fowler*, the judge identified three classes of information which an employee might acquire during his employment. First, there is information which is trivial or easily available to the public at large. This clearly does not give rise to any implied term of confidentiality. Second, there is information which is imparted to the employee, or which he learns, for the purpose of his employer's business. Clearly, during the course of his employment, this should not be the subject of unauthorised disclosure, but once the employment has ceased, it remains part of the employee's own skill and knowledge, and can be used by him for his own benefit – if necessary, in competition with his former employer. An employee may be restrained by a restrictive covenant not to disclose such information, but such a covenant can only give reasonable protection in limited circumstances (*Herbert Morris Ltd v Saxelby*). Third, there is information which clearly amounts to trade secrets, such as secret processes etc. This cannot be disclosed after the employment has ceased (*Lancashire Fires Ltd v SA Lyons & Co Ltd*), unless there is a public interest in disclosure (see below). In *Faccenda Chicken Ltd v Fowler*, the employer sought an injunction to restrain two former employees from using their knowledge of sales and prices information when they set up a competing business. It was held that this was not confidential information, and the application for the injunction was refused. Thus, subject to the above restrictions, an ex-employee is entitled to make use of his skill and knowledge which he has generally acquired in his previous employments (*United Sterling Corpn v Felton*), and may only be restrained by a validly worded restrictive covenant.

19.5–19.10 In the absence of an express covenant, there is no general restriction on an ex-employee canvassing or doing business with customers of his former employer, and no implied term prohibiting this (*Wallace Bogan & Co v Cove*). Nor is an ex-employee in breach of an implied term of confidentiality in disclosing information relating to his former employer's solvency, or other true statements which may be detrimental to that employer's interests, because the duty of confidentiality is much more restricted in scope after the end of the employment than that which is imposed by the general duty of good faith during the employment (*Brooks v Olyslager OMS (UK) Ltd*).

Disclosure of information

19.11 The ex-employee is under a duty not to disclose to any unauthorised person any confidential information he had obtained during his employment, or to use such information in an unauthorised manner. In *Robb v Green* an employee copied out a list of the employer's clients with a view to approaching them after his employment had ceased, and in *Wessex Dairies Ltd v Smith* a milk roundsman, during the last week of his employment, approached his customers to ask them if they would join a round of his own which he was proposing to start. In both cases it was held that there was a breach of contract.

19.12 It will be obvious that the rule is easier to state in theory than to enforce in practice, for it is not possible to wipe out from an employee's mind information which he has gained in the course of the employment and which he may properly place at the disposal of his new employer. A distinction must be drawn between trade secrets and confidential information on the one hand, and an employee's skill, knowledge and general familiarity with his former employer's business on the other hand (*Lock International plc v Beswick*). In *Printers and Finishers Ltd v Holloway* the claimants sought an injunction against their former works manager restraining him from disclosing certain confidential information which he had obtained during his employment. Some of this information was contained in documents which the defendant had taken with him, and an injunction was granted in respect of these and an enquiry was ordered to ascertain what damage, if any, had flowed from the defendant's breach of duty. So far as confidential matters which were in his memory were concerned, which related to the know-how and general processes of the claimant's business, these were not readily separable from his general knowledge of the whole trade, and it would not be unreasonable for him to recall particular skills of his former employer's business and use his skills for the benefit of his new employer. Consequently, an injunction relating to these matters was refused.

19.13 It is not necessary that the employer points out to the employee the precise nature or aspects of the production process for which protection as a trade secret is sought (*Lancashire Fires Ltd v SA Lyons & Co Ltd*).

19.14 However, if the information obtained, though confidential, relates to a breach of the law or wrongful act by the employer, then there is an entirely different situation, for 'there is no confidence as to the disclosure of an iniquity'. In *Initial Services Ltd v Putterill* the defendant was employed as a manager by the claimants. After leaving his employment he gave information to a newspaper concerning the conduct of the claimants' business, in particular alleging that they had violated the Restrictive Trade Practices Act 1956 by entering into agreements with other laundries which ought to have been registered under that Act, and that they had issued circulars which were misleading to the public. The newspaper proposed to publish an article which would have made detrimental allegations about the claimants' business, and an injunction was sought. It was held that the disclosure would be justified as being in the public interest, and there was no confidence attached thereto.

19.15 If an employee does disclose information relating to the commission of a fraud, crime or act of corruption by his former employer, he can rely on the defence of 'just cause' if the disclosure is made in the public interest. Thus in *Lion Laboratories Ltd v Evans* two ex-employees gave information to a newspaper which showed that there were doubts about the reliability of a breathalyser approved by the Home Office. It was held that the information disclosed was of grave public concern, and would not be restrained (see now para 10.139 for protected disclosures).

19.16–19.25 Nor can an employee be restrained from disclosing information to regulatory bodies (such as FIMBRA) which have a duty to investigate matters within their remit (in *Re A Company's Application*).

Garden leave clauses

19.26 We have noted (see para 19.2) that a distinction must be drawn between a contractual term which prohibits an employee from working for another employer (usually, but not necessarily, a competitor) during the subsistence of the contract, and a restrictive covenant which restrains an employee from working for a competitor for a certain period after the contract has ended. In the former case, such work would constitute a breach of the duty of faithful service (see para

10.121), which would warrant dismissal. However, there are cases where an employee resigns his employment, sometimes by giving due notice, sometimes by giving less notice than the contract requires, and then seeks to work for a competitor. Can he be restrained from so working in breach of contract?

19.27 It now seems clear that a garden leave requirement can only be enforced if there is an express term in the contract of employment to that effect. In the absence of such a clause, an employee (particularly one who is highly skilled) is entitled to be provided with work during his notice period, rather than stay at home in idleness. But even if there is such a clause in the contract, employers would have to justify the length of the period of garden leave by reference to the individual's access to confidential information, connection with customers and the effect the employee's absence will have on the stability of the remaining workforce. In other words, the approach of the courts to garden leave clauses will now be consistent with that applied to applications to enforce restrictive covenants (*William Hill Organisation Ltd v Tucker*).

19.28 In *Evening Standard Co Ltd v Henderson*, the employee agreed that during his contract he would not work for another employer. His contract also provided that one year's notice had to be given by either side. He decided to work for a rival newspaper, and gave two months' notice to terminate his employment. The employer applied for an injunction to restrain him from working for the rival newspaper until the full year's contractual notice had expired. In the circumstances of the case, the injunction was granted. The claimants were quite willing to pay the employee during the full year notice period, whether or not he worked for them. The balance of convenience was in favour of granting the injunction to enforce the very thing the contract was designed to prevent him from doing, namely working for a rival concern.

19.29 But if the employee gives lawful notice, can the employer require him not to work during the notice period, pay him his salary, and yet insist that he does not work for a rival concern during the notice period. The effect of such a 'garden leave' arrangement was considered in *Provident Financial Group plc v Hayward*, where the defendant was a financial director of an estate agency business. His contract provided that during his employment he would not work for any other person. He tendered his resignation on 1 July, and although he was bound to give 12 months' notice, it was mutually agreed that his employment would terminate at the end of December. He continued to work during the notice period until September, when the employers decided that he need no longer do any work, although they were prepared to pay him his salary until the end of December. In effect, he was on 'garden leave', at home, on full pay and with all his contractual benefits. In October, he announced that he intended starting work for another firm of estate agents, and the claimants sought an injunction to restrain him from doing so. The application was refused. There were only ten weeks of the unexpired notice period left, and there was no evidence of the prospect of serious damage resulting to the claimants' business if the employee took up the new job. His duties were more of an administrative nature, and he had very little confidential information in his possession which would cause the employers damage.

19.30 The matter is one for the court's discretion. In *Hayward*, the Court of Appeal made it clear that there were circumstances where it would be appropriate to restrain an employee from working during his notice period, particularly if the notice period is not excessive, and the employee is not being deprived of his opportunity to practise his skills. However, the insertion of long periods of 'garden leave' provisions in contracts of employment is capable of abuse. It is to be expected that senior employees will seek employment with someone in the same line of business, and will not take kindly to enforced idleness, even if they are being paid. Employers will also have exaggerated fears as to the damage likely to be caused to their business (see also *JA Mont (UK) Ltd v Mills*).

19.31   Garden leave clauses will only be enforced by the courts if they are reasonable in terms of the length of time, and if there is a genuine interest which the employer is entitled to protect (*Euro Brokers Ltd v Rabey*).

19.32–19.40   There is no reason why a restrictive covenant should not commence after the expiry of a garden leave period, in effect lengthening the period of time when the employee is prevented from approaching former customers etc. The one period cannot be 'set off' against the other. But the existence of a garden leave clause may be a factor to take into account when determining the validity of the restrictive covenant, and, if the garden leave is exceptionally long, the courts may, on grounds of public policy, refuse to enforce any further protection based on a restrictive covenant (*Crédit Suisse Asset Management Ltd v Armstrong*).

Covenants in restraint of trade

19.41   An employer cannot prevent an ex-employee from competing with him, nor using the knowledge, skill and experience gained during the employment. The employer can, however, extract a promise that the ex-employee will not use his personal influence over customers, or his knowledge of trade secrets, to the disadvantage of the employer (*Spafax Ltd v Harrison*), provided this is reasonably necessary for the protection of the employer's business. Thus, an employer who has a genuine interest to protect should get the employee to sign a covenant to this effect, so that the employee's future conduct is restricted once the employment comes to an end. Normally, this would be signed at the commencement of the employment, but though desirable, this is not essential. In *R S Components Ltd v Irwin* the employer asked a salesman, who was already in employment, to sign a covenant which would have prevented him from soliciting business from the firm's customers for a period of 12 months after leaving the employment. The employee refused to do so, and his consequent dismissal was held by the NIRC to have been fair on the grounds of 'some other substantial reason' (see Chapter 17).

19.42   There are several limitations on the right of the employer to impose such restraints, for the courts will look with a critical eye at any agreement which has the effect of restraining a person from earning his livelihood in the future. The employer cannot take away the employee's skill, experience and fund of knowledge which he has obtained during the employment, and, in particular, the employer cannot protect himself against future competition *per se*. For example, in *SW Strange Ltd v Mann*, the defendant was employed by a firm of bookmakers as a manager. Most of the betting was done by telephone, and hence the defendant had little personal contact with customers. He agreed that he would not, after leaving the employment, be engaged in a similar business within a radius of 12 miles. After leaving his job, he set up in business as a bookmaker within the prohibited area. It was held that the restriction was void. The purpose of the covenant was not to give legitimate protection to the business interests of the employer, but was a naked attempt to prevent future competition.

19.43   What, then, are the interests in respect of which the employer is entitled to have protection? Basically, there are four. The first relates to his trade secrets and confidential information, the second to his customers and connections, the third relates to working for competitors and the fourth relates to existing employees.

A. Trade secrets and confidential information

19.44   If an employer could not ensure that his employees would not pass on information concerning his secret processes, it might restrict the employment relationship to an extent where commercial initiative became impossible. The employer would not be able to trust the employee; furtive attempts would have to be made to disclose some information without disclosing all, industrial espionage would flourish, and employees would attempt to sell secrets by offering themselves on the labour market at the highest bidder. Research and development would be hampered and become unprofitable. So, at least, ran the economic theories of former ages, though with the advent of patent law the modern scene might be somewhat different. Nonetheless, the legal principles remain substantially the same. Thus if a trade secret, or a secret process, exists, the employer is entitled to have his employee's promise not to divulge that information to a future employer, at least, subject to possible limitations on time and area. In *Forster & Sons Ltd v Suggett* the defendant was a works engineer concerned with a secret process in the glass-making industry. He covenanted that he would not divulge any trade secret or manufacturing process, and would not be employed by a competitor anywhere in the United Kingdom for five years after leaving his employment with the plaintiffs. It was held that the covenant was reasonable and enforceable.

19.45   It is not possible to restrain an employee from disclosing to a future employer a special method of organisation, as opposed to a secret process, for one must draw a distinction between objective knowledge, such as trade secrets and lists of customers, which are part of the employer's property, and subjective knowledge which has been acquired by the employee, such as his general knowledge of the trade or industry, or his organisational ability. In *Herbert Morris Ltd v Saxelby* an engineer covenanted not to be engaged by a competitor for seven years after leaving his employment. This was held to be void, for it was a restraint on his technical skill and knowledge which he had acquired by his own industry, observation and intelligence, and this could not be taken away from him. On the other hand, in *SBJ Stephenson Ltd v Mandy*, a covenant against the disclosure of any information relating to the company's business affairs which had come into the employee's possession whilst employed by the company was held to be valid. The identity of customers, prices charged, renewal dates, market information and contractual arrangements were objective knowledge capable of being protected. But if an employer wishes to enforce a covenant against the disclosure of confidential information, he must be able to identify a perceived or actual harm from the disclosure which would justify the restraint (*Jack Allen Ltd v Smith*).

19.46   Another example is *Thomas Marshall Ltd v Guinle*, where the defendant was appointed managing director of the claimant company under a 10-year service contract, which contained clauses against disclosing confidential information relating to the affairs, customers or trade secrets of the company, during his employment or after it ceased. He resigned after five years and set up his own competing business. The court granted an injunction against him from acting in breach of the agreement.

B. Existing customers and connections

19.47   The nature of the employee's work may well lead him into close contact with the firm's customers, so as to build up a relationship which may lead those customers to follow the employee when he takes up new employment. This, then, is a legitimate field where the employer may seek protection. In *GW Plowman & Sons Ltd v Ash*, the defendant was employed as a sales representative. He covenanted not to canvass or solicit orders from any person who was a customer of the firm for a period of two years after leaving his employment. It was held that the restraint was valid, even though it extended to customers whom the employee did not know or with whom he had no contact during his period of employment. It was argued that the restraint was bad because it could apply to those customers who had ceased to do business with the firm, but the Court of Appeal thought that an employer was entitled not to abandon hope that such customers would return to do business once more.

19.48   On the other hand, if an employee does not come into contact with such customers, then it cannot be argued that he has built up a special relationship with them so as to entitle the employer to extract a covenant restraining the employee from approaching them with a view to taking business away from the employer. For example, if a firm is engaged mainly in trading in the south of England, and has few customers outside that area, a covenant restraining an employee from working in that type of business anywhere in the world must of necessity be void, as being wider than legitimately required for the protection of the employer's business (*Dowden and Pook Ltd v Pook*). In *Attwood v Lamont* a tailor's cutter in a department store agreed not to be employed by another firm which competed with his employer. Since it can hardly be said that in his position he had gained the trust and confidence of the customers so that they would follow him if he left the firm, the covenant was void. Again, if the business is such that it is not of a recurring nature, then the employer's interest in the customer ceases on the conclusion of a particular transaction, and he is not entitled to protection against poaching. In *Bowler v Lovegrove* the defendant was a negotiating clerk who worked for a firm of estate agents. He covenanted not to enter into a similar business for one year within a restricted area, but it was held that as the business was of a non-recurring nature, the employer had no interest to protect, and the covenant was void.

19.49   The position held by the employee may be relevant, too. An employer can scarcely claim that he fears competition from an ex-employee if, during the period of employment, he pays him a low wage, for this reflects the regard he has for his services (*M and S Drapers v Reynolds*). Nor is an employer entitled to restrain competition by preventing the ex-employee from approaching persons who are not his customers. In *Gledhow Autoparts v Delaney* the claimants employed the defendant as a commercial traveller. It was agreed that after leaving his employment, the defendant would not seek orders from any firm within the area in which he had previously operated. The restraint was held to be void, for as worded, it would have prevented him from calling on firms who were not then customers of the claimants, and was therefore a covenant designed to restrain competition. Nor can a covenant restrain an ex-employee from dealing with businesses which were not in competition with the employer (*Scully UK Ltd v Lee*).

19.50 Moreover, the personality, temperament and general make-up of an employee is his own possession, and there is thus no proprietary right in an employee's own personality which the employer can keep to himself as part of his own business (*Cantor Fitzgerald (UK) Ltd v Wallace*).

19.51 If there is a prima facie breach of a covenant not to deal with the employer's former customers, the employer is entitled to an injunction even though the customer has intimated that he will not do further business with the employer (*John Michael Design plc v Cooke*).

19.52 The employer's 'connections' are also a legitimate object for protection. Thus an employment agency which supplied temporary staff to business clients was held to be entitled to extract and enforce a restrictive covenant from its own staff who dealt with the temporary staff (the connection) and the clients (*Office Angels Ltd v Rainer-Thomas*).

C. Working for competitors

19.53 We have seen (para 10.1) that the courts will not grant an injunction to compel a person to work for a particular employer, for this would amount to compulsory labour. Thus if an employee agrees that after leaving his employment, he will not work for anyone the courts will rarely enforce such an agreement because the employee will be faced with the alternative of being forced to work for his former employer or starve! But if the latter alternative does not exist, the courts may be more willing to enforce the agreement.

19.54 In *Littlewoods Organisation Ltd v Harris*, the claimants ran a mail order business, their chief rivals being Great Universal Stores (GUS). The defendant worked for the claimants in a senior position, and had access to confidential information about how the business was operated. He agreed that on leaving his employment, he would not work for GUS for a period of 12 months. He then resigned his position in order to take employment with GUS, and the claimants sought an injunction to restrain him. For the defendant it was argued that the covenant was too wide, and therefore void, for, as worded, it would have prevented him from being employed by GUS anywhere in the world, or by one of their companies which was not concerned with mail order. Nonetheless, the restriction was held to be valid by a majority of the Court of Appeal. It was held that where a covenant in restraint of trade was drafted in general terms, which, without alteration could be construed in a sense which was not unreasonably wide in relation to the relevant confidential information or trade secrets for which the covenantee was seeking protection, the court could construe the covenant in that sense, thereby rendering it valid and enforceable. Accordingly, the covenant should not be construed as applying to the whole range of business carried on by GUS throughout the world, but only to the mail order business carried on in the

United Kingdom. So construed, it was no wider than was reasonably necessary to protect the confidential information about the mail order side of the claimants' business, and it was thus enforceable. There is little doubt that this case represents a major shift in the judicial approach to the interpretation of restrictive covenants, though it is arguable that the conclusion is warranted on the special facts.

19.55　But the protection taken out by the employer must be in respect of his specific interests, and if it is too wide for this purpose, it will be void. In *Commercial Plastics Ltd v Vincent*, the claimants employed the defendant to work on the production of PVC calendering sheeting for adhesive tape. The defendant agreed not to be employed by a competitor in the PVC calendering field for one year after leaving his employment. This restriction was held to be void. The protection legitimately required by the claimants could only be in respect of their own business, which was the production of adhesive tape. In fact, the covenant covered the whole field of calendering sheeting, and hence was too wide.

19.56　It should also be noted that if an employee has agreed to a restrictive covenant with his employers, which has the effect of restricting his activities after the employment has ended, then if the employer transfers the business in circumstances in which the Transfer of Undertakings (Protection of Employment) Regulations apply (see para 9.21), the new owner of the transferred business is entitled to enforce that covenant against the employee (*Morris Angel & Son Ltd v Hollande*, see para 9.57).

D. Enticing existing employees

19.57　A covenant which purports to restrict the right of an employee to solicit or entice other employees to leave the employer's employment and to work for another employer is generally void. Thus in *Hanover Insurance Brokers Ltd v Schapiro* the defendant entered into a restrictive covenant with his employers which provided, inter alia, that for a period of 12 months after leaving his employment he would not '... solicit or entice any employees of the company to the intent or effect that such employee terminates that employment.' When the defendant left his employment, the employers sought an injunction to restrain him from acting in breach of the clause quoted. It was held that an employee has the right to work for any employer who is willing to employ him. Thus employees are not part of the assets of an employer—like stock in trade or goodwill and customers. A restriction which sought to prevent a person from poaching employees—irrespective of their expertise, technical knowledge and/or juniority, and which could also apply to employees who were not in the particular employment when the defendant left, was clearly a restriction against competition, and therefore void (*TSC Europe UK Ltd v Massey*).

19.58　However, different considerations may apply if the covenant purports to restrain the poaching of 'an executive' or a person 'in a senior capacity', and, if necessary, the court will identify those who fall within such categories (*Alliance Paper Group plc v Prestwich*). Further, the Court of Appeal has recently held that an employer has a legitimate interest in maintaining a stable, trained workforce in a highly competitive business (*Ingham v ABC Contract Services Ltd*) which can be protected within the limits of reasonableness by means of a non-solicitation clause (*Dawnay Day Ltd v De Braconier D'Alphen*).

19.59–19.65 Employers cannot agree to a restraint among themselves which would not be enforced if it was entered into by their employees. In *Kores Manufacturing Co Ltd v Kolok Manufacturing Co Ltd* two companies, both engaged in the selling of carbon paper, agreed that they would not employ any person who had been employed by the other party for a period of five years after that person had left the other's employment. Had the restraint been imposed by a company on the employees, it would have been void. It was equally void having been made by the employers themselves.

Extent of the restraint

19.66 The legitimate interests of the employer can only be protected within their proper limits, and any restraint outside those limits will be void. Thus if the covenant is too wide in time, or too extensive in terms of the area covered, the courts will not enforce it. Covenants which are in restraint of trade will only be valid if they are reasonable, and this will depend on an examination of all the circumstances. In *Nordenfelt v Maxim Nordenfelt Guns and Ammunition Co Ltd* an inventor of guns and ammunition sold his business to a company for a substantial sum, and covenanted not to be engaged in any similar business anywhere in the world for 25 years. Considering the worldwide nature of the business, and the price which had been paid for his promise, the House of Lords held that the restraint was reasonable.

19.67 Time and area may be looked at together to assess the validity of the covenant. In *Fitch v Dewes* a solicitor's clerk was prohibited from entering into the employment of another solicitor within a radius of seven miles of Tamworth Town Hall. Although this was a lifetime restraint, the modest area enabled him to work quite openly outside the limit, and it was held to be valid. But if the covenant is too wide for its purpose, either in time or area, it will be void. In *Mason v Provident Clothing and Supply Co Ltd* a covenant restraining a canvasser from competing with his former employer anywhere within 25 miles from the centre of London was held to be void. And in *Herbert Morris v Saxelby* (above) a seven-year restraint on an engineer was equally bad.

19.68 The restriction cannot be worded in a manner which prevents the employee from obtaining non-competing employment (*Commercial Plastics Ltd v Vincent* (above)). For example, in *Fellowes & Son v Fisher* the defendant was a conveyancing clerk employed by a firm of solicitors in Walthamstow. He agreed that for five years after leaving his employment, he would not (a) be employed or concerned in the legal profession anywhere within the postal districts of Walthamstow and Chingford, or (b) solicit any person who had been a client of the firm whilst he had been with them. After leaving his employment, he commenced work with another firm of solicitors who had offices in Walthamstow. The Court of Appeal refused to grant an injunction to restrain him. A restraint of five years which covered such a thickly populated area was undoubtedly too wide in the circumstances. Further, clause (a), as worded, would have prevented him from being employed as an assistant to a justices' clerk, or in the legal department of the local authority. In *Greer v Sketchley Ltd*, the activities of the company were confined to the Midlands and London area. The employee agreed that after leaving his employment he would not work for any similar business anywhere in the United Kingdom. This was held to be void; the fact that there was a problematical and possible expansion by the company into other areas of the country was too vague to justify such a wide restraint.

19.69–19.75 An area restriction will always be considered critically by the courts, since it will frequently amount to a covenant against competition, which would generally be unenforceable. Thus if such a restriction will do little to protect the employer (eg, because most of the orders are placed on the telephone), or if there is no functional connection with the area covered by the restriction and the areas associated with the employee's work, the restraint is likely to be void (*Office Angels Ltd v Rainer-Thomas*).

Interpreting a covenant in restraint of trade

19.76 If a covenant is too restrictive, it will be totally void, and the courts will not enforce it or any part of it. They will not normally validate the agreement by altering it, for the test is whether the parties have in fact made a valid agreement, not whether they could have done so, and it must stand or fall on its own merits. Exceptionally, however, the courts may relax this strict interpretation by use of a device known as 'the blue pencil' rule.

19.77 The court must be satisfied (a) the unenforceable provision is capable of being removed without the necessity of adding to or modifying the wording of what remains, (b) the remaining terms continue to be supported by adequate consideration, (c) the removal of the unenforceable provision does not so change the character of the contract that it becomes different from that which the parties entered into, and (d) the severance must be consistent with public policy underlying the avoidance of the offending term (*Marshall v NM Financial Management Ltd*).

19.78 If there are terms which are too wide, and others which are valid and reasonable, then the former may be struck out of the agreement altogether. If those terms which thus remain are valid, then they may be enforced. In *T Lucas & Co Ltd v Mitchell* the defendant was employed by the claimants as a sales representative. He agreed that after leaving his employment he would not (a) deal in any goods similar to those which he had previously sold, or (b) solicit orders from or supply any such goods to any customer of the firm within the Manchester area. The first part of the covenant was clearly void, for this was a restraint on competition. The second part was clearly reasonable. Because there were two separate restraints, capable of being enforced separately, the excision of the first was possible without affecting the second.

19.79 Severance is possible if there is no grammatical difficulty in removing the offending words (*Business Seating Ltd v Broad*). If that which remains is reasonable, the covenant will be enforced (*Rex Stewart etc v Parker*). The courts will prefer an interpretation which gives effect to the parties' intentions, rather than invalidate it by using a literal interpretation (*Turner v Commonwealth and British Minerals Ltd*).

19.80 If, in the particular circumstances of the case, there is 'a want of accuracy of expression' the court may be prepared to permit an interpretation which would give some sensible meaning to a covenant. Thus in *Business Seating (Renovations) Ltd v Broad*, a clause forbade a sales representative from canvassing, soliciting or endeavouring to take away from the company the business of any client or customers. The nature of 'the business' was not defined, but its meaning could be inferred from the nature of the defendant's employment, and, as a matter of construction, it meant the business carried out by the company.

19.81 A clause in a restrictive covenant which states that the covenant will continue to apply when the contract is terminated 'for whatever reason', or 'whether the contract is lawfully terminated or not', or 'howsoever arising' or some other such phrase, is not, by itself, unreasonable. Not every stipulation in a contract falls when there has been a fundamental breach by one side which has been accepted by the innocent party. Thus if the employee is dismissed for reason of misconduct, or if he resigns his employment, the restrictive covenant may still be enforced. The fact that the offending term may apply to some circumstances, but not to others, will not invalidate the rest of the covenant (*Rock Refrigeration Ltd v Jones*).

19.82–19.90 However, a court will not rewrite a covenant so that it has a meaning which is different from that which it has when properly construed.

Injunctive relief

19.91 In considering whether or not to grant an injunction, the court will take account of the 'balance of convenience' in accordance with the principles laid down in *American Cyanamid v Ethicon Ltd*. Three questions need to be asked; (a) is there a serious issue to be tried, (b) would damages be an appropriate remedy if the injunction is not granted, and (c) what is the likelihood of the plaintiff succeeding at a full trial. In *Lansing Linde Ltd v Kerr* it was alleged that the defendant was in breach of a covenant which was designed to prevent him from working for a competitor for a period of 12 months after leaving his employment. The Court of Appeal held that an application for an injunction was rightly refused. The trial of the action would not have taken place until most of the period for which the injunction was sought would have expired. Thus the question was not only whether there was a serious issue to be tried, but also an assessment of the plaintiff's prospect of succeeding at that hearing. The injunction, if granted, would have effectively determined the case in the claimant's favour, and therefore the judge had been correct in considering as an additional factor the strength of the plaintiff's claim.

19.92 Even though an employee is in breach of his covenant, the granting of an injunction to restrain him from working for a competitor is a discretionary remedy, and will only be granted if, on the balance of convenience, it is necessary to do so. In *GFI Group Inc v Eaglestone* the defendant was required by his employment contract to give 20 weeks' notice of termination. He, and two other highly-paid employees, decided to resign and work for a competitor. The other two employees were only required to give four weeks' notice. The claimant sought an order to restrain the defendant from working in breach of his contract until the end of the 20-week notice period, but the court decided to uphold the restraint only for 13 weeks. The fact that two other employees had already commenced work for the competitor meant that the reality of the situation was that the damage had already been done. It was not necessary for the protection of the claimant's interests to hold the defendant to the full period of 20 weeks.

19.93–19.100   It should be noted that if an employer wrongfully dismisses an employee, he cannot at the same time claim the benefit of the restrictive covenant, for the whole contract will have been repudiated by the employer (*General Billposting Co v Atkinson*), distinguished in *Rock Refrigeration Ltd v Jones*). This is so even if there is an automatic termination of the employment (eg on the dissolution of a partnership (*Briggs v Oates*)). But if a contract provides that it may be terminated by an employer on giving six months' notice or six months' pay in lieu of notice, an employer who adopts the latter option is not acting in breach of contract (*Rex Stewart etc v Parker*).

Search orders

19.101   In addition (or as an alternative) to obtaining an injunction, the aggrieved employer may seek a search order. This permits the employer to search the employee's premises or home etc, and to remove documents, drawings, records, prototypes or other specified matter. The purpose is to prevent a defendant from destroying, hiding or removing vital evidence, and to enable the claimant to obtain inspection of any relevant matter in the defendant's possession. A refusal to permit the search, and/or the removal, destruction etc of the evidence not only enables the courts to draw an adverse conclusion, but may also amount to a contempt of court (*Anton Piller KG v Manufacturing Processes Ltd*). Before granting the order, the court must be satisfied (a) that there is a strong prima facie case, (b) the actual or potential damage to the plaintiff would be very serious, and (c) that there is clear evidence that the defendant has in his possession incriminating matter, and that there is a real possibility that he would destroy, hide, remove or otherwise dispose of it (*Lock International plc v Beswick*).

19.102–19.110   Search orders are not available in Scotland, although there is a separate procedure by way of letters of request, under which a court may grant a commission and a diligence for the recovery of documents relevant to pending litigation.

Training agreements

19.111   An employer may permit an employee to go on a training course (possibly with paid leave of absence) under an agreement whereby the employee agrees to serve the employer for a specified period after completing the course. Clearly, such an agreement can be for the mutual benefit of both parties. The problem arises when the employee fails to serve the employer for the specified period. In *Strathclyde Regional Council v Neil*, the defendant was employed by the claimants as a trainee social worker. She was given paid leave of absence to go on a training course, and signed an agreement to serve the council for two years after completing the course. The agreement also specified that if she left her employment before completing two years' service she would refund to the council a sum of money, proportionate to the unexpired period of the contractual two years. After completing the course, she worked for the council for 15 months, and resigned her employment. It was held that the council could recover a proportion of their expenditure in respect of her salary, course fees, examination fees and book allowance. The terms of the contract were not extravagant or unconscionable.

CHAPTER 20

Practice and procedure

Making a claim to an employment tribunal

20.1   An employee who wishes to seek the enforcement of a statutory right, or to obtain a remedy for a breach of that right must present his claim to an employment tribunal within the appropriate time limit. An application for interim relief must be made within seven days of the dismissal, and a claim for a redundancy payment must be made within six months from the relevant date, although the employment tribunal has a discretion to extend the period for a further six months in certain circumstances if it is just and equitable to do so (ERA s 164). Claims for equal pay must also be presented within six months from the termination of employment, as must a claim based on a dismissal connected with official industrial action (see para 21.116), and a claim against a trade union in respect of unlawful exclusion or expulsion.

20.2   All other claims must be presented within three months of the act complained of, unless it was not reasonably practicable to present the claim earlier, in which case it may be presented within such further period as the employment tribunal considers reasonable. So far as claims based on race or sex discrimination or disability are concerned, the employment tribunal must consider whether it is just and equitable to extend the time limit (*British Coal Corpn v Keeble*).

20.3   Generally, there are two separate issues to consider. The first is whether or not it was reasonably practicable to present the claim within the time limits. If it was, that will usually be the end of the matter. The second is whether the employment tribunal should exercise its discretion so as to permit the claim to be admitted within such further period as it considers is reasonable. Thus, if a claimant makes a claim which is outside the three-month limit, but subsequently discovers facts which lead him to believe that he has a further legitimate complaint, the employment tribunal may still exercise its discretion to allow the latter complaint, even though there is no jurisdiction to consider the former (*Marley (UK) Ltd v Anderson*).

20.4   If the employee was not aware of the facts which gave rise to a potential complaint until after the three-month time limit has expired (eg the alleged acts of race or sex discrimination, see *Berry v Ravensbourne National Health Service Trust*, or an alleged act of unfair dismissal, see *Marley (UK) Ltd v Anderson*), then it may be just and equitable or reasonable to allow the late submission of a claim.

20.5 If the act complained of is a continuing act (eg race or sex or disability discrimination) which extends over a period, time will run from the end of the period (*Barclays Bank plc v Kapur*). The date on which the cause of the action crystallised will depend on the facts of each case (see *Clarke v Hampshire Electro-Plating Co Ltd*, para 4.274). If a claimant is ill during the three-month period, attention should be focused on whether the illness falls in the earlier weeks or in the far more critical weeks leading up to the expiry of the limitation period if the employment tribunal is considering whether to permit the claim outside the three-month period (*Schulz v Esso Petroleum*).

20.6 In deciding whether or not to allow an application which is out of time, the employment tribunal must first enquire into the circumstances as to why it was not reasonably practicable to present it before the end of the relevant period. 'Practicable', in this connection, means 'feasible', and it is a question of fact for the employment tribunal to determine as to whether it was reasonably feasible to present the claim in time (*Palmer v Southend-on-Sea Borough Council*). Thus if the time limit expires on a non-working day (eg Sunday), an application will be out of time if it is presented on the following day (*Swainston v Hetton Victory Club Ltd*). However, the employment tribunal will consider whether to exercise their discretion to allow the complaint to be presented out of time, but this will only be permitted in exceptional circumstances (*Walls Meat Co v Khan*). Thus it may be just and equitable to extend the time limits where the reason for the late submission was that the employee was trying to resolve the issue by using the internal procedures (*Aniagwu v London Borough of Hackney*). But an offer of re-engagement, subsequently withdrawn, will not prevent the operation of the time limits (*London Underground Ltd v Noel*).

20.7 If an employee or his representatives (eg trade union official or solicitor) are at fault in not presenting the claim in time, then it is likely that the employment tribunal will refuse jurisdiction (*Times Newspapers v O'Regan*), but if an employee is blameless, it may be easier to infer that it was not reasonably practicable to present the claim in time (*Union Cartage Co Ltd v Blunden*). The fact that an internal appeal was being pursued by the claimant is not a ground on which he may claim that it was not reasonably practicable to present the claim earlier (*Palmer v Southend-on-Sea Borough Council*), but if the employer expressly requests that the application be delayed so that negotiations can take place with a view to reaching an amicable settlement, then it may not be practicable to present the claim within the time limit (*Owen v Crown House Engineering Ltd*). Ignorance of one's legal rights is not an excuse for not presenting the claim within the three-month period (*Avon County Council v Haywood-Hicks*), but mistaken advice given by a member of the staff of the employment tribunal may be a ground for extending the time limit (*London International College v Sen*).

20.8 All complaints must actually be received (*Secretary of State for Employment v Banks*) by the Central Office of Industrial Tribunals within the appropriate time limits (before midnight, see *Post Office v Moore*), although an application received by a Regional Office will be valid if presented in time (*Bengey v North Devon District Council*). If the application does not arrive in time because of an abnormal delay in the post, the claimant will have to rely on the escape clause (*Beanstalk Shelving Ltd v Horn*).

20.9 If an application is posted, then delivery in the ordinary course of the post may be expected:
(a) in the case of first class mail, on the second working day after posting;
(b) in the case of second class mail, on the fourth working day after posting.
Working days are Monday to Friday, excluding bank holidays.

20.10 Thus if an application is posted, but arrives one day after the time limits have expired, it is open to the employment tribunal to decide if the claimant could have reasonably expected the application to be delivered in the ordinary course of the post. This is a question of fact for the employment tribunal to determine on the evidence (*St Basil's Centre v McCrossan*).

20.11 If an employee is dismissed on the 14th of the month, his claim must be presented on or before the 13th day of the third month following. If the month in question has no corresponding date (ie because it is a shorter month) the three-month period will expire at the end of the relevant month. Thus if an employee is dismissed on 30 November, his claim must be presented by 28 February (or 29th, if it is a Leap Year); see *Pruden v Cunard Ellerman Ltd*.

20.12 But if, though posted in time, an application does not appear to have been received by COIT, prudence requires that the claimant (or his representative) should make further enquiries, because it should be obvious from the failure to receive an acknowledgment that something is amiss, and therefore confirmation should be sought as to its arrival. It follows that if nothing is done to check the receipt of an application which has in fact never arrived, a fresh application may well be out of time (*Capital Foods Retail Ltd v Corrigan*). Indeed, a solicitor who submits an application on behalf of a client is expected to have a proper system operating which enables him to find out, contemporaneously, whether the conduct of business is taking a normal course, and to check, at or near the time, that replies which should have been received at a given date have in fact been received. Thus in *Camden and Islington Community Services NHS Trust v Kennedy*, the claimant's claim for unfair dismissal had to be presented by 27 December. Her solicitor posted her application on 19 December, but although he expected to receive an acknowledgment by 5 January, he delayed checking with the tribunal office until 30 January, when he was told that it had not been received. He posted another application the following day. It was held that the claim was out of time. Solicitors practising in the field of employment law must be aware of the need to comply strictly with the appropriate time limits, and ensure that they have in place systems which ensure that time limits are complied with.

20.13 If, in error, a claimant names the wrong employer in his application, an employment tribunal may, at the request of the claimant or on its own motion, add any other person to be joined in the proceedings, even though this is done outside the normal time limit for presenting a claim. The employment tribunal may exercise its discretion to join the other party not only when the claimant has misnamed or misdescribed the respondent, but also when he has failed to identify the 'correct' employer (eg where his contract has been transferred by virtue of the Transfer of Undertakings (Protection of Employment) Regulations 1981 (see *Drinkwater Sabey Ltd v Burnett*).

20.14–20.20 The statutory time limits go to the employment tribunal's jurisdiction, and if a claim is presented out of time, the tribunal will be unable to hear the claim even though the employer fails to take the point (*Rogers v Bodfari (Transport) Ltd*). But there is no time limit as such when it is proposed to add a new respondent, or substitute another one, to an application which has been lodged in time (*Drinkwater Sabey Ltd v Burnett*). If the claimant's claim is for breach of contract under the Employment Tribunals Extension of Jurisdiction Order, which is out of time, the employer's counterclaim, presented in time, can be proceeded with (*Patel v RCMS Ltd*).

Time limits for enforcing Community rights

20.21 European law (ie the Treaty of Rome or EC directives) does not specify any particular time limits for bringing proceedings when an employee is seeking to enforce a Community right. The general principle to be adopted was laid down in *Fisscher v Voorhuis Hengelo B V* where the European Court held that national rules relating to time limits for bringing such actions were to be applied, providing that they are no less favourable than similar actions of a domestic nature, and do not render the exercise of rights conferred by Community law impossible in practice.

20.22 Thus, in principle, domestic time limits will apply, but the question arises, what are the time limits when it is discovered that UK law does not meet the requirements of EC law? Does time start to run from when the cause of action arose, or from when it is discovered that UK law is defective, or from when UK law is brought into line with EC law?

20.23 Part of the answer is to be found when considering the EC law which is being sought to enforce. Article 141 of the Treaty of Rome became effective from when the UK joined the Community in 1973. Time will start to run against an employee from the date when the UK Government fully implemented art 141. Thus in *Rankin v British Coal Corpn* the claimant was dismissed for reason of redundancy in 1987. She was then 61 years of age, and at that time women over the age of 60 were not entitled to a redundancy payment. The law was changed in January 1990 (Employment Act 1989 s 16(1)), and in April that year she applied to an employment tribunal for a redundancy payment, based on art 141 of the Treaty of Rome. The EAT held that her claim was timeous. The appropriate starting date from which time would run was the date when it became clear that a claim could properly be made.

20.24 A similar view was taken in *Methilhill Bowling Club v Hunter*, where a woman worked between 8 and 16 hours per week. In 1993 she was dismissed, and brought a claim for unfair dismissal. At a preliminary hearing, the employment tribunal held that there was no jurisdiction to hear her complaint, as she had not been employed for more than five years, as required by the provisions of the Employment Protection (Consolidation) Act 1978, then in force. In March 1994 The House of Lords decided (*R v Secretary of State for Employment, ex p Equal Opportunities Commission*) that those provisions which prevented part-time workers from receiving redundancy payments unless they had been employed for more than five years were contrary to art 141 of the Treaty of Rome. Two months after this decision, the claimant presented a claim to an employment tribunal, arguing that she had been unfairly dismissed, and seeking a remedy by virtue of art 141. It was held that she was entitled to pursue her claim. The earlier proceedings had been based on the 1978 Act, whereas the present proceedings, being based on art 141, were wholly different. The first tribunal had not made any findings of fact, and therefore could not be regarded as being *res judicata*. The second claim was presented within a reasonable time of the House of Lords' decision, and thus should be heard on its merits. (The EAT also followed an earlier decision in *Mediguard Services Ltd v Thame* to the effect that compensation for unfair dismissal is to be regarded as 'pay' within the meaning of art 141.)

20.25 However, contrary conclusions were reached by the EAT in two further cases. In *Biggs v Somerset County Council*, the claimant worked as a teacher for 14 hours per week. She was dismissed in 1976, after being employed for less than two years. Following the *EOC* case (above), in June 1994 she presented a claim for unfair dismissal, relying on art 141. The employment tribunal held that her claim was out of time, and the decision was confirmed by the EAT. It clearly was the duty of an employment tribunal to disapply the qualifying threshold condition, and, in practice, it was possible for the claimant to have invoked her rights under art 141 within three months of her dismissal. The time limits in UK law were not incompatible with Community law, they are of general application, and do not discriminate between claims based on domestic law and those based on Community law. The cases of *Rankin* and *Methilhill* were not followed.

20.26 The same conclusion was reached in *Setiya v East Yorkshire Health Authority* where the claimant worked for two half days (ie seven hours) per week for 20 years. His contract was terminated in 1991, and he brought a claim for unfair dismissal. The employment tribunal held that, on a preliminary point, since he worked for less than eight hours per week, he was precluded from complaining that he had been unfairly dismissed. Following the *EOC* case (above) he applied for an extension of time in which to appeal to the EAT. It was held that it would not be just to extend the time for appealing to the EAT. It had been open to the claimant to take the point which finally succeeded in the *EOC* case.

20.27 The decision of the EAT in *Biggs v Somerset County Council* was subsequently upheld by the Court of Appeal. Although, in 1976, when she was dismissed, the claimant would have been unaware of the impact of s 2 of the European Communities Act or the effect of the decision of the European Court of Justice in *Defrenne v Sabena*, her mistake as to her rights was a mistake of law, not of fact. There was no legal impediment which prevented her from presenting her claim and arguing that the restriction on part-time workers was indirectly discriminatory. The fact that the existing law at the relevant time had not been explained or was not fully understood was no ground for reopening past transactions. Further, the complaint was not presented within a reasonable time after the expiry of the time limits.

20.28–20.35 Similarly, in *Barber v Staffordshire County Council*, the Court of Appeal refused to permit a claimant to bring a new claim based on EU law where an earlier claim had already been dismissed by an employment tribunal. The doctrine of issue estoppel applies.

Effective date of termination (s 55(4))

20.36 So far as unfair dismissals are concerned, the claim must be presented within three months from the effective date of termination of employment. This date can be

a. if the employment is terminated with notice, the date on which that notice expires, or

b. if the employment is terminated without notice, the date on which the termination takes effect, or

c. in the case of a fixed term contract, the date on which the term expires.

20.37 Certain problems have arisen out of this. In *Dixon v Stenor Ltd* Sir John Donaldson pointed out that there were four situations commonly met. The first is where the employee is given notice, and works to the end of that notice. The second is where there is a summary dismissal, and the third is where the employee is given money in lieu of notice. These cases are fairly straightforward, but the fourth situation presented a problem. This was where the employee is dismissed with notice, but is not required to work the period of that notice. In effect, he is on paid leave, and his employment does not effectively terminate until the notice expires, even though he may not be working during that time. If he were to submit an application during this period, in effect it would be premature. However, ERA s 111(3) provides that if a dismissal is with notice, a tribunal may consider a complaint notwithstanding that it is presented before the effective date of termination of the employment. In other words, an employee may bring a complaint as soon as he receives his notice, or within three months from the effective date of termination of his employment.

20.38 If an employee is dismissed, and pursues an appeal through the domestic procedures, there are two possibilities. If the procedure provides for an immediate dismissal, with the possibility of reinstatement should the appeal be successful, the EDT is the date of dismissal (*J Sainsbury Ltd v Savage*). If the procedure provides for a suspension of the dismissal with the possibility of it being lifted following a successful appeal, the EDT is the date when the appeal was dismissed should the dismissal be confirmed (*Drage v Governers of Greenford High School*).

20.39 The fact that the employer retains the employee's P45 is irrelevant to the effective date of termination (*Newham London Borough v Ward*).

20.40 If an employer dismisses an employee without notice, but gives him a payment in lieu of notice, the effective date of termination is the date of dismissal (ERA s 97(1)). Consequently, if on that date the employee does not have the requisite length of continuous employment, he cannot pursue his claim for unfair dismissal, unless, of course, he can add on his statutory notice 'to pull him past the post' (s 97(2), see para 15.81). If notice of termination is given orally, the period of notice commences the day after it has been given, and the effective date of termination is calculated accordingly (*West v Kneels Ltd*).

20.41 The effective date of termination cannot be earlier than the date on which the employee receives notice of the dismissal. There is no room for a doctrine of 'presumed or constructive knowledge' of a dismissal (*McMaster v Manchester Airport plc*). On the other hand, the parties are free to determine for themselves the effective date of termination (*Lambert v Croydon College*).

20.42 It should be noted that s 97(2) will extend the effective date of termination by the requisite statutory notice for the purposes of s 92 (right to have written reasons for dismissal), s 94 (unfair dismissal), s 119(1) (calculation of the basic award) and s 227(3) (increases the maximum allowable week's pay), but not for the purpose of computing the time limit within which a claim must be brought under s 111(2).

20.43 If an employee's claim is based on a constructive dismissal, the effective date of termination is the date when the employee accepts the alleged breach of contract by the employer (*G W Stephens & Son v Fish*). But time will only run from when the resignation is actually communicated to the employer, whether by written or oral communication or by conduct (*Edwards v Surrey Police*).

20.44–20.50 If the employee resigns with notice, he may present his claim before that notice has expired (*Presley v Llanelli Borough Council*), but if he resigns without notice, he can rely on the provisions of s 97(4) to 'pull him past the post' if he lacks the necessary period of continuous employment.

Submitting a complaint

20.51 There is no requirement that a claimant shall complete Form IT1 (see Appendix D) although this is commonly used. A complaint merely has to be in writing, specifying the name and address of the claimant and respondent, and contain a statement of the grounds on which relief is sought and particulars thereof. In other words, it is not sufficient merely to allege 'I was unfairly dismissed'; the claimant must state why he thinks the dismissal was unfair. In his reply, the employer must set out sufficient particulars to show the grounds on which he intends to resist the claim. Tribunals will use their wide powers to allow amendments in order to ensure that justice is done, for the actual relief may be a technical matter to be decided by the tribunal, and claimants may not have the necessary legal knowledge (see *Chapman v Goonvean and Rostowrack China Clay Co Ltd*). In allowing amendments, the employment tribunal should consider whether there would be any hardship or injustice to the parties if the amendment was permitted (*British Newspaper Printing Corpn (North) Ltd v Kelly*).

20.52 It is the duty of the claimant to state (with as much precision as possible) the nature of the claim, but the employment tribunal will not investigate on its own motion every allegation made but not pursued by a party (*Mansah v East Herts NHS Trust*). Generally a claimant will be precluded from bringing fresh proceedings in respect of a matter which could and should have been litigated in earlier proceedings (*Divine-Bortey v Brent London Borough Council*).

20.53 Once the complaint has been made, copies will be sent to the respondent (the employer) and to the conciliation officer. The latter is under a statutory duty, either at the request of the parties or on his own initiative if he thinks he can be successful, to endeavour to promote a settlement without the matter going to a tribunal hearing, either by getting the parties to agree on reinstatement or re-engagement of the claimant, or securing agreement on the amount of compensation to be paid, or to get the claimant to withdraw his claim because it has little prospect of success (see para 1.7).

20.54 From the available figures, it would appear that more than half of the complaints are settled without a tribunal hearing, though the confidential nature of the work of the conciliation officer is such that we have little knowledge of the terms or circumstances. About 70 per cent of the cases referred to conciliation officers are settled on the basis of some form of monetary payment by the employer. The bulk of the remaining cases are settled because the claimant withdraws the claim, and in a few cases, there will be an agreement for reinstatement or re-engagement. Any communication to the conciliation officer is not admissible in evidence without the consent of the party who communicated it. In *M and W Grazebrook Ltd v Wallens* certain documents, which had been prepared by the personnel manager after the claimant had been dismissed, were shown to the conciliation officer. It was held that the documents were not covered by the privilege, for to find otherwise would enable a party to prevent disclosure of evidence by deliberately communicating it to the conciliation officer. On the other hand, if the documents had been specially prepared for the purpose of showing them to the conciliation officer then no disclosure can be ordered.

20.55 A claim under s 94 of ERA has two objects. First, the claimant will be seeking a finding that he has been unfairly dismissed and, second, he will be seeking compensation. Both those matters are justiciable before the employment tribunal. Thus, if the employers offer to pay the maximum compensation which would be payable, this does not prevent the claimant from proceeding with his claim in order to obtain a finding that the dismissal is unfair, where the employers are unwilling to concede this (*Telephone Information Services Ltd v Wilkinson*).

20.56–20.65 It will be seen (below) that an agreement reached whereby an employee agrees to waive his statutory rights is generally void, subject to certain exceptions, and hence the fact that the employee has accepted a sum in settlement (even though this may be in excess of the statutory compensation limits) does not preclude an employment tribunal from hearing the claim (*NRG Victory Reinsurance Ltd v Alexander*), and it is not vexatious or frivolous to pursue such a claim.

Restrictions on contracting out (ERA s 203)

20.66 Subject to the exceptions noted below, an employee cannot voluntarily surrender or contract out of his statutory rights, and any statement or agreement to that effect is void. A private settlement between the parties, even one purporting to be in full and final settlement of all or any outstanding claims cannot prevent an employee from pursuing the matter further in the employment tribunal, for an employee cannot opt out of his statutory rights.

20.67 Thus in *Council of Engineering Institutions v Maddison* the employee accepted £1,600 in consideration that he would forgo any claim against his former employers. This was held to be void. The object of the legislation is to prevent hasty and imprudent agreements being entered into by the employee. On the other hand, such an agreement, whilst void, can be taken account of by the employment tribunal, and if it provides for compensation at a level not less than that which would have been awarded by the tribunal, then the employee will not have suffered any loss, and no further award will be made. Further, it will be recalled (para 17.67) that an agreement for a financial settlement as a price for a resignation is not void under the Act (*Sheffield v Oxford Controls Co Ltd*). In practice, if an agreed settlement is reached, it is sound policy to call in the conciliation officer, thus turning the agreement into a binding one, although whether they will take action in such circumstances is a matter for conjecture (see para 1.12).

20.68 The exceptions to the rule are as follows:

(a) Any settlement made under the auspices of the conciliation office from ACAS acting under his statutory powers, whether the settlement is made orally or in writing, will be binding on the parties (*Gilbert v Kembridge Fibres Ltd*), and can be enforced. But the settlement, usually made on Form COT3, will only apply to the matters contained therein. Thus if a settlement is made to an unfair dismissal claim made under ERA, this will not bar a subsequent claim under other legislation, eg Sex Discrimination Act etc unless such claims have been specifically excluded (*Livingstone v Hepworth Refractories Ltd*),

Where a counsel, solicitor, CAB adviser or member of a law centre, who has been named as a representative, holds himself out as having authority to negotiate and reach a settlement on behalf of a claimant, then, in the absence of any notice to the contrary, the other party is entitled to assume that the adviser has such authority. Thus an agreement reached between the adviser and the conciliation officer will be binding on the claimant whether or not the adviser has actual authority to enter into it. Thus the ostensible authority of the adviser extends beyond the pleadings and presentation of the case, but includes all the actual and potential issues which are known to the parties (*Freeman v Sovereign Chicken Ltd*).

(b) A collective agreement which provides for guaranteed remuneration where all parties have applied to the minister for an Order excluding the right to receive guarantee pay under s 35. About 30 such Orders have been made.

(c) A dismissal procedure agreement which provides for remedies at least as effective as ERA which has been designated by the minister by Order on an application by all the parties. However, such exclusion from statutory rights does not apply to failure to permit a woman to return to work after childbirth, dismissal for reason of pregnancy or childbirth, dismissal of protected shop or betting workers, dismissal for asserting a statutory right, and an inadmissible reason for redundancy. Apparently only one industry (electrical contracting) has opted for this procedure.

(d) A collective agreement which provides for redundancy payments where all the parties have applied to the minister for an exemption Order. A few such Orders have been made under this provision.

(e) A fixed contract of two years or more where the employee has agreed in writing to exclude his right to a redundancy payment.

(f) A compromise agreement, which satisfied the following conditions:
   (i)   the agreement must be in writing;
   (ii) it must relate to a particular complaint;
   (iii) the employee must have received advice from a relevant independent adviser as to the terms of the proposed agreement and its effect. An independent legal adviser is a qualified lawyer (barrister, solicitor or advocate), official, employee or member of an independent trade union who has been certified in writing as being competent and authorised to give advice on behalf of the trade union, a worker at an advice centre who has been certified in writing as being competent to give advice on

behalf of the centre, or a person of a description specified in an order made by the Secretary of State;

(iv) the adviser must have a professional indemnity insurance policy or be covered by a contract of insurance;

(v) the agreement must identify the adviser; and

(vi) the agreement must state that the conditions regulating the compromise agreement under the Act are satisfied.

Compromise agreements may be made in respect of all those claims for which the employment tribunal has jurisdiction under s 18(1) of the Employment Tribunals Act 1996, which covers most, though not all, of the rights contained in ERA, TULR(C)A (except a failure to consult with a trade union on redundancies), Sex Discrimination Act, Equal Pay Act, Race Relations Act and Disability Discrimination Act. Compromise agreements are binding in respect of the particular complaints mentioned therein. A further claim may be made (within the appropriate time limits) in respect of matters not within the terms of the agreement (*Lunt v Merseyside TEC Ltd*). Thus the agreement should be drawn up in such a way that all matters which could be the subject of a complaint are effectively covered.

A compromise agreement cannot be set aside on the ground that one party has failed to disclose that there has been a breach of the duty of mutual trust and confidence (*BCCI SA v Ali*).

(g) An agreement to submit the dispute to arbitration under a scheme prepared by ACAS, which has been approved by the Secretary of State, under the provisions of s 212A of TULR(C)A. At the time of writing no such scheme has been prepared.

20.69–20.75 A compromise agreement is a contract connected with employment, and as such it may be enforced in an employment tribunal under the provisions of the Employment Tribunals Extension of Jurisdictions Order (*Rock-It Cargo Ltd v Green*), and see para 1.55.

Employer's reply

20.76 A copy of Form IT1 will be sent to the employer, who should reply on Form IT3 (see Appendix D) within 14 days, although it is permissible to apply for an extension of time. The response should state sufficient particulars to indicate the grounds upon which the application will be resisted. The 'label' attached to those grounds is generally irrelevant, for this is a matter which may well be determined on consideration of the factual evidence. Thus, if an employer submits that the reason for the dismissal was 'redundancy', and the facts are fully investigated by the employment tribunal, it is open to them to find that the reason was for 'some other substantial reason' (*Hannan v TNT-IPEC (UK) Ltd*). All relevant defences should be pleaded, if necessary in the alternative (*Church v Lancashire NHS Trust*).

Pre-hearing review

20.77 The Employment Tribunal (Constitution and Rules of Procedure) Regulations 1993 make provision for an employment tribunal, at the request of a party or on its own volition, to conduct a pre-hearing review. The parties are entitled to submit written representations and to give oral argument. If the employment tribunal considers that the claim or defence has no reasonable prospect of success, it may require a party to provide a deposit of up to £150 as a pre-condition of being permitted to pursue the matter further. If the party persists in pursuing the matter, and loses at the hearing, an award of costs against him may be made, and he may also lose his deposit. A failure to pay the deposit may result in the originating application or notice of appearance being struck out. No deposit may be ordered to be paid unless the employment tribunal has taken reasonable steps to ascertain the ability of the party concerned to pay.

Employment tribunal procedure

20.78 The tribunal will generally regulate its own procedure, and can issue directions to the parties as to how the case is to proceed (see generally, the cases cited in *Aberdeen Steak Houses Group plc v Ibrahim*). If a party is dissatisfied with the way the proceedings have been conducted by the chairman, he can only succeed on an appeal if it can be shown that he had been prejudiced thereby (*Barnes v BPC (Business Forms) Ltd*). The tribunal also has powers, at the request of one party or on its own volition, to order the other party to deliver further information of their case (*International Computers Ltd v Whitley*), and to disclose for inspection documents or other relevant evidence and to allow the other party to make any copies. However, in keeping with the non-legalistic approach of the tribunals, such orders are not made as a matter of routine procedure, but only if the party requiring the information can show that he will be prejudiced without such information (*White v University of Manchester*). In particular, disclosure of documents will not be ordered to enable a party to indulge in 'a fishing expedition', ie to search for material with which to establish a case (*British Aerospace plc v Green*). An employment tribunal cannot order a party to produce 'evidence', or to create documentary evidence which was not in existence. An order for discovery is limited to those documents which are in being (*Carrington v Helix Lighting Ltd*). Attendance orders, compelling witnesses to attend, may also be granted in appropriate circumstances. A tribunal cannot direct that a representative chosen by a party to the proceedings shall not act as such (*Bache v Essex County Council*).

20.79 Under the rules of procedure, a tribunal chairman, sitting alone can determine a number of preliminary issues, including jurisdictional matters (*Tsangacos v Amalgamated Chemicals Ltd*), and all matters in connection with the originating application (see para 1.42).

20.80 If an order for further particulars or discovery of documents is not complied with, the employment tribunal has the power to strike out the whole or part of the claim or defence, as appropriate (Employment Tribunals (Constitution and Rules of Procedure) Regulations, reg 4), but this punitive power should only be exercised if a fair trial is not possible due to the failure to comply. If there is a last-minute compliance, due to an acceptable explanation, it is not appropriate to strike out the claim or defence (*National Grid Co plc v Virdee*).

20.81 If one party is seeking the disclosure of documents which the other side regards as being of a confidential nature, such as references, confidential assessments on the applicant or other employees, and so forth, the chairman of the employment tribunal should himself inspect the document to satisfy himself that discovery is essential in order to dispose fairly of the proceedings. If he does decide that they should be disclosed, the interests of third parties can be protected by 'covering up', substituting names, and, in rare cases, hearing the proceedings in camera (*Science Research Council v Nassé*).

20.82 If privilege is claimed from disclosure, a balance must be held between the public interest in non-disclosure and that of justice in the production of the documents (*Halford v Sharples*). Communications between parties headed 'without prejudice' should be excluded from the evidence submitted, unless the matcrial was such that without them a dishonest case was being presented (*Independent Research Services Ltd v Catterall*).

20.83 Privilege from the disclosure of documents only applies to communications between clients and professional legal advisers, such as solicitors and barristers (*New Victoria Hospital v Ryan*).

20.84 There is no general duty on a party to disclose any documents in his possession or power, in the absence of any formal order to that effect. However, if he voluntarily discloses documents, there is a duty not to be selective in that disclosure, and he must not withhold other documents if there is a risk that the non-disclosure might convey a false or misleading impression as to the nature of any document disclosed (*Birds Eye Walls Ltd v Harrison*).

20.85 If there is no prior settlement or withdrawal, the employment tribunal will hear the case. A date, time and place for the hearing will be notified to the parties, although applications for adjournments will be considered on appropriate grounds. At the hearing, as a general rule, the burden of proof is on the claimant, and he should therefore give evidence first in order to support his allegations. This is true of race or sex discrimination claims, employment protection rights, claims made out of time, allegations by the respondent that the claimant was not an employee, or that he was not dismissed, etc.

20.86 If an employment tribunal is unable to come to a conclusion on a question of fact, they may apply the burden of proof. Thus in *Morris v London Iron and Steel Co Ltd* the tribunal could not decide whether an employee had been dismissed or resigned, and they held that he had not discharged the burden of proof which was on him to show that he was dismissed.

20.87 In unfair dismissal cases, if the dismissal is admitted, the employer will be required to give evidence first, and he must establish:
a. the reason for the dismissal (or, if there is more than one reason, the principal reason, see *Smith v Glasgow City District Council*), and
b. that it was a statutory reason.
He should then seek to show that he acted reasonably in the circumstances.

20.88 From a practical point of view, the employer should recognise that there are a number of matters within his knowledge about which the tribunal may wish to learn, and therefore should be prepared to give evidence on these matters. Thus it is not sufficient to show a reason for dismissal; the reasonableness of acting on that reason must also be shown. If an employee is dismissed because of redundancy, an employer should normally lead evidence to show that there was a fair selection system, full consultation with the individual concerned and trade union (if appropriate) and that efforts were made to find alternative employment, even if the applicant does not raise all these matters (*Langston v Cranfield University*). If the dismissal is for incompetence, the employer would need to show all those matters which a reasonable employer should have done before taking the decision to dismiss (see Chapter 17).

20.89 If one party is taken by surprise by the evidence of the other side, it will normally be possible to apply to introduce rebutting evidence, even if it is necessary to apply for an adjournment in order to produce the necessary evidence and/or witnesses. However, unreasonable applications for adjournments may be visited by an award of costs against the offending party although costs cannot be awarded as a pre-condition for resuming a hearing (*Cooper v Weatherwise (Roofing and Walling) Ltd*). An employment tribunal may permit a witness to be recalled for further examination, but should then give the other party an opportunity to make a further rebuttal (*Aberdeen Steak House Group v Ibrahim*).

20.90 If an employment tribunal, on its own volition, takes a point which was not taken by the parties, natural justice requires that the parties should be alerted to the fact, so that they can be given an opportunity to present further evidence on the matter, and/or make further submissions (*Laurie v Holloway*).

20.91 The standard of proof, ie the quantum of evidence which must be given in support of any particular allegation, must be sufficient to establish the balance of probabilities in that party's favour. The informality of tribunal procedure can sometimes mislead the parties into thinking that they can escape with a standard of proof which is in fact unacceptable. If the employer, for example, fails to prove the reason or the principal reason for the dismissal (*Smith v Glasgow City District Council*) or fails to show any reason, or gives a reason which the tribunal does not believe, then he will have failed to discharge the burden of proof which is placed on him, and the dismissal will be unfair. Although the tribunals will admit hearsay evidence in the proceedings, the weight which is given to such evidence is a matter for them to decide (*Coral Squash Clubs Ltd v Matthews*) and they will seldom base a decision in favour of an employer on such evidence, particularly if it is controverted by the direct evidence (or denials) of the claimant (*Mawson v Leadgate Engineering Ltd*). The tribunals will give such assistance as they can to a person who is not legally qualified or represented, but it is the duty of the parties to present all the relevant evidence before the tribunals, and applications of adjournments may be made if a party considers it necessary to call someone whose attendance was not thought necessary.

20.92 The evidential requirements in the employment tribunals are not the same as other courts. For example, in *Docherty v Reddy*, the claimant was dismissed for suspected theft. The tribunal permitted the employer to introduce evidence that the claimant had stolen on previous occasions. Such evidence would scarcely have been admissible in the criminal courts, as its probative value would have been exceeded by its prejudicial value, but the EAT held that the evidence was rightly admitted. The issues in the employment tribunals and the criminal courts are different; in this case, the tribunal had to decide if the employer had reasonable grounds for dismissing, and the claimant's previous conduct was a relevant factor to be taken into account.

20.93 Equally, whether a dismissal was fair or unfair can only be determined on the basis of the facts which were known to the employer at the time he dismissed the employee, and subsequent information which comes to light is only relevant if it confirms that reason. Such information cannot be admissible to show a separate and additional reason for dismissal, because when the employer dismissed the employee, he did not know of those facts. This can be illustrated by *W Devis & Sons Ltd v Atkins*, where the company dismissed a manager for failing to follow company directives. After he had left, it was alleged that facts were discovered which indicated that he had been guilty of gross misconduct, in that he had been taking secret commissions from customers, for which he could have been dismissed summarily. The employment tribunal refused to allow such evidence to be called on the issue of the fairness of the dismissal, and this was upheld on appeal to the House of Lords. It was permissible to adduce evidence which was discovered after the dismissal to prove the fairness of that reason, but not for the purpose of showing that the employers had discovered subsequently another reason which would have enabled them to dismiss fairly. However, if the dismissal is found to be unfair, the subsequent evidence can then be admitted for the purpose of determining the remedies which would be considered by the tribunal, whether by way of a refusal to make an order for reinstatement or re-engagement, a reduction in the amount of compensation to be paid, or an award of nil compensation (*Moncrieff v MacDonald*) or a reduction of the basic award (ERA s 122).

20.94 If, on the conclusion of the evidence of one party (be it applicant or respondent, as the case may be) the employment tribunal form the view that a prima facie case (or defence) has not been made out, they should nonetheless hear evidence from the other side, except in the most hopeless or frivolous cases (*Hackney London Borough Council v Usher*). Otherwise, after considering all the facts, hearing the witnesses, and studying any evidence tendered, the employment tribunal must determine the issue on the basis of the relevant legal requirement. Thus if the issue is whether or not the employer has acted reasonably, this does not mean that the tribunal must agree with the employer's decision, for in many cases more than one course of action is possible, and an employer is not to be criticised because he adopts one in preference to another. It is not the duty of the tribunal to decide if they would have come to the same conclusion as the employer based on the facts which were within the employer's knowledge (*Ferodo v Barnes*), nor should the tribunal substitute their own judgment for that of the employer (*Donn v Greater London Council*), and any temptation to interfere with management prerogatives should be resisted. In *St Anne's Board Mills Co Ltd v Brien* four employees refused to work with another employee, who they considered had been responsible for an accident. The employers investigated the matter, came to the conclusion that that employee was not to blame, and required the four to continue to work with him. They continued to refuse, and were dismissed. After considering the facts, the tribunal decided that the other employee had been responsible for the accident, and hence the four employees had not acted unreasonably in refusing to work with him. The dismissals were therefore unfair. On appeal, it was held that the question before the tribunal was not who was responsible for the accident, but whether the employers had acted reasonably in the circumstances. They had investigated the matter thoroughly and carefully, and come to certain conclusions. They had had the choice of dismissing an employee whom they considered to be blameless, or the four employees who were (in their view, wrongfully) refusing to work with him. In the circumstances, they had not acted unreasonably in dismissing the latter.

20.95 The paramount duty of the employment tribunal is to apply the law as laid down by Parliament. Account must be taken of the interpretation of that law as laid down by the EAT and other superior courts, but it is the statute which is paramount. In *Jowett v Earl of Bradford*, the employment tribunal refused to follow a test of selection for redundancy as laid down by the EAT in *Vickers v Smith*. It was held that this did not constitute an error of law on the part of the tribunal. When the language of a statute is unclear or ambiguous, then the duty of the courts is to interpret the statute and thus lay down binding precedents. But when the statute is clear and unambiguous, precedents are only guides, and do not bind (*Kearney & Trecker Marwin Ltd v Varndell*). The prime duty of the employment tribunal is to follow the words of the statute (*Anandarajah v Lord Chancellor's Department*).

20.96 About 95 per cent of all the decisions of the employment tribunals are unanimous, the remainder being majority decisions of 2–1, sometimes with the two 'wingmen' joining together to outvote the legal chairman. An unusual case was *R v Industrial Tribunal, ex p Cotswold Collotype*, where one tribunal member thought that the claimant was unfairly dismissed, a second member thought the claimant was not unfairly dismissed but redundant, and the third member thought the applicant was neither unfairly dismissed nor redundant! It was held that if the voting was so inconclusive that no decision was reached, the tribunal had an inherent power to refer the matter to a differently constituted tribunal.

20.97 If the claimant fails to appear at the hearing, and does not send a representative, the employment tribunal may adjourn to another date, or dismiss the claim (with or without an order for costs). A claim may also be struck out for want of prosecution on an application by the respondent or by the tribunal on its own motion (Employment Tribunals (Constitution and Rules of Procedure) Regulations, Sch 1) but only if the respondent would be seriously prejudiced thereby (*Evans v Metropolitan Police Comr*).

20.98 A claim may also be struck out on the ground that the manner in which the proceedings are conducted is scandalous, frivolous or vexatious, although before doing so an opportunity must be given to the party concerned to show cause why this should not be done.

20.99 It is the practice of some employment tribunals to give an oral decision immediately the hearing finishes, and then promulgate the decision in writing at a later date. In rare cases it is possible for the chairman, before such written promulgation, to announce his intention to recall the tribunal in order to reconsider some point of law which he has omitted to notice, or which was not drawn to his attention. While such practice is unusual, there is no legal objection to it (*Hanks v Ace High Productions Ltd*). However, it is not possible for an employment tribunal to depart from their oral decision when it is reduced to writing (*Arthur Guinness Son & Co (Great Britain) Ltd v Green*).

20.100–20.110 If, at the end of the oral hearing, both sides agree to put their submissions in writing, the employment tribunal must send a copy of each party's submission to the other party, and give a specified time in which any response is to be made. Such comments should be limited to the correction of factual errors and legal submissions on any new points of law raised (*Barking and Dagenham London Borough Council v Oguoko*).

Summary reasons

20.111 The Employment Tribunals (Constitution and Rules of Procedure) Regulations 1993 permit an employment tribunal to give summary reasons for their decision which, in effect, will be a shortened version of their decision. Either party may apply for full reasons, either at the conclusion of the hearing or within 21 days of receiving the summary reasons. The time for lodging an appeal against the decision will be 42 days from when the full reasons are entered in the employment tribunal register. Summary reasons will not be given in cases which relate to sex or race or disability discrimination, or equal pay claims.

Full reasons

20.112 In *Meek v City of Birmingham District Council*, Bingham LJ stated the duty of an industrial tribunal as follows:

> 'the decision of an industrial tribunal is not required to be an elaborate formalistic product of refined legal draftsmanship, but it must contain an outline of the story which has given rise to the complaint and a summary of the tribunal's basic factual conclusions and a statement of the reasons which have led them to reach the conclusion which they do on those basic facts. The parties are entitled to know why they won or lost. There should be sufficient account of the facts and of the reasoning to enable the EAT or, on further appeal, this court to see whether any question of law arises, and it is highly desirable that the decision of an industrial tribunal should give guidance both to the employers and trade unions as to practices which should or should not be adopted.'

Financial remedies

20.113 Monetary awards in respect of proceedings brought before an employment tribunal are subject to the special rules applicable in each case (see Appendix C). In particular, it should be noted that in race, sex and disability discrimination claims, there is no limit to the amount which may be awarded, and an award may also be made in respect of injury to feelings. Nor is there a limit to compensation awards in cases of health and safety and protected disclosure dismissals. Special rules are also applicable in claims brought under EU law (eg the Equal Treatment Directive) because 'full compensation' is required, and hence there is a difference in the stages at which percentage reductions are to be made for mitigation, contributory conduct, *ex gratia* payments, etc (see *Ministry of Defence v Hunt*).

Reviews

20.114   An application may be made to an employment tribunal within 14 days from the time the decision was sent to the parties, asking for a review of its decision. This is not an appeal, and there are limited circumstances in which the tribunal will accede to such a request. These are as follows:

a.   if the decision was wrongly made as a result of an error on the part of the tribunal's staff;

b.   if a party did not receive notice of the proceedings (*Hancock v Middleton*);

c.   if the decision was made in the absence of a party entitled to be heard. If an employer fails to reply to a complaint by not returning the appropriate defence within the stated time he may be denied the right to be heard unless he can show some valid reason for this. But if a party is prevented from attending a hearing through illness, then the tribunal should consider whether the absence was for a genuine reason, and it believes his story, a review should be granted (*Morris v Griffiths*). In addition to seeking a review, the person applying should state in writing his reasons not only for the application, but also for contending that the decision of the employment tribunal was wrong. In *Drakard & Sons Ltd v Wilton*, the employers did not attend a tribunal hearing as they believed that once having made an offer of settlement to the conciliation officer, they thought that they would be contacted if any further steps were required. The EAT held that the tribunal should have granted a review. They should have enquired into the circumstances surrounding the failure to attend the hearing;

d.   new evidence comes to light, which could not have been discovered before. For example, if, after the claimant has been awarded compensation for unfair dismissal, new evidence comes to light that he had been defrauding the employer during the period of employment, so that it would have been possible to have dismissed him summarily, then this will be taken into account by the tribunal when it reviews the decision, and any previous award of compensation may be altered accordingly (*McGregor v Gibbings Amusements Ltd*). It must be shown that the new evidence which has now become available could not have been presented at the original hearing, and the application should be accompanied by the substance of that new evidence, including, if possible, proofs of witnesses (*Simmons v Medway Welding Ltd*);

e.   the interests of justice require a review. This general power can be illustrated by the case of *Berkeley Garage Ltd v Edmunds* where the employers were told by officers from the Department of Employment that the claimant was bringing his case out of time. Consequently, they did not bother to attend the hearing. The tribunal found that it was not practicable for the claimant to have presented the case earlier, and proceeded to hear the case on its merits. When the employers discovered this, they applied for a review and a rehearing, which the tribunal refused. On appeal this was reversed, for the interests of justice clearly required that the employers be given an opportunity to present their side of the story. Similarly, in *Help the Aged Housing Association (Scotland) Ltd v Vidler* the claimant was awarded £4,700 compensation for unfair dismissal, mainly on the basis that he was 60 years of age, and the tribunal thought that it would be a considerable length of time before he obtained further employment. Within two weeks of the tribunal's decision, he obtained employment. It was held on appeal that the tribunal should have exercised its powers of review and reviewed the compensation in the light of the new situation, for the original assessment was totally wrong. Because the claimant had obtained alternative employment so quickly, this altered the substratum of the tribunal's reasoning in computing the loss likely to be suffered, and hence it was in the interests of justice that there should be a review.

20.115   Before refusing an application for review, the employment tribunal should give the claimant an opportunity to elaborate in writing the grounds which he intends to put forward (*Drakard & Sons Ltd v Wilton*).

20.116   The power to review only applies when the employment tribunal has made a decision. There is no power to review an actual settlement reached during or at the end of proceedings, where the tribunal has not made a finding on liability (*Larkfield of Cheptstow Ltd v Milne*).

20.117   An application for review may be made on the ground that there was an error in the proceedings, but not on the ground that the decision of the employment tribunal discloses an error of law, for that is a matter which must be dealt with on appeal to the EAT (*Trimble v Supertravel Ltd*).

20.118–20.125   An employment tribunal may also review its decision on its own motion.

Costs

20.126   An employment tribunal has the power to award costs against a party who has acted frivolously, vexatiously, abusively, disruptively or otherwise unreasonably in bringing or conducting the proceedings. Thus if a claimant or respondent knows that his case is hopeless, but still pursues it, an award of costs may be made (*Davidson v Jon Calder (Publishers) Ltd*). There is also a power to award costs against a claimant if his representative acts frivolously, vexatiously, abusively or otherwise unreasonably. Thus, if the representative knows that the claim has no reasonable prospect of success, or brings the claim with a collateral purpose (eg if a trade union does so in order to obtain recognition from the employer) costs against the claimant may properly be awarded. There is no absolute rule that the tribunal should take into account the means of the claimant or his representative (*Beynon v Scadden*). Costs may also be awarded if there is an unnecessary application for an adjournment or postponement, again at the discretion of the employment tribunal.

20.127   If the employment tribunal has previously required a deposit to be paid under the pre-hearing review procedure, an award of costs may be made against the losing party for unreasonably persisting with the case.

20.128–20.135   If an order for costs is made, this can be for a specific sum not exceeding £500, or an amount agreed between the parties, or the whole or specific part of the costs incurred by the other party to be taxed on the county court scale.

Appeals

20.136   It has already been noted (see Chapter 1) that the Employment Appeal Tribunal will hear appeals on points of law from employment tribunals, and on points of law and of fact from the decisions of the certification officer. An appeal on a point of law from the employment tribunals must be made within 42 days from the date when the document recording the full reasons for the decision was sent to the appellant (*Hammersmith London Borough Council v Ladejobe*), not from the date which in the normal postal rules they might be deemed to have been received (*Mock v IRC*), although it is possible in exceptional circumstances to apply for an extension of time, but a good reason for the delay must be shown (*Duke v Prospect Training Services Ltd*). Legal aid is available in the EAT, but it should be noted that a delay in obtaining legal aid, or the fact that the assistance of the Equal Opportunities Commission or the Commission for Racial Equality is being sought for the purpose of pursuing an appeal are not reasons for not adhering to the 42-day time limit. In particular, a Practice Direction issued by the EAT makes it clear that if an application for a review is made to an employment tribunal, this does not prevent the time for appealing from running (although this obviously does not prevent an appeal against the refusal of the tribunal to grant the review), and further, if an employment tribunal makes a finding of liability, but adjourns the question of compensation, the time for appealing runs from the date of the decision, and is not suspended until the final matter of compensation has been dealt with. The EAT will also consider the motives of the appellant, the tactics used, whether the delay was intentional, the length of the delay, the merits of the appeal, and whether there would be any injustice or prejudice to the party who was successful before the employment tribunal (see *Aziz v Bethnal Green City Challenge Co Ltd*).

20.137 Once an appeal to the EAT has been lodged, a preliminary hearing/directions (PHD) will take place. The appellant will be required to satisfy the EAT that it is reasonably arguable that the employment tribunal made an error of law. If so satisfied, the appeal will be allowed to proceed, and the EAT will make any appropriate directions to ensure that the appeal may be determined efficiently and effectively. A special PH/D form must be completed, enabling amendment to be made to the notice of appeal, giving time estimates for argument, and, if needed, requesting the chairman's notes of evidence. If the appeal does not raise an arguable point of law, it will be dismissed at the PHD stage. Only in very limited circumstances will an appellant be permitted to raise a point of law on appeal which was not canvassed before the employment tribunal (*Church v West Lancashire NHS Trust*).

20.138 An appeal from a decision of an employment tribunal can only hope to succeed if the employment tribunal have misdirected themselves in law, or entertained the wrong issue, or proceeded on a misapprehension or misconstruction of the evidence, or taken matters into account which were irrelevant to the decision, or reached a decision which no reasonable employment tribunal, properly directing themselves in law, could have arrived at. In *Neale v Hereford and Worcester County Council*, Lord Justice May propounded the so-called 'Biggles' test. He stated that the EAT should not interfere with the decision of the employment tribunal (except when they erred on a point of law) unless it was possible to say 'My goodness, that was certainly wrong!' Thus, if there is evidence to support their decision, the EAT will not normally interfere, particularly where the questions of fact and degree are at issue. The task of the EAT is to hear appeals only on points of law (*Spook Erection Ltd v Thackray*). It is not an error of law that the employment tribunal has misunderstood the facts (*British Telecommunications plc v Sheridan*).

20.139 In *Piggott Bros & Co Ltd v Jackson* the Court of Appeal stated that a decision of the employment tribunal can only be characterised as being perverse if it was not a permissible option. The EAT would have to identify a finding of fact which was unsupported by any evidence or a clear self-misdirection of law. However, in *East Berkshire Health Authority v Matadeen* the EAT held that in addition, 'perversity' was a free-standing basis for interfering with an employment tribunal's decision, if that decision 'was not a permissible option' or was 'a conclusion which offends reason' or 'so outrageous in its defiance of logic or of acceptable standards of industrial relations'. In particular, the EAT thought that the lay members were there to bring their experience and industrial judgment to the application of the law and to the decision to be reached on appeal. They were entitled to use that experience to ensure that employment tribunal decisions did not ignore generally acceptable standards.

20.140 The weight to be attached to the evidence is a matter for the employment tribunal, and it is not permissible for the EAT to substitute their own views on this (*Eclipse Blinds Ltd v Wright*). But an employment tribunal must consider whether a dismissal fell within the range of reasonable responses open to a reasonable employer, and not substitute their own judgment. A failure to adopt this approach may result in the decision not being a permissible option (*United Distillers v Conlin*).

20.141 The notice of appeal should state quite precisely what point of law is to be argued. It is not sufficient to make a bald statement that the employment tribunal misdirected itself on a point of law without specifying the error or misdirection to be appealed against. As Phillips J has pointed out, to say that something is an error of law does not, without further explanation, make it so. Indeed, if it turns out that there is in fact no arguable point of law involved in the appeal, the EAT is quite likely to make an award of costs against the unsuccessful party. Further, if no arguable point is disclosed in the notice of appeal, the notice itself can be rejected by the EAT, so that the appeal will never be heard.

20.142 In a Practice Direction issued in 1996 the EAT stated that copies of the notes taken by the chairman of the employment tribunal will not normally be made available in appeal proceedings except on cause shown and are necessary for the purpose of arguing a point of law on appeal. More latitude will be allowed to applicants who were not legally represented at the tribunal hearing (*Webb v Anglian Water Authority*). The facts of the case will be found in the tribunal's decision, and any appeal must be based on the law as applied to those facts. However, it is permissible in argument to refer to the chairman's notes for the purpose of clarifying any ambiguity in the case. If an appeal is based on the actual conduct of the case by the chairman, or some evidence contrary to that found by the tribunal, the claimant must first inform the Registrar of the EAT, so that this can be communicated to the respondent, and the views of the chairman sought. The EAT will not interfere with an award of compensation unless it is more than a trifling matter. If the question of the amount of compensation is alleged to be an error of law, it must be of a substantial nature for the EAT to interfere (*Fougère v Phoenix Motor Co Ltd*).

20.143 The EAT does have power to hear new evidence on appeal, but only if a reasonable explanation is produced as to why the evidence was not put before the employment tribunal. It must be shown that the existence of the new evidence could not have been known or foreseen, and that had it been available at the employment tribunal hearing, it would have had an important influence on either the outcome of the case or the award of compensation (*Photostatic Copiers (Southern) Ltd v Okuda*). The evidence must be credible, and of such a nature that it would have had a decisive effect on the tribunal's decision had they heard it (*International Aviation Services (UK) Ltd v Jones*). It is also possible to argue a new point of law, not canvassed before the employment tribunal, if the balance of justice so requires (*Russell v Elmdon Freight Terminal Ltd*).

20.144 If the decision of the employment tribunal is defective, because no reference or insufficient reference had been made to a particular aspect of the case, the EAT must not remit the case back to the employment tribunal for further amplification or clarification. The proper course is to allow the appeal and remit the case back for a further hearing (*Reuben v Brent London Borough Council*). Where the EAT remits a case back to the employment tribunal to consider certain specific issues, the tribunal has no jurisdiction to hear or determine matters outside the scope of those issues. In particular, there is no power to permit one party to amend its case so as to raise issues which were not previously before the employment tribunal (*Aparau v Iceland Frozen Foods Ltd (No 2)*).

20.145–20.155 If there is a complaint about the actual conduct of the employment tribunal proceedings (eg that a member is falling asleep) this should be raised with the chairman at the time, and not after the tribunal has reached its conclusions (*Red Bank Manufacturing Co Ltd v Meadows*), although more serious matters, such as allegations of bias, can be raised at any time (*Peter Simper & Co Ltd v Cooke*).

Reviews

20.156 The EAT has power to review its own decision on the grounds (a) that the order was wrongly made as a result of an error on the part of the tribunal or its staff, (b) a party did not receive proper notice of the proceedings, and (c) the interests of justice require such review. However, the purpose of review is not to allow appeals to be reheard and, in particular, a review will not be granted if an appeal has been lodged to the Court of Appeal (*Blockleys plc v Miller*).

Vexatious litigants (Employment Tribunals Act 1996 s 33)

20.157 If the EAT is satisfied that any person has habitually and persistently and without reasonable grounds instituted vexatious proceedings or made vexatious applications before an employment tribunal or the EAT, then, on an application by the Attorney General or the Lord Advocate, the EAT may make a restriction of proceedings order, the effect of which will be to debar that person from instituting proceedings or making applications without leave from the EAT. The hallmark of vexatious proceedings is that it has little or discernible basis in law, with the effect of subjecting the defendant to inconvenience, harassment and expense out of all proportion to any gain likely to accrue to the claimant (*A-G v Wheen*).

Further appeals

20.158   An appeal will lie from the EAT to the Court of Appeal (in Scotland the Court of Session). Leave to appeal must be given by the EAT, but if this is refused an application for leave to appeal must be made to the Court of Appeal or the Court of Session. It must be shown that there is a genuine point of law of practical consequence involved (*Campbell v Dunoon and Cowal Housing Association Ltd*). A further appeal will lie to the House of Lords.

CHAPTER 21

Individual trade union rights

21.1–21.10 In this chapter we shall consider the rights of an individual in respect of his trade union membership and/or non-membership. These rights exist vis-à-vis a trade union and against an actual or potential employer. The relevant statutory provisions are contained in the Trade Union and Labour Relations (Consolidation) Act 1992 (TULR(C)A), which has been amended by subsequent legislation, and reference will also be made to a number of legal decisions.

Rights vis-à-vis a trade union

A. Right not to be excluded from any trade union (TULR(C)A s 174)

21.11 An individual cannot be excluded or expelled from any trade union unless:
(a) he does not satisfy an enforceable membership requirement contained in the rules of the union. Enforceable means the restriction of membership solely by reference to employment in a specified trade, industry or profession, or occupational description, or the possession of a specified trade, industrial or professional qualification or work experience;
(b) he does not qualify for membership by reason of the union operating only in a particular part of Great Britain;
(c) the union negotiates with one particular employer (or a number of particular employers who are associated) and the applicant is no longer employed by that employer;
(d) the exclusion or expulsion is entirely attributable to the applicant's conduct. Conduct does not include being, or ceasing to be, a member of another trade union, or employment by a particular employer at a particular place, or membership of a political party, or conduct which would constitute unjustified discipline within the meaning of s 65 (below).

21.12 If a person's application for membership of a trade union is neither granted nor rejected within a reasonable period, he shall be treated as having been excluded from the union (s 177).

21.13 The significance of the new law is two-fold. First, at common law a trade union was entitled to lay down the description of persons who were eligible to join, and could specify any qualification for membership it desired (see *Boulting v ACTAT*), and exclude a person on any ground (see *Faramus v Film Artistes' Association*). The courts did take the view that a rule which operated arbitrarily and unreasonably was void as being against public policy (see *Nagle v Feilden*), but such cases were rare and, generally speaking, a trade union could control its own admissions, and the court had no power to order it to grant membership to any particular individual. Section 174 now overrides the common law in this respect. A trade union may lay down certain requirements for membership, as above, but otherwise must admit any person seeking to join.

21.14 The second significance of the new law is that the Bridlington Agreement, which used to govern inter-union disputes arising from competition for members, and applied to TUC affiliated unions, can no longer be activated. Previously, if a trade union commenced recruitment in an area in which another union already had a substantial membership, the TUC could order the interloper to surrender the members gained in the recruitment drive (see *Rothwell v APEX*). This is no longer possible, because the individual has an indefeasible right to join whichever union he pleases, and cannot be expelled as a result of any award made by the TUC Disputes Committee.

21.15 A union may still specify who is entitled to join as a member within the limits specified above, but it is submitted that even these requirements cannot be exercised in an arbitrary and unreasonable manner (see *Nagle v Feilden*). But if an applicant needs a trade union card because an actual or prospective employer operates a 'closed shop' he cannot otherwise be excluded from membership (*Clark v NATSOPA (SOGAT '82)*). In any case, the aggrieved person would have a right against the actual or potential employer under the 'unfair recruitment' provisions (see para 21.47).

21.16 The remedy for a failure to admit an applicant to membership is dealt with at para 21.29.

B. Right not to be unjustifiably disciplined (TULR(C)A s 64)

21.17 The power of a trade union to take disciplinary action against a member, and the procedural rules which should be followed, is noted in Chapter 22. In addition, a member has the right not to be unjustifiably disciplined by the trade union. A member is unjustifiably disciplined if the reason for the disciplinary action was conduct by him which was:

a. a failure to participate in or support a strike or other industrial action (whether by members of that union or by others) or indicate his opposition to or lack of support for any such strike or other industrial action; or

b. something required from him by virtue of an obligation imposed by his contract of employment or other agreement made with his employer; or

c. the making of an assertion that the union, or an official or representative or trustee of the union's property has contravened or is proposing to contravene a requirement of the union's rules or any other agreement or legal provision, or attempts to vindicate any such assertion; or

d. the encouraging of any person to perform an obligation imposed by virtue of a contract of employment or any other agreement; or

e. the contravention by him of any requirement imposed by a determination which itself constitutes an infringement of his rights or of the right of any other individual; or

f. failing to agree to, or withdrawing from, a check-off agreement; or

g. resigning from a union, becoming a member of another union, or refusing to join any other union; or

h. working with individuals who are not members of the union or any other union; or

i. working for an employer who employs individuals who are not members of the union, or who are or are not members of any other union; or

j. requiring the union to do something which the union is required to do on the requisition of any member; or

k. an approach to the certification officer for advice or assistance on any matter whatsoever, or involves any other person being asked for advice or assistance with respect to any assertion made under c. above; or

l. a proposal to engage in conduct outlined in paras a. to k. above, or preparatory conduct (s 65).

But a refusal to accept union policy that members should not take on additional work is not protected, because the policy is not 'other industrial action' (*Knowles v Fire Brigade Union*).

21.18 Discipline, for the purpose of this section, is a determination made under the union's rules by an official of the union, or by a number of persons including an official:

a. that an individual shall be expelled from the union (or branch or section). In *T & GWU v Webber*, it was held that a recommendation that the claimant be expelled was not a determination for the purpose of s 174. Until an appeal against the recommendation had been heard, he was still a member of the union;

b. that an individual shall pay any sum to the union (or branch or section) or to any other person whatsoever;

c. that sums tendered by that individual in respect of any obligation to pay a subscription or other sums to the union (or branch or section) should be treated as unpaid or as paid for a different purpose;

d. that that individual should be deprived of, or refused access to, benefits, services or facilities which would otherwise be available to him as a member of the union. Suspending a member involves depriving him of benefits which accrue from union membership (*NALGO v Killorn*);

e. that another trade union (or branch or section) should be encouraged or advised not to accept that individual as a member; or

f. that that individual should be subjected to any other detriment. Naming a person as a 'strike breaker' in a union circular, with the intention of causing him embarrassment is to subject that person to a detriment (*NALGO v Killorn*).

21.19 However, a member will not be unjustifiably disciplined if the reason for the disciplinary action was that he made an allegation that the union, an official, a representative or a trustee had contravened the union's rules or an agreement or an enactment or rule of law, and the assertion was false, and the member knew it was false or otherwise acted in bad faith.

21.20 If a complaint relating to an expulsion is brought under s 174, and is declared to be well-founded, no further complaint relating to that matter can be brought under s 64 (unjustifiable discipline).

C. Complaints of unjustifiable discipline (TULR(C)A s 64)

21.21 An individual who believes that he has been unjustifiably disciplined by a trade union may present a complaint to an employment tribunal, alleging that his rights have been infringed. The complaint must be presented within three months of the alleged infringement, unless the employment tribunal is satisfied that it was not reasonably practicable to present the complaint earlier, and that any delay in making the complaint was wholly or partially attributable to any reasonable attempts to appeal against the decision or to have it reconsidered or reviewed.

21.22 If the employment tribunal find that the claimant has been unjustifiably disciplined contrary to s 64, they will make a declaration that the complaint is well-founded. Thereafter, the claimant's remedies depend on what the trade union does about the situation. If, after four weeks but within six months from the date of the declaration, the determination which constituted the infringement of rights has not been revoked, (see *NALGO v Courtney-Dunn*), or the trade union fails to take such steps as are necessary for securing the reversal of anything done, an application must be made to the Employment Appeal Tribunal. If, on the other hand, the determination has been revoked, or the necessary steps have been taken to reverse anything done, the application may be made to the employment tribunal. The EAT or the employment tribunal may then make an award of compensation, and may also order the union to repay any sum paid to the union (or branch or section) or to any other person (eg by way of a fine or donation etc).

21.23 The amount of compensation to be awarded will be such as is considered to be just and equitable in all the circumstances, bearing in mind the duty of the applicant to mitigate against his loss, and any reduction which may be made on the ground of contributory conduct.

21.24 If the application has been made to an employment tribunal, the maximum compensation shall not exceed
a.   30 times one week's pay (maximum £230 per week), ie £6,900, plus
b.   £50,000.

21.25 If the application is made to the EAT, the above maximum figures apply, but there will be an irreducible minimum of £5,300 (TULR(C)A s 67; see *Bradley v NALGO*).

21.26 An appeal will lie from any decision of an employment tribunal on a point of law. Any provision in an agreement which purports to take away a person's rights under these sections shall be void, but this does not preclude any agreement made under the auspices of a conciliation officer, acting under the provisions of s 18 of the Employment Tribunals Act 1996.

D. Right to resign from a trade union (TULR(C)A s 69)

21.27 In every contract of membership of a trade union, whether made before or after the passing of the Act, there shall be an implied term conferring a right on the member, on giving reasonable notice and complying with any reasonable conditions, to terminate his membership of the union. In *Ashford v Association of Scientific, Technical and Management Staffs* (decided under the provisions of the Industrial Relations Act 1971) the claimant wrote a letter of resignation to the union, which was to take immediate effect. This was not in accordance with the union rules, and subsequently expulsion proceedings were commenced. It was held by the NIRC that as the member had failed to give reasonable notice, he was bound by the union's rules. It was suggested that although it might be reasonable to invite members to state their reasons for resignation, it would not be reasonable to make such a statement a condition of resignation.

E. Right not to be expelled from the union (TULR(C)A s 174)

21.28   The grounds upon which a person cannot be excluded from trade union membership (see para 21.11) apply equally to the right not to be expelled from a union. However, a person who resigns from the union because of dissatisfaction with the way the union is conducting its affairs cannot bring proceedings under s 174, for there is no such doctrine as 'constructive expulsion' (*McGhee v T & GWU*). If a member ceases to be a member of the union on the happening of an event specified in the rules of the union, he shall be treated as having been expelled from the union (s 177).

F. Remedies for wrongful exclusion or expulsion (TULR(C)A ss 175–176)

21.29   A person who claims that he has been wrongly excluded or expelled from a trade union may present a complaint to an employment tribunal within six months from the date of the exclusion or expulsion, or, where it was not reasonably practicable to do so, within such further period as the tribunal considers reasonable. If the tribunal find the complaint to be well-founded, it shall make a declaration to that effect. If the claimant has been admitted or re-admitted to the union, a further application may be made (after four weeks from the date of the declaration, but within six months) for compensation to be assessed by the employment tribunal. The amount shall be such as the tribunal considers to be just and equitable in all the circumstances, and may be reduced if the claimant caused or contributed towards the exclusion or expulsion (*Saunders v Bakers, Food and Allied Workers' Union*). If the claimant has not been admitted or readmitted to the union, an application may be made to the Employment Appeal Tribunal, within the same time limits, and the EAT will make an award of compensation on the same principles.

The amount of compensation shall not exceed the aggregate of:

a.   30 times the maximum amount of a week's pay for basic awards in unfair dismissal cases (£6,900); and

b.   the maximum compensation award of £50,000.

However, if the award is made by the EAT, the award shall not be less than £5,300.

G. Right of access to the courts (TULR(C)A s 63)

21.30   A member who is seeking a determination or conciliation of a dispute under the union's rules should first pursue his case through the union's internal disputes procedure before seeking recourse to the courts (*White v Kuzych*). But irrespective of any provision in the union's rules, the member has an indefeasible right to apply to the courts any time after six months from when the union first receives his application to have the matter determined or conciliated. However, if the delay is attributable to the unreasonable conduct of the union member, the court can extend the six-month period (ie to give the union more time to deal with the complaint).

21.31 The right to apply to the court after six months is of course without prejudice to a member's right to apply to the court at any time when, for example, an appeal cannot cure a defect because the action complained against is *ultra vires* or otherwise contrary to law.

H. Right to a ballot before industrial action (TULR(C)A s 62)

21.32 If a trade union calls on members to engage in a strike or other industrial action without the affirmative support of a ballot conducted in accordance with the stringent requirements of the Act, any member may apply to the court for an order seeking to have the authorisation or endorsement of the action withdrawn by the union. If the strike is not called by the specified person, or the Act's requirements relating to the functions of the independent scrutineer are not satisfied, or members have not been given an equal opportunity to vote, or a ballot has been held but a majority have not voted in favour, then the court will make such order as it considers appropriate for requiring the union to take steps for ensuring that there is no further inducement to take part in the action, and that no member engages in conduct after the making of the order by virtue of having been induced before the order to take part or continue to take part in the action.

21.33 The right to apply to the court for an order is thus available to an individual member of the union, whether or not the strike is actionable by anyone else (eg an employer, see para 23.82) and is additional to any right a member may have in respect of any breach which may have occurred of the trade union's rules. The right exists in respect of calls for any strike or other industrial action, whether or not the member is in breach of his contract of employment. Thus secondary action (see para 23.104) is covered.

21.34 A court may grant interlocutory or interim relief by ordering that the authorisation or endorsement of the industrial action is withdrawn, but it cannot order the union to hold a ballot. The right to bring an action under s 62 applies to self-employed persons, as well as to employees (s 62(8)).

21.35 Crown employees (who may not be employed under a contract of employment) are within the provisions of s 62 (see s 62(7)).

I. Other individual rights

21.36–21.45 A member of a trade union has the right to restrain the union from indemnifying unlawful conduct (see para 22.167), to bring an action against the union's trustees in respect of unlawful application of the union's property (see para 22.176), and to bring a complaint about the conduct of the ballot in respect of a political fund (see para 22.186). He has the right to inspect the register of members (see para 22.53) and examine the union's accounts, and can apply to the court if the union has failed to comply with the requirements relating to union elections, election addresses, appointment of a scrutineer, etc. These matters will be considered in Chapter 22.

Rights vis-à-vis an employer

21.46   An individual worker has a number of legal rights against an actual or potential employer, as follows.

A. Access to employment (TULR(C)A s 137)

21.47   It is unlawful to refuse a person employment:
a.   because he is, or is not, a member of a trade union; or
b.   because he is unwilling to accept a requirement:
   (i)   to take steps to become or cease to be, or to remain or not to become, a member of a trade union; or
   (ii)   to make payments or suffer deductions in the event of his not being a member of a trade union.

21.48   A person shall be taken to have been refused employment if the person to whom he is applying:
a.   refuses or deliberately omits to entertain and process his application or enquiry; or
b.   causes him to withdraw or cease to pursue his application or enquiry; or
c.   refuses or deliberately omits to offer him employment of that description; or
d.   makes him an offer of such employment the terms of which are such that no reasonable employer who wished to fill the post would offer, and which is not accepted; or
e.   makes him an offer of such employment but withdraws it or causes him not to accept it.

21.49   The law is aimed at preventing any form of discrimination against a worker on the ground of his trade union membership. The employer is quite entitled to refuse to employ someone because of that person's previous trade union activities (eg a well-known militant, see *Birmingham District Council v Beyer*), because the refusal is not based on trade union membership, but disruptive conduct in his previous employment. Whether the employer thus refuses employment because of past trade union membership or past trade union activities is a question of fact for the employment tribunal to determine in accordance with the evidence. However, once the worker has entered employment slightly different considerations may apply (see *Fitzpatrick v British Railways Board*, para 21.89).

21.50   The precise scope of s 137 is not clear. In *Harrison v Kent County Council* the claimant had previously been employed for some 14 years, during which time he was known to be the leader of a long and bitter industrial dispute. He then left the employment, and subsequently applied for an advertised vacancy. He was refused employment. He argued that the refusal was because of his trade union membership, and hence contrary to s 137. The employers argued that he was refused employment because of his unco-operative attitude and anti-management style. His claim failed before the employment tribunal, but this was reversed by the EAT, who held that there was an overlap between trade union membership and activities. If a person was refused employment because of his trade union activities, it was open to an employment tribunal to find that he was refused employment because of his trade union membership. However, it should be noted that the decision in this case was made prior to the House of Lords decisions in

Associated Newspapers Ltd v Wilson and *Associated British Ports v Palmer* where it was pointed out that there is a distinction between 'the purpose' and 'the effect' of an act, and thus the decision in *Harrison* must be regarded as being of doubtful authority.

Job advertisements (TULR(C)A s 137(3))

21.51 Where a job advertisement (including every form of advertisement or notice, whether to the public or not), is published, which indicates (or might reasonably be understood as indicating) that the employment is only open to a person who is, or who is not, a member of a trade union, or make payments or suffer deductions (see para 21.47 above), then if a person applies for a job, and he is refused employment, it will be conclusively presumed that he was refused employment for that reason. Thus it is clear that all references to trade union membership or non-membership should be eliminated from job advertisements. However, the job advertisement *per se* is not unlawful (unlike advertisements which seek to discriminate on grounds of race or sex, see paras 4.268 and 4.147), and the only remedy is for an individual who has been refused employment to bring a personal complaint.

Unfair practices (TULR(C)A s 137(4))

21.52 Where there is an arrangement or practice under which employment is only offered to persons put forward or approved by a trade union, a person who is not a member of the trade union, and who is refused employment because of that arrangement or practice, shall be taken to have been refused employment because he is not a member of the trade union.

Employment agencies (TULR(C)A s 138)

21.53 The Act covers employment agencies, defined as any person who provides services for the purpose of finding employment for workers or for supplying employers with workers. In so far as the employment agency acts as an agent for an employer, the provisions of s 137 (above) apply. In so far as the agency is acting in its own right, the identical provisions apply, and a person who has been refused the services of an employment agency (on grounds on his membership or non-membership of a trade union) will have a right to complain against the agency to an employment tribunal. Advertisements by employment agencies are also covered by identical provisions (s 138(3)).

Exceptions to the Act

21.54 The Act only deals with employment under a contract of service or apprenticeship. Thus it cannot apply to self-employed persons. Further, if a person is being considered for appointment or election to an office in a trade union, then s 137 does not prevent anything done for the purpose of securing the compliance with a condition that he be or become a member of the trade union, even though this would constitute employment. Thus it is not unlawful to insist that a trade union official becomes a member of the union concerned.

21.55 The unfair recruitment provisions do not apply to members of the armed forces, police, share fishermen, employees who work outside Great Britain, seamen registered on ships registered at ports outside Great Britain, or who are not ordinarily resident in Great Britain, and when the minister issues an exemption certificate on the ground of national security.

Remedies under the Act (ss 139–142)

21.56 A person who considers that his rights have been violated under the Act may make a complaint to an employment tribunal within three months from the date of the act complained of, with the usual extension of time if it was not reasonably practicable to present it earlier. If the tribunal uphold the complaint, they must make a declaration to that effect, may award compensation, and may make a recommendation that the respondent takes action to obviate or reduce the effect on the complainant of the conduct which is the subject of the complaint. If the complaint is made against an employment agency and a prospective employer, there are provisions which permit the joinder of both parties, and any award of compensation may be apportioned between them, as the tribunal think just and equitable. It is also possible to join a third party (eg a trade union or shop steward) if the act complained of came about by virtue of industrial pressure.

21.57 The practical effect of legislation is that the pre-entry and post-entry closed shop is no longer lawful in Great Britain.

B. Action short of dismissal (TULR(C)A s 146, as amended)

21.58 Every employee has the right not to be subjected to any detriment as an individual by any act, or any deliberate failure to act, by his employer, if the act or failure takes place for the purpose of
(a) preventing or deterring him from being a member of an independent trade union, or penalising him for being so; or
(b) preventing or deterring him from taking part in the activities of an independent trade union at an appropriate time, or penalising him for doing so; or
(c) compelling him to become a member of a trade union.
   Detriment, for the purpose of this section, is detriment short of dismissal.

21.59 The first matter to be determined whether the action was taken against the employee 'as an individual'. If action is taken against a trade union this may affect an individual employee, but the action was not necessarily taken against him as an individual. In *F W Farnworth Ltd v McCoid*, a collective agreement provided that the employer had the right to derecognise a shop steward if his conduct was called into question. The employer notified the union that they intended to derecognise the claimant because his conduct was such that he was not suited to hold the office of shop steward. The claimant claimed that this derecognition constituted a breach of s 146(1). For the employer, it was argued that the action had not been taken against him as an individual, because it only affected his status as a shop steward, not as an employee. The argument was rejected. The Court of Appeal held that the purpose of s 146(1) was to allow an individual (in whatever capacity) to bring a complaint before an employment tribunal. However, it was thought that the employer could still successfully defend the action if they could show that the action taken was not for the purpose of preventing or deterring him from taking part in the activities of an independent trade union, but for the purpose of removing someone from the office of shop steward who was not fit for that role.

21.60 The next matter to be determined under s 146 is to decide what is the purpose of the employer's action or omission. If the purpose is to change the relationship between him and all or any class of employees, this will not be a detriment under s 146 unless no reasonable employer would act in that manner. Thus an employer is free to make changes in bargaining arrangements, for example, following voluntary or statutory derecognition, or when changes have taken place in bargaining units, or by moving from collective bargaining arrangements to individual wage negotiation (s 148(3)). To this extent, the decision of the House of Lords in *Associated Newspapers Ltd v Wilson* is still good law, provided that there is no evidence that the employer took such action in order to prevent or deter trade union membership.

21.61 There is no breach of s 146 if the action taken (or omission) had the effect of so doing, if it was not done for that purpose. Thus in *Gallacher v Department of Transport*, the claimant was a civil servant, who spent most of his working time carrying out trade union duties. He put his name forward for promotion to a higher grade, but was turned down because of his lack of management skills. He was told that the only way he could acquire those skills was by taking a line job, and thus reduce the amount of time spent on trade union duties. He complained to an employment tribunal, who found that the advice given to him that he should spend more time gaining management experience was intended to deter him from spending time on trade union duties and activities. However, the EAT allowed the employer's appeal and that decision was upheld by the Court of Appeal. The employer's purpose was to ensure that only employees with sufficient line management experience were promoted. Thus any action taken was not for the purpose of deterring the applicant from exercising his statutory rights.

21.62 The 'appropriate time' for carrying out trade union activities means time which is outside his working hours, or at a time within his working hours at which, in accordance with arrangements agreed with or consent given by, his employer, it is permissible for him to take part in those activities. Such consent may be express, and will frequently be implied from the conduct of the parties. However, it would be rare that consent can be implied in the case of a shop steward who is not accredited (*Marley Tile Co Ltd v Shaw*). An employee cannot just engage in trade union activities in working hours when he feels like it. Thus in *Brennan and Ging v Ellward (Lancs) Ltd* the claimants left a site on which they were working to consult their trade union official, despite a warning that if they did so they would be dismissed. Although this may have amounted to trade union activities, it was not within the appropriate time for such activities.

21.63 In *Robb v Leon Motor Services* the claimant was a long distance coach driver. He was appointed shop steward. He was then told that he would have to drive other vehicles, because of all the trouble he was causing, and he claimed that by taking him off better paid and more important work, he was being deterred from carrying out his trade union activities at an appropriate time. It was held that even though this was action taken against him short of dismissal, and even though it was done for the purpose of deterring him from taking part in trade union activities, he could not succeed. There was no attempt to stop him from taking part in union activities outside his working hours, and the activities he was engaged in within working hours were not done with any arrangement or with the consent of the employers. Consequently, he was not being deterred from taking part in trade union activity at the appropriate time.

21.64 Whether the activities in question are the activities of an independent trade union is an issue of fact for the employment tribunal to determine (*Marley*

Tile Co Ltd v Shaw). There must be some institutional link, with the union or an accredited shop steward being involved. Individual requests or complaints, or group meetings which have no union connection, are outside the statutory protections (*Dixon and Shaw v West Ella Developments Ltd*).

21.65 If there is a requirement (whether contractual or not) that in the event of a failure by the employee to become or remain a member of a trade union, he must make a payment (usually to charity), and a deduction is made from the employee's wages in consequence, this shall be treated as a detriment. Further, where an employee notifies the employer that he has ceased or will cease to be a member of a trade union as from a certain date, the employer will ensure that no amount representing his trade union subscription shall be deducted from the employee's pay (TULR(C)A s 68, see below). If the employer fails to comply, the employee may seek a declaration in the county court. The court may make an order to ensure that the employer's actions are not repeated, but for any unlawful past deductions, the employee must seek a remedy in the employment tribunal under the provisions of s 23 of the Employment Rights Act 1996.

21.66 A complaint may be presented to a tribunal that an employer has taken action against an employee in violation of the above rights. The burden of proof is placed on the employer to show the purpose for which the action was taken. Moreover, no account is to be taken of any pressure which may have been exercised on the employer by way of strike or other industrial action (or threats of such), and the tribunal will determine the issue as if no such pressure has been exercised. But if the complaint is on the ground that the employer has taken action against the employee for the purpose of compelling him to be or become a member of a trade union, and the employer or employee claims that the employer was induced to take such action by such pressure, the employer or the employee may, before the hearing of the complaint, require the person who he claimed exercised the pressure to be joined as a party to the proceedings.

21.67 The employment tribunal may then make an award of compensation to the claimant either against the employer or the party who exercised the pressure, or partly against each of them as it thinks just and equitable in the circumstances (TULR(C)A s 150).

21.68 The complaint must be presented within three months from the date of the last action complained of (see *Adlam v Salisbury and Wells Theological College*), with the usual extension of time in cases where it was not reasonably practicable to present it earlier. If the tribunal upholds the complaint, it may make a compensation award as it considers just and equitable having regard to the claimant's loss, and the infringement of his rights, including any expenses incurred and any benefits he might have received but for that action. There is no limit (in theory) on the amount of compensation which can be awarded. The claimant must mitigate against his loss, and compensation is subject to a reduction on the ground of contributory conduct.

21.69 The basis of the award is to compensate the employee for any loss suffered, not for the purpose of imposing a fine on the employer. In *Brassington v Cauldon Wholesale Ltd* an employer threatened to close his business down if he was forced to recognise a trade union. The claimant claimed this was action short of dismissal taken against him for the purpose of preventing or deterring him from joining an independent trade union, and with some hesitation, the EAT agreed that this was so and remitted the appeal back to an employment tribunal to assess compensation under s 149(2) of TULR(C)A. Thus the infringement of a person's trade union rights will lead to an employment tribunal making a mandatory declaration, and compensation if the employee can show that he has suffered a loss. This could be, for example, stress causing ill-health (*Cheall v Vauxhall Motors Ltd*) injury to feelings as a result of being overlooked for promotion (*Cleveland Ambulance NHS Trust v Blane*) the loss of the benefit of trade union advice or assistance, and so on.

C. Detriment and dismissal in statutory recognition cases (TULR(C)A, Sch A1)

21.70 We shall see (Chapter 23) that the new Sch A1 inserted into TULR(C)A sets out a statutory procedure whereby a trade union may obtain recognition or suffer derecognition. The Schedule also (in Pt VIII) provides protection for any worker (see para 23.13) against suffering a detriment because he did or did not do any of a wide range of actions in connection with the statutory procedure for recognition or derecogniton, including supporting or opposing the application, influencing others to support or oppose the application, voting in a ballot, and so on (see para 156 of the Schedule). However, there will be no protection if what the worker did was unreasonable (query whether a breach of contract by the worker, eg a strike, is unreasonable conduct on his part). A worker may make a complaint to an employment tribunal, which may make a declaration, and may also award compensation to be paid by the employer in respect of the act or omission complained of; the amount shall be such as the tribunal consider to be just and equitable.

21.71 If the detriment amounts to the termination of the worker's contract, but that contract is not a contract of employment, the amount awarded by the tribunal may be the equivalent of the normal basic and compensatory awards which can be made in unfair dismissal cases under ss 119 and 124(1) of ERA.

21.72 So far as workers who are employees are concerned, if the detriment amounts to a dismissal, that dismissal shall be regarded as being automatically unfair under Pt X of ERA. It will also be unfair to select an employee for redundancy if the reason was any of the above specified reasons.

21.73 Similar protections are given to employees who are employed under a fixed-term contract (even though they have opted out of their redundancy rights), and the normal qualifying periods of employment and the age limits provisions do not apply to any of the above rights. Interim relief will also be available, as appropriate.

21.74 Workers who act or omit to act in circumstances which are outside the statutory procedure of Sch A1 must rely on those provisions which protect against detriment or dismissal in respect of trade union activities contained in ss 146 and 152 of TULR(C)A (see paras 21.58 and 21.89). Thus recruiting members, distributing literature, etc, with a view to obtaining recognition outside the statutory procedures, will constitute trade union activities under the existing TULR(C)A provisions, and are thus protected (*Lyon v St James Press Ltd*).

D. Time off work for trade union duties (TULR(C)A s 168)

21.75 An employer shall permit an employee of his who is an official of a recognised independent trade union to take time off work during his working hours, for the purpose of carrying out any duties as such official concerned with

(a) negotiations with the employer related to or connected with collective bargaining, or

(b) the performance on behalf of the employees of functions in relation to or in connection with matters falling within collective bargaining which the employer has agreed may be performed by the union, or

(c) the receipt of information from the employer and consultations by the employer concerned with redundancies (see para 18.113) and the transfer of an undertaking (see para 9.101).

21.76 The employer will also permit the employee to have time off work during working hours to undergo training in aspects of industrial relations which is relevant to the carrying out of those duties, and which has been approved by the TUC or by his union.

21.77 Time off work for this purpose is not confined to face-to-face meetings with the employers, but can also include preparatory or co-ordinating meetings in order to discuss forthcoming negotiations, as long as these are in connection with the collective bargaining purposes outlined in s 178 (*London Ambulance Service v Charlton*).

21.78 A trade union official wishing to take time off work for training should show a copy of the syllabus to the employer. In *Menzies v Smith & McLaurin Ltd* the claimant wished to go on a course relating to job security. The union sent a copy of the syllabus to the employers, showing that topics to be covered included import controls, North Sea Oil, EEC policies, and so on. The company decided that all this was not relevant to his trade union duties, but agreed to give him time off work (without pay) for trade union activities. He went on the course and then claimed his pay. It was held that he was not entitled to be paid. The syllabus clearly indicated that the course was not relevant to his duties as a trade union official.

21.79 The amount of time off, the purposes for which, the occasions on which, and any conditions subject to which time off may be taken are those that are reasonable in all the circumstances having regard to the relevant provisions of the code of practice issued by ACAS. The employer shall pay an employee who has taken time off for these purposes in accordance with his usual rate of remuneration. A failure to permit an employee to have time off under this section, or a failure to pay him for time off, may be the subject of a complaint to an employment tribunal by the aggrieved employee. In *Blower v CEGB* the claimant, who was a night shift worker, was a member of a works committee which met during the day. His day shift colleagues were paid for attending, whereas he was not. It was held that he was not entitled to be paid. It was part of his union work that his leisure time would be eaten into; the law only requires time off to be paid for if it is during his normal working hours, not for time spent on trade union duties outside his working hours (see *Hairsine v Kingston upon Hull City Council*).

21.80   Whether it is reasonable to have time off under s 168 is a question of fact for the employment tribunal, and its findings cannot be challenged in the EAT unless it took into account matters which ought not to be taken into account (*Thomas Scott & Sons (Bakers) Ltd v Allen*).

E. Time off work for trade union activities (TULR(C)A s 170)

21.81   An employer shall permit an employee who is a member of a recognised independent trade union to take time off during the employee's working hours for the purpose of taking part in:
a.   any activities of that trade union; and
b.   any activities in relation to which the employee is acting as a representative of that union. This might include, for example, attendance at a conference as a union delegate, etc, but the activities for which permission is to be granted do not include anything which involved the taking of industrial action, whether or not in contemplation or furtherance of a trade dispute. Nor does the lobbying of Parliament to protest against proposed legislation come within the definition of 'trade union activities', even if the lobby is organised by a trade union, because it is intended to convey political and ideological objections to the proposed legislation, and is not as such a trade union activity (*Luce v London Borough of Bexley*).

21.82   Again, the amount of time off, the purposes, the occasions and the conditions are those that are reasonable in all the circumstances having regard to the relevant provisions in the Code of Practice issued (see *Depledge v Pye Telecommunications Ltd*). It will be noted that the employer does not have to pay an employee for time taken off for trade union activities. A failure to permit time off for these purposes may be the subject of a complaint to an employment tribunal by the aggrieved employee.

F. Check-off arrangements (TULR(C)A s 68)

21.83   If a trade union and an employer have an agreement whereby the employer will deduct the union subscriptions from the worker's wages and pay this direct to the union (ie a check-off agreement) the employer shall ensure that the worker has authorised the deduction in a document which is signed and dated, that the amount of the deduction does not exceed the permitted amount, and that the authorisation is current on the day of the deduction. An authorisation once made will be operative until the worker withdraws it in writing. The permitted amount to be deducted is the amount of the union subscription. It is no longer necessary for the employer to give one month's notice in writing before deducting an increase in the union subscription, but the amount of the deduction will still have to be shown on the regular itemised pay statement, and the worker is free to withdraw from the check-off arrangement at any time (Deregulation (Deduction from Pay of Union Subscriptions) Order 1998).

21.84   The fact that the worker has given his authorisation to the deductions does not give rise to any obligation on the part of the employer to continue to make the deductions (s 68(9)). That is clearly a matter between the employer and the trade union.

21.85   A worker may bring a complaint before an employment tribunal that his employer has made a deduction in contravention of s 68. The complaint must be presented within three months from the date of the last deduction, with the usual extension of time if it was not reasonably practicable to present the claim earlier.

21.86   If the tribunal find the complaint to be well-founded, it shall make a declaration to that effect, and also order the employer to pay to the worker the unauthorised deduction (or unauthorised increase in subscription).

G. Deductions for the political fund of the union (s 86)

21.87   If a member of a trade union informs the employer in writing that he is exempt from paying the levy to the political fund of the union, the employer shall ensure that no amount representing the contribution to the political fund is deducted from the employee's wages.

21.88   If a person alleges that his employer has wrongly deducted a political fund contribution, or has refused to deduct union dues, he may make a complaint to an employment tribunal within three months, and the tribunal may make a declaration, order the employer to pay the applicant the amount deducted in contravention of s 87, or make an order requiring the employer to take steps specified in relation to emoluments payable. In the latter case, if there is still a failure to comply, there is an ultimate sanction of two weeks' pay (TULR(C)A s 87).

H. Dismissal on the ground of trade union membership or non-membership, or trade union activities (TULR(C)A s 152)

21.89   The dismissal of an employee will be unfair if the reason (or principal reason) was because the employee:
a.   was, or proposed to become, a member of an independent trade union; or
b.   had taken part, or proposed to take part, in the activities of an independent trade union at an appropriate time. 'Appropriate time' means time which is outside his working hours, or time within his working hours at which, in accordance with arrangements agreed with or consent given by his employer it is permissible to take part in those activities. 'Working hours' means any time when the employee is required to work. A person is not taking part in trade union activities merely because he is a trade union activist, for one must distinguish between individual and trade union activities (*Chant v Aquaboats Ltd*). Nor do the activities of an unofficial strike committee constitute trade union activities. But enlisting the help of a trade union official to assist in negotiations of terms and conditions of employment may constitute trade union activities (*Discount Tobacco and Confectionery Ltd v Armitage*), (but see *Speciality Care plc v Pachela*). Going on strike does not constitute trade union activities, but leading an official strike will (*Britool Ltd v Roberts*).
   If the employee is dismissed because the employer learns of his trade union activities in a previous employment (eg as a trade union activist), it would be inevitable that the employer was dismissing him because of the belief that he would be involved in trade union activities in his current employment, and thus the principal reason for the dismissal would be that the employee

proposed to take part in trade union activities, and hence the dismissal is unfair (*Fitzpatrick v British Railways Board*). But if the trade union activist has obtained employment by deceit (eg by changing his name) then a dismissal for that deceit may be fair, and the reason is not because of past or proposed trade union activities (*Birmingham City District Council v Beyer*);

c. was not a member of any trade union, or a particular trade union, or had refused or proposed to refuse to become or remain a member (*Crosville Motor Services Ltd v Ashfield*). This provision gives general rights to non-unionists not to be dismissed because of their non-membership of a trade union.

A distinction may be drawn between the fact of involvement in trade union activities and the manner of such involvement. Thus if, in the course of such activities, the trade unionist makes statements which are malicious, untruthful or irrelevant to the matter in hand, his manner of conducting those activities may take him outside the protection of s 152 (*Bass Taverns Ltd v Burgess*).

21.90 If a person is dismissed for any of the above reasons, it will be an unfair dismissal, and thus it is not necessary for him to have the normal qualifying period of employment of one year before he can bring his claim (TULR(C)A s 154, and see *Carrington v Therm-A-Stor Ltd*.) Taking part in a strike may be trade union activity, but it is not at an appropriate time (see para 21.95).

21.91 It is also an unfair dismissal to select a person for redundancy because of his trade union membership/non-membership, or his trade union activities (TULR(C)A ss 152(1)–153).

21.92 To select an employee for redundancy because of his trade union membership or non-membership or trade union activities would, of course, be manifestly unfair, but it must be shown that the circumstances constituting the redundancy applied equally to other employees who held positions similar to that employee, and that they were not dismissed. This in *O'Dea v ISC Chemical Ltd*, the claimant, who was a senior shop steward, was paid as a technical services operator, although in fact he spent half of his working time working as a packaging operator and the other half on trade union activities. He was dismissed for reason of redundancy, although two other technical service operators were retained. It was held that his dismissal was not unfair. When considering his 'position' account had to be taken of his status as an employee, the nature of his work and his terms and conditions of employment. The claimant could not compare himself with technical service operators because he did not do that job.

21.93 It does not need to be shown that the employer acted maliciously or with a deliberate desire to get rid of a trade union activist. Thus if an employee spends a major part of his working hours on trade union duties, with the result that he is given a poor assessment when redundancy selection procedures are being implemented, 'the reason' for his selection is his trade union activities, carried out at an appropriate time with the consent (albeit reluctantly given) of the employer, and hence his dismissal falls within s 152(1) (*Dundon v GPT Ltd*).

21.94 Finally, it should be noted that the employment tribunal has no right to go into an investigation as to the reasons which have brought about the redundancies, or to require the employers to justify them on economic grounds. In *Moon v Homeworthy Furniture (Northern) Ltd*, a factory was closed down after a series of labour disputes. It was held that TULRA had taken away any right of the courts or tribunals to interfere in industrial relations matters, and the tribunals refused to entertain an argument that the closure was unnecessary.

I. Dismissal in connection with industrial action (TULR(C)A ss 237–239)

21.95   The law on dismissal for taking part in industrial action is somewhat complicated, and needs careful consideration. There are five different situations to consider.

21.96   The first situation arises when the employer conducts a lock-out. Here, the provisions of s 238(1)(a) apply, and if there is a dismissal, the 'no picking and choosing' rule applies.

21.97   The second situation arises when employees, who may be all union members, or some of whom are union members (and some are not), go on strike, and the strike has not been authorised or endorsed by the trade union to which they belong. This is an unofficial strike, and the provisions of s 237 apply.

21.98   The third situation arises when none of those who go on strike are union numbers. This is not an unofficial strike (nor, for that matter, is it official!), and therefore the provisions of s 238 (1)(b) apply, together with the 'no picking and choosing' rule.

21.99   The fourth situation arises when the union authorises or endorses a strike, but the strike is not protected industrial action by virtue of s 219 (because, for example, the balloting provisions have not been complied with, or the strike is secondary action, etc). Again, s 238(1)(b) applies.

21.100   The fifth situation arises when the union calls a protected strike, ie one that is protected by s 219 of TULR(C)A (immunity from actions in tort, see para 23.76) and the union has not lost its immunity through a failure to comply with the rules which would lead to such loss (see ss 222–235). Here, the new provisions of s 238A apply.

21.101   There is a further subtle distinction between the above sections. Sections 237 and 238 are both concerned with a dismissal *while* taking part in industrial action, whereas s 238A deals with a dismissal *for* taking part in industrial action. In other words, ss 237 and 238 apply whenever an employee is dismissed during the actual industrial action, whereas s 238A will apply if the participation in the industrial action was the reason for the dismissal.

(a) Dismissal in connection with a lock-out (TULR(C)A s 238(1)(a))
21.102   A lock-out is the closing of a place of employment, or a suspension of the work, or the refusal by the employer to continue to employ his employees, done with a view to compelling those employees to accept terms and conditions of or affecting employment (ERA s 235(4)). A lock-out by an employer is not necessarily a breach of contract by him (*Express and Star Ltd v Bunday*). If an employee claims that he has been dismissed by virtue of the lock-out, an employment tribunal is precluded from determining whether or not such dismissal is fair or unfair unless it can be shown that (a) one or more of the relevant employees were not dismissed, or (b) if they were dismissed, they were re-engaged within

three months from the date of dismissal, but the applicant was not offered re-engagement. The relevant employees are those who were directly interested in the dispute on the day of the lock-out (*H Campey & Sons Ltd v Bellwood*).

(b) Dismissal of unofficial strikers (TULR(C)A s 237)

21.103 An employee has no right to claim that he has been unfairly dismissed if at the time of the dismissal he was taking part in an unofficial strike or other industrial action.

A strike or other industrial action will be unofficial unless

(a) he is a member of the trade union, and the strike or other industrial action was authorised or endorsed by his trade union, or

(b) he is not a member of the trade union, but there are others who are taking part in the strike who are members of the trade union by which the strike or other industrial action has been authorised or endorsed.

21.104 If either of the above two cases apply, then if the strike is not protected industrial action, s 238 (below) applies, or if the strike is protected industrial action, s 238A (below) will apply. A strike or other industrial action cannot be either official or unofficial if none of those taking part are members of a trade union, and in such circumstances, s 238 will apply. A strike will only be unofficial if some of those taking part are union members, but the action has not been authorised or endorsed by the trade union. If a trade union authorises or endorses the action, but then repudiates it, the action will become unofficial the next working day after the repudiation takes place. In other words, s 237 only applies when trade union members go on an unofficial strike, or where non-union members and union members take part in a strike or other industrial action which has not been authorised or endorsed by the union.

(c) Dismissal in connection with a strike or other industrial action (TULR(C)A s 238(1)(b))

21.105 Subject to s 238A (below), if an employee is dismissed because he was taking part in a strike or other industrial action, the tribunal shall not determine whether the dismissal was fair or unfair unless it is shown that (a) one or more of those employees at the establishment where the complainant works who were taking part in the strike or other industrial action at the time of the claimant's dismissal were not dismissed, or (b) that any such employee who was dismissed was offered re-engagement within three months of the complainant's dismissal, but that he was not offered re-engagement (TULR(C)A s 238(2)). There is no requirement that the offer to re-engage must be in writing (*Marsden v Fairey Stainless Ltd*).

21.106 Whether or not an employee is taking part in a strike or other industrial action must be determined as an objective fact. In other words, the test is 'what is the employee doing or omitting to do?' The subjective knowledge of the employer is not relevant (*Manifold Industries v Sims*).

21.107 An employee who is dismissed for taking part in a strike is not entitled to a redundancy payment, even though it can be shown that a subsequent redundancy situation is revealed. In *Baxter v Limb Group of Companies*, dock workers refused to work overtime following a dispute with the employers over bonus payments. They were dismissed, and subsequently the employers discontinued using direct labour and contracted the work out. The dismissed employees argued that the employers had decided to dispense with direct labour, and had manoeuvred the employees into a position where it appeared that they were dismissed for taking part in a strike or other industrial action, whereas the real reason for the dismissal was redundancy. The Court of Appeal dismissed their claim. The industrial action was the reason for the dismissal and for the decision to use contract labour. Section 238 of TULR(C)A prohibits an employment tribunal from considering whether a dismissal is fair or unfair if, at the date of dismissal, the employee *was taking part* in a strike or other industrial action. It does not say that the employee was dismissed *because* he was taking part in such action. In other words, if the dismissals caused the redundancy, a redundancy payment cannot be made (*Sanders v Ernest A Neale Ltd*).

21.108   It will be recalled that a strike is a breach of contract by the employee which entitles the employer to dismiss him. Provided the employer dismisses all the strikers, or offers all of them re-engagement after the strike is over within three months, the employment tribunal has no jurisdiction to hear any complaint. This is the 'no picking and choosing' rule (see *McCormick v Horsepower Ltd*). But if an employer is selective in his dismissals or offers of re-engagement, those employees who have been excluded may bring claims in the employment tribunals. To avoid a finding of unfair dismissal, the employer must show that he has acted reasonably in not taking back those strikers who were not offered re-engagement. The question will be determined by the circumstances, having regard to the equity and substantial merits of the case (*Edwards v Cardiff City Council*).

21.109   Further, the employer can re-engage an employee who has been dismissed for striking any time after three months from the time another striker was dismissed without exposing himself to a claim for unfair dismissal from the latter.

21.110   But if the employer (or an associated employer) re-engages a striker by mistake (eg in ignorance of the fact that he had been on strike) this gives the employment tribunal jurisdiction to consider a claim from a striker who has not been offered re-engagement (*Bigham v GKN Kwikform Ltd*).

21.111   The three-month period is in the nature of a 'cooling off' period, designed to enable industrial disputes to be settled on honourable terms. As long as the offer of re-engagement is made within that period, the employment tribunal has no jurisdiction to hear a claim by a person who does not wish to accept that offer (*Highland Fabricators Ltd v McLaughlin*).

21.112   But the employer will lose the protection of s 238 if he seeks to dismiss before the strike has begun or after the strike is over. In *Heath v Longman (Meat Salesmen) Ltd* employees went out on strike, but subsequently decided to return to work. One of them informed the employer that the strike was over, but when they returned to work they were dismissed. The NIRC held that since they had returned to work, they were no longer on strike, and hence the dismissals were unfair. In *Midland Plastics Ltd v Till*, a letter was sent to the company management stating that unless certain demands were met, industrial action would commence at 11 am. At 9.30 am, the managing director spoke to four employees, who confirmed that they would abide by the decision, and they were immediately dismissed. It was held that the employment tribunal were not precluded by s 238 from entertaining a complaint of unfair dismissal. The threat to take part in a strike was a mere display of power by one side to a dispute which is a substantial feature of industrial relations negotiations. As the dismissals took place before the strike, s 238 did not apply.

21.113 The offer of re-engagement must be made to the striking employee. A general advertising campaign offering employment to those who apply does not amount to an offer of employment to any particular individual. Such a campaign merely makes available the opportunity to be offered employment (*Crosville Wales Ltd v Tracey*).

21.114 TULR(C)A does not define what is meant by 'other industrial action', and it is assumed that the term includes traditional industrial techniques such as work-to-rule campaigns, a go-slow, sit-ins, and, possibly, 'working without enthusiasm'. In *Thompson v Eaton Ltd* employees were standing around a new machine so as to prevent the employers from testing it. They refused to return to their normal place of work, and were dismissed. It was held that they were engaged in 'other industrial action', and consequently the employment tribunal had no jurisdiction to hear the case. In *Power Packing Casemakers v Faust* the claimants were dismissed for refusing to do overtime, even though there was no contractual requirement to do so. The refusal occurred because of a dispute about wages. It was held that the claimants had been carrying out industrial action, and the employment tribunal had no jurisdiction to hear the claim. Other examples include a 'go slow' (*Drew v St Edmundsbury Borough Council*), a 'work to rule' (*Secretary of State for Employment v ASLEF*), imposing sanctions on normal working (*Williams v Western Mail*), etc. However, a mere threat to take other industrial action is not sufficient (*Midland Plastics Ltd v Till*). Whether or not employees are taking part in other industrial action is a question of fact for the employment tribunal to determine (*Lewis and Britton v E Mason & Sons*).

21.115 If a dismissal is unfair because the employer has re-engaged some of the strikers contrary to s 238 of TULR(C)A, compensation is not to be reduced on the ground of contributory conduct merely because the employees who were not re-engaged took part in the strike. There must have been some other sufficiently blameworthy conduct which makes it just and equitable to reduce their compensation, for example if the strikers' leaders were over-hasty or indulged in inflammatory language. The circumstances of each claimant must be examined to see whether *his* compensation should be reduced because of *his* conduct other than the mere fact that he was on strike (*Tracey v Crosville Wales Ltd*).

(d) Protected industrial action (TULR(C)A s 238A)
21.116 Protected industrial action is industrial action in respect of which the trade union will be immune from liability in tort by virtue of s 219 of TULR(C)A, and has not lost that immunity. Thus if the strike was called to enforce union membership (s 222), or because of the dismissal of unofficial strikers (s 223) or was secondary action (s 224), or to impose union recognition requirements (s 225), or there was a breach of the balloting provisions (s 226–234) or notice of the strike action was not given to the (s 234A) employer, the industrial action will cease to be protected. If the strike is called by the union in accordance with the legal rules, the union will be immune from legal action by virtue of s 219, and those who take part in such action will have the additional protection conferred by s 238A.

21.117 We have seen that s 238 of TULR(C)A protects an employee against selective dismissal when taking part in an official strike. The new s 238A goes further, and gives additional protection to all employees who take part in protected industrial action. They will have protection against dismissal if the dismissal takes place

(i) within a period of eight weeks beginning with the day on which the employee started to take industrial action, or

(ii) after the end of the eight-week period, but the employee had ceased to take part in the industrial action before the end of that period, or

(iii) after the end of the eight-week period, but the employer had not taken such procedural steps as would have been reasonable for the purposes of ending the dispute.

21.118 Any such dismissal is automatically unfair, and there is no qualifying period of employment or upper age limit which would otherwise defeat a claim. A claim may be presented before the end of six months from the date of dismissal, with the usual extension of time provisions. It will equally unfair to select an employee for redundancy if the selection was because the employee took part in protected industrial action as defined in the above three categories (s 105(7C) of ERA). The action taken must be an official strike called by a trade union which itself would be protected under s 219 of TULR(C)A (see Chapter 23). If the union repudiates the official action, and thus the strike changes from being official to unofficial, employees are given a day's grace in which to cease their action, ie if they continue to be on strike beyond the next working day after the day on which the repudiation took place, they will lose their protection of s 238A.

21.119 To determine whether the employer has taken reasonable steps to resolve the dispute, regard shall be had to

(i) whether the employer or the union have complied with procedures established by any collective agreement or other agreement;

(ii) whether the employer or the union offered or agreed to commence or resume negotiations after the start of the protected industrial action;

(iii) whether the employer or the union unreasonably refused, after the start of the protected industrial action, a request for conciliation services to be used;

(iv) whether the employer or the union unreasonably refused, after the start of the protected industrial action, a request that mediation services be used.

21.120 In determining whether the employer has taken those steps, no regard shall be had to the merits of the dispute. If there is a dismissal contrary to s 238A, an employment tribunal cannot make an order for reinstatement or re-engagement until after the conclusion of the protected industrial action. Additional powers are given to tribunals to carry out pre-hearing reviews and to adjourn proceedings if they become aware that legal actions are being brought challenging the legitimacy of the industrial action in question.

(e) Exceptions in certain cases (s 237(1A) and s 238(2A))
21.121 We have seen that if a strike is unofficial (s 237), or official but not protected (s 238), striking employees have limited rights. However, those limitations do not apply if the reason for the dismissal (or selection for redundancy) was a protected reason, ie pregnancy or maternity, parental leave, health and safety case, working time, employee representative, protected disclosure (s 237(1A) only), or assertion of statutory right to have time off work

for dependants. In these circumstances, the employment tribunal will have jurisdiction to hear a complaint.

J. Dismissal due to industrial pressure (ERA s 10)

21.122 If an employer is forced to dismiss an employee because of actual, or the threat of, industrial pressure by other employees, this may amount to an unfair dismissal. The reason is that s 107 of ERA provides that for the purpose of determining whether the employer has a statutory reason for dismissing, or whether the employer acted reasonably in dismissing, no account shall be taken of any industrial pressure (ie strike or other industrial action) which was put on the employer, and the question must be determined as if no such pressure had been exercised. In *Hazells Offset v Luckett*, the claimant was dismissed from his managerial post after trade union representatives had indicated that they would not co-operate with him. Clearly, the principal reason for the dismissal was the industrial pressure, but this could not be advanced as a reason. Since there was no other reason, the dismissal was unfair. The tribunal thought that this did not seem right, nor fair, but it was clearly what Parliament had decided. But if the employee was partly responsible for the threat of industrial action, this could amount to contributory conduct so as to warrant a reduction in the compensation awarded. Thus if the industrial pressure is exercised because of some personal animosity, and the employee is unco-operative in a difficult situation, and, for example, refuses to move to another job, he may well have contributed to his dismissal (*Ford Motor Co Ltd v Hudson*).

21.123 However, if on a claim for unfair dismissal the employer or the claimant claims that the employer was induced to dismiss the claimant because of pressure which a trade union or other person exercised on him by way of calling, organising, procuring or financing a strike, or threatening to do so, and the pressure was exercised because the claimant was not a member of any trade union or a particular trade union, then the employer or the claimant may, before the hearing of the complaint, join that person as a party to the proceedings before the employment tribunal. If the latter decides to make an award of compensation in favour of the claimant, but also finds that the employer was induced to dismiss him because of the pressure, the tribunal may make an award against that person instead of the employer, or partly against that person and partly against the employer. The amount shall be such as the tribunal consider to be just and equitable in all the circumstances ((TULR(C)A s 160).

K. Selection for dismissal on grounds of redundancy (TULR(C)A s 153)

21.124 We have seen that to select a person for dismissal on grounds of redundancy will be unfair if the reason for the selection was his membership or non-membership of a trade union. No qualifying period of continuous employment is required and the age limit does not apply.

L. Compensations for dismissals (TULR(C)A ss 155–158)

21.125 In respect of compensation for dismissals for trade union membership or non-membership, there are rules relating to a minimum basic award, an additional award, as well as the usual compensation award (see Chapter 17).

M. Interim relief for dismissed trade unionists or non-unionists (TULR(C)A ss 161–166)

21.126 If an employee considers that he was unfairly dismissed because he was, or proposed to become a member of an independent trade union, or had taken or proposed to take part in the activities of that union, or he was not a member of a trade union, he may present a complaint to an employment tribunal asking for an order that he be reinstated or re-engaged by the employer or, if this cannot be agreed upon, that he be suspended on full pay pending a settlement or a determination of the complaint. The employee must present the complaint before the end of seven days from the effective date of the termination of his employment, and must, if he is claiming he was dismissed because of his trade union membership or activities, accompany his complaint with a certificate signed by an authorised official of the trade union concerned, stating that the employee was or had proposed to become a member, and that there were reasonable grounds for believing that the reason for the dismissal was the one alleged in the complaint. The signature of a trade union official is prima facie evidence that he is duly authorised to sign the certificate, but if this is challenged, the onus is on the employee to show that the official had actual or implied authority to sign it (*Sulemany v Habib Bank Ltd*).

21.127 The tribunal will give the employer seven days' notice before the hearing, but shall thereupon hear the complaint as soon as is practicable. If the tribunal comes to the conclusion that it is likely that it would uphold a complaint of unfair dismissal on one of the above grounds, it shall announce this preliminary finding and explain to the parties its powers. It will then ask the employer if he is willing to reinstate the employee, or re-engage him on terms and conditions which are no less favourable than he formerly enjoyed, pending the determination or settlement of the complaint. If the employer is willing to re-engage the employee in another job, and specifies the terms and conditions, the tribunal will ask the employee if he is willing to accept, and if so, an order to that effect will be made. If the employee is unwilling to accept the job on those terms and conditions, then, if his refusal is reasonable, the tribunal will make an order for the continuation of his contract of employment, but if his refusal is regarded as being unreasonable, no order will be made. If the employer fails to attend the hearing, or states that he is unwilling to reinstate or re-engage the employee, the tribunal will make an order for the continuation of the employee's contract of employment.

21.128 The effect of an order for continuation of the contract of employment is that if the employment has ceased, it will continue in force, or if it has not yet ceased, it will continue when it does so cease, until, in either case, the determination or settlement of the complaint, for the purposes of pay, seniority, pension rights, and other similar rights, and for determining for any purpose the period for which the employee has been continuously employed. The tribunal will also specify the pay due to the employee from the time of dismissal until the complaint is finally settled, but it will take into account any lump sum received in lieu of wages. At any time after making the order and before the determination by the tribunal, the employer or the employee may apply for a revocation or variation of the order on the ground that there has been a relevant change in circumstances. Also, the employee may apply to the tribunal on the ground that the employer has not complied with the terms of the order. If his complaint is that the employer has not paid the amount specified, the tribunal will determine the amount due, and make it as a separate award for any other sum it gives by way of compensation. If the complaint relates to any other breach by the employer, then it shall make an award of compensation as it thinks just and equitable having regard to the loss suffered by the complainant.

21.129 An order for continuation of employment merely preserves the employee's rights; the employer does not have to permit him to come back to work, or to allow him on the premises.

21.130 On an application for interim relief, the employment tribunal must decide if the claimant can establish that he has a good chance of succeeding at a full hearing. This is a higher degree of certainty than a mere reasonable chance of success. 'Likely' means more than 'probable', and probable itself suggests more than an even chance (*Taplin v C Shippam Ltd*).

21.131 It will be extremely rare that an employer will admit that a person was dismissed because he engaged in trade union activity, and doubtless some other reason will be advanced. In *Forsyth v Fry's Metals Ltd* the tribunal considered the evidence under four headings: (a) the extent of the alleged behaviour, (b) the extent of the employer's dissatisfaction with the employee, (c) the coincidence in time between the alleged behaviour and the initial steps taken towards dismissal, and (d) the coincidence in time between the behaviour and the actual dismissal. In this case, the claimant was dismissed for alleged poor work performance. There was little direct evidence of this; on the other hand he had been instrumental in persuading most of the employees to join a trade union, and had been elected shop steward. On the facts, there was a likelihood that he would succeed in establishing his claim, and interim relief was granted.

21.132 On an application for interim relief, it is possible to join a person who is exercising pressure to bring about the dismissal (see TULR(C)A s 160), and such a person shall be given notice of the time, date and place of the hearing as soon as reasonably practicable (s 162(3)).

CHAPTER 22

The law relating to trade unions

22.1–22.5 In this chapter we shall concentrate on the law as it affects the running of a trade union. All the relevant law has now been consolidated by the Trade Union and Labour Relations (Consolidation) Act 1992, as amended. In so far as earlier reported decisions were based on provisions in earlier (now replaced) legislation, references to the relevant statutory provisions have, for the sake of convenience, been transposed to the corresponding provisions of the 1992 Act.

Definition of a trade union (TULR(C)A s 1)

22.6 A trade union is an organisation (whether permanent or temporary) which either:

a. consists wholly or mainly of workers of one or more descriptions and whose principal purposes include the regulation of relations between workers and employers or employers' associations; or
b. consists wholly or mainly of:
   i. constituent or affiliated organisations which have those purposes; or
   ii. representatives of such constituent or affiliated organisations, and in either case whose principal purposes include the regulation of relations between workers and employers or workers' and employers' associations, or include the regulation of relations between the constituent or affiliated organisations.

This definition discloses two functional bodies:

a. a single trade union; and
b. confederated organisations, such as the Confederation of Shipbuilding and Engineering Unions or the Trades Union Congress.

22.7 Whether or not a trade union has a 'legal personality' of its own was always a matter of some controversy. Section 10 provides that a trade union shall not be a body corporate, but shall nonetheless be capable of making contracts, suing and being sued in its own name, and capable of being prosecuted for any offences committed in its name. As, however, it has no 'legal' existence, property must be held by its trustees, and any judgment, order or award shall be enforced against the property held by the trustees. This does not apply to those organisations which were on the special register created by the Industrial Relations Act 1971 (see TULR(C)A s 117) for these were professional organisations which engaged in collective bargaining on behalf of their members, and their legal personality stemmed from their charter of incorporation, or by virtue of incorporation under the Companies Acts. Such legal personality is to continue, but other than these, any registration by a trade union under the Companies Acts, or as a friendly society or an industrial and provident society, is void.

22.8–22.15 Between 1901 and 1971, a series of legal decisions had laid down that a trade union had some form of quasi-legal personality, but this status has been clearly removed by s 10. In *EEPTU v Times Newspapers*, it was held that a trade union, not having a legal personality, could not therefore sue for libel in respect of its reputation, for s 10 states that a trade union shall not be 'or treated as if it were', a body corporate, and hence the claimant trade union did not have the personality which could be protected by an action for defamation.

Definition of employers' association (TULR(C)A s 122)

22.16 An employers' association is defined as an organisation which either:
a. consists wholly or mainly of employers or individual proprietors, and whose principal purposes include the regulation of relations between employers and workers or trade unions; or
b. consists wholly or mainly of constituent or affiliated organisations with those purposes or representatives of such constituents or affiliated organisations, whose principal objects include the regulation of relations between employers and workers or between the constituent or affiliated organisations.

22.17–22.25 An employers' association may be incorporated under the Companies Acts, or may be an unincorporated association. In the latter case it shall nonetheless be capable of making contracts, or suing and being sued in its own name, and of being prosecuted in its own name. Its property, however, will have to be held by trustees, and any judgment, award or order would have to be enforced against that property. A trade association, which is largely concerned with the business interests of employers, is not an employers' association within the statutory definition, but if it did have as one of its purposes collective bargaining objectives, or if it regulated the relations between organisations which have such objectives, it could be an employers' association. This is because the Act requires the principal objects of an employers' association to 'include' the statutory objects, not that the principal objects 'shall be' the statutory objects.

Listing of employers' associations (TULR(C)A s 123)

22.26 The Act permits the employers' associations to be entered on the appropriate list, but there are few advantages of doing so. Many employers' associations are incorporated under the Companies Act, and therefore do not require trustees to hold property. They do not have provident funds, and do not require certificates of independence. Not surprisingly, less than half of employers' associations have bothered to become listed.

Listing of trade unions (TULR(C)A s 2)

22.27   The certification officer (a post created in 1975 by the Employment Protection Act—see Chapter 1) has taken over and maintains a list of trade union organisations which were formerly held by the Registrar of Friendly Societies (s 257). On this list there will be organisations which were registered under the pre-1971 law (or formed as a result of an amalgamation of two or more bodies which were registered), all organisations registered under the Industrial Relations Act 1971, and all TUC affiliated trade unions. Any organisation (including employers' associations) which is not listed may apply for inclusion, submitting the appropriate fee, a copy of its rules, a list of officers, the address of its head office, and details of its name. The certification officer will refuse to enter on the list any organisation the name of which is the same as a previously registered or listed organisation, or a name which so closely resembles any such organisation as to be likely to deceive the public. If it appears to the certification officer that an organisation whose name is on the list is not a trade union he may remove it from the list, but not without giving notice of his intention to do so, and considering any representations which may be made. An organisation which is aggrieved by the decision of the certification officer to refuse to enter it on the list, or a decision to remove it from the list, may appeal either on a question of law or of fact, to the Employment Appeal Tribunal. Copies of the list shall be available for public inspection.

22.28–22.35   There are certain advantages of being a 'listed' trade union. First, it is evidence that the body concerned satisfied the statutory definition without further proof being required. Second, there are tax reliefs on income in the union's provident funds. Third, there are procedural advantages in connection with the passing of property consequent on the change of trustees. Fourth, and perhaps the most significant of all, only a listed trade union can apply for a certificate of independence.

Certification of trade unions (TULR(C)A s 6)

22.36   Any trade union which is on the list may apply to the certification officer for a certificate that it is an independent trade union. A union is independent if:
a.   it is not under the domination or control of an employer or groups of employers or an employers' association; and
b.   it is not liable to interference by an employer or any such group or association arising out of the provision of financial or material support or by any other means whatsoever tending towards such control (s 5).
If, after making enquiries the certification officer decides that the union is independent he will issue a certificate accordingly; otherwise he will refuse to do so, but must give reasons for his refusal. Even if he grants the certificate, he may withdraw it if he is of the opinion that the union is no longer independent, but he must notify the trade union concerned of his intention, and may take into account any relevant information supplied by any person. An appeal will lie on a point of law or fact to the Employment Appeal Tribunal against the decision of the certification officer to refuse to grant, or to withdraw, a certificate.

22.37   Only a trade union aggrieved by the decision not to grant a certificate may appeal. There is no general right of appeal by anyone who is aggrieved. In

General and Municipal Workers Union v Certification Officer, a trade union objected to a decision of the Certification Officer to grant a certificate to another organisation, but it was held that the trade union had no right to appeal against that decision.

22.38 Once granted, the certificate is conclusive evidence of the independence of the trade union, and in any proceedings before any court, the Employment Appeal Tribunal, the Central Arbitration Committee, or an employment tribunal, where the independence of the trade union is in issue and there is no certificate in force and no refusal, withdrawal or cancellation recorded, the proceedings shall be stayed until a certificate has been issued or refused by the certification officer.

22.39 To understand the arguments about certification, it is necessary to make a short excursus into industrial relations. Some years ago there was an expansion of unionisation, particular among the so-called 'white collar' workers and management. A considerable number of staff associations have sprung up in order to exercise the sort of industrial pressure hitherto reserved for the blue collar workers. These staff associations are looked upon as not being 'proper' trade unions, and are sometimes referred to in a derogatory tone as being 'sweetheart unions' or 'house unions'. The test of independence for certification purposes is to permit through the net those unions which can demonstrate that they are truly independent, and not just the tame adjuncts of management. A considerable number of such staff associations have applied for and obtained certificates of independence; many have not bothered, on the ground that they can obtain by negotiation all the advantages which certification confers. Those that have succeeded in obtaining a certificate are criticised for bringing about a proliferation of trade unions (at a time when a reduction in the number of unions is thought to be desirable) and for not joining in with the existing established (ie TUC) trade unions.

22.40 The first case to be challenged under this branch of the law was *Blue Circle Staff Association v Certification Officer*. In 1971 the staff association was formed for salaried staff at the instigation of higher management. Subsequently, changes were made to the association's constitution and an application was made for certification. It was held by the EAT that the certification officer was right in his refusal to grant a certificate. The association had not yet attained the freedom from domination by the employer under which it had lived since its formation. There is a heavy burden to show that it had shaken off such paternal control.

22.41 A different view of the realities of the scene was taken in *Association of HSD (Hatfield) Employees v Certification Officer*, where the association was formed with the active encouragement of the employers, who shared the opposition of the association to proposals for nationalisation. After the decision to nationalise was taken, the new head of the industry visited the factory, and was met by a hostile demonstration organised by the association. A subsequent application for a certificate of independence was refused by the certification officer, and the association appealed to the EAT. It was held that the certificate should be granted. Under s 5(a) the organisation must show that it is not under the domination or control of the employer. This involves an examination of the factual situation, including finance, the extent (if any) of employer assistance or interference, the history, rules, organisation, membership base and general attitude. Under s 5(b) there is inevitably a degree of speculation, but the certification officer ought not to be unduly anxious about future possibilities as he always has the power to revoke the certificate if he thinks he should do so. On the facts of the case, the EAT was clearly impressed by the hostile demonstration, and held that as the association had demonstrated that it was 'fiercely independent of management' a certificate should be granted.

22.42 The fact that an association is company based is not fatal to the association's independence, for there are many trade unions in industry which negotiate with a single employer (eg the Post Office, or civil service unions). Nor is the fact that the employer makes facilities available to a trade union destructive of its independence, for this may be seen as good industrial relations practice, and is in accordance with the Code of Practice on Time Off for Trade Union Duties and Activities. In *Squibb UK Staff Association v Certification Officer*, a certificate of independence was refused because of fears of vulnerability to employer interference. This was based largely on the extensive facilities which were provided by the employer, which included time off with pay for the officials of the association when performing their duties, free use of office accommodation and rooms for meetings, the provision of free stationery, free use of the employer's telephone, photocopying and internal mailing system, and a free check-off system. In view of the obvious limited resources of the association, and its narrow membership base, the certification officer thought that it would be very difficult to function effectively if these were withdrawn by the employer. The EAT held that nonetheless the certificate should be granted, but this decision was reversed by the Court of Appeal, and the original ruling of the certification officer was confirmed. The test of 'liability to interference' by the employer, which would be fatal to the association's independence, meant vulnerable to, or at risk of, interference. The degree of the likelihood of the risk was irrelevant as long as it was not insignificant.

22.43–22.50 If the continued existence of the staff association is dependent on the approval of the employer, then it is 'liable to interference' and hence cannot be an independent trade union (*Government Communications Staff Federation v Certification Officer*).

Advantages of certification

22.51 The advantages of having a certificate of independence are to be found mainly in the 1992 Act, and are as follows:
a. representatives of recognised independent trade unions are entitled to receive information for collective bargaining purposes (s 181);
b. the rights of employees not to have discriminatory action taken against them (short of dismissal) apply only to members of independent trade unions (s 146);
c. employees who are officials of recognised independent trade unions are entitled to have time off work to carry out their duties as such, or for the purpose of undergoing training in industrial relations. In doing so, they are entitled to their normal remuneration (s 168);
d. employees who are members of recognised independent trade unions are entitled to have time off work for trade union activities, though not necessarily with pay (s 170);

e.   an employer must consult with representatives of recognised independent trade unions in the event of redundancies arising (s 188);

f.   an application for interim relief if a dismissal is alleged to be for trade union membership may be made by a member of an independent trade union (s 161);

g.   it is unfair to dismiss a person because he wishes to join an independent trade union, or take part in its activities (s 152);

h.   a recognised independent trade union is entitled to be given information and be consulted under the Transfer of Undertakings (Protection of Employment) Regulations 1981;

i.   a recognised independent trade union is entitled to receive information from an employer concerning occupational pension schemes (Social Security Act 1975 s 56A);

j.   an independent trade union may enter into an agreement to exclude statutory rights of unfair dismissal and substitute a dismissal procedure (ERA s 110);

k.   an independent trade union is entitled to appoint safety representatives (Health & Safety at Work etc Act 1974 s 2).

Register of members (s 24)

22.52   A trade union shall maintain a register of the names and addresses of its members. The register shall be accurate, up to date, and may be kept by means of a computer.

22.53–22.60   A member is entitled to know whether there is an entry in the register relating to him, and be supplied with a copy of that entry. The person who has been appointed as an independent scrutineer for election purposes must also be permitted to inspect the register and be provided with an up-to-date copy of it (see para 22.133).

Confidentiality of the register of members (s 24A)

22.61   A trade union shall impose a duty of confidentiality on the independent scrutineer who has been appointed to oversee any ballot held on an election for office, political resolution or resolution to approve an instrument of amalgamation or transfer. The scrutineer or independent person must not disclose any name or address on the register (except in permitted circumstances), and must take all reasonable steps to ensure that no such disclosure takes place. Disclosure will be permitted (a) when the member consents, (b) where required for the purposes of the discharge of functions by the certification officer or of the scrutineer under the terms of his appointment, or (c) where required for the purpose of investigating crime or of criminal proceedings.

Remedies (ss 25–26)

22.62   A member of a trade union who claims that the union has failed to comply with ss 24 or 24A may apply to the certification officer for a declaration to that effect (s 25), or, in the alternative, to the court (s 26). The certification officer can make an enforcement order requiring the union to remedy the breach and/or abstain from acts which might lead to a future recurrence of the same breach. Any member of the union (who was a member at the time of the declared failure) may apply to the court to force the union to comply with the order. An appeal against the decision of the certification officer may be made to the EAT.

Membership of a trade union

22.63   In principle, it is for the trade union to lay down the description of persons who are eligible to join, and this will usually be laid down in the union's rules (*Boulting v ACAT*). It follows that it cannot accept for membership someone who is not within the prescribed class, and cannot create a category of membership not provided for in the rules (*Martin v Scottish Transport and General Workers' Union*). The rules may also specify a class of person who is not eligible to join (*Faramus v Film Artistes' Association*). However, a trade union cannot exclude a person from membership on arbitrary and unreasonable grounds (*Nagle v Feilden*). It is unlawful to discriminate against a woman in the terms on which it is prepared to accept her for membership, or by refusing or deliberately omitting to accept her application (Sex Discrimination Act 1975 s 12) or to discriminate against her in the way in which it affords her access to any benefits, facilities or other services, to deprive her of membership, or subject her to any other detriment (other than benefits on death or retirement). Similar provisions relating to unlawful discrimination on grounds of race etc are contained in the Race Relations Act 1976 s 12.

22.64   However, notwithstanding anything contained in the union's rules, a person cannot be excluded (or expelled) from a trade union unless this is permitted by the provisions of s 174 of TULR(C)A (see para 21.11), and a person who is so excluded or expelled has the right to bring a complaint before an industrial tribunal or the EAT as appropriate.

22.65–22.75   There is no statutory definition of who is a 'member' of a trade union, and the term has to be looked at in its context. Thus, if a trade union has a class of 'limited members', who have restricted rights, precisely defined in the union's rules, then they may not be 'members' for the purpose of voting in certain elections (eg on a proposal for the transfer of engagements, see *National Union of Mineworkers (Yorkshire Area) v Millward*).

Rules of a trade union

22.76   At common law, a trade union was tainted with illegality because its rules and/or objects were in 'restraint of trade'. In the nineteenth century this led to certain problems; the trade unionists were prosecuted for criminal conspiracy, and the rules of the unions were generally unenforceable. The effect of the doctrine against restraint of trade on trade unions, was nullified by the 1871 Trade Union Act, (see now TULR(C)A s 11) which provides that the purposes of a trade union or an employers' association shall not, by reason of being in restraint of trade, make any member liable for criminal conspiracy, or make any agreement or trust void or voidable, nor shall the rules be unlawful or unenforceable by virtue of their being in restraint of trade (see *Goring v British Actors Equity Association*). This also applies to incorporated employers' associations and special register bodies in so far as the purposes or rules relate to the regulation of relations between employers or employers' organisations and workers.

22.77–22.85 As long as a trade union complies with the various statutory requirements, there are no general restrictions on the rules which it may adopt. But the rules constitute a contract between the union and its members, and must be strictly observed.

Disciplinary action

22.86 If the trade union wishes to take disciplinary action, by way of fines or forfeitures, or wishes to expel a member, such powers must be contained in the rules, otherwise they cannot be exercised. In *Spring v National Amalgamated Stevedores and Dockers' Society* the plaintiff was enrolled as a member of the defendant union contrary to the Bridlington Agreement, which was designed to prevent poaching of members among TUC affiliated unions. The TUC ordered the union to expel the members, which it did, but the expulsion was held to be void when it was discovered that the union rules contained no power of expulsion.

22.87 However, it is possible for the court to imply into the union's rules a power to discipline a member, although since such a power is penal and could involve serious consequences which would affect the reputation and livelihood of the member, an implied disciplinary power would only arise when there are compelling circumstances to justify it. In *McVitae v UNISON* the claimant was a member of the National and Local Government Officers' Association (NALGO). Various complaints of intimidation, oppressive and sexist conduct were made against him and disciplinary proceedings were arranged. However, before they could take place, NALGO amalgamated with two other unions, to form Unison, and, following an investigation into the original complaints, Unison decided to re-institute the disciplinary proceedings. The claimant sought an injunction to prevent Unison from taking disciplinary action against him in respect of conduct which occurred prior to the union coming into existence.

There was no power in the instrument of amalgamation or the rules of the new union to discipline members in respect of conduct which occurred before its inception, but in the circumstances of the case, the court was prepared to imply such a power. The conduct in question was contrary to the rules of NALGO and Unison, and it could not have been intended that there should be a complete amnesty for conduct which occurred before the new union was created out of the amalgamation of the three unions.

22.88 If the rules specify the grounds on which disciplinary action may be taken, then the union must adhere to these grounds, and not proceed on others. Moreover, the courts have in the past exercised the power to interpret the rules of the union in accordance with the courts' understanding of the rules, not the union's. In *Lee v Showmen's Guild*, the claimant was expelled from the defendant guild for violating a rule designed to prevent 'unfair competition'. It was held that since the guild had misconstrued the meaning of this term, the court could substitute its own interpretation, and the expulsion was declared void. This interpretative power is particularly important in those cases where the rules are somewhat vague (eg 'conduct detrimental to the union' in *Kelly v NATSOPA*), although the legitimate interests of the union will be upheld. In *Evans v National Union of Bookbinding and Printing Workers*, the rules provided that a member who acted contrary to the interests of the union might be expelled. The claimant absented himself from work on several occasions, contrary to an agreement between the union and the employers. As a result of such conduct, he was expelled. It was held that the expulsion was valid, for it was designed to uphold the success of the collective bargaining arrangements.

22.89 If the union rules provide for a procedure to be adopted in disciplinary cases, then that procedure must be strictly adhered to, and the smallest irregularity will be as fatal as the greatest. The rules cannot be so framed as to oust the jurisdiction of the courts by declaring that the decision of the union shall be final and binding (*Chapple v ETU*), and if there is an appeal procedure which is denied to the aggrieved member, the expulsion will be invalid (*Braithwaite v Electrical Electronics and Telecommunications Union*). If the expulsion is void because of lack of authority or some other reason, then, as the appeal procedure cannot cure the defect, the aggrieved member may apply to the courts nonetheless, without exhausting the internal machinery. In *Porter v National Union of Journalists*, the union called a strike of provincial journalists without holding a ballot as required by its rules. An injunction was granted to restrain the union from taking disciplinary action against those members who refused to comply with the instruction, for the strike call was unconstitutional.

22.90 Although the statutory requirements that a trade union must act in accordance with the rules of natural justice have been repealed, it is submitted that the common law position remains unchanged. This means that a trade union, in the exercise of what is essentially a quasi-judicial function, cannot expel a member without giving him a hearing, notifying him of the charges against him, and giving him an opportunity to rebut them (*Lawlor v Union of Post Office Workers*). It also means that the officials of the union should avoid being placed in the position of being prosecutor, judge and jury. In *Taylor v National Union of Seamen*, the general secretary of the union dismissed the claimant for insubordination. When the claimant appealed to the executive council, the general secretary was the chairman of the meeting, and after the claimant had withdrawn, the meeting was treated to a long statement of matters which were not the subject of the charge, but which were prejudicial to him, and he had no opportunity of rebutting. It was held that the hearing of the appeal offended against the rules of natural justice.

22.91 However, the withdrawal of a privilege, granted outside the rules is not disciplinary action. In *Hudson v GMB*, a federated trade union nominated the claimant to attend a regional conference of the Labour Party. It was then alleged that she was a member of 'Militant', an organisation proscribed by the Labour Party, and so her nomination was withdrawn. She claimed that this was disciplinary action in violation of the rules of the union, as she had not been allowed to state her case. Further, she claimed that her nomination was a privilege which could not be withdrawn without proceedings taken in accordance with the principles of natural justice. Her claim failed. The withdrawal of the nomination was not a disciplinary measure relating to an office within the union's rules. Nor was the nomination made in respect of any permanent position which would involve a financial advantage. The union had no rules concerning such delegates, and the nomination could therefore be withdrawn at will.

22.92   A member who has been wrongfully expelled may apply for a declaration that he is still a member, an injunction restraining the union and its officials from acting on the purported expulsion, and damages for wrongful expulsion. In *Bonsor v Musicians' Union*, the appellant was expelled by the branch secretary, when this power could only be exercised by the branch committee. In consequence, he could not get work, and was reduced to earning a living by scraping rust off Brighton Pier. It was held that as the expulsion was void, he could recover damages for wrongful expulsion.

22.93–22.100   In addition (as already indicated) whatever the rules may or may not state, a member of a trade union has a statutory right not to be unjustifiably disciplined (see para 21.17) or expelled from a trade union (see para 21.11) unless the discipline or expulsion is not prohibited by the statute, and may seek an appropriate remedy before an employment tribunal.

Conduct of union affairs

22.101   Membership of a trade union confers certain rights and privileges on the members, and they are entitled to damages if these are not forthcoming. If the rules provide that members shall be entitled to legal advice, then a union which fails to provide that advice, or negligently provides incorrect advice, may be sued for the loss which flows from that breach. The tremendous increase in the statutory rights of employees is bound to throw an additional burden on trade union officials, who now need to be as familiar with those rights as management. Thus it is submitted that if a trade union fails to apply for a protective award in appropriate circumstances, or negligently delays the presentation of a claim to an employment tribunal so that it becomes out of time, the aggrieved member will have a right of action against that union for damages. No breach of contract arises if the member fails to show that his action had a reasonable prospect of success (*Buckley v NUGMW*), and in any case the union can fulfil the duty to use ordinary care and skill by handing over a potential claim to a firm of competent solicitors (*Friend v Institution of Professional Managers and Specialists*).

22.102   In the conduct of union affairs, the officials can only act within the confines of the rules. Thus in *Weakley v AEUW* the president of the union exercised a casting vote on a motion when the committee was equally divided. An injunction was granted restraining the union from acting on the motion, for, on a true construction of the rules, the president was not entitled to exercise a casting vote. But the officials may have implied power to do certain things which are in the interests of the union. In *Hill v Archbold*, two union officials brought an action in respect of matters which arose out of their employment. The actions were dismissed, but the union sought to pay the legal costs on behalf of the officials, though there was no provision in the rules for such expenditure. It was held that the union had implied power to do so, for the matter was incidental to their work as officials of the union.

22.103–22.110   A trade union which pays out strike pay which is not authorised by the rules (*Taylor v NUM (Derbyshire Area)*) or imposes a levy for a purpose which is *ultra vires* (*Hopkins v National Union of Seamen*) can be restrained from so doing by an injunction. However, allegations of electoral irregularities can be pursued under the provisions of s 54, (see para 22.146).

Copy of the rules (s 27)

22.111 A trade union shall supply, at the request of any person, a copy of its rules, either free or on payment of a reasonable charge.

Executive committee (TULR(C)A s 46)

22.112 Every member of the principal executive committee of a trade union (including those members who are members by virtue of holding an office) shall be elected by a ballot at least every five years. A person who holds his membership of the principal executive committee as a result of an election may continue as a member or official for such period as may be necessary (not exceeding six months) to give effect to an election result. In such a ballot, every member of the union shall be entitled to vote, except:
a. those members who as a class are excluded by the rules from voting;
b. members not in employment;
c. members in arrears; and
d. members who are students, trainees, apprentices or new members.
If the rules permit, it is possible to have voting restricted to special classes of membership, determined by reference to:
a. trade or occupation;
b. geographical area;
c. separate sections of the union; or
d. any combination of these.
Voting at an election must be made by the marking of a ballot paper by the person voting, and every person entitled to vote (a) must be allowed to do so without interference or constraint imposed by the union or any of its members, officials or employees, and (b) so far as is reasonably practicable, be able to do so without incurring any direct cost. So far as is reasonably practicable, voting papers must be sent to voters by post, containing or accompanied by a list of candidates, and the voter must be given a convenient opportunity to vote by post. So far as is reasonably practicable, voting shall be in secret, and the result shall be determined by the counting of the number of votes cast for each candidate (with or without the transferable vote) and votes shall be fairly and accurately counted.

22.113 The above provisions do not apply to trade unions which consist of representatives of constituent or affiliated organisations, merchant seamen who are ordinarily resident outside the United Kingdom, newly formed trade unions, or to members of the principal executive committee who are near retirement.

22.114 The president and general secretary (or persons who hold equivalent positions) shall be deemed to be members of the principal executive committee (and hence subject to the balloting provisions) as will be any other persons, notwithstanding anything in the rules of the union, if they are permitted to attend and speak at the meeting of that committee, other than for the purpose of providing the committee with factual information or technical or professional advice.

22.115 However, a person who is the president or general secretary of the union, and who is neither a voting member of the principal executive committee, nor an employee of the union, is not required to be elected in the above manner if he holds his office for a period of less than 13 months.

22.116 Elections for the members of the principal executive committee shall be by means of postal ballot, and no other method, except that there is no need to hold a ballot if the election is uncontested.

Election of candidates (TULR(C)A s 47)

22.117 No member of a trade union may be unreasonably excluded from standing as a candidate for election to any position unless he belongs to a class of which all members are excluded by the rules of the union. The rules of the union may give the executive committee of the union a discretion to decide certain prescribed qualifications for a union post, but not having the confidence of the executive committee is not a qualification (*Ecclestone v National Union of Journalists*). No candidate shall be required to be a member of any political party.

Election addresses (TULR(C)A s 48)

22.118 Every candidate in an election for the principal executive committee must be provided with an opportunity of preparing an election address, in his own words, and submitting it to the union to be distributed to those who are entitled to vote. Such election addresses are to be sent out with the voting paper, and the candidates are not required to bear any expense for the production of these copies. The election address shall be sent out without any modification except at the request of or with the consent of the candidate, or where the modification is necessarily incidental to the method adopted for the production of the copy. The same method of production is to be used for the election addresses of all candidates. A trade union may determine that election addresses may not exceed a certain length (but must permit a minimum of 100 words), and may incorporate only such photographs or other matter as the union may determine. So far as is reasonably practicable, the union must ensure that the same facilities and restrictions with respect to the preparation, submission, length and modifications, and the incorporation of photographs or other matter not in words are provided or applied equally to each of the candidates.

22.119–22.130 No person other than the candidate himself shall be subject to any criminal or civil liability in respect of the publication of a candidate's election address made under s 48.

Independent scrutineer (ss 49, 75, 100A, 226B)

22.131 Before an election is held for positions in the principal executive committee, or a ballot is held on the approval of a political fund, or approving an instrument of amalgamation or transfer, or a ballot on the holding of industrial action, the trade union must appoint a qualified independent person as a scrutineer, who will carry out his functions without interference. A person will be eligible for such appointment if he satisfies the conditions laid down in the Trade Union Ballots and Elections (Independent Scrutineers' Qualifications) Order 1988.

22.132 However, a scrutineer need not be appointed if there is a ballot on the holding of industrial action, and the number of members entitled to vote does not exceed 50 (s 226C).

22.133 The union will supply the scrutineer with a copy of the register of members, which he will inspect as appropriate, and in particular if requested to do so by a member or candidate who suspects that it was not accurate or up to date. The name of the independent scrutineer must be sent to every member of the union by notice, or communicated to members in the same manner as when matters of general interest are brought to their attention. His name must also appear on any ballot paper.

22.134 The storage, distribution and counting of ballot papers must be undertaken by an independent person, who may be the scrutineer or other person whose competence and independence is not in doubt (s 51A). The scrutineer must supervise the production and distribution of all voting papers, which are to be returned to him by those voting. He will retain them for one year after the announcement of the result of the election or ballot or, if the result is challenged before the certification officer or a court, until disposal is authorised.

22.135 As soon as is reasonably practicable after the last date for the return of the voting papers, the scrutineer shall make a report to the union, stating:
a.   the number of voting papers distributed;
b.   the number of voting papers returned to him;
c.   the number of valid votes cast in the election for each candidate, or, in a ballot, for each proposition;
d.   the number of invalid or spoiled votes returned; and
e.   the name of the person (if any) appointed as an independent person to count the votes.

22.136 The report will also state if he is satisfied that there was no contravention of any requirement imposed by law, that the arrangements for the ballot or election (including any security arrangements) minimised the risk of any unfairness or malpractice, and that he was able to carry out his functions without interference or anyone calling his independence into question. He will also state if he has inspected the register of members, and whether any such inspection has revealed any matter which should be brought to the attention of the union in order to ensure that it is accurate and up to date (s 52).

22.137–22.145 Within three months of receiving the scrutineer's report on an election (s 52(4)), on a political fund resolution (s 78(4)), or on an amalgamation or transfer resolution (s 100E(6)), the trade union shall send a copy to every member to whom it is reasonably practicable to send such a copy, or take all such steps for notifying the contents of the report to members of the union as it is the practice for the union to take when matters of general interest need to be brought to the members' attention. So far as ballots on industrial action are concerned, any person entitled to vote in the ballot, and the employer of any such person, is entitled to be supplied with a copy of the scrutineer's report on request. This may be supplied free of charge or on the payment of a reasonable fee.

Remedies (s 54)

22.146 Any member may apply to the High Court (or Court of Session) or the certification officer (but not both) for a declaration that the trade union has failed to comply with any requirement of the Act relating to secret ballots for trade union elections or relating to election addresses or to scrutineers. The court may make an enforcement order specifying the action which the trade union shall take in consequence of its failure to comply with the Act (s 56). The certification officer may grant the declaration, and, if necessary, make an enforcement order requiring the union to hold a fresh election (s 55). An appeal from the order of the Certification Officer may be made to the EAT.

Accounts, records, etc (TULR(C)A s 28)

22.147 Every trade union and employers' association shall keep proper records, and establish a satisfactory system of control over its cash holdings, receipts and remittances. An annual return must be sent to the certification officer, with accounts duly audited. There are provisions in ss 32–42 detailing the matters which must be contained in the annual return including the salaries paid to, and the benefits provided for, the president, general secretary and members of the executive committee, together with the qualifications, appointment, functions, and removal of auditors, and for the control over members' superannuation schemes. Any person who refuses or wilfully neglects to perform a duty imposed by these provisions, or who alters a document required for those purposes, shall be guilty of an offence, punishable by a fine of up to level 3 and 5 on the standard scale respectively.

22.148–22.155 An annual statement must be sent to all members of the union (or otherwise communicated to them) giving details of the union's income and expenditure, salaries paid to the president, general secretary and executive members, and the income and expenditure of the political fund. The statement will also include prescribed information on the remedies to members who are concerned about any irregularities in the conduct of the union's affairs (s 32A).

Right to inspect accounts (ss 29–31)

22.156 A trade union shall keep its accounting records available for inspection for six years from 1 January following the end of the period to which those records relate.

22.157 Any member of a trade union may request to be permitted access to those records in respect of any period when he was a member. Such access shall be permitted within 28 days of the request and, unless otherwise agreed, at a reasonable hour and at the place where the records are normally kept. The member is entitled to take an accountant with him, and to take, or be supplied with, such copies or extracts from those records as he may require. The trade union may make a charge in respect of reasonable administrative expenses incurred (s 30).

22.158   If the trade union fails to comply with the member's request for access to the accounting records, the member may apply to the court or the certification officer (but not both), who may make such order as is considered appropriate for ensuring that that person:
a.   is allowed to inspect the records;
b.   is allowed to be accompanied by an accountant; and
c.   is allowed to take, or is supplied with, such copies of or extracts from those records as he may require (s 31).

22.159–22.165   The certification officer has the power to require the production of documents, take copies etc and appoint an inspector to investigate the financial affairs of the union, if he suspects that the financial affairs of the union have been conducted in a fraudulent manner, or a person managing its affairs has been guilty of fraud, or the union has failed to comply with a provision of the Act or its own rules with relation to the conduct of its financial affairs (TULR(C)A s 37B). The inspector has wide powers of investigation, and will report back to the certification officer.

Offences (ss 45–45C)

22.166   If a trade union refuses to supply a copy of its rules (s 27), fails to keep accounting records (s 28), fails to keep records available for inspection (s 29), fails to give members access to the accounts (s 30), fails to make an annual return (s 32), make an annual statement to members (s 32A), breaches the auditing requirements (s 33–37), or breaches the requirements relating to members' superannuation schemes (ss 38–42), it commits an offence. The offence will also be committed by every officer who is bound by the rules to discharge any of those duties, or, if there is no such officer, every member of the management committee. It will be a defence for the officer or member of the management committee to prove that he had reasonable cause to believe that some other competent person was authorised to discharge that duty. It is also an offence wilfully to alter a document, fail to produce a document, destroy, mutilate or falsify a document relating to the financial affairs of the union, or fraudulently alter or delete anything in such document, or to make a false statement. The offences may be punishable by a fine or, in some circumstances, up to six months' imprisonment. A person who has been convicted under these provisions shall not hold office as a member of the executive, president or general secretary for a period of five or ten years, depending on the offence.

Indemnifying unlawful conduct (s 15)

22.167   It is unlawful for any property of a trade union to be applied towards the payment for any individual, or towards the provision of anything for indemnifying an individual, in respect of any penalty which has been imposed on him for a relevant offence, or for contempt of court. A 'relevant offence' is any offence other than one which has been designated as an offence by the Secretary of State in relation to which s 15 does not apply.

22.168–22.175 If property has been so applied in contravention of this section, the equal amount of any payment is recoverable from the individual concerned by the trade union, and in the case of property, the individual shall be liable to account for its value. If the trade union unreasonably fails to make a claim against the individual, any member may apply to the court for authorisation to bring or continue proceedings on the union's behalf and at the union's expense.

Remedies against trustees (s 16)

22.176 If a member of a trade union considers that the trustees of the union's property are carrying out their functions so as to permit an unlawful application of the union's property, or are complying with an unlawful direction which has been given to them under the union's rules, he may apply to the court for an order. If the court is satisfied that the application is well-founded, it may make such orders as it deems appropriate, including:
a. requiring the trustees of the union to take all such steps as may be specified for the purpose of protecting or recovering the union's property;
b. appointing a receiver (or judicial factor) of/on the union's property;
c. the removal of one or more trustees.

22.177–22.185 Should the trustees act in contravention of the court's order, the court may remove all the trustees except those who can satisfy the court that there is good reason to allow them to remain a trustee.

Political fund and political objects (TULR(C)A ss 71–74)

22.186 The Act lays down the necessary requirements before a trade union can have a political fund and pursue political objects. A resolution to establish a political fund must be passed at least every ten years by a ballot of all the union's members, and if approved, a separate political fund may be created. The ballot must be by the use of a voting paper, and every person entitled to vote must be allowed to do so without interference from or constraint imposed by the trade union or any of its members, officials or employees. The member must be able to vote without incurring any direct cost.

22.187 So far as is reasonably practicable, every person who is entitled to vote on a ballot concerning the establishment of a political fund must have the voting papers sent to him at his home or postal address, and be given a convenient opportunity to vote by post. The voting must be in secret, and the votes fairly and accurately counted (s 77).

22.188 If the political fund is established, no property of the trade union shall be added to that fund other than sums representing contributions made to the fund by the members or any other person and property accruing to the fund in the course of administering its assets. No liability of the political fund shall be met out of any other fund of the trade union. If there is no resolution in force establishing the political fund, no property shall be added to an existing fund (other than that which accrues in the course of administering the fund) and no union rule shall require any member to contribute towards the fund. The union may transfer the whole or part of the assets of an existing fund to such other fund of the trade union as it thinks fit. Where a resolution is passed rescinding an existing fund, the trade union may use the fund for a period of six months, but not so as to put the fund in deficit.

22.189   If a resolution to have a political fund ceases to have effect, the union shall take such steps to ensure that the collection of contributions to the fund is discontinued as soon as is reasonably practicable, and any contribution collected after the resolution ceases to have effect may be paid to any other fund of the trade union. If the trade union continues to collect contributions these are refundable at the members' request.

22.190   Any member of a trade union who wishes to contract out of a political fund must be free to do so, and if he does, he shall not in consequence be excluded from any benefit or disqualified from holding any office other than a position connected with the management of the political fund. Contributing towards the fund must not be a condition of membership.

22.191   The TUC has issued a 'Statement of Guidance' on political funds. It advises trade unions to draw up 'information sheets' about their political funds, and inform members why it has a fund, make clear members' legal rights to opt out, state the current amount of the levy, and provide information on how members may contract out.

22.192   The political fund may be used for the following purposes:
a.   any contribution to the funds of, or the payment of any expense incurred by, a political party;
b.   the provision of any services or property for the use by or on behalf of a political party;
c.   the registration of electors, the candidature of any person, the selection of any candidate, or the holding of a ballot by the union in connection with any election to a political office;
d.   the maintenance of any holder of a political office;
e.   the holding of any conference or meetings by or on behalf of a political party, or any other meetings the main purpose of which is the transaction of business in connection with a political party;
f.   the production, publication or distribution of any literature, document, film, sound recording or advertisement the main purpose of which is to persuade people to vote for a political party or candidate or not to vote for it or him.

22.193   An allegation that a trade union has broken a rule as to the use to which the political fund may be put may be the subject of an investigation by the certification officer. In *Richards v NUM* a complaint was made that the union had spent money from the general fund sending members on a lobby of Parliament organised by the Labour Party, and had also paid money to a trade union consortium which was developing Labour Party headquarters. It was held by the certification officer that such expenditure was in furtherance of political objects, and he ordered that the money should come from the political funds of the union, not the general funds.

22.194–22.200   A member who claims that the union has applied its funds in breach of s 71 may apply to the certification officer for a declaration. After making the necessary enquiries, the certification officer may grant the declaration, specifying the amount of funds applied in breach of s 71 and any remedial action to be taken, and specify any steps to be taken to ensure that the same or similar breach does not take place in the future (s 72A).

Complaints over political fund ballots (TULR(C)A ss 79–81)

22.201   A member of a trade union who complains that a ballot on the political fund was taken otherwise than in accordance with the rules approved by the certification officer, or that there has been a failure to comply with those rules, may apply to the certification officer or to the court (but not both) for a declaration. The application must be made within one year from the date when the result of the ballot was announced.

22.202–22.210   The court may make an enforcement order, specifying the action which the trade union shall take in consequence of its failure to comply with the Act.

Breach of union rules (s 108A–108B)

22.211   A member of the union who claims that there has been a breach of other rules of the union rules may apply to the certification officer for a declaration. The rules in question are
(a) the appointment or election of a person to, or the removal of a person from, any office
(b) disciplinary proceedings by the union (including expulsion)
(c) the balloting of members on any issue other than industrial action
(d) the constitution or proceedings of any executive committee or of any decision-making meeting
(e) such other matters as may be specified in an order make by the Secretary of State.

22.212   The application must be made within six months from the day when the breach occurred, or, if an internal complaints procedure was invoked, six months from when it was concluded. The certification officer is not entitled to consider a complaint about the discipline or dismissal of an employee of the union, as these are matters capable of being dealt with under the general law on individual employment rights.

22.213–22.220   The certification officer may refuse to consider the complaint unless reasonable steps were taken to resolve the issue by use of the internal complaints procedure, but if he hears the complaint he may make a declaration, and, if appropriate, an enforcement order, requiring the union to remedy the breach, or abstain from specified acts. An appeal from any proceedings under this section will lie to the EAT on a point of law.

Amalgamation and transfers (ss 97–105)

22.221   Two or more trade unions may decide to amalgamate into one union, or a union may wish to transfer its engagements to another union. In both cases, the instrument of amalgamation or transfer must first be submitted to the certification officer for approval, and then voted upon by the members of the amalgamating unions or transferor union, as the case may be. The union must give the members a notice in writing, which either sets out the instrument of amalgamation or transfer, or gives an account of it so as to enable the member to form a reasonable judgment of its main effects. Section 100 of the Act provides that the instrument may be approved by a simple majority of votes recorded, unless the rules of the union specifically exclude this provision, in which case some other specified proportion of members will be required to approve.

22.222   An independent scrutineer must be appointed, who will supervise the production and distribution of the voting papers, inspect the register of members, and generally report to the union after the ballot has been concluded. Voting in the ballot shall be accorded equally to all members of the union, the ballot papers will be numbered consecutively, and sent to members' homes or postal address. The notice sent to members shall not contain any statement making a recommendation or expressing an opinion about the proposed transfer or amalgamation. A copy of the scrutineer's report must be sent to every member or otherwise suitably published.

22.223   A complaint about the procedure relating to an amalgamation or transfer may be made to the certification officer, who may make a declaration, and an order specifying the steps, to be taken before he will entertain the application (s 103).

CHAPTER 23

Law relating to industrial relations

23.1   Since 1871, when trade unions were legalised by the Trade Union Act of that year, the history of industrial relations in the United Kingdom has been somewhat turbulent. This is partly due to conflicting ideologies, sometimes of a political nature, but mainly due to a conflict between those who favour individual as opposed to collective bargaining arrangements. A consideration of the extent to which the law should play a role in the control of industrial relations, and the precise nature of that law, has always been a subject for political controversy. Various governments of differing political persuasions have made their impact throughout the years, but, mainly due to the reforms pushed through in the Thatcher era (see Appendix G) trade unions have now achieved a respectability and a role recognised by employers and confirmed by law. The whole story, though interesting from a legal and philosophical point of view, need not detain us in this book, but history has left its mark, and it is not possible to understand the present legal position without some reference to the previous law on this topic, though it is intended to keep such excursus to a minimum, In particular, it will be necessary to examine certain common law rules which, though they may now be only of historical importance, have shaped the legislative provisions.

23.2   Freedom of association, ie the right of an individual to join a trade union, is guaranteed by the European Convention on Human Rights (see para 1.166) and is now accepted in the United Kingdom as axiomatic. However, the right of a trade union to bargain and/or negotiate on behalf of its members is initially dependent on the willing co-operation of employers. Thus an employer may refuse to recognise a trade union, may recognise it for some purposes only (eg representation) or for all purposes (eg negotiations). Whether an employer recognises a trade union, and the extent of that recognition, are questions of fact; there need not be a formal agreement to confirm this (see para 23.11). Once recognition has been granted, various legal consequences will flow, including the right to receive information for collective bargaining purposes (para 23.28), the right to be consulted on redundancies (Chapter 18) and transfers of the undertaking (Chapter 9) etc. Members of independent trade unions which are recognised by the employer are entitled to certain benefits, including time off work for union duties and activities, and have various protections from dismissal and detriment (Chapter 21).

23.3–23.10   One of the reasons for industrial unrest in the past was the reluctance of some employers to recognise a trade union for any purpose, for whatever reason. An attempt to force employers to recognise a trade union was made in the Employment Protection Act 1975, but this was not a success, and the provisions were subsequently repealed. Whether the new law (below) will achieve more success is a matter which time only will tell.

Voluntary recognition

23.11   Employment tribunals appear to operate under the general rule that it is for the trade union to show that there is some formal agreement (not necessarily in writing) that it is recognised for collective bargaining purposes (*T & GWU v Dyer*). The mere fact that there are employees who are trade union members, and that one of them negotiates, but without specific trade union authority, will not constitute recognition (*AUEW v Sefton Engineering*). Negotiations which may lead to recognition do not themselves constitute recognition (*T & GWU v Stanhope Engineering*). Nor can recognition be inferred if a full-time union official represents an individual in a disciplinary proceeding, for the purpose of collective bargaining (*T & GWU v Courtenham Products*). The fact that an employer is a member of an association which negotiates with a trade union does not mean that the individual employer recognises the union (*NUGSAT v Albury Bros Ltd*). Nor does recognition by a former employer by itself constitute recognition by a successor (*UCATT v Burrage*). In *NUTGW v Charles Ingram & Co Ltd* five propositions were established: (1) recognition is a mixed question of law and fact; (2) recognition requires mutuality; (3) there must be an express or implied agreement for recognition; (4) if the agreement was implied, there must be clear and unequivocal acts or conduct, usually over a period of time; (5) there may be partial recognition, for some, but not all purposes. Recognition for representation purposes only is not the same thing as recognition for negotiating purposes (*USDAW v Sketchley Ltd*).

Statutory recognition (TULR(C)A; Sch A1

23.12   The Employment Relations Act 1999 lays down a new complex statutory procedure for recognition and derecognition of trade unions, which can be found in the new Sch A1 TULR(C)A. The detailed provisions, including time limits and balloting procedures can be found in some 172 paragraphs of the Schedule, which additionally deal with semi-voluntary recognition, derecognition procedures, and protection of workers from detriments or dismissal on grounds relating to trade union membership or non-membership. However, the provisions do not apply where an employer employs fewer than 21 workers.

23.13   Schedule A1 is divided into eight parts, as follows:
Part I: statutory recognition;
Part II: voluntary recognition following a request for statutory recognition;
Part III: changes affecting the bargaining unit;
Part IV: derecognition, general;
Part V: automatic derecognition;
Part VI: derecognition of non-independent trade union;
Part VII: derecognition when a trade union loses its certificate of independence;

Part VIII: detriment and dismissal;
Part IX: general matters.

23.14   An independent trade union can apply to CAC for a declaration requiring the employer to recognise it for collective bargaining purposes in respect of workers in a particular bargaining unit. CAC will grant the declaration if a majority of workers in the bargaining unit already belong to the trade union, or where the union obtains the support of a majority of those voting in a secret ballot, which consists of at least 40 per cent of those entitled to vote. The employer and the union should then agree to a method of collective bargaining, although if they fail to do so, an application may be made by either party to CAC, who will impose one. Recognition, thus obtained, will last for a minimum of three years, and cannot be ended unilaterally by the employer even after the end of that time, unless the derecognition procedure has been followed (Pt I, paras 1–51). The manner is which collective bargaining is to be conducted is set out in the Trade Union Recognition (Method of Collective Bargaining) Order 2000, which is legally binding, and can be enforced by an order for specific performance.

23.15   An alternative method is an agreement for recognition, which will arise when the union makes an application to CAC for recognition, but then abandons it because the employer agrees voluntarily to recognise the union. Nonetheless, either side may still request CAC to impose a method of collective bargaining. An agreement for recognition will last for three years, but does not require the derecognition procedure to be followed to terminate it (Pt II, paras 52–63).

23.16   It should be noted that neither of the above two procedures in any way affects existing voluntary collective bargaining arrangements, which will no doubt continue without the necessity of being underpinned by a statutory procedure.

23.17   If, for whatever reason, the original bargaining unit is no longer considered to be appropriate, either side may apply to CAC to select a new bargaining unit. There are provisions which are designed to ensure that the new unit does not overlap with an existing bargaining unit (including balloting if necessary), and CAC can make arrangements for workers who consequently fall outside the original unit into a residual unit (Pt III, paras 64–95).

23.18–23.25   An employer may derecognise the union if the number of workers falls below 21, or if an application is made to CAC (by the employer or by the workers) for a secret ballot to be held, at any time after three years from a CAC declaration. There is a further procedure for the workforce to apply for the derecognition of a non-independent trade union (which had achieved voluntary recognition), and for dealing with the situation which arises if a trade union loses its independent status (Pts 4, 5, 6, 7, paras 96–155).

Employers' training policies (TULR(C)A s 70B)

23.26   If a trade union has obtained recognition for collective bargaining purposes under Sch A1, and CAC has imposed a method of collective bargaining (and the parties have not agreed that the imposed method should not be legally binding) a trade union will be entitled to be consulted about the employer's policy on training for workers within the bargaining unit, the plans for training those workers during the following six months, and to receive information about training provided since the previous meeting. Two weeks before a meeting is held for this purpose, the employer must provide the union with whatever information is required to ensure that the union's representative can participate meaningfully in the meeting, and which it would be in accordance with good industrial relations practice for the employer to disclose. The employer shall take account of any written representations made by the union within four weeks from the date of the meeting. If the employer fails to comply with s 70B, the trade union may present a complaint to an employment tribunal, which may make a declaration, and award compensation of up to two weeks' pay to each person who was a member of the bargaining unit.

Collective bargaining (TULR(C)A, Sch AI, para 94)

23.27   The existing definition of collective bargaining refers to negotiations between a trade union and an employer on a wide variety of matters, including terms and conditions of employment, termination and suspension of employment, allocation of work, discipline and physical conditions of work (TULR(C)A s 178). However, for the purposes of Sch A1, the definition is more restrictive, with the following result.
(a) So far as existing voluntary arrangements are concerned, collective bargaining refers to those matters listed in s 178 of TULR(C)A.
(b) Where statutory recognition is awarded under Pt I of Sch Al, collective bargaining refers to the three core issues of pay, hours and holidays.
(c) If the parties agree matters as the subject of collective bargaining (eg if there is an agreement for recognition under Pt II, or an agreement to change the agenda in relation to a new unit under Pt III), the matters referred to in the agreement.
(d) If there is a new unit, or a residual unit under Pt III (with certain exceptions, see para 94(2)), collective bargaining means negotiations on the matters which were the subject of collective bargaining in the corresponding or parent unit.

Disclosure of information (TULR(C)A s 181)

23.28   For the purpose of all stages of collective bargaining it shall be the duty of the employer, on request, to disclose to representatives of a recognised independent trade union all such information relating to his undertaking as is in his possession, and is information without which the representatives would to a material extent be impeded in carrying on such bargaining, and is information which it would be in accordance with good industrial relations practice that he should disclose. In one of its earliest findings, the CAC held that the test of 'materially impeded' meant that the information should be both relevant and important (*Institute of Journalists v Daily Telegraph*). The employer need only make the disclosure to unions which are recognised by him. In determining what is good industrial relations practice, regard will be had to any Code of Practice issued by ACAS. If the trade union representatives so request the employer will disclose or confirm the information in writing, but he need not disclose:

a. information the disclosure of which would be contrary to the national interest;
b. any information which he could not disclose without breaking the law;
c. information which he received in confidence;
d. information relating to an individual, unless he has consented to the disclosure;
e. information the disclosure of which would cause substantial injury to the employer's business for reasons other than its effect on collective bargaining;
f. information obtained by the employer for the purpose of bringing or defending any legal proceedings.

23.29 The employer is not bound to produce, or allow the inspection of, any document, or to compile information where this would involve an amount of work or expenditure out of all reasonable proportion to its value in the conduct of collective bargaining.

23.30 If an independent trade union wishes to make a complaint that an employer has failed to disclose information which he is required to produce, it may report the matter to the Central Arbitration Committee. If that body thinks that the complaint can be settled by conciliation it will refer the matter to ACAS, which will try to promote a settlement. If this does not prove possible, or if the complaint is not so referred, the committee will hear and determine the complaint. If it finds the complaint is wholly or partly well-founded, it will issue a declaration, stating:
a. the information in respect of which the complaint is well-founded;
b. the date on which the employer refused or failed to disclose the information; and
c. a period (being more than one week from the date of the declaration) within which the employer ought to disclose the information. If, at the end of that period, the employer still fails to disclose, a further complaint may be made by the trade union.

23.31–23.40 The complaint may be accompanied by a claim relating to the terms and conditions of the employees, and if the employer still persists in his refusal, the committee may make an award that in respect of the employees of any description specified in the claim, the employer shall observe the terms and conditions demanded, or other terms and conditions which the committee considers to be appropriate. These will form part of the contracts of employment of those employees from a date specified in the award, until varied or superseded by a further award or a subsequent collective agreement, or an express or implied agreement made between the employer and the employees which is an improvement on the award. As a general rule, CAC would consider the likely loss which flows from the failure to give the union the relevant information, and make an award accordingly.

Legal liabilities and legal proceedings

23.41 At common law it is impossible for a trade union to engage in any effective industrial relations activity without falling foul of some well-established legal rule. An understanding of those liabilities is necessary in order to understand and appreciate the statutory protections which have been developed over the years.

A. Inducing or procuring a breach of contract

23.42   It is a tort (civil wrong) for a person to induce another to break a contract to which the other is a party, or to procure a breach of that contract. In *Lumley v Gye*, an opera singer contracted to sing at a theatre owned by the claimant. The defendant induced her to break that contract and sing for him instead. Clearly, the singer was liable for her own breach of contract, but it was held that the claimant could successfully sue the defendant for inducing her to break the contract. In terms of industrial relations, the tort is peculiarly appropriate (see, for example, the recent county court decision in *Falconer v ASLEF and NUR*). An employer has a contract (of employment) with an employee. If a trade union official calls upon that employee to strike, the employee is breaking the contract (for which he can be dismissed—but see Chapter 21) but the union official (and possibly the union also) could be held liable for inducing a breach of that contract. Equally, if a trade union was to call for a secondary boycott, it may be furthering strike action, but it is also inducing (or procuring) a breach of a commercial contract. In *Torquay Hotel Co Ltd v Cousins*, a trade union was in dispute with a hotel. A union official informed a company which was supplying oil to the hotel of the existence of the dispute, and instructed its members not to deliver oil supplies. It was held that an injunction would lie restraining the union officials from causing any fuel supplier to breach its contract to supply oil.

23.43   If a shop steward has express or implied authority to act on behalf of a trade union, then the union may be responsible for his actions unless it can shelter behind some legal protection (*Heatons Transport (St Helens) Ltd v T & GWU*). But a union cannot be responsible for activities of unofficial committees of shop stewards, particularly when they are pursuing policies which are contrary to those of the union, and where union officials are trying to solve problems through machinery for negotiation and conciliation, while the shop stewards are taking militant industrial action (*General Aviation Services (UK) Ltd v T & GWU*). However, in such a situation, the union must repudiate the activities in question (see para 23.113) if it wishes to retain its immunities.

23.44   For the tort of inducing or procuring or otherwise wrongfully interfering with contractual rights to be made out, five conditions must be satisfied: (1) it must be shown that the defendant persuaded or procured or induced a third party to break its contract with the claimant; (2) when the defendant so acted he had knowledge of the existence of the contract, if not its precise terms; (3) it must be shown that the defendant intended to persuade, induce or procure a breach of that contract; (4) the claimant must show more than nominal damage; (5) if the defendant puts forward the defence of justification, the claimant has to rebut that defence (*Timeplan Education Group Ltd v National Union of Teachers*).

B. Conspiracy

23.45   A conspiracy is a combination of two or more persons to do an unlawful act, or a lawful act by unlawful means. Such acts could lead to a prosecution for criminal conspiracy (ie where the conspirators combine in order to pursue criminal objects) or an action for civil conspiracy where the alleged act constitutes a tort. Since trade unions are by necessity combinations, it is not surprising that they are particularly vulnerable to this form of legal constraint. For example, in *Quinn v Leathem*, Leathem was a butcher who employed non-union labour. The union called upon him to dismiss them, but he refused to do so. Instead, he offered to pay the men's arrears of subscriptions if they were admitted into the union. This offer was rejected by the union officials, who wanted to teach the non-unionists a lesson 'and make them walk the streets for 12 months'. Munce supplied meat to Leathem, and the union threatened to call a strike of Munce's men unless supplies of meat to Leathem were cut off, and Munce complied with this request. It was held that the union officials had conspired together to cause harm to Leathem without lawful jurisdiction. Their legitimate trade union objectives could have been achieved by accepting Leathem's offer and admitting the men to membership, but in fact their subsequent conduct had been motivated by vindictiveness.

23.46   But the mere fact that an act causes harm does not, by itself, amount to a conspiracy. Clearly, a strike causes harm to an employer, but if the object is a legitimate one, eg obtaining higher wages, no actionable conspiracy exists (*Crofter Hand Woven Harris Tweed Co v Veitch*). In *Scala Ballroom (Wolverhampton) Ltd v Ratcliffe,* the claimants operated a colour bar at their dance hall. Officials of the Musicians' Union placed a boycott on the premises in protest. It was held that this was not a conspiracy to injure, for the combination was a legitimate furtherance of the union's interests.

C. Intimidation

23.47   This 'obscure and unfamiliar' tort was resurrected from oblivion in the controversial case of *Rookes v Barnard*, where a shop steward threatened to call a strike at Heathrow Airport unless the claimant, a non-unionist, was dismissed. This 'threat' constituted a breach of contract, which was held to be an unlawful act (ie in the same way that a threat to commit an act of violence would be unlawful) and the defendants were held liable for intimidation.

D. Other tort liabilities

23.48   There are a number of other possible headings of legal liabilities which trade unions may run up against, including such headings as unlawful interference with trade business or employment, interference with future contracts, and so forth. Such torts are to be found in judicial hints rather than actuality, and the fear was of their emergence rather than their existence. With the increased statutory control over the conduct of trade unions, it is unlikely that these obscure torts will be revived.

23.49–23.55   But if there are unlawful acts committed by a trade union, an injured party may apply for an injunction to restrain the commission of such acts, and sue for damages in respect of any loss suffered, including, if necessary, exemplary damages (*Messenger Newspapers Group Ltd v NGA*). A trade union can only defend itself if it can rely on the statutory protections.

Legal protections

23.56   It is clear from the above that if trade unions are to carry out their legitimate functions in industrial relations, they require protection from these headings of common law liability, and arguably against judicial ingenuity in developing new case law which would restrict their activities. This has been the object of statute law since 1906; it was a process which was carried on by the Industrial Relations Act 1971, and has been continued in TULR(C)A. But the statutory immunities are not a licence to do anything; they only provide a protective cover for trade unions when legitimate objectives are being pursued. These objectives are limited to acts done in furtherance or contemplation of a trade dispute, and it is to the wide meaning of this phrase that we must now turn.

A. 'Trade dispute' (TULR(C)A s 244)

23.57 A trade dispute means a dispute between workers and their employers which relates wholly or mainly to one or more of the following:
a. terms and conditions of employment, or the physical conditions in which any workers are required to work;
b. the engagement or non-engagement or termination or suspension of employment or the duties of employment, of one or more workers;
c. the allocation of work or the duties of employment between workers or groups of workers;
d. matters of discipline;
e. membership or non-membership of a trade union on the part of a worker;
f. facilities for officials of trade unions;
g. machinery for negotiations or consultation, and other matters relating to the foregoing (ie a–f above), including recognition by employers or employers' associations of the right of a trade union to represent workers in any such negotiations or consultations or in the carrying out of such procedures.

23.58 The important change made by the Employment Act 1982 is that the dispute must relate 'wholly or mainly' to the above matters. In *Mercury Communications Ltd v Scott-Garner*, the claimants were granted a licence by the Government to run a telecommunications system (the 'liberalisation' agreement), which effectively broke the Post Office monopoly. The Government also proposed to privatise British Telecommunications. The Post Office Engineering Union opposed both the liberalisation and privatisation of the work, and gave instructions to its members not to do work which would enable the plaintiffs to connect to the British Telecommunications network. The claimants applied for an injunction to restrain the union from inducing a breach of contractual relations between themselves and British Telecommunications. The Court of Appeal granted the injunction. It was unlikely that the union would be able to establish at the trial that there was a trade dispute within the statutory definition. There was little evidence to support the union's contention that there was a dispute about the risk of loss of jobs. The reality was that the union was waging a campaign against the political decisions to liberalise and privatise the industry.

23.59 In addition, there are three other circumstances to consider. First, a trade dispute will exist between a minister of the Crown and a group of workers notwithstanding that the minister is not the employer of those workers, if the dispute relates to matters which have been referred for consideration to a joint body on which that minister is bound by statute to be represented, and which cannot be settled without the minister exercising a power.

23.60 For example, in *Wandsworth London Borough Council v National Association of Schoolmasters Union of Women Teachers*, the defendants wished to ballot their members to protest against the excessive workload caused by the assessment requirements of the national curriculum, which had been imposed by the Government. A local authority sought an injunction against the unions, arguing that the dispute was not about terms and conditions of employment, but about the very idea of the national assessment, and this was a matter which could only be resolved by the Secretary of State exercising a power conferred by statute. It was held that the dispute was wholly or mainly about the workload imposed on teachers and, therefore, since it was about the terms and conditions of employment, the statutory protection (see below) applied, and the application for an injunction was refused.

23.61 Second, there is a trade dispute even though it relates to matters occurring outside the United Kingdom as long as the persons who are taking action are likely to be affected in respect of one or more of the matters mentioned above. The third situation is more curious. In *Cory Lighterage Ltd v T & GWU*, a lighterman named Shute decided to leave the union, and the employers were informed that none of the crew would sail if he did not pay his union dues. The employers had no quarrel with the union, for they accepted the principle of 100 per cent unionisation, but they could not dismiss Shute under the Dock Workers Employment Scheme, so they sent him home on full pay. It was held that as there was no dispute between the employers and the union, the statutory protections did not apply. The employers did not resist the demands of the union, but rather acceded to them by taking Shute off the lighter. In line with the policy of giving the widest possible protection to trade unions in all actual and potential conflict situations, TULR(C)A s 244(4) provides that an act, threat or demand done or made by one party or organisation against another which, if resisted, would have led to a trade dispute with that other, shall, notwithstanding that because that other submits to the act or threat or accedes to the demand no dispute arises, be treated as done or made in contemplation or furtherance of a trade dispute.

23.62 There is no trade dispute if a strike is called about the terms and conditions of employment of employees of a third party who have never been employed by the employer with whom the union is in dispute, nor is there a trade dispute if it concerns the employment of the employees with a future unidentified employer. In *University College London Hospitals NHS Trust v Unison* the claimant entered into a contract with a consortium for the latter to build and run a new hospital. The union was opposed to the scheme, and sought to persuade the claimant to enter into a contractual agreement with the consortium whereby the terms and conditions of staff who were transferred to the new hospital would receive equivalent terms and conditions of employment to those who were not transferred. When the claimant refused to accede to the demand, the union called a strike, which was approved in a ballot of members. An injunction to restrain the strike was confirmed by the Court of Appeal. The dispute was about the terms and conditions which would apply to another employer, and in respect of employees who may at some future stage be employed by that other employer. The dispute was not between 'workers and their employer', because, at this stage, neither the future employer nor the workers employed by him could be identified.

23.63 But a strike called for political reasons is not a trade dispute. In *BBC v Hearn*, the Association of Broadcasting Staff threatened to stop a transmission of the Cup Final by satellite to South Africa, in protest of the alleged racist policies of the Government of that country. This would also have affected a number of other countries throughout the world. The Court of Appeal held that there was no trade dispute, and granted an injunction restraining the union from telling its members to break their contracts of employment, and from inducing the BBC to break its contracts with other countries. In *Express Newspapers v Keys*, three trade unions instructed their members to strike in response to a call sent out by the TUC for a one day national stoppage in protest against Government policies. It was held that this was a political strike, not in connection with a trade dispute, and injunctions were granted restraining the unions from inducing or procuring breaches of contract between the claimants and their employees.

23.64 In *Examite Ltd v Whittaker*, a trade union called a strike against a firm called Baldwins Industrial Services, with the result that the company's business came to a standstill. A new company called Examite was formed, with two shares being issued, and it took over the business of Baldwins and engaged some of its former employees. The union continued the strike against the new company, as it was considered to be a sham, and the company sought an injunction to restrain the union officials from intimidating the employees and to restrain them from procuring a breach of contract. It was held that a trade dispute existed between the union and Examite. There was sufficient evidence to show that the company had been formed to take over the business formerly carried on by Baldwins. The 'hat' worn by the employer was irrelevant. The truth was that the new company was carried on by the same people who ran the old one, and the legal form it took was irrelevant.

B. 'In contemplation of'

23.65 Having obtained the formula for a trade dispute, for an act to come within the statutory protection, it must be in contemplation of that dispute. The act may be so done if it is committed before the dispute arises, but is imminent. However, the dispute must be more than a mere possibility. In *Bents Brewery Co Ltd v Hogan* managers of a brewery were asked by a trade union official to obtain information about the firm's salaries, sales, etc. In providing this, the managers were in breach of their contract not to disclose confidential information to unauthorised persons (see Chapter 10). The union official was clearly inducing a breach of that contract, and it was held that his action was not in contemplation of a trade dispute, even though one may well have arisen at some future date. His actions may have been preparatory to the dispute, but were not in contemplation of one.

C. 'In furtherance of'

23.66 The act committed must also be in furtherance of the trade dispute, and not in furtherance of some other issue. In *Conway v Wade* a union official informed employers that unless a worker was dismissed there would be a strike. This was untrue, and the union official's actions were prompted by his desire to get the worker to pay a fine which was due to the union. It was held that although a trade dispute existed, the act was not done in furtherance of that dispute, but for some other motive. A more difficult problem arises when there is more than one motive for the acts in question, and some of the pre-1971 cases, which were decided on a much narrower definition of the term 'trade dispute' must now be viewed with greater care. For example, in *Huntley v Thornton* the claimant was recommended for expulsion by the branch committee of a trade union, but this was not upheld by the national executive. Nonetheless, the local officials regarded him as being expelled, and took steps to ensure that he did not obtain employment. The judge thought that there was no trade dispute, but such conduct would nowadays clearly be covered by the new, wider definition. More interesting was the finding that some of the officials were not acting in furtherance of a trade dispute, but in furtherance of a personal grudge, and their actions were in the nature of a vendetta. In other words, if protection is sought for acts done in furtherance of a trade dispute, the predominant motive must be the advancement of legitimate objects, and trade unionists cannot use the cover of the statutory protection to pursue improper aims.

23.67 But not every action which flows from a trade dispute is necessarily in furtherance of that dispute. In *Beaverbrook Newspapers Ltd v Keys*, a trade dispute existed between the *Daily Mirror* newspaper and a trade union, which resulted in a complete stoppage of production. The *Daily Express* decided to print more copies to cater for the increase in demand, but the general secretary of the printing union told his members not to handle the additional copies. The claimants applied for an injunction to restrain the union from inducing their employees to break their contracts of employment. It was held that the injunction would be granted. There was no trade dispute between the members of the defendant's union and the claimants, and the action would not further the dispute between the *Daily Mirror* and its employees.

23.68–23.75 Armed with the 'golden formula', we can now consider those statutory protections, and consider when the immunities will be lost.

Statutory protection and loss of immunities

A. The provisions of TULR(C)A s 219

23.76 Subsection (1) provides that an act done by a person in contemplation or furtherance of a trade dispute shall not be actionable in tort on the ground only (a) that it induces another person to break a contract or interferes or induces any other person to interfere with its performance; or (b) that it consists of his threatening that a contract (whether one to which he is party or not) will be broken or its performance interfered with, or that he will induce another person to break a contract or to interfere with its performance.

23.77 This subsection does three things. First, it gives immunity against legal action to anyone who calls a strike or other industrial action and thus induces a breach of contract (of employment) by the strikers, or a breach of a commercial contract by any other person. It also covers any inducement which interferes with the performance of a contract. Second, the subsection provides immunity where a threat of strike or other industrial action is made, whether this is done by the actual strikers or some other person, eg a trade union official. Thus, the threat to call a strike—the unlawful act in *Rookes v Barnard*—is no longer actionable. Third, it protects those who threaten to induce a breach of contract or to interfere with its performance.

23.78 Section 219(2) provides that an agreement or combination of two or more persons to do or procure the doing of an act in contemplation or furtherance of a trade dispute shall not be actionable in tort if the act is one which, if done without such agreement or combination, would not be so actionable. This subsection is designed to nullify the law of conspiracy as applied to trade disputes (above). If an act in contemplation or furtherance of a trade dispute would be actionable if done by one person, then a civil conspiracy would be committed if a group of persons did it. For example, if strikers commit a trespass by engaging in a sit-in, or commit a nuisance, or libel someone by picketing with defamatory placards, such conduct would be actionable if done by one person, and therefore no statutory protection exists.

23.79 Thus, in *News Group Newspapers Ltd v SOGAT '82* the defendants were responsible for organising mass picketing at the claimant's premises at Wapping. This was held to be a public nuisance, intimidation and an interference with commercial contracts, and injunctive relief was granted. But if the act was lawful if done by one person, it does not become an actionable conspiracy merely because a group of persons do it. Thus it is not unlawful for one person to threaten to strike or to go on strike. It therefore cannot be a conspiracy if more than one person does so. It is unlawful for one person to use violence; it will be a conspiracy for a group of persons to agree to use violence or actually to use it in a strike situation, and civil, as well as potential criminal liability, may arise.

23.80 However, it was suggested in *Meade v Haringey London Borough Council* that the immunity of a trade union from actions in tort based on conspiracy may not apply if there is an inducement to break a duty laid down by statute. Thus, if a local authority is forced to close a school (which it is under a statutory duty to keep open) because of trade union pressure, the union officials may be liable for inducing a breach of statutory duty and will not be protected by TULR(C)A. But if the statutory duty can be re-arranged so that it can still be carried out, injunctive relief will not be granted (*Barretts & Baird (Wholesale) Ltd v IPCS*). Also, if there is no statutory obligation to break, a trade union cannot be liable for inducing an alleged breach (*Associated British Ports v T & GWU*).

B. Loss of immunities

23.81 In recent years, the tactics adopted by trade unions in industrial disputes have not always attracted universal approval, and Parliament has intervened to place restrictions on certain types of activities, by limiting the immunity conferred by s 219 of TULR(C)A. The objects are twofold: first, to ensure greater democracy in trade unions by requiring secret ballots to be held before strikes or other industrial action are called, so as to negate decisions made at mass meetings by show of hands, or calls for action which may be unsupported by the rank and file; second, to prevent unnecessary hardship caused by industrial action to third parties who are in no way involved with or connected with the dispute. The primary purpose is to regulate official trade union action; unofficial action, though covered by the law, is seldom the subject of court proceedings (but see para 23.103).

Consequently, the immunity provided by s 219 of TULR(C)A will be lost unless the following legal hurdles can be surmounted.

(1) Secret ballots before strike action (TULR(C)A ss 226–234A)
23.82 There is no legal requirement which insists that a ballot be called by the union before strike action can be taken. However, a failure to do so will have the following legal consequences:

(a) industrial action which is authorised or endorsed by the union will not have the statutory immunity under s 219 from actions in tort, and an employer affected by the strike will be able to obtain an injunction and sue for damages;

(b) members of the trade union will be able to apply to the court for an order restraining the union from calling for strike action (TULR(C)A s 62, see Chapter 21);

(c) any member of the public who suffers a reduction or delay in the quality or supply of goods or services may apply to the court for an injunction to restrain the strike (s 235A);

(d) employees who go on strike will not have the protection afforded by s 238A (para 21.116) although they will have the protection contained in s 238(1)(b) (para 21.105).

23.83 The balloting provisions contained in TULR(C)A ss 226–235 have been amended by the Employment Relations Act 1999, and a new Code of Practice on Industrial Action Ballots and Notice to Employers has been issued (see Appendix H). The requirements apply only to official industrial action.

23.84 An act done by a trade union to induce a person to take part in industrial action will not be protected unless the industrial action has the support of a ballot, and the other detailed requirements of TULR(C)A are satisfied (s 226) . These are that, not later than seven days before the opening day of the ballot, the union must take reasonable steps to notify the employer of persons who are entitled to vote:

(i) that a ballot is to be held

(ii) the date of the opening day of the ballot

(iii) of information in the union's possession as would help the employer to make plans and bring information to the attention of those employees whom it is reasonable for the union to believe will be entitled to vote in the ballot. The information in question is (at least) the number, category and workplace of the employees concerned. There is no longer a requirement to name the actual employees who are to be balloted (s 226A(3A)).

23.85 A sample voting paper is to be sent to the employer at least three days before the opening of the ballot. If there is more than one employer involved, and different forms of voting paper used, the union need only ensure that each employer receives the voting paper sent to his own employees (s 226A(3B)). Before the ballot is held, the union must appoint a scrutineer (see paras 22.131) unless the number of those to be balloted is less than 50.

23.86 All those members of the trade union whom it is reasonable to believe (at the time of the ballot, see *London Underground Ltd v National Union of Rail Maritime and Transport Workers*) will be induced to take part in the industrial action must be balloted, and no other person (s 227(1)). But if the union acquires new members, or if existing members transfer from employments which are not in dispute into the area of a dispute, immunity will not be lost, because it would hardly be reasonable for the union to believe that they would be induced to take part in the industrial action (s 232A). So far as is reasonably practicable, a voting paper must be sent to the home address of the member, and he must be given a reasonable opportunity to vote by post (s 230(2)). If a member is denied the opportunity to vote, and is subsequently induced to take part in the industrial action, the trade union will lose its statutory immunity (s 232A), but the inadvertent failure to supply a ballot paper to union members will be disregarded if the failure was accidental and not likely to affect the result of the ballot (s 232B).

(I) SEPARATE WORKPLACE BALLOTS (TULR(C)A ss 228–228A)

23.87 The general rule about balloting is that a separate ballot shall be held for each workplace (s 228(3)), and industrial action will not be protected unless a majority of workers at that workplace voted in favour (s 226(3)). A person's workplace is a single set of premises (if that is where he works) or premises with which the person's employment has the closest connection (s 228, and see *InterCity West Coast Ltd v National Union of Rail Maritime and Transport Workers*). This requirement does not apply where the union reasonably believes that all the members who are entitled to vote have the same workplace (s 228(2)).

23.88 If the union wishes to call an aggregate ballot of a genuine bargaining unit (instead of separate ballots), certain conditions must be satisfied. The entitlement to vote must be limited to all members of the union who, according to the union's reasonable belief, have an occupation of a particular kind, and are employed by a particular employer or any number of employers with whom the union is in dispute. There must be at least one of its members at each of the workplaces directly affected by the dispute, or the union must be balloting members of a particular occupational category who are employed by a particular employer or by a group of employers, or balloting all of its members who are so employed (s 228A).

(II) BALLOTS FOR OVERSEAS MEMBERS (TULR(C)A s 232)

23.89 Generally, a trade union can elect whether or not to ballot overseas members (ie a person who is not a merchant seaman or offshore worker), who is outside Great Britain during the period of the ballot (s 232(3)) (Great Britain means England, Scotland and Wales). However, if the ballot relates to industrial action involving Great Britain and Northern Ireland, or if a member is temporarily seconded to Northern Ireland, members in both countries must be balloted. If a trade union reasonably believes that a merchant seaman will be at sea or a place outside Great Britain at the time of the ballot, then, if it is reasonably practicable, he is entitled to have a voting paper made available while on ship or at the place where the ship is.

(III) VOTING REQUIREMENTS (TULR(C)A ss 229–231A)

23.90 Voting must be by means of marking a voting paper. This must state the name of the independent scrutineer, specify the address to which and the date by which it is to be returned, and be given one of a series of consecutive numbers, and marked with that number. The voting paper must contain the question (however framed) which requires the member to answer 'Yes' or 'No' whether he is prepared to take part in (or continue to take part in) a strike. A similar question must be posed if the issue is industrial action short of a strike, and for this purpose an overtime ban and a call-out ban will constitute industrial action short of a strike (*Connex South Eastern Ltd v National Union of Rail Maritime and Transport Workers* being thus overruled). The requisite majority must be on each of the relevant questions, not the combined voting figures on both ballots (if two questions are being posed) (*West Midlands Travel Ltd v T & GWU*). After all, a member might be willing to take part in industrial action short of a strike, but not a strike, and vice versa (*Post Office v Union of Communication Workers*).

23.91 The question on the ballot paper must relate to a trade dispute (within the statutory definition) and not to matters in respect of which no statutory immunity applies (*London University Ltd v National Union of Railwaymen*).

23.92 The voting paper must also specify who, in the event of the vote being in favour of industrial action, is authorised to call upon members to take the industrial action. It is not necessary to name the individual in question, but he must be a person duly authorised either by the rules of the union, or the principal executive committee, or president or general secretary, or any other committee or official of the union (including shop stewards) (s 229(3), s 230(2)).

23.93 The ballot paper must contain the following statement 'If you take part in a strike or other industrial action, you may be in breach of your contract of employment. However, if you are dismissed for taking part in a strike or other industrial action which is called officially and is otherwise lawful, the dismissal will be unfair if it takes place fewer than eight weeks after you started to take part in the action, and depending on the circumstances may be unfair if it takes place later.' There must be no further comment or qualification on this statement.

23.94 Every person who is entitled to vote must be allowed to do so without interference from, or constraint imposed by the union, or any of its members, officials or employees, and without direct cost. So far as is reasonably practicable, he must have the voting paper sent to his home address or other address as may be requested, and be given a convenient opportunity to vote by post (s 230(2)). The ballot shall be so conducted as to ensure that, so far as is reasonably practicable, voting is done in secret. The votes must be fairly and accurately counted, but accidental inaccuracies, which could not affect the result of the ballot, may be disregarded.

23.95 As soon as is reasonably practicable after the holding of the ballot, the trade union shall inform all persons entitled to vote of the number of
(a) votes cast
(b) individuals answering 'yes'
(c) individuals answering 'no', and
(d) spoilt papers.

23.96 The union will also ensure that every relevant employer receives this information (s 231A), ie every employer who it is reasonable for the union to believe was the employer of any persons entitled to vote. A failure to do so would make subsequent industrial action unlawful.

23.97 A scrutineer's report will also be prepared, stating whether there were grounds for believing that the statutory grounds for holding the ballot were contravened, that the arrangements with respect to the production, storage, distribution return or handling of the voting papers, and the arrangements for the counting of the votes, including all security arrangements, were such as to minimise the risk of unfairness or malpractice, and that he was able to carry out his functions without interference from the trade union, or any of its members, officials or employees.

(IV)   EFFECTIVENESS OF THE BALLOT (TULR(C)A SS 233–4)
23.98 A ballot will not be effective in so far as it relates to a call for a strike or other industrial action before the date of the ballot, or any such call after the

ballot ceases to be effective (s 233(3)). In other words, industrial action cannot be subsequently validated by a ballot. But this does not require a union to adopt a neutral stance on the matter, and urging members to vote in favour of strike action is not the same thing as calling them to strike (*Newham London Borough Council v NALGO*).

23.99 A ballot will also cease to be effective after the end of four weeks, or such longer period not exceeding eight weeks, from the date of the ballot, as may be agreed between the employer and the trade union. Industrial action which takes place after that time will not be supported by a ballot (*RJB Mining (UK) Ltd v National Union of Mineworkers*). If, during the four or eight-week period, industrial action is prohibited by a court order (eg on an application for a temporary injunction), and the order is subsequently discharged, or it lapses, the trade union may request the court to order that the period during which the prohibition took effect shall not count towards the four or eight-week period. Once industrial action has started, it may continue indefinitely if necessary, and if at any time it is suspended (eg to enable negotiations to take place), a new ballot will not be required if the resumption of industrial action was part of the original dispute (*Monsanto plc v T & GWU*), although if there is a fresh dispute a new ballot will be required (*Post Office v Union of Communication Workers*).

(2) Notice of industrial action (TULR(C)A s 234A)
23.100 An act done by a trade union to induce a person to take part in industrial action shall not be prevented from being actionable in tort by s 219 unless the union takes such steps as are reasonably necessary to ensure that the employer receives a relevant notice of the industrial action within the appropriate period, ie the period beginning with the day when the union informed the employer of the result of the ballot, and ending with the seventh day before the day specified in the notice for industrial action to commence. The notice must be in writing, and must contain such information in the union's possession as would help the employer to make plans and bring information to the attention of those of his employees whom the union intend to induce to take part in the industrial action. If the union possesses information as to the number, category or workplace of the employees concerned, the notice must contain at least that information. There is no need for the union to identify by name the employees concerned. The notice must state whether the industrial action is to be continuous or discontinuous, and if continuous, the date when it will commence, and if discontinuous, the dates when the action will take place.

23.101 Technically, if the union suspended industrial action (to enable negotiations to take place) a further seven days' notice would be required before the action could be resumed. However, s 234A(7B) now provides that if the union agrees with the employer that it will cease to authorise industrial action from a specified date (the suspension date) but that it may be again authorised with effect from a date not earlier than a specified date (the resumption date), then if the action is suspended, it may be resumed without the necessary notice being required.

(3) Industrial action to enforce a closed shop (TULR(C)A s 222)
23.102 Section 219 shall not provide an immunity in tort for acts done in furtherance or contemplation of a trade dispute if the reason for the act is that the

employer is employing or proposes to employ a person who is not a member of a trade union or of a particular trade union. Immunity is also removed if the action is designed to put pressure on an employer into treating persons less favourably on grounds of their non-membership of a trade union.

(4) Industrial action in support of unofficial strikers (TULR(C)A s 223)

23.103 We have noted that if a person goes on unofficial strike, and is dismissed, he has no right to claim that he has been unfairly dismissed (see para 21.103). Section 223 provides that s 219 will not prevent an act from being actionable in tort, if the reason for the action was that an employer had lawfully dismissed unofficial strikers.

(5) Secondary action (TULR(C)A s 224))

23.104 The immunities conferred by s 219 will only apply when a trade union takes industrial action (supported by the appropriate ballot) vis-à-vis an employer with whom there is a trade dispute. In recent years, it became an increasingly popular technique to strengthen the effectiveness of such action by extending it to employers who were not themselves parties to the dispute, in the hope that pressure (direct or indirect) would be thereby exerted on the employer with whom there was a dispute. This is known as secondary action (see, eg *Duport Steels Ltd v Sirs*).

23.105 Secondary action is defined as when a person:
a.   induces another to break a contract of employment; or
b.   interferes or induces another to interfere with its performance; or
c.   threatens that a contract of employment under which he or another is employed will be broken, or its performance interfered with; or
d.   threatens that he will induce another to break a contract of employment, or to interfere with its performance;
and the employer under the contract of employment is not the employer party to the dispute (s 224(2)).

23.106 In these circumstances, nothing in s 219 shall prevent an act from being actionable in tort where one of the facts relied upon for the purpose of establishing such liability amounts to secondary action which is not lawful picketing.

23.107 The current definition of secondary action is wider than the original definition contained in the Employment Act 1980, and thus there are greater pitfalls for those who engage in such action. Secondary action must result in a breach of a contract of employment, whether or not there is a breach of a commercial contract. Further, the present definition extends the meaning of contract of employment to include the contract of a self-employed person who contracts personally to do work or perform services for another, thus closing a loophole revealed in *Shipping Co Uniform Inc v ITWF*.

23.108 The only type of secondary action which now remains lawful is peaceful picketing, as laid down in s 220 of TULR(C)A (see para 23.181), ie by workers who are (or were) employed by the employer who is a party to the dispute, and by a trade union official whose attendance is lawful by virtue of s 220(4) of the Act. Secondary picketing (ie at the gate of an employer who is a customer or supplier to the employer who is a party to the dispute) is not lawful.

(6) Pressure to impose union recognition requirement (s 225)

23.109 An act will not be protected by s 219 if it constitutes an inducement of a person to incorporate into a contract a term requiring a party to a contract for goods or services to recognise a trade union for the purpose of negotiating on behalf of workers employed by him, or to negotiate or consult with an official of a trade union (such a contract term would be void by reason of s 186, see para 23.216). Nor will an act be protected if it interferes with the supply of goods or services, by inducing another person to break a contract of employment, and the reason being that the supplier does not recognise or negotiate or consult with a trade union (see para 23.206).

Immunity of trade unions (TULR(C)A s 20)

23.110 Section 14 of TULRA 1974 (which re-enacted provisions dating from the Trade Disputes Act 1906) conferred total legal immunity on trade unions in respect of most actions in tort. This immunity was repealed by the Employment Act 1982, and nowadays a trade union will be liable in tort if the protection of s 219 of TULR(C)A is not available. However, a trade union cannot be responsible for everything which is done in its name by its members, shop stewards or officers, but only for those actions which have been authorised or endorsed.

23.111 A trade union will only be liable for inducing breaches of contract, or threatening that a contract will be broken, or for actions for conspiracy, if the act in question is authorised or endorsed by the union. An act shall be taken to have been endorsed or authorised by the trade union if it was done or authorised or endorsed by:

a. any person empowered by the rules to do, authorise or endorse the act; or
b. the principal executive committee or the president or general secretary of the union; or
c. by any other committee of the union, or any other official of the union (whether employed by the union or not).

23.112 Thus, under the current law, a trade union may be held to be legally liable not only for the acts of its full-time officials, but also for its shop stewards if they are authorised to do an act. Further, the liability arises for the acts of any committee (set up in accordance with the union's rules) and also for the acts of any group of members of which a shop steward was a member, and the purpose of which included the organising or co-ordinating of industrial action (TULR(C)A s 20(4)). This is so notwithstanding anything in the rules of the union, or any contract or rule of law subject to the repudiation provisions, below.

23.113 However, the union will not be liable if the act was repudiated by the principal executive committee or president or general secretary as soon as was reasonably practicable. Written notice must be given to the committee or official in question, without delay, and the union must do its best to give written notice of the fact and date of repudiation, without delay, to every member whom the union believes is taking part in the industrial action, and to the employer of every such member (s 21).

23.114 The written notice must be in the following form: 'Your union has repudiated the call (or calls) for industrial action to which this notice relates and will give no support to unofficial industrial action taken in response to it (or them). If you are dismissed while taking industrial action, you will have no right to complain of unfair dismissal.'

23.115   The repudiation will not be effective if the principal executive, president or general secretary behave in a manner inconsistent with the repudiation (see *Richard Read (Transport) Ltd v National Union of Mineworkers (South Wales Area)*). If, within three months of the purported repudiation, a person who is a party to a commercial contract which has been interfered with by the unofficial industrial action so requests, the union must confirm the repudiation in writing.

The effect of the Act

23.116–23.125   If a trade union calls for a strike or other industrial action in violation of the balloting provisions of the Act, or for a reason which is not permitted by the Act, it can be sued, and will not have the immunity conferred by s 219. An application may be made by an aggrieved person to the court for an injunction (*Solihull Metropolitan Borough Council v NUT*) and a failure to comply constitutes contempt of court, which would lead to a fine or imprisonment being imposed (*Express and Star Ltd v NGA*) or sequestration of property (*Kent Free Press v NGA*). Additionally, an action for damages could be brought against the trade union, subject to the limits on the amount which can be awarded, depending on the size of the trade union.

Amount of damages (TULR(C)A s 22)

23.126   If a trade union is sued successfully in tort, there are limits to the amount of damages which may be awarded. These limits are dependent on the size of the union's membership and are as follows:

> less than 5,000 members, the limit is £10,000
> 5,000 or more, but less than 25,000, the limit is £50,000
> 25,000 or more, but less than 100,000, the limit is £125,000
> 100,000 or more, the limit is £250,000.

23.127   These limits are applicable in each claim brought against the union, and are not global limits on each incident. Thus, if a trade union calls a strike in circumstances where it lacks legal immunity under s 219, each employee who has suffered damage may sue the union for the maximum sum, depending on the number of members it has. In addition, interest may be added to the award (*Boxfoldia Ltd v NGA*).

23.128   The limits do not apply to any action in tort in respect of personal injury caused by negligence, nuisance or breach of statutory duty, nor to any breach of duty in connection with the ownership, occupation, possession, control or use of property.

23.129–23.135   If damages, costs or expenses are awarded against a trade union, these cannot be enforced against the 'protected property' ie property which belongs to trustees other than in their capacity as trustees of the union, property owned by members in association with other members (ie common property), the property of an official who is not a member or trustee, political funds and provident benefit funds.

Injunctions and interdicts (TULR(C)A s 221)

23.136 An injunction without notice is an application for a temporary injunction to restrain the commission of some act. It is usually made in great haste, and thus only the party applying will have the time and opportunity to argue the case and be represented. Section 221 states that the court shall not grant such an application if the party against whom the injunction is sought claims, or the court thinks he might claim, that the act was done in contemplation or furtherance of a trade dispute, unless all reasonable steps have been taken to give that person notice of the hearing and an opportunity has been given for that party to be heard.

23.137–23.145 If an application is made for an interlocutory injunction (ie restraining an act until the matter comes to trial), and the party against whom the injunction is sought claims that he acted in contemplation or furtherance of a trade dispute, the court shall, in exercising its discretion whether or not to grant the injunction, assess the likelihood of success of any defence which may be raised that the act complained of will be protected by the statutory immunities (s 221(2)). This provision does not apply in Scotland.

Injunctive relief (TULR(C)A s 20(6))

23.146 If a trade union is responsible for official or unofficial strike action under the provisions of s 20 then in any court proceedings arising out of the act in question, the court may grant an injunction requiring the trade union to take such steps as the court thinks appropriate for ensuring:
a. that there is no, or no further, inducement of persons to take part in industrial action; and
b. that no person engage in any conduct after the granting of the injunction because he was induced to take part in industrial action before the injunction was granted.

23.147 This appears to give the court power to order a trade union to take disciplinary action against those who continue to induce or take part in industrial action after it has been repudiated by the union. However, no court shall make an order of specific performance or grant an injunction if the effect is to compel an employee to work or attend any place for the doing of any work (s 236).

23.148–23.155 A failure by a trade union (or any other person) to observe the terms of an injunction amounts to contempt of court, in respect of which a fine and/or imprisonment or sequestration of property may be ordered (*Kent Free Press v NGA*).

Industrial action affecting an individual (s 235A)

23.156 Any individual, who claims that industrial action has been called by a trade union which is actionable in tort or which has not been supported by a ballot under s 226, and the effect of which is to prevent or delay the supply of goods or services, or reduce their quality, may make an application to the High Court or Court of Session. It is immaterial that the individual in question is entitled to be supplied with the goods or services in question. If the court is satisfied that the claim is well-founded, it shall make such order as it considers appropriate for requiring the union to take steps for ensuring that no further act is done by him to induce any person to take part in the industrial action, and that no person engages in any conduct before the making of the order because he has been induced before the making of the order to take part in industrial action. This section also applies to Crown employment even though no contract of employment may exist.

23.157–23.165 The situation may sometimes arise where a trade union calls for industrial action which would otherwise be actionable in tort because the various statutory provisions have not been complied with, but, (for whatever reason) the employer (or union members) are unwilling to seek to restrain the industrial action. In such circumstances, any individual, whether affected by the industrial action or not, can bring an application to the court, seeking an appropriate order.

Legal effect of collective agreements (TULR(C)A ss 178–179)

23.166 A collective agreement is any agreement or arrangement made by or on behalf of a trade union on the one part, and one or more employers or employers' associations on the other part, relating to one or more of the matters contained above in the definition of a trade dispute. In essence, a collective agreement performs two functions. First, it lays down the guiding procedures which will govern the relationship between the signatory parties, by providing, for example, for the constitution of any joint body, or the procedure to be adopted in the event of a dispute or disagreement. Second, it will lay down patterns of terms and conditions of employment which are to cover union members, and possibly others as well, and which are to be observed by all federated and some assenting non-federated firms. Such terms and conditions are usually the minimum, not the maximum rate, so if national bargaining results in a particular award, this may frequently be supplemented at a local level by a further bout of negotiations.

23.167 So far as legal enforceability of these agreements is concerned, s 179 provides that any agreement shall be conclusively presumed not to have been intended by the parties to be a legally enforceable contract, unless the agreement is in writing, and contains a provision stating that the parties do intend the agreement to be legally binding (*Universe Tankships Inc of Monrovia v International Transport Workers' Federation*). It is possible for the parties to state expressly that only part of the agreement is intended to be legally binding, and part not, in which case, the parties' intentions will be given effect to, though it is possible to look at a non-legally binding part for the purpose of interpreting a part which is legally binding.

23.168   There must be an express statement to the effect that the parties intend the collective agreement to be legally enforceable. If the agreement states that the parties intend to be bound by it, this may indicate that it is intended to be binding in honour only, which would not satisfy the provisions of s 179 of TULR(C)A (*National Coal Board v NUM*).

23.169   The extent to which, and the circumstances in which, the terms of a collective agreement can be incorporated into the contract of employment of an individual employee have already been examined in Chapter 3. Section 180 lays down one further important rule. If a collective agreement, whether legally binding or not, contains a clause prohibiting or restricting the right of workers to engage in a strike or other industrial action, this particular clause shall not be incorporated into the individual contract of employment of any worker, unless the collective agreement:

a.   is in writing;
b.   contains a provision expressly stating that such term shall be or may be incorporated into such contract;
c.   is reasonably accessible at the place of work of such a worker, and is available for him to consult during working hours; and
d.   is one made by an independent trade union.

It should have been noted that this rule applies notwithstanding any agreement to the contrary, whether contained in a collective agreement or an individual contract of employment.

23.170   Thus, if a collective agreement provides that 'the union will not call a strike until the disputes procedure is exhausted', a breach of this clause would be governed by the law relating to the legal effect of the agreement, as mentioned above. If the collective agreement states: 'The employees will not go on strike until the disputes procedure is exhausted', then this clause will only form part of the individual contract of employment if the above conditions are fulfilled. The matter, however, is not really important, for a strike is likely to be a breach of most individuals' contracts of employment (whether or not it is in breach of the terms of a collective agreement) as it is a breach of the duty of faithful service (see Chapter 10) and a breach of contract of such importance that a striker may be dismissed.

23.171–23.180   However, if CAC grants a declaration imposing a statutory collective bargaining framework (see para 23.14) the procedure to be followed is legally binding, and can be enforced by specific performance (Trade Union Recognition (Method of Collective Bargaining) Order 2000).

Peaceful picketing (TULR(C)A s 220)

23.181   It shall be lawful for a person in contemplation or furtherance of a trade dispute to attend:

a.   at or near his own place of work; or
b.   if he is an official of a trade union, at or near the place of work of a member of that union whom he is accompanying and whom he represents;

for the purpose only of peacefully obtaining or communicating information, or peacefully persuading any person to work or to abstain from working. If a person works at more than one place, or at a place where it is impracticable to picket because of its location, his place of work shall be any premises from which he works, or from which his work is administered. A person whose employment has been terminated because of a trade dispute is allowed to picket at his former place of work.

23.182 A trade union official who has been elected or appointed to represent some of the members shall be regarded as representing only those members. Otherwise, a union official shall be regarded as representing all its members (s 220(4)). The purpose of this provision is to draw a distinction between officials who are shop stewards and full-time officials.

23.183 An employee's 'place of work' means his principal place of work or base. It does not refer to premises which, during his work, he may visit from time to time (*Union Traffic Ltd v T & GWU*).

23.184 Whether the picketing has taken place at or near the place of work is a question of fact and degree. In *Rayware Ltd v T & GWU*, pickets stood at the entrance of a private estate, about $3/10$th of a mile from the employers' premises. An application by the employers for an injunction to restrain unlawful picketing failed. The pickets could not get any nearer to their place of work without trespassing, and thus they were picketing lawfully near their place of work.

23.185 Section 220 only makes lawful the above acts. If something else is done, the section provides no protection. Thus in *Piddington v Bates*, a policeman wished to restrict the number of pickets who were outside a factory. When a striker tried to join the picket line, he was arrested, and charged with obstructing the policeman in the course of his duty. A conviction was upheld, for the policeman had acted on reasonable grounds that a breach of the peace might have occurred. In *Tynan v Balmer*, a group of pickets walked in a circle at the entrance of a factory in order to prevent traffic from entering and this was held to be an obstruction of the highway and a nuisance.

23.186 Nor do pickets have the power to stop vehicles, for traffic control is a matter for the police. In *Broome v DPP* a trade union official stood in front of a lorry and attempted to persuade the driver not to deliver goods to a factory where a dispute was on. The police told him to get out of the way, but he refused, and he was arrested and charged with obstructing the highway, an offence under the Highways Act 1959. It was held that he was guilty of the offence. Views were expressed in *Broome's* case that the law gave no right to pickets to stop persons or vehicles, for that would indicate that those persons were under a duty to stop and listen. The purpose of the statute was to make attendance at a picket line lawful, and then only for the statutory purposes of peacefully communicating information, etc.

23.187 Mass picketing can also amount to the tort of public nuisance (unreasonable obstruction of the highway), private nuisance (interference with access to the highway) and intimidation (see *News Group Newspapers Ltd v SOGAT '82*). Thus under the new law, 'flying pickets' and mass demonstrations are clearly unlawful, the former because they will not normally be picketing at their own place of work, the latter because it is unlikely that it is for the purpose of peacefully persuading. In *Thomas v National Union of Mineworkers (South Wales Area)*, it was held that mass picketing constituted a common law nuisance (as well as an offence under TULR(C)A s 241(1)), for all citizens had the right to use the highway without harassment or unreasonable interference. Accordingly, injunctions were granted against various trade union officials to prevent them from organising, encouraging, etc, members of the union congregating at coal mines, other than for the statutory purpose of peacefully communicating information, numbers in such cases being restricted to six.

23.188 Section 219(3) of TULR(C)A now provides that if an act is done in the course of picketing which is not lawful then s 219 will not provide a defence to any action which may be brought. Thus, if a picket induces workers to break their contracts of employment, and he is picketing at some place other than his own place of work, he can be sued in tort, and the statutory immunity of s 219 will not be available to him. Thus, unlawful picketing may now attract civil, as well as criminal liabilities. A Code of Practice on picketing has been approved by Parliament laying down the parameters for peaceful picketing (see Appendix I).

23.189–23.195 If a tort is committed by picketing, s 220 will provide a trade union with legal protection provided the picketing is lawful within that section. But if no tort has been committed, the statutory rules are basically irrelevant. Thus, in *Middlebrook Mushrooms Ltd v T & GWU*, the employers were mushroom producers, employing some 300 workers. They wished to introduce certain cost-saving measures, but these were not agreed to, and the union called a strike. The employer then dismissed all those employees who went on strike.

The union then urged its members to attend at supermarkets which were supplied with the mushrooms by the employers, and hand out leaflets to members of the public, asking them not to buy the employers' mushrooms. The employers brought an action for an interlocutory injunction restraining the union and its officials from organising the 'pickets' outside the supermarkets. The judge held that there was a direct interference with the contracts between the employers and the supermarkets, and granted the injunction.

However, the Court of Appeal reversed the decision. There was nothing in the leaflets which were handed out to members of the public which was aimed at the managers of the supermarket who placed orders with the employers. Thus the union was not seeking to persuade a party to the contract (ie the employers and the supermarkets) but members of the public, who, of course, had no contractual relations with the employers. It may well be that the managers of the supermarket might react to the reaction of the public (not to the picketing), but this, at most, would amount to an indirect inducement not to enter into future contracts, and, as no unlawful means had been used, the application for an injunction was dismissed.

Sit-in

23.196 Workers who engage in a sit-in or work-in are in breach of their contractual licence to remain on the employers' premises (*City and Hackney Health Authority v National Union of Public Employees*), and as such, if they refuse to leave after being given reasonable notice to do so are committing the tort of trespass and interfering with business by unlawful means (*Norbrook Laboratories Ltd v King*). It is possible to obtain an injunction against those involved, and also an employer may use the special expedited procedure to obtain possession of the property (see Ord 113 of the Rules of the Supreme Court).

23.197–23.205   If a trade union called for or authorised the sit-in or work-in, it would not be protected by the immunity conferred by s 219, even if a ballot was held, because the immunity in respect of interference with business by unlawful means was removed with the repeal of earlier legislation.

Union or non-union members only contracts (TULR(C)A s 144)

23.206   Any term or condition in a contract for the supply of goods or services shall be void in so far as it purports to require that the whole or part of the work shall be done by persons who are not members of a trade union (or a particular trade union), or who are members of a trade union (or a particular trade union).

23.207   It will be a tort of breach of statutory duty if, on the grounds of union membership or non-membership, a person:
a.   fails to include a particular person's name on a list of approved suppliers of goods or services;
b.   terminates a contract for the supply of goods or services;
c.   excludes a person from tendering for the supply of goods or services;
d.   fails to permit a person to submit a tender; or
e.   otherwise determines not to enter into a contract for the supply of goods or services.

23.208–23.215   Thus any person who suffers damage through the failure or refusal of another to enter into a contract with him for the supply of goods or services on the grounds of union membership or non-membership may sue for breach of statutory duty, and will be able to recover damages (subject to any general defences which may exist to such an action). Further, if there is pressure from any person to induce another to incorporate into a contract to which that other is a party any term or condition which would be void by the above provisions then s 219 shall not be a defence. Nor will s 219 be a defence if a person induces or threatens to induce another person to break a duty imposed by s 144. Thus if trade unionists threaten to strike unless an employer enters into a union labour only contract, or unless he removes non-union sub-contractors from a site, such acts will be actionable despite the general immunity of s 219 (see s 222(3)).

Prohibition on union recognition requirements (TULR(C)A s 186)

23.216   Any term or condition of a contract for the supply of goods or services shall be void in so far as it purports to require any party to the contract
a.   to recognise one or more trade unions, or
b.   to negotiate or consult with any official of a trade union.

Refusal to deal on union exclusion grounds (TULR(C)A s 187)

23.217   If a person maintains a list of approved suppliers of goods or services, or list of persons from whom tenders may be invited, and fails to include on that list a person who does not recognise trade unions, or terminates a contract for the supply of goods or services on that ground, or does other acts which prevent a person from being able to enter into a contract for the supply of goods or services because he does not recognise trade unions, such action will amount to a breach of statutory duty, and is actionable accordingly (subject to any relevant defences) by the person against whom the action was taken or by any other person adversely affected.

23.218–23.225 An act will not be protected by s 219 if it consists of inducing a person to impose a union recognition requirement contrary to ss 186–187 (see s 225).

Criminal liabilities

23.226 Members of the armed forces and policemen have no right to strike, and it is unlawful to induce a member of the prison service to strike or commit a breach of discipline, which effectively prevents them from taking part in an official strike (Criminal Justice and Public Order Act 1994 s 127). Merchant seaman may lawfully terminate their contracts and give 48 hours' notice of strike action provided their ship is in a safe berth in the United Kingdom. Industrial action by post office workers may involve criminal liability (see *Gouriet v Union of Post Office Workers*) and there are restrictions on aliens who promote industrial action.

23.227 Sections 240–241 of TULR(C)A enacts two provisions which may be relevant in trade disputes generally. The first is contained in s 240 of the Act, which provides that where any person wilfully and maliciously breaks a contract of service of hiring, knowing or having reasonable cause to believe that the probable consequences of his doing so, either alone or in combination with others, will be to endanger human life, or cause serious bodily injury, or to expose valuable property whether real or personal to destruction or serious injury, he shall, on conviction, be liable to a fine or to imprisonment for a term not exceeding three months.

23.228 The second provision is contained in s 241 of the Act. This states that every person who, with a view to compelling any person to abstain from doing an act which he has a legal right to do:
a.   uses violence to or intimidates such other person or his wife or children, or injures his property; or
b.   persistently follows such other persons from place to place; or
c.   hides any tools, clothes or other property owned or used by such other person, or deprives him of or hinders him in the use thereof; or
d.   watches or besets the house or other place where such person resides, or works, or carries on business, or happens to be, or the approach to such house or place; or
e.   follows such other person with two or more other persons in a disorderly manner along any street or road,
then he shall be liable to a fine not exceeding level 5 on the standard scale or a term of imprisonment not exceeding six months, or both.

23.229 Section 241 was considered in the recent case of *Galt v Philp*, where workers engaged in a 'sit-in', during which they locked and barricaded laboratories, thus preventing other employees from entering the rooms. This was held to be 'besetting' within the meaning of s 241(1)(a) and the individuals concerned were found guilty of an offence under the Act.

23.230–23.240 It must be remembered that s 219 of TULR(C)A only protects a person from civil liability, and does not give any immunity in respect of criminal acts.

Public Order Act 1986

23.241 This Act abolished the common law offences of riot, rout, unlawful assembly and affray, and repealed the provisions of the Public Order Act 1936, relating to threatening behaviour likely to provoke a breach of the peace. A number of statutory criminal offences have been introduced by the new Act, which may be invoked when the conduct of industrial disputes gets out of hand. These are:
a. *Riot* (s 1). This is where 12 or more people use or threaten to use violence for a common purpose which would cause a person of reasonable firmness to fear for his personal safety;
b. *Violent disorder* (s 2). This has the same elements as *riot*, except that it applies when three or more persons are taking part;
c. *Affray* (s 3). This also has the same elements as *riot*, except that only one person need be involved, and threats, by themselves, would not be sufficient;
d. *Fear or provocation of violence* (s 4). It is an offence to use threatening, abusive or insulting words or behaviour or to distribute or display any visual representation which is threatening, abusive or insulting, where the act is intended or likely to make a person fear immediate violence, or to provoke immediate violence;
e. *Harassment, alarm or distress* (s 5). This has almost the same elements as *fear or provocation of violence*, but the accused may defend himself by arguing that he had no reason to believe that a person alarmed was within his hearing or sight, or that his conduct was reasonable.

23.242–23.250 The Act also lays down new rules for marches, processions, demonstrations and public assemblies.

Intentional harassment

23.251 The Criminal Justice and Public Order Act 1994 s 154 creates a new criminal offence of intentional harassment. This is committed if a person, with intent to cause another person harassment, alarm or distress:
(a) uses threatening, abusive or insulting behaviour, or disorderly behaviour;
(b) displays any writing, sign or visible representation which is threatening, abusive or insulting
so that the other person feels harassment, alarm or distress.

23.252–23.260 It is believed that this offence could be committed in a number of employment situations, including verbal or written abuse etc to those who cross picket lines, and harassment on grounds of race, sex, sexual orientation, disabilities, religion, and so on.

European Works Councils

23.261 The Transnational Information and Consultation of Employees Regulations 1999 came into force in January 2000, and implement the European Works Council Directive 94/45/EC. The regulations apply to undertakings and groups of undertakings with at least 1,000 employees in the European Economic Area (ie, the 15 member states of the EU and Norway, Liechtenstein and Iceland), and at least 150 employees in each of two or more states. Employee numbers are calculated by adding together the number of employees in each month in a two-year period, and dividing the total by 24 (reg 6). An employee (or employee representative) may request information from the management for the purpose of determining whether the establishment or undertaking is part of a European-scale undertaking, and if there is a failure to supply the information, a complaint may be made to the Central Arbitration Committee, which can order the disclosure of the relevant information (reg 8), or, if it considers the matter to be beyond doubt, declare that the undertaking is a Community-scale organisation, ie within the scope of the Regulations.

23.262 If there is a valid request by employees or their representatives (see reg 9) management shall set up a special negotiating body, charged with the task of determining the scope, composition, functions, and term of office of a European Works Council, or, as an alternative, the arrangements for an information and consultation procedure (regs 11–17). The members of the special negotiating body must be elected by ballot, organised by management, and an employee or employee representative may complain to CAC if there is dissatisfaction with the balloting plans. CAC can require that the ballot arrangements be modified so as to reflect the interests of UK employees. However, if there is already in existence a consultative committee which has been elected by ballot and represents all UK employees, that committee may nominate its own members to be members of the special negotiating body.

23.263 Negotiations between management and the special negotiating body must be carried out in a spirit of co-operation, with a view to reaching agreement, either by establishing a European Works Council or an information and consultation procedure. If necessary, one or more experts may be engaged to assist. If a Works Council is established, the agreement will determine the undertakings covered, the composition of the Works Council, its functions, venue, frequency and duration of meetings, financial and material resources to be allocated, and the duration of the agreement and procedure for renegotiation. If an information and consultation procedure is adopted, the agreement will specify a method by which the representatives are to meet to discuss the information conveyed to them, which must in particular relate to transnational questions which significantly affect the interests of the employees (reg 17).

23.264 If management fails to establish a European Works Council or an information and consultation procedure, or if the terms of the agreement are not complied with by management, a complaint may be made to the EAT, which can make an order specifying the steps which central management shall take, with the ultimate sanction of a penalty notice (up to £75,000) if there is a failure to take the required steps.

23.265   A person who is or was a member of the European Works Council or information and consultation representative (or an expert who was assisting) shall not disclose any information or document which has been in his possession by virtue of his position as such, which central management has entrusted to him on terms requiring it to be held in confidence. A breach of this duty is actionable, although not in respect of a protected disclosure (see para 10.139). Disputes as to whether it was reasonable for management to impose a requirement of confidentiality, as well as complaints that management have improperly withheld information which ought to be disclosed, may be referred for settlement to CAC.

Time off work for members of a European Works Council (regs 25–27)

23.266   An employee who is
(a) a member of a special negotiating body;
(b) a member of a European Works Council;
(c) an information and consultation representative; or
(d) a candidate for election as a member or representative

is entitled to take reasonable time off work, with pay (at the appropriate hourly rate), during working hours, in order to perform his functions as a member, representative or candidate. He may bring a claim to an employment tribunal, that
(a) his employer has unreasonably refused to permit him to take time off work, or
(b) has failed to pay him for taking time off work.
   The complaint must be made within the usual time limit of three months (with the usual extension if it was not reasonably practicable to present it earlier). If the complaint is well founded, the tribunal will make a declaration, and order the employer to pay the amount to which the employee was entitled, or would have been had he taken the time off work.

Protection from detriment and dismissal (regs 28–33)

23.267   An employee who is
(a) a member of a special negotiating body;
(b) a member of a European Works Council;
(c) an information and consultation representative; or
(d) a candidate for election as a member or representative

has the right not to be subjected to any detriment by an act or deliberate failure to act, or to be dismissed, on the ground that the employee performed any functions or activities as a member, representative or candidate, or made a request for time off work or for pay for time off work to perform those functions or activities.

23.268   Any employee (whether or not he is one of the above categories) has the right not to be subjected to any detriment, or to be dismissed because
(a) he took proceedings before an employment tribunal to enforce a right or secure an entitlement under the regulations;
(b) he exercised an entitlement to complain to an appeal tribunal or CAC;

(c) he requested information from management to ascertain whether the establishment is part of a Community-scale undertaking (see reg 7);
(d) acted with a view to securing that a special negotiating body, or European Works Council or an information and consultation procedure, did or did not come into existence;
(e) indicated that he supported or did not support any of those institutions;
(f) stood as a candidate for membership of a special negotiating body, or European Works Council or as an information and consultation representative;
(g) influenced the way in which votes were to be cast by other employees in a ballot under the regulations;
(h) voted in such ballot;
(i) expressed doubts as to whether the ballot was properly conducted; or
(j) proposed to do or declined to do any of the things mentioned in paras (d)–(i) above.

23.269 A complaint may be made to an employment tribunal by a person who alleges that he has suffered a detriment or been dismissed on any of the above grounds. The complaint must be made within the usual time limits. If the complaint relates to a detriment, and is well-founded, the tribunal will make a declaration, and may award compensation, as it thinks just and equitable. If the complaint relates to a dismissal, reinstatement or re-engagement can be ordered, or the usual basic and compensation awards will be made (see Chapter 20).

Appendices

Appendices

Penalties under the Health and Safety at Work etc Act

	Offence	Summary conviction	On indictment
1.	Failure to discharge a duty under ss 2-6	£20,000	Fine
2.	Contravening ss 7-9	£5,000	Fine
3.	Contravening Health and Safety Regulations	£5,000	Fine
4.	Contravening any requirement made by regulations relating to investigations or enquiries made by the Commission, etc under s 14, or obstructing anyone exercising his powers	£5,000	
5.	Contravening any requirement under s 20 (powers of inspectors)	£5,000	
6.	Contravening any requirement under s 25 (power of the inspector to seize and render harmless articles or substances likely to cause imminent danger)	£5,000	Fine
7.	Preventing a person from appearing before an inspector or from answering questions under s 20(2)(j) (examinations and investigations)	£5,000	
8.	Contravening a requirement or prohibition imposed by an improvement notice	£20,000 and/or six months' imprisonment	Fine and/or 2 years' imprisonment
9.	Contravening a requirement or prohibition imposed by a prohibition notice	£20,000 and/or 6 months' imprisonment	Fine and/or 2 years' imprisonment

	Offence	Summary conviction	On indictment
10.	Intentionally obstructing an inspector or obstructing a customs officer in the exercise of his powers under s 25A	£5,000	
11.	Contravening a notice served by the Commission under s 27(1) requiring information	£5,000	Fine
12.	Using or disclosing information in contravention of s 27(4) (disclosure by the Crown or certain Government agencies of information to the Commission or Executive)	£5,000	Fine and/or 2 years' imprison-ment
13.	Disclosure of information obtained under s 27(1) or pursuant to any statutory provision, not within the exceptions of s 28	£5,000	Fine
14.	Making a false or reckless statement in purported compliance with a statutory provision, or for the purpose of obtaining the issuance of a document under any statutory provision	£5,000	Fine
15.	Intentionally making a false entry in any register, book, or other document required to be kept, or to making use of such entry, knowing it to be false	£5,000	Fine
16.	Forging document, or, with intent to deceive, using a forged document	£5,000	Fine
17.	Pretending to be an inspector	£5,000	
18.	Failing to comply with an order of the court under s 42 (order to remedy)	£20,000 and/or six months' imprison-ment	Fine and/or 2 years' imprison-ment
19.	Acting without a licence which is necessary under a relevant statutory provision	£5,000	Fine and/or 2 years' imprison-ment
20.	Contravening the terms of such licence	£5,000	Fine and/or 2 years' imprison-ment

	Offence	Summary conviction	On indictment
21.	Acquiring, using or possessing explosives contrary to the relevant statutory provisions	£5,000	Fine and/or 2 years' imprisonment
22.	Breach of regulations made under the Offshore Safety Act	£5,000	Fine and/or 2 years' imprisonment
23.	Working Time Regulations	£5,000	Fine

Redundancy pay calculation table

1. Read off the employee's age and number of complete years' employment.
2. Multiply the relevant factor by the employee's week's pay (current maximum to be applied is £230 per week).
3. For men and women over the age of 64, reduce the entitlement by $1/12$th for each month over that age, until entitlement ceases altogether at the age of 65.
4. The table may be used to calculate the Basic Award, it being noted that there is no lower age limit, and employment below the age of 18 will therefore count.

Service (years)

Age (years)	2	3	4	5	6	7	8	9	10	11	12	13	14	15	16	17	18	19	20
20	1	1	1	1	—														
21	1	1½	1½	1½	1½	—													
22	1	1½	2	2	2	2	—												
23	1½	2	2½	3	3	3	3	—											
24	2	2½	3	3½	4	4	4	4	—										
25	2	3	3½	4	4½	5	5	5	5	—									
26	2	3	4	4½	5	5½	6	6	6	6	—								
27	2	3	4	5	5½	6	6½	7	7	7	7	—							
28	2	3	4	5	6	6½	7	7½	8	8	8	8	—						
29	2	3	4	5	6	7	7½	8	8½	9	9	9	9	—					
30	2	3	3	4	5	6	7	8	8½	9	9½	10	10	10	10	—			
31	2	3	4	5	6	7	8	9	9½	10	10½	11	11	11	11	—			
32	2	3	4	5	6	7	8	9	10	10½	11	11½	12	12	12	12	—		
33	2	3	4	5	6	7	8	9	10	11	11½	12	12½	13	13	13	13	—	
34	2	3	4	5	6	7	8	9	10	11	12	12½	13	13½	14	14	14	14	—
35	2	3	4	5	6	7	8	9	10	11	12	13	13½	14	14½	15	15	15	15
36	2	3	4	5	6	7	8	9	10	11	12	13	14	14½	15	15½	16	16	16
37	2	3	4	5	6	7	8	9	10	11	12	13	14	15	15½	16	16½	17	17
38	2	3	4	5	6	7	8	9	10	11	12	13	14	15	16	17	17½	18	
39	2	3	4	5	6	7	8	9	10	11	12	13	14	15	16	17	17½	18	18½
40	2	3	4	5	6	7	8	9	10	11	12	13	14	15	16	17	18	18½	19
41	2	3	4	5	6	7	8	9	10	11	12	13	14	15	16	17	18	19	19½
42	2½	3½	4½	5½	6½	7½	8½	9½	10½	11½	12½	13½	14½	15½	16½	17½	18½	19½	20½
43	3	4	5	6	7	8	9	10	11	12	13	14	15	16	17	18	19	20	21
44	3	4½	5½	6½	7½	8½	9½	10½	11½	12½	13½	14½	15½	16½	17½	18½	19½	20½	21½
45	3	4½	6	7	8	9	10	11	12	13	14	15	16	17	18	19	20	21	22
46	3	4½	6	7½	8½	9½	10½	11½	12½	13½	14½	15½	16½	17½	18½	19½	20½	21½	22½
47	3	4½	6	7½	9	10	11	12	13	14	15	16	17	18	19	20	21	22	23
48	3	4½	6	7½	9	10½	11½	12½	13½	14½	15½	16½	17½	18½	19½	20½	21½	22½	23½

Service (years)

Age (years)	2	3	4	5	6	7	8	9	10	11	12	13	14	15	16	17	18	19	20
49	3	4½	6	7½	9	10½	12	13	14	15	16	17	18	19	20	21	22	23	24
50	3	4½	6	7½	9	10½	12	13½	14½	15½	16½	17½	18½	19½	20½	21½	22½	23½	24½
51	3½	4½	6	7½	9	10½	12	13½	15	16	17	18	19	20	21	22	23	24	25
52	3	4½	6	7½	9	10½	12	13½	15	16½	17½	18½	19½	20½	21½	22½	23½	24½	25½
53	3	4½	6	7½	9	10½	12	13½	15	16½	18	19	20	21	22	23	24	25	26
54	3	4½	6	7½	9	10½	12	13½	15	16½	18	19½	20½	21½	22½	23½	24½	25½	26½
55	3	4½	6	7½	9	10½	12	13½	15	16½	18	19½	21	22	23	24	25	26	27
56	3	4½	6	7½	9	10½	12	13½	15	16½	18	19½	21	22½	23½	24½	25½	26½	27½
57	3	4½	6	7½	9	10½	12	13½	15	16½	18	19½	21	22½	24	25	26	27	28
58	3	4½	6	7½	9	10½	12	13½	15	16½	18	19½	21	22½	24	25	26½	27½	28½
59	3	4½	6	7½	9	10½	12	13½	15	16½	18	19½	21	22½	24	25½	27	28	29
60	3	4½	6	7½	9	10½	12	13½	15	16½	18	19½	21	22½	24	25½	27	28½	29½
61	3	4½	6	7½	9	10½	12	13½	15	16½	18	19½	21	22½	24	25½	27	28½	30
62	3	4½	6	7½	9	10½	12	13½	15	16½	18	19½	21	22½	24	25½	27	28½	30
63	3	4½	6	7½	9	10½	12	13½	15	16½	18	19½	21	22½	24	25½	27	28½	30
64	3	4½	6	7½	9	10½	12	13½	15	16½	18	19½	21	22½	24	25½	27	28½	30

Monetary awards (as at 1 February 2000)

Statutory reference	Statutory right	Maximum rate	Maximum award
1. ERA s 12(4)	Itemised pay statement	none	Unnotified deduction for 13 weeks prior to application to an employment tribunal
2. ERA s 31(1)	Guarantee pay	£16.10 per day	£80.50 in any period of three months
3. ERA s 69(1)	Medical suspension pay	none	26 weeks' pay
4. TULR(C)A 1992 s 149(2)	Action short of dismissal	none	Just and equitable
5. TULR(C)A 1992 s 172(2)	Time off work	none	Just and equitable (refusal to allow) or normal pay or average hourly earnings (failure to pay)
6. ERA s 54(3)	Time off to look for work or arrange for retraining	none	Two fifths of a week's pay
7. SSCBA 1992 ss 164–171	Maternity pay	none	Nine tenths of a week's pay for six weeks and 12 weeks at 'lower rate'
8. ERA s 93(2)	Written reasons for dismissal	none	Two weeks' pay
9. ERA ss 118–124	Unfair dismissal	£230 per week	Basic award £6,900 Compensation award £50,000 Additional award £5,980–£11,960

Statutory reference	Statutory right	Maximum rate	Maximum award
10. TULR(C)A 1992 s 158(1) and (2)	Unfair dismissal for trade union membership or non-membership		(a) Re-instatement/re-engagement not sought
		£230 per week	(i) Basic award £6,900 (minimum £3,100
			(ii) Compensation award £50,000
			(b) Re-instatement/re-engagement sought, but IT makes no order
		£230 per week	(i) Basic award £6,900 (minimum £3,100
			(ii) Compensation award £50,000
			(c) Re-instatement/re-engagement ordered but not complied with
		£230 per week	(i) Basic award £6,900 (minimum £3,100
			(ii) Compensation award £50,000
		£230 per week	(iii) Additional award £5,980–£11,960
			(d) Re-instatement/re-engagement ordered and complied with
			Compensation award— loss made good
11. ERA s 162	Redundancy pay	£230 per week	£6,900
12. ERA s 184	Rights on employer's insolvency	£230 per week	Arrears of pay £1,840
		£230 per week	Statutory notice £2,760
		£230 per week	Holiday pay £1,380
		£230 per week	Basic award £6,900

Statutory reference	Statutory right	Maximum rate	Maximum award
13. Sex Discrimination Act 1975 s 65	Sex discrimination	none	Just and equitable
14. Race Relations Act 1976 s 56	Race discrimination	none	Just and equitable
15. Disability Discrimination Act 1996 s 8	Disability discrimination	none	Just and equitable
16. TULR(C)A 1992 s 67(8)	Right not to be unjustifiably disciplined	£230 per week	£56,900
17. TULR(C)A 1992 s 176(6)	Unreasonable expulsion/exclusion from trade union membership	£230 per week	£56,900
18. TULR(C)A 1992 s 189(4)	Protective award	none	Up to 90 days' pay
19. ET Extension of Jurisdiction Order 1994	Breach of contract	none	£25,000

Employment Tribunal Forms

Application to an Employment Tribunal

- If you fax this form you do not need to send one in the post.
- This form has to be photocopied. Please use CAPITALS and black ink (if possible).
- Where there are tick boxes, please tick the one that applies.

For office use

Received at ET

Case number	
Code	
Initials	

1 Please give the type of complaint you want the tribunal to decide (for example, unfair dismissal, equal pay). A full list is available from the tribunal office. If you have more than one complaint list them all.

2 Please give your details

Mr ☐ Mrs ☐ Miss ☐ Ms ☐ Other _____

First names
Surname
Date of birth
Address

Postcode

Phone number
Daytime phone number

Please give an address to which we should send documents if different from above

Postcode

3 If a representative is acting for you please give details
(all correspondence will be sent to your representative)

Name
Address

Postcode

Phone	Fax
Reference	

4 Please give the dates of your employment

From _____ to _____

5 Please give the name and address of the employer, other organisation or person against whom this complaint is being brought

Name
Address

Postcode

Phone number

Please give the place where you worked or applied to work if different from above

Address

Postcode

6 Please say what job you did for the employer (or what job you applied for). If this does not apply, please say what your connection was with the employer

IT1(E/W)

<table>
<tr><td>

7 Please give the number of normal basic hours worked each week

Hours per week

</td><td>

9 If your complaint is not about dismissal, please give the date when the matter you are complaining about took place

</td></tr>
</table>

---

8 Please give your earning details

Basic wage or salary

£   ·   per

Average take home pay

£   :   per

Other bonuses or benefits

£   :   per

---

10 Unfair dismissal applicants only

Please indicate what you are seeking at this stage, if you win your case

☐ Reinstatement: to carry on working in your old job as before (an order for reinstatement normally includes an award of compensation for loss of earnings).

☐ Re-engagement: to start another job or new contract with your old employer (an order for re-engagement normally includes an award of compensation for loss of earnings).

☐ Compensation only: to get an award of money

---

11 Please give details of your complaint

If there is not enough space for your answer, please continue on a separate sheet and attach it to this form.

SPECIMEN

---

12 Please sign and date this form, then send it to the appropriate address on the back cover of this booklet, (see postcode list on pages 13-16).

Signed   Date

IT1(E/W)

THE EMPLOYMENT TRIBUNALS
NOTICE OF APPEARANCE BY RESPONDENT

In the application of:

Case Number:
(please quote in all correspondence)

---

* This form has to be photocopied, if possible please use Black Ink and Capital letters
* If there is not enough space for your answer, please continue on a separate sheet and attach it to this form

1. Full name and address of the Respondent:

Post Code:

Telephone number:

2. If you require documents and notices to be sent to a representative or any other address in the United Kingdom please give details:

Post Code:

Reference:

Telephone number:

3. Do you intend to resist the application? (Tick appropriate box)

YES   NO

4. Was the applicant dismissed? (Tick appropriate box)

YES   NO

Please give reason below

Reason for dismissal:

5. Are the dates of employment given by the applicant correct? (Tick appropriate box)

YES   NO

please give correct dates below

Began on:

Ended on:

6. Are the details given by the applicant about wages/salary, take home or other bonuses correct? (Tick appropriate box)

YES   NO

Please give correct details below

Basic Wages/Salary	£	per
Average Take Home Pay	£	per
Other Bonuses/Benefits	£	per

PLEASE TURN OVER

for office use only
Date of receipt   Initials

Form IT3 E&W - 1/95

7. Give particulars of the grounds on which you intend to resist the application.

8. Please sign and date the form.

Signed   Dated

SPECIMEN

DATA PROTECTION ACT 1984
We may put some of the information you give on this form on to a computer. This helps us to monitor progress and produce statistics. We may also give information to:
* the other party in the case
* other parts of the Employment Department Group and organisations such as ACAS (Advisory Conciliation and Arbitration Service), the Equal Opportunities Commission or the Commission for Racial Equality.

Please post or fax this form to : The Regional Secretary 19-29 Woburn Place, LONDON, WC1H 0LU

* IF YOU FAX THE FORM, DO NOT POST A COPY AS WELL
* IF YOU POST THE FORM, TAKE A COPY FOR YOUR RECORDS

Form IT3 E&W - 1/95

Names and addresses

Advisory, Conciliation and Arbitration Service
Brandon House
180 Borough High Street
London SE1 1LW

020 7396 5100

(Regional offices can be found in Newcastle-upon-Tyne, Leeds, London, Bristol, Birmingham, Fleet, Manchester, Glasgow and Cardiff)

Central Office of the Industrial Tribunals
Southgate Street
Bury St Edmunds
Suffolk IP33 2AQ

01284 762300
Fax: 01284 766334

Central Office of the Industrial Tribunals
Eagle Building
215 Bothwell Street
Glasgow G2 7TS

0141 204 0730
Fax: 0141 204 0732

Central Arbitration Committee
39 Grosvenor Place
London SW1X 7BD

020 7210 3738

Certification Officer
Brandon House
180 Borough High Street
London SE1 1LW

020 7210 3734

Commission for Racial Equality
Elliot House
10–12 Allington Street
London SW1E 5EH

020 7828 7022

Department of Trade and Industry
Caxton House
Tothill Street
London SW1H 9NA

020 7273 3000

Employment Appeal Tribunal
58 Victoria Embankment
London EC4Y 0DS

020 7273 1041
Fax: 020 7273 1045

52 Melville Street
Edinburgh EH3 7HF

0131 225 3963
Fax: 0131 220 6694

Equal Opportunities Commission
Overseas House
Quay Street
Manchester M3 3HN
0161 833 9244

Health and Safety Commission
Rose Court
2–10 Southwark Bridge Road
London SE1 9HS

020 7273 3000

Improvement and Prohibition Notices

HSE
Health & Safety
Executive

Health and Safety at Work etc Act 1974, Sections 21, 23, and 24

Serial Number

I _____

Improvement notice

Name

Address

Trading as*

Inspector's full name   I,

Inspector's official designation   one of Her Majesty's Inspectors of
Being an Inspector appointed by an instrument in writing made pursuant to section 19 of the said Act and entitled
to issue the notice

Official address   of

Telephone number

hereby give you notice that I am of the opinion that

Location of premises
or place of activity   at

you, as an employer / self employed person / person wholly or partly in control of the premises / other*

are contravening / have contravened in circumstances that make it likely that the contravention will continue or
be repeated* the following statutory provisions:

The reasons for my said opinion are:

SPECIMEN

and I hereby require you to remedy the said contraventions or, as the case may be, the matters occasioning them by
(and I direct that the measures specified in the Schedule
which forms part of this notice shall be taken to remedy the said contraventions or matters)*

Signature   Date

* An Improvement Notice is also being served on

of

related to the matters contained in this notice.

Environment and Safety
Information Act 1988   This is a relevant notice for the purposes of the Environment and Safety Information Act 1988   YES/NO*
This page only will form the register entry.*

Signature   Date

LP 1 (rev 05.97)   *SEE NOTES OVERLEAF*   * delete as appropriate

1   Failure to comply with this Improvement Notice is an offence as provided by section 33(1) (g) of the Health and Safety at Work etc Act 1974 and section 33(2A) of this Act renders the offender liable on summary conviction to imprisonment for a term not exceeding 6 months, or to a fine not exceeding £20,000, or both, or, on conviction on indictment, to imprisonment for a term not exceeding 2 years, or a fine, or both.

2   An Inspector has power to withdraw an Improvement Notice or to extend the period specified in the notice, before the end of the period specified in it. If you wish this to be considered you should apply to the Inspector who issued the notice, but you must do so before the end of the period given in it. Such an application is not an appeal against this notice.

3   The issue of this notice does not relieve you of any legal liability for failing to comply with any statutory provisions referred to in the notice or to perform any other statutory or common law duty resting on you.

4   You can appeal against this notice to an Industrial Tribunal. Details of the method of making an appeal, a form to use, and information about where to send it are contained in booklet ITL 19 which will be provided by the Inspector with this notice. Copies are also available from the Industrial Tribunal Enquiry Line (Tel: 0345 959775).

Time limit for appeal

A notice of appeal must be sent to the Industrial Tribunal within 21 days from the date of service on the appellant of the notice, or notices, appealed against, or within such further period as the tribunal considers reasonable in a case where it is satisfied that it was not reasonably practicable for the notice of appeal to be presented within the period of 21 days. If posted the appeal should be sent by recorded delivery.

The entering of an appeal suspends the Improvement Notice until the appeal has been determined, but does not automatically alter the date given in this notice by which the matters contained in it must be remedied.

The rules for the hearing of an appeal are given in The Industrial Tribunals (Constitution and Rules of Procedure) Regulations 1993 (SI 1993 No 2687), as amended, for England and Wales and The Industrial Tribunals (Constitution and Rules of Procedure) (Scotland) Regulations 1993 (SI 1993 No 2688), as amended, for Scotland.

PUBLIC REGISTERS OF ENFORCEMENT NOTICES UNDER THE ENVIRONMENT AND SAFETY INFORMATION ACT 1988

1. Under the requirements of the Environment and Safety Information Act 1988, the Health and Safety Executive (HSE) maintains at its Offices public registers of information on notices which do not impose requirements or conditions solely for the protection of persons at work. These are called "relevant notices" under this Act and will be identified by the inspector serving the notice (see overleaf). Entries will be kept in the public register for a period of at least 3 years.

2. The entry in the register will be made within 14 days either of the expiry of the right of appeal or of the disposal of an appeal. Where a notice is cancelled on appeal no entry will be made. Where an inspector is satisfied that a notice has been complied with, a further entry will be made in the register within 7 days to show this. If a notice is withdrawn or amended the entry on the register will be withdrawn or amended within 7 days.

3. The entry on the register will normally be the front page of the notice form. If you think that the entry for this notice would disclose information about a trade secret or secret manufacturing process, you should give written notice to HSE **within 14 days.** HSE will then draft an entry which it believes will not reveal the secret and serve this on you. In the meantime the entry in the register will specify only your name and address, any place involved and the relevant legal provisions.

4. If you are not satisfied with the redrafted entry you have a further right of appeal to the Secretary of State within 14 days. HSE will give you further information about appeals to the Secretary of State at this time.

PUBLIC AVAILABILITY OF INFORMATION ON OTHER NOTICES

1. Under the Code of Practice on Access to Government Information HSE is committed to make available on request information about its actions and decisions, which includes information about the notices it has issued. In general the information that HSE will make available about a notice is the information on the front page.

2. Information on a notice will not be made available until the right of appeal against the notice has expired or the appeal has been disposed of. Where an inspector is satisfied that a notice has been complied with, this information will be made available at the same time as the information on the front page of the notice.

3. If you think that the information in the notice would disclose commercially confidential information you should give written notification to HSE **within 14 days.** HSE will then redraft the information in such a way that it believes will not reveal the commercially confidential information. In the meantime the only information that HSE would make available would be your name and address, any place involved and the relevant legal provisions.

4. If you are not satisfied with the redrafted information there is no further appeal. However, HSE will make every effort to agree with you a form of words which would not reveal any commercially confidential information.

Some Local Authorities use this form and references to **HSE and** disclosure provisions will not apply.

HSE
Health & Safety
Executive

Health and Safety at Work etc Act 1974, Sections 22, 23, and 24

Serial Number

P

Prohibition notice

Name

Address

Trading as*

Inspector's full name	I,
	one of Her Majesty's Inspectors of
Inspector's official designation	Being an Inspector appointed by an instrument in writing made pursuant to section 19 of the said Act and entitled to issue the notice
Official address	of

Telephone number

hereby give you notice that I am of the opinion that the following activities namely :

which are being carried on by you / likely to be carried on by you / under your control* at

Location of premises
or place of activity

involve, or will involve, a risk of serious personal injury, and that the matters which give rise / will give rise* to the said risks are :

and that the said matters involve / will involve* contravention of the following statutory provisions :

because

SPECIMEN

and I hereby direct that the said activities shall not be carried on by you or under your control immediately / after*
unless the said contraventions and matters have been remedied.
I further direct that the measures specified in the schedule which forms part of this notice shall be taken to remedy the said contraventions or matters.*

Signature   Date

* A Prohibition Notice is also being served on

of

related to the matters contained in this notice.

Environment and Safety
Information Act 1988

This is a relevant notice for the purposes of the Environment and Safety Information Act 1988   YES/NO*
This page only will form the register entry.*

Signature   Date

LP 2 (rev 05.98)   *SEE NOTES OVERLEAF*   * delete as appropriate

1   Failure to comply with this Prohibition Notice is an offence as provided by section 33(1) (g) of the Health and Safety at Work etc Act 1974 and section 33(2A) of this Act renders the offender liable on summary conviction to imprisonment for a term not exceeding 6 months, or to a fine not exceeding £20,000, or both, or, on conviction on indictment, to imprisonment for a term not exceeding 2 years, or a fine, or both.

2   Except for an immediate Prohibition Notice, an Inspector has power to withdraw a notice or extend the period specified in the notice, before the end of the period specified in it. If you wish this to be considered you should apply to the Inspector who issued the notice, but you must do so before the end of the period given in it. Such an application is not an appeal against this notice.

3   The issue of this notice does not relieve you of any legal liability for failing to comply with any statutory provisions referred to in the notice or to perform any other statutory or common law duty resting on you.

4   You can appeal against this notice to an Industrial Tribunal. Details of the method of making an appeal, a form to use, and information about where to send it are contained in booklet ITL 19 which will be provided by the Inspector with this notice. Copies are also available from the Industrial Tribunal Enquiry Line (Tel: 0345 959775).

Time limit for appeal

A notice of appeal must be sent to the Industrial Tribunal within 21 days from the date of service on the appellant of the notice, or notices, appealed against, or within such further period as the tribunal considers reasonable in a case where it is satisfied that it was not reasonably practicable for the notice of appeal to be presented within the period of 21 days. If posted the appeal should be sent by recorded delivery.

The entering of an appeal does not have the effect of suspending this notice. Application can be made for the suspension of this notice to the Industrial Tribunal, but the notice continues in force until a tribunal otherwise directs.

An application for suspension of the notice must be in writing and must set out :

(a)   the case number of the appeal, if known, or particulars sufficient to identify it; and

(b)   the grounds on which the application is made. (It may accompany the appeal).

The rules for the hearing of an appeal are given in The Industrial Tribunals (Constitution and Rules of Procedure) Regulations 1993 (SI 1993 No 2687), as amended, for England and Wales and The Industrial Tribunals (Constitution and Rules of Procedure) (Scotland) Regulations 1993 (SI 1993 No 2688), as amended, for Scotland.

PUBLIC REGISTERS OF ENFORCEMENT NOTICES UNDER THE ENVIRONMENT AND SAFETY INFORMATION ACT 1988

1. Under the requirements of the Environment and Safety Information Act 1988, the Health and Safety Executive (HSE) maintains at its Offices public registers of information on notices which do not impose requirements or conditions solely for the protection of persons at work. These are called "relevant notices" under this Act and will be identified by the inspector serving the notice (see overleaf). Entries will be kept in the public register for a period of at least 3 years.

2. The entry in the register will be made within 14 days either of the expiry of the right of appeal or of the disposal of an appeal. Where a notice is cancelled on appeal no entry will be made. Where an inspector is satisfied that a notice has been complied with, a further entry will be made in the register within 7 days to show this. If a notice is withdrawn or amended the entry on the register will be withdrawn or amended within 7 days.

3. The entry on the register will normally be the front page of the notice form. If you think that the entry for this notice would disclose information about a trade secret or secret manufacturing process, you should give written notice to HSE **within 14 days.** HSE will then draft an entry which it believes will not reveal the secret and serve this on you. In the meantime the entry in the register will specify only your name and address, any place involved and the relevant legal provisions.

4. If you are not satisfied with the redrafted entry you have a further right of appeal to the Secretary of State within 14 days. HSE will give you further information about appeals to the Secretary of State at this time.

PUBLIC AVAILABILITY OF INFORMATION ON OTHER NOTICES

1. Under the Code of Practice on Access to Government Information HSE is committed to make available on request information about its actions and decisions, which includes information about the notices it has issued. In general the information that HSE will make available about a notice is the information on the front page.

2. Information on a notice will not be made available until the right of appeal against the notice has expired or the appeal has been disposed of. Where an inspector is satisfied that a notice has been complied with, this information will be made available at the same time as the information on the front page of the notice.

3. If you think that the information in the notice would disclose commercially confidential information you should give written notification to HSE **within 14 days.** HSE will then redraft the information in such a way that it believes will not reveal the commercially confidential information. In the meantime the only information that HSE would make available would be your name and address, any place involved and the relevant legal provisions.

4. If you are not satisfied with the redrafted information there is no further appeal. However, HSE will make every effort to agree with you a form of words which would not reveal any commercially confidential information.

Some Local Authorities use this form and references to HSE and disclosure provisions will not apply.

Main legislative provisions 1980–1999

1. Employment Act 1980

Enabled the payment of public funds to be made for ballots held by trade unions (since repealed); independent trade unions were entitled to hold ballots on an employer's premises; the Secretary of State was empowered to issue codes of practice (Codes on Picketing and Trade Union Ballots have been issued; the Code on Closed Shop Agreements and Arrangements has been revoked); there is a right not to be unreasonably excluded or expelled from a trade union, but this applied only where there was a union membership agreement in force—somewhat limited because of the provisions of the Employment Act 1990, see below; the burden of proof in unfair dismissal cases was neutralised as between the parties; a dismissal for non-membership of a trade union where there was a union membership agreement was to be unfair unless a ballot was held, or if the employee objected to joining on grounds of conscience or deeply-held conviction (this provision has since been repealed); minor changes were made to the provisions on unfair dismissal and maternity leave of absence and guarantee payments; the Act provided for time off work for ante-natal care, redefined peaceful picketing, and dealt with liability in tort for secondary action (since repealed).

2. Employment Act 1982

Companies were required to deal with the employee involvement in their annual reports; new rules were laid down when a person was dismissed because of union or non-union membership, and on ballots for union membership agreement (since repealed); the Act provided for a minimum basic award and a special award and for a contribution against third parties when dismissal was on the ground of trade union membership or non-membership; changes were made when dismissal was in connection with a strike or other industrial action, and terms in contracts requiring work to be done by union or non-union workers were stated to be void; the immunity of trade unions from actions in tort was removed, but a trade union would only be liable if the act was authorised or endorsed by a responsible person (since amended); the Act provided for limits on damages awarded against trade unions, and the definition of 'trade dispute' was altered.

3. Trade Union Act 1984

Trade unions are required to hold ballots for certain posts, and the immunity of trade unions from actions in tort was removed unless the industrial action was supported by a secret ballot (since amended); ballots have to be held to establish the political fund.

4. Sex Discrimination Act 1986

The first six sections of this Act altered the Sex Discrimination Act 1975 and the Equal Pay Act 1970 in consequence of rulings by the European Court of Justice to the effect that British law did not comply with the Equal Treatment Directive (76/207/EEC). The exemption in favour of an employer who employed five or fewer employees was repealed, and the definition of genuine occupational qualification for private household employment was altered; the upper age limit for unfair dismissal was equalised; discriminatory terms of employment in collective agreements were declared to be void, and certain restrictions on working hours and conditions of employment of women were removed.

5. Wages Act 1986

Repealed the Truck Acts 1831–1940 and other legislation relating to the payment of wages. The Act provides for a remedy in respect of unlawful deductions from wages, with special provisions for retail employment; the functions of Wages Councils were restricted; redundancy rebates were limited to employers who employed less than 10 employees (since repealed).

6. Employment Act 1988

A trade union member can obtain a court order restraining the union from calling a strike without holding a ballot; he also has the right not to be unjustifiably disciplined by the union; other provisions gave greater control to members of the affairs of the union; it became thus automatically unfair to dismiss a person because he was not a member of a trade union; industrial action to enforce a closed shop would no longer attract immunity; changes were made to the law on trade union ballots and elections; the post of Commissioner for the Rights of Trade Union Members was created, and given power to provide assistance to trade union members in taking certain legal actions; there must be an independent scrutineer appointed for certain ballots, and mandatory postal ballots for union elections and political fund ballots.

7. Employment Act 1989

This Act further amended the Sex Discrimination Act, so as to bring British law in line with the European directive on the implementation of the principle of equal treatment for men and women as regards access to employment, vocational training, promotion and working conditions; it repealed many provisions of protective legislation which laid down different treatment for men and women, and removed restrictions relating to the employment of young persons; Sikhs were exempted from the requirement to wear safety helmets on construction sites; minor changes were made to the Employment Protection (Consolidation) Act (written statement under s 1, time off for trade union duties, two years' qualifying employment for written reasons for dismissal), and the age up to which women and men could receive redundancy payment was assimilated; the redundancy rebate was abolished altogether; the Secretary of State was given power to provide for pre hearing assessment); the Training Commission was dissolved.

8. Employment Act 1990

This Act made it unlawful to refuse a person employment because he was or was not a member of a trade union (being the final nail in the coffin of the closed shop); immunity in respect of secondary action was abolished, minor amendments were made to the law on trade union ballots and the responsibility of a trade union for the acts of its officials; a ballot on industrial action ceases to be effective after four weeks, though this period is extended if there are court proceedings; unofficial strikers lost their right to bring a claim for unfair dismissal, the powers of the Commissioner for the Rights of Trade Union Members were increased; the Act made provision for the revision of codes of practice.

9. Trade Union and Labour Relations (Consolidation) Act 1992

This Act consolidates all the relevant law on trade unions and labour relations, including provisions from the Conspiracy and Protection of Property Act 1875, Trade Union Act 1913, Trade Union (Amalgamations etc) Act 1964, Trade Union and Labour Relations Act 1974, Employment Protection Act 1975, Trade Union and Labour Relations (Amendment) Act 1976, Employment Protection (Consolidation) Act 1978, Trade Union Act 1984, and the Employment Acts of 1980, 1982, 1988, 1989 and 1990.

10. Trade Union Reform and Employment Rights Act 1993

This Act amends the Employment Protection (Consolidation) Act 1978 and the Trade Union and Labour Relations (Consolidation) Act 1992, and makes further changes in the law. The independent scrutineer appointed for trade union elections and ballots is given more powers, voting is to be fully postal, funds for trade union ballots are to be phased out, and ballots may no longer be carried out on employers' premises. An individual cannot be excluded or expelled from a trade union except on specific grounds, employers must not make unauthorised deductions from a worker's pay in respect of union subscriptions, and the right not to be unjustifiably disciplined is extended. To be protected from being sued in respect of industrial action, a trade union must send a copy of the ballot paper to the employer before the date of the ballot, and inform the employer of the result. Notice of industrial action must be given to an employer. Any individual may apply to the High Court claiming that industrial action is unlawful, and he may receive assistance from a new Commissioner for Protection against Unlawful Industrial Action. There is a new general right to maternity leave for pregnant employees, and a woman dismissed on grounds connected with pregnancy or childbirth no longer requires two years' qualifying employment before she can present a claim of unfair dismissal. Protection is given to persons in health and safety cases, consultations with trade unions on redundancies must be carried out with a view to reaching agreement. Amendments are made to the written statement to be given to every employee within eight weeks of commencing employment. Wages Councils are abolished. The constitution and jurisdiction of industrial tribunals and the Employment Appeal Tribunal is altered. ACAS is given power to make charges for advice, women dismissed on grounds of pregnancy or childbirth are to be given written reasons for their dismissal without the need to request them, certain compensation awards are increased, and interim relief will apply in health and safety cases. It is unfair to dismiss an employee on the ground that he asserted a statutory right.

11. Disability Discrimination Act 1995

This Act makes it unlawful to discriminate against a person who has a physical or mental disability as defined. A National Disability Council is created to advise the Secretary of State on related matters. Codes of practice are to be produced. The Act will be brought into force by stages, and will be subject to regulations to be made.

12. Employment Rights Act 1996

This Act consolidates all the main statutory provisions on employment law, including those provisions which were formerly contained in the Employment Protection (Consolidation) Act 1978, Wages Act 1986, Sunday Trading Act 1994, and the relevant parts of other legislation.

13. Industrial Tribunals Act 1996

This Act consolidates those earlier legislative provisions which deal with the constitution and procedures of industrial tribunals and the Employment Appeal Tribunal. The Act has now been renamed the 'Employment Tribunals Act 1996'.

14. Employment Rights (Dispute Resolution) Act 1998

This Act renamed industrial tribunals 'employment tribunals', and makes certain provisions designed to speed up the hearing of complaints before them (eg cases which can heard by a chairman alone, interlocutory matters to be dealt with a by a legal officer). Non-lawyers (duly insured) can enter into compromise agreements. Empowers ACAS to draw up an arbitration scheme.

15. National Minimum Wage Act 1998

Creates the Low Pay Commission, and sets out the procedures for ensuring and enforcing a national minimum wage for all workers.

16. Employment Relations Act 1999

This Act made a number of changes in the law relating to trade unions, by introducing a new statutory framework for collective bargaining, alterations in the balloting procedures, and increased protections for trade union members, in particular when taking part in official industrial action. The maternity leave provisions were simplified, and new provisions on time off work for domestic emergencies, to care for dependants and parental leave were introduced. An employee has the right to be accompanied in grievance or disciplinary proceedings, the service qualification was reduced to one year for unfair dismissal claims etc, and the compensation limit for unfair dismissal claims was raised to £50,000. The offices of Commissioner for the Rights of Trade Union Members and Commissioner for Protection against Unlawful Industrial Action were abolished.

Codes of Practice

(a) ACAS Code of Practice I
Disciplinary and Grievance Procedures

Preamble

This Code from pages 4 to 23 is issued under section 201 of the Trade Union and Labour Relations (Consolidation) Act 1992 and was laid before both Houses of Parliament on   . The Code comes into effect by order of the Secretary of State on   .

A failure on the part of any person to observe any provision of this Code of Practice does not of itself render that person liable to any proceedings. In any proceedings before an employment tribunal any Code of Practice issued under sections 199 and 201 of the Trade Union and Labour Relations (Consolidation) Act 1992 is admissible in evidence and any provision of the Code which appears to the tribunal to be relevant to any question arising in the proceedings is required to be taken into account in determining that question. (Trade Union and Labour Relations (Consolidation) Act 1992, section 207) This Code has also to be taken into account by the arbitrators appointed by ACAS to determine cases brought under the ACAS Arbitration Scheme (see Section 212A of the Trade Union and Labour Relations (Consolidation) Act 1992).

Some of the provisions referred to in this code only apply by statute to employees. But others, such as the right to be accompanied at disciplinary and grievance hearings, apply to all workers. This Code is about good employment practice. Therefore where workers are involved in grievance and disciplinary proceedings, it would be good practice to apply the standards set out in the guidelines in sections one and two to those proceedings.

For ease of reference, text in bold type in this code summarises statutory provisions, whilst practical guidance is set out in ordinary type. Whilst every effort has been made to ensure that the explanations included in the Code are accurate, only the Courts or Tribunals can give authoritative interpretations of the law.

Introduction

This code aims to help employers, workers and their representatives by giving practical guidance on how to deal with disciplinary and grievance issues in employment. It also provides guidance on the statutory right of a worker to be accompanied at a disciplinary or grievance hearing. In small establishments it may not be practicable to adopt all the detailed provisions relating to disciplinary and grievance procedures, but most of the essential features listed in paragraphs 9 and 38 to 41 could be adopted and incorporated into a simple procedure.

Disciplinary issues arise when problems of conduct or capability are identified by the employer and management seeks to address them through well recognised procedures. In contrast, grievances are raised by individuals bringing to management's attention concerns or complaints about their working environment, terms and conditions and work-place relationships.

The code is divided into three sections as follows

Section 1 - deals with disciplinary practice and procedures;

Section 2 - considers the handling of grievances

Section 3 - is concerned with the statutory right to be accompanied at disciplinary and grievance hearings.

Section I - Disciplinary practice and procedures in employment

Why have disciplinary rules and procedures?

1.   Disciplinary rules and procedures are necessary for promoting orderly employment relations as well as fairness and consistency in the treatment of individuals. They enable organisations to influence the conduct of workers and deal with problems of poor performance and attendance thereby assisting organisations to operate effectively. Rules set standards of conduct and performance at work; procedures help ensure that the standards are adhered to and also provide a fair method of dealing with alleged failures to observe them.

2.   It is important that workers know what standards of conduct and performance are expected of them. The Employment Rights Act 1996 requires employers to provide written information for their employees about certain aspects of their disciplinary rules and procedures.[1] Managers should also know and be able to apply the rules and the procedures they are required to follow.

---

1   Section 1 of the Employment Rights Act 1996 requires employers to provide employees with a written statement of particulars of employment. Such statements must also specify any disciplinary rules applicable to them and indicate the person to whom they should apply if they are dissatisfied with any disciplinary decision. The statement should explain any further steps which exist in any procedure for dealing with disciplinary decisions. The employer may satisfy certain of these requirements by referring the employees to a reasonably accessible document which provides the necessary information. The statutory requirements relating to disciplinary rules and procedures do not apply where on the day the employee's employment began the total number of employees employed by the employer and any associated employer was less than twenty.

3.   The importance of having disciplinary rules and procedures and ensuring that they are followed has also been recognised by the law relating to dismissals, since the grounds for dismissal and the way in which the dismissal has been handled can be challenged before an employment tribunal or an ACAS-appointed arbitrator.[2] Where either of these is found by a tribunal or arbitrator to have been unfair, the employer may be ordered to re-instate or re-engage the employees concerned where requested and may be liable to pay compensation to them. In coming to a decision about the fairness or otherwise of a dismissal, the tribunal, or arbitrator, will consider whether the employer acted reasonably in all the circumstances, having regard to the size and administrative resources of the undertaking.

Formulating policy

4.   Management is responsible for maintaining discipline and setting standards of performance within the organisation and for ensuring that there are appropriate disciplinary rules and procedures covering issues of worker conduct and capability. If they are to be fully effective, however, the rules and procedures need to be accepted as reasonable both by those who are covered by them and those who operate them. Management should therefore aim to secure the involvement of workers and where appropriate their representatives and all levels of management when formulating new or revising existing rules and procedures. Where trade unions are recognised, trade union officials[3] may, or may not, wish to participate in the formulation of the rules but they should participate fully with management in agreeing the procedural arrangements which will apply and in seeing that these arrangements are used properly, fairly and consistently.

Rules

5.   When drawing up disciplinary rules, the aim should be to specify clearly and concisely those that are necessary for the efficient and safe performance of work and for the maintenance of satisfactory relations within the workforce and between workers and management. It is unlikely that any set of disciplinary rules can cover all circumstances that may arise. However, it is usual that rules would cover issues such as misconduct, sub-standard performance (where not covered by a separate capability procedure), harassment or victimisation, misuse of company facilities including computer facilities (eg, e-mail and the Internet), poor timekeeping and unauthorised absences. The rules required will necessarily vary according to particular circumstances, such as the type of work, working conditions and size and location of the workplace. Whatever set of rules are eventually drawn up they should not be so general as to be meaningless.

6.   Rules should be set out clearly and concisely in writing and be readily available to all workers, for example in handbooks or on company Intranet sites. Management should make every effort to ensure that all workers know and

2   Section 111 (2) of the Employment Rights Act 1996 specifies that a complaint of unfair dismissal has to be presented to an employment tribunal before the end of the three month period beginning with the effective date of termination.

3   Throughout this code, trade union official has the meaning assigned to it by section 119 of the Trade Union and Labour Relations (Consolidation) Act 1992 and means, broadly, officers of the union, its branches and sections, and anyone else, including fellow employees, appointed or elected under the union's rules to represent members.

understand the rules including those whose first language is not English or who have a disability or impairment (eg, the inability to read). This may best be achieved by giving every worker a copy of the rules and explaining them orally. In the case of new workers this might form part of any induction programme . It is also important that managers at all levels and worker representatives are fully conversant with the disciplinary rules and that the rules are regularly checked and updated where necessary.

7.   Workers should be made aware of the likely consequences of breaking disciplinary rules or failing to meet performance standards. In particular, they should be given a clear indication of the type of conduct, often referred to as gross misconduct, which may warrant summary dismissal (ie, dismissal without notice). Summary is not necessarily synonymous with instant and incidents of gross misconduct will usually still need to be investigated as part of a formal procedure. Acts which constitute gross misconduct are those resulting in a serious breach of contractual terms and will be for organisations to decide in the light of their own particular circumstances. However, they might include the following:
i)   theft, fraud and deliberate falsification of records;
ii)   physical violence;
iii) serious bullying or harassment;
iv)   deliberate damage to property;
v)   serious insubordination;
vi)   misuse of an organisation's property or name;
vii) bringing the employer into serious disrepute;
viii) serious incapability whilst on duty brought on by alcohol or illegal drugs;
ix)   serious negligence which causes or might cause unacceptable loss, damage or injury;
x)   serious infringement of health and safety rules;
xi)   serious breach of confidence (subject to the Public Interest (Disclosure) Act 1998).

As indicated earlier this list is not intended to be exhaustive.

Essential features of disciplinary procedures

8.   Disciplinary procedures should not be viewed primarily as a means of imposing sanctions. Rather they should be seen as a way of helping and encouraging improvement amongst workers whose conduct or standard of work is unsatisfactory. Some organisations may prefer to have separate procedures for dealing with issues of conduct and capability but it is important to remember that any hearing which might result in a formal warning or some other action will be covered by the provisions on accompaniment set out in the Employment Relations Act 1999 (see section three). Smaller organisations may wish to deal with issues of conduct and capability within one disciplinary procedure.

9.   When drawing up and applying disciplinary procedures employers should have regard to the requirements of natural justice. This means workers should be informed in advance of any disciplinary hearing of the allegations that are being made against them together with the supporting evidence and be given the opportunity of challenging the allegations and evidence before decisions are reached. Workers should also be given the right of appeal against any decisions taken. Consequently good disciplinary procedures should:

i)   be in writing;

ii)   specify to whom they apply;

iii)   be non-discriminatory;

iv)   provide for matters to be dealt with without undue delay;

v)   provide for proceedings, witness statements and records to be kept confidential;

vi)   indicate the disciplinary actions which may be taken;

vii)   specify the levels of management which have the authority to take the various forms of disciplinary action;

viii)   provide for workers to be informed of the complaints against them and where possible all relevant evidence before any hearing;

ix)   provide workers with an opportunity to state their case before decisions are reached;

x)   provide workers with the right to be accompanied (see also section three for information on the statutory right to be accompanied);

xi)   ensure that, except for gross misconduct, no worker is dismissed for a first breach of discipline;

xii)   ensure that disciplinary action is not taken until the case has been carefully investigated;

xiii)   ensure that workers are given an explanation for any penalty imposed;

xiv)   provide a right of appeal - normally to a more senior manager - and specify the procedure to be followed.

10.   It is important to ensure that all managers and, where appropriate, worker representatives understand the organisation's disciplinary procedure. Training in the use and operation of the procedure may also be appropriate. There can be benefits in undertaking such training on a joint basis.

The procedure in operation

11.   When a disciplinary matter arises, the relevant supervisor or manager should first establish the facts promptly before recollections fade, and where appropriate obtain statements from any available witnesses. It is important to keep a record for later reference. Having investigated all the facts the manager or supervisor should decide whether to, drop the matter; arrange informal coaching or counselling; or arrange for the matter to be dealt with under the disciplinary procedure.

12.   Minor cases of misconduct and most cases of poor performance may best be dealt with by informal advice, coaching and counselling rather than through the disciplinary procedure. Sometimes managers may issue informal oral warnings - but they need to ensure that problems are discussed with the objective of encouraging and helping workers to improve. It is important that workers understand what needs to be done, how performance or conduct will be reviewed and over what period. Workers should also be made aware of what action will be taken if they fail to improve either their performance or conduct. Informal warnings and/or counselling are not part of the formal disciplinary procedure and the worker should be informed of this.

13.   In certain circumstances, for example in cases involving gross misconduct, where relationships have broken down or where it is considered there are risks to an employer's property or responsibilities to other parties, consideration should

be given to a brief period of suspension with pay whilst an unhindered investigation is conducted. Such a suspension should only be imposed after careful consideration and should be reviewed to ensure it is not unnecessarily protracted. It should be made clear that the suspension is not considered as disciplinary action.

14. Before a decision is reached or any disciplinary action taken there should be a disciplinary hearing at which workers have the opportunity to state their case and to answer the allegations that have been made. Wherever possible the hearing should be arranged at a mutually convenient time and in advance of the hearing the worker should be advised of any rights under the disciplinary procedure including the statutory right to be accompanied (see section three). Prior to this stage, where matters remain informal, the statutory right of accompaniment does not arise.

15. Where the facts of a case appear to call for formal disciplinary action a formal procedure should be followed. The type of procedure will vary according to the circumstances of the organisation. Depending on the outcome of the procedure some form of disciplinary action may be taken as follows:–

First Warning:
Oral – In the case of minor infringements the worker should be given a formal oral warning. Workers should be advised of the reason for the warning, that it constitutes the first step of the disciplinary procedure and of their right of appeal. A note of the oral warning should be kept but should be disregarded for disciplinary purposes after a specified period (eg, six months).

Or

Written – If the infringement is regarded as more serious the worker should be given a formal written warning giving details of the complaint, the improvement or change in behaviour required, the timescale allowed for this and the right of appeal. The warning should also inform the worker that a final written warning may be considered if there is no sustained satisfactory improvement or change. A copy of the written warning should be kept on file but should be disregarded for disciplinary purposes after a specified period (eg, 12 months).

Final written warning – Where there is a failure to improve or change behaviour during the currency of a prior warning, or where the infringement is sufficiently serious, the worker should normally be given a final written warning. This should give details of the complaint, warn the worker that failure to improve or modify behaviour may lead to dismissal or to some other action short of dismissal and refer to the right of appeal. The final written warning should normally be disregarded for disciplinary purposes after a specified period (eg, 12 months).

Dismissal or other sanction – If the worker's conduct or performance still fails to improve the final step might be disciplinary transfer, disciplinary suspension without pay[4], demotion, loss of seniority, loss of increment (provided these penalties are allowed for in the contract) or dismissal. The decision to dismiss

4   Where a disciplinary suspension without pay is imposed it should not exceed any period allowed by the contract of employment.

should be taken only by the appropriate designated manager and the worker should be informed as soon as reasonably practicable of the reasons for the dismissal, the date on which the contract between the parties will terminate, the appropriate period of notice (or pay in lieu of notice) and information on the right of appeal including how to make the appeal and to whom. The decision to dismiss should be confirmed in writing. Employees with one year's continuous service or more have the right, on request, to have a 'written statement of particulars of reasons for dismissal[5] '.

16.   When deciding whether a disciplinary penalty is appropriate and what form it should take it is important to bear in mind the need to act reasonably in all the circumstances. Factors which might be relevant include, the extent to which standards have been breached, precedent, the worker's general record, position, length of service and special circumstances which might make it appropriate to adjust the severity of the penalty.

17.   When operating disciplinary procedures employers should be particularly careful not to discriminate on the grounds of race, gender or disability, eg, whilst it is not unlawful to take disciplinary action against a pregnant woman for some reason unconnected with her pregnancy it is unlawful sex discrimination and automatically unfair to dismiss a woman on the grounds of her pregnancy.

18.   In the course of a disciplinary case a worker might sometimes raise a grievance about the behaviour of the manager handling the case. Where this happens, and depending on the circumstances it may be appropriate to suspend the disciplinary procedure for a short period until the grievance can be considered. Consideration might also be given, where possible, to bringing in another manager to deal with the disciplinary case.

Dealing with absence

19.   When dealing with absence a distinction should always be made between absences on grounds of medically certificated illness, both physical and mental, and those which may call for disciplinary action. All unexpected absences should be investigated promptly and the worker asked to give an explanation[6]. If, after investigation, it appears that there were no acceptable reasons for the absence the matter should be treated as a conduct issue and be dealt with under the disciplinary procedure. It is important that the worker is told what improvement in attendance is expected and warned of the likely consequences if this does not happen.

20.   Where the absence is due to medically certificated illness the issue becomes one of capability and employers should take a sympathetic and considerate approach to these sort of absences. In deciding what action to take in these cases

---

5   The right to a written statement of reasons for dismissal applies automatically to employees dismissed while pregnant or during ordinary maternity leave without them having to request it.

6   When considering the reasons for absence or sub-standard performance employers should bear in mind the provisions of the Disability Discrimination Act 1995. In particular employers should note the obligations placed on them by the Act to make reasonable adjustments when dealing with sickness related absences.

employers will need to take into account, the likelihood of an improvement in health and subsequent attendance (based where appropriate on professional medical advice), the availability of suitable alternative work, the effect of past and likely future absences on the organisation, how similar situations have been handled in the past and whether the illness is a result of a disability as defined in the Disability Discrimination Act 1995. Even though employers may have a separate procedure for dealing with illness any hearing which could result in a formal warning or some other action will attract the statutory right of accompaniment (see section three).

21. In cases of extended sick leave both statutory and contractual issues will need to be addressed and specialist advice may be necessary.

Dealing with poor performance

22. Individuals have a contractual responsibility to perform to a satisfactory level and should be given every help and encouragement to do so. Employers have a responsibility for setting realistic and measurable standards of performance and for explaining these standards carefully to employees.

23. Where workers are found to be failing to perform to the required standard the matter should be investigated before any action is taken[6] . Where the reason for the sub standard performance is found to be a lack of the required skills the worker should, wherever practicable, be assisted through training or coaching and given reasonable time to reach the required standard. Where the sub standard performance is due to negligence or lack of application on the part of the worker then some form of disciplinary action will normally be appropriate. Failures to perform to the required standard can either be dealt with through the normal disciplinary procedure or through a separate capability procedure.

24. A worker should not normally be dismissed because of a failure to perform to the required standard unless warnings and an opportunity to improve (with reasonable targets and timescales) have been given. However, where a worker commits a single error due to negligence and the actual or potential consequences of that error are, or could be, extremely serious, warnings may not be appropriate. The disciplinary or capability procedure should indicate that summary dismissal action may be taken in such circumstances.

25. Employers may need to have special arrangements for dealing with poor performance of workers on short-term contracts or new workers during their probationary period.

Dealing with special situations

26. Certain situations will require special consideration.

Workers to whom the full procedure is not immediately available. Special provisions may be necessary for the handling of disciplinary matters among nightshift workers, workers in isolated locations or depots or others who may pose particular problems.

Trade union officials. Disciplinary action against a trade union official can lead to a serious dispute if it is seen as an attack on the union's functions. Although normal disciplinary standards should apply to their conduct as workers, if disciplinary action is contemplated then the case should be discussed with a senior trade union representative or full-time official.

Criminal charges or convictions outside employment. These should not be treated as automatic reasons for dismissal. The main consideration should be whether the offence is one that makes workers unsuitable for their type of work. In all cases employers, having considered the facts, will need to consider whether the conduct is sufficiently serious to warrant instituting the disciplinary procedure. For instance, workers should not be dismissed solely because a charge against them is pending or because they are absent as a result of being remanded in custody.

Appeals

27.   The opportunity to appeal against a disciplinary decision is essential to natural justice. Workers may choose to raise appeals on a number of grounds which could include the perceived unfairness of the judgement, the severity of the penalty, new evidence coming to light or procedural irregularities. These grounds need to be considered when deciding the extent of any new investigation or re-hearing in order to remedy previous defects in the disciplinary process.

28.   Appeals should be dealt with as promptly as possible. A time limit should be set within which appeals should be lodged. This time limit may vary between organisations but five working days for lodging an appeal is usually appropriate. A time limit should also be set for hearing the appeal.

29.   Wherever possible the appeal should be heard by an appropriate individual, usually a senior manager, not previously involved in the disciplinary procedure. In small organisations it may not be possible to find such an individual and in these circumstances the person dealing with the appeal should act as impartially as possible. Independent arbitration is sometimes an appropriate means of resolving disciplinary issues and where the parties concerned agree it may constitute the appeals stage of procedure.

30.   Individuals should be informed of the arrangements for appeal hearings and also of their statutory or other right to be accompanied at these hearings (see section three). Where new evidence arises during the appeal the worker, or their representative, should be given the opportunity to comment before any action is taken. It may be more appropriate to adjourn the appeal to investigate or consider such points.

31.   The worker should be informed of the results of the appeal and the reasons for the decision as soon as possible and this should be confirmed in writing. If the decision constitutes the final stage of the organisation's appeals procedure this should be made clear to the worker.

Records

32.   Records should be kept detailing the nature of any breach of disciplinary rules or unsatisfactory performance, the worker's defence or mitigation, the action

taken and the reasons for it, whether an appeal was lodged, its outcome and any subsequent developments. These records should be kept confidential and retained in accordance with the disciplinary procedure and the Data Protection Act 1998 which requires the release of certain data to individuals on their request. Copies of any meeting records should be given to the individual concerned although in certain circumstances some information may be withheld, for example to protect a witness.

Further action

33.   Rules and procedures should be reviewed periodically in the light of any developments in employment legislation or good employment practice and if necessary, revised in order to ensure their continuing relevance and effectiveness. Any amendments and additional rules imposing new obligations should be introduced only after reasonable notice has been given to all workers and, where appropriate, their representatives have been consulted. Except in very exceptional circumstances, where legal advice should be sought, changes to individual contracts may only be made with agreement.

Section 2 - Grievance procedures

Why have a grievance procedure?

34.   In any organisation workers may have problems or concerns about their work, working environment or working relationships that they wish to raise and have addressed. A grievance procedure provides a mechanism for these to be dealt with fairly and speedily, before they develop into major problems and potentially collective disputes.

35.   Whilst employers are not required by statute to have a grievance procedure it is good employment relations practice to provide workers with a reasonable and prompt opportunity to obtain redress of any grievance. Employers are statutorily required in the written statement of terms and conditions of employment to specify, by description or otherwise, a person to whom the employee can apply if they have a grievance and they are also required by statute to allow a worker to be accompanied at certain grievance hearings (see section three).

36.   In circumstances where a grievance may apply to more than one person and where a trade union is recognised it may be appropriate for the problem to be resolved through collective agreements between the trade union(s) and the employer.

Formulating procedures

37.   It is in everyone's best interest to ensure that workers' grievances are dealt with quickly and fairly and at the lowest level possible within the organisation at which the matter can be resolved. Management is responsible for taking the initiative in developing grievance procedures which, if they are to be fully effective, need to be acceptable to both those they cover and those who have to

operate them. It is important therefore that senior management aims to secure the involvement of workers and their representatives, including trade unions where they are recognised, and all levels of management when formulating or revising grievance procedures.

Essential features of grievance procedures

38.   Grievance procedures enable individuals to raise issues with management about their work, or about their employers', clients' or their fellow workers' actions that affect them. It is impossible to provide a comprehensive list of all the issues that might give rise to a grievance but some of the more common include: terms and conditions of employment; health and safety; relationships at work; new working practices; organisational change and equal opportunities.

39.   Procedures should be simple, set down in writing and rapid in operation. They should also provide for grievance proceedings and records to be kept confidential.

40.   It is good practice for individuals to be accompanied at grievance hearings (see also section three for information on the statutory right to be accompanied).

41.   In order for grievance procedures to be effective it is important that all workers are made aware of them and understand them and if necessary that supervisors, managers and worker representatives are trained in their use. Wherever possible every worker should be either given a copy of the procedures or provided with access to it (eg, in the personnel handbook or on the company intranet site) and have the detail explained to them. For new employees this might best be done as part of any induction process. Special allowance should be made for individuals whose first language is not English or who have a visual impairment or some other disability.

The procedure in operation

42.   Most routine complaints and grievances are best resolved informally in discussion with the worker's immediate line manager. Dealing with grievances in this way can often lead to speedy resolution of problems and can help maintain the authority of the immediate line manager who may well be able to resolve the matter directly. Both manager and worker may find it helpful to keep a note of such an informal meeting.

43.   Where the grievance cannot be resolved informally it should be dealt with under the formal grievance procedure. The number of stages contained in the procedure will depend on the size of organisation, its management structure and the resources it has available. In larger organisations the procedure might contain all the following stages, but for the smaller business the first and final stages might be sufficient :-

First Stage: Workers should put their grievance, preferably in writing, to their immediate line manager. Where the grievance is against the line manager the matter should be raised with a more senior manager. If the grievance is contested the manager should invite the worker to attend a hearing in order to discuss the grievance and should inform the worker of his or her statutory right to be accompanied depending on the nature of the grievance (see section three) The manager should respond in writing to the grievance within a specified time (eg, within five working days of the hearing or, where no hearing has taken place, within five working days of receiving written notice of the grievance). If it is not possible to respond within the specified time period the worker should be given an explanation for the delay and told when a response can be expected.

Second Stage: If the matter is not resolved at Stage 1 the worker should be permitted to raise the matter in writing with a more senior manager. The choice of this person will depend on the organisation but could be a departmental, divisional or works' manager. The manager should arrange to hear the grievance within a specified period (eg, five working days) and should inform the worker of the statutory right to be accompanied (see section three). Following the hearing the manager should, where possible, respond to the grievance in writing within a specified period (eg, ten working days). If it is not possible to respond within the specified time period the worker should be given an explanation for the delay and told when a response can be expected.

Final Stage: Where the matter cannot be resolved at Stage 2 the worker should be able to raise their grievance in writing with a higher level of manager than for Stage 2. The choice of this person will depend on the organisation but could include directors or in certain cases the chief executive or managing director. Workers should be permitted to present their case at a hearing and should be informed of their statutory right to be accompanied (see section three). The manager dealing with the grievance should give a decision on the grievance within a specified period (eg, ten working days). If it is not possible to respond within the specified time period the worker should be given an explanation and told when a response can be expected.

44.   In most organisations it should be possible to have at least a two stage grievance procedure. However, where there is only one stage, for instance in very small firms where there is only a single owner/manager, it is especially important that the person dealing with the grievance acts impartially.

45.   In certain circumstances it may, with mutual agreement, be helpful to seek external advice and assistance during the grievance procedure. For instance where relationships have broken down an external facilitator might be able to help resolve the problem. Where the grievance is against the chief executive or managing director an external stage using some form of alternative dispute resolution might be helpful.

Special considerations

46.   Some organisations may wish to have specific procedures for handling grievances about unfair treatment eg, discrimination or bullying and harassment, as these subjects are often particularly sensitive.

47.   Organisations may also wish to consider whether they need a whistleblowing procedure in the light of the Public Interest Disclosure Act 1998. This provides strong protection to workers who raise concerns about wrongdoing (including frauds, dangers and cover-ups). While the Act reassures workers that it is safe to raise such a concern internally, it also protects disclosures to key

regulatory authorities and - provided they are reasonable and made with good cause - wider disclosures.

48.   Sometimes a worker may raise a grievance about the behaviour of a manager during the course of a disciplinary case. Where this happens and depending on the circumstances, it may be appropriate to suspend the disciplinary procedure for a short period until the grievance can be considered. Consideration might also be given to bringing in another manager to deal with the disciplinary case.

Records

49.   Records should be kept detailing the nature of the grievance raised, the employers response, any action taken and the reasons for it. These records should be kept confidential and retained in accordance with the Data Protection Act 1998 which requires the release of certain data to individuals on their request. Copies of any meeting records should be given to the individual concerned although in certain circumstances some information may be withheld, for example to protect a witness.

Section 3 - The statutory right to be accompanied at disciplinary and grievance hearings

What is the right?

50.   Workers have a statutory right to be accompanied by a fellow worker or trade union official[7] where they are required or invited by their employer to attend certain disciplinary or grievance hearings and when they make a reasonable request to be so accompanied. This right is additional to any contractual rights.

To whom does the right apply?

51.   The statutory right to be accompanied applies to all workers, not just employees working under a contract of employment. 'Worker' is defined in the legislation and includes anyone who performs work personally for someone else, but is not genuinely self-employed, as well as agency workers and home workers, workers in Parliament and Crown employees other than members of the armed forces[8] . There are no exclusions for part-time or casual workers, those on short term contracts or for people who work overseas (subject to any jurisdictional rules).

Application of the statutory right

52.   The statutory right applies where a worker:–
i)   is required or invited to attend a disciplinary or grievance hearing, and
ii)   reasonably requests to be accompanied at the hearing.

---

7   See paragraph for more information on who can accompany a worker at a disciplinary or grievance hearing.
8   See Section 13 (1), (2) and (3) of the Employment Relations Act 1999 for definitions of 'worker' 'agency worker' and 'home worker'.

What is a disciplinary hearing?

53. Whether a worker has a statutory right to be accompanied at a disciplinary hearing will depend on the nature of the hearing. Employers often choose to deal with disciplinary problems in the first instance by means of an informal interview or counselling session. So long as the informal interview or counselling session does not result in a formal warning or some other action it would not generally be good practice for the worker to be accompanied as matters at this informal stage are best resolved directly by the worker and manager concerned. Equally, employers should not allow an investigation into the facts surrounding a disciplinary case to extend into a disciplinary hearing. If it becomes clear during the course of the informal or investigative interview that formal disciplinary action may be needed then the interview should be terminated and a formal hearing convened at which the worker should be afforded the statutory right to be accompanied.

54. The statutory right to be accompanied applies specifically to hearings which could result in:
i)   the administration of a formal warning to a worker by his employer (ie, a warning, whether about conduct or capability, that will be placed on the worker's record);
ii) the taking of some other action in respect of a worker by his employer (eg, suspension without pay, demotion or dismissal); or
iii) the confirmation of a warning issued or some other action taken.[9]

What is a grievance hearing?

55. The statutory right to accompaniment applies only to grievance hearings which concern the performance of a 'duty by an employer in relation to a worker'[10]. This means a legal duty arising from statute or common law (eg, contractual commitments). Ultimately, only the courts can decide what sort of grievances fall within the statutory definition but the individual circumstances of each case will always be relevant. For instance:–
i)   An individual's request for a pay rise is unlikely to fall within the definition unless specifically provided for in the contract. On the other hand a grievance about equal pay would be included as this is covered by a statutory duty imposed on employers.
ii) Grievances about the application of a grading or promotion exercise are likely to be included if they arise out of the contract but not grievances arising out of requests for new terms and conditions of employment, for instance a request for subsidised health care or travel loans where these are not already provided for in the contract.
iii) Equally an employer may be under no duty to provide car parking facilities and thus a grievance on the issue would not attract the right to be accompanied. However, if the worker was disabled and needed parking facilities in order to attend work the employer's duty of care becomes relevant and the worker is likely to have a statutory right to be accompanied.
iv) Grievance arising out of day to day friction between fellow workers may not involve the breach of a legal duty unless the friction develops into incidents

9   See section 13(4) of the Employment Relations Act 1999
10 See section 13(5) of the Employment Relations Act 1999.

of bullying or harassment which would be included as they arise out of the employer's duty of care.

What is a reasonable request?

56.   In order for workers to exercise their statutory right to be accompanied they must make a reasonable request to their employer. It will be for the Courts to decide what is reasonable in all the circumstances. There is no test of reasonableness associated with the choice of companion and workers are therefore free to choose any one fellow worker or trade union official (within the limitations of paragraph 57). However, in making their choice workers should bear in mind that it would not be appropriate to insist on being accompanied by a colleague whose presence would prejudice the hearing or who might have a conflict of interest. Nor would it be sensible for a worker to request accompaniment by a colleague from a geographically remote location when someone suitably qualified was available on site. The request to be accompanied need not be in writing.

The accompanying person

57.   A worker has a statutory right to be accompanied at a disciplinary or grievance hearing by a single companion who is either a:
i)   Fellow worker, ie, another of the employer's workers;
ii)   A full-time official employed by a trade union[11] ; or a lay trade union official, so long as they have been reasonably certified in writing by their union as having experience of, or as having received training in, acting as a worker's companion at disciplinary or grievance hearings. Such certification may take the form of a card or letter.

Workers may, however, have contractual rights to be accompanied by persons other than those listed above, for instance a partner, spouse or legal representative.

58.   Workers are free to choose an official from any trade union to accompany them at a disciplinary or grievance hearing regardless of whether the union is recognised or not. However where a trade union is recognised in a workplace it is good practice for an official from that union to accompany the worker at a hearing.

59.   There is no duty on a fellow worker or trade union official to accept a request to accompany a worker and no pressure should be brought to bear on a person if they do not wish to act as a companion.

60.   Accompanying a worker at a disciplinary or grievance hearing is a serious responsibility and it is important therefore that trade unions ensure their officials are trained in the role. Even where a trade union official has experience of acting in the role there may still be a need for periodic refresher training.

61.   A worker who has been requested to accompany a colleague employed by the same employer and has agreed to do so is entitled to take a reasonable amount

11   As defined in sections 1 and 119 of the Trade Union and Labour Relations (Consolidation) Act 1992.

of paid time off to fulfil this responsibility. The time off should not only cover the hearing but should also allow a reasonable amount of time off for the accompanying person to familiarise themselves with the case and confer with the worker before and after the hearing. A lay trade union official is permitted to take a reasonable amount of paid time off to accompany a worker at a hearing so long as the worker is employed by the same employer.[12]

The statutory right in operation

62.   It is good practice for an employer to try to agree a mutually convenient date for the disciplinary or grievance hearing with the worker and their companion. This is to ensure that hearings do not have to be delayed or postponed at the last minute. Where the chosen companion cannot attend on the date proposed the worker can offer an alternative time and date so long as it is reasonable and falls before the end of the period of five working days[13] beginning with the first working day after the day proposed by the employer. In proposing an alternative date the worker should have regard to the availability of the relevant manager. For instance it would not normally be reasonable to ask for a new date for the hearing where it was known the manager was going be absent on business or on leave unless it was possible for someone else to act for the manager at the hearing. The location and timing of any alternative hearing should be convenient to both worker and employer.

63.   Both the employer and worker should prepare carefully for the hearing. The employer should ensure that a suitable venue is available and that, where necessary, arrangements are made to cater for any disability the worker or their companion may have. Where English is not the worker's first language there may also be a need for translation facilities. The worker should think carefully about what is to be said at the hearing and should discuss with their chosen companion their respective roles at the meeting. Before the hearing the worker should inform the employer of the identity of their chosen companion. In certain circumstances, for instance where the chosen companion is an official of a non-recognised trade union, it might also be helpful for the employer and chosen companion to make contact with each other before the hearing.

64.   The chosen companion has a statutory right to address the hearing but no statutory right to answer questions on the worker's behalf. Companions have an important role to play in supporting a worker and to this end should be allowed to ask questions and should, with the agreement of the employer, be allowed to participate as fully as possible in the hearing. The companion should also be permitted reasonable time to confer privately with the worker, either in the hearing room or outside.

What if the right to be accompanied is infringed?

65.   If an employer fails to allow a worker to be accompanied at a disciplinary or grievance hearing or fails to re-arrange a hearing to a reasonable date proposed

---

12   Time off for a lay official to accompany a worker at another employer is a matter for agreement by the parties concerned.
13   See section 13(6) of the Employment Relations Act 1999 for a definition of 'working day'.

by the worker when a companion cannot attend on the date originally proposed, the worker may present a complaint to an employment tribunal. If the tribunal finds in favour of the worker the employer may be liable to pay compensation of up to two weeks pay as defined in statute[14] . Where the failure leads to a finding of unfair dismissal greater legal remedies might be involved.

66.　Employers must be careful not to place any worker at a disadvantage for exercising or seeking to exercise their right to be accompanied as such detriment is unlawful and may lead to a claim to an employment tribunal. Equally employers must not place at a disadvantage those who act or seek to act as the accompanying person.

14　See Chapter II of Part XIV of the Employment Rights Act 1996.

(b) ACAS Code of Practice 2
Disclosure of Information to Trade Unions for Collective Bargaining Purposes

Introduction

1 Under the Trade Union and Labour Relations (Consolidation) Act 1992 the Advisory, Conciliation and Arbitration Service (ACAS) may issue the Codes of Practice containing such practical guidance as the Service thinks fit for the purpose of promoting the improvement of industrial relations. In particular, the Service has a duty to provide practical guidance on the application of sections 181 and 182 of the Act in relation to the disclosure of information by employers to trade unions for the purpose of collective bargaining.

2 The Act and the Code apply to employers operating in both the public and private sectors of industry. They do not apply to collective bargaining between employers' associations and trade unions, although the parties concerned may wish to follow the guidelines contained in the Code.

3 The information which employers may have a duty to disclose under section 181 is information which it would be in accordance with good industrial relations practice to disclose. In determining what would be in accordance with good industrial relations practice regard is to be had to any relevant provisions of the Code. However, the Code imposes no legal obligations on an employer to disclose any specific item of information. Failure to observe the Code does not by itself render anyone liable to proceedings, but the Act requires any relevant provisions to be taken into account in proceedings before the Central Arbitration Committee.[1]

This Code replaces the Code of Practice on Disclosure of Information to Trade Unions for Collective Bargaining Purposes, issued by the Service in 1977.

Provisions of the Act

4 The Act places a general duty on an employer who recognises an independent trade union to disclose for the purposes of all stages of collective bargaining about matters, and in relation to description of workers, in respect of which the union is recognised by him, information requested by representatives of trade unions. The representative of the union is an official or other person authorised by the union to carry on such collective bargaining.

5 The information requested has to be in the employer's possession, or in the possession of any associated employer, and must relate to the employer's undertaking. The information to be disclosed is that without which a trade union representative would be impeded to a material extent in bargaining and which it would be in accordance with good industrial relations practice to disclose for the purpose of collective bargaining. In determining what is in accordance with good industrial relations practice, any relevant provisions of this Code are to be taken into account.

---

1   Trade Union and Labour Relations (Consolidation) Act 1992, ss 181(2)(b), 181(4) and 207(1) and (2).

6 No employer is required to disclose any information which: would be against the interests of national security; would contravene a prohibition imposed by or under an enactment; was given to an employer in confidence, or was obtained by the employer in consequence of the confidence reposed in him by another person; relates to an individual unless he has consented to its disclosure; would cause substantial injury to the undertaking (or national interest in respect of Crown employment) for reasons other than its effect on collective bargaining; or was obtained for the purpose of any legal proceedings.

7 In providing information the employer is not required to produce original documents for inspection or copying. Nor is he required to compile or assemble information which would entail work or expenditure out of reasonable proportion to the value of the information in the conduct of collective bargaining. The union representative can request that the information be given in writing by the employer or be confirmed in writing. Similarly, an employer can ask the trade union representative to make the request for information in writing or confirm it in writing.

8 If the trade union considers that an employer has failed to disclose to its representatives information which he was required to disclose by section 181 of the Act, or to confirm such information in writing in accordance with that section, it may make a complaint to the Central Arbitration Committee. The Committee may ask the Advisory, Conciliation and Arbitration Service to conciliate. If conciliation does not lead to a settlement of the complaint, the Service shall inform the Committee accordingly who shall proceed to hear and determine the complaint. If the complaint is upheld by the Committee, it is required to specify the information that should have been disclosed or confirmed in writing, the date the employer failed to disclose, or confirm in writing, any of the information and a period of time within which the employer ought to disclose the information, or confirm it in writing. If the employer does not disclose the information, or confirm it in writing, within the specified time the union (except in relation to Crown employment and Parliamentary staff) may present a further complaint to the Committee and may also present a claim for improved terms and conditions. If the further complaint is upheld by the Committee an award, which would have effect as part of the contract of employment, may be made against the employer on the terms and conditions specified in the claim, or other terms and conditions which the Committee considers appropriate.

Providing information

9 The absence of relevant information about an employer's undertaking may to a material extent impede trade unions in collective bargaining, particularly if the information would influence the formulation, presentation or pursuance of a claim, or the conclusion of an agreement. The provision of relevant information in such circumstances would be in accordance with good industrial relations practice.

10 To determine what information will be relevant, negotiators should take account of the subject-matter of the negotiations and the issues raised during them; the level at which negotiations take place (department, plant, division, or company level); the size of the company; and the type of business the company is engaged in.

11   Collective bargaining within an undertaking can range from negotiations on specific matters arising daily at the work place affecting particular sections of the workforce, to extensive periodic negotiations on terms and conditions of employment affecting the whole workforce in multi-plant companies. The relevant information and the depth, detail and form in which it could be presented to negotiators will vary accordingly. Consequently, it is not possible to compile a list of terms that should be disclosed in all circumstances. Some examples of information relating to the undertaking which could be relevant in certain collective bargaining situations are given below:

(i)   *Pay and benefits*: principles and structure of payment systems; job evaluation systems and grading criteria; earnings and hours analysed according to work-group, grade, plant, sex, out-workers and homeworkers, department or division, giving where appropriate, distributions and make-up of pay showing any additions to basic rate or salary; total pay bill; details of fringe benefits and non-wage labour costs.

(ii)   *Conditions of service*: policies of recruitment, redeployment, redundancy, training, equal opportunity, and promotion; appraisal systems; health, welfare and safety matters.

(iii) *Manpower*: numbers employed analysed according to grade, department, location, age and sex; labour turnover; absenteeism; overtime and short-time; manning standards; planned changes in work methods, materials, equipment or organisation; available manpower plans; investment plans.

(iv) *Performance*: productivity and efficiency data; savings from increased productivity and output; return on capital investment; sales and state of order book.

(v)   *Financial*: cost structures; gross and net profits; sources of earnings; assets; liabilities; allocation of profits; details of government financial assistance; transfer prices; loans to parent or subsidiary companies and interest charged.

12   These examples are not intended to represent a check list of information that should be provided for all negotiations. Nor are they meant to be an exhaustive list of types of information as other items may be relevant in particular negotiations.

Restrictions on the duty to disclose

13   Trade unions and employers should be aware of the restrictions on the general duty to disclose information for collective bargaining.[2]

14   Some examples of information which if disclosed in particular circumstances might cause substantial injury are: cost information on individual products; detailed analysis of proposed investment; marketing or pricing policies; and price quotas or the make-up of tender prices. Information which has to be made available publicly, for example under the Companies Acts, would not fall into this category.

---

2   Trade Union and Labour Relations (Consolidation) Act 1992, s 182. See paras 6 and 7 of this Code.

15 Substantial injury may occur if, for example, certain customers would be lost to competitors, or suppliers would refuse to supply necessary materials, or the ability to raise funds to finance the company would be seriously impaired as a result of disclosing certain information. The burden of establishing a claim that disclosure of certain information would cause substantial injury lies with the employer.

Trade union's responsibilities

16 Trade unions should identify and request the information they require for collective bargaining in advance of negotiations whenever practicable. Misunderstandings can be avoided, costs reduced, and time saved, if requests state as precisely as possible all the information required, and the reasons why the information is considered relevant. Requests should conform to an agreed procedure. A reasonable period of time should be allowed for employers to consider a request and to reply.

17 Trade unions should keep employers informed of the names of the representatives authorised to carry on collective bargaining on their behalf.

18 Where two or more trade unions are recognised by an employer for collective bargaining purposes they should co-ordinate their requests for information whenever possible.

19 Trade unions should review existing training programmes or establish new ones to ensure negotiators are equipped to understand and use information effectively.

Employers' responsibilities[3]

20 Employers should aim to be as open and helpful as possible in meeting trade union requests for information. Where a request is refused, the reasons for the refusal should be explained as far as possible to the trade union representatives concerned and be capable of being substantiated should the matter be taken to the Central Arbitration Committee.

21 Information agreed as relevant to collective bargaining should be made available as soon as possible once a request for the information has been made by an authorised trade union representative. Employers should present information in a form and style which recipients can reasonably be expected to understand.

Joint arrangements for disclosure of information

22 Employers and trade unions should endeavour to arrive at a joint understanding on how the provisions on the disclosure of information can be implemented most effectively. They should consider what information is likely to be required, what is available, and what could reasonably be made available. Consideration should also be given to the form in which the information will be

---

3   The Stock Exchange has drawn attention to the need for employers to consider any obligations which they may have under their Listing Agreement.

presented, when it should be presented and to whom. In particular, the parties should endeavour to reach an understanding on what information could most appropriately be provided on a regular basis.

23 Procedures for resolving possible disputes concerning any issues associated with the disclosure of information should be agreed. Where possible such procedures should normally be related to any existing arrangements within the undertaking or industry and the complaint, conciliation and arbitration procedure described in the Act.[4]

4   Trade Union and Labour Relations (Consolidation) Act 1992, ss 183 to 185. See para 8 of this Code.

(c) ACAS Code of Practice 3
Time off for Trade Union Duties and Activities

Introduction

1 Under section 199 of the Trade Union and Labour Relations (Consolidation) Act 1992 the Advisory, Conciliation and Arbitration Service (ACAS) has a duty to provide practical guidance on the time off to be permitted by an employer:
(a) to a trade union official in accordance with section 168 of the Trade Union and Labour Relations (Consolidation) Act 1992; and
(b) to a trade union member in accordance with section 58 of the Act. This Code is intended to provide such guidance.

This Code, which replaces the Code of Practice issued by the Service in 1991, is intended to provide such guidance.

The background
2 The Employment Protection Act 1975 gave trade union officials a statutory right to reasonable paid time off from employment to carry out trade union duties and to undertake trade union training. Union officials and members were also given a statutory right to reasonable unpaid time off when taking part in trade union activities. These rights were subsequently re-enacted as sections 27 and 28 of the Employment Protection (Consolidation) Act 1978 and then as sections 168–170 of the Trade Union and Labour Relations (Consolidation) Act 1992.

3 Section 14 of the Employment Act 1989, which came into force on 26th February 1990, and which is now consolidated into section 168 of the Trade Union and Labour Relations (Consolidation) Act 1992 amended the statutory provisions. In particular, it introduced restrictions on the range of issues for which paid time off for trade union duties can be claimed to those covered by recognition agreements between employers and trade unions. Additionally union duties must relate to the official's own employer and not, for example, to any associated employer.

General purpose of the Code
4 The general purpose of the statutory provisions and this Code of Practice is to aid and improve the effectiveness of relationships between employers and trade unions. Employers and unions have a joint responsibility to ensure that agreed arrangements seek to specify how reasonable time off for union duties and activities and for training can work to their mutual advantage.

Structure of the Code
5 Section 1 of this Code provides guidance on time off for trade union duties. Section 2 deals with time off for training of trade union officials. Section 3 considers time off for trade union activities. In each case the amount and frequency of time off, and the purposes for which and any conditions subject to which time off may be taken, are to be those that are reasonable in all the circumstances. Section 4 describes the responsibilities which employers and trade unions share in considering reasonable time off. Section 5 notes the advantages of reaching formal agreements on time off. Section 6 deals with industrial action and section 7 with methods of appeal.

6 The annex to this Code reproduces the relevant statutory provisions on time off. To help differentiate between these and practical guidance, the summary of statutory provisions relating to time off which appears in the main text of the Code is in **bold type**. Practical guidance is in ordinary type. While every effort has been made to ensure that the summary of the statutory provisions included in this Code is accurate, only the courts can interpret the law authoritatively.

Status of the Code
7 The provisions of this Code are admissible in evidence and may be taken into account in determining any question arising during industrial tribunal proceedings relating to time off for trade union duties and activities. However, failure to observe any provision of the Code does not of itself render a person liable to any proceedings.

Section I – TIME OFF FOR TRADE UNION DUTIES

Entitlement
8 **Employees who are officials of an independent trade union recognised by their employer are to be permitted reasonable time off during working hours to carry out certain trade union duties.**

9 **An official is an employee who has been elected or appointed in accordance with the rules of the union to be a representative of all or some of the union's members in the particular company or workplace.**

10 **Officials are entitled to time off where the duties are concerned with:**
* **negotiations with the employer about matters which fall within section 178(2) of the Trade Union and Labour Relations (Consolidation) Act 1992 (TULR(C)A) and for which the union is recognised for the purposes of collective bargaining by the employer; or**
* **any other functions on behalf of employees of the employer which are related to matters falling within section 178(2) TULR(C)A and which the employer has agreed the union may perform.**

Matters falling within section 178(2) TULR(C)A are listed in the sub-headings of paragraph 12 below.

11 **An independent trade union is recognised by an employer when it is recognised to any extent for the purposes of collective bargaining. Where a trade union is not so recognised by an employer, employees have no statutory right to time off to undertake any duties.**

EXAMPLES OF TRADE UNION DUTIES
12 **Subject to the recognition or other agreement, trade union officials should be allowed to take reasonable time off for duties concerned with negotiations or, where their employer has agreed, for duties concerned with other functions related to or connected with:**
(a) **terms and conditions of employment, or the physical conditions in which workers are required to work.**
    Examples could include:
    * pay
    * hours of work
    * holidays and holiday pay
    * sick pay arrangements

- pensions
- vocational training
- equal opportunities
- notice periods
- the working environment
- utilisation of machinery and other equipment;

(b) **engagement or non-engagement, or termination or suspension of employment or the duties of employment, of one or more workers.** Examples could include:
  - recruitment and selection policies
  - human resource planning
  - redundancy and dismissal arrangements;

(c) **allocation of work or the duties of employment as between workers or groups of workers**. Examples could include:
  - job grading
  - job evaluation
  - job descriptions
  - flexible working practices;

(d) **matter of discipline.** Examples could include:
  - disciplinary procedures
  - arrangements for representing trade union members at internal interviews
  - arrangements for appearing on behalf of trade union members, or as witnesses, before agreed outside appeal bodies or industrial tribunals;

(e) **trade union membership or non-membership.** Examples could include:
  - representational arrangements
  - any union involvement in the induction of new workers;

(f) **facilities for officials of trade unions.** Examples could include agreed arrangements for the provision of:
  - accommodation
  - equipment
  - names of new workers to the union;

(g) **machinery for negotiation or consultation and other procedures.** Examples could include arrangements for:
  - collective bargaining
  - grievance procedures
  - joint consultation
  - communicating with members
  - communicating with other union officials also concerned with collective bargaining with the employer.

13 The duties of an official of a recognised trade union must be connected with or related to negotiations or the performance of functions both in time and subject matter. Reasonable time off may be sought, for example, to:
- prepare for negotiations
- inform members of progress
- explain outcomes to members
- prepare for meetings with the employer about matters for which the trade union has only representational rights.

Payment for time off for trade union duties
14 An employer who permits officials time off for trade union duties must pay them for the time off taken. The employer must pay either the amount

that the officials would have earned had they worked during the time off taken or, where earnings vary with the work done, an amount calculated by reference to the average hourly earnings for the work they are employed to do. There is no statutory requirement to pay for time off where the duty is carried out at a time when the official would not otherwise have been at work.

Section 2 – TRAINING OF OFFICIALS IN ASPECTS OF INDUSTRIAL RELATIONS

Entitlement
15   Employees who are officials of an independent trade union recognised by their employer are to be permitted reasonable time off during working hours to undergo training relevant to the carrying out of their trade union duties. These duties must be concerned with:
* negotiations with the employer about matters which fall within section 178(2) TULR(C)A and for which the union is recognised to any extent for the purposes of collective bargaining by the employer; or
* any other functions on behalf of employees of the employer which are related to matters falling within section 178(2) TULR(C)A and which the employer has agreed the union may perform.

Matters falling within section 178(2) TULR(C)A are set out in paragraph 12 above.

WHAT IS RELEVANT INDUSTRIAL RELATIONS TRAINING?
16   **Training should be in aspects of industrial relations relevant to the duties of an official**. There is no one recommended syllabus for training as an official's duties will vary according to:
* the collective bargaining arrangements at the place of work, particularly the scope of the recognition or other agreement
* the structure of the union
* the role of the official.

17   **The training must also be approved by the Trades Union Congress or by the independent trade union of which the employee is an official.**

18   Trade union officials are more likely to carry out their duties effectively if they possess skills and knowledge relevant to their duties. In particular, employers should be prepared to consider releasing trade union officials for initial training in basic representational skills as soon as possible after their election or appointment, bearing in mind that suitable courses may be infrequent. Reasonable time off could also be considered, for example:
* for further training particularly where the official has special responsibilities
* where there are proposals to change the structure and topics of negotiation about matters for which the union is recognised; or where significant changes in the organisation of work are being contemplated
* where legislative change may affect the conduct of industrial relations at the place of work and may require the reconsideration of existing agreements.

Payment for time off for training
19   **An employer who permits time off for officials to attend training relevant to their duties at the workplace must pay them for the time off taken. The employer must pay either the amount that the officials would have earned had**

they worked during the time off taken or, where earnings vary with the work done, an amount calculated by reference to the average hourly earnings for the work that they are employed to do. There is no statutory requirement to pay for time off where training is undertaken at a time when the official would not otherwise have been at work.

Section 3 – TIME OFF FOR TRADE UNION ACTIVITIES

Entitlement

20   To operate effectively and democratically, trade unions need the active participation of members. It can also be very much in employers' interests that such participation is assured. **An employee who is a member of an independent trade union recognised by the employer in respect of that description of employee is to be permitted reasonable time off during working hours to take part in any trade union activity.**

WHAT ARE EXAMPLES OF TRADE UNION ACTIVITIES?

21   The activities of a trade union member can be, for example:
* attending workplace meetings to discuss and vote on the outcome of negotiations with the employer
* meeting full-time officials to discuss issues relevant to the workplace
* voting in union elections.

22   Where the member is acting as a representative of a recognised union activities can be, for example, taking part in:
* branch, area or regional meetings of the union where the business of the union is under discussion
* meetings of official policy making bodies such as the executive committee or annual conference
* meetings with full-time officials to discuss issues relevant to the workplace.

23   **There is no right to time off for trade union activities which themselves consist of industrial action.**

Payment for time off for trade union activities

24   **There is no requirement that union members or representatives be paid for time off taken on trade union activities.** Nevertheless employers may want to consider payment in certain circumstances, for example to ensure that workplace meetings are fully representative.

Section 4 – THE RESPONSIBILITIES OF EMPLOYERS AND TRADE UNIONS

General considerations

25   **The amount and frequency of time off should be reasonable in all the circumstances.** Although the statutory provisions apply to all employers without exception as to size and type of business or service, trade unions should be aware of the wide variety of difficulties and operational requirements to be taken into account when seeking or agreeing arrangements for time off, for example:
* the size of the organisation and the number of workers
* the production process

- the need to maintain a service to the public
- the need for safety and security at all times.

26 Employers in turn should have in mind the difficulties for trade union officials and members in ensuring effective representation and communications with, for example:
- shift workers
- part-time workers
- those employed at dispersed locations
- workers with particular domestic commitments.

27 For time off arrangements to work satisfactorily trade unions should:
- ensure that officials are aware of their role, responsibilities and functions
- inform management, in writing, as soon as possible of appointments or resignations of officials
- ensure that officials receive any appropriate written credentials promptly.

28 Employers should consider making available to officials the facilities necessary for them to perform their duties efficiently and communicate effectively with their members, fellow lay officials and full-time officers. Where resources permit the facilities could include:
- accommodation for meetings
- access to a telephone and other office equipment
- the use of notice boards
- where the volume of the official's work justifies it, the use of dedicated office space.

Requesting time off
29 Trade union officials and members requesting time off to pursue their industrial relations duties or activities should provide management with as much notice as possible and give details of:
- the purpose of such time off
- the intended location
- the timing and duration of time off required.

30 In addition, officials who request paid time off to undergo relevant training should:
- give at least a few weeks' notice to management of nominations for training courses
- if asked to do so, provide a copy of the syllabus or prospectus indicating the contents of the training course.

31 When deciding whether requests for paid time off should be granted, consideration would need to be given as to their reasonableness, for example to ensure adequate cover for safety or to safeguard the production process or the provision of service. Similarly managers and unions should seek to agree a mutually convenient time which minimises the effect on production or services. Where workplace meetings are requested consideration should be given to holding them, for example:
- towards the end of a shift or the working week
- before or after a meal break.

32   Employers need to consider each application for time off on its merits; they might also need to consider the reasonableness of the request in relation to agreed time off already taken or in prospect.

Section 5 – AGREEMENTS ON TIME OFF

33   To take account of the wide variety of circumstances and problems which can arise, there can be positive advantages for employers and trade unions in establishing agreements on time off in ways which reflect their own situations. A formal agreement can help to:
*   provide clear guidelines against which applications for time off can be determined
*   avoid misunderstanding
*   facilitate better planning
*   ensure fair and reasonable treatment.

34   Agreements could specify:
*   the amount of time off permitted
*   the occasions on which time off can be taken
*   in what circumstances time off will be paid
*   to whom time off will be paid
*   the procedure for requesting time off.

35   In addition, it would be sensible for agreements to make clear:
*   arrangements for the appropriate payment to be made when time off relates in part to union duties and in part to union activities
*   whether payment (to which there would be no statutory entitlement) might be made to shift and part-time employees undertaking trade union duties outside their normal working hours.

36   Agreements for time off and other facilities for union representation should be consistent with wider agreements which deal with such matters as constituencies, number of representatives and the election of officials.

37   In smaller organisations, it might be thought more appropriate for employers and unions to reach understanding about how requests for time off are to be made; and more broadly to agree flexible arrangements which can accommodate their particular circumstances.

38   The absence of a formal agreement on time off, however, does not in itself deny an individual any statutory entitlement. Nor does any agreement supersede statutory entitlement to time off.

Section 6 – INDUSTRIAL ACTION

39   Employers and unions have a responsibility to use agreed procedures to settle problems and avoid industrial action. Time off may therefore be permitted for this purpose particularly where there is a dispute. **There is no right to time off for trade union activities which themselves consist of industrial action.** However, where an official is not taking part in industrial action but represents members involved, normal arrangements for time off with pay for the official should apply.

Section 7 – MAKING A COMPLAINT

40 Every effort should be made to resolve any dispute or grievance in relation to time off work for union duties or activities. There is advantage in agreeing ways in which such disputes can be settled and any appropriate procedures to resolve disputes should be followed. **Where the grievance remains unresolved, trade union officials or members have a right to complain to an industrial tribunal that their employer has failed to allow reasonable time off or, in the case of an official, has failed to pay for all or part of the time off taken. Such complaints may be resolved by conciliation by ACAS and, if this is successful, no tribunal hearing will be necessary.** ACAS assistance may also be sought without the need for a formal complaint to a tribunal.

Annex – THE LAW ON TIME OFF FOR TRADE UNION DUTIES AND ACTIVITIES

Section 168 of the Trade Union and Labour Relations (Consolidation) Act 1992 states:
(1) An employer shall permit an employee of his who is an official of an independent trade union recognised by the employer to take time off during his working hours for the purpose of carrying out any duties of his, as such an official, concerned with –
  (a) negotiations with the employer related to or connected with matters falling within section 178(2) (collective bargaining) in relation to which the trade union is recognised by the employer, or
  (b) the performance on behalf of employees of the employer of functions related to or connected with matters falling within that provision which the employer has agreed may be so performed by the trade union.
(2) He shall also permit such an employee to take time off during his working hours for the purpose of undergoing training in aspects of industrial relations–
  (a) relevant to the carrying out of such duties as are mentioned in subsection (1), and
  (b) approved by the Trades Union Congress or by the independent trade union of which he is an official.
(3) The amount of time off which an employee is to be permitted to take under this section and the purposes for which, the occasions on which and any conditions subject to which time off may be so taken are those that are reasonable in all the circumstances having regard to any relevant provisions of a Code of Practice issued by ACAS.
(4) An employee may present a complaint to an industrial tribunal that his employer has failed to permit him to take time off as required by this section.

Section 169 of the Trade Union and Labour Relations (Consolidation) Act 1992 states:
(1) An employer who permits an employee to take time off under section 168 shall pay him for the time taken off pursuant to the permission.
(2) Where the employee's remuneration for the work he would ordinarily have been doing during that time does not vary with the amount of work done, he shall be paid as if he had worked at that work for the whole of that time.
(3) Where the employee's remuneration for the work he would ordinarily have been doing during that time varies with the amount of work done, he shall

be paid an amount calculated by reference to the average hourly earnings for that work.

The average hourly earnings shall be those of the employee concerned or, if no fair estimate can be made of those earnings, the average hourly earnings for work of that description of persons in comparable employment with the same employer or, if there are no such persons, a figure of average hourly earnings which is reasonable in the circumstances.

(4) A right to be paid an amount under this section does not affect any right of an employee in relation to remuneration under his contract of employment, but –
   (a) any contractual remuneration paid to an employee in respect of a period of time off to which this section applies shall go towards discharging any liability of the employer under this section in respect of that period, and
   (b) any payment under this section in respect of a period shall go towards discharging any liability of the employer to pay contractual remuneration in respect of that period.

(5) An employee may present a complaint to an industrial tribunal that his employer has failed to pay him in accordance with this section.

Section 170 of the Trade Union and Labour Relations (Consolidation) Act 1992 states:
(1) An employer shall permit an employee of his who is a member of an independent trade union recognised by the employer in respect of that description of employee to take time off during his working hours for the purpose of taking part in –
   (a) any activities of the union, and
   (b) any activities, in relation to which the employee is acting as a representative of the union.

(2) The right conferred by subsection (1) does not extend to activities which themselves consist of industrial action, whether or not in contemplation or furtherance of a trade dispute.

(3) The amount of time off which an employee is to be permitted to take under this section and the purposes for which, the occasions on which and any conditions subject to which time off may be so taken are those that are reasonable in all the circumstances having regard to any relevant provisions of a Code of Practice issued by ACAS.

(4) An employee may present a complaint to an industrial tribunal that his employer has failed to permit him to take time off as required by this section.

Section 178(1) – (3) of the Trade Union and Labour Relations (Consolidation) Act 1992 states:
(1) In this act 'collective agreement' means any agreement or arrangement made by or on behalf of one or more trade unions and one or more employers or employers' associations and relating to one or more of the matters specified below; and 'collective bargaining' means negotiations relating to or connected with one or more of those matters.

(2) The matters referred to above are –
   (a) terms and conditions of employment, or the physical conditions in which any workers are required to work;
   (b) engagement or non-engagement, or termination or suspension of employment or the duties of employment, of one or more workers;

(c) allocation of work or the duties of employment as between workers or groups of workers;

(d) matters of discipline;

(e) a worker's membership or non-membership of a trade union;

(f) facilities for officials of trade unions; and

(g) machinery for negotiation or consultation, and other procedures, relating to any of the above matters, including the recognition by employers or employers' associations of the right of a trade union to represent workers in such negotiation or consultation or in the carrying out of such procedures.

(3) In this Act 'recognition', in relation to a trade union, means the recognition of the union by an employer, or two or more associated employers, to any extent, for the purpose of collective bargaining; and 'recognised' and other related expressions shall be construed accordingly.

Section 173(1) of the Trade Union and Labour Relations (Consolidation) Act 1992 states:

For the purposes of sections 168 and 170 the working hours of an employee shall be taken to be any time when in accordance with his contract of employment he is required to be at work.

Section 119 of the Trade Union and Labour Relations (Consolidation) Act 1992 states:

'Official' means –

(a) an officer of the union or of a branch or section of the union, or

(b) a person elected or appointed in accordance with the rules of the union to be a representative of its members or of some of them,

and includes a person so elected or appointed who is an employee of the same employer as the members or one or more of the members whom he is to represent.

(d) EOC Code of Practice
For the elimination of sex and marriage discrimination

Introduction

1   The EOC issues this Code of Practice for the following purposes:
a.   for the elimination of discrimination in employment
b.   to give guidance as to what steps it is reasonably practicable for employers to take to ensure that their employees do not in the course of their employment act unlawfully contrary to the Sex Discrimination Act (SDA)
c.   for the promotion of equality of opportunity between men and women in employment.

   The SDA prohibits discrimination against men, as well as against women. It also requires that married people should not be treated less favourably than single people of the same sex.

   It should be noted that the provisions of the SDA—and therefore of this Code—apply to the UK-based subsidiaries of foreign companies.

2   The Code gives guidance to employers, trade unions and employment agencies on measures which can be taken to achieve equality. The chances of success of any organisation will clearly be improved if it seeks to develop the abilities of all employees, and the Code shows the close link which exists between equal opportunities and good employment practice. In some cases, an initial cost may be involved, but this should be more than compensated for by better relationships and better use of human resources.

Small businesses

3   The Code has to deal in general terms and it will be necessary for employers to adapt it in a way appropriate to the size and structure of their organisations. Small businesses, for example, will require much simpler procedures than organisations with complex structures and it may not always be reasonable for them to carry out all the Code's detailed recommendations. In adapting the Code's recommendations, small firms should, however, ensure that their practices comply with the Sex Discrimination Act.

Employers' responsibility

4   **The primary responsibility at law rests with each employer to ensure that there is no unlawful discrimination**. It is important, however, that measures to eliminate discrimination or promote equality of opportunity should be understood and supported by all employees. Employers are therefore recommended to involve their employees in equal opportunity policies.

Individual employee's responsibility

5   While the main responsibility for eliminating discrimination and providing equal opportunity is that of the employer, individual employees at all levels have responsibilities too. They must not discriminate or knowingly aid their employer to do so.

TRADE UNION RESPONSIBILITY

6 The full commitment of trade unions is essential for the elimination of discrimination and for the successful operation of an equal opportunities policy. Much can be achieved by collective bargaining and throughout the Code it is assumed that all the normal procedures will be followed.

7 It is recommended that unions should co-operate in the introduction and implementation of equal opportunities policies where employers have decided to introduce them, and should urge that such policies be adopted where they have not yet been introduced.

8 Trade unions have a responsibility to ensure that their representatives and members do not unlawfully discriminate on grounds of sex or marriage in the admission or treatment of members. The guidance in this Code also applies to trade unions in their role as employers.

Employment agencies

9 Employment agencies have a responsibility as suppliers of job applicants to avoid unlawful discrimination on the grounds of sex or marriage in providing services to clients. The guidance in this Code also applies to employment agencies in their role as employers.

Definitions

10 For ease of reference, the main employment provisions of the Sex Discrimination Act, including definitions of direct and indirect sex and marriage discrimination, are provided in a Legal Annex to this Code.

PART I

The role of good employment practices in eliminating sex and marriage discrimination

11 This section of the Code describes those good employment practices which will help to eliminate unlawful discrimination. It recommends the establishment and use of consistent criteria for selection, training, promotion, redundancy and dismissal which are made known to all employees. Without this consistency, decisions can be subjective and leave the way open for unlawful discrimination to occur.

Recruitment

12 It is unlawful: UNLESS THE JOB IS COVERED BY AN EXCEPTION*: TO DISCRIMINATE DIRECTLY OR INDIRECTLY ON THE GROUNDS OF SEX OR MARRIAGE
— IN THE ARRANGEMENTS MADE FOR DECIDING WHO SHOULD BE OFFERED A JOB

---

* There are a number of exceptions to the requirements of the SDA, that employers must not discriminate against their employees or against potential employees. The main exceptions are mentioned on pages 17/18 of the Legal Annex.

— IN ANY TERMS OF EMPLOYMENT
— BY REFUSING OR OMITTING TO OFFER A PERSON EMPLOYMENT
[*Section* 6(1)(a); 6(1)(b); 6(1)(c)]°

13 It is therefore recommended that:

a. each individual should be assessed according to his or her personal capability to carry out a given job. It should not be assumed that men only or women only will be able to perform certain kinds of work;

h any qualifications or requirements applied to a job which effectively inhibit applications from one sex or from married people should be retained only if they are justifiable in terms of the job to be done:

[*Section* 6(1)(a), *together with section* 1(1)(b) *or* 3(1)(b)];

c. any age limits should be retained only if they are necessary for the job. An unjustifiable age limit could constitute unlawful indirect discrimination, for example, against women who have taken time out of employment for child-rearing;

d. where trade unions uphold such qualifications or requirements as union policy, they should amend that policy in the light of any potentially unlawful effect.

Genuine occupational qualifications (GOQs)

14 It is unlawful: EXCEPT FOR CERTAIN JOBS WHEN A PERSON'S SEX IS A GENUINE OCCUPATIONAL QUALIFICATION (GOQ) FOR THAT JOB to select candidates on the ground of sex.
[*Section* 7(2); 7(3) *and* 7(4)]

15 There are very few instances in which a job will qualify for a GOQ on the ground of sex. However, exceptions may arise, for example, where considerations of privacy and decency or authenticity are involved. The SDA expressly states that the need of the job for strength and stamina does not justify restricting it to men. When a GOQ exists for a job, it applies also to promotion, transfer, or training for that job, but cannot be used to justify a dismissal.

16 In some instances, the GOQ will apply to some of the duties only. A GOQ will not be valid, however, where members of the appropriate sex are already employed in sufficient numbers to meet the employer's likely requirements without undue inconvenience. For example, in a job where sales assistants may be required to undertake changing room duties, it might not be lawful to claim a GOQ in respect of all the assistants on the grounds that any of them might be required to undertake changing room duties from time to time.

17 It is therefore recommended that:

— A job for which a GOQ was used in the past should be re-examined if the post falls vacant to see whether the GOQ still applies. Circumstances may well have changed, rendering the GOQ inapplicable.

° For the full text of section 6 or other sections of the Sex Discrimination Act referred to in this Code, readers are advised to consult a copy of the Act which is available from Her Majesty's Stationery Office.

Source of recruitment

18 It is unlawful: UNLESS THE JOB IS COVERED BY AN EXCEPTION:
— TO DISCRIMINATE ON GROUNDS OF SEX OR MARRIAGE IN THE ARRANGEMENTS MADE FOR DETERMINING WHO SHOULD BE OFFERED EMPLOYMENT WHETHER RECRUITING BY ADVERTISEMENTS, THROUGH EMPLOYMENT AGENCIES, JOBCENTRES, OR CAREER OFFICES.
— TO IMPLY THAT APPLICATIONS FROM ONE SEX OR FROM MARRIED PEOPLE WILL NOT BE CONSIDERED.
[*Section* 6(1)(a)]
— TO INSTRUCT OR PUT PRESSURE ON OTHERS TO OMIT TO REFER FOR EMPLOYMENT PEOPLE OF ONE SEX OR MARRIED PEOPLE UNLESS THE JOB IS COVERED BY AN EXCEPTION.
[*Section* 39 *and* 40]

It is also unlawful WHEN ADVERTISING JOB VACANCIES,
— TO PUBLISH OR CAUSE TO BE PUBLISHED AN ADVERTISEMENT WHICH INDICATES OR MIGHT REASONABLY BE UNDERSTOOD AS INDICATING AN INTENTION TO DISCRIMINATE UNLAWFULLY ON GROUNDS OF SEX OR MARRIAGE.
[*Section* 38]

19 It is therefore recommended that:

Advertising
a. job advertising should be carried out in such a way as to encourage applications from suitable candidates of both sexes. This can be achieved both by wording of the advertisements and, for example, by placing advertisements in publications likely to reach both sexes. All advertising materials and accompanying literature relating to employment or training issues should be reviewed to ensure that it avoids presenting men and women in stereotyped roles. Such stereotyping tends to perpetuate sex segregation in jobs and can also lead people of the opposite sex to believe that they would be unsuccessful in applying for particular jobs;
b. where vacancies are filled by promotion or transfer, they should be published to all eligible employees in such a way that they do not restrict applications from either sex;
c. recruitment solely or primarily by word of mouth may unnecessarily restrict the choice of applicants available. The method should be avoided in a workforce predominantly of one sex, if in practice it prevents members of the opposite sex from applying;
d. where applicants are supplied through trade unions and members of one sex only come forward, this should be discussed with the unions and an alternative approach adopted.

Careers service/schools
20 When notifying vacancies to the Careers Service, employers should specify that these are open to both boys and girls. This is especially important when a job has traditionally been done exclusively or mainly by one sex. If dealing with single sex schools, they should ensure, where possible, that both boys' and girls'

schools are approached; it is also a good idea to remind mixed schools that jobs are open to boys and girls.

Selection methods

Tests

21 a. If selection tests are used, they should be specifically related to a job and/or career requirements and should measure an individual's actual or inherent ability to do or train for the work or career.

    b. Tests should be reviewed regularly to ensure that they remain relevant and free from any unjustifiable bias, either in content or in scoring mechanism.

Applications and interviewing

22 It is unlawful: UNLESS THE JOB IS COVERED BY AN EXCEPTION:

TO DISCRIMINATE ON GROUNDS OF SEX OR MARRIAGE BY REFUSING OR DELIBERATELY OMITTING TO OFFER EMPLOYMENT.
[*Section 6(1)(c)*]

23 It is therefore recommended that:

a. employers should ensure that personnel staff, line managers and all other employees who may come into contact with job applicants, should be trained in the provisions of the SDA, including the fact that it is unlawful to instruct or put pressure on others to discriminate;

b. applications from men and women should be processed in exactly the same way. For example, there should not be separate lists of male and female or married and single applicants. All those handling applications and conducting interviews should be trained in the avoidance of unlawful discrimination and records of interviews kept, where practicable, showing why applicants were or were not appointed;

c. questions should relate to the requirements of the job. Where it is necessary to assess whether personal circumstances will affect the performance of the job (for example, where it involves unsocial hours or extensive travel) this should be discussed objectively without detailed questions based on assumptions about marital status, children and domestic obligations. Questions about marriage plans or family intentions should not be asked, as they could be construed as showing bias against women. Information necessary for personnel records can be collected after a job offer has been made.

Promotion, transfer and training

24 It is unlawful: UNLESS THE JOB IS COVERED BY AN EXCEPTION FOR EMPLOYERS TO DISCRIMINATE DIRECTLY OR INDIRECTLY ON THE GROUNDS OF SEX OR MARRIAGE IN THE WAY THEY AFFORD ACCESS TO OPPORTUNITIES FOR PROMOTION, TRANSFER OR TRAINING.
[*Section 6(2)(a)*]

25 It is therefore recommended that:

a. where an appraisal system is in operation, the assessment criteria should be examined to ensure that they are not unlawfully discriminatory and the scheme monitored to assess how it is working in practice;

b. when a group of workers predominantly of one sex is excluded from an appraisal scheme, access to promotion, transfer and training and to other benefits should be reviewed, to ensure that there is no unlawful discrimination;

c. promotion and career development patterns are reviewed to ensure that the traditional qualifications are justifiable requirements for the job to be done. In some circumstances, for example, promotion on the basis of length of service could amount to unlawful indirect discrimination, as it may unjustifiably affect more women than men;

d. when general ability and personal qualities are the main requirements for promotion to a post, care should be taken to consider favourably candidates of both sexes with differing career patterns and general experience;

e. rules which restrict or preclude transfer between certain jobs should be questioned and changed if they are found to be unlawfully discriminatory. Employees of one sex may be concentrated in sections from which transfers are traditionally restricted without real justification;

f. policies and practices regarding selection for training, day release and personal development should be examined for unlawful direct and indirect discrimination. Where there is found to be an imbalance in training as between sexes, the cause should be identified to ensure that it is not discriminatory;

g. age limits for access to training and promotion should be questioned.

Health and safety legislation

26 Equal treatment of men and women may be limited by statutory provisions which require men and women to be treated differently. For example, the Factories Act 1961 places restrictions on the hours of work of female manual employees, although the Health and Safety Executive can exempt employers from these restrictions, subject to certain conditions. The Mines and Quarries Act 1954 imposes limitation on women's work and there are restrictions where there is special concern for the unborn child (eg lead and ionising radiation). However, the broad duties placed on employers by the Health and Safety at Work etc Act, 1974 makes no distinction between men and women. Section 2(1) requires employers to ensure, so far as is reasonably practicable, the health and safety and welfare at work of *all* employees.

SPECIFIC HEALTH AND SAFETY REQUIREMENTS UNDER EARLIER LEGISLATION ARE UNAFFECTED BY THE ACT.

(It is therefore recommended that:
— company policy should be reviewed and serious consideration given to any significant differences in treatment between men and women, and there should be well-founded reasons if such differences are maintained or introduced.

Terms of employment, benefits, facilities and services

27 It is unlawful: UNLESS THE JOB IS COVERED BY AN EXCEPTION TO DISCRIMINATE ON THE GROUNDS OF SEX OR MARRIAGE, DIRECTLY OR

INDIRECTLY, IN THE TERMS ON WHICH EMPLOYMENT IS OFFERED OR IN AFFORDING ACCESS TO ANY BENEFITS*, FACILITIES OR SERVICES.
[*Sections* 6(1)(*b*); 6(2)(*a*); 29]

28 It is therefore recommended that:

a.   all terms of employment, benefits, facilities and services are reviewed to ensure that there is no unlawful discrimination on grounds of sex or marriage. For example, part-time work, domestic leave, company cars and benefits for dependants should be available to both male and female employees in the same or not materially different circumstances.

29 In an establishment where part-timers are solely or mainly women, unlawful indirect discrimination may arise if, as a group, they are treated less favourably than other employees without justification.

It is therefore recommended that:

b.   where part-time workers do not enjoy pro-rata pay or benefits with full-time workers, the arrangements should be reviewed to ensure that they are justified with regard to sex.

Grievances, disciplinary procedures and victimisation

30 It is unlawful: TO VICTIMISE AN INDIVIDUAL FOR A COMPLAINT MADE IN GOOD FAITH ABOUT SEX OR MARRIAGE DISCRIMINATION OR FOR GIVING EVIDENCE ABOUT SUCH A COMPLAINT.
[*Section* 4(1); 4(2); *and* 4(3)]

31 It is therefore recommended that:

a.   particular care is taken to ensure that an employee who has in good faith taken action under the Sex Discrimination Act or the Equal Pay Act does not receive less favourable treatment than other employees, for example by being disciplined or dismissed;

b.   employees should be advised to use the internal procedures, where appropriate, but this is without prejudice to the individual's right to apply to an industrial tribunal within the statutory time limit, ie before the end of the period of three months beginning when the act complained of was done;

c.   particular care is taken to deal effectively with all complaints of discrimination, victimisation or harassment. It should not be assumed that they are made by those who are over-sensitive.

Dismissals, redundancies and other unfavourable treatment of employees

32 It is unlawful: TO DISCRIMINATE DIRECTLY OR INDIRECTLY ON GROUNDS OF SEX OR MARRIAGE IN DISMISSALS OR BY TREATING AN EMPLOYEE UNFAVOURABLY IN ANY OTHER WAY.
[*Section* 6(2)(*b*)]

It is therefore recommended that:

---

*   Certain provisions relating to death and retirement are exempt from the Act.

a. care is taken that members of one sex are not disciplined or dismissed for performance or behaviour which would be overlooked or condoned in the other sex;

b. redundancy procedures affecting a group of employees predominantly of one sex should be reviewed, so as to remove any effect which could be disproportionate and unjustifiable;

c. conditions of access to voluntary redundancy benefit* should be made available on equal terms to male and female employees in the same or not materially different circumstances;

d. where there is down-grading or short-time working (for example, owing to a change in the nature or volume of an employer's business) the arrangements should not unlawfully discriminate on the ground of sex;

e. all reasonably practical steps should be taken to ensure that a standard of conduct or behaviour is observed which prevents members of either sex from being intimidated, harassed or otherwise subjected to unfavourable treatment on the ground of their sex.

PART 2

The role of good employment practices in promoting equality of opportunity

33 This section of the Code describes those employment practices which help to promote equality of opportunity. It gives information about the formulation and implementation of equal opportunities policies. While such policies are not required by law, their value has been recognised by a number of employers who have voluntarily adopted them. Others may wish to follow this example.

Formulating an equal opportunities policy

34 An equal opportunities policy will ensure the effective use of human resources in the best interests of both the organisation and its employees. It is a commitment by an employer to the development and use of employment procedures and practices which do not discriminate on grounds of sex or marriage and which provide genuine equality of opportunity for all employees. The detail of the policy will vary according to the size of the organisation.

Implementing the policy

35 An equal opportunities policy must be seen to have the active support of management at the highest level. To ensure that the policy is fully effective, the following procedure is recommended:

a. the policy should be clearly stated and, where appropriate, included in a collective agreement;

b. overall responsibility for implementing the policy should rest with senior management;

c. the policy should be made known to all employees and, where reasonably practicable, to all job applicants.

---

* Certain provisions relating to death and retirement are exempt from the Act.

36 Trade unions have a very important part to play in implementing genuine equality of opportunity and they will obviously be involved in the review of established procedures to ensure that these are consistent with the law.

Monitoring

37 It is recommended that the policy is monitored regularly to ensure that it is working in practice. Consideration could be given to setting up a joint Management/Trade Union Review Committee.

38 In a small firm with a simple structure it may be quite adequate to assess the distribution and payment of employees from personal knowledge.

39 In a large and complex organisation a more formal analysis will be necessary, for example, by sex, grade and payment in each unit. This may need to be introduced by stages as resources permit. Any formal analysis should be regularly updated and available to Management and Trade Unions to enable any necessary action to be taken.

40 Sensible monitoring will show, for example, whether members of one sex:
a. do not apply for employment or promotion, or that fewer apply than might be expected;
b. are not recruited, promoted or selected for training and development or are appointed/selected in a significantly lower proportion than their rate of application;
c. are concentrated in certain jobs, sections or departments.

Positive Action

Recruitment, training and promotion
41 Selection for recruitment or promotion must be on merit, irrespective of sex. However, the Sex Discrimination Act does allow certain steps to redress the effects of previous unequal opportunities. Where there have been few or no members of one sex in particular work in their employment for the previous 12 months, the Act allows employers to give special encouragement to and provide specific training for the minority sex. Such measures are usually described as Positive Action.
[*Section* 48]

42 Employers may wish to consider positive measures such as:
a. training their own employees (male and female) for work which is traditionally the preserve of the other sex, for example, training women for skilled manual or technical work;
b. positive encouragement to women to apply for management posts—special courses may be needed;
c. advertisements which encourage applications from the minority sex, but make it clear that selection will be on merit without reference to sex;
d. notifying job agencies, as part of a Positive Action Programme that they wish to encourage members of one sex to apply for vacancies, where few or no members of that sex are doing the work in question. In these circumstances, job agencies should tell both men and women about the posts and, in addition, let the under-represented sex know that applications from them are

particularly welcome. Withholding information from one sex in an attempt to encourage applications from the opposite sex would be unlawful.

Other working arrangements

43   There are other forms of action which could assist both employer and employee by helping to provide continuity of employment to working parents, many of whom will have valuable experience or skills.

Employers may wish to consider with the employees whether:

a.   certain jobs can be carried out on a part-time or flexi-time basis;
b.   personal leave arrangements are adequate and available to both sexes. It should not be assumed that men may not need to undertake domestic responsibilities on occasion, especially at the time of child-birth;
c.   child-care facilities are available locally or whether it would be feasible to establish nursery facilities on the premises or combine with other employers to provide them;
d.   residential training could be facilitated for employees with young children. For example, where this type of training is necessary, by informing staff who are selected well in advance to enable them to make childcare and other personal arrangements; employers with their own residential training centres could also consider whether childcare facilities might be provided;
e.   the statutory maternity leave provisions could be enhanced, for example, by reducing the qualifying service period, extending the leave period, or giving access to part-time arrangements on return.

These arrangements, and others, are helpful to both sexes but are of particular benefit to women in helping them to remain in gainful employment during the years of child-rearing.

(e) Code of Practice
Race Relations

Introduction

I The purpose of this status of the Code

1.1   This Code aims to give practical guidance which will help employers, trade unions, employment agencies and employees to understand not only the provisions of the Race Relations Act and their application, but also how best they can implement policies to eliminate racial discrimination and to enhance equality of opportunity.

s 47(1)
s 47(10)
s 47(11)
s 32

1.2   The Code does not impose any legal obligations itself, nor is it an authoritative statement of the law—that can only be provided by the courts and tribunals. If, however, its recommendations are not observed this may result in breaches of the law where the act or omission falls within any of the specific prohibitions of the Act. Moreover its provisions are admissible in evidence in any proceedings under the Race Relations Act before an Industrial Tribunal and if any provision appears to the Tribunal to be relevant to a question arising in the proceedings it must be taken into account in determining that question. If employers take the steps that are set out in the Code to prevent their employees from doing acts of unlawful discrimination they may avoid liability for such acts in any legal proceedings brought against them.

References to the appropriate sections of the Race Relations Act 1976 are therefore given in the margin to the Code.

1.3   Employees of all racial groups have a right to equal opportunity. Employers ought to provide it. To do so is likely to involve some expenditure, at least in staff time and effort. But if a coherent and effective programme of equal opportunity is developed it will help industry to make full use of the abilities of its entire workforce. It is therefore particularly important for all those concerned—employers, trade unions and employees alike—to co-operate with goodwill in adopting and giving effect to measures for securing such equality. We welcome the commitment already made by the CBI and TUC to the principle of equal opportunity. The TUC has recommended a model equal opportunity clause for inclusion in collective agreements and the CBI has published a statement favouring the application by companies of constructive equal opportunity policies.

1.4   A concerted policy to eliminate both race and sex discrimination often provides the best approach. Guidance on equal opportunity between men and women is the responsibility of the Equal Opportunities Commission.

2. The application of the Code

2.1   The Race Relations Act applies to all employers. The Code itself is not restricted to what is required by law, but contains recommendations as well. Some of its detailed provisions may need to be adapted to suit particular circumstances. Any adaptations that are made, however, should be fully consistent with the Code's general intentions.

2.2 Smaller firms

In many small firms employers have close contact with their staff and there will therefore be less need for formality in assessing whether equal opportunity is being achieved, for example, in such matters as arrangements for monitoring. Moreover it may not be reasonable to expect small firms to have the resources and administrative systems to carry out the Code's detailed recommendations. In complying with the Race Relations Act, small firms should, however, ensure that their practices are consistent with the Code's general intentions.

3. Unlawful discrimination

3.1 The Race Relations Act 1976 makes it unlawful to discriminate against a person, directly or indirectly, in the field of employment.   s 4

Direct discrimination consists of treating a person, on racial grounds*, less favourably than others are or would be treated in the same or similar circumstances.   s 1(1)(a)

Segregating a person from others on racial grounds constitutes less favourable treatment.   s 1(2)

3.2 Indirect discrimination consists of applying in any circumstances covered by the Act a requirement or condition which, although applied equally to persons of all racial groups, is such that a considerably smaller proportion of a particular racial group can comply with it and it cannot be shown to be justifiable on other than racial grounds. Possible examples are: s 1(2)
— a rule about clothing or uniforms which disproportionately disadvantages a racial group and cannot be justified;
— an employer who requires higher language standards than are needed for safe and effective performance of the job.

3.3 The definition of indirect discrimination is complex, and it will not be spelt out in full in every relevant Section of the Code. Reference will be only to the terms 'indirect discrimination' or 'discriminate indirectly'.

3.4 Discrimination by victimisation is also unlawful under the Act. For example, a person is victimised if he or she is given less favourable treatment than others in the same circumstances because it is suspected or known that he or she has brought proceedings under the Act, or given evidence or information relating to such proceedings, or alleged that discrimination has occurred.   s 2

4. The Code and good employment practice

Many of the Code's provisions show the close link between equal opportunity and good employment practice. For example, selection criteria which are relevant to job requirements and carefully observed selection procedures not only help to ensure that individuals are appointed according to their suitability for the job

---

*   *Racial grounds are the grounds of race, colour, nationality—including citizenship—or ethnic or national origins and groups defined by reference to these grounds are referred to as racial groups.*

and without regard to racial group; they are also part of good employment practice. In the absence of consistent selection procedures and criteria, decisions are often too subjective and racial discrimination can easily occur.

5. Positive action

Opportunities for employees to develop their potential through encouragement, training and careful assessment are also part of good employment practice. Many employees from the racial minorities have potential which, perhaps because of previous discrimination and other causes of disadvantage, they have not been able to realise, and which is not reflected in their qualifications and experience. Where members of particular racial groups have been under-represented over the previous twelve months in particular work, employers and specified training bodies are allowed under the Act to encourage them to take advantage of opportunities for doing that work and to provide training to enable them to attain the skills needed for it. In the case of employers, such training can be provided for persons currently in their employment (as defined by the Act) and in certain circumstances for others too, for example if they have been designated as training bodies. This Code encourages employers to make use of these provisions, which are covered in detail in paragraphs 1.44 and 1.45.

s 37 &
s 38

6. Guidance papers

The guidance papers referred to in the footnotes contain additional guidance on specific issues but do not form part of the statutory Code.

PART I THE RESPONSIBILITIES OF EMPLOYERS

1.1   Responsibility for providing equal opportunity for all job applicants and employees rest primarily with employers. To this end it is recommended that they should adopt, implement and monitor an equal opportunity policy to ensure that there is no unlawful discrimination and that equal opportunity is genuinely available.*

1.2   This policy should be clearly communicated to all employees—eg through notice boards, circulars, contracts of employment or written notifications to individual employees.

Equal opportunity policies

1.3   An equal opportunity policy aims to ensure:
a.   *that no job applicant or employee receives less favourable treatment than another on racial grounds;*
b.   *that no applicant or employee is placed at a disadvantage by requirements or conditions which have a disproportionately adverse effect on his or her racial group and which cannot be shown to be justifiable on other than racial grounds;*

---

*   *The CRE has issued guidance papers on equal opportunity policies: 'Equal Opportunity in Employment' and 'Monitoring an Equal Opportunity Policy'.*

c. *that where appropriate and where permissible under the Race Relations Act, employees of under-represented racial groups are given training and encouragement to achieve equal opportunity within the organisation.*

1.4 In order to ensure that an equal opportunity policy is fully effective, the following action by employers is recommended:

a. allocating overall responsibility for the policy to a member of senior management;
b. discussing and, where appropriate, agreeing with trade union or employee representatives the policy's contents and implementation;
c. ensuring that the policy is known to all employees and if possible, to all job applicants;
d. providing training and guidance for supervisory staff and other relevant decision makers, (such as personnel and line managers, foremen, gatekeepers and receptionists) to ensure that they understand their position in law and under company policy;
e. examining and regularly reviewing existing procedures and criteria and changing them where they find that they are actually or potentially unlawfully discriminatory;
f. making an initial analysis of the workforce and regularly monitoring the application of the policy with the aid of analyses of the ethnic origins of the workforce and of job applicants in accordance with the guidance in paragraphs 1.34–1.35.

Recruitment, promotion, transfer, training & dismissal

Sources of recruitment

Advertisements

1.5 *When advertising job vacancies it is unlawful for employers:*
to publish an advertisement which indicates, or could reasonably be understood as indicating, an intention to discriminate against applicants from a particular racial group. (For exceptions see the Race Relations Act.) s 29

1.6 It is therefore recommended that:
a. employers should not confine advertisements unjustifiably to those areas of publications which would exclude or disproportionately reduce the numbers of applicants of a particular racial group; s 30
b. employers should avoid prescribing requirements such as length of residence or experience in the UK and where a particular qualification is required it should be made clear that a fully comparable qualification obtained overseas is as acceptable as a UK qualification. s 31

1.7 In order to demonstrate their commitment to equality of opportunity it is recommended that where employers send literature to applicants, this should include a statement that they are equal opportunity employers.

Employment agencies

1.8 When recruiting through employment agencies, job centres, careers offices and schools, it is unlawful for employers:

a. *to give instructions to discriminate, for example by indicating that certain groups will or will not be preferred. (For exceptions see the Race Relations Act)*;
b. *to bring pressure on them to discriminate against members of a particular racial group. (For exceptions, as above).*

1.9   In order to avoid indirect discrimination it is recommended that employers should not confine recruitment unjustifiably to those agencies, job centres, careers office and schools which, because of their particular source of applicants, provide only or mainly applicants of a particular racial group.

Other sources

1.10   *It is unlawful to use recruitment methods which exclude or disproportionately reduce the numbers of applicants of a particular racial group and which cannot be shown to be justifiable.* It is therefore recommended that employers should not recruit through the following methods:
a. recruitment, solely or in the first instance, through the recommendations of existing employees where the workforce concerned is wholly or predominantly white or black and the labour market is multi-racial;
b. procedures by which applicants are mainly or wholly supplied through trade unions where this means that only members of a particular racial group, or a disproportionately high number of them, come forward.

Sources for promotion and training

1.11   *It is unlawful for employers to restrict access to opportunities for promotion or training in a way which is discriminatory.* It is therefore recommended that:
— job and training vacancies and the application procedure should be made known to all eligible employees, and not in such a way as to exclude or disproportionately reduce the numbers of applicants from a particular racial group.

s 4 & s 28

Selecion for recruitment, promotion, transfer, training & dismissal

1.12   *It is unlawful to discriminate*, not only in recruitment, promotion, transfer and training, but also in the arrangements made for recruitment and in the ways of affording access to opportunities for promotion, transfer or training.*

Selection criteria and tests

s 24 & s 28

1.13   In order to avoid direct or indirect discrimination it is recommended the selection criteria and tests are examined to ensure that they are related to job requirements and are not unlawfully discriminatory (see Introduction para. 3.2). For example:
a. a standard of English higher than that needed for the safe and effective performance of the job or clearly demonstrable career pattern should not be required, or a higher level of educational qualification than is needed;

*   *It should be noted that discrimination in selection to achieve 'racial balance' is not allowed. The clause in the 1968 Race Relations Act which allowed such discrimination for the purpose of securing or preserving a reasonable balance of persons of different racial groups in the establishment is not included in the 1976 Race Relations Act.*

b. in particular, employers should not disqualify applicants because they are
    unable to complete an application form unassisted unless personal
    completion of the form is a valid test of the standard of English required for
    safe and effective performance of the job;

c. overseas degrees, diplomas and other qualifications which are comparable
    with UK qualifications should be accepted as equivalents, and not simply
    be assumed to be of an inferior quality;

d. selection tests which contain irrelevant questions or exercises on matters
    which may be unfamiliar to racial minority applicants should not be used
    (for example, general knowledge questions on matters more likely to be
    familiar to indigenous applicants);

e. selection tests should be checked to ensure that they are related to the job's
    requirements, ie an individual's test markings should measure ability to do
    or train for the job in question.

Treatment of applicants: shortlisting, interviewing and selection

1.14 In order to avoid direct or indirect discrimination it is recommended that:

a. gate, reception and personnel staff should be instructed not to treat casual or
    formal applicants from particular racial groups less favourably than others.
    These instructions should be confirmed in writing:

b. in addition, staff responsible for shortlisting, interviewing and selection of
    candidates should be:
    — clearly informed of selection criteria and of the need for their consistent
       application;
    — given guidance or training on the effects which generalised assumptions
       and prejudices about race can have on selection decisions;
    — made aware of the possible misunderstandings that can occur in
       interviews between persons of different cultural backgrounds;

c. where possible, shortlisting and interviewing should not be done by one
    person alone but should at least be checked at a more senior level.

Genuine occupational qualification

1.15 *Selection on racial grounds is allowed in certain jobs where being of a
particular racial group is a genuine occupational qualification for that job.*
An example is where the holder of a particular job provides persons of a racial
group with personal services promoting their welfare, and those services cannot
effectively be provided by a person of that group.

s 5

s 5(2)(d)

Transfers and training

1.16 In order to avoid direct or indirect discrimination it is recommended that:

a. staff responsible for selecting employees for transfer to other jobs should be
    instructed to apply selection criteria without unlawful discrimination;

b. industry or company agreements and arrangements of custom and practice
    on job transfers should be examined and amended if they are found to contain
    requirements or conditions which appear to be indirectly discriminatory. For
    example, if employees of a particular racial group are concentrated in
    particular sections, the transfer arrangements should be examined to see if
    they are unjustifiably and unlawfully restrictive and amended if necessary;

c. staff responsible for selecting employees for training, whether induction,
    promotion or skill training should be instructed not to discriminate on racial
    grounds;

d. selection criteria for training opportunities should be examined to ensure that they are not indirectly discriminatory.

Dismissal (including redundancy) and other detriment

s 4(2)(c) **1.17** *It is unlawful to discriminate on racial grounds in dismissal, or other detriment to an employee.* It is therefore recommended that:

a. staff responsible for selecting employees for dismissal, including redundancy, should be instructed not to discriminate on racial grounds;
b. selection criteria for redundancies should be examined to ensure that they are not indirectly discriminatory.

Performance appraisals

s 4(2)(b) **1.18** *It is unlawful to discriminate on racial grounds in appraisals of employee performance.*

1.19 It is recommended that:

a. staff responsible for performance appraisals should be instructed not to discriminate on racial grounds;
b. assessment criteria should be examined to ensure that they are not unlawfully discriminatory.

Terms of employment, benefits, facilities and services

s 4(2) **1.20** *It is unlawful to discriminate on racial grounds in affording terms of employment and providing benefits, facilities and services for employees.* It is therefore recommended that:

a. all staff concerned with these aspects of employment should be instructed accordingly;
b. the criteria governing eligibility should be examined to ensure that they are not unlawfully discriminatory.

1.21 In addition, employees may request extended leave from time to time in order to visit relations in their countries of origin or who have emigrated to other countries. Many employers have policies which allow annual leave entitlement to be accumulated, or extra unpaid leave to be taken to meet these circumstances. Employers should take care to apply such policies consistently and without unlawful discrimination.

Grievance, disputes and disciplinary procedures

s 4(2) &
s 2
1.22 It is unlawful to discriminate in the operation of grievance, disputes and disciplinary procedures, for example by victimising an individual through disciplinary measures because he or she has complained about racial discrimination, or given evidence about such a complaint. Employers should not ignore or treat lightly grievances from members of particular racial groups on the assumption that they are over-sensitive about discrimination.

1.23 It is recommended that in applying disciplinary procedures consideration should be given to the possible effect on an employee's behaviour of the following:
— racial abuse or other racial provocation;
— communication and comprehension difficulties;
— differences in cultural background or behaviour.

Cultural and religious needs

1.24   Where employees have particular cultural and religious needs which conflict with existing work requirements, it is recommended that employers should consider whether it is reasonably practicable to vary or adapt these requirements to enable such needs to be met. For example, it is recommended that they should not refuse employment to a turbanned Sikh because he could not comply with unjustifiable uniform requirements. Other examples of such needs are:

a.   observance of prayer times and religious holidays*;
b.   wearing of dress such as sarees and trousers worn by Asian women.

1.25   *Although the Act does not specifically cover religious discrimination, work requirements would generally be unlawful if they have a disproportionately adverse effect on particular racial groups and cannot be shown to be justifiable.*[+]   s 4 & s 28

Communications and language training for employees

1.26   Although there is no legal requirement to provide language training, difficulties in communications can endanger equal opportunity in the workforce. In addition, good communications can improve efficiency, promotion prospects and safety and health and create a better understanding between employer, employees and unions. Where the workforce includes current employees whose English is limited it is recommended that steps are taken to ensure that communications are as effective as possible.

1.27   These should include, where reasonably practicable:

a.   provision of interpretation and translation facilities, for example, in the communication of grievance and other procedures, and of terms of employment;
b.   training in English language and in communication skills[‡];
c.   training for managers and supervisors in the background and culture of racial minority groups;
d.   the use of alternative or additional methods of communication, where employees find it difficult to understand health and safety requirements for example:
 —   safety signs, translations of safety notices;
 —   instructions through interpreters;
 —   instructions combined with industrial language training.

Instructions and pressure to discriminate

1.28   *It is unlawful to instruct or put pressure on others to discriminate on racial grounds.*

---

*   *The CRE has issued a guidance paper entitled—'Religious Observance by Muslim Employees'.*
+   *Genuinely necessary safety requirements may not constitute unlawful discrimination.*
‡   *Industrial language training is provided by a network of Local Educational Authority units throughout the country. Full details of the courses and the comprehensive services offered by these units are available from the National Centre for Industrial Language Training, The Havelock Centre, Havelock Road, Southall, Middx.*

a. An example of an unlawful instruction is:
    — an instruction from a personnel or line manager to junior staff to restrict the number of employees from a particular racial group in any particular work;
b. An example of pressure to discriminate is:
    — an attempt by a shop steward or group of workers to induce an employer not to recruit members of particular racial groups, for example by threatening industrial action.

1.29 It is also unlawful to discriminate in response to such instructions or pressure.

1.30 The following recommendations are made to avoid unlawful instructions and pressure to discriminate:
a. guidance should be given to all employees, and particularly those in positions of authority or influence on the relevant provisions of the law;
b. decision-makers should be instructed not to give way to pressure to discriminate;
c. giving instructions or bringing pressure to discriminate should be treated as a disciplinary offence.

Victimisation

1.31 *It is unlawful to victimise individuals who have made allegations or complaints of racial discrimination or provided information about such discrimination, for example, by disciplining them or dismissing them.* (See Introduction, para. 3.4).

1.32 It is recommended that:
— guidance on this aspect of the law should be given to all employees and particularly to those in positions of influence or authority.

Monitoring equal opportunity*

1.33 It is recommended that employers should regularly monitor the effects of selection decisions and personnel practices and procedures in order to assess whether equal opportunity is being achieved.

1.34 The information needed for effective monitoring may be obtained in a number of ways. It will best be provided by records showing the ethnic origins of existing employees and job applicants. It is recognised that the need for detailed information and the methods of collecting it will vary according to the circumstances of individual establishments. For example, in small firms or in firms in areas with little or no racial minority settlement it will often be adequate to assess the distribution of employees from personal knowledge and visual identification.

1.35 It is open to employers to adopt the method of monitoring which is best suited to their needs and circumstances, but whichever method is adopted, they should be able to show that it is effective. In order to achieve the full commitment

---

*   *See the CRE's guidance paper on 'Monitoring an Equal Opportunity Policy'.*

of all concerned the chosen method should be discussed and agreed, where appropriate, with the trade union or employee representatives.

1.36 Employers should ensure that information on an individual's ethnic origins is collected for the purpose of monitoring equal opportunity alone and is protected from misuse.

1.37 The following is the comprehensive method recommended by the CRE[+].

Analyses should be carried out of:
a.   the ethnic composition of the workforce of each plant, department, section, shift and job category, and changes in distribution over periods of time;
b.   selection decisions for recruitment, promotion, transfer and training, according to the racial group of candidates, and reasons for these decisions.

1.38 Except in cases where there are large numbers of applicants and the burden on resources would be excessive, reasons for selection and rejection should be recorded at each stage of the selection process, eg initial shortlisting and final decisions. Simple categories of reasons for rejection should be adequate for the early sifting stages.

1.39 Selection criteria and personnel procedures should be reviewed to ensure that they do not include requirements or conditions which constitute or may lead to unlawful indirect discrimination.

1.40 This information should be carefully and regularly analysed and, in order to identify areas which may need particular attention, a number of key questions should be asked.

1.41 Is there evidence that individuals from any particular racial group:

a.   do not apply for employment or promotion, or that fewer apply than might be expected?
b.   are not recruited or promoted at all, or are appointed in a significantly lower proportion than their rate of application?
c.   are under-represented in training or in jobs carrying higher pay, status or authority?
d.   are concentrated in certain shifts, sections or departments?

1.42 If the answer to any of these questions is yes, the reasons for this should be investigated. If direct or indirect discrimination is found action must be taken to end it immediately.

1.43 It is recommended that deliberate acts of unlawful discrimination by employees are treated as disciplinary offences.

Positive action*

1.44 *Although they are not legally required, positive measures are allowed by the law to encourage employees and potential employees and provide training*

+   *This is outlined in detail in 'Monitoring an Equal Opportunity Policy'.*
*   *The CRE has issued a guidance paper on Positive Action, entitled 'Equal Opportunity in Employment—Why Positive Action?'.*

for employees who are members of particular racial groups which have been under-represented[+] *in particular work.* (See Introduction, para. 5). Discrimination at the point of selection for work, however, is not permissible in these circumstances.

1.45 Such measures are important for the development of equal opportunity. It is therefore recommended that, where there is under-representation of particular racial groups in particular work, the following measures should be taken wherever appropriate and reasonably practicable:

a. job advertisements designed to reach members of these groups and to encourage their applications: for example, through the use of the ethnic minority press, as well as other newspapers;
b. use of the employment agencies and careers offices in areas where these groups are concentrated;
c. recruitment and training schemes for school leavers designed to reach members of these groups;
d. encouragement to employees from these groups to apply for promotion or transfer opportunities;
e. training for promotion or skill training for employees of these groups who lack particular expertise but show potential: supervisory training may include language training.

PART 2 The responsibilities of individual employees

2.1 While the primary responsibilities for providing equal opportunity rests with the employer, individual employees at all levels and of all racial groups have responsibilities too. Good race relations depend on them as much as on management, and so their attitudes and activities are very important.

2.2 *The following actions by individual employees would be unlawful*:

s 4 & s 33

a. *discrimination in the course of their employment against fellow employees or job applicants on racial grounds*, for example, in selection decisions for recruitment, promotion, transfer and training;
b. *inducing, or attempting to induce other employees, unions or management to practise unlawful discrimination.* For example, they should not refuse to accept other employees from particular racial groups or refuse to work with a supervisor of a particular racial group;

s 31

c. *victimising individuals who have made allegations or complaints of racial discrimination or provided information about such discrimination.* (See Introduction, para. 3.4).

2.3 To assist in preventing racial discrimination and promoting equal opportunity it is recommended that individual employees should:

a. co-operate in measures introduced by management designed to ensure equal opportunity and non-discrimination;
b. where such measures have not been introduced, press for their introduction (through their trade union where appropriate);

+ *A racial group is under-represented in trade union membership if at any time during the previous twelve months no persons of that group were in membership, or disproportionately few in comparison with the proportion of persons of that group among those eligible for membership. Under-representation in trade union posts applies under the same twelve month criteria, where there were no persons of a particular racial group in those posts or disproportionately few in comparison with the proportion of that group in the organisation.*

c.   draw the attention of management and, where appropriate, their trade unions   s 2
to suspected discriminatory acts or practices;
d.   refrain from harassment or intimidation of other employees on racial grounds,
for example, by attempting to discourage them from continuing employment.
Such action may be unlawful if it is taken by employees against those subject
to their authority.

2.4   In addition to the responsibilities set out above individual employees from
the racial minorities should recognise that in many occupations advancement is
dependent on an appropriate standard of English. Similarly an understanding of
the industrial relations procedures which apply is often essential for good working
relationships.

2.5   They should therefore:
a.   where appropriate, seek means to improve their standards of English;
b.   co-operate in industrial language training schemes introduced by employers
and/or unions;
c.   co-operate in training and other schemes designed to inform them of industrial
relations procedures, company agreements, work rules, etc;
d.   where appropriate, participate in discussions with employers and unions, to
find solutions to conflicts between cultural or religious needs and production
needs.

PART 3 The responsibilities of trade unions

3.1   Trade unions, in common with a number of other organisations, have a dual
role as employers and providers of services specifically covered by the Race
Relations Act.

3.2   In their role as employer, unions have the responsibilities set out in Part 1
of the Code. They also have a responsibility to ensure that their representatives   s 11
and members do not discriminate against any particular racial group in the
admission or treatment of members, or as colleagues, supervisors or subordinates.

3.3   In addition, trade union officials at national and local level and shopfloor
representatives at plant level have an important part to play on behalf of their
members in preventing unlawful discrimination and in promoting equal
opportunity and good race relations. Trade unions should encourage and press
for equal opportunity policies so that measures to prevent discrimination at the
workplace can be introduced with the clear commitment of both management
and unions.

Admission of members

3.4   *It is unlawful for trade unions to discriminate on racial grounds*:
a.   *by refusing membership*;
b.   *by offering less favourable terms of membership.*
                                                                    s 11

Treatment of members

3.5   *It is unlawful for trade unions to discriminate on racial grounds against*   s 11(3)
existing members:

a. *by varying their terms of membership, depriving them of membership or subjecting them to any other detriment*;
b. *by treating them less favourably in the benefits, facilities or services provided.* These may include:
   training facilities;
   welfare and insurance schemes;
   entertainment and social events;
   processing of grievances;
   negotiations;
   assistance in disciplinary or dismissal procedures.

3.6 In addition, it is recommended that unions ensure that in cases where members of particular racial groups believe that they are suffering racial discrimination, whether by the employer or the union itself, serious attention is paid to the reasons for this belief and that any discrimination which may be occurring is stopped.

Disciplining union members who discriminate

3.7 It is recommended that deliberate acts of unlawful discrimination by union members are treated as disciplinary offences.

Positive action

s 38
(4) & (5)

3.8 *Although they are not legally required, positive measures are allowed by the law to encourage and provide training for members of particular racial groups which have been under-represented* in trade union membership or in trade union posts.* (Discrimination at the point of selection, however, is not permissible in these circumstances.)

3.9 It is recommended that, wherever appropriate and reasonably practicable, trade unions should:
a. encourage individuals from these groups to join the union. Where appropriate, recruitment material should be translated into other languages;
b. encourage individuals from these groups to apply for union posts and provide training to help fit them for such posts.

Training and information

3.10 Training and information play a major part in the avoidance of discrimination and the promotion of equal opportunity. It is recommended that trade unions should:
a. provide training and information for officers, shop stewards and representatives on their responsibilities for equal opportunity. This training and information should cover:
   the Race Relations Act and the nature and causes of discrimination;

---

*

s 38(4)

&

s 38(4)

A racial group is under-represented in trade union membership if at any time during the previous twelve months no persons of that group were in membership, or disproportionately few in comparison with the proportion of persons of that group among those eligible for membership. Under-representation in trade union posts applies under the same twelve month criteria, where there were no persons of a particular racial group in those posts or disproportionately few in comparison with the proportion of that group in the organisation.

the backgrounds of racial minority groups and communication needs;
the effects of prejudice;
equal opportunity policies;
avoiding discrimination when representing members.

b. ensure that members and representatives, whatever their racial group, are informed of their role in the union, and of industrial relations and union procedures and structures. This may be done, for example:
through translation of material;
through encouragement to participate in industrial relations courses and industrial language training.

Pressure to discriminate

3.11 *It is unlawful for trade union members or representatives to induce or to attempt to induce those responsible for employment decisions to discriminate*:   s 31
a. *in the recruitment, promotion, transfer, training or dismissal of employees*;
b. *in terms of employment, benefits, facilities or services.*

3.12 For example, they should not:
a. restrict the numbers of a particular racial group in a section, grade or department;
b. resist changes designed to remove indirect discrimination, such as those in craft apprentice schemes, or in agreement concerning seniority rights or mobility between departments.

Victimisation

3.13 *It is unlawful to victimise individuals who have made allegations or complaints of racial discrimination or provided information about such discrimination.* (See Introduction, para 3.4.)   s 2

Avoidance of discrimination

3.14 *Where unions are involved in selection decisions for recruitment, promotion, training or transfer, for example through recommendation or veto, it is unlawful for them to discriminate on racial grounds.*   s 31 & s 33

3.15 It is recommended that they should instruct their members accordingly and examine their procedures and joint agreements to ensure that they do not contain indirectly discriminatory requirements or conditions, such as:
unjustifiable restrictions on transfers between departments or irrelevant and unjustifiable selection criteria which have a disproportionately adverse effect on particular racial groups.

Union involvement in equal opportunity policies

3.16 It is recommended that:
a. unions should co-operate in the introduction and implementation of full equal opportunity policies, as defined in paras. 1.3 and 1.4;
b. unions should negotiate the adoption of such policies where they have not been introduced or the extension of existing policies where these are too narrow;

c.   unions should co-operate with measures to monitor the progress of equal opportunity policies, or encourage management to introduce them where they do not already exist. Where appropriate (see paras. 1.33–1.35) this may be done through analysis of the distribution of employees and job applicants according to ethnic origin;

d.   where monitoring shows that discrimination has occurred or is occurring, unions should co-operate in measures to eliminate it;

e.   although positive action* is not legally required, unions should encourage management to take such action where there is under-representation of particular racial groups in particular jobs, and where management itself introduces positive action representatives should support it;

f.   similarly, where there are communication difficulties management should be asked to take whatever action is appropriate to overcome them.

PART 4 The responsibilities of employment agencies

4.1   Employment agencies, in their role as employers, have the responsibilities outlined in Part 1 of the Code. In addition, they have responsibilities as suppliers of job applicants to other employers.

4.2   *It is unlawful for employment agencies: (for exceptions see Race Relations Act)*

s 14(1)   a.   *to discriminate on racial grounds in providing services to clients;*

s 29   b.   *to publish job advertisements indicating, or which might be understood to indicate that applications from any particular group will not be considered or will be treated more favourably or less favourably than others;*

s 14(1)   c.   *to act on directly discriminatory instructions from employers to the effect that applicants from a particular racial group will be rejected or preferred so that their numbers should be restricted;*

s 14(1) &   d.   *to act on indirectly discriminatory instructions from employers ie that*
s 1(1)(b)   *requirements or conditions should be applied that would have a disproportionately adverse effect on applicants of a particular racial group and which cannot be shown to be justifiable.*

4.3   It is recommended that agencies should also avoid indicating such conditions or requirements in job advertisements unless they can be shown to be justifiable. Examples in each case may be those relating to educational qualifications or residence.

4.4   It is recommended that staff should be given guidance on their duty not to discriminate and on the effect which generalised assumptions and prejudices can have on their treatment of members of particular racial groups.

4.5   In particular staff should be instructed:

a.   not to ask employers for racial preferences;

b.   not to draw attention to racial origin when recommending applicants unless the employer is trying to attract applicants of a particular racial group under the exceptions in the Race Relations Act;

---

*   *See 1.44—Positive Action recommendations.*

c. to report a client's refusal to interview an applicant for reasons that are directly or indirectly discriminatory to a supervisor, who should inform the client that discrimination is unlawful. If the client maintains this refusal the agency should inform the applicant of his or her right to complain to an industrial tribunal and to apply to the CRE for assistance. An internal procedure for recording such cases should be operated;

d. to inform their supervisor if they believe that an applicant, though interviewed, has been rejected on racial grounds. If the supervisor is satisfied that there are grounds for this belief, he or she should arrange for the applicant to be informed of the right to complain to an industrial tribunal and to apply to the CRE for assistance. An internal procedure for recording such cases should be operated;

e. to treat job applicants without discrimination. For example, they should not send applicants from particular racial groups to only those employers who are believed to be willing to accept them, or restrict the range of job opportunities for such applicants because of assumptions about their abilities based on race or colour.

4.6 It is recommended that employment agencies should discontinue their services to employers who give unlawful discriminatory instructions and who refuse to withdraw them.

4.7 It is recommended that employment agencies should monitor the effectiveness of the measures they take for ensuring that no unlawful discrimination occurs. For example, where reasonably practicable they should make periodic checks to ensure that applicants from particular racial groups are being referred for suitable jobs for which they are qualified at a similar rate to that for other comparable applicants.

(f) Code of Practice
Picketing

Section B   Picketing and the Civil Law

9.   The law sets out the basic rules which must be observed if picketing is to be carried out, or organised, lawfully. To keep to these rules, attendance for the purpose of picketing may only:
(i) be undertaken in contemplation or furtherance of a trade dispute;
(ii) be carried out by a person attending at or near his own place of work; a trade union official, in addition to attending at or near his own place of work, may also attend at or near the place of work of a member of his trade union whom he is accompanying on the picket line and whom he represents.

Furthermore, the only purpose involved must be peacefully to obtain or communicate information, or peacefully to persuade a person to work or not to work.

10.   Picketing commonly involves persuading workers to break, or interfere with the performance of, their contacts of employment by not going to work. Picketing can also disrupt the business of the employer who is being picketed by interfering with the performance of a commercial contract which the employer has with a customer or supplier. If pickets follow the rules outlined in paragraph 9, however, they may have the protection against civil proceedings afforded by the 'statutory immunities'. These rules, and immunities, are explained more fully in paragraphs 11 to 30 below.

In contemplation or furtherance of a trade dispute
11.   Picketing is lawful only if it is carried out in contemplation or furtherance of a 'trade dispute'. A 'trade dispute' is defined in law so as to cover the matters which normally occasion disputes between employers and workers—such as terms and conditions of employment, the allocation of work, matters of discipline, trade union recognition.

'Secondary' action
12.   The 'statutory immunities' do not apply to protect a threat of, or a call for or other inducement of 'secondary' industrial action. The law defines 'secondary' action—which is sometimes referred to as 'sympathetic' or 'solidarity' action—as that by workers whose employer is not a party to the trade dispute to which the action relates.

13.   However, a worker employed by a party to a trade dispute, picketing at his own place of work may try to persuade another worker, not employed by that employer, to break, or interfere with the performance of, the second worker's contract of employment, and/or to interfere with the performance of a commercial contract. This could happen, for example, if a picket persuaded a lorry driver employed by another employer not to cross the picket line and deliver goods to be supplied, under a commercial contract, to the employer in dispute. Such an act by a picket would be an unlawful inducement to take secondary action unless provision was made to the contrary.

14.   Accordingly, the law contains provisions which make it lawful for a peaceful picket, at the picket's own place of work, to seek to persuade workers other than those employed by the picket's own employer not to work, or not to work normally. To have such protection, the peaceful picketing must be done:
a.   by a worker employed by the employer who is party to the dispute[1]; or
b.   by a trade union official whose attendance is lawful (see paragraphs 22–23 below).

15.   Where an entrance or exit is used jointly by the workers of more than one employer, the workers who are not involved in the dispute to which a picket relates should not be interfered with by picketing activities. Particular care should be taken to ensure that a picketing does not involve calls for a breach, or interference with the performance, of contracts by employees of the other employer(s) who are not involved in the dispute. Observing this principle will help avoid consequences which might otherwise be damaging and disruptive to good industrial relations.

Attendance at or near a picket's own place of work
16.   It is lawful for a person to induce breach, or interference with the performance, of a contract in the course of attendance for the purpose of picketing only if he pickets at or near his own place of work.

17   The expression 'at or near his own place of work' is not further defined in statute law. The provisions mean that, except for those covered by paragraphs 22 and 23 below, lawful picketing must be limited to attendance at, or near, an entrance to or exit from the factory, site or office at which the picket works. Picketing should be confined to a location, or locations, as near as practicable to the place of work.

18   The law does not enable a picket to attend lawfully at an entrance to, or exit from, *any* place of work other than his own. This applies even, for example, if those working at the other place of work are employed by the same employer, or are covered by the same collective bargaining arrangements as the picket.

19.   The law identifies two specific groups in respect of which particular arrangements apply. These groups are:
•   those (eg mobile workers) who work at more than one place; and
•   those for whom it is impracticable to picket at their own place of work because of its location.
The law provides that it is lawful for such workers to picket those premises of their employer from which they work, or those from which their work is administered. In the case of lorry drivers, for example, this will usually mean, in practice, the premises of their employer from which their vehicles operate.

20.   Special provisions also apply to people who are not in work, and who have lost their jobs for reasons connected with the dispute which has occasioned the picketing. This might arise, for example, where the dismissal of a group of employees has led directly to the organisation of a picket, or where an employer has dismissed employees because they refuse to work normally, and some or all

1   However, the peaceful picketing may be done by a worker who is not in employment but was last employed by the employer in dispute in certain circumstances—see paragraph 20.

of those dismissed then wish to set up a picket. In such cases the law provides that it is lawful for a worker to picket at his former place of work. This special arrangement ceases to apply, however to any worker who subsequently takes a job at another place of work.

21.   The law does not protect anyone who pickets without permission on or inside any part of premises which are private property. The law will not, therefore, protect pickets who trespass, or those who organise such trespass, from being sued in the civil courts.

Trade union officials

22.   For the reasons described in Section F of this Code, it may be helpful to the orderly organisation and conduct of picketing for a trade union official[2] to be present on a picket line where his members are picketing. The law provides that it is lawful for a trade union official to picket at any place of work provided that:
(i)   he is accompanying members of his trade union who are picketing lawfully at or near their own place of work; and
(ii) he personally represents those members.

23.   If these conditions are satisfied, then a trade union official has the same legal protection as other pickets who picket lawfully at or near their own place of work. However, the law provides that an official—whether a lay official or an employee of the union—is regarded for this purpose as representing only those members of his union whom he has been specifically appointed or elected to represent. An official cannot, therefore, claim that he represents a group of members simply because they belong to his trade union. He must represent and be responsible for them in the normal course of his trade union duties. For example, it is lawful for an official at a particular place of work—such as a shop steward— who represents members at a particular place of work to be present on a picket line where those members are picketing lawfully; for a branch official to be present only where members of his branch are lawfully picketing; for a regional official to be present only where members of his region are lawfully picketing; for a national official who represents a particular trade group or section within the union, to be present wherever members of that trade group or section are lawfully picketing; and for a national official such as a general secretary or president who represents the whole union to be present wherever any members of his union are picketing lawfully.

Lawful purposes of picketing

24.   In no circumstances does a picket have power, under the law, to require other people to stop, or to compel them to listen or to do what he asks them to do. A person who decides to cross a picket line *must* be allowed to do so. In addition, the law provides a remedy for any union member who is disciplined by his union because he has crossed a picket line.[3]

2   The law defines an 'official of the union' as a person who is an officer of the union (or of a branch or section of the union), or who, not being such an officer, is a person elected or appointed in accordance with the rules of the union to be a representative of its members (or some of them), including any person so elected or appointed who is an employee of the same employer as the members, or one or more of the members, whom he is elected to represent. This could include, for example, a shop steward.
3   A member disciplined for crossing a picket line is 'unjustifiably disciplined'; the remedy for unjustifiable discipline is by complaint to an industrial tribunal. (See also paragraphs 60–61 in Section F of this Code.)

25.   The **only** purposes of picketing declared lawful in statute are:
*   peacefully obtaining and communicating information; and
*   peacefully persuading a person to work or not to work.

26.   The law allows pickets to seek to explain their case to those entering or leaving the picketed premises, and/or to ask them not to enter or leave the premises where the dispute is taking place. This may be done by speaking to people, or it may involve the distribution of leaflets or the carrying of banners or placards putting the pickets' case. **In all cases, however, any such activity must be carried out** *peacefully.*

27.   The law protects peaceful communication and persuasion. It does not give pickets, anyone organising or participating in any activity associated with picketing, or anyone organising a picket, protection against civil proceedings being brought against them for any conduct occurring during the picketing, or associated activity, which amounts to a separate civil wrong such as:
*   unlawful threat or assault;
*   harassment (ie threatening or unreasonable behaviour causing fear or apprehension to those in the vicinity);
*   obstruction of a path, road, entrance or exit to premises;
*   interference (eg because of noise or crowds) in the rights of those in neighbouring properties (ie 'private nuisance');
*   trespassing on private property.

28.   Both individual pickets, and anyone—including a union—organising a picket or associated activity, should be careful not to commit such civil wrongs. It is possible, for example, that material on placards carried by pickets—or, for that matter, by those involved in activities associated with picketing—could be defamatory or amount to a threat or harassment. Pickets will also have no legal protection if they do or say things, or make offensive gestures at people, which amount to unlawful threat or harassment. Section C of this Code explains that such actions may also give rise to prosecution under the criminal law.

29.   Similarly, if the noise or other disturbance caused to residents of an area by pickets, or by those associated with picketing activity, amounts to a civil wrong, those involved or responsible are not protected by the law from proceedings being brought against them.

30.   Similar proceedings apply in respect of any breach of the criminal law by pickets, or their organiser. As explained in Section C of this Code, a picket, or anyone involved in an associated activity, who threatens or intimidates someone, or obstructs an entrance to a workplace, or causes a breach of the peace, commits a criminal offence. Where pickets commit a criminal offence, then in many circumstances they will not be acting peacefully; consequently, any immunity under the civil law will be lost.

Seeking redress
31.   An employer, a worker, or anyone else who is party to a contract which is, or may be, broken or interfered with by unlawful picketing has a civil law remedy. He may apply to the court for an order[4] preventing, or stopping, the unlawful

4   An injunction in England and Wales; an interdict in Scotland.

picketing, or its organisation. Such a person may also claim damages from those responsible where the activities of the unlawful picket have caused him loss. An order can be sought against the person—which could include a particular trade union or unions—on whose instructions or advice the unlawful picketing is taking place, or will take place.

32.   In making an order, the court has authority to require a trade union which has acted unlawfully to take such steps as are considered necessary to ensure that there is no further call for, or other organisation of, unlawful picketing. An order may be granted by the court on an interim basis, pending a full hearing of the case.

33.   If a court order is made, it can apply not only to the person or union named in the order, but to anyone else acting on his behalf or on his instructions. Thus an organiser of unlawful picketing cannot avoid liability, for example, merely by changing the people on the unlawful picket line from time to time.

34.   Similarly, anyone who is wronged in any other way by a picket can seek an order from the court to get the unlawful act stopped or prevented, and/or for damages. Thus, for example, if picketing, or associated activities, give rise to unlawful disturbance to residents in the vicinity, one or more of the residents so affected can apply to the court for such an order and/or for damages. Such proceedings might be taken against individual pickets, or the person—including a union where applicable—responsible for the unlawful act.

35.   If a court order is not obeyed, or is ignored, those who sought it can go back to court and ask to have those concerned declared in contempt of court. Anyone who is found to be in contempt of court may face heavy fines, or other penalties, which the court may consider appropriate. For example, a union may be deprived of its assets through sequestration, where the union's funds are placed in the control of a person appointed by the court who may, in particular, pay any fines or legal costs arising from the court proceedings. Similarly, if a person knows that such an order has been made against someone, or some union, and yet aids and abets that person to disobey or ignore the order, he may also be found to be acting in contempt of court and liable to be punished by the court.

Determining whether a union is responsible
36.   Pickets will usually attend at a place of work for the purpose of persuading others not to work, or not to work normally, and may thereby be inducing them to breach, or interfere with the performance of, contracts. The law lays down rules which determine whether a union will be held liable for any such acts of inducement which are unlawful.

37.   The law provides that a union will be held responsible for such an unlawful act if it is done, authorised or endorsed by:
a.   the union's principal executive committee, president, or general secretary;
b.   any person given power under the union's own rules to do, authorise or endorse acts of the kind in question; or
c.   any other committee of the union, or any official of the union[5]—including

---

5   See footnote to paragraph 22 for the relevant definition of 'official'. In this case, however, an act will also be taken to have been done by an 'official of the union' if it was done (or authorised

those who are employed by the union, and those, like shop stewards, who are not.[6]

A union will be held responsible for such an act by such a body or person regardless of any provisions to the contrary in its own rules, or anything in any other contract or rule of law.

38.   Pickets may, of course, commit civil wrongs other than inducing breach, or interference with the performance, of contracts. The question of whether a union will be held responsible for those wrongs will be determined according to common law principles of liability, rather than by reference to the rules described in paragraph 37 above.

The need for a ballot

39.   If what is done in the course of picketing amounts to a call for industrial action, and is an act for which the union is responsible in law, the union can only have the protection of statutory immunity if it has first held a properly-conducted secret ballot.

40.   The law requires that entitlement to vote in such a ballot must be given to all the union's members who it is reasonable at the time of the ballot for the union to believe will be called upon to take part in, or continue with, the industrial action, and to no other member. The ballot must produce a majority of those voting which is in favour of taking, or continuing with, industrial action. These, and other requirements of the law in respect of such ballots, are restated in the statutory Code of Practice 'Trade Union Ballots on Industrial Action (1st Revision).'

Section C   Picketing and the criminal law

41.   If a picket commits a criminal offence he is just as liable to be prosecuted as any other member of the public who breaks the law. The immunity provided under the civil law does not protect him in any way.

42.   The criminal law protects the right of every person to go about his lawful daily business free from interference by others. No one is under any obligation to stop when a picket asks him to do so, or if he does stop, to comply with a request, for example, not to go into work. Everyone has the right, if he wishes to do so, to cross a picket line in order to go into his place of work or to deliver or collect goods. A picket may exercise peaceful persuasion, but if he goes beyond that and tries by means other than peaceful persuasion to deter another person from exercising those rights he may commit a criminal offence.

---

or endorsed) by a group of persons, or any member of a group, to which such an official belonged at the relevant time if the group's purposes included organising or co-ordinating industrial action.

6   However, if an act which is done (or authorised or endorsed) by a union committee or official is 'effectively repudiated' by the union's principal executive committee, president or general secretary, the union will not be held responsible in law. In order to avoid liability in this way, the act concerned must be repudiated by any of these as soon as reasonably practicable after it has come to their knowledge. In addition, the union must, without delay:

   a.   give written notice of the repudiation to the committee or official in question; and
   b.   do its best to give individual written notice of the fact and date of the repudiation to: (i) every member of the union who it has reason to believe is taking part—or might otherwise take part—in industrial action as a result of the act; and (ii) the employer of every such member.

43.   Among other matters, it is a criminal offence for pickets (as for others):

*   to use threatening, abusive or insulting words or behaviour, or disorderly behaviour within the sight or hearing of any person—whether a worker seeking to cross a picket line, an employer, an ordinary member of the public, or the police—likely to be caused harassment, alarm or distress by such conduct;

*   to use threatening, abusive or insulting words or behaviour towards any person with intent to cause fear of violence or to provoke violence;

*   to use or threaten unlawful violence;

*   to obstruct the highway or the entrance to premises or to seek physically to bar the passage of vehicles or persons by lying down in the road, linking arms across or circling in the road, or jostling or physically restraining those entering or leaving the premises;

*   to be in possession of an offensive weapon;

*   intentionally or recklessly to damage property;

*   to engage in violent, disorderly or unruly behaviour or to take any action which is likely to lead to a breach of the peace;

*   to obstruct a police officer in the execution of his duty.

44.   A picket has no right under the law to require a vehicle to stop or to be stopped. The law allows him only to ask a driver to stop by words or signals. A picket may not physically obstruct a vehicle if the driver decides to drive on or, indeed, in any other circumstances. A driver must—as on all other occasions—exercise due care and attention when approaching or driving past a picket line, and may not drive in such a manner as to give rise to a reasonably foreseeable risk of injury.

Section D   Role of the police

45.   It is not the function of the police to take a view of the merits of a particular dispute. They have a general duty to uphold the law and keep the peace, whether on the picket line or elsewhere. The law gives the police discretion to take whatever measures may reasonably be considered necessary to ensure that picketing remains peaceful and orderly.

46.   The police have **no** responsibility for enforcing the **civil law**. An employer cannot require the police to help in identifying the pickets against whom he wishes to seek an order from the civil court, nor is the job of the police to enforce the terms of an order. Enforcement of an order on the application of a plaintiff is a matter for the court and its officer. The police may, however, decide to assist the officers of the court if they think there may be a breach of the peace.

47.   As regards the criminal law the police have considerable discretionary powers to limit the number of pickets at any one place where they have reasonable cause to fear disorder.[7] The law does not impose a specific limit on the number of people who may picket at any one place; nor does this Code affect in any way the discretion of the police to limit the number of people on a particular picket

---

7   In *Piddington v Bates* (1960) the High Court upheld the decision of a police constable in the circumstances of that case to limit the number of pickets to two.

line. It is for the police to decide, taking into account all the circumstances, whether the number of pickets at any particular place provides reasonable grounds for the belief that a breach of the peace is likely to occur. If a picket does not leave the picket line when asked to do so by the police, he is liable to be arrested for obstruction either of the highway or of a police officer in the execution of his duty if the obstruction is such as to cause, or be likely to cause, a breach of the peace.

Section E   Limiting numbers of pickets

48.   Violence and disorder on the picket line is more likely to occur if there are excessive numbers of pickets. Wherever large numbers of people with strong feelings are involved there is a danger that the situation will get out of control, and that those concerned will run the risk of committing an offence, with consequent arrest and prosecution, or of committing a civil wrong which exposes them, or anyone organising them, to civil proceedings.

49.   This is particularly so whenever people seek by sheer weight of numbers to stop others going into work or delivering or collecting goods. In such cases, what is intended is not peaceful persuasion, but obstruction or harassment—if not intimidation. Such a situation is often described as 'mass picketing'. In fact, it is not picketing in its lawful sense of an attempt at peaceful persuasion, and may well result in a breach of the peace or other criminal offences.

50.   Moreover, anyone seeking to demonstrate support for those in dispute should keep well away from any picket line so as not to create a risk of breach of the peace or other criminal offence being committed on that picket line. Just as with a picket itself, the numbers involved in any such demonstration should not be excessive, and the demonstration should be conducted lawfully. Section 14 of the Public Order Act 1986 provides the police with the power to impose conditions (for example, as to numbers, location and duration) on public assemblies of 20 or more people where the assembly is likely to result in serious public disorder; or serious damage to property; or serious disruption to the life of the community; or if its purpose is to coerce.

51.   Large numbers on a picket line are also likely to give rise to fear and resentment amongst those seeking to cross that picket line, even where no criminal offence is committed. They exacerbate disputes and sour relations not only between management and employees but between the pickets and their fellow employees. **Accordingly pickets and their organisers should ensure that in general the number of pickets does not exceed six at any entrance to, or exit from, a workplace; frequently a smaller number will be appropriate.**

Section F   Organisation of picketing

52.   Sections B and C of this Code outline aspects of the civil law and the criminal law, as they may apply to pickets, and to anyone, including a trade union, who organises a picket. While it is possible that a picket may be entirely 'spontaneous', it is much more likely that it will be organised by an identifiable individual or group.

53.   Paragraphs 36–38 in Section B of this Code describe how to identify whether a trade union is, in fact, responsible in terms of civil law liability, for certain acts. As explained in these paragraphs, the law means, for example, that if such an act takes place in the course of picketing, and if a trade union official has done, authorised or endorsed the act, then the official's union will be responsible in law unless the act is 'effectively repudiated' by the union's national leadership.

Functions of the picket organiser

54.   Wherever picketing is 'official' (ie organised by a trade union), an experienced person, preferably a trade union official who represents those picketing, should always be in charge of the picket line. He should have a letter of authority from his union which he can show to the police officers or to people who want to cross the picket line. Even when he is not on the picket line himself he should be available to give the pickets advice if a problem arises.

55.   A picket should not be designated as an 'official' picket unless it is actually organised by a trade union. Nor should pickets claim the authority and support of a union unless the union is prepared to accept the consequent responsibility. In particular, union authority and support should not be claimed by the pickets if the union has, in fact, repudiated calls to take industrial action made, or being made, in the course of the picketing.

56.   Whether a picket is 'official' or 'unofficial', an organiser of pickets should maintain close contact with the police. Advance consultation with the police is always in the best interests of all concerned. In particular the organiser and the pickets should seek directions from the police on the number of people who should be present on the picket line at any one time and on where they should stand in order to avoid obstructing the highway.

57.   The other main functions of the picket organiser should include ensuring that:
- the pickets understand the law and are aware of the provisions of this Code, and that the picketing is conducted peacefully and lawfully;
- badges or armbands, which authorised pickets should wear so that they are clearly identified, are distributed to such pickets and are worn while they are picketing;
- workers from other places of work do not join the picket line, and that any offers of support on the picket line from outsiders are refused;
- the number of pickets at any entrance to, or exit from, a place of work is not so great as to give rise to fear and resentment amongst those seeking to cross that picket line (see paragraph 51 in Section E of this Code);
- close contact with his own union office (if any), and with the offices of other unions if they are involved in the picketing, is established and maintained;
- such special arrangements as may be necessary for essential supplies, services or operations (see paragraphs 62–64 in Section G of this Code) are understood and observed by the pickets.

Consultation with other trade unions

58.   Where several unions are involved in a dispute, they should consult each other about the organisation of any picketing. It is important that they should

agree how the picketing is to be carried out, how many pickets there should be from each union, and who should have overall responsibility for organising them.

Right to cross picket lines

59. Everyone has the right to decide for himself whether he will cross a picket line. Disciplinary action should not be taken or threatened by a union against a member on the grounds that he has crossed a picket line.

60. If a union disciplines any member for crossing a picket line, the member will have been 'unjustifiably disciplined'. In such a case, the individual can make a complaint to an industrial tribunal. If the tribunal finds the complaint well-founded, it will make a declaration to that effect.

61. If the union has not lifted the penalty imposed on the member, or if it has not taken all necessary steps to reverse anything done in giving effect to the penalty, an application for compensation should be made to the Employment Appeal Tribunal (EAT). In any other case, the individual can apply to an industrial tribunal for compensation. The EAT or tribunal will award whatever compensation it considers just and equitable in all the circumstances, subject to a specified maximum amount. Where the application is made to the EAT, there will normally be a specified minimum award.

Section G   Essential supplies, services and operations

62. Pickets, and anyone organising a picket should take very great care to ensure that their activities do not cause distress, hardship or inconvenience to members of the public who are not involved in the dispute. Particular care should be taken to ensure that the movement of essential goods and supplies, the carrying out of essential maintenance of plant and equipment, and the provision of services essential to the life of the community are not impeded, still less prevented.

63. The following list of essential supplies and services is provided as an illustration of the kind of activity which requires special protection to comply with the recommendations in paragraph 62 above. However, **the list is not intended to be comprehensive**. The supplies and services which may need to be protected in accordance with these recommendations could cover different activities in different circumstances. Subject to this *caveat*, 'essential supplies, services and operations' include:

- the production, packaging, marketing and/or distribution of medical and pharmaceutical products;
- the provision of supplies and services essential to health and welfare institutions, eg hospitals, old peoples' homes;
- the provision of heating fuel for schools, residential institutions, medical institutions and private residential accommodation;
- the production and provision of other supplies for which there is a crucial need during a crisis in the interests of public health and safety (eg chlorine, lime and other agents for water purification; industrial and medical gases; sand and salt for road gritting purposes);
- activities necessary to the maintenance of plant and machinery;
- the proper care of livestock;
- necessary safety procedures (including such procedures as are necessary to maintain plant and machinery);

- the production, packaging, marketing and/or distribution of food and animal feeding stuffs;
- the operation of essential services, such as police, fire, ambulance, medical and nursing services, air safety, coastguard and air sea rescue services, and services provided by voluntary bodies (eg Red Cross and St John's ambulances, meals on wheels, hospital car services), and mortuaries, burial and cremation services.

64. Arrangements to ensure these safeguards for essential supplies, services and operations should be agreed in advance between the pickets, or anyone organising the picket, and the employer, or employers, concerned.

(g) Code of Practice
Industrial Action Ballots and Notice to Employers

Preamble

The legal framework for the operation of this Code is explained in Annex 1 and in its main text. While every effort has been made to ensure that explanations included in the Code are accurate, only the courts can give authoritative interpretations of the law.

The Code's provisions apply equally to men and to women, but for simplicity the masculine pronoun is used throughout. Wherever it appears in the Code the word 'court' is used to mean the High Court in England and Wales and the Court of Session in Scotland, but without prejudice to the Code's relevance to any proceedings before any other court.

Passages in this Code which are printed in bold are re-statements of provisions in primary legislation.

Section A   Introduction

1.   This Code provides practical guidance to trade unions and employers to promote the improvement of industrial relations and good practice in the conduct of trade union industrial action ballots.

2.   A union is legally responsible for organising industrial action only if it 'authorises or endorses' the action. Authorisation would take place before the industrial action starts, and endorsement after it has previously started as unofficial action[1].

3.   Apart from certain small accidental failures that are unlikely to affect the result, a failure to satisfy the statutory requirements[2] relating to the ballot or giving employers notice of industrial action will give grounds for proceedings against a union by an employer, a customer or supplier of an employer, or an individual member of the public claiming that an effect or likely effect of the industrial action would be to prevent or delay the supply of goods or services to him or to reduce the quality of goods or services so supplied. With the exception of failures to comply with the requirements to give notice to employers, these will also give grounds for action by the union's members.

4.   The Code does not deal with other matters which may affect a union's liability in respect of industrial action. For example, the law will give no protection against proceedings to a union which organises secondary action, intimidatory or violent

---

1   *A note on trade union legal liability for the organisation of industrial action is set out in*
    Annex 1 to this Code.
2   *Set out in sections 226-232A and section 234A of the Trade Union and Labour Relations*
    (Consolidation) Act 1992 as amended by the Trade Union Reform and Employment Rights
    Act 1993 and the Employment Relations Act 1999.

picketing, industrial action which is not 'in contemplation or furtherance of a trade dispute'[3], industrial action to establish or maintain any closed shop practice or in support of a worker dismissed while taking part in unofficial industrial action. Nor does it apply to union election ballots, ballots on union political funds or ballots on union recognition or derecognition arranged for by the Central Arbitration Committee under section 70A of and Schedule A1 to the Trade Union and Labour Relations (Consolidation) Act 1992 ('the 1992 Act')[4]. These are subject to separate statutory requirements.

Legal status

5. The Code itself imposes no legal obligations and failure to observe it does not by itself render anyone liable to proceedings. But section 207 of the 1992 Act provides that any provisions of the Code are to be admissible in evidence and are to be taken into account in proceedings before any court where it considers them relevant.

Section B   Whether a ballot as appropriate

Observing procedural agreements

6.   An industrial action ballot should not take place until any agreed procedures, whether formal or otherwise, which might lead to the resolution of a dispute without the need for industrial action have been completed and consideration has been given to resolving the dispute by other means, including seeking assistance from the Advisory, Conciliation and Arbitration Service (ACAS). A union should hold a ballot on industrial action only if it is contemplating the organisation of industrial action.

Balloting by more than one union

7.   Where more than one union decides that it wishes to ballot members working for the same employer in connection with the same dispute, the arrangements for the different ballots should be co-ordinated so that, as far as practicable, they are held at the same time and the results are announced simultaneously.

Section C   Preparing for an industrial action ballot

Arranging for independent scrutiny of the ballot

8.   For a ballot where more than 50 members are given entitlement to vote (see paragraph 21below), the union must appoint a qualified person as the scrutineer of the ballot[5]. For a person to be qualified for appointment as scrutineer of an industrial action ballot, he must be among those specified in an

---

3   *The term 'trade dispute' is defined in section 244 of the 1992 Act.*
4   *Inserted by the Employment Relations Act 1999.*
5   *Where separate workplace ballots are required, the scrutiny procedures must be followed in respect of each separate ballot if the number of members given entitlement to vote aggregated across all of the ballots is more than 50.*

order made by the Secretary of State[6] and the union must not have grounds for believing that he will carry out the functions which the law requires other than competently or that his independence in relation to the union might reasonably be called into question.

9.   The scrutineer's terms of appointment must require him to take such steps as appear appropriate to him for the purpose of enabling him to make a report to the union as soon as reasonably practicable after the date of the ballot (ie the last day on which votes may be cast, if they may be cast on more than one day), and in any event not later than four weeks after that date.

10.   The union must ensure that the scrutineer carries out the functions required to be part of his terms of appointment, and that there is no interference with this from the union, or any of its members, officials or employees; and comply with all reasonable requests made by the scrutineer for the purpose of carrying out those functions.

11.   It may be desirable to appoint the scrutineer before steps are taken to satisfy any of the other requirements of the law to make it easier for the scrutineer to satisfy himself whether what is done conforms to the legal requirements.

12.   In some circumstances, it may help ensure adequate standards for the conduct of the ballot or simplify the balloting process if a union gives the scrutineer additional tasks to carry out on the union's behalf, such as:-
•   supervising the production and distribution of voting papers;
•   being the person to whom the voting papers are returned by those voting in the ballot; and
•   retaining custody of all returned voting papers for a set period after the ballot.

13.   Although the scrutiny requirement does not apply to ballots where 50 or fewer members are entitled to vote, a union may want to consider whether the appointment of a scrutineer would still be of benefit in enabling it to demonstrate compliance with the statutory requirements more easily.

Providing ballot notice to employers

14.   The union must take such steps as are reasonably necessary to ensure that any employer who it is reasonable for the union to believe will be the employer of any of its members who will be given entitlement to vote receives written notice of the ballot not later than the seventh day before the intended opening day of the ballot (ie the first day on which a voting paper is sent to any person entitled to vote). That notice must:-
•   state that the union intends to hold the ballot;
•   specify the date which the union reasonably believes will be the opening day of the ballot; and
•   contain such information in the union's possession as would help the employer to make plans (for example, as appropriate, to enable him to warn

6   *In broad terms, the current order (SI 1993 No. 1909) covers practising solicitors, qualified accountants and three named bodies (Electoral Reform Ballot Services Limited; The Industrial Society; and Unity Security Balloting Services Limited, now called Election.Com Limited).*

his customers of the possibility of disruption so that they can make alternative arrangements or to take steps to ensure the health and safety of his employees or the public or to safeguard equipment which might otherwise suffer damage from being shut down or left without supervision) **and bring information to the attention of those of his employees who it is reasonable for the union to believe (at that time) will be entitled to vote. In particular, the union must provide as a minimum any information which it possesses as to the number, category or workplace of the employees concerned. But a notice will not fail to satisfy the requirements simply because it does not name any employees.**

15.   To avoid the risk of legal action, the union should allow sufficient time for delivery, use a suitable means of transmission (such as first class post, courier, fax, email or hand delivery) and consider obtaining confirmation that the employer has received the notice, by using recorded delivery or otherwise.

16.   It may also reduce the risk of litigation for a union to check that an employer accepts that the information provided complies with the requirements of section 226A(2)(c) of the 1992 Act. Similarly, it would be in the interests of good industrial relations for an employer who believes the notice he has received does not contain sufficient information to comply with the statutory requirements to raise that with the union promptly before pursuing the matter in the court.

17.   It is for the union to satisfy the requirement to provide sufficient notice. In reaching a decision on what information needs to be provided, the union may find it helpful to consider what information an employer is likely to have available, apart from that in the notice itself, which could help it make plans and bring information to those entitled to vote. Depending on the circumstances, factors such as the size and turnover rate of the employer's workforce; the variety of work done for the employer; the number of locations at which it is carried out; and any previous experience of ballot notifications concerning the same employer may be relevant to a decision about how much detail needs to be included.

18.   In some circumstances the requirement is likely to be satisfied by indicating to the employer that entitlement to vote will be given to all of the union's members engaged on, for example, a specified kind of work activity, or in a certain grade, or at a particular location. In some cases, if the employer would otherwise be left in doubt, more specific information, such as a combination of these items of information, may be needed, but in no case will a union be required to give employees' names. Ultimately, it will always be a question on the facts of a particular case whether the notice gives an employer the required details.

Providing sample voting paper(s) to employers

19.   **The union must take such steps as are reasonably necessary to ensure that any employer who it is reasonable for the union to believe will be the employer of any of its members who will be given entitlement to vote receives a sample voting paper (and a sample of any variant of that voting paper) not later than the third day before the opening day of the ballot. Where more than one employer's workers are being balloted, it is sufficient to send each employer only the voting paper or papers which will be sent to his employees.**

20.   If the sample voting paper is available in time, the union may wish to include it with the notice of intention to ballot. As with the ballot notice, the risk of non-compliance can be reduced by allowing enough time, using appropriate means of transmission and, possibly, by obtaining confirmation of receipt.

Establishing entitlement to vote (the 'balloting constituency')

21.   Entitlement to vote in the ballot must be given to all the union's members who it is reasonable at the time of the ballot for the union to believe will be induced (whether that inducement will be successful or not) to take part in or continue with the industrial action, and to no other members[7].

22.   The validity of the ballot will not however be affected if the union subsequently induces members to take part in or continue with industrial action who at the time of the ballot:-
- **were not members; or**
- **were members but who it was not reasonable to expect would be induced to take action** (for example because they changed jobs after the ballot)**.**

23.   It should also be noted that accidental failures to comply with the requirements on:
- **who is given entitlement to vote,**
- **the dispatch of voting papers,**
- **giving members the opportunity to vote conveniently by post, and**
- **balloting merchant seamen employed in a ship at sea or outside Great Britain at some time during the voting period**

will be disregarded if, taken together, they are on a scale unlikely to affect the ballot's result.

Balloting members at more than one workplace

24.   Where the members of a union with different workplaces are to be balloted, a separate ballot will be necessary for each workplace unless one of the conditions set out below is met. It will be unlawful for the union to organise industrial action at any such workplace where a majority of those voting in the ballot for that workplace have not voted 'Yes' in response to the relevant required question (or questions) (see paragraph 30 below). (If an employee works at or from a single set of premises, his workplace is those premises. If not, it is the premises with which his employment has the closest connection.)

---

7   *The union may choose whether or not to give a vote to any 'overseas member', ie any member (other than a merchant seaman or offshore worker) who is outside Great Britain for the whole of the voting period. However, members who may be called upon to take part in or continue with the industrial action, and will be in Northern Ireland for the whole of the voting period, must be given entitlement to vote in a ballot where: (i) the ballot is a workplace ballot at their workplace in Great Britain; or (ii) they work in Northern Ireland but it is intended that they should be called upon to take part in the industrial action alongside their counterparts in Britain, and the ballot is a general ballot covering places of work in both Northern Ireland and Great Britain.*

25.   In summary, the conditions for holding a single ballot for more than one workplace are:-

- **at each of the workplaces covered by the single ballot there is at least one member of the union affected[8] by the dispute; or**
- **entitlement to vote in the single ballot is given, and limited, to all of a union's members who, according to the union's reasonable belief, are employed in a particular occupation or occupations by one employer or any of a number of employers with whom the union is in dispute; or**
- **entitlement to vote in the single ballot is given, and limited, to all of a union's members who are employed by a particular employer or any of a number of employers with whom the union is in dispute.**

It is possible for a union to hold more than one ballot on a dispute at a single workplace. If the conditions above are met, some or all of those ballots may also cover members in other workplaces.

The balloting method

26.   Votes must be recorded by the individual voter marking a voting paper. Voting papers must be sent out by post and members must be enabled conveniently to return them by post at no direct expense to themselves[9]. In practice, this means that those properly entitled to vote should be supplied with pre-paid reply envelopes in which to return the voting paper.

27.   The period between sending out voting papers (ie the opening day of the ballot) and the date by which completed voting papers should be returned should be long enough for the voting papers to be distributed and returned and for the members concerned to consider their vote. The appropriate period may vary according to such factors as the geographical dispersion of the workforce, their familiarity or otherwise with the issues in the dispute, the class of post used and whether the ballot is being held at a time of year when members are more than usually likely to be away from home or the workplace, for example during the summer holidays. Generally, seven days should be the minimum period where voting papers are sent out and returned by first class post and fourteen days where second class post is used, although – very exceptionally – shorter periods may be possible for ballots with very small, concentrated constituencies who can be expected to be familiar with the terms of the dispute.

28.   In order to reduce the likelihood of dispute over whether or not sufficient time has been allowed, the union may wish to consider obtaining one or more certificates of posting to confirm the date when voting papers were actually put into the post, and the number sent out.

8   *Section 228A(5) of the 1992 Act defines for this purpose which members are affected by a dispute.*

9   *There is a limited exception for the balloting of union members who are merchant seamen, where the union reasonably believes that they will be employed in a ship at sea (or outside Great Britain) at some time in the period during which votes may be cast and that it will be convenient for them to vote while on the ship or where the ship is. So far as reasonably practicable, the union must ensure that, in these circumstances, those members get a voting paper while on board ship (or at the place where the ship is located), and an opportunity to vote on board ship (or at that place). The recommendations in this Code should be applied to such ballots, however, save to the extent that they are irrelevant because the dispatch of voting papers is not by post.*

Voting papers

29. The voting paper must:-
* where applicable, state the name of the independent scrutineer;
* clearly specify the address to which, and the date by which, it is to be returned;
* be marked with a number, which is one of series of consecutive numbers used to give a different number to each voting paper;
* make clear whether voters are being asked if they are prepared to take part in industrial action which consists of a strike, or in industrial action short of a strike, which for this purpose includes overtime bans and call-out bans; and
* specify the person or persons (and/or class or classes of person/s) who the union intends to have authority to make the first call for industrial action to which the ballot relates, in the event of a vote in favour of industrial action[10].

30. While the question (or questions) may be framed in different ways, the voter must be asked to say by answering 'Yes' or 'No' whether he is willing to take part in or continue with the industrial action. If the union has not decided whether the industrial action would consist of a strike or action short of a strike (including overtime bans or call-out bans), separate questions in respect of each type of action must appear on the voting paper.

31. The relevant required question (or questions) should be simply expressed. Neither they, nor anything else which appears on the voting paper, should be presented in such a way as to encourage a voter to answer one way rather than another as a result of that presentation. It is not in general good practice for the union to include additional questions on the voting paper (for example, asking if voters agree with the union's opinion on the merits of the dispute or are prepared to 'support' industrial action), but if it chooses to do so they should be clearly separate from the required question(s).

32. The following words must appear on every voting paper:-

'If you take part in a strike or other industrial action, you may be in breach of your contract of employment. However, if you are dismissed for taking part in a strike or other industrial action which is called officially and is otherwise lawful, the dismissal will be unfair if it takes place fewer than eight weeks after you started taking part in the action, and depending on the circumstances may be unfair if it takes place later.'

This statement must not be qualified or commented upon by anything else on the voting paper.

33. An example voting paper containing the information required by law and other useful information is set out in Annex 2 to this Code. Factual information as

---

10 *Where a person who has not been not specified on the voting paper calls industrial action before it is first called by a specified person, then – in order to be certain that the ballot will give protection against legal proceedings – the union should if possible ensure that the call by the unspecified person is effectively repudiated.*

indicated would appear in the square brackets and either or both questions could be used as appropriate.

Printing and distribution of the voting papers

34.   The union will wish to ensure that arrangements for producing and distributing voting papers will prevent mistakes which might invalidate the ballot. If in doubt, the independent scrutineer may be able to provide useful advice.

35.   If there is no independent scrutineer, or if a union decides that it cannot follow the advice offered by the scrutineer, it should consider:-
*   printing the voting papers on a security background to prevent duplication;
*   whether the arrangements proposed for printing (or otherwise producing) the voting papers, and for their distribution to those entitled to vote in the ballot, offer all concerned sufficient assurance of security.

Communication with members

36.   A union should give relevant information to its members entitled to vote in the ballot, including (so far as practicable):-
*   the background to the ballot and the issues to which the dispute relates;
*   the nature and timing of the industrial action the union proposes to organise if a majority vote 'Yes';
*   any considerations in respect of turnout or size of the majority vote in the ballot that will be taken into account in deciding whether to call for industrial action; and
*   the possible consequences for workers if they take industrial action.

In doing so, the union should ensure that any information it gives to members in connection with the ballot is accurate and not misleading.

Section D   Holding an industrial action ballot

37.   In an industrial action ballot:-
*   **every person entitled to vote must be allowed to do so without interference from, or constraint imposed by, the union or any of its members, officials or employees;**
*   **as far as reasonably practicable, every person entitled to vote must be:-**
    -   sent a voting paper by post to his home address, or another address which he has asked the union (in writing) to treat as his postal address;
    -   given a convenient opportunity to vote; and
    -   allowed to do so without incurring any direct cost to himself (see also paragraph 26); and
*   **as far as reasonably practicable, the ballot must be conducted in such a way as to ensure that those voting do so in secret.**

Checks on number of voting papers for return

38.   In order to reduce the risk of failures to satisfy the statutory requirements and invalidating the ballot, the union should establish an appropriate checking system so that:-

- no-one properly entitled to vote is accidentally disenfranchised, for example through the use of an out of date or otherwise inaccurate membership list; and
- votes from anyone not properly entitled to vote are excluded.

The independent scrutineer may provide advice on this.

Ensuring secrecy of voting

39. Any list of those entitled to vote should be compiled, and the voting papers themselves handled, so as to preserve the anonymity of the voter so far as this is consistent with the proper conduct of the ballot.

40. Steps should be taken to ensure that a voter's anonymity is preserved when a voting paper is returned. This means, for example, that:-
- envelopes in which voting papers are to be posted should have no distinguishing marks from which the identity of the voter could be established; and
- the procedures for counting voting papers should not prejudice the statutory requirement for secret voting.

Section E   Following an industrial action ballot

41.   The union must:-
- **ensure that the votes given in an industrial action ballot are fairly and accurately counted;**
- **observe its obligations in connection with the notification of details of the result of an industrial action ballot to all those entitled to vote in the ballot and their employers; and**
- **provide a copy of the scrutineer's report on the ballot to anyone entitled to receive it.**

An inaccuracy in the counting of the votes is to be disregarded if it is both accidental and on a scale which could not affect the result of the ballot. Whether an accidental inaccuracy meets this test in practice will depend on the closeness of the ballot result.

Counting votes accurately and fairly

42. Where the union itself is conducting the ballot, it may wish to apply some or all of the following procedures to secure that the statutory requirements have been complied with:-
- ensuring all unused or unissued voting papers are retained only for so long as is necessary after the time allowed for voting has passed to allow the necessary information for checking the number of voting papers issued and used to be prepared, and that a record is kept of such voting papers when they are destroyed;
- rejection of completed voting papers received after the official close of voting or the time set for receipt of voting papers;
- settlement well in advance of the actual ballot of the organisational

arrangements for conducting the count of votes cast, and making available equipment or facilities needed in the conduct of the count to those concerned;
- storage of all voting papers received at the counting location under secure conditions from when they arrive until they are counted;
- setting clear criteria to enable those counting the votes to decide which voting papers are to be rejected as 'spoiled', and designating someone who is neither directly affected by the dispute to which the ballot relates nor a union official who regularly represents any of those entitled to vote in the ballot to adjudicate on any borderline cases;
- locking and securing the counting room during the period during which votes are to be counted whenever counting staff are not actually at work; and
- storage of voting papers, once counted, under secure conditions (ie so that they cannot be tampered with in any way and are available for checking if necessary) for at least 6 months after the ballot.

The union may wish to consider putting the counting exercise as a whole into the hands of the independent scrutineer.

Announcing details of the result of a ballot

43.   A union must, as soon as reasonably practicable after holding an industrial action ballot, take steps to inform all those entitled to vote[11], and their employer(s), of the number of:-
- **votes cast in the ballot;**
- **individuals answering 'Yes' to the required question (or questions);**
- **individuals answering 'No' to the required question (or questions); and**
- **spoiled voting papers.**

Where separate workplace ballots are required (see paragraphs 24 and 25 above), these details must be notified separately for each such workplace to those entitled to vote there.

44.   To help ensure that its result can be notified as required, the union may wish to consider, for example:-
- designating a 'Returning Officer' for the centralised count of votes cast in the ballot (or separate 'Returning Officers' for counts conducted at different locations) to whom the results will be notified in the form required prior to their announcement;
- organising the counting of votes in such a way that the information required to satisfy the relevant statutory requirements can be easily obtained after the counting process is over;

---

1 1   *If overseas members of a trade union have been given entitlement to vote in an industrial action ballot the detailed information about its result need not be sent to them, but the information supplied to non-overseas members in accordance with the statutory requirements must distinguish between votes cast, individuals voting, and spoiled ballot papers to show which details relate to overseas, and which to non-overseas, members. (For these purposes members in Northern Ireland given entitlement to vote do not count as 'overseas' members.)*

- using its own journals, local communications news-sheets, company or union branch noticeboards to publicise the details of the ballot result to its members; and
- checking with relevant employers that the ballot result details notified to them have arrived.

45.   Before giving the seven-day notice to employers of intended industrial action, the union must have taken the required steps to notify the relevant employer(s) of the ballot result details. Where the employees of more than one employer have been balloted, a failure to provide the required ballot result details to a particular employer or employers will mean that if the union organises industrial action by the workers of that employer or those employers it will not have the support of a ballot.

46.   If the inducement of industrial action to which the ballot relates is to be capable of being protected by the law, some part of the action must be induced and start to take place within four weeks from the date of the ballot (ie the last day on which votes may be cast in the ballot) or such longer period not exceeding eight weeks as the union and employer may agree[12]. (To reduce the risk of misunderstanding, both parties may find it helpful for such agreements to be in writing.) **If a ballot results in a 'Yes' vote for both a strike and action short of a strike and action short of a strike is induced and starts to take place within the relevant period, the ballot would also continue to protect strike action subsequently, and vice versa.**

Obtaining, and providing copies of, the scrutineer's report

47.   Where more than 50 members are given entitlement to vote, a union must appoint an independent scrutineer, whose terms of appointment must include the production of a report on the conduct of the ballot. This report must be produced as soon as reasonably practicable after the date of the ballot, and in any event not later than four weeks after that date.

48.   The union must provide a copy of the scrutineer's report to any union member who was entitled to vote in the ballot, or any employer of such a member, who requests one within six months of the date of the ballot. The copy must be

---

12   *A union may be allowed to make its first call for industrial action more than four weeks after the date of the ballot if either (a) the employer and union agree on an extension, for example to enable talks which are making progress to continue, of up to eight weeks after the date of the ballot or (b) an injunction granted by a court or an undertaking given by the union to the court prohibits the union from calling for industrial action during some part, or the whole, of the four weeks following the date of the ballot, and the injunction subsequently lapses or is set aside or the union is released from its undertaking. In the latter case, a union may forthwith apply to the court for an order which, if granted, would provide that the period during which the prohibition had effect would not count towards the four week period for which ballots are normally effective. However, if the court believes that the result of a ballot no longer represents the views of union members, or that something has happened or is likely to happen which would result in union members voting against taking, or continuing with, action if there were a fresh ballot, it may not make such an order. In any case, a ballot can never be effective if a union's first call for industrial action is made more than twelve weeks after the date of the ballot.*

supplied as soon as reasonably practicable, and free of charge (or on payment of a reasonable fee specified by the union).

49.   In order to reduce the risk of challenge to a ballot's compliance with the statutory requirements, a union may wish to delay any call for industrial action, following a ballot, until it has obtained the scrutineer's report on the ballot.

If the union decides to authorise or endorse industrial action

50.   If the union decides to authorise or endorse industrial action following a ballot, it must take such steps as are reasonably necessary to ensure that any employer who it is reasonable for the union to believe employs workers who will be, or have been, called upon to take part in the action receives no less than seven days before the day specified in the notice as the date on which workers are intended to begin to take part in continuous action or as the first date on which they are intended to take part in discontinuous action a written notice from the union which:-
*   is given by any officer, official or committee of the union for whose act of inducing industrial action the union is responsible in law (an indication of whom this might cover is given in Annex 1 to this Code);
*   specifies: (i) whether the union intends the action to be 'continuous' or 'discontinuous'[13]; and (ii) the date on which any of the workers concerned are intended to begin to take part in the action (where it is continuous action), or all the dates on which any of them are intended to take part (where it is discontinuous action);
*   contains such information in the union's possession as would help the employer to make plans and bring information to the attention of those of his employees who the union intends should take part in the action; and
*   states that it is a notice given for the purposes of section 234A of the 1992 Act.

Changes in the union's intentions, for example as to the dates on which action is to be taken, require further notices to be given accordingly.

51.   With the exception of the requirements relating to continuous and discontinuous action and to the need to give further notices in the event of changes in the union's intentions, the statutory requirements applying to notice of industrial action are for the most part the same as those applying to notice of industrial action ballots and the guidance in paragraphs 15-18 will be of relevance, taking account of the different circumstances.

52.   **Where continuous industrial action is suspended,** for example for further negotiations between the employer and union, **the union must normally give the employer a further notice as in paragraphs 50 and 51 above before resuming the action. There is an exception to this requirement to give further notice, however, where the union agrees with the employer that the industrial action**

13   *For these purposes, industrial action is 'discontinuous' if it is to involve action other than on all the days when action might be taken by those concerned.* An indefinite strike would, therefore, be 'continuous'; an overtime ban might be 'continuous' or 'discontinuous', depending on whether the ban applied to overtime working on all the days on which overtime would otherwise be worked or to overtime working on only some of those days.

will cease to be authorised or endorsed with effect from a date specified in the agreement but may be authorised or endorsed again on or after another date specified in the agreement and the union:-

- ceases to authorise or endorse the action with effect from the specified date; and
- subsequently re-authorises or re-endorses the action from a date on or after the originally specified date or such later date as may be agreed with the employer.

For this exception to apply, the resumed industrial action must be of the same kind as covered in the original notice. That will not be so if, for example, the later action is taken by different or additional descriptions of workers. In order to avoid misunderstanding, both parties may find it helpful for such agreements to be in writing.

Seeking union members' views after a union has authorised or endorsed industrial action

53.   There is no statutory obligation on a union to ballot, or otherwise consult, its members before it decides to call off industrial action. However, if a union decides to seek its members' views about continuing with industrial action, it may wish to apply the same standards to the process of seeking their views as are set out in this Code.

Annex I   Trade union liability

1.   Section 20 of the Trade Union and Labour Relations (Consolidation) Act 1992 lays down when a union is to be held responsible for the act of inducing, or threatening, a breach or interference with a contract when there is no immunity. The union will be held liable for any such act which is done, authorised or endorsed by:-
- **its Executive Committee, General Secretary, President;**
- **any person given power under the union's rules to do, authorise or endorse acts of the kind in question; or**
- **any committee or official of the union (whether employed by it or not).**

A union will be held responsible for such an act by such a body or person regardless of any term or condition to the contrary in its own rules, or in any other contractual provision or rule of law.

2.   For these purposes:-
- **a 'committee of the union' is any group of persons constituted in accordance with the rules of the union;**
- **an 'official of the union' is any person who is an officer of the union or of a branch or section of the union or any person who is elected or appointed in accordance with the union's own rules to be a representative of its members, including any person so elected or appointed who is an employee of the same employer as the members, or one or more of the members, he is elected to represent** (eg` a shop steward); **and**
- **an act will be treated to have been done (or authorised or endorsed) by an official if it was so done (or authorised or endorsed) by a group of persons, or any member of a group, to which an official belonged at the relevant time if the group's purposes included organising or co-ordinating industrial action.**

3.   A union will not be held liable for such an act of any of its committees or officials, however, if its Executive Committee, President or General Secretary repudiates the act as soon as reasonably practicable after it has come to the attention of any of them, and the union takes the steps which the law requires to make that repudiation effective. But the union will not be considered to have 'effectively repudiated' an act if the Executive Committee, President or General Secretary subsequently behave in a manner which is inconsistent with the repudiation.

4.   The fact that a union is responsible for organising industrial action to which immunity does not apply does not prevent legal action also being taken against the individual organisers of that action.

'Immunity'

5.   A trade union which organises (ie authorises or endorses) industrial action without satisfying the requirements of section 226 (for balloting on industrial action), or 234A (for notice to employers of official industrial action), of the 1992 Act will have no 'immunity'. Without immunity the trade union will be at risk of legal action by (i) an employer (and/or a customer or supplier of such an employer)

who suffers (or may suffer) damage as a consequence of the trade union's unlawful inducement to his workers to break or interfere with the performance of contracts; and/or (ii) any individual who is (or is likely to be) deprived of goods or services because of the industrial action. Such legal proceedings might result in a court order requiring the trade union not to proceed with, and/or desist from, the unlawful inducement of its members to take part or continue with the action, and that no member does anything after the order is made as a result of unlawful inducement prior to the making of the order.

6.   Under section 62 of the 1992 Act, a member of a trade union who claims that members of the union, including himself, are likely to be or have been induced by the union to take industrial action which does not have the support of a ballot may apply to the court for an order, which may require the trade union to take steps to ensure that there is no, or no further, unlawful inducement to members to take part or continue to take part in the action, and that no member does anything after the order is made as a result of unlawful inducement prior to the making of the order.

Contempt and other proceedings

7.   If a court order issued following legal proceedings as described in paragraphs 5 and 6 above is not obeyed, anyone who sought it can go back to court and ask that those concerned be declared in contempt of court. A union found in contempt of court may face heavy fines, or other penalties which the court may consider appropriate.

8.   In addition, any member of the union may have grounds for legal action against the union's trustees if they have caused or permitted the unlawful application of union funds or property.

Annex 2   Example of voting paper for ballot on taking industrial action

[VOTING PAPER NUMBER]

[NAME OF THE TRADE UNION]

ARE YOU PREPARED TO TAKE PART IN INDUSTRIAL ACTION CONSISTING OF A STRIKE?[14]

YES [ ]   NO [ ]

ARE YOU PREPARED TO TAKE PART IN INDUSTRIAL ACTION SHORT OF A STRIKE (which for this purpose is defined to include overtime and call-out bans)?[14]

YES [ ]   NO [ ]

Your union intends the following to have authority to make the call for industrial action to which this ballot relates: [**DETAILS OF RELEVANT PERSON, PERSONS, AND/OR CLASS OR CLASSES OF PERSONS**]

If your vote is to count, this voting paper must be returned to [**FULL ADDRESS OF LOCATION TO WHICH THE VOTING PAPER IS TO BE RETURNED**] by [**FULL DATE AND TIME AS APPROPRIATE**]. Please use the enclosed pre-paid envelope provided for this purpose.

The independent scrutineer for this ballot is [**DETAILS OF RELEVANT PERSON**].

The law requires your union to ensure that your vote is accurately and fairly counted and that you are able to vote without interference from the union or any of its members, officials or employees and, so far as is reasonably practicable, in secret.

If you take part in a strike or other industrial action, you may be in breach of your contract of employment. However, if you are dismissed for taking part in a strike or other industrial action which is called officially and is otherwise lawful, the dismissal will be unfair if it takes place fewer than eight weeks after you started taking part in the action, and depending on the circumstances may be unfair if it takes place later.

14   *Either question or both should be included as appropriate.*

Annex 3   Information to be given to employers

The following paragraphs of the Code deal with requirements to provide information to employers:-

(h) Code of Practice
Equal Pay

Equal pay legislation

1. This chapter provides a basic outline of current equal pay legislation. Subsequent chapters expand on the main legal concepts and explain their implications for pay practices:
a) The law relating to sex discrimination in pay is contained in both UK statute and European Community law. The former is required to conform with the latter and UK legislation is interpreted by domestic courts in the light of European law. Claims may be taken under domestic law where possible, but because this is more limited in scope than European law, in some circumstances claims can be made directly under European law.
b) The law applies to both men and women but to avoid repetition throughout this Draft Code it is assumed that the claimant is a woman comparing herself with a man, as in practice most claimants are women.

Domestic Law

2. The relevant law is contained in the Equal Pay Act 1970 and the Sex Discrimination Act 1975, (each as amended) and the Pensions Act 1995. Despite its name, the Equal Pay Act covers all contractual terms and not simply those relating to pay. The Sex Discrimination Act covers claims which do not relate to contractual issues. Claims under both Acts are taken initially to an Industrial Tribunal. Those under the Sex Discrimination Act must be taken within 3 months of the act complained of. Those under the Equal Pay Act can be taken at any time up to 6 months after leaving the employment to which the claim relates. The Pensions Act 1995 allows claims in relation to the terms of, and access to, occupational pension schmes.

3. The Equal Pay Act 1970, as amended by the Equal Pay (Amendment) Regulations 1983, provides for equal pay between women and men in the same employment by giving a woman the right to equality in the terms of her contract of employment where she is employed on:
•   like work to that of a man, or
•   work rated as equivalent to that of a man, or
•   work of equal value to that of a man,
hereafter referred to as equal work.

4. The employer can defeat a claim under the Equal Pay Act by proving that the difference between the woman's contractual terms and those of the man is genuinely due to a material factor other than sex.

5. Where a claim under the Equal Pay Act is successful at Tribunal, equal pay is achieved by raising the pay of the woman to that of the man. This means that any term which is in the man's contract but missing from the woman's is to be treated as if it is in her contract, and/or any term in the woman's contract which is less favourable to her than the same term in the man's contract, is improved so that it is as good.

6. This legislation applies to:
•   all employees, whether on full-time, part-time, casual or temporary contracts, regardless of length of service.

- other workers (eg self-employed) whose contracts require personal performance of the work,
- employment carried out wholly or mainly in Great Britain,
- employment carried out in British registered ships or UK registered aircraft operated by someone based in Great Britain unless the employee works wholly outside Great Britain.

Great Britain includes such of the territorial waters of the UK as are adjacent to Great Britain and certain areas designated in relation to employment in the off-shore oil and gas industry.

7. The employment provisions of the Sex Discrimination Act 1975 prohibit sex discrimination in, among other things, access to benefits and in grading schemes.

8. Employees victimised for taking an equal pay claim or giving information or acting as a witness or comparator in the course of a claim, can make a claim under the Sex Discrimination Act.

9. Also, if a woman considers that a term in a collective agreement or employer's rule provides for the doing of an unlawful discriminatory act, and that the term or rule may at some time have effect in relation to her, she can challenge that term or rule under the Sex Discrimination Act 1986 as amended by section 32 of the Trade Union Reform and Employment Rights Act 1993.

European Community Law

10. The relevant principles of European equal pay law are contained in Article 119 of the Treaty of Rome and the Equal Pay Directive 75/117.

a) Article 119 of the Treaty of Rome establishes the principle that men and women should receive equal pay for equal work. It defines pay as:
  - the ordinary basic or minimum wage of salary and
  - any other consideration, in cash or in kind, which the employee receives directly or indirectly from her employer in respect of her employment.

b) The Equal Pay Directive 75/117 states that the principle of equal pay outlined in Article 119 means that, for the same work or for work to which equal value is attributed, all discrimination on grounds of sex must be eliminated in all aspects and conditions of remuneration. It also states that where a job classification system is used for determining pay, it must be based on the same criteria for men and women and exclude any discrimination on grounds of sex.

Meaning of Pay

11. The legislation has established that a woman may bring a complaint under the Equal Pay Act in relation to any term or condition contained in her contract whether or not it relates to money. This Act excludes non-contractual benefits, even if they relate to money and those relating to death or retirement. Claims concerning non-contractual benefits may be taken under the Sex Discrimination Act.

12. The definition of pay under Article 119 as interpreted by the ECJ is very broad and not limited to contractual terms.

Implications of the law for employers

13. Sex discrimination in pay is unlawful. The law provides a procedure by which an individual can take a claim for equal pay to an Industrial Tribunal. In the course of an equal pay claim employers may be called upon to explain and justify their pay practices and arrangements. This section looks at the grounds on which an employer can defend a claim.

Burden of Proof

14. The burden of proof is initially on the employee to show on the balance of probabilities that her male comparator is doing the same or broadly similar work, or that her work has been rated as equivalent to his, or that her work is of equal value; and that his contract contains a more favourable term. If the employee succeeds in this, equal pay will be awarded unless the employer can prove that the difference between the contracts is genuinely due to a material factor which is not the difference of sex.

Material Factor Defence

15. The material factor defence is the reason put forward by the employer to explain why the comparator, although doing equal work, is paid more than the applicant. To be successful this factor must be significant and relevant; that is it must be an important cause of the difference and apply to the jobs in question. The difference in pay must be genuinely due to the material factor which must not be tainted by sex discrimination. For example, if the reason given for paying the comparator more is that he has certain skills which the applicant does not have, then the employer would have to demonstrate that these skills are necessary for the job, and genuinely applied during the performance of the job, and are not simply rewarded because past pay agreements recognised and rewarded skills which are no longer applicable.

16. To succeeed in a defence, the employer needs to show that the material factor accounts for the whole of the difference in pay. Where it accounts for only part of the difference equal pay can be awarded for the rest. For example, if the material factor defence relates to rates of pay determined by skill shortages, but on examination it is found that these shortages can only justify part of the higher pay of the comparator, then the Tribunal will award the applicant the difference.

Objective Justification

17. In circumstances where a particular pay practice results in an adverse impact on substantially more members of one or other sex, the ECJ has introduced a test of objective justification. This means that the employer must be able to justify the pay practice in question objectively, in terms unrelated to sex. In practice he or she must show that the practice which causes the difference in pay corresponds to a business need on the part of the organisation, is appropriate with a view to achieving the objective pursued and is necessary to that end. For example, where a firm excludes part-time workers from an occupational pension scheme and this exclusion affects a far greater proportion of women than men, the employer would need to show that the exclusion is based on objectively justified factors unrelated to any discrimination on grounds of sex. If the ground for the exclusion is that the firm seeks to employ as few part-time workers as possible then the exclusion must be shown to correspond to a real need on the part of the undertaking and be appropriate and necessary to achieving that need.

18. Both the material factor defence and the objective justification test are essentially explanations for how the difference in pay arises and are closely related.

Transparency

19. It is important that the pay system is clear and easy to understand; this has become known as transparency. A transparent pay system is one where employees understand not only their rate of pay but also the components of their individual pay packets and how each component contributes to total earnings in any pay period. Transparency is an advantage to the employer as it will avoid uncertainty and perceptions of unfairness and reduce the possibility of individual claims.

20. The ECJ has held that where the organisation concerned applies a system of pay which is wholly lacking in transparency and appears to operate to the substantial disadvantage of one sex, then the onus is on the employer to show that the pay differential is not in fact discriminatory. An employer should therefore ensure that any elements of a pay system which could contribute to pay differences between employers are readily understood and free of sex bias.

Sex discrimination in pay systems

21. Sex discrimination in pay now occurs primarily because women and men tend to do different jobs or to have different work patterns. As a result it is easy to undervalue the demands of work performed by one sex compared with the demands associated with jobs typically done by the other. Such differences can be reinforced by discriminatory recruitment, training, selection and promotion procedures which may restrict the range of work each sex performs; for example, by allocating the full-time, higher paid, bonus-earning jobs mainly to men.

Different Jobs

22.
a)   There is some degree of job segregation in most employing organisations. Frequently the jobs done mainly by men have a higher status and are more highly rewarded than those done by women. Commonly men and women do different types of work within an organisation. It is also common for men to be in the majority at managerial level and women to occupy lower graded jobs. In certain occupations there is further segregation to the extent that there is an even greater concentration of ethnic minority women in lower status, lower paid jobs.
b)   Gender segregation in employment is often historical. Consequently it may be difficult to recognise the discriminatory effects of past pay and grading decisions based on traditional values ascribed to 'male' and 'female' work. In addition, the pay and conditions of 'male' and 'female' jobs within a firm might have been bargained separately by different unions. It is not sufficient to explain how the difference in pay came about. Arguments based on 'tradition' or separate bargaining would not justify paying women less than men when their work is of equal value.
c)   The fact that certain jobs are associated with one sex can affect the level of wages for those jobs which in turn can result in discrimination.
d)   Past discriminatory assumptions about the value of what has been regarded as men's or women's work may be reflected in current grading schemes. For example, men and women may be doing the same or very similar work but

have different job titles and consequently be in separate grades, with the women's jobs being graded lower. They may, on the other hand, be doing quite different jobs which are actually of equal value though the women are in lower grades. In both examples the grading scheme could result in discrimination and fail to value the actual work done.

Different Work Patterns
23.
a) Many women take time out of work for pregnancy and maternity. Women also tend to carry the main responsibility for family care. As a result women in general have shorter periods of service than men and more women than men work part-time. This difference in work patterns has contributed to the gender segregation of jobs.
b) There has been a tendency for payment systems to be designed to reward work patterns traditionally associated with men's employment and fail to recognise the different pattern of 'female' work. For example, a performance pay scheme which relies on an annual appraisal could mean that a woman who begins maternity leave before the appraisal, but has performed well for part of the year, will be denied a performance pay increase altogether. Another example is where pay benefits, such as occupational pensions or sick pay, are available only to full-time employees. This rule may mean that a group of female employees, ie those who work part-time, are denied access to important benefits.

24. Most of the discrimination in pay systems takes the form of indirect or hidden discrimination. This occurs where pay rules and agreements appear to be neutral between men and women but the effect of their application is to disadvantage substantially more of one sex than the other. Whatever the cause of the discrimination and regardless of whether it was intentional or not, once an applicant has established that someone of the opposite sex is paid more for equal work, the employer will be required to show that the difference is not based on sex, using the criteria set out under 'material factor defence' and 'Objective Justification'.

Review of pay systems for sex bias

25.
a) Pay arrangements are frequently complicated and the features which can give rise to sex discrimination are not always obvious. Although pay reviews are not required by law, they are recommended as the most appropriate method of ensuring that a pay system delivers equal pay free from sex bias.
b) A pay systems review also provides an opportunity to investigate the amount of information employees receive about their pay. Pay systems should be clear and easy to understand. Where they are not and where pay differentials exist, these may be inferred to be due to sex discrimination. It is therefore in an employer's interest to have transparent pay systems to prevent unnecessary equal pay claims.
c) The Equal Opportunities Commission recommends that a pay systems review should involve the following stages:

Stage One
Undertake a thorough analysis of the pay system to produce a breakdown of all employees, which covers for example, sex, job title, grade, whether part-time or

full-time, with basic pay, performance ratings and all other elements of remuneration.

Stage Two
Examine each element of the pay system against the data obtained in stage one. (see paragraph 27).

Stage Three
Identify any elements of the pay system which the review indicates may be the source of any discrimination.

Stage Four
Change any rules or practices including those in collective agreements which stages 1 to 3 have identified as likely to give rise to discrimination in pay. It is recommended that this should be done in consultation with employees, trade unions where appropriate. Stages 1 to 3 may reveal that practices and procedures in relation to recruitment, selection and access to training have contributed to discrimination in pay; in that event, these matters should also be addressed.

Stage Five
Analyse the likely effects of any proposed changes in practice to the pay system before implementation, to identify and rectify any discrimination which could be caused.

Stage Six
Give equal pay to current employees. Where the review shows that some employees are not receiving equal pay for equal work and the reasons cannot be shown to be free of sex bias, then a plan must be developed for dealing with this.

Stage Seven
Set up a system of regular monitoring to allow checks to be made to pay practices.

Stage Eight
Draw up and publish an equal pay policy with provision for assessing the new pay system or modification to a system in terms of sex discrimination. Also, in the interests of transparency, provide pay information where this is not already usual practice.

The pay review process

The following section provides guidance on carrying out stages 1 to 3 of the review process.

Initial Analysis
26. Undertake a thorough analysis of pay systems. This will require a breakdown of all employees to include for example, sex, job title, and grade, whether part-time or full-time, with performance ratings and the distribution of basic pay and all other elements of the remuneration package, to identify potential vulnerability to claims of pay discrimination. This will reveal whether there are any vulnerabilities and what their extent is, and enable a plan to be developed to correct any problems.

Identification of Discriminatory Elements
27.
a) Pay systems vary in complexity. Some have more elements than others. In the process of a review, each element will require examination against the statistical data generated at the initial analysis stage. Investigation may show discrimination in written rules and agreements, for example, limiting profit-related pay to employees who work above a minimum number of hours; or in the way processes are interpreted and applied, for example, failure to obtain adequate job descriptions during a job evaluation exercise.
b) Some of the more common pay elements are set out below, with examples of facts which could indicate problems of discrimination in pay and suggestions of further questions to be asked to reveal the cause of the pay difference and whether it can be shown to be free of sex bias in the terms explained under 'Material Factor Defence' and 'Objective Justification'.

Basic Pay
28.

A) PROBLEM:
Women are consistently appointed at lower points on the pay scale than men.

RECOMMENDED ACTION:
* Check the criteria which determine promotion or recruitment starting pay. Are these spelt out clearly?
* Examine recruitment and promotion records for evidence of criteria which appear to be disadvantaging women. Can these criteria, eg qualification requirements, be justified objectively in terms of the demands of the job?
* Check the records for evidence of sex bias in the application of managerial discretion.

B) PROBLEM:
Women are paid less per hour than men for doing virtually the same job, but with different job and grade titles.

RECOMMENDED ACTION:
Check whether there are any reasons other than custom and practice for the difference; if so are these reasons justified objectively?

C) PROBLEM:
Women progress more slowly through incremental salary scales and seldom reach higher points.

RECOMMENDED ACTION:
* Investigate the criteria applied for progression through the scale. Are these clearly understood? Does any particular criterion, eg length of service, work to the detriment of women more than men? If so can the use of that criterion or the extent to which it is relied on be justified objectively?
* Review the length of the incremental scale. Is the scale longer than it need be? Are there good practical reasons for a scale of that length?

D) PROBLEM:
Women progress more slowly through non-incremental salary ranges and seldom reach higher points.

RECOMMENDED ACTION:
- Check the criteria that applied when the structure was introduced and the current criteria for new recruits/promotees to each salary.
- Check whether there is a clear, well-understood mechanism for progressing through the salary range.
- Investigate the criteria for progression through the salary range and whether there are performance, qualification or other bars to upward movement. Can these be justified?
- Review the length of the salary range. Can this be justified by real need?

Bonus/Premium Rates/Plus Elements
29.

A) PROBLEM:
Female and male manual workers receive the same basic pay but only jobs mainly done by men have access to bonus earnings and those mainly done by women do not.

RECOMMENDED ACTION:
Check the reason why. Does this reflect real differences, for example, in the value of the work or in productivity? Can it be justified objectively on grounds unrelated to sex?

B) PROBLEM:
Where shift and overtime work is available and paid at a premium rate, fewer full-time women have access to this higher rated work.

RECOMMENDED ACTION:
Check that women and men employees have equal access to this work and, if not, that the reasons can be justified objectively.

C) PROBLEM:
A smaller percentage of women employees receive enhanced rates for weekend and unsocial hours work.

RECOMMENDED ACTION:
Check the eligibility requirements for this work. Do any of these, for example, requiring that employees must be working full-time, work to the disadvantage of women? Can these requirements be objectively justified?

D) PROBLEM:
Average female earnings under a variable payment system are lower than average male earnings (even where some women may have higher earnings than most men).

RECOMMENDED ACTION:
- Review the design and operation of the variable payment system. Do these genuinely reflect the demands of the jobs and the productivity needs of the organisation?
- In particular, check how factors such as down-time and personal needs breaks are dealt with in a variable payment system covering men and women.

Performance Pay
30.

A) PROBLEM:
The performance pay system is applied largely to employees of one sex only and results in a pay discrepancy to the advantage of that group.

RECOMMENDED ACTION:
Investigate the reasons why employees of the other sex are largely excluded from performance pay awards. Are these justified objectively for reasons unrelated to sex?

B) PROBLEM:
Women receive lower performance ratings on average than men.

RECOMMENDED ACTION:
*   Investigate the performance rating system. Is it really likely that women would on average perform less well than men? What are the possible reasons for this?
*   Review the criteria for performance rating. Do employees and managers know what these are? Do any of these disadvantage women? Do any of these disadvantage ethnic minority women in particular? If so, are these criteria justified objectively?
*   Monitor the ratings of individual managers. Do the results of the monitoring suggest a stereotypical interpretation of criteria? Are there appropriate controls on managerial discretion?

C) PROBLEM:
Although women and men receive similar ratings, men achieve higher performance pay awards.

RECOMMENDED ACTION:
Investigate the reasons for this. Is it linked to managerial discretion? Are potentially discriminatory criteria being applied in the linking of ratings to pay? Can these be justified objectively?

Pay Based on Additional Skills or Training
31.

PROBLEM:
In practice only or mainly male employees receive this supplement.

RECOMMENDED ACTION:
*   Investigate the reasons for this. Are 'female' skills not recognised? Do women have the same access to any skills or training modules offered?
*   Review the training/skills/qualifications criteria. Do they genuinely reflect enhanced ability to carry out the job duties?
*   Review the procedures for implementing the supplement. Are managers and employees aware of the procedure? Are they operated fairly as between men and women?

Pay Based on an Assessment of Individual Competencies
32.

PROBLEM:
There is a pay gap between the male and female employees who are assessed in this way.

RECOMMENDED ACTION:
- Review the competencies assessed. Are women and men assessed for the same set of competencies? Are the competencies being interpreted in a consistent way?
- Are potentially indirectly discriminatory criteria being applied? If so are these justified objectively?
- Monitor the assessment of individual managers.

Pay Benefits
33.

A) PROBLEM:
A smaller percentage of women employees than men are covered by the organisation's sick pay, pensions, low interest loans, share option schemes.

RECOMMENDED ACTION:
- Check eligibility requirements. Are there restrictions which impact negatively on women? For example, are any of these limited to employees working over a minimum number of hours?
- Can these requirements be justified objectively?

B) PROBLEM:
Proportionately fewer women than men are in receipt of contractual benefits, for example, cars, telephone rentals and bills, rent and rates on tied accommodation, reimbursement of council tax in residential occupations.

RECOMMENDED ACTION:
- Review the criteria for such benefits and any differences in treatment between male and female dominated groups. Can these differences be justified in terms of the needs of the work?
- Review policies for the payment of such benefits between departments within the organisation. Are they consistent and can any differences be justified?

Grading
34.

1) PROBLEM:
Jobs predominantly occupied by women are graded lower than jobs predominantly occupied by men.

RECOMMENDED ACTION:
Review the method of grading. Was it devised for the current jobs? Is it adapted from a scheme used in a different organisation? What was the method used to

determine job size? Some methods, eg felt-fair or whole job comparison, are potentially more discriminatory than others, eg analytical job evaluation. Are separate grading schemes used for jobs predominantly done by women and those predominantly done by men? If so, why, and is this difference objectively justified?

B) PROBLEM:
Some jobs held mainly by men are in higher grades because of 'recruitment and retention' problems.

RECOMMENDED ACTION:
*   Check that there is genuine evidence of a current 'recruitment and retention' problem.
*   Check that the whole of the difference in pay is attributable to market pressure. If not, investigate the reasons for the rest of the difference.
*   Consider amending the grading/pay structure so that the 'labour market' element of pay is 'transparent'.

C) PROBLEM:
Red circling, for example, where salary is protected when a job has been downgraded, is mainly applied to male employees.

RECOMMENDED ACTION:
*   Check the criteria for red circling. Why do they favour male jobs? Can this be justified objectively?
*   Investigate whether other criteria which are more equitable could be used.
*   Ensure the difference in pay is phased out as soon as possible so that unequal pay is not perpetuated.

Job Evaluation Method of Grading
35.

A) PROBLEM:
An analytical job evaluation scheme has resulted in jobs predominantly done by women being graded lower than those predominantly done by men.

RECOMMENDED ACTION:
Check that all features of the scheme's design and implementation took full account of the need to avoid sex bias. Was the job information collected consistently and accurately? Do the factors and weighting favour characteristics typical of jobs dominated by one sex? If so, is this justified objectively? Was training in the avoidance of sex bias given to those responsible for implementing the scheme?

B) PROBLEM:
Jobs which have been evaluated as the same have widely differing salaries to the detriment of jobs largely held by women.

RECOMMENDED ACTION:
*   Investigate the possible causes, for example, how were the jobs assimilated to the evaluated structure?

- Are different pay scales in use?
- Could elements like additional skills payments or performance pay awards be responsible? What part do market rate or productivity considerations play? Can the cause of the difference be justified objectively?

Monitoring

36. Once the current pay systems have been reviewed it is important that periodic checks are made to ensure that discrimination does not creep in. This is best done by incorporating statistics on pay broken down by sex into the existing management information package, so that the necessary information can be checked regularly.

A policy on equal pay

37. Good equal opportunities practice in employment not only helps to avoid unlawful or unfair discrimination but is also good for business and the right and fair thing to do. Many employers have adopted Equal Opportunities Policies in order to signal to employees and clients or customers that the organisation takes equality issues seriously. Equal pay is an important part of equality at work because pay is the most direct way an organisation values the contribution made by employees and should be covered in any Equal Opportunities Policy.

38. An Equal Pay Policy is an important way of showing commitment to achieving equal pay free of sex bias. The Policy should set out clear objectives which enable priorities for action to be identified and an effective programme to achieve them to be implemented. The internal pay review described above would apply the identification of priorities.

39. It is good employment practice for employees to understand how their rate of pay is determined. Information about priorities and proposed action could be communicated to employees as part of the process of informing them about how the pay system affects them individually. This will serve to assure employees that any sex bias in the payment system is being addressed.

40. Experience shows that the effectiveness of any Equal Pay Policy depends on the following:
- A commitment to the policy by senior management.
- A recognition by all staff involved in decisions about pay that they share responsibility for the proper implementation of the policy.
- Effective training in identifying sex discrimination in pay for all staff who take decisions about the pay and grading of other employees.
- Moving beyond a statement of intent to include a provision for a review of the payment system and periodic monitoring to ensure continuing effectiveness.
- Information given to employees about the review and any plan of action drawn up as a result.

A suggested Equal Pay Policy is to be found at Annex A.

Annex A: Suggested equal pay policy

Equal Pay Statement
This organisation supports the principle of equal opportunities in employment and believes as part of that principle that male and female staff should receive equal pay for the same or broadly similar work, for work rated as equivalent and for work of equal value.

We understand that a right to equal pay between men and women free of sex bias is a fundamental principle of European Community law and is conferred by United Kingdom legislation.

We believe it is in our company's interest and good business practice that pay is awarded fairly and equitably.

We recognise that in order to achieve equal pay for employees doing equal work we should operate a pay system which is transparent, based on objective criteria and free from sex bias.

Action to implement policy
In order to put our commitment to equal pay into practice we will:
- examine our existing and future pay practices for all our employees including those in non-standard employment and those who are absent on pregnancy and maternity leave.
- carry out regular monitoring of the impact of our practices.
- inform employees of how these practices work and how their own pay is arrived at.
- provide training and guidance for managers and supervisory staff involved in decisions about pay and benefits.
- discuss and agree the equal pay policy with employees, trade unions or staff representatives where appropriate.

We intend through the above action to avoid unfair discrimination, to reward fairly the skills, experience and potential of all staff and thereby to increase efficiency, productivity and competitiveness and enhance the organisation's reputation and image.

(i) Code of Practice

For the elimination of discrimination in the field of employment against disabled persons or persons who have had a disability

3   General guidance to help avoid discrimination

Be flexible

3.1   There may be several ways to avoid discrimination in any one situation. Examples in this Code are *illustrative only*, to indicate what should or should not be done in those and other broadly similar types of situations. They cannot cover every possibility, so it is important to consider carefully how the guidance applies in any specific circumstances. **Many ways of avoiding discrimination will cost little or nothing.** The Code should not be read narrowly; for instance, its guidance on recruitment might help avoid discrimination when promoting employees.

Do not make assumptions

3.2   It will probably be helpful to talk to each disabled person about what the real effects of the disability might be or what might help. There is less chance of a dispute where the person is involved from the start. Such discussions should not, of course, be conducted in a way which would itself give the disabled person any reason to believe that he was being discriminated against.

Consider whether expert advice is needed

3.3   It is possible to avoid discrimination using personal, or in-house, knowledge and expertise, particularly if the views of the disabled person are sought. The Act does not oblige anyone to get expert advice but it could help in some circumstances to seek independent advice on the extent of a disabled person's capabilities. This might be particularly appropriate where a person is newly disabled or the effects of someone's disability become more marked. It may also help to get advice on what might be done to change premises or working arrangements, especially if discussions with the disabled person do not lead to a satisfactory solution. Annex 2 gives information about getting advice or help.

Plan ahead

3.4   Although the Act does not require an employer to make changes in anticipation of ever having a disabled applicant or employee, nevertheless when planning for change it could be cost-effective to consider the needs of a range of possible future disabled employees and applicants. There may be helpful improvements that could be built into plans. For example, a new telecommunications system might be made accessible to deaf people even if there are currently no deaf employees.

Promote equal opportunities

3.5   If an employer has an equal opportunities policy or is thinking of introducing one, it would probably help to avoid a breach of the Act if that policy covered disability issues. Employers who have, and follow, a good policy – including monitoring its effectiveness – are likely to have that counted in their favour by a tribunal if a complaint is made. But employers should remember that treating people equally will not always avoid a breach of the Act. An employer may be under a duty to make a reasonable adjustment. This could apply at any time in the recruitment process or in the course of a disabled person's employment.

4   The main employment provisions of the Act

Discrimination

WHAT DOES THE ACT SAY ABOUT DISCRIMINATION?

4.1   *The Act makes it unlawful* for an employer to discriminate against a disabled person in the field of employment (s 4). The Act says 'discrimination' occurs in two ways.

4.2   One way in which discrimination occurs is when:
❏   for a reason which relates to a disabled person's disability, the employer treats that disabled person less favourably than the employer treats or would treat others to whom the reason does not or would not apply; *and*
❏   the employer cannot show that this treatment is justified (s 5(1)).

A woman with a disability which requires use of a wheelchair applies for a job. She can do the job but the employer thinks the wheelchair will get in the way in the office. He gives the job to a person who is no more suitable for the job but who does not use a wheelchair. The employer has therefore treated the women *less favourably* than the other person because he did not give her the job. The treatment was *for a reason related to the disability* – the fact that she used a wheelchair. And the reason for treating her less favourably *did not apply to the other person* because that person did not use a wheelchair.

If the employer could not justify his treatment of the disabled woman then he would have unlawfully discriminated against her.

An employer decides to close down a factory and makes all the employees redundant, including a disabled person who works there. This is not discrimination as the disabled employee is not being dismissed for a reason which relates to the disability.

4.3   A disabled person may not be able to point to other people who were actually treated more favourably. However, it is still 'less favourable treatment' if the employer would give better treatment to someone else to whom the reason for the treatment of the disabled person did not apply. This comparison can also be made with other disabled people, not just non-disabled people. For example, an employer might be discriminating by treating a person with a mental illness less favourably than he treats or would treat a physically disabled person.

4.4   The other way **the Act says** that discrimination occurs is when:
❏   an employer fails to comply with a duty of reasonable adjustment imposed on him by section 6 in relation to the disabled person; *and*
❏   he cannot show that this failure is justified (s 5(2)).

4.5   The relationship between the duty of reasonable adjustment and the need to justify less favourable treatment is described in paragraphs 4.7–4.9. The duty itself is described from paragraph 4.12 onwards and the need to justify a failure to comply with it is described in paragraph 4.34.

WHAT WILL, AND WHAT WILL NOT, BE JUSTIFIED TREATMENT?

4.6 **The Act says** that less favourable treatment of a disabled person will be justified only if the reason for it is both material to the circumstances of the particular case *and* substantial (s 5(3)). This means that the reason has to relate to the individual circumstances in question and not just be trivial or minor.

Someone who is blind is not shortlisted for a job involving computers because the employer thinks blind people cannot use them. The employer makes no effort to look at the individual circumstances. A general assumption that blind people cannot use computers would not in itself be a material reason – it is not related to the particular circumstances.

A factory worker with a mental illness is sometimes away from work due to his disability. Because of that he is dismissed. However, the amount of time off is very little more than the employer accepts as sick leave for other employees and so is very unlikely to be a substantial reason.

A clerical worker with a learning disability cannot sort papers quite as quickly as some of his colleagues. There is very little difference in productivity but he is dismissed. That is very unlikely to be a substantial reason.

An employer seeking a clerical worker turns down an applicant with a severe facial disfigurement solely on the ground that other employees would be uncomfortable working alongside him. This will be unlawful because such a reaction by other employees will not in itself justify less favourable treatment of this sort – it is not substantial. The same would apply if it were thought that a customer would feel uncomfortable.

An employer moves someone with a mental illness to a different workplace solely because he mutters to himself while he works. If the employer accepts similar levels of noise from other people, the treatment of the disabled person would probably be unjustified – that level of noise is unlikely to be a substantial reason.

Someone who has psoriasis (a skin condition) is rejected for a job involving modelling cosmetics on a part of the body which in his case is severely disfigured by the condition. That would be lawful if his appearance would be incompatible with the purpose of the work. This is a substantial reason which is clearly related – material – to the individual circumstance.

4.7 **The Act says** that less favourable treatment cannot be justified where the employer is under a duty to make a reasonable adjustment but fails (without justification) to do so, *unless* the treatment would have been justified even after that adjustment (s 5(5)).

An employee who uses a wheelchair is not promoted, solely because the work station for the higher post is inaccessible to wheelchairs – though it could readily be made so by rearrangement of the furniture. If the furniture had been re-arranged, the reason for refusing promotion would not have applied. The refusal of promotion would therefore not be justified.

An applicant for a typing job is not the best person on the face of it, but only because her typing speed is too slow due to arthritis in her hands. If a reasonable adjustment – perhaps an adapted keyboard – would overcome this, her typing speed would not in itself be a substantial reason for not employing her. Therefore the employer would be unlawfully discriminating if on account of her typing speed he did not employ her and provide the adjustment.

An employer refuses a training course for an employee with an illness which is very likely to be terminal within a year because, even with a reasonable adjustment to help in the job after the course, the benefits of the course could not be adequately realised. This is very likely to be a substantial reason. It is clearly material to the circumstances. The refusal of training would therefore very likely be justified.

Someone who is blind applies for a job which requires a significant amount of driving. If it is not reasonable for the employer to adjust the job so that the driving duties are given to someone else, the employer's need for a driver might well be a substantial reason for not employing the blind person. It is clearly material to the particular circumstances. The non-appointment could therefore be justified.

How DOES AN EMPLOYER AVOID UNLAWFUL DISCRIMINATION?
4.8   An employer should not treat a disabled employee or disabled job applicant less favourably, for a reason relating to the disability, than others to whom that reason does not apply, unless that reason is material to the particular circumstances and substantial. If the reason is material and substantial, the employer may have to make a reasonable adjustment to remove it or make it less than substantial. (s 5(3) and (5)).

4.9   Less favourable treatment is therefore justified if the disabled person cannot do the job concerned, and no adjustment which would enable the person to do the job (or another vacant job) is practicable (s 5(3) and (5)). (See paragraph 4.20 for examples of adjustments which employers may have to make.)

4.10   *The Act says* that some charities (and Government-funded supported employment) are allowed to treat some groups of disabled people more favourably than others. But they can do this only if the group being treated more favourably is one with whom the charitable purposes of the charity are connected and the more favourable treatment is in pursuance of those purposes (or, in the case of supported employment, those treated more favourably are severely disabled people whom the programme aims to help) (s 10).

WHAT DOES THE ACT SAY ABOUT HELPING OTHERS TO DISCRIMINATE?
4.11   **The Act says** that a person who knowingly helps another to do something made unlawful by the Act will also be treated as having done the same kind of unlawful act (s 57(1)).

A recruitment consultant engaged by an engineering company refuses to consider a disabled applicant for a vacancy, because the employer has told the consultant that he does not want the post filled by someone who is 'handicapped'. Under the Act the consultant could be liable for aiding the company.

Reasonable adjustment
WHAT DOES THE ACT SAY ABOUT THE DUTY OF 'REASONABLE ADJUSTMENT'?
4.12   **The Act says** that the duty applies where any physical feature of premises occupied by the employer, or any arrangements made by or on behalf of the

employer, cause a substantial disadvantage to a disabled person compared with non-disabled people. An employer has to take such steps as it is reasonable for him to have to take in all the circumstances to prevent that disadvantage – in other words the employer has to make a 'reasonable adjustment' (s 6(1)).

> A man who is disabled by dyslexia applies for a job which involves writing letters within fairly long deadlines. The employer gives all applicants a test of their letter-writing ability. The man can generally write letters very well but finds it difficult to do so in stressful situations. The *employer's arrangements* would mean he had to begin his test immediately on arrival and to do it in a short time. He would be *substantially disadvantaged compared to non-disabled people* who would not find such arrangements stressful or, if they did, would not be so affected by them. The employer therefore gives him a little time to settle in and longer to write the letter. These new arrangements do not inconvenience the employer very much and only briefly delay the decision on an appointment. These are *steps that it is reasonable for the employer to have to take in the circumstances to prevent the disadvantage* – a 'reasonable adjustment'.

4.13 If a disabled person cannot point to an existing non-disabled person compared with whom he is at a substantial disadvantage, then the comparison should be made with how the employer would have treated a non-disabled person.

4.14 How to comply with this duty in recruitment and during employment is explained in paragraphs 5.1–5.29 and 6.1–6.21. The following paragraphs explain how to satisfy this duty more generally.

WHAT 'PHYSICAL FEATURES' AND 'ARRANGEMENTS' ARE COVERED BY THE DUTY?
4.15 **Regulations define** the term 'physical features' to include anything on the premises arising from a building's design or construction or from an approach to, exit from or access to such a building; fixtures, fittings, furnishings, furniture, equipment or materials; and any other physical element or quality of land in the premises. All of these are covered whether temporary or permanent.

4.16 **The Act says** that the duty applies to 'arrangements' for determining to whom employment should be offered and any term, condition or arrangement on which employment, promotion, transfer, training or any other benefit is offered or afforded (s 6(2)). The duty applies in recruitment and during employment; for example, selection and interview procedures and the arrangements for using premises for such procedures as well as job offers, contractual arrangements, and working conditions.

> The design of a particular workplace makes it difficult for someone with a hearing impairment to hear. That is a disadvantage caused by the *physical features*. There may be nothing that can reasonably be done in the circumstances to change these features. However, requiring someone to work in such a workplace is an *arrangement made by the employer* and it might be reasonable to overcome the disadvantage by a transfer to another workplace or by ensuring that the supervisor gives instructions in an office rather than in the working area.

WHAT 'DISADVANTAGES' GIVE RISE TO THE DUTY?

4.17   **The Act says** that only substantial disadvantages give rise to the duty (s 6(1)). Substantial disadvantages are those which are not minor or trivial.

> An employer is unlikely to be required to widen a particular doorway to enable passage by an employee using a wheelchair if there is an easy alternative route to the same destination.

4.18   An employer cannot be required to prevent a disadvantage caused by premises or by non-pay arrangements by increasing the disabled person's pay. (see paragraph 5.29).

4.19   The duty of reasonable adjustment does not apply in relation to benefits under occupational pension schemes or certain benefits under other employment-related benefits schemes although there is a duty not to discriminate in relation to such benefits (see paragraphs 6.9–6.16).

WHAT ADJUSTMENTS MIGHT AN EMPLOYER HAVE TO MAKE?

4.20   **The Act gives** a number of examples of 'steps' which employers may have to take, if it is reasonable for them to have to do so in all the circumstances of the case (s 6(3)). Steps other than those listed here, or a combination of steps, will sometimes have to be taken. The steps in the Act are:

❑ making adjustments to premises

> An employer might have to make structural or other physical changes such as: widening a doorway, providing a ramp or moving furniture for a wheelchair user; relocating light switches, door handles or shelves for someone who has difficulty in reaching; providing appropriate contrast in decor to help the safe mobility of a visually impaired person.

❑ allocating some of the disabled person's duties to another person.

> Minor or subsidiary duties might be reallocated to another employee if the disabled person has difficulty in doing them because of the disability. For example, if a job occasionally involves going onto the open roof of a building an employer might have to transfer this work away from an employee whose disability involves severe vertigo.

❑ transferring the person to fill an existing vacancy

> If an employee becomes disabled, or has a disability which worsens so she cannot work in the same place or under the same arrangements and there is no reasonable adjustment which would enable the employee to continue doing the current job, then she might have to be considered for any suitable alternative posts which are available. (Such a case might also involve reasonable retraining.)

❑ altering the person's working hours

> This could include allowing the disabled person to work flexible hours to enable additional breaks to overcome fatigue arising from the disability, or changing the disabled person's hours to fit with the availability of a carer.

❏ assigning the person to a different place of work

This could mean transferring a wheelchair user's work station from an inaccessible third floor office to an accessible one on the ground floor. It could mean moving the person to other premises of the same employer if the first building is inaccessible.

❏ allowing the person to be absent during working hours for rehabilitation, assessment or treatment

For example, if a person were to become disabled, the employer might have to allow the person more time off during work, than would be allowed to non-disabled employees, to receive physiotherapy or psychoanalysis or undertake employment rehabilitation. A similar adjustment might be appropriate if a disability worsens or if a disabled person needs occasional treatment anyway.

❏ giving the person, or arranging for him to be given, training

This could be training in the use of particular pieces of equipment unique to the disabled person, or training appropriate for all employees but which needs altering for the disabled person because of the disability. For example, all employees might need to be trained in the use of a particular machine but an employer might have to provide slightly different or longer training for an employee with restricted hand or arm movements, or training in additional software for a visually impaired person so that he can use a computer with speech output.

❏ acquiring or modifying equipment

An employer might have to provide special equipment (such as an adapted keyboard for a visually impaired person or someone with arthritis), or an adapted telephone for someone with a hearing impairment or modified equipment (such as longer handles on a machine). There is no requirement to provide or modify equipment for personal purposes unconnected with work, such as providing a wheelchair if a person needs one in any event but does not have one: the disadvantage in such a case does not flow from the employer's arrangements or premises.

❏ modifying instructions or reference manuals

The way instruction is normally given to employees might need to be revised when telling a disabled person how to do a task. The format of instructions or manuals may need to be modified (eg produced in braille or on audio tape) and instructions for people with learning disabilities may need to be conveyed orally with individual demonstration.

❏ modifying procedures for testing or assessment

This could involve ensuring that particular tests do not adversely affect people with particular types of disability. For example, a person with restricted manual dexterity might be disadvantaged by a written test, so an employer might have to give that person an oral test.

❏ providing a reader or interpreter

This could involve a colleague reading mail to a person with a visual impairment at particular times during the working day or, in appropriate circumstances, the hiring of a reader or sign language interpreter.

❑ providing supervision

This could involve the provision of a support worker, or help from a colleague, in appropriate circumstances, for someone whose disability leads to uncertainty or lack of confidence.

WHEN IS IT 'REASONABLE' FOR AN EMPLOYER TO HAVE TO MAKE AN ADJUSTMENT?

4.21 Effective and practicable adjustments for disabled people often involve little or no cost or disruption and are therefore very likely to be reasonable for an employer to have to make. **The Act lists** a number of factors which may, in particular, have a bearing on whether it will be reasonable for the employer to have to make a particular adjustment (s 6(4)). These factors make a useful checklist, particularly when considering more substantial adjustments. The effectiveness and practicability of a particular adjustment might be considered first. If it is practicable and effective, the financial aspects might be looked at as a whole – cost of the adjustment and resources available to fund it. Other factors might also have a bearing. The factors in the Act are listed below.

The effectiveness of the step in preventing the disadvantage

4.22 It is unlikely to be reasonable to an employer to have to make an adjustment involving little benefit to the disabled employee.

A disabled person is significantly less productive than his colleagues and so is paid less. A particular adjustment would improve his output and thus his pay. It is more likely to be reasonable for the employer to have to make that adjustment if it would significantly improve his pay, than if the adjustment would make only a relatively small improvement.

The practicability of the step

4.23 It is more likely to be reasonable for an employer to have to take a step which is easy to take than one which is difficult.

It might be impracticable for an employer who needs to appoint an employee urgently to have to wait for an adjustment to be made to an entrance. How long it might be reasonable for the employer to have to wait would depend on the circumstances. However, it might be possible to make a temporary adjustment in the meantime, such as using another, less convenient entrance.

The financial and other costs of the adjustment and the extent of any disruption caused

4.24 If an adjustment costs little or nothing and is not disruptive, it would be reasonable unless some other factor (such as practicability or effectiveness) made it unreasonable. The costs to be taken into account include staff and other resource costs. The significance of the cost of a step may depend in part on what the employer might otherwise spend in the circumstances.

It would be reasonable for an employer to have to spend at least as much on an adjustment to enable the retention of a disabled person – including any retraining – as might be spent on recruiting and training a replacement.

4.25   The significance of the cost of a step may also depend in part on the value of the employee's experience and expertise to the employer.

Examples of the factors that might be considered as relating to the value of an employee would include:

❑   the amount of resources (such as training) invested in the individual by the employer;
❑   the employee's length of service;
❑   the employee's level of skill and knowledge;
❑   the employee's quality of relationship with clients;
❑   the level of the employee's pay.

4.26   It is more likely to be reasonable for an employer to have to make an adjustment with significant costs for an employee who is likely be in the job for some time than for a temporary employee.

4.27   An employer is more likely to have to make an adjustment which might cause only minor inconvenience to other employees or the employer than one which might unavoidably prevent other employees from doing their job, or cause other significant disruption.

The extent of the employer's financial or other resources

4.28   It is more likely to be reasonable for an employer with substantial financial resources to have to make an adjustment with a significant cost, than for an employer with fewer resources. The resources in practice available to the employer as a whole should be taken into account as well as other calls on those resources. The reasonableness of an adjustment will depend, however, not only on the resources in practice available for the adjustment but also on all other relevant factors (such as effectiveness and practicability).

4.29   Where the resources of the employer are spread across more than one 'business unit' or 'profit centre' the calls on them should also be taken into account in assessing reasonableness.

A large retailer probably could not show that the limited resources for which an individual shop manager is responsible meant it was not reasonable for the retailer to have to make an adjustment at that shop. Such an employer may, however, have a number – perhaps a large number – of other disabled employees in other shops. The employer's expenditure on other adjustments, or his potential expenditure on similar adjustments for other existing disabled employees, might then be taken into account in assessing the reasonableness of having to make a new adjustment for the disabled employee in question.

4.30   It is more likely to be reasonable for an employer with a substantial number of staff to have to make certain adjustments, than for a smaller employer.

It would generally be reasonable for an employer with many staff to have to make significant efforts to reallocate duties, identify a suitable alternative post or provide supervision from existing staff. It could also be reasonable for a small company covered by the Act to have to make any of these adjustments but not if it involved disproportionate effort.

The availability to the employer of financial or other assistance to help make an adjustment.
4.31   The availability of outside help may well be a relevant factor.

> An employer, in recruiting a disabled person, finds that the only feasible adjustment is too costly for him alone. However, if assistance is available eg from a Government programme or voluntary body, it may well be reasonable for him to have to make the adjustment after all.

A disabled person is not required to contribute to the cost of a reasonable adjustment. However, if a disabled person has a particular piece of special or adapted equipment which he is prepared to use for work, this might make it reasonable for the employer to have to take some other step (as well as allowing use of the equipment).

> An employer requires his employees to use company cars for all business travel. One employee's disability means she would have to use an adapted car or an alternative form of transport. If she has an adapted car of her own which she is willing to use on business, it might well be reasonable for the employer to have to allow this and pay her an allowance to cover the cost of doing so, even if it would not have been reasonable for him to have to provide an adapted company car, or to pay an allowance to cover alternative travel arrangements in the absence of an adapted car.

Other factors
4.32   Although the Act does not mention any further factors, others might be relevant depending on the circumstances. For example:

❏ effect on other employees

> Employees' adverse reaction to an adjustment being made for the disabled employee which involves something they too would like (such as a special working arrangement) is unlikely to be significant.

❏ adjustments made for other disabled employees

> An employer may choose to give a particular disabled employee, or group of disabled employees, an adjustment which goes beyond the duty – that is, which is more than it is reasonable for him to have to do. This would not mean he necessarily had to provide a similar adjustment for other employees with a similar disability.

❏ the extent to which the disabled person is willing to cooperate

> An employee with a mobility impairment works in a team located on an upper floor, to which there is no access by lift. Getting there is very tiring for the employee, and the employer could easily make a more accessible location available for him (though the whole team could not be relocated). If that was the only adjustment which it would be reasonable for the employer to have to make but the employee refused to work there then the employer would not have to make any adjustment at all.

COULD AN EMPLOYER HAVE TO MAKE MORE THAN ONE ADJUSTMENT?
4.33   Yes, if it is reasonable for the employer to have to make more than one.

A woman who is deafblind is given a new job with her employer in an unfamiliar part of the building. The employer (i) arranges facilities for her guide dog in the new area, (ii) arranges for her new instructions to be in Braille and (iii) suggests to visitors ways in which they can communicate with her.

DOES AN EMPLOYER HAVE TO JUSTIFY NOT MAKING AN ADJUSTMENT?

4.34   **The Act says** that it is discrimination if an employer fails to take a step which it is reasonable for him to have to take, and he cannot justify that failure (s 5(2)). However, if it is unreasonable (under s 6) for an employer to have to make any, or a particular, adjustment, he would not then also have to justify (under s 5) not doing so. Failure to comply with the duty of reasonable adjustment can only be justified if the reason for the failure is material to the circumstances of the particular case and substantial (s 5(4)).

An employer might not make an adjustment which it was reasonable for him to have to make because of ignorance or wrong information about appropriate adjustments or about the availability of help with making an adjustment. He would then need to justify failing in his duty. It is unlikely that he could do so unless he had made a reasonable effort to obtain good information from a reputable source such as contracting the local Placing Assessment and Counselling Team or an appropriate disability organisation.

If either of two possible adjustments would remove a disadvantage, but the employer has cost or operational reasons for preferring one rather than the other, it is unlikely to be reasonable for him to have to make the one that is not preferred. If, however, the employee refuses to cooperate with the proposed adjustment the employer is likely to be justified in not providing it.

A disabled employee refuses to follow specific occupational medical advice provided on behalf of an employer about methods of working or managing his condition at work. If he has no good reason for this and his condition deteriorates as a result, the refusal may justify the employer's subsequent failure to make an adjustment for the worsened condition.

Building regulations, listed buildings, leases

HOW DO BUILDING REGULATIONS AFFECT REASONABLE ADJUSTMENTS?

4.35   A building or extension to a building may have been constructed in accordance with Part M of the building regulations (or the Scottish parallel, Part T of the Technical Standards) which is concerned with access and facilities for disabled people. **Regulations provide** in these circumstances that the employer does not have to alter any physical characteristic of the building or extension which still complies with the building regulations in force at the time the building works were carried out.

Where the building regulations in force at the time of a building's construction required that a door should be a particular width, the employer would not have to alter the width of the door later. However, he might have to alter other aspects of the door (eg the type of handle).

4.36   Employers can only rely upon this defence if the feature still satisfies the requirement of the building regulations that applied when the building or extension was constructed.

WHAT ABOUT THE NEED TO OBTAIN STATUTORY CONSENT FOR SOME BUILDING CHANGES?

4.37 Employers might have to obtain statutory consent before making adjustments involving changes to premises. Such consents include planning permission, listed building consent, scheduled monument consent and fire regulations approval. The Act does not override the need to obtain such consents (s 59). Therefore an employer does not have to make an adjustment if it requires a statutory consent which has not been given.

4.38 The time it would take to obtain consent may make a particular adjustment impracticable and therefore one which it is not reasonable for the employer to have to make. However, the employer would then also need to consider whether it was reasonable to have to make the temporary adjustment – one that does not require consent – in the meantime.

4.39 Employers should explore ways of making reasonable adjustments which either do not require statutory consent or are likely to receive it. They may well find it useful to consult their local planning authority (in England and Wales) or planning authority (in Scotland).

> An employer needs statutory consent to widen an internal doorway in a listed building for a woman disabled in an accident who returned to work in a wheelchair. The employer considers using a different office but this is not practicable. In the circumstances the widening would be a reasonable adjustment. The employer knows from the local planning authority that consent is likely to be given in a few weeks. In the meantime the employer arranges for the woman to share an accessible office which is inconvenient for both employees, but does not prevent them doing their jobs and is tolerable for that limited period.

WHAT HAPPENS WHERE A LEASE SAYS THAT CERTAIN CHANGES TO PREMISES CANNOT BE MADE?

4.40 Special provisions apply where a lease would otherwise prevent a reasonable adjustment involving an alteration to premises. **The Act modifies** the effect of the lease so far as necessary to enable the employer to make the alteration if the landlord consents, and to provide that the landlord must not withhold consent unreasonably but may attach reasonable conditions to the consent (s 16).

HOW WILL ARRANGEMENTS FOR GETTING THE LANDLORD'S CONSENT WORK?

4.41 **The Act says** that the employer must write to the landlord (called the 'lessor' in the Act) asking for consent to make the alteration. If an employer fails to apply to the landlord for consent, anything in the lease which would prevent that alteration must be ignored in deciding whether it was reasonable for the employer to have to make that alteration (Sch 4 para 1). If the landlord consents, the employer can then carry out the alteration. If the landlord refuses consent the employer must notify the disabled person, but then has no further obligation. Where the landlord fails to reply within 21 days or a reasonable period after that he is deemed to have withheld his consent. In those circumstances the withholding of the consent will be unreasonable (see paragraph 4.44).

4.42 If the landlord attaches a condition to the consent and it is reasonable for the employer to have to carry out the alteration on that basis, the employer must then carry out the alteration. If it would not be reasonable for the employer to have to carry out the alteration on that basis, the employer must notify the disabled person, but then has no further obligation.

WHEN IS IT UNREASONABLE FOR A LANDLORD TO WITHHOLD CONSENT?
4.43   This will depend on the circumstances but a trivial or arbitrary reason would almost certainly be unreasonable. Many reasonable adjustments to premises will not harm a landlord's interests and so it would generally be unreasonable to withhold consent for them.

> A particular adjustment helps make a public building more accessible generally and is therefore likely to benefit the landlord. It would very probably be unreasonable for consent to be withheld in these circumstances.

4.44   **Regulations provide** that withholding consent will be unreasonable where:
❏   a landlord has failed to act within the time limits referred to in paragraph 4.41 above (ie 21 days of receipt of the employer's application or a reasonable period after that); or
❏   the lease says that consent will be given to alterations of that type or says that such consent will be given if it is sought in a particular way and it has been sought in that way.

WHEN IT IS REASONABLE FOR A LANDLORD TO WITHHOLD CONSENT?
4.45   This will depend on the particular circumstances.

> A particular adjustment is likely to result in a substantial permanent reduction in the value of the landlord's interest in the premises. The landlord would almost certainly be acting reasonably in withholding consent.

> A particular adjustment would cause significant disruption or inconvenience to other tenants (for example, where the premises consist of multiple adjoining units). The landlord would be likely to be acting reasonably in withholding consent.

WHAT CONDITIONS WOULD IT BE REASONABLE FOR A LANDLORD TO MAKE WHEN GIVING CONSENT?
4.46   This will depend on the particular circumstances. However, Regulations provide that it would be reasonable for the landlord to require the employer to meet any of the following conditions:
❏   obtain planning permission and other statutory consents;
❏   submit any plans to the landlord for approval (provided that the landlord then confirms that approval will not be withheld unreasonably);
❏   allow the landlord a reasonable opportunity to inspect the work when completed;
❏   reimburse the landlord's reasonable costs incurred in connection with the giving of his consent;
❏   reinstate the altered part of the premises to its former state when the lease expires but only if it would have been reasonable for the landlord to have refused consent in the first place.

WHAT HAPPENS IF THE LANDLORD HAS A 'SUPERIOR' LANDLORD?
4.47   The employer's landlord may also hold a lease which prevents him from consenting to the alteration without the consent of the 'superior' landlord. The statutory provisions have been modified by regulations to cover this. The

employer's landlord will be acting reasonably by notifying the employer that consent will be given if the superior landlord agrees. The employer's landlord must then apply to the superior landlord to ask for agreement. The provisions in paragraphs 4.41–4.46, including the requirements not to withhold consent unreasonably and not to attach unreasonable conditions, then apply to the superior landlord.

WHAT IF SOME AGREEMENT OTHER THAN A LEASE PREVENTS THE PREMISES BEING ALTERED?
4.48   An employer or landlord may be bound by the terms of an agreement or other legally binding obligation (for example, a mortgage or charge or restrictive covenant or, in Scotland, a feu disposition) under which the employer or landlord cannot alter the premises without someone else's consent. In these circumstances **Regulations provide** that it is always reasonable for the employer or landlord to have to take steps to obtain the necessary consent so that a reasonable adjustment can be made. Unless or until that consent is obtained the employer or landlord is not required to make the alteration in question. The step of seeking consent which it is always reasonable to have to take does not extend to having to apply to a court or tribunal. Whether it is reasonable for the employer or landlord to have to apply to a court or tribunal would depend on the circumstances of the case.

Agreements which breach the Act's provisions
CAN A DISABLED PERSON WAIVE RIGHTS, OR AN EMPLOYER'S DUTIES, UNDER THE ACT?
4.49   **The Act says** that any term in a contract of employment or other agreement is 'void' (ie not valid) to the extent that it would require a person to do anything that would breach any of the Act's employment provisions, or exclude or limit the operation of those provisions (s 9).

4.50   An employer should not include in an agreement any provision intended to avoid obligations under the Act, or to prevent someone from fulfilling obligations. An agreement should not, therefore, be used to try to justify less favourable treatment or deem an adjustment unreasonable. Moreover, even parts of agreements which have such an effect (even though unintended) are made void if they would restrict the working of the employment provisions in the Act. However, special arrangements cover leases and other agreements which might prevent a change to premises which could be an adjustment under the Act but where the possible restrictions to the Act's working were unintentional. These are described in paragraphs 4.40–4.48.

4.51   The Act also says that a contract term is void if it would prevent anyone from making a claim under the employment provisions in an industrial tribunal (s 9). Further information is given in Annex 3 about such agreements.

WHAT ABOUT PERMITS ISSUED IN ACCORDANCE WITH THE AGRICULTURAL WAGES ACTS?
4.52   Under the Agricultural Wages Act 1948 and the Agricultural Wages (Scotland) Act 1949 minimum wages, and terms and conditions, can be set for agricultural workers. Permits can be issued to individuals who are 'incapacitated' for the purposes of those Acts and they can then be paid such lower minimum rates or be subject to such revised terms and conditions of employment that the permit specifies. Regulations provide that the treatment of a disabled person in accordance with such a permit would be taken to be justified. This would not prevent the employer from having to comply with the duty not to discriminate,

including the duty of reasonable adjustment, for matters other than those covered by the permit.

Victimisation
WHAT DOES THE ACT SAY ABOUT VICTIMISATION?

4.53   Victimisation is a special form of discrimination covered by the Act. The **Act makes** it unlawful for one person to treat another (the victim) less favourably than he would treat other people in the same circumstances because the 'victim' has.

❑   brought, or given evidence or information in connection with, proceedings under the Act (whether or not proceedings are later withdrawn);

❑   done anything else under the Act; or

❑   alleged someone has contravened the Act (whether or not the allegation is later dropped);

or because the person believes or suspects that the victim has done or intends to do any of these things (s 55).

It is unlawful for an employer to victimise either disabled or non-disabled people.

> A disabled employee complains of discrimination. It would be unlawful for the employer to subject non-disabled colleagues to any detriment (eg suspension) for telling the truth about the alleged discrimination at an industrial tribunal hearing or in any internal grievance procedures.

4.54   It is not victimisation to treat a person less favourably because that person has made an allegation which was false and not made in good faith (s 55(4)).

(Harassment is covered in paragraphs 6.22–6.23.)

Setting up management systems to help avoid discrimination
WHAT MANAGEMENT SYSTEMS MIGHT BE SET UP TO HELP AVOID DISCRIMINATION?

4.55   The Act says that employers are responsible for the actions done by their employees in the course of their employment. In legal proceedings against an employer based on actions of an employee, it is a defence that the employer took such steps as were reasonably practicable to prevent such actions. It is not a defence for the employer simply to show the action took place without his knowledge or approval. Employers who act through agents will also be liable for the actions of their agents done with the employer's express or implied authority (s 58).

> An employer makes it clear to a recruitment agency that the company will not take kindly to recruits with learning disabilities being put forward by the agency. The agency complies by not putting such candidates forward. Both the employer and the agency will be liable if such treatment cannot be justified in an individual case.

4.56   Employers should communicate to their employees and agents any policy they may have on disability matters, and any other policies which have elements relevant to disabled employees (such as health, absenteeism or equal opportunities). All staff should be made aware that it is unlawful to discriminate against disabled people, and be familiar with the policies and practices adopted by their employer to ensure compliance with the law. Employers should provide guidance on non-discriminatory practices for all employees, so they will be aware what they should do and how to deal with disabled colleagues and disabled applicants for vacancies in the organisation, and should ensure so far as possible that these policies and practices are implemented. Employers should also make it clear to their agents what is required of them with regard to their duties under the Act, and the extent of their authority.

4.57　**The Act says** that an employer is not under an obligation to make an adjustment if he does not know, and could not reasonably be expected to know, that a person has a disability which is likely to place the person at a substantial disadvantage (s 6(6)). An employer must therefore do all he could reasonably be expected to do to find out whether this is the case.

> An employee has a disability which sometimes causes him to cry at work although the cause of this behaviour is not known to the employer. The employer's general approach on such matters is to tell staff to leave their personal problems at home and to make no allowance for such problems in the work arrangements. The employer disciplines the employee without giving him any opportunity to explain that the problem in fact arises from a disability. The employer would be unlikely to succeed in a claim that he could not reasonably be expected to have known of the disability or that it led to the behaviour for which the employee was disciplined.

> An employer has an annual appraisal system which specifically provides an opportunity to notify the employer in confidence if any employees are disabled and are put at a substantial disadvantage by the work arrangements or premises. This practice enables the employer to show that he could not reasonably be expected to know that an employee was put at such a disadvantage as a result of disability, if this was not obvious and was not brought to the employer's attention through the appraisal system.

4.58　In some cases a reasonable adjustment will not work without the co-operation of other employees. Employees may therefore have an important role in helping to ensure that a reasonable adjustment is carried out in practice.

> It is a reasonable adjustment for an employer to communicate in a particular way to an employee with autism (a disability which can make it difficult for someone to understand normal social interaction among people). As part of the reasonable adjustment it is the responsibility of that employer to seek the co-operation of other employees in communicating in that way.

4.59　It may be necessary to tell one or more of a disabled person's colleagues (in confidence) about a disability which is not obvious and/or whether any special assistance is required. This may be limited to the person's supervisor, or it may be necessary to involve other colleagues, depending on the nature of the disability and the reason they need to know about it.

> In order for a person with epilepsy to work safely in a particular factory, it may be necessary to advise fellow workers about the effects of the condition, and the methods for assisting with them.

> An office worker with cancer says that he does not want colleagues to know of his condition. As an adjustment he needs extra time away from work to receive treatment and to rest. Neither his colleagues nor the line manager needs to be

told the precise reasons for the extra leave but the latter will need to know that the adjustment is required in order to carry it out effectively.

4.60   The extent to which an employer is entitled to let other staff know about an employee's disability will depend at least in part on the terms of employment. An employer could be held to be discriminating in revealing such information about a disabled employee if the employer would not reveal similar information about another person for an equally legitimate management purpose; or if the employer revealed such information without consulting the individual, whereas the employer's usual practice would be to talk to an employee before revealing personal information about him.

4.61   The Act does not prevent a disabled person keeping a disability confidential from an employer. But this is likely to mean that unless the employer could reasonably be expected to know about the person's disability anyway, the employer will not be under a duty to make a reasonable adjustment. If a disabled person expects an employer to make a reasonable adjustment, he will need to provide the employer – or, as the case may be, someone acting on the employer's behalf – with sufficient information to carry out that adjustment.

> An employee has symptomatic HIV. He prefers not to tell his employer of the condition. However, as the condition progresses, he finds it increasingly difficult to work the required number of hours in a week. Until he tells his employer of his condition –or the employer becomes or could reasonably be expected to be aware of it – he cannot require the employer to change his working hours to overcome the difficulty. However, once the employer is informed he may then have to make a reasonable adjustment.

4.62   If an employer's agent or employee (for example, an occupational health officer, a personnel officer or line manager) knows in that capacity of an employee's disability, then the employer cannot claim that he does not know of that person's disability, and that he is therefore excluded from the obligation to make a reasonable adjustment. This will be the case even if the disabled person specifically asked for such information to be kept confidential. Employers will therefore need to ensure that where information about disabled people may come through different channels, there is a means – suitably confidential – for bringing the information together, so the employer's duties under the Act are fulfilled.

> In a large company an occupational health officer is engaged by the employer to provide him with information about his employees' health. The officer becomes aware of an employee's disability, which the employee's line manager does not know about. The employer's working arrangements put the employee at a substantial disadvantage because of the effects of her disability and she claims that a reasonable adjustment should have been made. It will not be a defence for the employer to claim that he did not know of her disability. This is because the information gained by the officer on the employer's behalf is imputed to the employer. Even if the person did not want the line manager to know that she had a disability, the occupational health officer's knowledge means that the employer's duty under the Act applies. It might even be necessary for the line manager to implement reasonable adjustments without knowing precisely why he has to do so.

4.63   Information will not be imputed to the employer if it is gained by a person providing services to employees independently of the employer. This is the case even if the employer has arranged for those services to be provided.

> An employer contracts with an agency to provide an independent counselling service to employees. The contract says that the counsellors are not acting on the employer's behalf while in the counselling role. Any information about a person's disability obtained by a counsellor during such counselling would not be imputed to the employer and so could not itself place a duty of reasonable adjustment on the employer.

WHAT IF SOMEONE SAYS THEY HAVE A DISABILITY AND THE EMPLOYER IS NOT CONVINCED?
4.64   If a candidate asks for an adjustment to be made because of an impairment whose effects are not obvious, nothing in the Act or Regulations would prohibit the employer from asking for evidence that the impairment is one which gives rise to a disability as defined in the Act.

> An applicant says she has a mental illness whose effects require her to take time off work on a frequent, but irregular, basis. If not satisfied that this is true, the employer would be entitled to ask for evidence that the woman has a mental illness which was likely to have the effects claimed and that it is clinically well recognised (as required by the Act).

Effects of other legislation
WHAT ABOUT THE EFFECTS OF OTHER LEGISLATION?
4.65   An employer is not required to make an adjustment – or do anything under the Act – that would result in a breach of statutory obligations (s 59).

> If a particular adjustment would breach health and safety or fire legislation then an employer would not have to make it. However, the employer would still have to consider whether he was required to make any other adjustment which would not breach any legislation. For instance, if someone in a wheelchair could not use emergency evacuation arrangements such as a fire escape on a particular floor, it might be reasonable for the employer to have to relocate that person's job to an office where that problem did not arise.

> An employer shortlisting applicants to fill a junior office post is considering whether to include a blind applicant who the employer believes might present a safety risk moving around the crowded office. A reasonable adjustment might be to provide mobility training to familiarise the applicant with the work area, so removing any risk there might otherwise be.

WHAT ABOUT LEGISLATION WHICH PLACES RESTRICTIONS ON WHAT EMPLOYERS CAN DO TO RECRUIT DISABLED PEOPLE?
4.66   The Disability Discrimination Act does not prevent posts being advertised as open only to disabled candidates. However, the requirement, for example, under Section 7 of the Local Government and Housing Act 1989 that every appointment to local authorities must be made on merit means that a post cannot be so advertised. Applications from disabled people can nevertheless be encouraged. However, this requirement to appoint 'on merit' does not exclude the duty under the 1995 Act to make adjustments so a disabled person's 'merit' must be assessed taking into account any such adjustments which would have to be made.

5   Recruitment

Discrimination against applicants
HOW DOES THE ACT AFFECT RECRUITMENT?
5.1   **The Act says** that it is unlawful for an employer to discriminate against a disabled person:

❑   in the arrangements made for determining who should be offered employment;
❑   in the terms on which the disabled person is offered employment; or
❑   by refusing to offer, or deliberately not offering, the disabled person employment (s 4(1))

5.2   The word 'arrangements' has a wide meaning. Employers should avoid discrimination in, for example, specifying the job, advertising the job, and the processes of selection, including the location and timing of interviews, assessment techniques, interviewing, and selection criteria.

Specifying the job
DOES THE ACT AFFECT HOW AN EMPLOYER SHOULD DRAW UP A JOB SPECIFICATION?
5.3   Yes. The inclusion of unnecessary or marginal requirements in a job specification can lead to discrimination.

> An employer stipulates that employees must be 'energetic', when in fact the job in question is largely sedentary in nature. This requirement could unjustifiably exclude some people whose disabilities result in them getting tired more easily than others.

> An employer specifies that a driving licence is required for a job which involves limited travelling. An applicant for the job has no driving licence because of the particular effects in his case of cerebral palsy. He is otherwise the best candidate for that job, he could easily and cheaply do the travelling involved other than by driving and it would be a reasonable adjustment for the employer to let him do so. It would be discriminatory to insist on the specification and reject his application solely because he had no driving licence.

5.4   Blanket exclusions (ie exclusions which do not take account of individual circumstances) may lead to discrimination.

> An employer excludes people with epilepsy from all driving jobs. One of the jobs, in practice, only requires a standard licence and normal insurance cover. If, as a result, someone with epilepsy, who has such a licence and can obtain such cover, is turned down for the job then the employer will probably have discriminated unlawfully in excluding her from consideration.

> An employer stipulates that candidates for a job must not have a history of mental illness, believing that such candidates will have poor attendance. The employer rejects an applicant solely because he has had a mental illness without checking the individual's probable attendance. Even if good attendance is genuinely essential for the job, this is not likely to be justified and is therefore very likely to be unlawful discrimination.

CAN AN EMPLOYER STIPULATE ESSENTIAL HEALTH REQUIREMENTS?
5.5   Yes, but the employer may need to justify doing so, and so show that it would not be reasonable for him to have to waive them, in any individual case.

5.6 Stating that a certain personal, medical or health-related characteristic is desirable may also lead to discrimination if the characteristic is not necessary for the performance of the job. Like a requirement, a preference may be decisive against an otherwise well-qualified disabled candidate and may have to be justified in an individual case.

> An employer prefers all employees to have a certain level of educational qualification. A woman with a learning disability, which has prevented her from obtaining the preferred qualification, is turned down for a job because she does not have that qualification. If the qualification is not necessary in order to do the job and she is otherwise the best candidate, then the employer will have discriminated unlawfully against her.

Publicising the vacancy
WHAT DOES THE ACT SAY ABOUT HOW AN EMPLOYER CAN ADVERTISE VACANCIES?
5.7 Where a job is advertised, and a disabled person who applies is refused or deliberately not offered it and complains to an industrial tribunal about disability discrimination, the Act requires the tribunal to assume (unless the employer can prove otherwise) that the reason the person did not get the job was related to his disability if the advertisement could reasonably be taken to indicate:
- ❏ that the success of a person's application for the job might depend to any extent on the absence of a disability such as the applicant's; or
- ❏ that the employer is unwilling to make an adjustment for a disabled person (s 11).

> An employer puts in an advertisement for an office worker, 'Sorry, but gaining access to our building can be difficult for some people'. A man, who as a result of an accident some years previously can only walk with the aid of crutches but can do office work, applies for the job and is turned down. He complains to an industrial tribunal. Because of the wording of the advertisement, the tribunal would have to assume that he did not get the job for a reason relating to his disability unless the employer could prove otherwise.

WHAT IS AN 'ADVERTISEMENT' FOR THE PURPOSES OF THE ACT?
5.8 **According to the Act** 'advertisement' includes every form of advertisement or notice, whether to the public or not (s 11(3)). This would include advertisements internal to a company or office.

DOES AN EMPLOYER HAVE TO PROVIDE INFORMATION ABOUT JOBS IN ALTERNATIVE FORMATS?
5.9 In particular cases, this may be a reasonable adjustment.

> A person whom the employer knows to be disabled asks to be given information about a job in a medium that is accessible to her (in large print, in braille, on tape or on computer disc). It is often likely to be a reasonable adjustment for the employer to comply, particularly if the employer's information systems, and the time available before the new employee is needed, mean it can easily be done.

CAN AN EMPLOYER SAY THAT HE WOULD WELCOME APPLICATIONS FROM DISABLED PEOPLE?
5.10 Yes. **The Act does not prevent** this and it would be a positive and public statement of the employer's policy.

CAN AN EMPLOYER INCLUDE A QUESTION ON AN APPLICATION FORM ASKING WHETHER SOMEONE IS
DISABLED?
5.11   Yes. **The Act does not prevent** employers including such a question on
application forms. Employers can also ask whether the individual might need an
adjustment and what it might be.

Selection
DOES THE DUTY OF REASONABLE ADJUSTMENT APPLY TO APPLICANTS?
5.12   **The Act says** that the duty to make a reasonable adjustment does not apply
where the employer does not know, and could not reasonably be expected to
know, that the disabled person in question is or may be an applicant for the post,
or, that a particular applicant has a disability which is likely to place him at a
disadvantage (s 6(6)).

DOES AN EMPLOYER HAVE TO TAKE SPECIAL CARE WHEN CONSIDERING APPLICATIONS?
5.13   Yes. Employers and their staff or agents must not discriminate against
disabled people in the way in which they deal with applications. They may also
have to make reasonable adjustments.

> Because of his disability, a candidate asks to submit an application in a
> particular medium, different from that specified for candidates in general (eg
> typewritten, by telephone, or on tape). It would normally be a reasonable
> adjustment for the employer to allow this.

WHOM CAN AN EMPLOYER SHORTLIST FOR INTERVIEW?
5.14   If an employer knows that an applicant has a disability and is likely to be
at a substantial disadvantage because of the employer's arrangements or premises,
the employer should consider whether there is any reasonable adjustment which
would bring the disabled person within the field of applicants to be considered
even though he would not otherwise be within that field because of that
disadvantage. If the employer could only make this judgement with more
information it would be discriminatory for him not to put the disabled person on
the shortlist for interview if that is how he would normally seek additional
information about candidates.

WHAT SHOULD AN EMPLOYER DO WHEN ARRANGING INTERVIEWS?
5.15   Employers should think ahead for interviews. Giving applicants the
opportunity to indicate any relevant effects of a disability and to suggest
adjustments to help overcome any disadvantage the disability may cause, could
help the employer avoid discrimination in the interview and in considering the
applicant, by clarifying whether any reasonable adjustments may be required.

5.16   Nevertheless, if a person, whom the employer previously did not know,
and could not have known, to be disabled, arrives for interview and is placed at
a substantial disadvantage because of the arrangements, the employer may still
be under a duty to make a reasonable adjustment from the time that he first learns
of the disability and the disadvantage. However, what the employer has to do in
such circumstances might be less extensive than if advance notice had been given.

WHAT CHANGES MIGHT AN EMPLOYER HAVE TO MAKE TO ARRANGEMENTS FOR INTERVIEWS?
5.17   There are many possible reasonable adjustments, depending on the
circumstances.

A person has difficulty attending at a particular time because of a disability. It will very likely be reasonable for the employer to have to rearrange the time.

A hearing impaired candidate has substantial difficulties with the interview arrangements. The interviewer may simply need to ensure he faces the applicant and speaks clearly or is prepared to repeat questions. The interviewer should make sure that his face is well lit when talking to someone with a hearing or visual impairment. It will almost always be reasonable for an employer to have to provide such help with communication support if the interviewee would otherwise be at a substantial disadvantage.

An employer who pays expenses to candidates who come for interview could well have to pay additional expenses to meet any special requirements of a disabled person arising from any substantial disadvantage to which she would otherwise be put by the interview arrangements. This might include paying travelling expenses for a support worker or reasonable cost of travel by taxi, rather than by bus or train, if this is necessary because of the disability.

A job applicant does not tell an employer (who has no knowledge of her disability) in advance that she uses a wheelchair. On arriving for the interview she discovers that the room is not accessible. The employer did not know of the disability and so could not have been expected to make changes in advance. However, it would still be a reasonable adjustment for the employer to hold the interview in an alternative accessible room, if a suitable one was easily available at the time with no, or only an acceptable level of, disruption or additional cost.

SHOULD AN EMPLOYER CONSIDER MAKING CHANGES TO THE WAY THE INTERVIEW IS CARRIED OUT?
5.18   Yes, although whether any change is needed – and, if so, what change – will depend on the circumstances.

It would almost always be reasonable to allow an applicant with a learning disability to bring a supportive person such as a friend or relative to assist when answering questions that are not part of tests.

It would normally be reasonable to allow a longer time for an interview to someone with a hearing impairment using a sign language interpreter to communicate.

DOES AN EMPLOYER HAVE TO MAKE CHANGES TO ANTICIPATE ANY DISABLED PERSON APPLYING FOR A JOB?
5.19   No. An employer is not required to make changes in anticipation of applications from disabled people in general. It is only if the employer knows or could be reasonably expected to know that a particular disabled person is, or may be, applying and is likely to be substantially disadvantaged by the employer's premises or arrangements, that the employer may have to make changes.

SHOULD AN EMPLOYER ASK ABOUT A DISABILITY?
5.20   The Act does not prohibit an employer from seeking information about a disability but an employer must not use it to discriminate against a disabled person. An employer should ask only about a disability if it is, or may be, relevant to the person's ability to do the job – after a reasonable adjustment, if necessary.

Asking about the effects of a disability might be important in deciding what adjustments ought to be made. The employer should avoid discriminatory questions.

> An applicant whose disability has left him using a wheelchair but healthy, is asked by an employer whether any extra leave might be required because of the condition. This is unlikely to be discriminatory because a need for extra time off work may be a substantial factor relevant to the person's ability to do the job. Therefore such a question would normally be justified. Similarly, a reasonable question about whether any changes may need to be made to the workplace to accommodate the use of the wheelchair would probably not be discriminatory.

DOES THE ACT PREVENT EMPLOYERS CARRYING OUT APTITUDE OR OTHER TESTS IN THE RECRUITMENT PROCESS?

5.21   No, but routine testing of all candidates may still discriminate against particular individuals or substantially disadvantage them. If so, the employer would need to revise the tests – or the way the results of such tests are assessed – to take account of specific disabled candidates, except where the nature and form of the test were necessary to assess a matter relevant to the job. It may, for instance, be a reasonable adjustment to accept a lower 'pass rate' for a person whose disability inhibits performance in such a test. The extent to which this is required would depend on how closely the test is related to the job in question and what adjustments the employer might have to make if the applicant were given the job.

> An employer sets a numeracy test for prospective employees. A person with a learning disability takes the test and does not achieve the level the employer normally stipulates. If the job in fact entails very little numerical work and the candidate is otherwise well suited for the job it is likely to be a reasonable adjustment for the employer to waive the requirement.

> An employer sets candidates a short oral test. An applicant is disabled by a bad stammer, but only under stress. It may be a reasonable adjustment to allow her more time to complete the test, or to give the test in written form instead, though not if oral communication is relevant to the job and assessing this was the purpose of the test.

CAN AN EMPLOYER SPECIFY QUALIFICATIONS?

5.22   An employer is entitled to specify that applicants for a job must have certain qualifications. However, if a disabled person is rejected for the job because he lacks a qualification, the employer will have to justify that rejection if the reason why the person is rejected (i.e. the lack of a qualification) is connected with his disability. Justification will involve showing that the qualification is relevant and significant in terms of the particular job and the particular applicant, and that there is no reasonable adjustment which would change this. In some circumstances it might be feasible to reassign those duties to which the qualification relates, or to waive the requirement for the qualification if this particular applicant has alternative evidence of the necessary level of competence.

> An employer seeking someone to work in an administrative post specifies that candidates must have the relevant NVQ Level 4 qualification. If Level 4 fairly reflects the complex and varied nature and substantial personal responsibility of the work, and these aspects of the job cannot reasonably be altered, the

employer will be able to justify rejecting a disabled applicant who has only been able to reach Level 3 because of his disability and who cannot show the relevant level of competence by other means.

An employer specifies that two GCSEs are required for a certain post. This is to show that a candidate has the general level of ability required. No particular subjects are specified. An applicant whose dyslexia prevented her from passing written examinations cannot meet this requirement, but the employer would be unable to justify rejecting her on this account alone if she could show she nevertheless had the skill and intelligence called for in the post.

CAN AN EMPLOYER INSIST ON A DISABLED PERSON HAVING A MEDICAL EXAMINATION?

5.23   Yes. However, if an employer insists on a medical check for a disabled person and not others, without justification, he will probably be discriminating unlawfully. The fact that a person has a disability is unlikely in itself to justify singling out that person to have a health check, although such action might be justified in relation to some jobs.

An employer requires all candidates for employment to have a medical examination. That employer would normally be entitled to include a disabled person.

An applicant for a job has a disabling heart condition. The employer routinely issues a health questionnaire to job applicants, and requires all applicants who state they have a disability to undergo a medical examination. Under the Act, the employer would not be justified in requiring a medical examination whenever an applicant states he has a disability – for example, this would not normally be justified if the disability is clearly relevant neither to the job nor to the environment in which the job is done. However, the employer would probably be justified in asking the applicant with the disabling heart condition to have a medical examination restricted to assessing its implications for the particular job in its context. If, for example, the job required lifting and carrying but these abilities were limited by the condition, the employer would also have to consider whether it would be reasonable for him to have to make a change such as providing a mechanical means of lifting and/or carrying, or arranging for the few items above the person's limit to be dealt with by another person, whilst ensuring that any health and safety provisions were not breached.

HOW CAN AN EMPLOYER TAKE ACCOUNT OF MEDICAL EVIDENCE?

5.24   In most cases, having a disability does not adversely affect a person's general health. Medical evidence about a disability can justify an adverse employment decision (such as dismissing or not promoting). It will not generally do so if there is no effect on the person's ability to do the work (or any effect is less than substantial), however great the effects of the disability are in other ways. The condition or effects must be relevant to the employer's decision.

An applicant for a post on a short-term contract has a progressive condition which has some effects, but it likely to have substantial adverse effects only in the long term. The likelihood of these long-term effects would not itself be a justifiable reason for the employer to reject him.

An employer requires all candidates for a certain job to be able to work for at least two years to complete a particular work project. Medical evidence shows that a particular candidate is unlikely to be able to continue working for that long. It would e lawful to reject that candidate if the two-year requirement was justified in terms of the work, and if it would not be reasonable for the employer to have to waive it in the particular circumstances.

Advice from an occupational health expert simply that an employee was 'unfit for work' would not mean that the employer's duty to make a reasonable adjustment was waived.

WHAT WILL HELP AN EMPLOYER DECIDE TO SELECT A PARTICULAR DISABLED PERSON?
5.25   The employer must take into account any adjustments that it is reasonable for him to have to make. Suggestions made by the candidate at any stage may assist in identifying these.

WHAT IF A DISABLED PERSON JUST ISN'T THE RIGHT PERSON FOR THE JOB?
5.26   An employer must not discriminate against a disabled candidate, but there is no requirement (aside from reasonable adjustment) to treat a disabled person more favourably than he treats or would treat others. An employer will have to assess an applicant's merits as they would be if any reasonable adjustments required under the Act had been made. If, after allowing for those adjustments, a disabled person would not be the best person for the job the employer would not have to recruit that person.

Terms and conditions of service
ARE THERE RESTRICTIONS ON THE TERMS AND CONDITIONS AN EMPLOYER CAN OFFER A DISABLED PERSON?
5.27   Terms and conditions of service should not discriminate against a disabled person. The employer should consider whether any reasonable adjustments need to be made to the terms and conditions which would otherwise apply.

An employer's terms and conditions state the hours an employee has to be in work. It might be a reasonable adjustment to change these hours for someone whose disability means that she has difficulty using public transport during rush hours.

DOES THAT MEAN THAT AN EMPLOYER CAN NEVER OFFER A DISABLED PERSON A LESS FAVOURABLE CONTRACT?
5.28   No. Such a contract may be justified if there is a material and substantial reason and there is no reasonable adjustment which can be made to remove that reason.

A person's disability means she has significantly lower output than other employees doing similar work, even after an adjustment. Her work is of neither lower nor higher quality than theirs. The employer would be justified in paying her less in proportion to the lower output if it affected the value of her work to the business.

CAN EMPLOYERS STILL OPERATE PERFORMANCE-RELATED PAY?
5.29   **Regulations provide** that this is justified so long as the scheme applies equally to all employees, or all of a particular class of employees. There would be no requirement to make a reasonable adjustment to an arrangement of this kind to ensure (for example) that a person's pay was topped up if a deteriorating

condition happened to lead to lower performance. However, there would still be a duty to make a reasonable adjustment to any aspect of the premises or work arrangements if that would prevent the disability reducing the employee's performance.

6 Employment

Discrimination against employees
DOES THE ACT COVER ALL AREAS OF EMPLOYMENT?
6.1   Yes. **The Act** says that it is unlawful for an employer to discriminate against a disabled person whom he employs:
- ❏   in the terms of employment which he affords him;
- ❏   in the opportunities which he affords him for promotion, a transfer, training or receiving any other benefit;
- ❏   by refusing to afford him, or deliberately not affording him, any such opportunity; or
- ❏   by dismissing him, or subjecting him to any other detriment (s 4(2)).

6.2   Therefore, an employer should not discriminate in relation to, for example: terms and conditions of service, arrangements made for induction, arrangements made for employees who become disabled (or who have a disability which worsens), opportunities for promotion, transfer, training or receiving any other benefit, or refusal of such opportunities, pensions, dismissal or any detriment.

Induction
WHAT IS THE EFFECT ON INDUCTION PROCEDURES?
6.3   Employers must not discriminate in their induction procedures. The employer may have to make adjustments to ensure a disabled person is introduced into a new working environment in a clearly structured and supported way with, if necessary, an individually tailored induction programme (s 4(2) and s 6(1)).

> An employer runs a one day induction course for new recruits. A recruit with a learning disability is put at a substantial disadvantage by the way the course is normally run. The employer might have to make an alternative arrangement: for example running a separate, longer course for the person, or permitting someone to sit in on the normal course to provide support, assistance or encouragement.

Promotion and transfer
WHAT ARE AN EMPLOYER'S DUTIES AS FAR AS PROMOTION AND TRANSFER ARE CONCERNED?
6.4   Employers must not discriminate in assessing a disabled person's suitability for promotion or transfer, in the practical arrangements necessary to enable the promotion or transfer to take place, in the operation of the appraisal, selection and promotion or transfer process, or in the new job itself – and may have to make a reasonable adjustment (s 4(2)(b) and (c) and s 6(1)).

> A garage owner does not consider for promotion to assistant manager a clerk who has lost the use of her right arm, because he wrongly and unreasonably believes that her disability might prevent her performing competently in a managerial post. The reason used by the employer to deny the clerk promotion has meant that she was discriminated against.

An employer considering a number of people for a job on promotion is aware that one of the candidates for interview has a hearing impairment, but does not find out whether the person needs any special arrangements for the interview, for example a sign language interpreter. If the candidate requires such an adjustment, and it would be reasonable for the employer to have to make it, the employer would fail in his duty if he did not make that adjustment.

A civil engineer whose disability involves kidney dialysis treatment, is based in London and regularly visits hospital for the treatment. She wishes to transfer to a vacant post in her company's Scottish office. She meets all the requirements for the post, but her transfer is turned down on the ground that her need for treatment would mean that, away from the facilities in London, she would be absent from work for longer. The employer had made no attempt to discuss this with her or get medical advice. If the employer had done so, it would have been clear that similar treatment would be equally available in the new locality. In these circumstances, the employer probably could not show that relying on this reason was justified.

Someone disabled by a back injury is seeking promotion to supervisor. A minor duty involves assisting with the unloading of the weekly delivery van, which the person's back injury would prevent. In assessing her suitability for promotion, the employer should consider whether reallocating this duty to another person would be a reasonable adjustment.

WHAT SHOULD AN EMPLOYER DO TO CHECK THAT PROMOTION AND TRANSFER ARRANGEMENTS DO NOT DISCRIMINATE?

6.5   The employer should review the arrangements to check that qualifications required are justified for the job to be done. He should also check that other arrangements, for example systems which determine other criteria for a particular job, do not exclude disabled people who may have been unable to meet those criteria because of their disability but would be capable of performing well in the job.

Training and other benefits provided by the employer
DOES THE ACT APPLY TO THE PROVISION OF TRAINING?

6.6   Yes. Employers must not discriminate in selection for training and must make any necessary reasonable adjustments (s 4(2)(b) and (c) and s 6(1)).

An employer wrongly assumes that a disabled person will be unwilling or unable to undertake demanding training or attend a residential training course, instead of taking an informed decision. He may well not be able to justify a decision based on that assumption.

An employer may need to alter the time or the location of the training for someone with a mobility problem, make training manuals, slides or other visual media accessible to a visually impaired employee, perhaps by providing braille versions or having them read out, or ensure that an induction loop is available for someone with a hearing impairment.

An employer refuses to allow a disabled employee to be coached for a theory examination relating to practical work which the disability prevented the employee from doing. The employer would almost always be justified in refusing to allow the coaching because it was designed to equip employees for an area of work for which, because of the disability, the person could not be suited even by a reasonable adjustment.

6.7 An employer must not discriminate in providing disabled people with opportunities for receiving benefits (which include 'facilities' and 'services') which are available to other employees (s 4(2)(b) and (c)). The employer must make any necessary reasonable adjustment to the way the benefits are provided (s 6(1)) although this does not apply to benefits under occupational pension schemes or certain other employment related benefit schemes (paragraph 6.16).

> Benefits might include canteens, meal vouchers, social clubs and other recreational activities, dedicated car parking spaces, discounts on products, bonuses, share options, hairdressing, clothes allowances, financial services, healthcare, medical assistance/insurance, transport to work, company car, education assistance, workplace nurseries, and rights to special leave.

> If physical features of a company's social club would inhibit a disabled person's access it might be a reasonable adjustment for the employer to make suitable modifications.

> An employer provides dedicated car parking spaces near to the workplace. It is likely to be reasonable for the employer to have to allocate one of these spaces to a disabled employee who has significant difficulty getting from the public car parks further away that he would otherwise have to use.

6.8 If an employer provides benefits to the public, or to a section of the public which includes the disabled employee, provision of those benefits will normally fall outside the duty not to discriminate in employment. Instead, the duty in the Act not to discriminate in providing goods, facilities and services will apply. However, the employment duty will apply if the benefit to employees is materially different (eg at a discount), is governed by the contract of employment, or relates to training (s 4(2) and (3)).

> A disabled employee of a supermarket chain who believes he has been discriminated against when buying goods as a customer at any branch of the supermarket would have no claim under the employment provisions. However, if that employee were using a discount card provided only to employees, then the employment provisions would apply if any less favourable treatment related to his use of the card.

Occupational pension schemes and insurance
6.9 **The Act inserts** into every scheme a 'non-discrimination' rule. The trustees or managers of the scheme are prohibited by that rule from doing – or omitting to do – anything to members or non-members of schemes that would be unlawful discrimination if done by an employer (s 17). References to employers in paragraphs 6.11–6.15 should therefore be read as if they also apply to trustees or managers when appropriate.

6.10 Less favourable treatment for a reason relating to a disability can be justified only if the reason is material and substantial.

Trustees of a pension scheme would not be justified in excluding a woman simply because she had a visual impairment. That fact, in itself, would be no reason why she should not receive the same pension benefits as any other employee.

6.11 There are circumstances when a disabled person's health or health prognosis is such that the cost of providing benefits under a pension scheme is substantially greater than it would be for a person without the disability. In these circumstances **Regulations provide** that an employer is regarded as justified in treating a disabled person less favourably in applying the eligibility conditions for receiving the benefit. Employers should satisfy themselves, if necessary with actuarial advice and/or medical evidence, of the likelihood of there being a substantially greater cost.

WHEN COULD THE JUSTIFICATION BE USED?
6.12 The justification would be available whenever the disabled person is considered for admission to the scheme. However, the justification cannot be applied to a disabled member, unless a term was imposed at the time of admission which allowed this.

WHICH BENEFITS DOES THIS JUSTIFICATION APPLY TO?
6.13 The justification can apply to the following types of benefits provided by an occupational pension scheme: termination of service, retirement, old age or death, accident, injury, sickness or invalidity.

WOULD A MINOR DEGREE OF EXTRA COST AMOUNT TO A JUSTIFICATION FOR LESS FAVOURABLE TREATMENT?
6.14 No. Only the likelihood of a substantial additional cost should be taken to be a justification. Substantial means something more than minor or trivial.

An employer receives medical advice that an individual with multiple sclerosis is likely to retire early on health grounds. The employer obtains actuarial advice that the cost of providing that early retirement benefit would be substantially greater than an employee without MS and so the individual is refused access to the scheme. This is justified.

WHAT HAPPENS TO AN EMPLOYEE'S RATE OF CONTRIBUTIONS IF THE EMPLOYER IS JUSTIFIED IN REFUSING THE EMPLOYEE ACCESS TO SOME BENEFITS BUT NOT OTHERS?
6.15 **Regulations provide** that if the employer sets a uniform rate of contribution the employer would be justified in applying it to a disabled person. A disabled person could therefore be required to pay the same rate of contributions as other employees, even if not eligible for some of the benefits.

DOES THE DUTY TO MAKE A REASONABLE ADJUSTMENT APPLY?
6.16 No. The duty of reasonable adjustment does not apply to the provision of benefits under an occupational pension scheme or any other benefit payable in money or money's worth under a scheme or arrangement for the benefit of employees in respect of:
❑ termination of service;
❑ retirement, old age or death; or

❑ accident, injury, sickness or invalidity (s 6(11)). (Although there is power to add other matters to this list by regulations, none have been added at the date of this Code).

Therefore, neither the employer nor the scheme's trustees or managers need to make any adjustment for a disabled person who, without that adjustment, will be justifiably denied access either to such a scheme or to a benefit under the scheme. Nor will they have to make an adjustment for someone receiving less benefit because they justifiably receive a lower rate of pay.

DOES THE ACT COVER THE PROVISION OF INSURANCE SCHEMES FOR INDIVIDUAL EMPLOYEES?

6.17 The Act also applies to provision of group insurance, such as permanent health insurance or life insurance, by an insurance company for employees under an arrangement with their employer. A disabled person in, or who applies or is considering applying to join, a group of employees covered by such an arrangement is protected from discrimination in the provision of the insurance services in the same way as if he were a member of the public seeking the services of that insurance company under the part of the Act relating to the provision of goods, facilities and services. However, the right of redress in this case would be exercised through an industrial tribunal (and not the courts) (s 18).

DOES THE ACT COVER THE PROVISION OF INSURANCE TO AN EMPLOYER?

6.18 The employer may have to make reasonable adjustments to remove any disadvantage caused to a disabled person which arose from the arrangements made by the employer to provide himself with insurance cover. Such adjustments could include measures which would reduce any risk otherwise posed by the disabled person, so that the insurer would then provide cover, or seeking alternative cover. If cover could not be obtained at all at realistic cost it is most unlikely that the employer would have to bear the risk himself.

> It comes to an employer's attention that someone who works for his antiques business has epilepsy. The employer is obliged to notify his insurance company who refuse to cover the employer against damage caused by the disabled person. To avoid dismissing the employee, it might be reasonable for the employer to have to bar the person from contact with valuable items, if this would mean the insurance company then provided cover.

Retention of disabled employees

6.19 An employer must not discriminate against an employee who becomes disabled, or has a disability which worsens (s 4(2)). The issue of retention might also arise when an employee has a stable impairment but the nature of his employment changes.

6.20 If as a result of the disability an employer's arrangements or a physical feature of the employer's premises place the employee at a substantial disadvantage in doing his existing job, the employer must first consider any reasonable adjustment that would resolve the difficulty. The employer may also need to consult the disabled person at appropriate stages about what his needs are and what effect the disability might have on future employment, for example, where the employee has a progressive condition. The nature of the reasonable adjustments which an employer may have to consider will depend on the circumstances of the case.

It may be possible to modify a job to accommodate an employee's changed needs. This might be by rearranging working methods or giving another employee certain minor tasks the newly disabled person can no longer do, providing practical aids or adaptations to premises or equipment, or allowing the disabled person to work at different times or places from those with equivalent jobs (for instance, it may be that a change to part-time work might be appropriate for someone who needed to spend some time each week having medical treatment).

A newly disabled employee is likely to need time to readjust. For example, an employer might allow: a trial period to assess whether the employee is able to cope with the current job, or a new one; the employee initially to work from home; a gradual build-up to full time hours; or additional training for a person with learning disabilities who moves to another workplace.

It may be a reasonable adjustment for an employer to move a newly disabled person to a different post within the organisation if a suitable vacancy exists or is expected shortly.

Additional job coaching may be necessary to enable a disabled person to take on a new job.

In many cases where no reasonable adjustment would overcome a particular disability so as to enable the disabled person to continue with similar terms or conditions, it might be reasonable for the employer to have to offer a disabled employee a lower-paying job, applying the rate of pay that would apply to such a position under his usual pay practices.

If new technology (for instance a telephone or information technology system) puts a disabled person at a substantial disadvantage compared with non-disabled people, then the employer would be under a duty to make a reasonable adjustment. For example, some telephone systems may interfere with hearing aids for people with hearing impairments and the quality of the inductive coupler may need to be improved.

TERMINATION OF EMPLOYMENT

6.21 Dismissal – including compulsory early retirement – of a disabled person for a reason relating to the disability would need to be justified and the reason for it would have to be one which could not be removed by any reasonable adjustment.

It would be justifiable to terminate the employment of an employee whose disability makes it impossible for him any longer to perform the main functions of his job, if an adjustment such as a move to a vacant post elsewhere in the business is not practicable or otherwise not reasonable for the employer to have to make.

It would be justifiable to terminate the employment of an employee with a worsening progressive condition if the increasing degree of adjustment necessary to accommodate the effects of the condition (shorter hours of work or falling productivity, say) became unreasonable for the employer to have to make.

An employer who needs to reduce the workforce would have to ensure that any scheme which was introduced for choosing candidates for redundancy did not discriminate against disabled people. Therefore, if a criterion for redundancy would apply to a disabled person for a reason relating to the disability, that criterion would have to be 'material' and 'substantial' and the employer would have to consider whether a reasonable adjustment would prevent the criterion applying to the disabled person after all.

Harassment
WHAT DOES THE ACT SAY ABOUT HARASSMENT?
6.22   The Act does not refer to harassment as a separate issue. However, harassing a disabled person on account of a disability will almost always amount to a 'detriment' under the Act. (Victimisation is covered in paragraphs 4.53–4.54).

ARE EMPLOYERS LIABLE FOR HARASSMENT BY THEIR EMPLOYEES?
6.23   An employer is responsible for acts of harassment by employees in the course of their employment unless the employer took such steps as were reasonable practicable to prevent it. As a minimum first step harassment because of disability should be made a disciplinary matter and staff should be made aware that it will be taken seriously.

7   Particular provisions

Discrimination against contract workers
7.1   The Act deals specifically with work which is carried out by individuals ('contract workers') for a person (a 'principal') who hires them under contract from their employer (generally an employment business) – referred to below as the 'sending' employer.

WHAT DOES THE ACT SAY ABOUT CONTRACT WORKERS?
7.2   **The Act says** that it is unlawful for a principal to discriminate against a disabled person:
- ❏   in the terms on which the person is allowed to do the contract work;
- ❏   by not allowing the person to do, or continue to do, the contract work;
- ❏   in the way he affords the person access to, or by failing to afford him access to, benefits in relation to contract work; or
- ❏   by subjecting the person to any other detriment in relation to contract work (s 12(1)).

7.3   **The Act and Regulations apply**, generally speaking, as if the principal were, or would be, the actual employer of the contract worker. Therefore, the same definition of 'discrimination' – including the need to justify less favourable treatment – applies as for employers (s 12(3)).

> The employer of a labourer, who some years ago was disabled by clinical depression but has since recovered, proposes to supply him to a contractor to work on a building site. Although his past disability is covered by the Act, the site manager refuses to accept him because of his medical history. Unless the contractor can show that the manager's action is justified, the contractor would be acting unlawfully.

WHAT WILL BE THE EFFECT OF THE DUTY TO MAKE ADJUSTMENTS FOR PRINCIPALS?
7.4   The duty to make a reasonable adjustment applies to a principal as to an employer (s 12(3)).

7.5   In deciding whether any, and if so, what, adjustment would be reasonable for a principal to have to make, the period for which the contract worker will work for the principal is important. It might well be unreasonable for a principal to have to make certain adjustments if the worker will be with the principal for only a short time.

> An employment business enters into a contract with a firm of accountants to provide an assistant for two weeks to cover an unexpected absence. The employment business wishes to put forward a person who, because of his disability, finds it difficult to travel during the rush hour and would like his working hours to be modified accordingly. It might not be reasonable for the firm to have to agree given the short time in which to negotiate and implement the new hours.

WILL THE PRINCIPAL AND THE 'SENDING' EMPLOYER BOTH HAVE DUTIES TO MAKE REASONABLE ADJUSTMENTS?

7.6   Both the 'sending' employer and the principal may separately be under a duty of reasonable adjustment in the case of a contract worker who is disabled. If the 'sending' employer's own premises or arrangements place the contract worker at a substantial disadvantage, then the 'sending' employer may have a duty to make a reasonable adjustment (s 6(1)). The 'sending' employer may also have a duty to make a reasonable adjustment where a similar substantial disadvantage is likely to affect a contract worker as a result of the arrangements or premises of all or most of the principals to whom he might be supplied. The employer would not have to take separate steps in relation to each principal, but would have to make any reasonable adjustment within his power which would overcome the disadvantage wherever it might arise. The principal would not have to make any adjustment which the employer should make. However, subject to that the principal would be responsible only for any additional reasonable adjustment which is necessary solely because of the principal's own arrangements or premises (s 6(1) applied by s 12(3)). It would also usually be reasonable for a principal and a 'sending' employer to have to cooperate with any steps taken by the other to assist a disabled contract worker.

> A travel agency hires a clerical worker from an employment business to fulfil a three month contract to file travel invoices during the busy summer holiday period. The contract worker is a wheelchair user, and is quite capable of doing the job if a few minor, temporary changes are made to the arrangement of furniture in the office. It would be reasonable for the travel agency to make this adjustment.

> A bank hires a blind word processor operator as a contract worker from an employment business. The employment business provides her with a specially adapted portable computer because she would otherwise be at a similar substantial disadvantage in doing the work wherever she does it. (In such circumstances the bank would not have to provide a specially adapted computer if the employment business did not.) The bank would have to cooperate by letting the contract worker use her computer whilst working for the bank if it is compatible with the bank's systems. If not, it could be a reasonable adjustment for the bank to make the computer compatible and for the employment business to allow that change to be made.

WHAT ABOUT CONTRACT WORKERS IN SMALL FIRMS?

7.7   The Act applies to any employment business which has 20 or more employees (including people currently employed by it but hired out to principals). It also applies to any principal who has 20 or more workers (counting both the principal's own employees and any contract workers currently working for the principal). It does not apply to employment businesses or principals with fewer than 20 employees. Note the extended definition of 'employment' in the Act (see paragraph 2.8).

> An employment business has 15 employees (including people currently hired out to others) and enters a contract to provide a worker in a shop. The shop employs 29 people. Neither the duty not to discriminate nor the duty to make a reasonable adjustment applies to the employment business, but both duties apply to the owner of the shop. However, the length of time the worker was contracted to work at the shop would be an important factor in assessing whether the shop-owner had to make any significant adjustment.

> A deaf individual is employed by an employment business that has 100 employees (including people currently hired out to others). He is hired regularly to do contract work and, as a reasonable adjustment, the business provides a portable induction loop for assignments. If he works for a principal with, say, 17 workers, (counting both employees and contract workers) that principal would not be required to cooperate with use of the induction loop. However, if the principal has 20 or more such workers the principal would be obliged to cooperate.

WHAT ABOUT THE SUPPORTED PLACEMENT SCHEME (SPS)?

7.8   These arrangements also apply to the Employment Service's Supported Placement Scheme (SPS) for severely disabled people. The 'contractor' under the scheme (usually a local authority or voluntary body) is the equivalent of the 'sending' employer, and the 'host employer' is the equivalent of the principal. A local authority can even be both the contractor and the host employer at the same time (as can a voluntary body) in which case the duty not to discriminate and the duty of reasonable adjustment would apply to it as to an employer.

Provisions applying to trade organisations

WHAT DOES THE ACT SAY ABOUT TRADE ORGANISATIONS?

7.9   A trade organisation is defined as an organisation of workers or of employers, or any other organisation whose members carry on a particular profession or trade for the purposes of which the organisation exists (s 13(4)). Therefore trade unions, employers' associations, and similar bodies like the Law Society and chartered professional institutions, for example, must comply with the legislation.

7.10   **The Act says** that it is unlawful for a trade organisation to discriminate against a disabled person:
❑   in the terms on which it is prepared to admit the person to membership; or
❑   by refusing to accept, or deliberately not accepting, an application for membership.
It is also unlawful for a trade organisation to discriminate against a disabled member of the organisation:
❑   in the way it affords the person access to any benefits or by refusing or deliberately omitting to afford access to them;

❏   by depriving the person of membership, or varying the terms of membership; or

❏   by subjecting the person to any other detriment (s 13).

Trade organisations should therefore check that they do not discriminate as regards, for example, training facilities, welfare or insurance schemes, invitations to attend events, processing of grievances, assistance to members in their employers' disciplinary or dismissal procedures.

7.11   The Act defines discrimination by a trade organisation in similar terms to the definition relating to discrimination by an employer. Therefore, the need to justify less favourable treatment for a reason relating to disability applies as in the case of an employer (s 14(3)).

> A trade organisation is arranging a trip to some of its members' workplaces but it decides to exclude a member in a wheelchair because too many of the sites are inaccessible to make participation worthwhile. This could well be justified. (Note, however, paragraph 7.12)

Do trade organisations have a duty to make adjustments?
7.12   The Act includes a requirement on trade organisations to make reasonable adjustments (s 15). However, this duty will not be brought into force until after the other employment provisions, at a date which will be subject to consultation.

What about the actions of employees or representatives of trade organisations?
7.13   Individual employees or agents of trade organisations who have dealings with members or applicants are treated in the same way as individual employees or agents of employers who deal with job applicants or employees: the trade organisation is responsible for their actions (s 58).

8   Resolving disagreements within the employing organisation

What does the Act say about resolving disagreements?
8.1   The Act does not require employers to resolve disputes within their organisations. However, it is in an employer's interests to resolve problems as they arise where possible. This should be in a non-discriminatory way to comply with the Act's general provisions.

8.2   One method might be the use of a grievance procedure. Grievance procedures provide an open and fair way for employees to make known their concerns and enable grievances to be resolved quickly before they become major difficulties. Use of the procedures can highlight areas where the employer's duty of reasonable adjustment may not have been observed, and can prevent misunderstandings in this area leading to tribunal complaints.

Do existing grievance and disciplinary procedures need changing?
8.3   Where grievance or disciplinary procedures are in place, the employer might wish to review, and where necessary adapt, them to ensure that they are flexible enough to be used by disabled employees. Where a formal grievance (or disciplinary) procedure operates, it must be open, or applied, to disabled employees on the same basis as to others. Employers will have to ensure that grievance (or disciplinary) procedures do not, in themselves, discriminate against disabled employees and may have to make reasonable adjustments to enable some

disabled employees to use grievance procedures effectively or to ensure disciplinary procedures have the same impact on disabled employees as on others.

> An employee with a learning disability has to attend an interview under the employer's disciplinary procedures. The employee would like his guardian or a friend to be present. The employer agrees to this but refuses to rearrange the interview to a time which is more convenient to the guardian or friend. The employer may be in breach of the duty to make a reasonable adjustment.

(See Annex 3 for information about industrial tribunals.)

Annex I What is meant by disability

1   This Annex is included to aid understanding about who is covered by the Act and should provide sufficient information on the definition of disability to cover the large majority of cases. The definition of disability in the Act is designed to cover only people who would generally be considered to be disabled. A Government publication *'Guidance on matters to be taken into account in determining questions relating to the definition of disability'*, is also available.

When is a person disabled?
2   A person has a disability if he has a physical or mental impairment which has a substantial and long-term adverse effect on his ability to carry out normal day-to-day activities.

What about people who have recovered from a disability?
3   People who have had a disability within the definition are protected from discrimination even if they have since recovered.

What does 'impairment' cover?
4   It covers physical or mental impairments; this includes sensory impairments, such as those affecting sight or hearing.

Are all mental impairments covered?
5   The term 'mental impairment' is intended to cover a wide range of impairments relating to mental functioning, including what are often known as learning disabilities. However, the Act states that it does not include any impairment resulting from or consisting of a mental illness, unless that illness is a clinically well-recognised illness. A clinically well-recognised illness is one that is recognised by a respected body of medical opinion.

What is a 'substantial' adverse effect?
6   A substantial adverse effect is something which is more than a minor or trivial effect. The requirement that an effect must be substantial reflects the general understanding of disability as a limitation going beyond the normal differences in ability which might exist among people.

What is a 'long-term' effect?
7   A long-term effect of an impairment is one:
❑   which has lasted at least 12 months; or
❑   where the total period for which it lasts is likely to be at least 12 months; or

❏   which is likely to last for the rest of the life of the person affected.

8   Effects which are not long-term would therefore include loss of mobility due to a broken limb which is likely to heal within 12 months and the effects of temporary infections, from which a person would be likely to recover within 12 months.

What if the effects come and go over a period of time?
9   If an impairment has had a substantial adverse effect on normal day-to-day activities but that effect ceases, the substantial effect is treated as continuing if it is likely to recur; that is if it is more probable than not that the effect will recur. To take the example of a person with rheumatoid arthritis whose impairment has a substantial adverse effect, which then ceases to be substantial (ie the person has a period of remission). The effects are to be treated as if they are continuing, and are likely to continue beyond 12 months, if:
❏   the impairment remains; and
❏   at least one recurrence of the substantial effect is likely to take place 12 months or more after the initial occurrence.
This would then be a long-term effect.

What are 'normal day-to-day activities'?
10   They are activities which are carried out by most people on a fairly regular and frequent basis. The term is not intended to include activities which are normal only for a particular person or group of people, such as playing a musical instrument, or a sport, to a professional standard or performing a skilled or specialised task at work. However, someone who is affected in such a specialised way but is also affected in normal day-to-day activities, would be covered by this part of the definition. The test of whether an impairment affects normal day-to-day activities is whether it affects one of the broad categories of capacity listed in Schedule 1 to the Act. They are:
❏   mobility;
❏   manual dexterity;
❏   physical co-ordination;
❏   continence;
❏   ability to lift, carry or otherwise move everyday objects;
❏   speech, hearing or eyesight;
❏   memory or ability to concentrate, learn or understand; or
❏   perception of the risk of physical danger.

What about treatment?
11   Someone with an impairment may be receiving medical or other treatment which alleviates or removes the effects (though not the impairment). In such cases, the treatment is ignored and the impairment is taken to have the effect it would have had without such treatment. This does not apply if substantial adverse effects are not likely to recur even if the treatment stops (ie the impairment has been cured).

Does this include people who wear spectacles?
12   No. The sole exception to the rule about ignoring the effects of treatment is the wearing of spectacles or contact lenses. In this case, the effect while the person is wearing spectacles or contact lenses should be considered.

Are people who have disfigurements covered?
13   People with severe disfigurements are covered by the Act. They do not need to demonstrate that the impairment has a substantial adverse effect on their ability to carry out normal day-to-day activities.

What about people who know their condition is going to get worse over time?
14   Progressive conditions are conditions which are likely to change and develop over time. Examples given in the Act are cancer, multiple sclerosis, muscular dystrophy and HIV infection. Where a person has a progressive condition he will be covered by the Act from the moment the condition leads to an impairment which has *some* effect on ability to carry out normal day-to-day activities, even though not a *substantial* effect, if that impairment is likely eventually to have a substantial adverse effect on such ability.

What about people who are registered disabled?
15   Those registered as disabled under the Disabled Persons (Employment) Act 1944 both on 12 January 1995 and 2 December 1996 will be treated as being disabled under the Disability Discrimination Act 1995 for three years from the latter date. At all times from 2 December 1996 onwards they will be covered by the Act as people who have had a disability. This does not preclude them from being covered as having a current disability any time after the three year period has finished. Whether they are or not will depend on whether they – like anyone else – meet the definition of disability in the Act.

Are people with genetic conditions covered?
16   If a genetic condition has no effect on ability to carry out normal day-to-day activities, the person is not covered. Diagnosis does not in itself bring someone within the definition. If the condition is progressive, then the rule about progressive conditions applies.

Are any conditions specifically excluded from the coverage of the Act?
17   Yes. Certain conditions are to be regarded as not amounting to impairments for the purposes of the Act. These are:
❑   addiction to or dependency on alcohol, nicotine, or any other substance (other than as a result of the substance being medically prescribed);
❑   seasonal allergic rhinitis (eg hayfever), except where it aggravates the effect of another condition;
❑   tendency to set fires;
❑   tendency to steal;
❑   tendency to physical or sexual abuse of other persons;
❑   exhibitionism;
❑   voyeurism.
Also, disfigurements which consist of a tattoo (which has not been removed), non-medical body piercing, or something attached through such piercing, are to be treated as not having a substantial adverse effect on the person's ability to carry out normal day-to-day activities.

Annex 2   How to get further information, help and advice

1   A range of leaflets about various aspects of the Act is available. To obtain copies, call 0345 622 633 (local rate), or textphone 0345 622 644. Copies of the leaflets are also available in braille and audio cassette.

2   Statutory Guidance on the definition of disability is produced separately. This can be obtained from HMSO bookshops – see back cover of this Code. This Guidance should prove helpful where it is not clear whether or not a person has or has had a disability.

3   There is a wide range of practical help and advice available to assist employers in the recruitment and employment of people, including disabled people, for example from Jobcentres, Careers Service offices, Training and Enterprise Councils (in England and Wales) and Local Enterprise Companies (in Scotland). Addresses and telephone numbers are available in local telephone directories.

4   Where necessary, specialist help and advice for disabled people and for employers who might, or do, employ disabled people is available from the Employment Service through its local Placing, Assessment and Counselling Teams (PACTs). PACTs can help with issues related to employing disabled people, but cannot advise on an employer's specific legal obligations.

5   PACTs may be able to provide help with special aids, equipment and other measures to overcome the effects of disability in the working environment.

6   The addresses and telephone numbers of PACTs are listed in local telephone directories under 'Employment Service', or can be obtained from the nearest Jobcentre.

7   Many specialist organisations for disabled people also offer a range of employment help and advice. The Employment Service publish a booklet called *Sources of Information and Advice* (Ref: PGP6) which lists many of the specialist organisations offering help to employers on employment and disability issues. The booklet can be obtained from PACTs.

8   The Advisory, Conciliation and Arbitration Service (ACAS) can help employers and individuals with factual information on the legislation and assistance related to its effects on industrial relations practices and procedures. The address and telephone numbers of ACAS offices are listed in local telephone directories under 'ACAS'.

9   Employers working in historic buildings, or other heritage properties, may also wish to obtain a copy of Easy Access to Historic Properties from English Heritage at 23 Savile Row, London W1X 1AB. Tel: 0171 973 3434.

10   Disability can take a very large number of forms and the action an employer may be required to take will depend to a very large extent on the particular circumstances of the case. Any advice and information employers receive should be considered in that light. In some circumstances employers may wish to consider whether they should seek legal advice.

Annex 3   Complaints under the employment provisions

What does the Act say about making complaints?
1   **The Act says** that a person who believes that an employer has unlawfully discriminated or failed to make a reasonable adjustment, or that a person has aided an employer to do such an act, may present a complaint to an industrial tribunal (s 8(1)).

What does the Act say about conciliation?
2   When a formal complaint has been made to an industrial tribunal **the Act places a duty** on the Advisory, Conciliation and Arbitration Service's (ACAS) conciliation officers to try to promote settlement of the dispute without a tribunal hearing (Sch 3, para 1). ACAS can also assist in this way without a formal application to a tribunal being made.

What does the Act say about obtaining a remedy for unlawful discrimination?
3   **The Act says** that a disabled person who believes someone has unlawfully discriminated against him or failed to make a reasonable adjustment, in breach of the employment provisions of the Act or Regulations, may present a complaint to an industrial tribunal (s 8(1)).

4   If the tribunal upholds the complaint it may:
- declare the rights of the disabled person (the complainant), and the other person (the respondent) in relation to the complaint;
- order the other person to pay the complainant compensation; and
- recommend that, within a specified time, the other person take reasonable action to prevent or reduce the adverse effect in question (s 8(2)).

5   **The Act allows** compensation for injury to feelings to be awarded whether or not other compensation is awarded (s 8(4)).

6   **The Act says** that if a respondent fails, without reasonable justification, to comply with an industrial tribunal's recommendation, the tribunal may:
- increase the amount of compensation to be paid; or
- order the respondent to pay compensation if it did not make such an order earlier (s 8 (5)).

Who can be taken to an Industrial Tribunal?
7   The tribunal complaints procedure applies to anyone whom, it is claimed, has discriminated in the employment field – employers (and their employees and agents for whose acts they are responsible), trade organisations, people who hire contract workers and people who aid any of these to discriminate.

COMPLAINTS INVOLVING LANDLORDS
8   If a reasonable adjustment requiring the consent of the employer's landlord (or a superior landlord) is not made, for whatever reason, the disabled person may bring a complaint against the employer in an industrial tribunal. Either the disabled person or the employer may ask the tribunal to make the landlord a party to the proceedings. If the industrial tribunal finds that the landlord acted unreasonably in withholding consent, or gave consent but attached an unreasonable condition, it can make any appropriate declaration, order that the

669

alteration may be made, or award compensation against the landlord (s 27 and Sch 4 para 2).

COMPLAINING ABOUT PENSION SCHEMES

9 A disabled person who considers that the trustees or managers of a pension scheme have discriminated against him, may complain through the pensions dispute resolution mechanism. Information about the scheme should give details about this. If necessary, a complaint may be made to the Pensions Ombudsman.

10 From April 1997, all occupational pension schemes will be required to set up and operate procedures for resolving disputes between individual pension scheme members and the trustees or managers.

11 The Occupational Pensions Advisory Service (OPAS) can provide an advice and conciliation service for members of the public who have problems with their occupational pension. OPAS can be contacted at 11 Belgrave Road, London SW1U 1RB. Tel: 0171 233 8080.

12 A disabled person who considers that an employer has discriminated against him in providing access to a pension scheme can complain to an industrial tribunal following the same process for other complaints against employers.

What is the 'Questionnaire Procedure'?

13. **The Act provides** for a procedure (the questionnaire procedure) to assist a person who believes that discrimination has occurred, to decide whether or not to start proceedings and, if the person does, to formulate and present a case in the most effective manner (s 56). Questionnaire forms will be obtainable from Jobcentres.

Can compromise agreements be an alternative to making tribunal complaints?

14 **The Act says** that, in general, the terms of an agreement (such as a contract of employment) cannot prevent a disabled person from complaining to an industrial tribunal, or force a complaint to be stopped (s 9). However, **the Act also says** that in some circumstances a disabled person can make an agreement not to make a complaint or to stop one (s 9).

15 These circumstances are if:
❑ an ACAS conciliation officer has acted under the Act on the matter; *or* the following conditions apply:
❑ the disabled person must have received independent legal advice from a qualified lawyer about the terms and effects of the agreement, particularly its effect on his ability to complain to a tribunal;
❑ the adviser must have an insurance policy covering any loss arising from the advice; and
❑ the agreement must be in writing, relate to the complaint, identify the adviser and say that these conditions are satisfied.

16 It may be in the interests of some disabled people to make such 'compromise' agreements instead of pursuing complaints to industrial tribunal hearings, but care should be taken to ensure that the above conditions are met.

How is a complaint made to an Industrial Tribunal?
17 Complaints to an industrial tribunal can be made on an application form (IT 1). Forms are obtainable from Jobcentres. Completed applications should be returned to the Industrial Tribunals Central Office. The address is on the form.

18 Applications to an industrial tribunal must be made within three months of the time when the incident being complained of occurred. The time limit will not normally be extended to allow for the time it might take to try to settle the dispute within the organisation eg. by way of internal grievance procedures (see paragraphs 8.1–8.3). A tribunal may, however, consider a complaint which is out of time, if it considers, in all the circumstances of the case, that it is just and equitable to do so (Sch 3, para 3).

What does the Act say about reporting restrictions?
19 **The Act empowers** a tribunal to make 'restricted reporting orders' if it considers that evidence of a personal nature is likely to be heard by the tribunal. Such orders prohibit the publication, for example in a newspaper, of any matter likely to lead members of the public to identify the complainant or any other person mentioned in the order, until the tribunal's decision is promulgated.

(J) Code of Practice
Access to Workers during Recognition and Derecogniton Ballots

Preamble

The legal framework within which this Code will operate is explained in its text. While every effort has been made to ensure that explanations included in the Code are accurate, only the courts can give authoritative interpretations of the law.

The Code's provisions apply equally to men and to women, but for simplicity the masculine pronoun is used throughout.

Unless the text specifies otherwise, (i) the term 'union' should be read to mean 'unions' in cases where two or more unions are seeking to be jointly recognised; (ii) the term 'workplace' should be read to mean 'workplaces' in cases where a recognition application covers more than one workplace; and (iii) the term 'working day' should be read to mean any day other than a Saturday or a Sunday, Christmas Day or Good Friday, or a day which is a bank holiday.

Passages in this Code which appear in italics are extracts from, or re-statements of, provisions in primary legislation.

Section A   Introduction

Background
1   Schedule A1 of the Trade Union and Labour Relations (Consolidation) Act 1992, inserted by the Employment Relations Act 1999, sets out the statutory procedure for the recognition and derecognition of trade unions for the purpose of collective bargaining.

Recognition
2   Where an employer and a trade union fail to reach agreement on recognition voluntarily, the statute provides for the union to apply to the Central Arbitration Committee (CAC) to decide whether it should be recognised for collective bargaining purposes. In certain cases, the CAC may award recognition, or dismiss the application, without a ballot. In other cases, the CAC will be obliged to hold a secret ballot of members of the bargaining unit to determine the issue. If a ballot takes place, the CAC will decide whether it should be held at the workplace, by post, or, if special factors make it appropriate, by a combination of the two methods. The ballot must be conducted by a qualified independent person appointed by the CAC.

3   Paragraph 26(2) of Schedule A1 places a duty on the employer *to co-operate generally, in connection with the ballot, with the union and the independent person appointed to conduct the ballot.*

4   Paragraph 26(3) of Schedule A1 places a duty on the employer to give a union applying for recognition *such access to the workers constituting the bargaining unit as is reasonable to enable the union to inform the workers of the object of the ballot and to seek their support and their opinions on the issues involved.*

5   Section 203(1)(a) of the Trade Union and Labour Relations (Consolidation) Act 1992 gives a general power to the Secretary of State to issue Codes of Practice containing practical guidance for the purpose of promoting the improvement of industrial relations. Paragraph 26(8)(b) of Schedule A1 specifies that this general power includes the particular power to issue a Code of Practice giving practical guidance about reasonable access during recognition ballots for the purposes of paragraph 26(3).

Derecognition
6   The CAC can also call a derecognition ballot in cases where an employer, or his workers, are seeking to end recognition arrangements with a union. Paragraph 118(3) of Schedule A1 contains identical wording to paragraph 26(3) of Schedule A1, placing a duty on the employer to give the recognised union reasonable access to the workers comprising the bargaining unit where the CAC is holding a ballot on derecognition. Paragraph 118(8)(b) contains a similar provision to paragraph 26(8)(b) enabling the Secretary of State to issue a Code of Practice giving practical guidance about reasonable access during derecognition ballots.

7   The guidance contained in this Code applies equally to cases where the ballot is about recognition or derecognition.

General purpose of the Code
8   This Code gives practical guidance about the issues which arise when an employer receives a request by a union to be granted access to his workers at their workplace and/or during their working time. It does not cover other forms of access outside the employer's control away from the workplace or outside working hours. For example, it does not discuss how the union might use other means, such as local newspapers or media, to put across its message to the workers involved. This Code deals with the specific circumstances of access during the period of recognition or derecognition ballots. It does not provide guidance on access at other times.

9   Access can take many and varied forms depending largely on the type of workplace involved and the characteristics of the balloted workforce. The overall aim is to ensure that the union can reach the workers involved, but local circumstances will need to be taken into account when deciding what form the access should take. Each case should be looked at on the facts. This Code therefore aims to help the employer and the union arrive at agreed arrangements for access, which can take full account of the circumstances of each individual case.

10   This Code also aims to encourage reasonable and responsible behaviour by both the employer and the union. This should ensure that acrimony between the parties is avoided and individual workers are not exposed to intimidation or threat. As regards the treatment of individuals, both parties should note that the law provides protections against dismissal or detriment for workers who campaign either for or against recognition.

11.   In order for a ballot to take place, the union must have satisfied the CAC that at least 10% of the proposed bargaining unit are already members of the union, and that a majority of the workers in the proposed bargaining unit would be likely to favour recognition. There is therefore a good chance that recognition

will be granted to the union, and that a working relationship between the parties will have to be sustained after the ballot. This longer term perspective should encourage both the employer and the union to behave responsibly and in a co-operative spirit during the balloting period.

Legal status of the Code

12   *Under paragraphs 27 and 119 of Schedule A1 to the Trade Union and Labour Relations (Consolidation) Act 1992, the CAC may order employers who are breaching their duty to allow reasonable access, to take specified, reasonable steps to do so, and can award recognition without a ballot, or can refuse to award derecognition where applied for by the employer, if an employer fails to abide by its orders to remedy a breach.*

13   *This Code itself imposes no legal obligations and failure to observe it does not in itself render anyone liable to proceedings. But section 207 of the Trade Union and Labour Relations (Consolidation) Act 1992 provides that any provisions of this Code are to be admissible in evidence and are to be taken into account in proceedings before any court, tribunal or the CAC where they consider them relevant.*

Section B   Preparing for access

When should preparations for access begin?

14   Preparations for access should begin as soon as possible. The CAC is required to give notice to the employer and the union that it intends to arrange for the holding of a ballot. There then follows a period of ten working days before the CAC proceeds with arrangements for the ballot. The parties should make full use of this notification period to prepare for access. The union should request an early meeting with the employer in this period to discuss access arrangements. The employer should agree to arrange the meeting on an early date and at a mutually convenient time. The employer and the union should ensure that the individual or individuals representing them at the meeting are expressly authorised by them to take all relevant decisions regarding access, or are authorised to make recommendations directly to those who take such decisions.

Joint applications by two or more unions

15   Where there is a joint application for recognition by two or more unions acting together, the unions should act jointly in preparing and implementing the access arrangements. Therefore, unless the employer and the unions agree otherwise, the unions should have common access arrangements. The amount of time needed for access would normally be the same for single or joint applications.

Establishing an access agreement

16   It would be reasonable for the employer to want to give his prior permission before allowing a full time union official to enter his workplace and talk to his workers. In particular, the employer may have security and health and safety issues to consider. The parties should discuss practical arrangements for the union's activities at the workplace, in advance of the period of access actually beginning.

17   Consideration should be given to establishing an agreement, preferably in written form, on access arrangements. Such an agreement could include:

- the union's programme for where, when and how it will access the workers on site and/or during their working time; and
- a mechanism for resolving disagreements, if any arise, about implementing the agreed programme of access.

18   In seeking to reach an agreement, the union should put its proposals for accessing the workers to the employer. The employer should not dismiss the proposals unless he considers the union's requirements to be unreasonable in the circumstances. If the employer rejects the proposals, he should offer alternative arrangements to the union at the earliest opportunity, preferably within three working days of receiving the union's initial proposals. In the course of this dialogue the union will need to reveal its plans for on-site access.

19   It is reasonable for the union to request information from the employer to help it formulate and refine its access proposals. In particular, the employer should disclose to the union information about his typical methods of communicating with his workforce and provide such other practical information as may be needed about, say, workplace premises or patterns of work. Where relevant to the union in framing its plans, the employer should also disclose information about his own plans to put across his views, directly or indirectly, to the workers about the recognition (or derecognition) of the union. The employer should not, however, disclose to the union the names or addresses (postal or e-mail) of the workers who will be balloted, unless the workers concerned have authorised the disclosure.

Amending the access agreement
20   Every effort should be made to ensure access agreements are faithfully implemented. However, in some cases, the agreement may need to be changed if circumstances alter. For example, a union official selected to enter the workplace may be unexpectedly called away by his union on other urgent business. Likewise, the employer might wish to re-arrange an event if the selected meeting-room is unexpectedly and unavoidably needed for other important business purposes. If such circumstances arise, the union, or the employer if his situation changes, should notify the other party at the earliest opportunity that a change will need to be made to the agreed access arrangements, and offer alternative suggestions. The other party should generally accept the alternative arrangements, if they are of an equivalent nature to those already agreed.

Resolving differences about agreeing access arrangements
21   Where the employer and the union fail to agree access arrangements voluntarily, either party, acting separately or together, may ask the Advisory, Conciliation and Arbitration Service (ACAS) to conciliate. Given the limited time available, ACAS will respond to the conciliation request as soon as possible, and preferably within one working day of receiving the request. Both parties should give all reasonable assistance to ACAS to enable it to help the parties overcome their difficulties through conciliation.

22   Every effort should be made to resolve any procedural difficulties remaining, but, ultimately, where it remains deadlocked, the CAC may be asked to assist. The CAC could, in appropriate circumstances, consider delaying the arrangement of the ballot for a limited period to give extra time for the parties to settle their differences. However, where no agreement is forthcoming, the CAC may be asked to adjudicate and to make an order.

Section C Access in operation

What is the access period?

23   *Following the notification period, and providing it does not receive a contrary request from the trade union, the CAC will be required to arrange the holding of the ballot. As soon as is reasonably practicable, the CAC must inform the parties of the fact that it is arranging the ballot, the name of the qualified independent person appointed to conduct the ballot, and the period within which the ballot must be conducted. The ballot must be held within 20 working days from the day after the appointment of the independent person, or longer if the CAC should so decide.*

24   The period of access will begin as soon as the parties have been informed of the arrangements for the ballot as in paragraph 23 above. The CAC will endeavour to inform both parties as soon as the independent person has been appointed. This may be achieved by a telephone call to both parties, followed by a letter of confirmation.

25   If the ballot is to be conducted by post, the period of access will come to an end on the closing date of the balloting period. If the ballot is to be conducted at the workplace, access will continue until the ballot has closed. However, where the ballot is to be conducted at the workplace, and where the union has already had adequate access opportunities, both the employer and the union should largely confine their activities during the actual hours of balloting to the encouragement of workers to vote. They should reduce or cease other campaigning activity at this time. For example, both the employer and the union should avoid scheduling large meetings at such times. This should ensure that the ballot is conducted in a calm and orderly fashion, with minimum disruption to the normal functioning of the workplace.

Who may be granted access?

26   The access agreement should specify who should be given access to the workers who will be balloted. Employers should be prepared to give access to:
(a) individual union members employed by the employer, who are nominated by the union as the lead representative of their members at workplaces where the bargaining unit is situated;
(b) individual union members employed by the employer, who are nominated by the union as the lead representative of their members at other workplaces in the employer's business, provided that it is practicable for them to attend events at workplaces where the bargaining unit is situated. The costs of travelling from other workplaces should be met by the individuals or the union; and
(c) 'full-time' union officials. (That is, individuals employed by the union, who are officials of the union within the meaning of the sections 1 and 119 of the Trade Union and Labour Relations (Consolidation) Act 1992).

The number of union representatives entitled to gain access should be proportionate to the scale and nature of the activities or events organised within the agreed access programme.

Where will the access take place?

27   Where practicable in the circumstances, a union should be granted access

to the workers at their actual workplace. However, each case will depend largely on the type of workplace concerned, and the union will need to take account of the wide variety of circumstances and operational requirements that are likely to be involved. In particular, consideration will need to be given to the employer's responsibility for health and safety and security issues. In other words, access arrangements should reflect local circumstances and each case should be examined on the facts.

28 Where they are suitable for the purpose, the employer's typical methods of communicating with his workforce should be used as a benchmark for determining how the union should communicate with members of the same workforce during the access period. If the employer follows the custom and practice of holding large workforce meetings in, for example, a meeting room or a canteen, then the employer should make the same facilities available to the union. However, in cases where the workplace is more confined, and it is therefore the employer's custom and practice to hold only small meetings at the workplace, then the union will also be limited to holding similar small meetings at that workplace. In exceptional circumstances, due to the nature of the business or severe space limitations, access may need to be restricted to meetings away from the workplace premises, and the union will need to consider finding facilities off-site at its own expense unless it agrees otherwise with the employer. In these circumstances, the employer should give all reasonable assistance to the union in notifying the workers in advance of where and when such off-site events are to take place. Where such exceptional circumstances exist, it would normally be expected that the employer would not hold similar events at the workplace.

When will the access take place?
29 The union should ensure that disruption to the business is minimised, especially for small businesses which might find it more difficult to organise cover for absent workers. The union's access to the workers should usually take place during normal working hours but at times which minimise any possible disruption to the activities of the employer. This will ensure that the union is able to communicate with as large a number of the workers as possible. Again, the arrangements should reflect the circumstances of each individual case. Consideration should be given to holding events, particularly those involving a large proportion of the workers in the bargaining unit, during rest periods or towards the end of a shift. In deciding the timing of meetings and other events, the union and the employer should be guided by the employer's custom and practice when communicating with his workforce. If, due to exceptional circumstances, access must be arranged away from the workplace, it might be practicable to arrange events in work time if they are held nearby, within easy walking distance. Otherwise, off-site events should normally occur outside work time.

The frequency and duration of union activities
30 The parties will need to establish agreed limits on the duration and frequency of the union's activities during the access period. Subject to the circumstances discussed in paragraphs 27–29 above, the employer should allow the union to hold one meeting of at least 30 minutes in duration for every 10 days of the access period, or part thereof, which all workers or a substantial proportion of them are given the opportunity to attend. In circumstances where the employer or others organise similar large-scale meetings in work time against the recognition

application (or in favour of derecognition), then it would be reasonable for the union to hold additional meetings, if necessary, to ensure that in total it has the same number of large-scale meetings as the employer and his supporters.

31   Where they would be appropriate having regard to all the circumstances, union 'surgeries' could be organised at the workplace during working hours at which each worker would have the opportunity, if they wish, to meet a union representative for fifteen minutes on an individual basis or in small groups of two or three. The circumstances would include whether there was a demand from the workforce for surgeries, whether the surgeries could be arranged off-site as effectively, whether the holding of surgeries would lead to an unacceptable increase in tension at the workplace and whether the employer, line managers or others use similar one-to-one or small meetings to put across the employer's case. The union should organise surgeries in a systematic way, ensuring that workers attend meetings at pre-determined times, thereby avoiding delays before workers are seen and ensuring that they promptly return to their work stations afterwards. Wherever practicable, the union should seek to arrange surgeries during periods of down-time such as rest or meal breaks. Where surgeries do not take place, the minimum time allowed for each larger scale meeting should be 45 minutes.

32   An employer should ensure that workers who attend a meeting or a 'surgery' organised by the union with his agreement during work time, should be paid, in full, for the duration of their absence from work. The employer will not be expected to pay the worker if the meeting or surgery takes place when the worker would not otherwise have been at work, and would not have been receiving payment from the employer.

33   Where the union wishes one of the employer's workers within the meaning of paragraphs 26(a) and 26(b) above to conduct a surgery, the employer should normally give time off with pay to the worker concerned. The worker should ensure that he provides the employer with as much notice as possible, giving details about the timing and location of the surgery. Exceptionally, it may be reasonable for the employer to refuse time off. This will apply if unavoidable situations arise where there is no adequate cover for the worker's absence from the workplace and the production process, or the provision of a service cannot otherwise be maintained. Before refusing permission, the employer should discuss the matter with the union and the worker to explore alternative arrangements.

What about written communication?
34   The union may want to display written material at the place of work. Employers, where practicable, should provide a notice board for the union's use. This notice board should be in a prominent location in the workplace and the union should be able to display material, including references to off-site meetings, without interference from the employer. Often, an existing notice-board could be used for this purpose. The union should also be able to place additional material near to the notice-board including, for example, copies of explanatory leaflets, which the workers may read or take away with them. If there are no union representatives within the meaning of paragraphs 26(a) and 26(b) above present at the workplace, the employer should allow access to a full time official of the union to display the material.

35   The union may also wish to make use of its web-site pages on the Internet for campaigning purposes. An employer should allow his workers access to the union's material in the same way that he explicitly, or tacitly, allows his workers to down-load information in connection with activities not directly related to the performance of their job. If an employer generally disallows all such Internet use, he should consider giving permission to one of his workers nominated by the union to down-load the material, and it would be this person's responsibility to disseminate it more widely among other workers.

36   A nominated union representative employed by the employer may also want to make use of internal electronic communication, such as electronic mail or intranets, for campaigning purposes. For example, he may want to remind workers of forthcoming union meetings or surgeries. The employer should allow the representative to make reasonable use of these systems if the employer explicitly, or tacitly, allows his workers to use them for matters which are not directly related to the performance of their job. In cases where such use is disallowed, it would still be reasonable for the representative to use them, if the employer uses such forms of communication to send to the workers information against the union's case. When sending messages in this capacity, the representative should make it clear that the advice comes from the union and not the employer.

What about small businesses?
37   Access arrangements for small businesses need not necessarily create difficulties. For example, it may be easier to arrange for a smaller number of workers to meet together. On the other hand, there may be difficulties providing cover for workers in smaller organisations, or in finding accommodation for meetings. In such cases, the employer and the union should try to reach an understanding about how access arrangements can be organised to ensure minimum disruption. Agreements may need to be flexible to accommodate any particular needs of the employer.

Arrangements for non-typical workers
38   Many, or sometimes most, workers in a bargaining unit may not work full time in a standard Monday-Friday working week. Others might rarely visit the employer's premises. The employer should bear in mind the difficulties faced by unions in communicating with :
- shift workers
- part-time workers
- homeworkers
- a dispersed or peripatetic workforce
- those on maternity or parental leave
- those on sick leave.

39   The employer should be receptive to a union's suggestions for securing reasonable access to such 'non-typical workers', and allow them, where practicable, to achieve a broadly equivalent level of access to those workers as to typical workers. It would be reasonable for the union to organise its meetings or surgery arrangements on a more flexible basis to cover shift workers or part-time workers. An employer should agree to the maximum flexibility of arrangements, where reasonable in the circumstances. This would not extend to an employer being obliged to meet the travel costs of his workers attending meetings arranged by the union.

679

40   In addition, the union will be able to make use of the independent person to distribute information to home addresses via the postal service. This will ensure that literature will be received by any workers who are not likely to attend the workplace during the access period, for example those on maternity or sick leave. The CAC will supply the name, address and telephone number of the independent person to both the union and the employer.

What about joint employer/union activities?
41   There may be scope for the union and the employer to undertake joint activities where they both put across their respective views about recognition or derecognition in a non-confrontational way. Such joint activities can be an efficient method of providing information, minimising business disruption and costs. For example, the parties may wish to consider:
*   the arrangement of joint meetings with each party allocated a period of thirty minutes to address the workers; and
*   the use of a joint notice-board where an equal amount of space is devoted to the employer and the union.

Section D   General responsibilities of employers and trade unions

Observing an access agreement
42   Both parties should ensure they keep to agreements about access arrangements. For example, if the parties agree to hold a meeting lasting 30 minutes in duration, every effort should be made to ensure that the meeting does not over-run its allocated time. Likewise, neither party should remove, or tamper with, material placed on a notice board by the other party, unless they are obliged to do so for legal reasons.

Avoiding acrimonious situations
43   Both parties should endeavour to ensure that, wherever possible, potentially acrimonious situations are avoided throughout the period of access. In particular, the parties should avoid:
*   using defamatory material or provocative propaganda;
*   personal attacks or personalised negative campaigning against individuals;
*   the harassment or intimidation of individuals;
*   issuing threats;
*   placing pressure on workers to reveal their voting intentions; and
*   behaviour likely to cause unnecessary offence.

44   The employer and the union should also dissociate themselves from material containing personal attacks or allegations which is circulated on an anonymous basis. The party whose case appears to be favoured by the anonymous material should formally repudiate it, informing all workers in the bargaining unit accordingly.

Behaving responsibly
45   For access arrangements to work satisfactorily, the employer and the union should behave responsibly, and give due consideration to the requirements of the other party throughout the access period. For example, neither the union nor the employer should seek to disrupt or interfere with meetings being held by the other party. If one party is holding a large meeting, the other should avoid the

scheduling of other conflicting meetings or events, and should not attempt to distract attention from the business of the meeting.

46   Where it is practicable to hold meetings or surgeries at the workplace, the employer should provide appropriate accommodation, fit for the purpose, which should include adequate heating and lighting, and arrangements to ensure that the meeting is held in private. In turn, the union should ensure that business costs and business disruption are minimised. Unions should be aware of the needs of the employer to maintain the production process, to maintain a level of service, and to ensure safety and security at all times.

Section E   Non-compliance with access provisions

Intervention by the CAC

47   Disputes may arise between the parties during the access period about the failure to allow reasonable access or to implement access agreements. If these disputes cannot be resolved, the union may ask the CAC to decide whether the employer has failed to perform his statutory duties in relation to the ballot.

48   *If the CAC is satisfied that the employer has failed to perform one or more of its three duties:*
a)   to co-operate generally with the union and the independent person on the ballot;
b)   to give the union such access to the workers constituting the bargaining unit as is reasonable to inform them of the object of the ballot and to seek their support and opinions; and
c)   to provide the CAC with the names and home addresses of those workers,

and the ballot has not been held, the CAC may order the employer to take such steps to remedy the failure as the CAC considers reasonable, and within a time that the CAC considers reasonable. Where the CAC is asked to make an order very shortly before the end of the access period, it may be impracticable for the CAC to consider the request and for the employer and the union to remedy any failure in the short time before the ballot is held. In such circumstances, the CAC may extend the access period by ordering the ballot to be rescheduled for a later date to ensure that access is achieved.

49   *If the employer fails to comply with the CAC's order within the time specified, and the ballot has still not been held, the CAC may issue a declaration that the union is recognised, or that the union is not derecognised.*

50   The law does not provide for employers to complain to the CAC about the union's behaviour in relation to access. However, in deciding whether the employer has complied with his duty to give the union access, the CAC may take into account all relevant circumstances. This may include the behaviour of the union. The CAC may therefore decide that the employer has complied with the duty in circumstances where, because the union has acted unreasonably, he denies the union access or refuses to implement agreed access arrangements.

Minor disputes

51   Some disputes may be minor by nature. For example, the employer may be aggrieved that a meeting has over-run somewhat. On the other hand, a union might

have cause to complain if it regards the meeting room provided by the employer as being too small to accommodate everyone in comfort. In such cases, both parties should avoid taking hasty action which might prejudice the implementation of other access arrangements. The union should generally avoid taking minor complaints to the CAC as a first course of action.

52   Instead, the parties should make every effort to resolve the dispute between themselves. They should make full use of any mechanism to resolve such disputes which they may have established in the access agreement, and consider the use of ACAS's conciliation services. It would generally be a good practice if both the employer and the union nominated a person to act as their lead contact if disagreements or questions arose about the implementation of access arrangements.

53   The period of access will be limited in duration, given that the balloting period will normally be a maximum of 20 working days, and the parties should therefore ensure that disputes are swiftly resolved. The parties should endeavour to inform each other immediately if a dispute arises, and should seek to resolve any disputes as a matter of priority, preferably within one working day of their occurrence.

The independent person

54   The prime duties of the independent person are to ensure that:
- the names and addresses of the workers comprising the balloting constituency are accurate;
- the ballot is conducted properly and in secret; and
- the CAC is promptly informed of the ballot result.

It is not the function of the independent person to adjudicate disputes about access. That is the CAC's role. However, the independent person may have wide experience and knowledge of balloting arrangements in different settings. The parties might consider informing the independent person about their problems and draw on his experience to identify possible options to resolve their difficulties.

European Commission recommendation No 92/131/EEC on the protection of the dignity of women and men at work

Article 1

It is recommended that the Member States take action to promote awareness that conduct of a sexual nature, or other conduct based on sex affecting the dignity of women and men at work, including conduct of superiors and colleagues, is unacceptable if:

(a) such conduct is unwanted, unreasonable and offensive to the recipient;

(b) a person's rejection of, or submission to, such conduct on the part of employers of workers (including superiors or colleagues) is used explicitly or implicitly as a basis for a decision which affects that person's access to vocational training, access to employment, continued employment, promotion, salary or any other employment decisions; and/or

(c) such conduct creates an intimidating, hostile or humiliating work environment for the recipient;

and that such conduct may, in certain circumstances, be contrary to the principle of equal treatment within the meaning of Articles 3, 4 and 5 of Directive 76.207.EEC.

Article 2

It is recommended that Member States take action, in the public sector, to implement the Commission's code of practice on the protection of the dignity of women and men at work, annexed hereto. The action of the Member States, in thus initiating and pursuing positive measures designed to create a climate at work in which women and men respect one another's human integrity, should serve as an example to the private sector.

Article 3

It is recommended that Member States encourage employers and employee representatives to develop measures to implement the Commission's code of practice on the protection of the dignity of women and men at work.

Article 4

Member States shall inform the Commission within three years of the date of this recommendation of the measures taken to give effect to it, in order to allow the

Commission to draw up a report on all such measures. The Commission shall, within this period, ensure the widest possible circulation of the code of practice. The report should examine the degree of awareness of the Code, its perceived effectiveness, its degree of application and the extent of its use in collective bargaining between the social partners.

Article 5

This recommendation is addressed to the Member States.

Done at Brussels, 27 November 1991.

Annex
Protecting the dignity of women and men at work
A code of practice on measures to combat sexual harassment

I. Introduction

This code of practice is issued in accordance with the resolution of the Council of Ministers on the protection of the dignity of women and men at work, and to accompany the Commission's recommendation on this issue.

Its purpose is to give practical guidance to employers, trade unions, and employees on the protection of the dignity of women and men at work. The code is intended to be applicable in both the public and the private sector and employers are encouraged to follow the recommendations contained in the code in a way which is appropriate to the size and structure of their organisation. It may be particularly relevant for small and medium-sized enterprises to adapt some of the practical steps to their specific needs.

The aim is to ensure that sexual harassment does not occur and, if it does occur, to ensure that adequate procedures are readily available to deal with the problem and prevent its recurrence. The code thus seeks to encourage the development and implementation of policies and practices which establish working environments free of sexual harassment and in which women and men respect one another's human integrity.

The expert report carried out on behalf of the Commission found that sexual harassment is a serious problem for many working women in the European Community and research in Member States has proven beyond doubt that sexual harassment at work is not an isolated phenomenon. On the contrary, it is clear that for millions of women in the European Community, sexual harassment is an unpleasant and unavoidable part of their working lives. Men too may suffer sexual harassment and should, of course, have the same rights as women to the protection of their dignity.

Some specific groups are particularly vulnerable to sexual harassment. Research in several Member States, which documents the link between the risk of sexual harassment and the recipient's perceived vulnerability, suggests that divorced and separated women, young women and new entrants to the labour market and those with irregular or precarious employment contracts, women in non-traditional jobs, women with disabilities, lesbians and women from racial minorities are disproportionately at risk. Gay men and young men are also vulnerable to harassment. It is undeniable that harassment on grounds of sexual orientation undermines the dignity at work of those affected and it is impossible to regard such harassment as appropriate workplace behaviour.

Sexual harassment pollutes the working environment and can have a devastating effect upon the health, confidence, morale and performance of those affected by it. The anxiety and stress produced by sexual harassment commonly leads to those subject to it taking time off work due to sickness, being less efficient at work, or leaving their job to seek work elsewhere. Employees often suffer the adverse consequences of the harassment itself and short- and long-term damage to their employment prospects if they are forced to change jobs. Sexual harassment may also have a damaging impact on employees not themselves the object of unwanted behaviour but who are witness to it or have a knowledge of the unwanted behaviour.

There are also adverse consequences arising from sexual harassment for employers. It has a direct impact on the profitability of the enterprise where staff take sick leave or resign their posts because of sexual harassment, and on the economic efficiency of the enterprise where employees' productivity is reduced by having to work in a climate in which individuals' integrity is not respected.

In general terms, sexual harassment is an obstacle to the proper integration of women into the labour market and the Commission is committed to encouraging the development of comprehensive measures to improve such integration.

2. Definition

Sexual harassment means unwanted conduct of a sexual nature, or other conduct based on sex affecting the dignity of women and men at work. This can include unwelcome physical, verbal or non-verbal conduct.

Thus, a range of behaviour may be considered to constitute sexual harassment. It is unacceptable if such conduct is unwanted, unreasonable and offensive to the recipient; a person's rejection of or submission to such conduct on the part of employers or workers (including superiors or colleagues) is used explicitly or implicitly as a basis for a decision which affects that person's access to vocational training or to employment, continued employment, promotion, salary or any other employment decisions; and/or such conduct creates an intimidating, hostile or humiliating working environment for the recipient.

The essential characteristic of sexual harassment is that it is unwanted by the recipient, that it is for each individual to determine what behaviour is acceptable to them and what they regard as offensive. Sexual attention becomes sexual harassment if it is persisted in once it has been made clear that it is regarded by the recipient as offensive, although one incident of harassment may constitute sexual harassment if sufficiently serious. It is the unwanted nature of the conduct which distinguishes sexual harassment from friendly behaviour, which is welcome and mutual.

3. The law and employers' responsibilities

Conduct of a sexual nature or other based on sex affecting the dignity of women and men at work may be contrary to the principle of equal treatment within the meaning of Articles 3, 4 and 5 of Council Directive 76/207/EEC of 9 February 1976 on the implementation of the principle of equal treatment for men and women as regards access to employment, vocational training and promotion, and working conditions. This principle means that there shall be no discrimination whatsoever on grounds of sex either directly or indirectly by reference in particular to marital or family status.

In certain circumstances, and depending upon national law, sexual harassment may also be a criminal offence or may contravene other obligations imposed by the law, such as health and safety duties, or a duty, contractual or otherwise, to be a good employer. Since sexual harassment is a form of employee misconduct, employers have a responsibility to deal with it as they do with any other form of employee misconduct as well as to refrain from harassing employees themselves. Since sexual harassment is a risk to health and safety, employers have a responsibility to take steps to minimise the risk as they do with other hazards. Since sexual harassment often entails an abuse of power, employers may have a responsibility for the misuse of the authority they delegate.

This code, however, focuses on sexual harassment as a problem of sex discrimination. Sexual harassment is sex discrimination because the gender of the recipient is the determining factor in who is harassed. Conduct of a sexual nature or other conduct based on sex affecting the dignity of women and men at work in some Member States already has been found to contravene national equal treatment laws and employers have a responsibility to seek to ensure that the work environment is free from such conduct.

As sexual harassment is often a function of women's status in the employment hierarchy, policies to deal with sexual harassment are likely to be most effective where they are linked to a broader policy to promote equal opportunities and to improve the position of women. Advice on steps which can be taken generally to implement an equal opportunities policy is set out in the Commission's guide to positive action.

Similarly, a procedure to deal with complaints of sexual harassment should be regarded as only one component of a strategy to deal with the problem. The prime objective should be to change behaviour and attitudes, to seek to ensure the prevention of sexual harassment.

4. Collective bargaining

The majority of the recommendations contained in this code are for action by employers, since employers have clear responsibilities to ensure the protection of the dignity of women and men at work.

Trade unions also have responsibilities to their members and they can and should play an important role in the prevention of sexual harassment in the workplace. It is recommended that the question of including appropriate clauses in agreements be examined in the context of the collective bargaining process, with the aim of achieving a work environment free from unwanted conduct of a sexual nature or other conduct based on sex affecting the dignity of women and men at work and free from victimisation of a complainant or of a person wishing to give, or giving, evidence in the event of a complaint.

5. Recommendations to employers

The policies and procedures recommended below should be adopted, where appropriate, after consultation or negotiation with trade unions or employee representatives. Experience suggests that strategies to create and maintain a working environment in which the dignity of employees is respected are most likely to be effective where they are jointly agreed.

It should be emphasised that a distinguishing characteristic of sexual harassment is that employees subjected to it often will be reluctant to complain. An absence of complaints about sexual harassment in a particular organisation, therefore, does not necessarily mean an absence of sexual harassment. It may mean that the recipients of sexual harassment think that there is no point in complaining because nothing will be done about it, or because it will be trivialised or the complainant subjected to ridicule, or because they fear reprisals. Implementing the preventative and procedural recommendations outlined below should facilitate the creation of a climate at work in which such concerns have no place.

A. Prevention

(I) POLICY STATEMENTS
As a first step in showing senior management's concern and their commitment to dealing with the problem of sexual harassment, employers should issue a policy statement which expressly states that all employees have a right to be treated with dignity, that sexual harassment at work will not be permitted or condoned and that employees have a right to complain about it should it occur.

It is recommended that the policy statement make clear what is considered inappropriate behaviour at work, and explain that such behaviour, in certain circumstances, may be unlawful. It is advisable for the statement to set out a positive duty on managers and supervisors to implement the policy and to take corrective action to ensure compliance with it. It should also place a positive duty on all employees to comply with the policy and to ensure that their colleagues are treated with respect and dignity.

In addition, it is recommended that the statement explain the procedure which should be followed by employees subjected to sexual harassment at work in order to obtain assistance and to whom they should complain; that it contain an undertaking that allegations of sexual harassment will be dealt with seriously, expeditiously and confidentially, and that employees will be protected against victimisation or retaliation for bringing a complaint of sexual harassment. It should also specify that appropriate disciplinary measures will be taken against employees found guilty of sexual harassment.

(II) COMMUNICATING THE POLICY
Once the policy has been developed, it is important to ensure that it is communicated effectively to all employees, so that they are aware that they have a right to complain and to whom they should complain; that their complaint will be dealt with promptly and fairly; and that employees are made aware of the likely consequences of engaging in sexual harassment. Such communication will highlight management's commitment to eliminating sexual harassment, thus enhancing a climate in which it will not occur.

(III) RESPONSIBILITY
All employees have a responsibility to help to ensure a working environment in which the dignity of employees is respected and managers (including supervisors) have a particular duty to ensure that sexual harassment does not occur in work areas for which they are responsible. It is recommended that managers explain the organisation's policy to their staff and take steps to positively promote the policy. Managers should also be responsive and supportive to any member of staff who complains about sexual harassment, provide full and clear advice on

the procedure to be adopted, maintain confidentiality in any cases of sexual harassment and ensure that there is no further problem of sexual harassment or any victimisation after a complaint has been resolved.

(iv) TRAINING

An important means of ensuring that sexual harassment does not occur and that, if it does occur, the problem is resolved efficiently is through the provision of training for managers and supervisors. Such training should aim to identify the factors which contribute to a working environment free of sexual harassment to familiarise participants with their responsibilities under the employer's policy and any problems they are likely to encounter

In addition, those playing an official role in any formal complaints procedure in respect of sexual harassment should receive specialist training, such as that outlined above.

It is also good practice to include information as to the organisation's policy on sexual harassment and procedures for dealing with it as part of appropriate induction and training programmes.

B. Procedures

The development of clear and precise procedures to deal with sexual harassment once it has occurred is of great importance. The procedures should ensure the resolution of problems in an efficient and effective manner. Practical guidance for employees on how to deal with sexual harassment when it occurs and with its aftermath will make it more likely that it will be dealt with at an early stage. Such guidance should of course draw attention to an employee's legal rights and to any time limits within which they must be exercised.

(i) RESOLVING PROBLEMS INFORMALLY

Most recipients of harassment simply want the harassment to stop. Both informal and formal methods of resolving problems should be available.

Employees should be advised that, if possible, they should attempt to resolve the problem informally in the first instance. In some cases, it may be possible and sufficient for the employee to explain clearly to the person engaging in the unwanted conduct that the behaviour in question is not welcome, that it offends them or makes them uncomfortable, and that it interferes with their work.

In circumstances where it is too difficult or embarrassing for an individual to do this on their own behalf, an alternative approach would be to seek support from, or for an initial approach to be made by, a sympathetic friend or confidential counsellor.

If the conduct continues or if it is not appropriate to resolve the problem informally, it should be raised through the formal complaints procedure.

(ii) ADVICE AND ASSISTANCE

It is recommended that employers designate someone to provide assistance to employees subjected to sexual harassment, where possible with responsibilities to assist in the resolution of any problems, whether through informal or formal means. It may be helpful if the officer is designated with the agreement of the trade unions or employees, as this is likely to enhance their acceptability. Such officers could be selected from personnel departments or equal opportunities departments for example. In some organisations they are designated as 'confidential counsellors' or 'sympathetic friends'. Often such a role may be played by someone from the employee's trade union or women's support groups.

Whatever the location of this responsibility in the organisation, it is recommended that the designated officer receives appropriate training in the best means of resolving problems and in the detail of the organisation's policy and procedures, so that they can perform their role effectively. It is also important that they are given adequate resources to carry out their function, and protection against victimisation for assisting any recipient of sexual harassment.

(III) COMPLAINTS PROCEDURE

It is recommended that, where the complainant regards attempts at informal resolution as inappropriate, where informal attempts at resolution have been refused, or where the outcome has been unsatisfactory, a formal procedure for resolving the complaint be provided. The procedure should give employees confidence that the organisation will take allegations of sexual harassment seriously.

By its nature sexual harassment may make the normal channels of complaint difficult to use because of embarrassment, fears of not being taken seriously, fears of damage to reputation, fears of reprisal or the prospect of damaging the working environment. Therefore, a formal procedure should specify to whom the employee should bring a complaint, and it should also provide an alternative if in the particular circumstances the normal grievance procedure may not be suitable, for example because the alleged harasser is the employee's line manager. It is also advisable to make provision for employees to bring a complaint in the first instance to someone of their own sex, should they so choose.

It is good practice for employers to monitor and review complaints of sexual harassment and how they have been resolved, in order to ensure that their procedures are working effectively.

(IV) INVESTIGATIONS

It is important to ensure that internal investigations of any complaints are handled with sensitivity and with due respect for the rights of both the complainant and the alleged harasser. The investigation should be seen to be independent and objective. Those carrying out the investigation should not be connected with the allegation in any way, and every effort should be made to resolve complaints speedily—grievances should be handled promptly and the procedure should set a time limit within which complaints will be processed, with due regard for any time limits set by national legislation for initiating a complaint through the legal system.

It is recommended as good practice that both the complainant and the alleged harasser have the right to be accompanied and/or represented, perhaps by a representative of their trade union or a friend or colleague; that the alleged harasser be given full details of the nature of the complaint and the opportunity to respond, and that strict confidentiality be maintained throughout any investigation into an allegation. Where it is necessary to interview witnesses, the importance of confidentiality should be emphasised.

It must be recognised that recounting the experience of sexual harassment is difficult and can damage the employee's dignity. Therefore, a complainant should not be required repeatedly to recount the events complained of where this is unnecessary.

The investigation should focus on the facts of the complaint and it is advisable for the employer to keep a complete record of all meetings and investigations.

(V) DISCIPLINARY OFFENCE

It is recommended that violations of the organisation's policy protecting the dignity of employees at work should be treated as a disciplinary offence and the disciplinary rules should make clear what is regarded as inappropriate behaviour at work. It is also good practice to ensure that the range of penalties to which offenders will be liable for violating the rule is clearly stated and also to make it clear that it will be considered a disciplinary offence to victimise or retaliate against an employee for bringing a complaint of sexual harassment in good faith.

Where a complaint is upheld and it is determined that it is necessary to relocate or transfer one party, consideration should be given, wherever practicable, to allowing the complaint to choose whether he or she wishes to remain in their post or be transferred to another location. No element of penalty should be seen to attach to a complainant whose complaint is upheld and in addition, where a complaint is upheld, the employer should monitor the situation to ensure that the harassment has stopped.

Even where a complaint is not upheld, for example because the evidence is regarded as inconclusive, consideration should be given to transferring or re-scheduling the work of one of the employees concerned rather than requiring them to continue to work together against the wishes of either party.

6. Recommendations to trade unions

Sexual harassment is a trade union issue as well as an issue for employers. It is recommended as good practice that trade unions formulate and issue clear policy statements on sexual harassment and take steps to raise awareness of the problem of sexual harassment in the workplace, in order to help create a climate in which it is neither condoned or ignored. For example, trade unions could aim to give all officers and representatives training on equality issues, including dealing with sexual harassment, and include such information in union-sponsored or approved training courses, as well as information on the union's policy. Trade unions should consider declaring that sexual harassment is inappropriate behaviour and educating members and officials about its consequences is recommended as good practice.

Trade unions should also raise the issue of sexual harassment with employers and encourage the adoption of adequate policies and procedures to protect the dignity of women and men at work in the organisation. It is advisable for trade unions to inform members of their right not to be sexually harassed at work and provide members with clear guidance as to what to do if they are sexually harassed, including guidance on any relevant legal rights.

Where complaints arise, it is important for trade unions to treat them seriously and sympathetically and ensure that the complainant has an opportunity of representation if a complaint is to be pursued. It is important to create an environment in which members feel able to raise such complaints knowing they will receive a sympathetic and supportive response from local union representatives. Trade unions could consider designating specially trained officials to advise and counsel members with complaints of sexual harassment and act on their behalf if required. This will provide a focal point for support. It is also a good idea to ensure that there are sufficient female representatives to support women subjected to sexual harassment.

It is recommended too, where the trade union is representing both the complainant and the alleged harasser for the purpose of the complaints procedure, that it be made clear that the union is not condoning offensive behaviour by providing representation. In any event, the same official should not represent both parties.

It is good practice to advise members that keeping a record of incidents by the harassed worker will assist in bringing any formal or informal action to a more effective conclusion, that the union wishes to be informed of any incident of sexual harassment and that such information will be kept confidential. It is also good practice for the union to monitor and review the union's record in responding to complaints and in representing alleged harassers and the harassed, in order to ensure its responses are effective.

7. Employees' responsibilities

Employees have a clear role to play in helping to create a climate at work in which sexual harassment is unacceptable. They can contribute to preventing sexual harassment through an awareness and sensitivity towards the issue and by ensuring that standards of conduct for themselves and for colleagues do not cause offence.

Employees can do much to discourage sexual harassment by making it clear that they find such behaviour unacceptable and by supporting colleagues who suffer such treatment and are considering making a complaint.

Employees who are themselves recipients of harassment should, where practicable, tell the harasser that the behaviour is unwanted and unacceptable. Once the offender understands clearly that the behaviour is unwelcome, this may be enough to put an end to it. If the behaviour is persisted in, employees should inform management and/or their employee representative through the appropriate channels and request assistance in stopping the harassment, whether through informal or formal means.

Index

References are to paragraph numbers except those which
relate to the Appendices, which refer to page numbers.